Itazura Na Kiss ⑧

イタズラな キッス

KAORU TADA

MAMA

PAPA

NAOKI

KOTOKO

ZINKO

SATOMI

CHRIS

KINNOSUKE

DMP

DIGITAL MANGA
PUBLISHING

Itazura Na Kiss 8

Translation	Sachiko Sato
Lettering	Replibooks
Graphic Design	Amy Lee Koga
Senior Editing	Stephanie Donnelly
Japan Relations	Yoshio Ogura
Sales & Distribution	Yoko Tanigaki
Editor in Chief	Fred Lui
Publisher	Hikaru Sashara

English Edition Published by
DIGITAL MANGA PUBLISHING
A division of DIGITAL MANGA, Inc.
1487 W 178th Street, Suite 300
Gardena, CA 90248

www.dmpbooks.com

First Edition: March 2012
ISBN-10: 1-56970-246-2
ISBN-13: 978-1-56970-246-8

1 3 5 7 9 10 8 6 4 2

Printed in Canada

 More titles available at
www.akadot.com

 Become our fan on Facebook
Digital Manga Inc.

 Follow us on Twitter
@DigitalManga

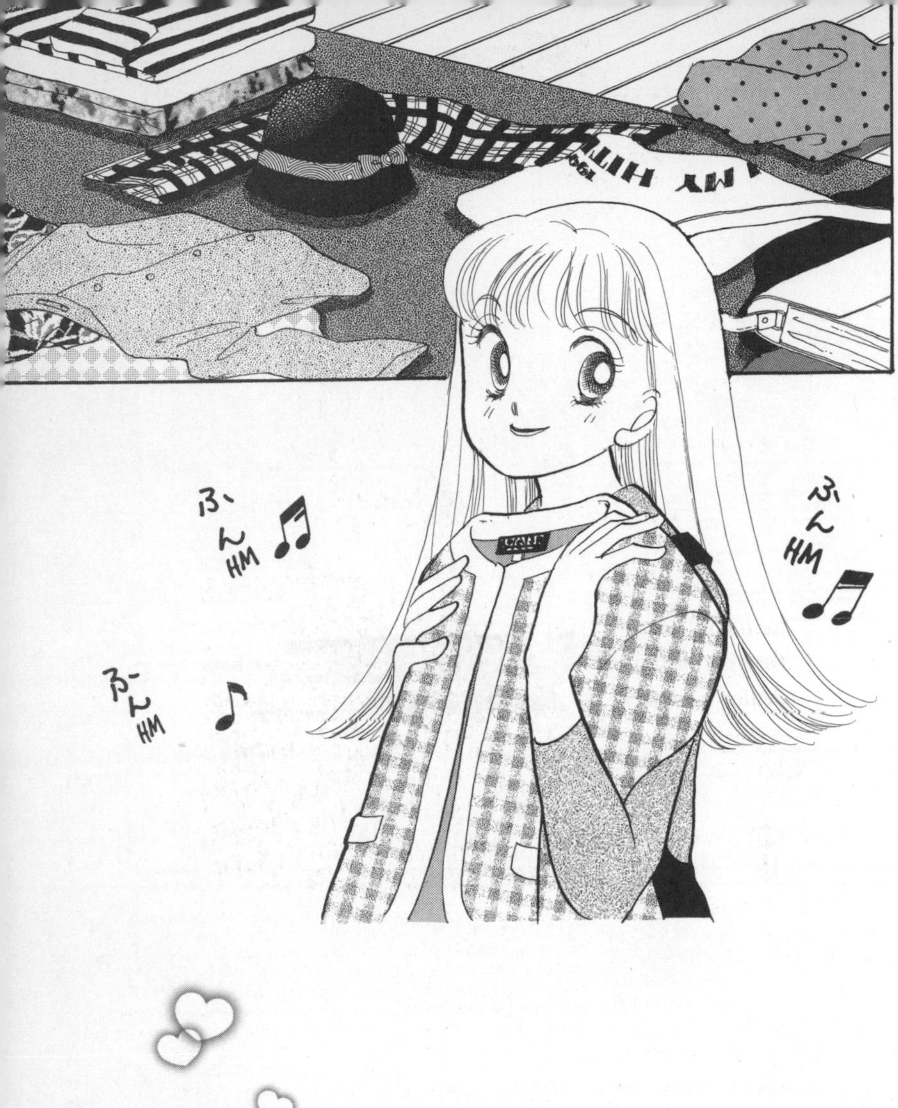
ふん HM
ふん HM
ふ〜ん HM

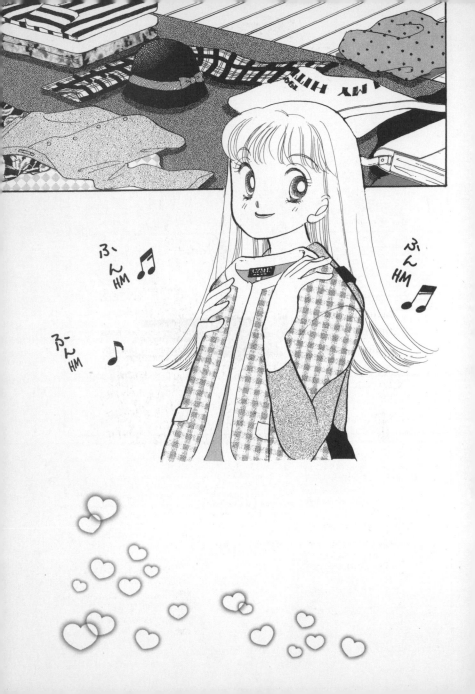

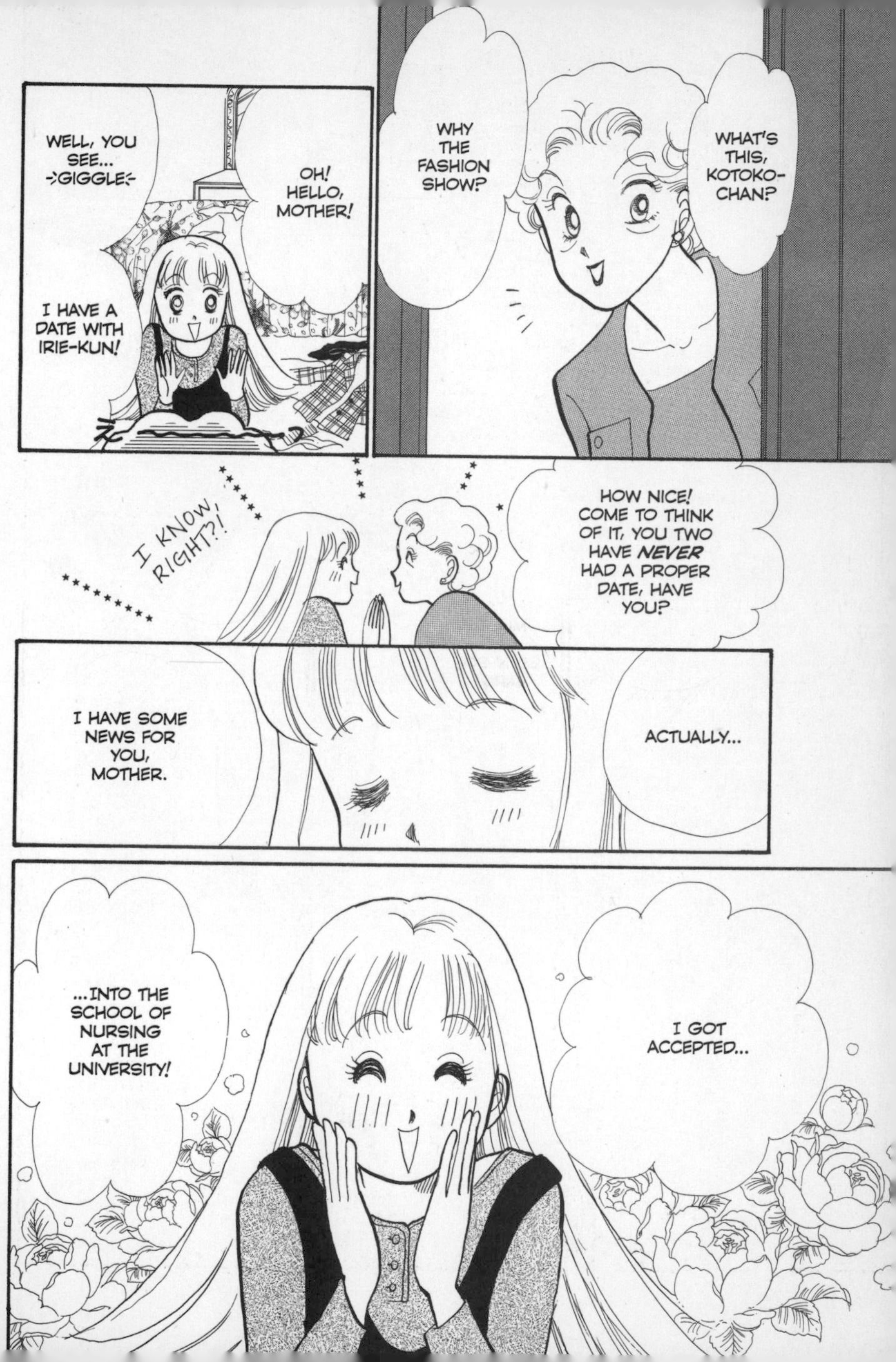
WHAT'S THIS, KOTOKO-CHAN?
WHY THE FASHION SHOW?
OH! HELLO, MOTHER!
WELL, YOU SEE... -GIGGLE-
I HAVE A DATE WITH IRIE-KUN!
HOW NICE! COME TO THINK OF IT, YOU TWO HAVE NEVER HAD A PROPER DATE, HAVE YOU?
I KNOW, RIGHT?!
ACTUALLY...
I HAVE SOME NEWS FOR YOU, MOTHER.
I GOT ACCEPTED...
...INTO THE SCHOOL OF NURSING AT THE UNIVERSITY!

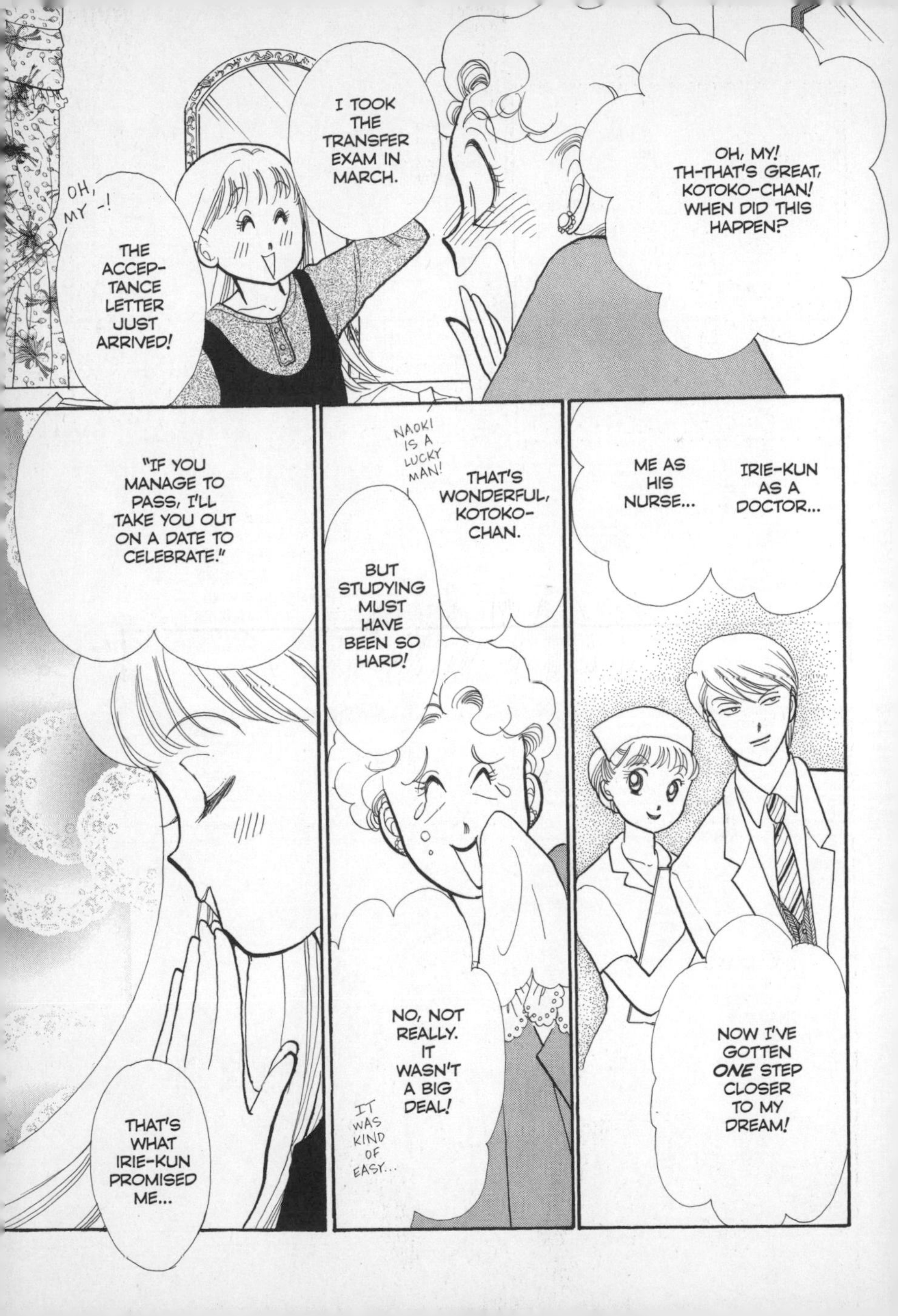
OH, MY! TH-THAT'S GREAT, KOTOKO-CHAN! WHEN DID THIS HAPPEN?
I TOOK THE TRANSFER EXAM IN MARCH.
OH, MY -!
THE ACCEPTANCE LETTER JUST ARRIVED!
IRIE-KUN AS A DOCTOR...
ME AS HIS NURSE...
NOW I'VE GOTTEN *ONE* STEP CLOSER TO MY DREAM!
THAT'S WONDERFUL, KOTOKO-CHAN.
NAOKI IS A LUCKY MAN!
BUT STUDYING MUST HAVE BEEN SO HARD!
NO, NOT REALLY. IT WASN'T A BIG DEAL!
IT WAS KIND OF EASY...
"IF YOU MANAGE TO PASS, I'LL TAKE YOU OUT ON A DATE TO CELEBRATE."
THAT'S WHAT IRIE-KUN PROMISED ME...

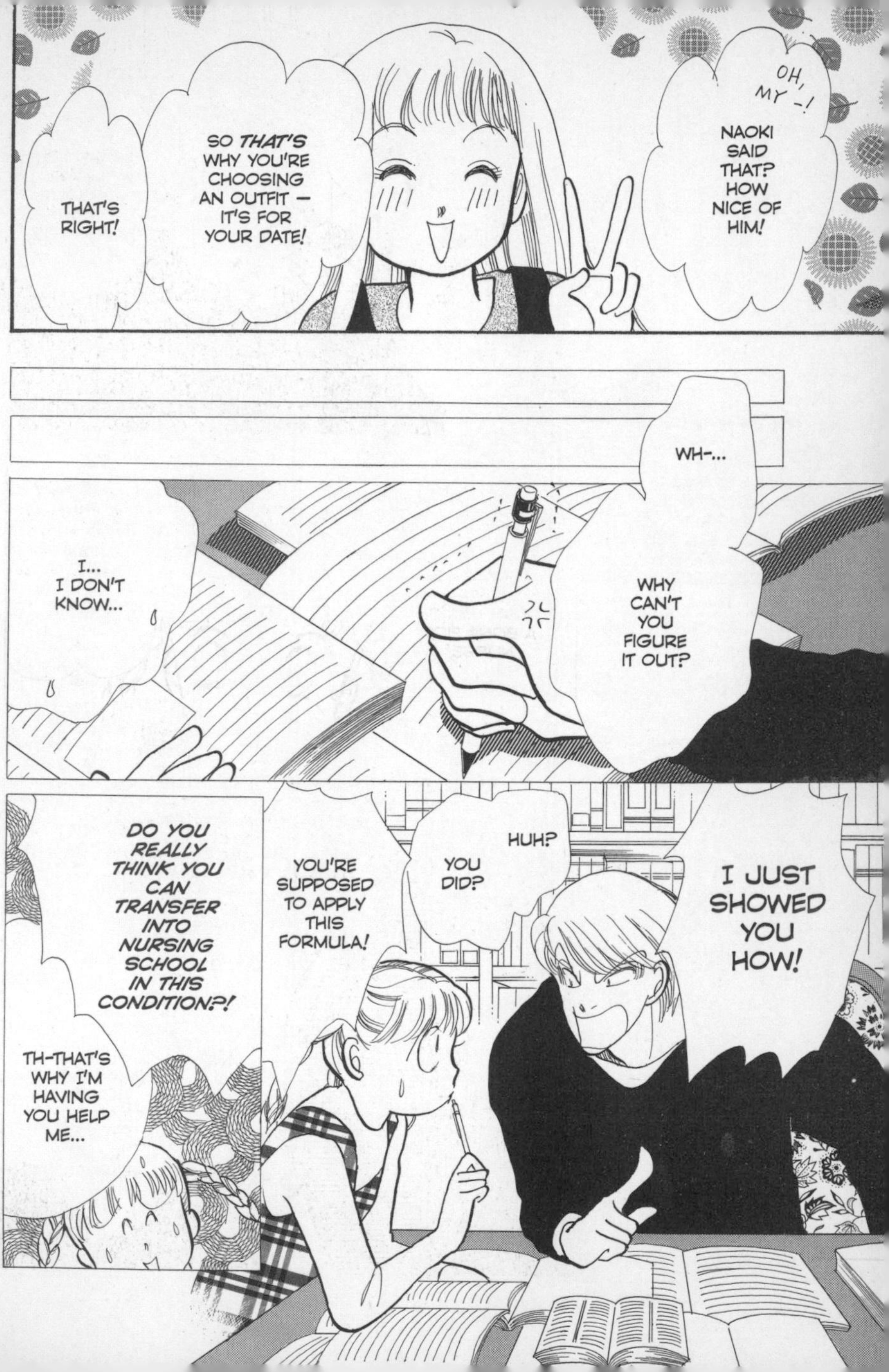
OH, MY –!
NAOKI SAID THAT? HOW NICE OF HIM!
SO THAT'S WHY YOU'RE CHOOSING AN OUTFIT – IT'S FOR YOUR DATE!
THAT'S RIGHT!
WH-...
WHY CAN'T YOU FIGURE IT OUT?
I... I DON'T KNOW...
I JUST SHOWED YOU HOW!
HUH? YOU DID?
YOU'RE SUPPOSED TO APPLY THIS FORMULA!
DO YOU REALLY THINK YOU CAN TRANSFER INTO NURSING SCHOOL IN THIS CONDITION?!
TH-THAT'S WHY I'M HAVING YOU HELP ME...

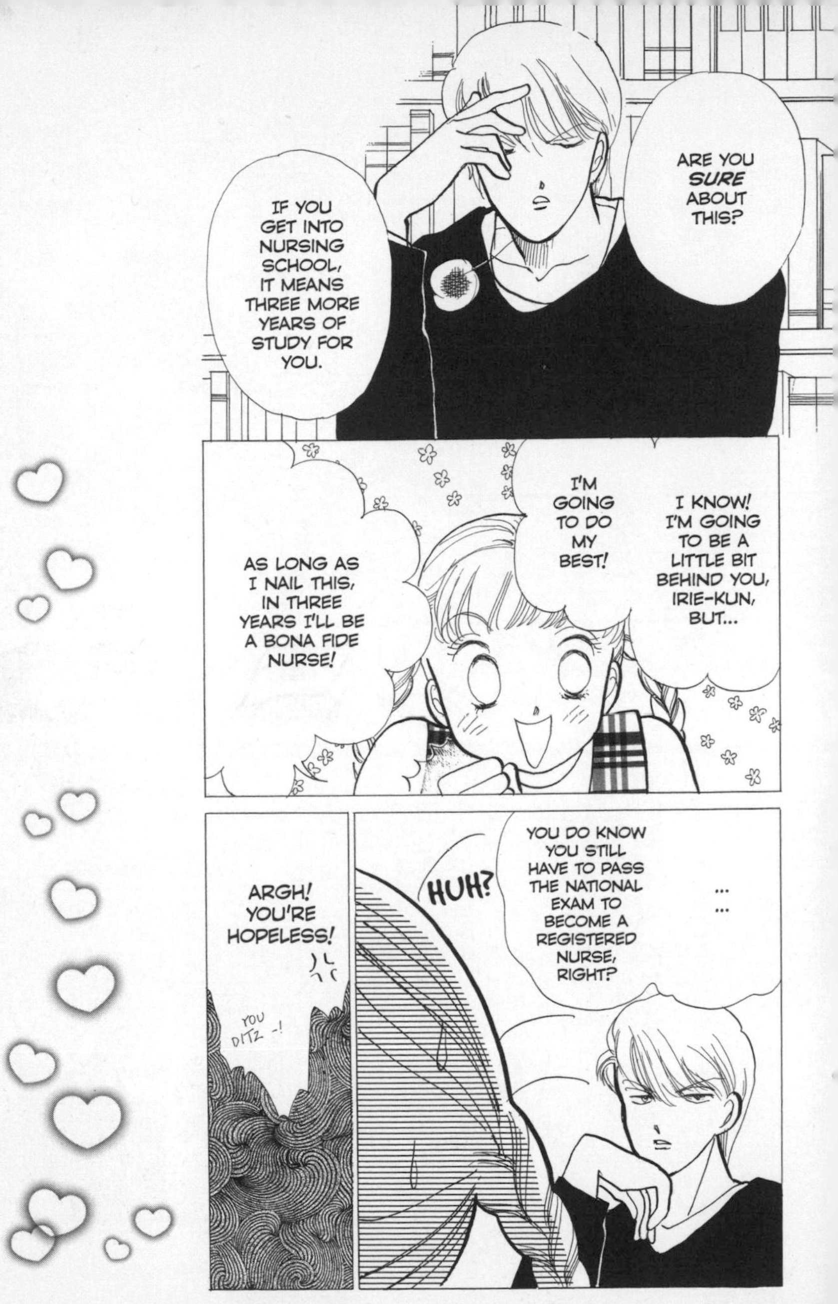
ARE YOU SURE ABOUT THIS?
IF YOU GET INTO NURSING SCHOOL, IT MEANS THREE MORE YEARS OF STUDY FOR YOU.
I KNOW! I'M GOING TO BE A LITTLE BIT BEHIND YOU, IRIE-KUN, BUT...
I'M GOING TO DO MY BEST!
AS LONG AS I NAIL THIS, IN THREE YEARS I'LL BE A BONA FIDE NURSE!
...
...
YOU DO KNOW YOU STILL HAVE TO PASS THE NATIONAL EXAM TO BECOME A REGISTERED NURSE, RIGHT?
HUH?
ARGH! YOU'RE HOPELESS!
YOU DITZ -!

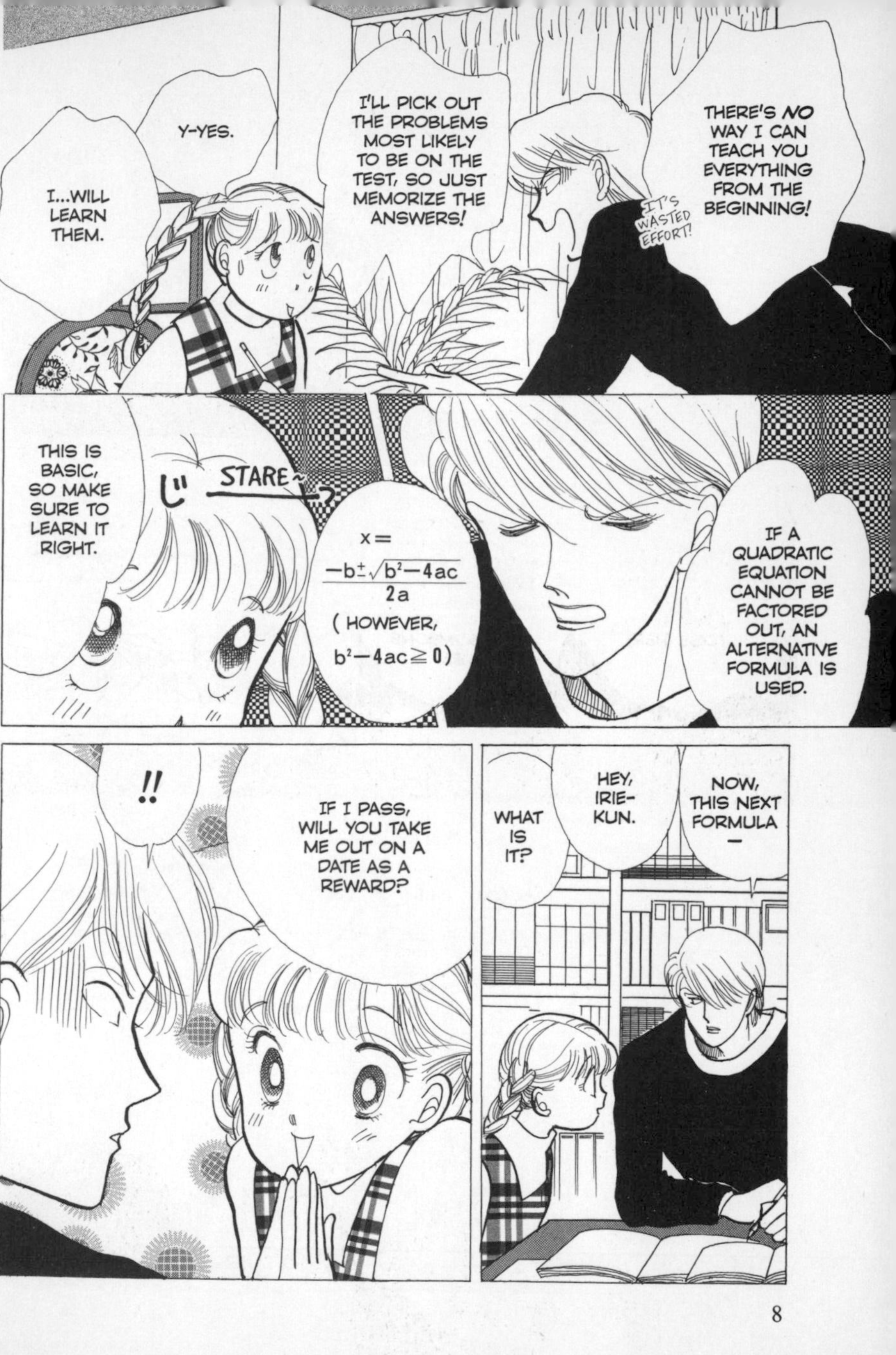
THERE'S NO WAY I CAN TEACH YOU EVERYTHING FROM THE BEGINNING!
IT'S WASTED EFFORT!
I'LL PICK OUT THE PROBLEMS MOST LIKELY TO BE ON THE TEST, SO JUST MEMORIZE THE ANSWERS!
Y-YES.
I...WILL LEARN THEM.
IF A QUADRATIC EQUATION CANNOT BE FACTORED OUT, AN ALTERNATIVE FORMULA IS USED.
$x = \frac{-b \pm \sqrt{b^2-4ac}}{2a}$ (HOWEVER, $b^2-4ac \geq 0$)
じ STARE~
THIS IS BASIC, SO MAKE SURE TO LEARN IT RIGHT.
NOW, THIS NEXT FORMULA—
HEY, IRIE-KUN.
WHAT IS IT?
IF I PASS, WILL YOU TAKE ME OUT ON A DATE AS A REWARD?
!!

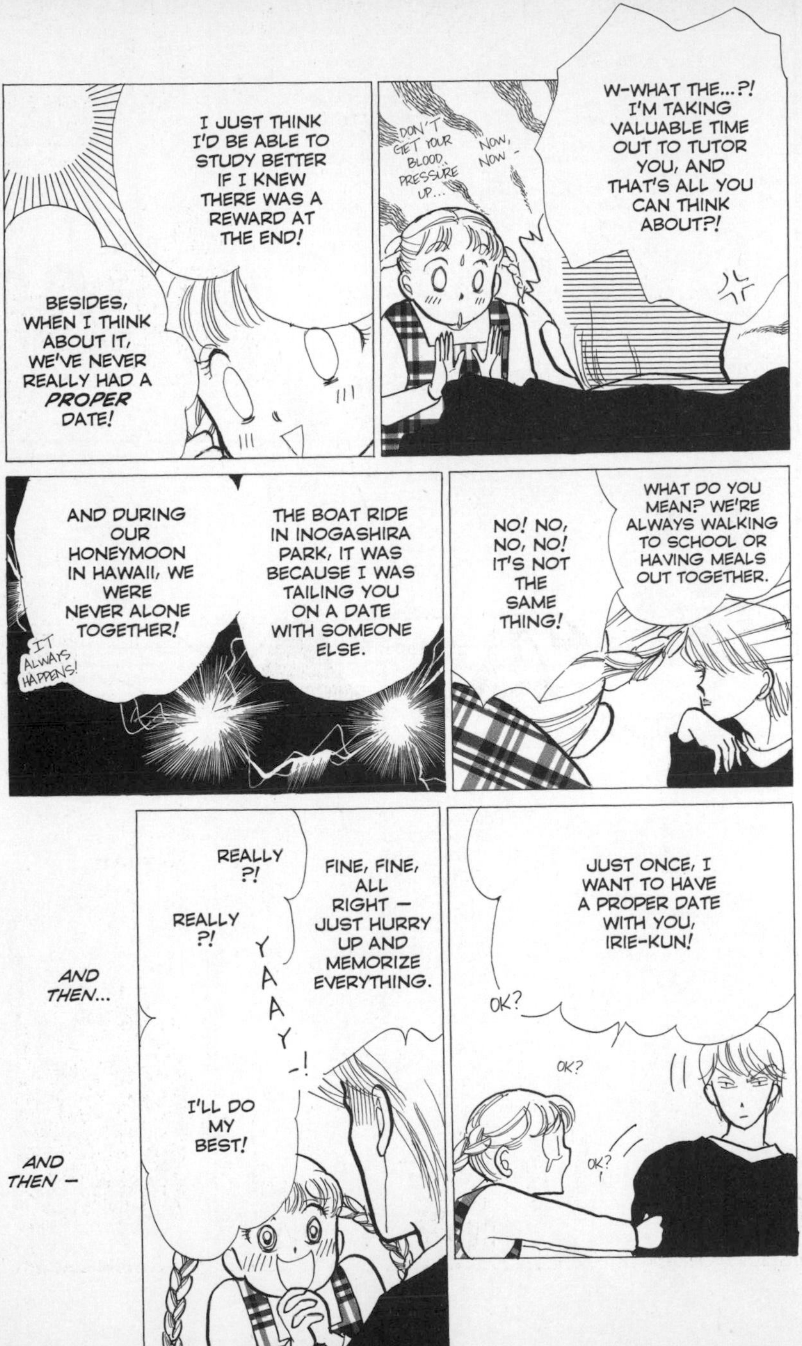
W-WHAT THE...?! I'M TAKING VALUABLE TIME OUT TO TUTOR YOU, AND THAT'S ALL YOU CAN THINK ABOUT?!
NOW, NOW –
DON'T GET YOUR BLOOD PRESSURE UP...
I JUST THINK I'D BE ABLE TO STUDY BETTER IF I KNEW THERE WAS A REWARD AT THE END!
BESIDES, WHEN I THINK ABOUT IT, WE'VE NEVER REALLY HAD A *PROPER* DATE!
WHAT DO YOU MEAN? WE'RE ALWAYS WALKING TO SCHOOL OR HAVING MEALS OUT TOGETHER.
NO! NO, NO, NO! IT'S NOT THE SAME THING!
THE BOAT RIDE IN INOGASHIRA PARK, IT WAS BECAUSE I WAS TAILING YOU ON A DATE WITH SOMEONE ELSE.
AND DURING OUR HONEYMOON IN HAWAII, WE WERE NEVER ALONE TOGETHER!
IT ALWAYS HAPPENS!
JUST ONCE, I WANT TO HAVE A PROPER DATE WITH YOU, IRIE-KUN!
OK?
OK?
OK?
FINE, FINE, ALL RIGHT – JUST HURRY UP AND MEMORIZE EVERYTHING.
REALLY ?!
REALLY ?!
YAAY–!
I'LL DO MY BEST!
AND THEN...
AND THEN –

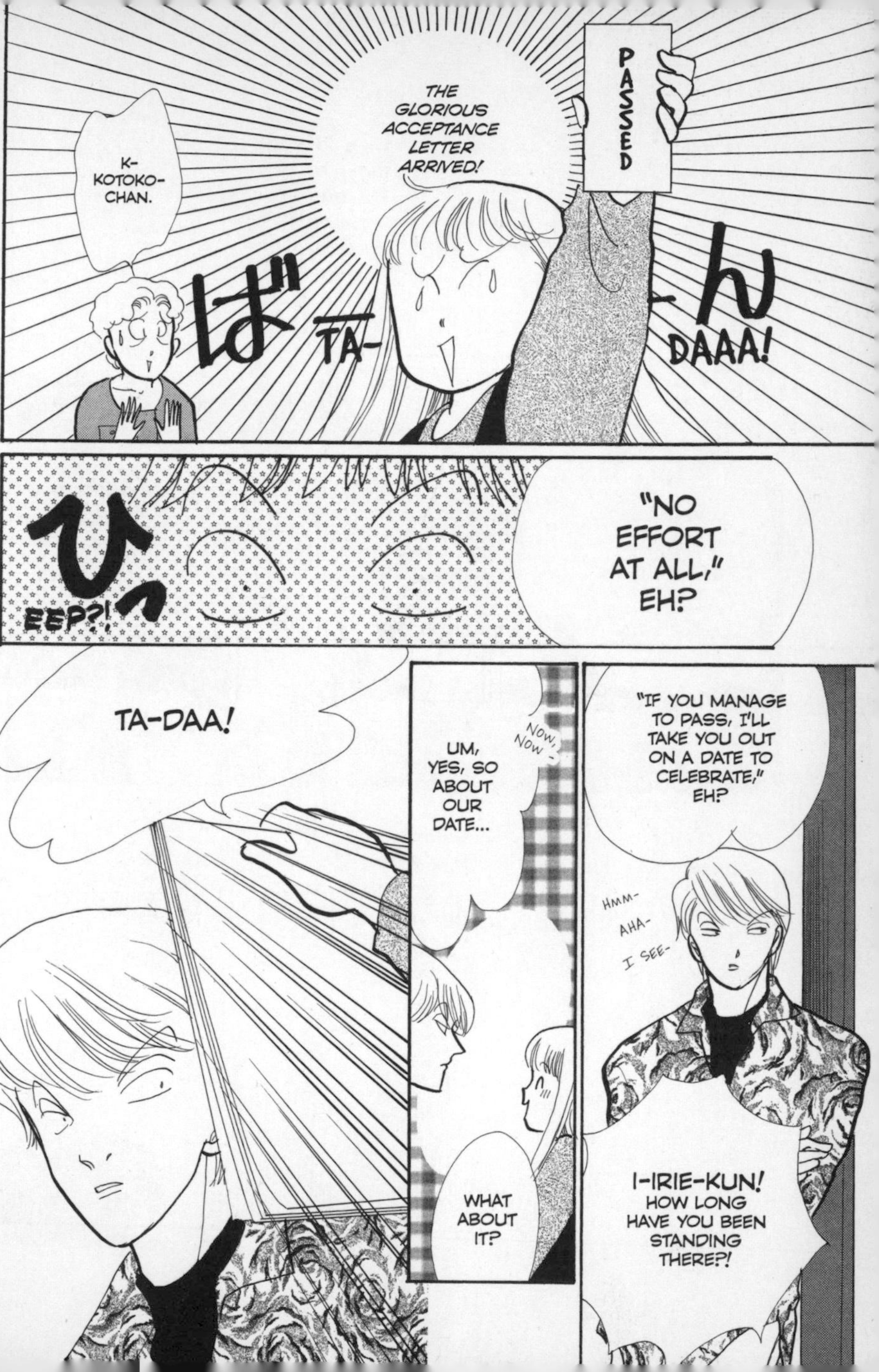
PASSED
THE GLORIOUS ACCEPTANCE LETTER ARRIVED!
ばん
TA-DAAA!
K-KOTOKO-CHAN.
"NO EFFORT AT ALL," EH?
ひっ
EEP?!
"IF YOU MANAGE TO PASS, I'LL TAKE YOU OUT ON A DATE TO CELEBRATE," EH?
HMM-AHA-I SEE-
I-IRIE-KUN! HOW LONG HAVE YOU BEEN STANDING THERE?!
NOW, NOW-
UM, YES, SO ABOUT OUR DATE...
WHAT ABOUT IT?
TA-DAA!

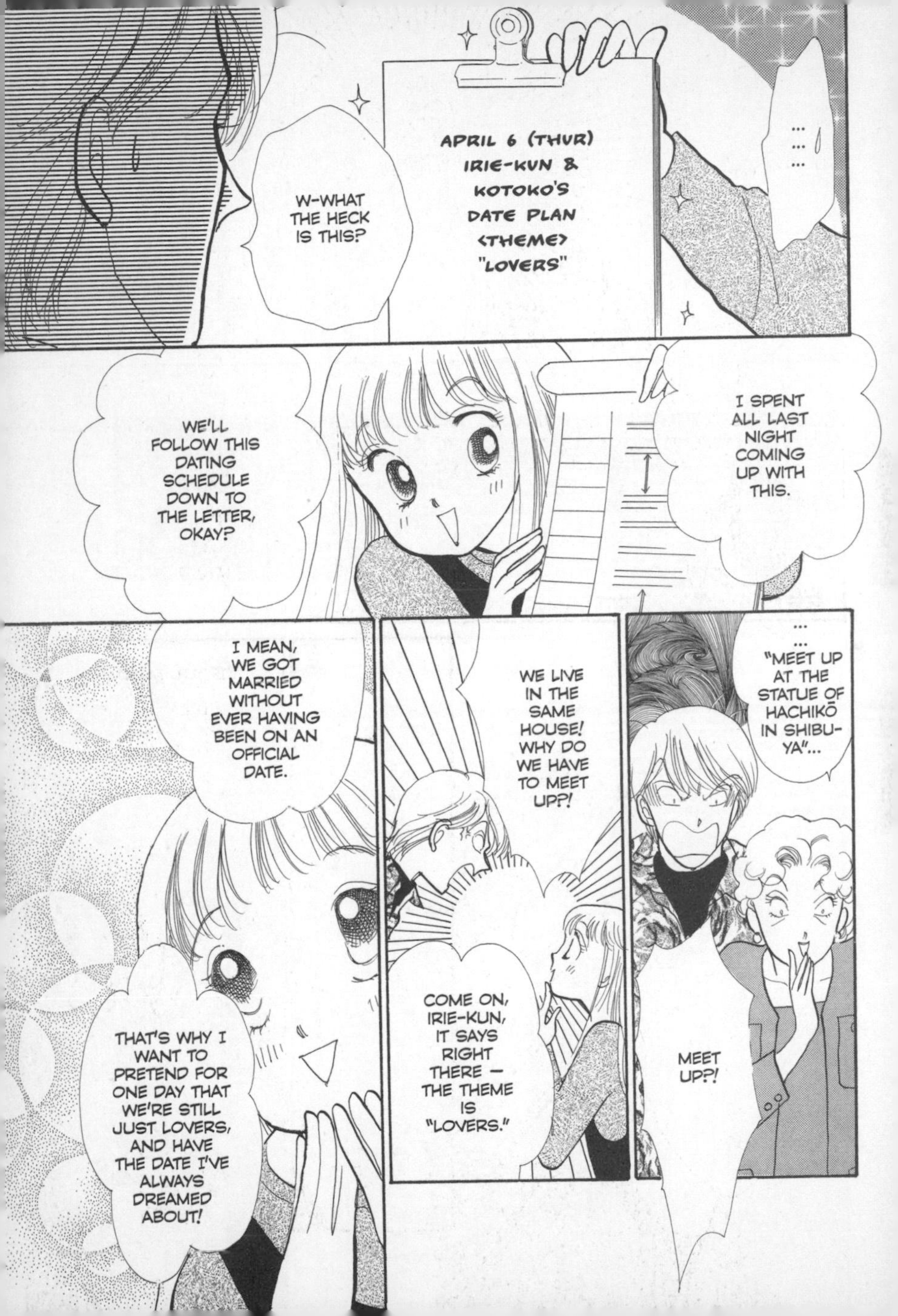
...
...
...
APRIL 6 (THUR)
IRIE-KUN &
KOTOKO'S
DATE PLAN
<THEME>
"LOVERS"
W-WHAT THE HECK IS THIS?
I SPENT ALL LAST NIGHT COMING UP WITH THIS.
WE'LL FOLLOW THIS DATING SCHEDULE DOWN TO THE LETTER, OKAY?
... ... "MEET UP AT THE STATUE OF HACHIKŌ IN SHIBU-YA"...
MEET UP?!
WE LIVE IN THE SAME HOUSE! WHY DO WE HAVE TO MEET UP?!
COME ON, IRIE-KUN, IT SAYS RIGHT THERE — THE THEME IS "LOVERS."
I MEAN, WE GOT MARRIED WITHOUT EVER HAVING BEEN ON AN OFFICIAL DATE.
THAT'S WHY I WANT TO PRETEND FOR ONE DAY THAT WE'RE STILL JUST LOVERS, AND HAVE THE DATE I'VE ALWAYS DREAMED ABOUT!

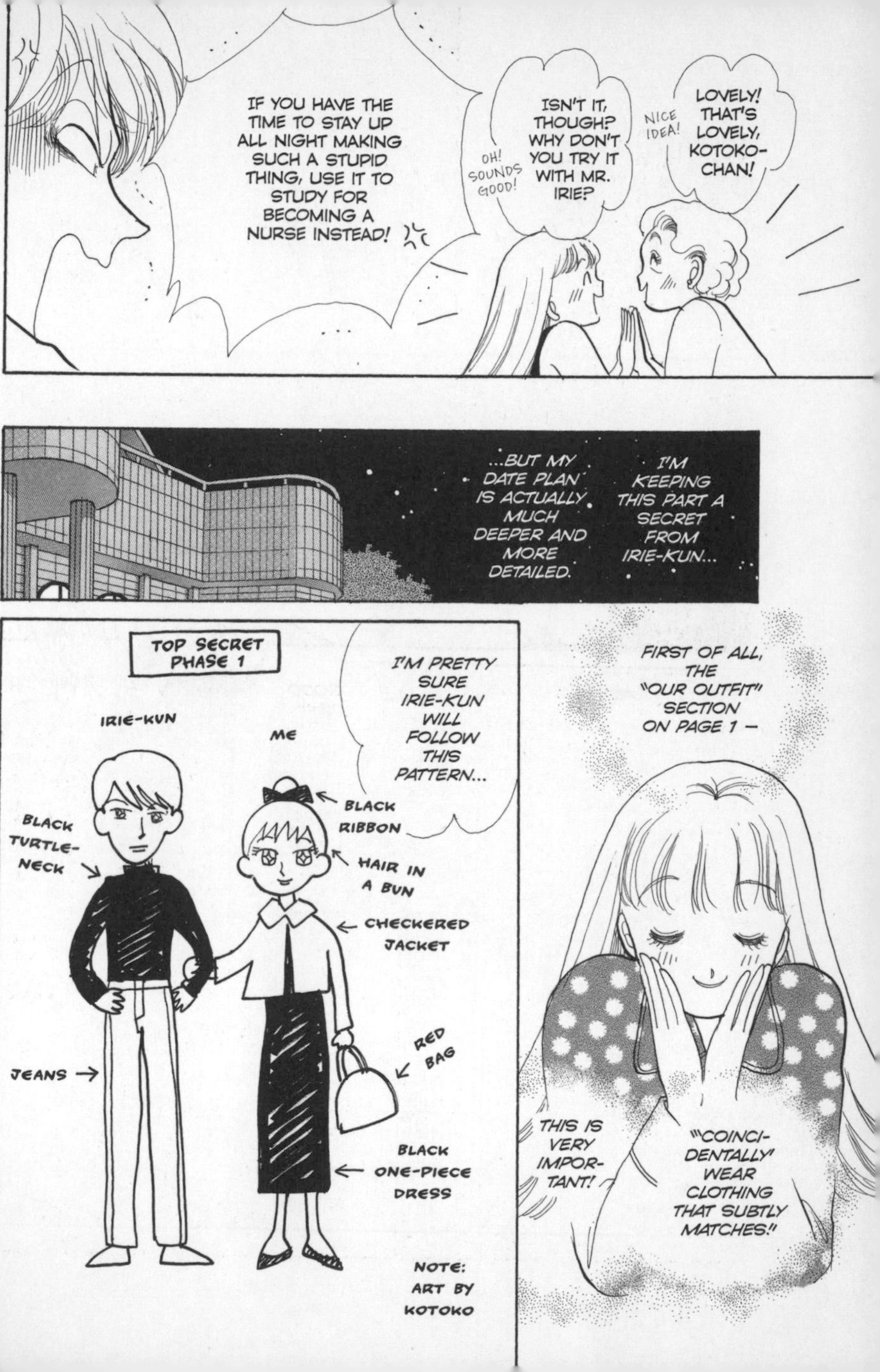

LOVELY! THAT'S LOVELY, KOTOKO-CHAN!
NICE IDEA!
ISN'T IT, THOUGH? WHY DON'T YOU TRY IT WITH MR. IRIE?
OH! SOUNDS GOOD!
IF YOU HAVE THE TIME TO STAY UP ALL NIGHT MAKING SUCH A STUPID THING, USE IT TO STUDY FOR BECOMING A NURSE INSTEAD!
I'M KEEPING THIS PART A SECRET FROM IRIE-KUN...
...BUT MY DATE PLAN IS ACTUALLY MUCH DEEPER AND MORE DETAILED.
FIRST OF ALL, THE "OUR OUTFIT" SECTION ON PAGE 1 —
"COINCIDENTALLY" WEAR CLOTHING THAT SUBTLY MATCHES!"
THIS IS VERY IMPORTANT!
I'M PRETTY SURE IRIE-KUN WILL FOLLOW THIS PATTERN...
TOP SECRET PHASE 1
IRIE-KUN
ME
BLACK RIBBON
HAIR IN A BUN
CHECKERED JACKET
BLACK TURTLE-NECK
RED BAG
JEANS
BLACK ONE-PIECE DRESS
NOTE: ART BY KOTOKO

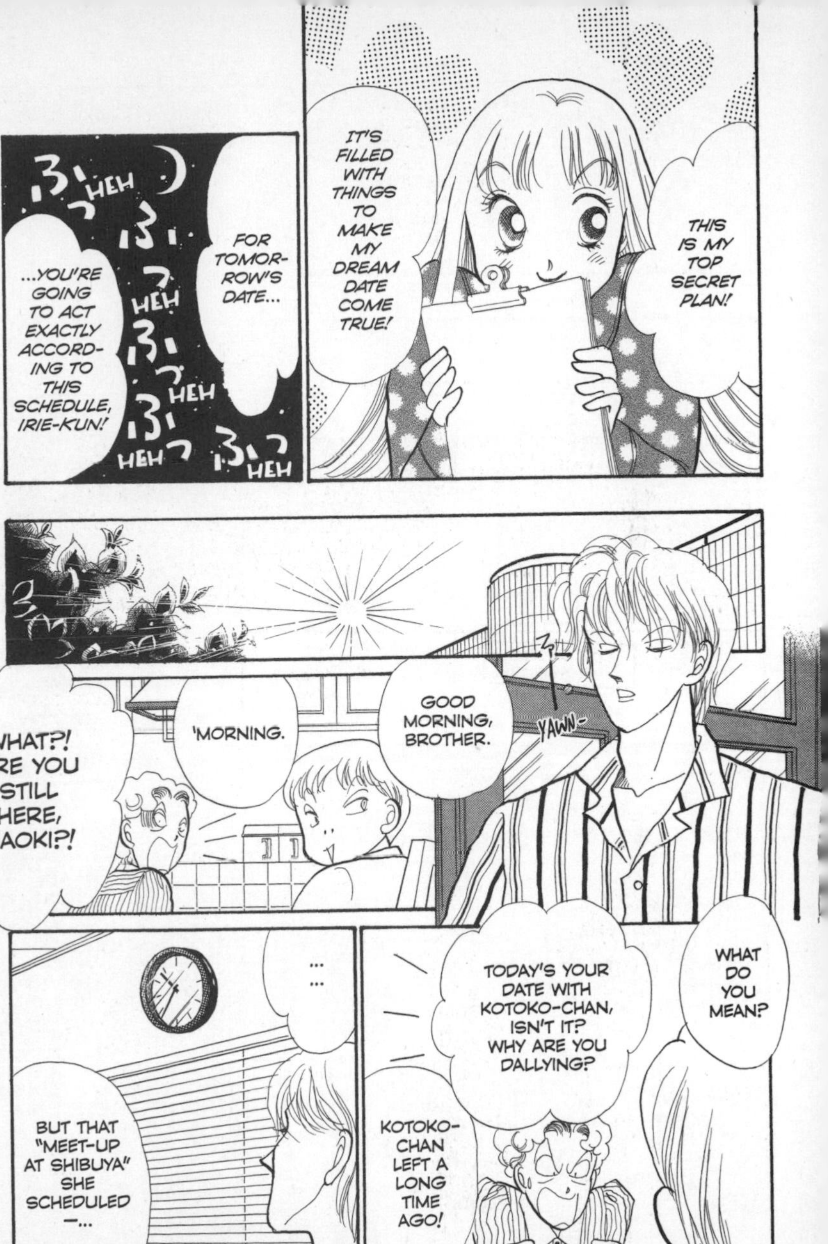
THIS IS MY TOP SECRET PLAN!
IT'S FILLED WITH THINGS TO MAKE MY DREAM DATE COME TRUE!
FOR TOMORROW'S DATE...
...YOU'RE GOING TO ACT EXACTLY ACCORDING TO THIS SCHEDULE, IRIE-KUN!
HEH HEH HEH HEH HEH
YAWN-
GOOD MORNING, BROTHER.
'MORNING.
WHAT?! ARE YOU STILL HERE, NAOKI?!
WHAT DO YOU MEAN?
TODAY'S YOUR DATE WITH KOTOKO-CHAN, ISN'T IT? WHY ARE YOU DALLYING?
KOTOKO-CHAN LEFT A LONG TIME AGO!
... ...
BUT THAT "MEET-UP AT SHIBUYA" SHE SCHEDULED —...

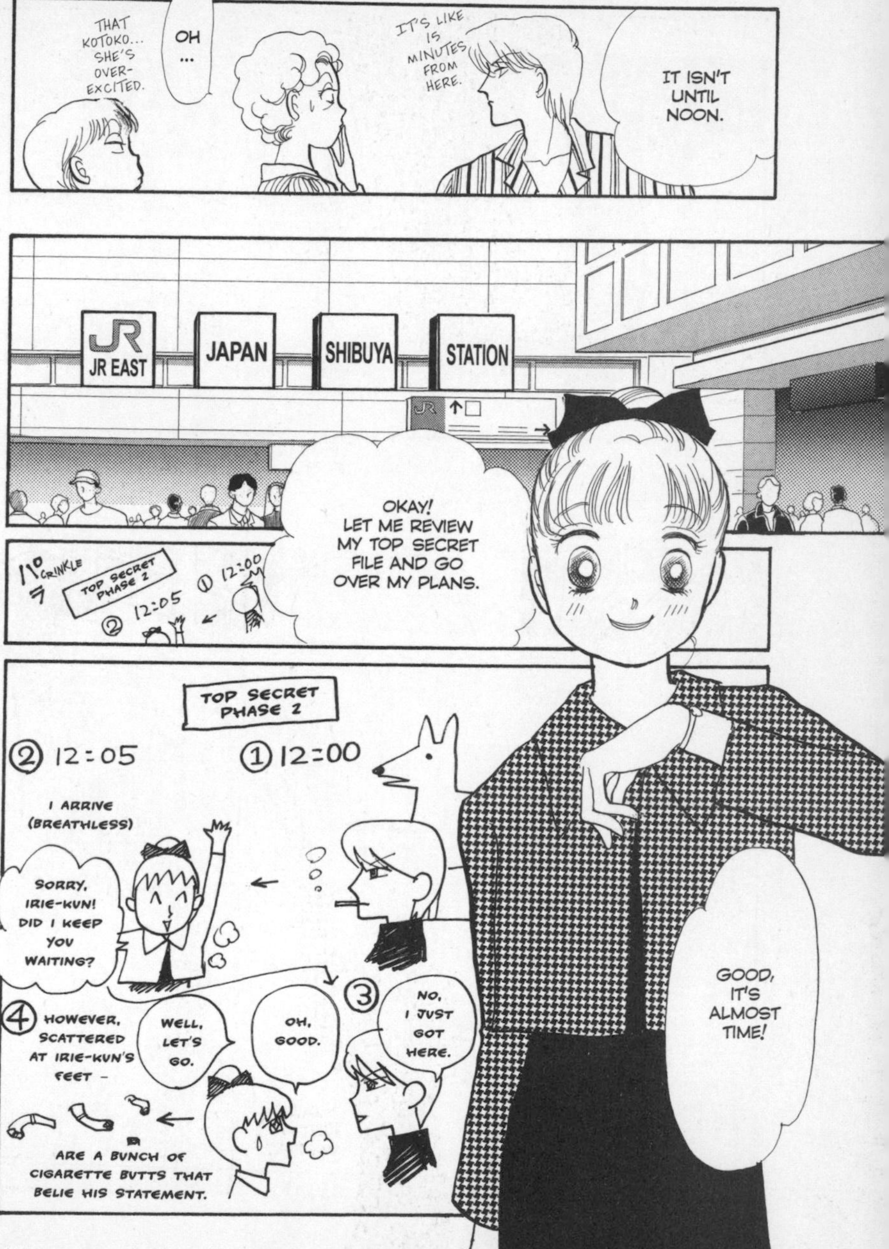
IT ISN'T UNTIL NOON.
IT'S LIKE 15 MINUTES FROM HERE.
OH ...
THAT KOTOKO... SHE'S OVER-EXCITED.
JR
JR EAST
JAPAN
SHIBUYA
STATION
OKAY! LET ME REVIEW MY TOP SECRET FILE AND GO OVER MY PLANS.
CRINKLE
TOP SECRET PHASE 2
① 12:00
② 12:05
GOOD, IT'S ALMOST TIME!
TOP SECRET PHASE 2
① 12:00
② 12:05
I ARRIVE (BREATHLESS)
SORRY, IRIE-KUN! DID I KEEP YOU WAITING?
③
NO, I JUST GOT HERE.
OH, GOOD.
WELL, LET'S GO.
④ HOWEVER, SCATTERED AT IRIE-KUN'S FEET -
ARE A BUNCH OF CIGARETTE BUTTS THAT BELIE HIS STATEMENT.

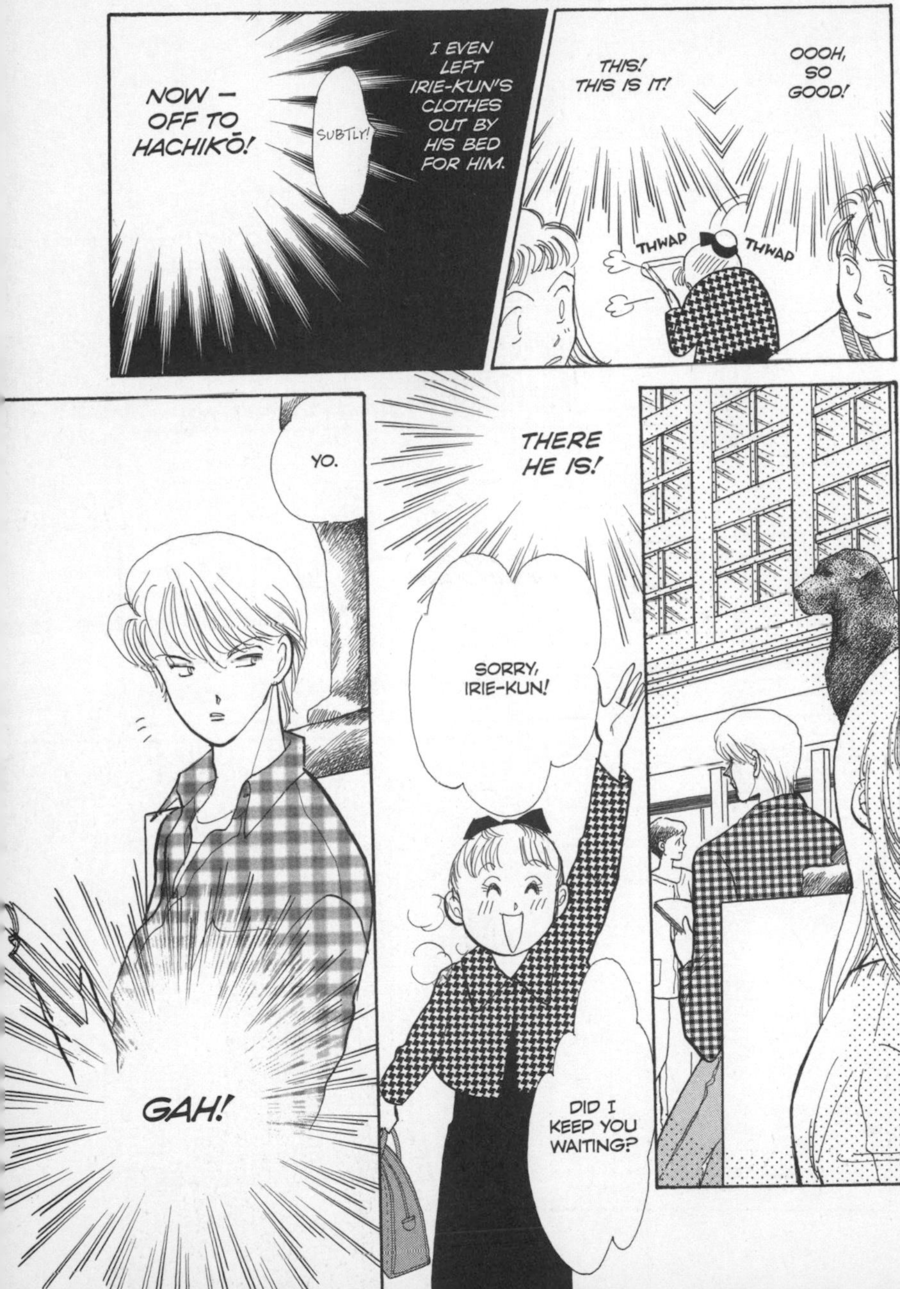
OOOH, SO GOOD!
THIS! THIS IS IT!
THWAP
THWAP
I EVEN LEFT IRIE-KUN'S CLOTHES OUT BY HIS BED FOR HIM.
SUBTLY!
NOW – OFF TO HACHIKŌ!
THERE HE IS!
SORRY, IRIE-KUN!
DID I KEEP YOU WAITING?
YO.
GAH!

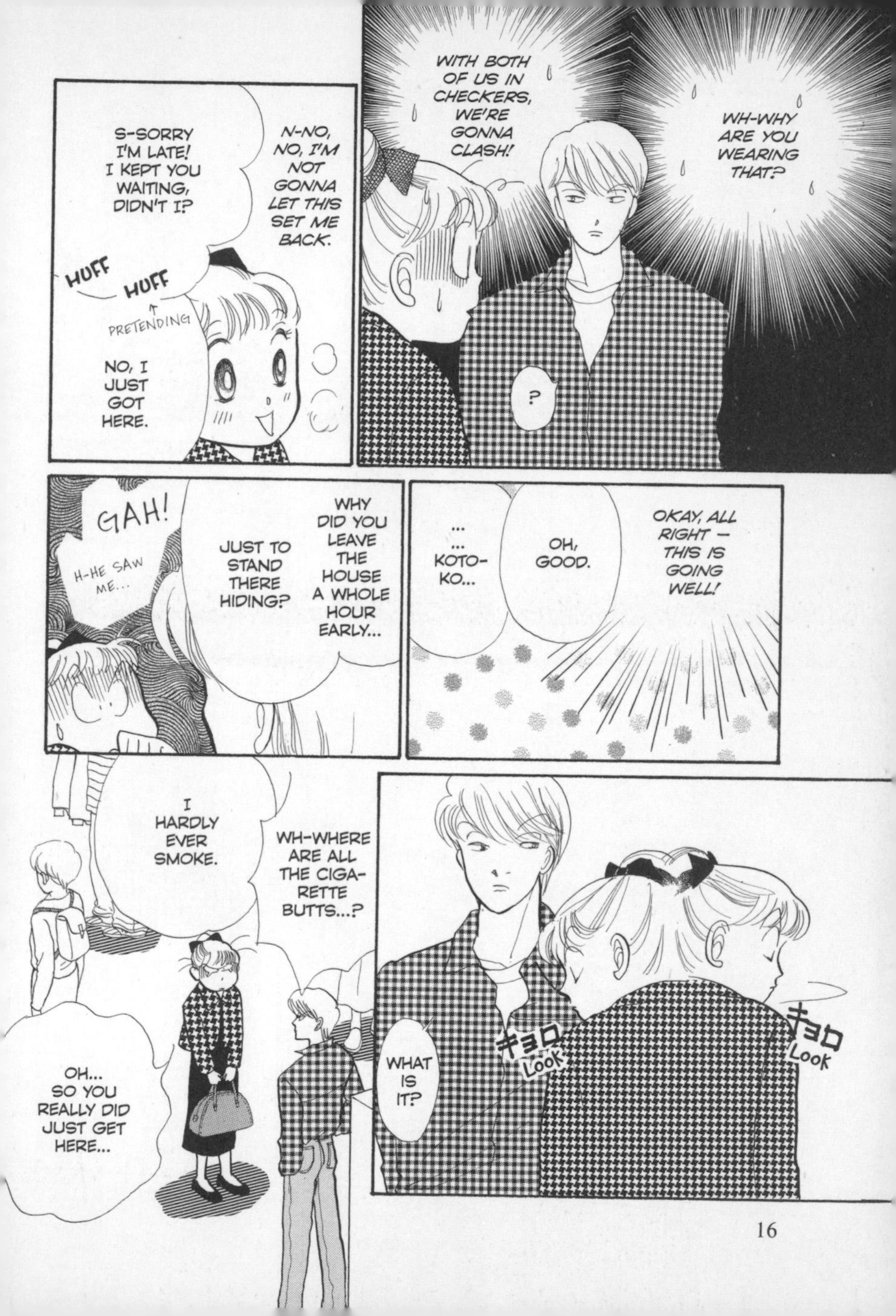
WH-WHY ARE YOU WEARING THAT?
WITH BOTH OF US IN CHECKERS, WE'RE GONNA CLASH!
?
N-NO, NO, I'M NOT GONNA LET THIS SET ME BACK.
S-SORRY I'M LATE! I KEPT YOU WAITING, DIDN'T I?
HUFF HUFF
PRETENDING
NO, I JUST GOT HERE.
OKAY, ALL RIGHT — THIS IS GOING WELL!
OH, GOOD.
... ... KOTO-KO...
WHY DID YOU LEAVE THE HOUSE A WHOLE HOUR EARLY...
JUST TO STAND THERE HIDING?
GAH!
H-HE SAW ME...
キョロ Look
キョロ Look
WHAT IS IT?
WH-WHERE ARE ALL THE CIGA-RETTE BUTTS...?
I HARDLY EVER SMOKE.
OH... SO YOU REALLY DID JUST GET HERE...

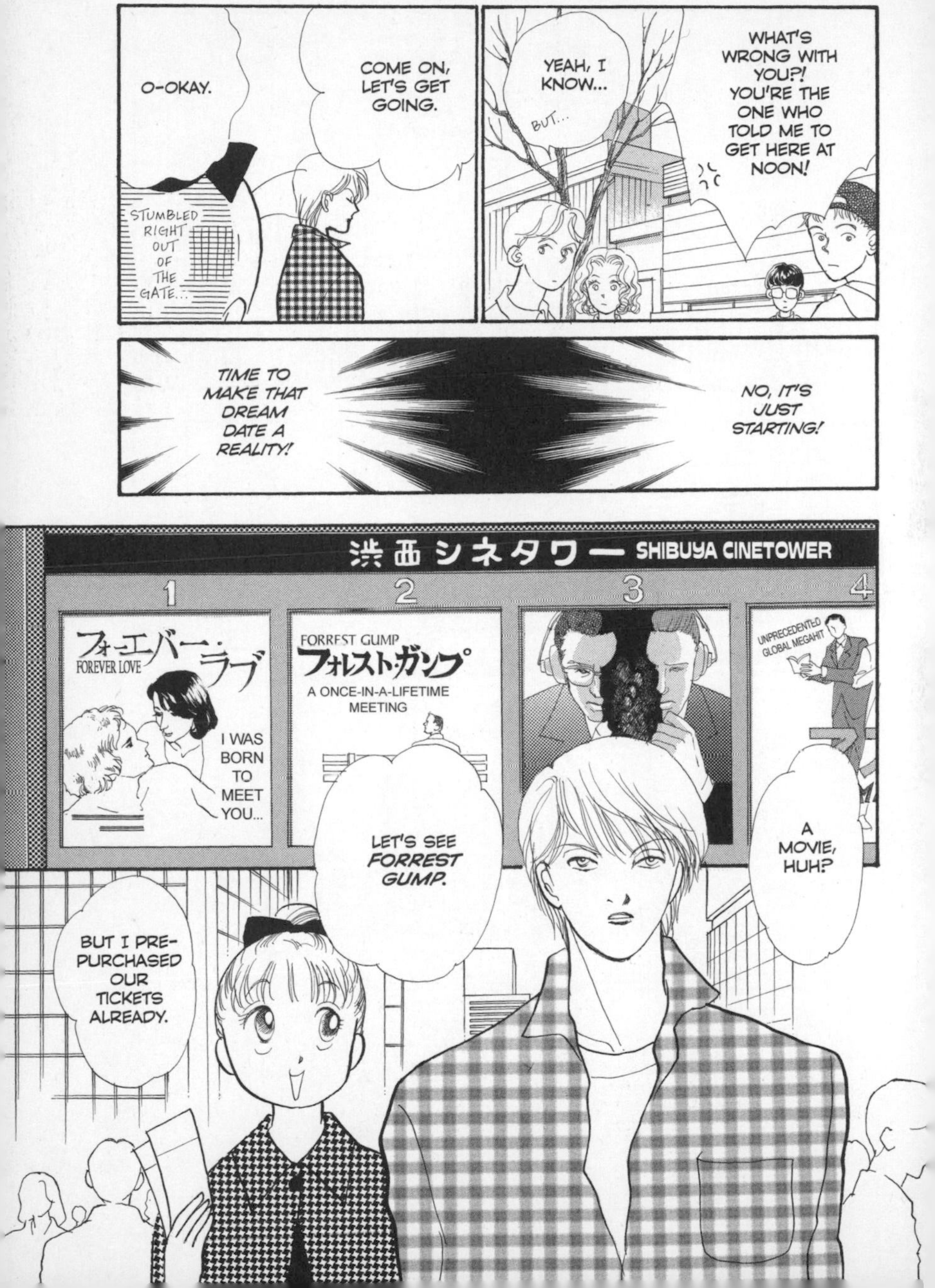

WHAT'S WRONG WITH YOU?! YOU'RE THE ONE WHO TOLD ME TO GET HERE AT NOON!
YEAH, I KNOW...
BUT...
COME ON, LET'S GET GOING.
O-OKAY.
STUMBLED RIGHT OUT OF THE GATE...
NO, IT'S JUST STARTING!
TIME TO MAKE THAT DREAM DATE A REALITY!
渋西シネタワー SHIBUYA CINETOWER
1
2
3
4
フォーエバー・ラブ
FOREVER LOVE
I WAS BORN TO MEET YOU...
FORREST GUMP
フォレスト・ガンプ
A ONCE-IN-A-LIFETIME MEETING
UNPRECEDENTED GLOBAL MEGAHIT
A MOVIE, HUH?
LET'S SEE FORREST GUMP.
BUT I PRE-PURCHASED OUR TICKETS ALREADY.

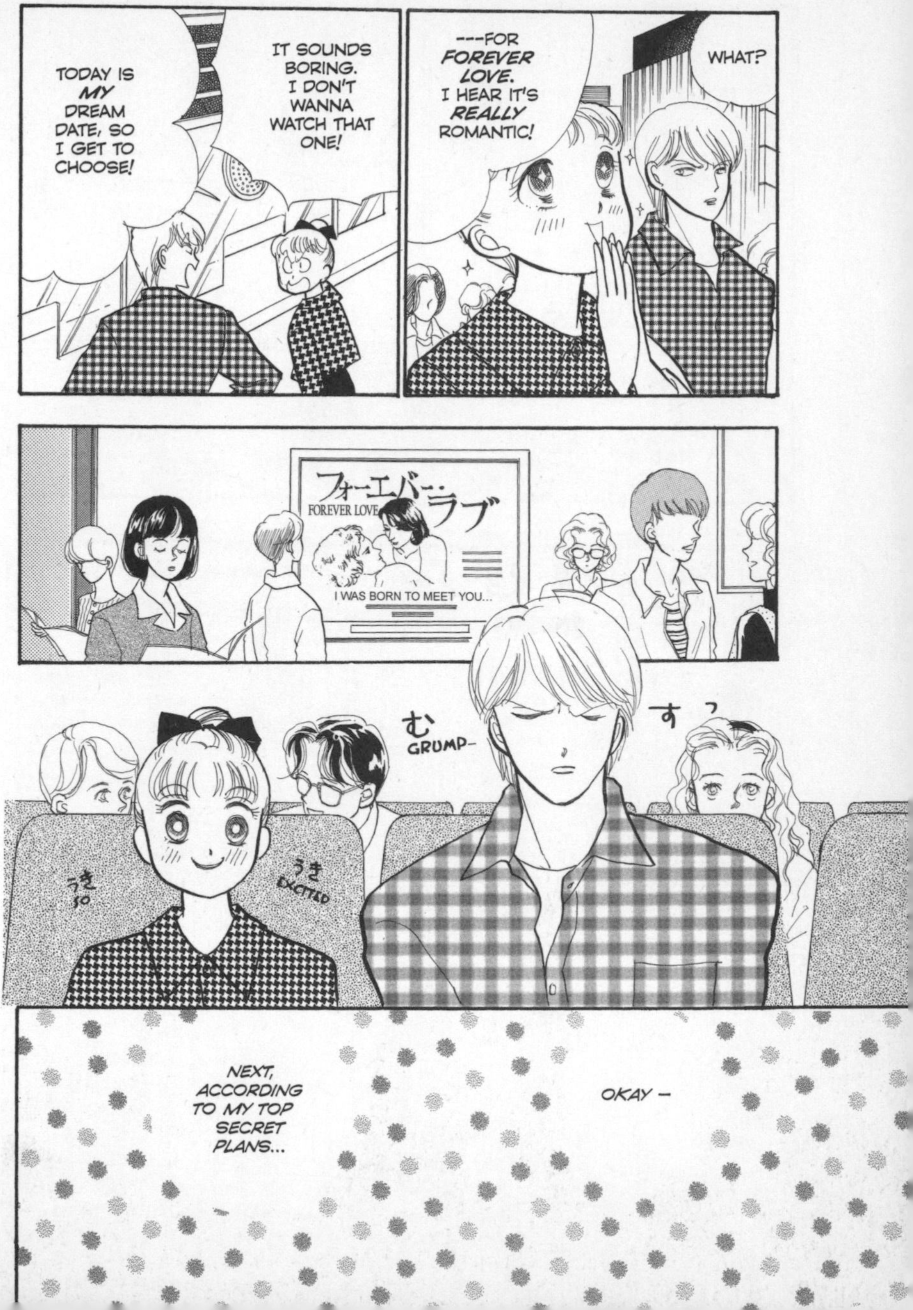
WHAT?
---FOR FOREVER LOVE. I HEAR IT'S REALLY ROMANTIC!
IT SOUNDS BORING. I DON'T WANNA WATCH THAT ONE!
TODAY IS MY DREAM DATE, SO I GET TO CHOOSE!
フォーエバー・ラブ
FOREVER LOVE
I WAS BORN TO MEET YOU...
すっ
む GRUMP-
うき EXCITED
うき SO
OKAY –
NEXT, ACCORDING TO MY TOP SECRET PLANS...

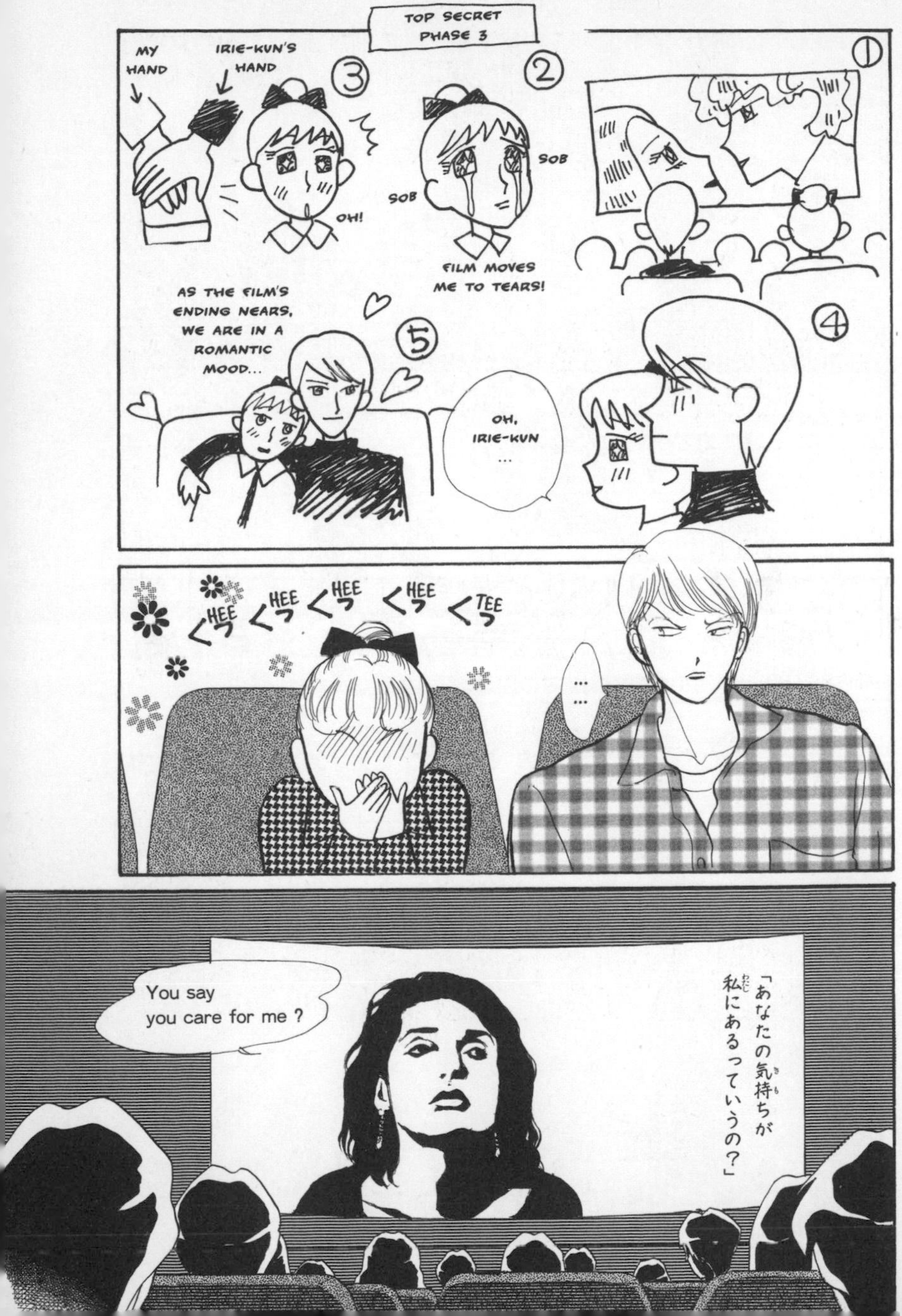
TOP SECRET PHASE 3
SOB
SOB
FILM MOVES ME TO TEARS!
MY HAND
IRIE-KUN'S HAND
OH!
OH, IRIE-KUN …
AS THE FILM'S ENDING NEARS, WE ARE IN A ROMANTIC MOOD…
……
くっ TEE
くっ HEE
くっ HEE
くっ HEE
くっ HEE
「あなたの気持ちが私にあるっていうの?」
You say you care for me ?

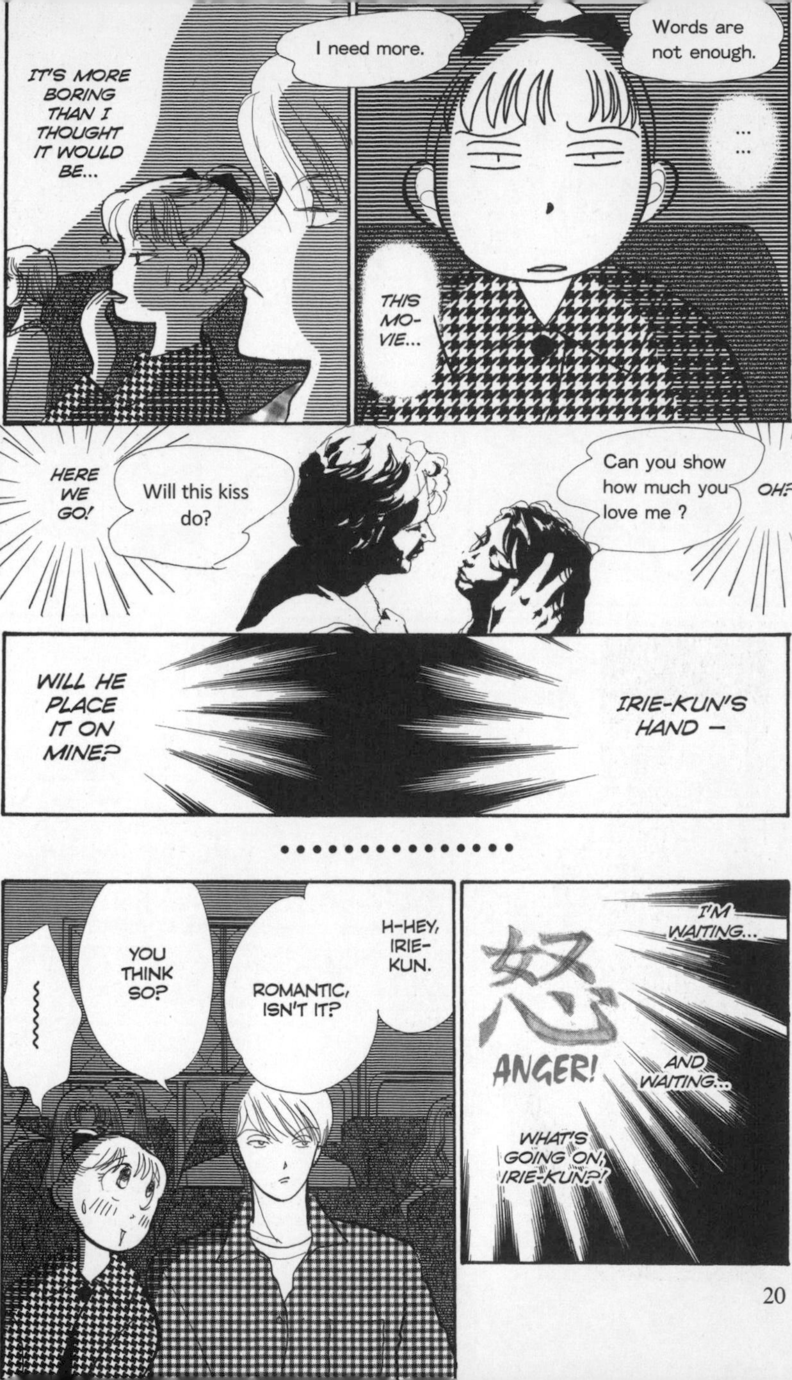

Words are not enough.
...
...
THIS MOVIE...
I need more.
IT'S MORE BORING THAN I THOUGHT IT WOULD BE...
OH?
Can you show how much you love me ?
Will this kiss do?
HERE WE GO!
IRIE-KUN'S HAND —
WILL HE PLACE IT ON MINE?
I'M WAITING...
怒
ANGER!
AND WAITING...
WHAT'S GOING ON, IRIE-KUN?!
H-HEY, IRIE-KUN.
ROMANTIC, ISN'T IT?
YOU THINK SO?

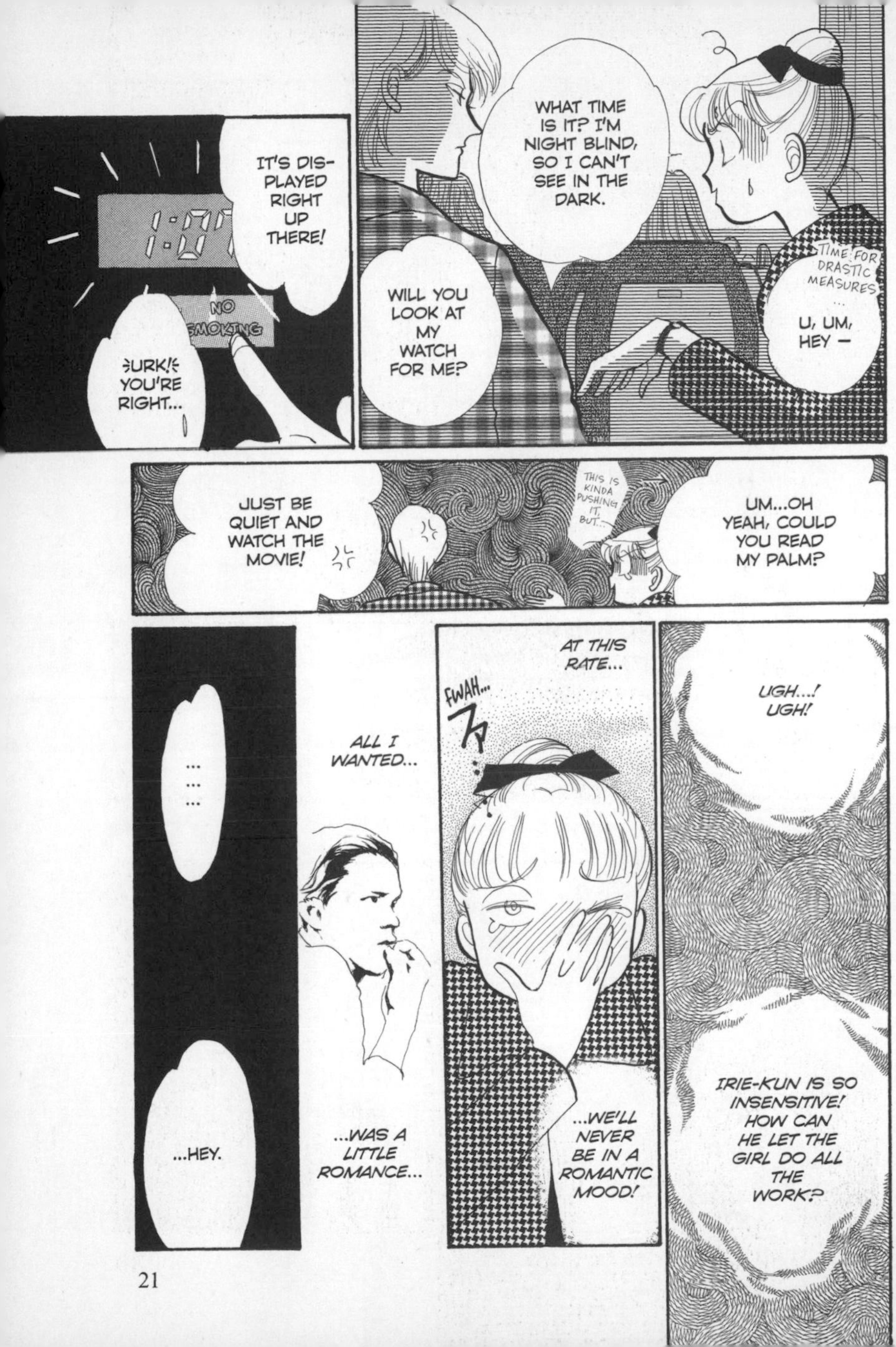
TIME FOR DRASTIC MEASURES...
U, UM, HEY —
WHAT TIME IS IT? I'M NIGHT BLIND, SO I CAN'T SEE IN THE DARK.
WILL YOU LOOK AT MY WATCH FOR ME?
IT'S DIS-PLAYED RIGHT UP THERE!
NO SMOKING
URK! YOU'RE RIGHT...
THIS IS KINDA PUSHING IT, BUT...
UM...OH YEAH, COULD YOU READ MY PALM?
JUST BE QUIET AND WATCH THE MOVIE!
UGH...! UGH!
IRIE-KUN IS SO INSENSITIVE! HOW CAN HE LET THE GIRL DO ALL THE WORK?
AT THIS RATE...
FWAH...
...WE'LL NEVER BE IN A ROMANTIC MOOD!
ALL I WANTED...
...WAS A LITTLE ROMANCE...
......
...HEY.

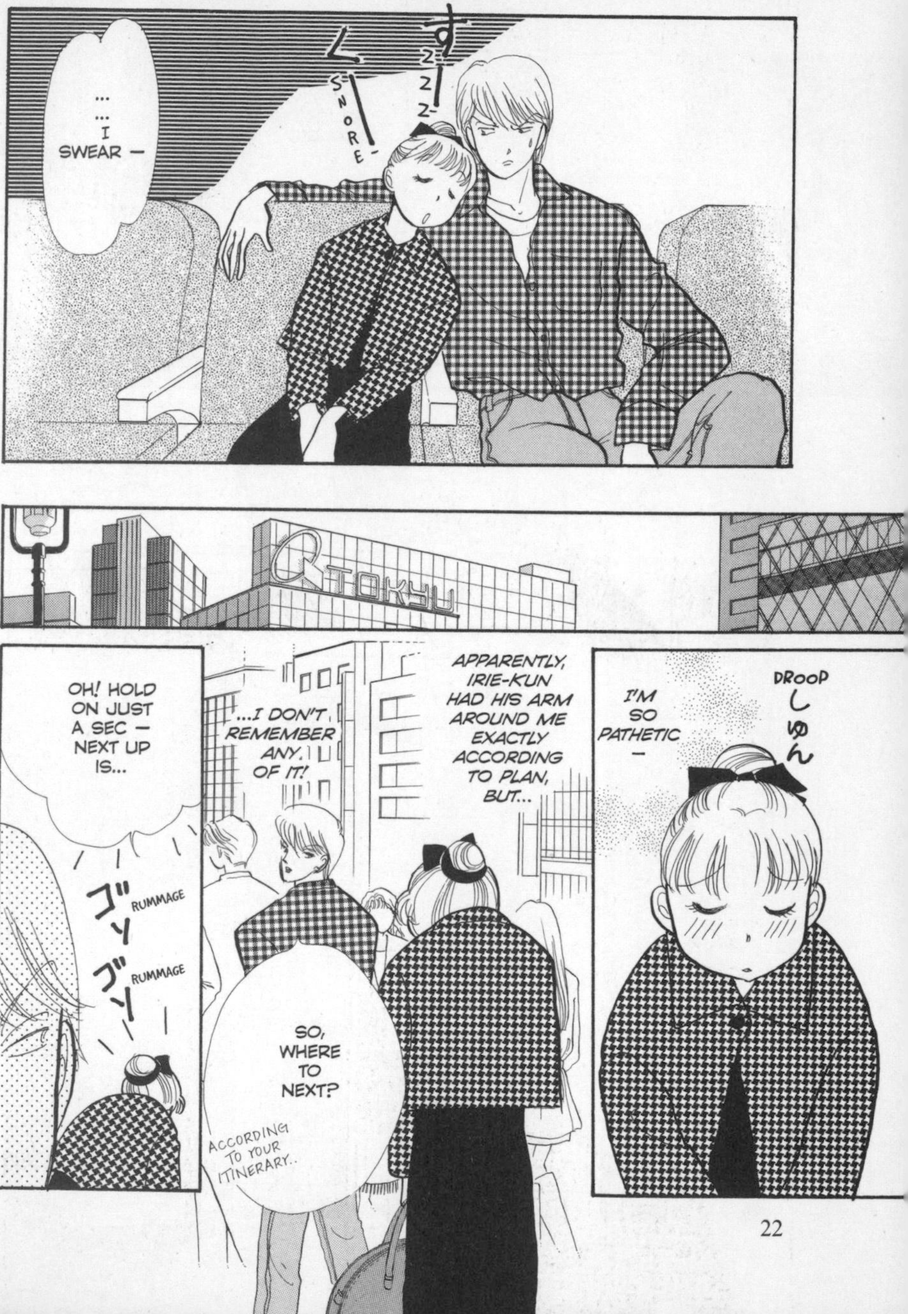
すー
ZZZ-
く
SNORE-
... ... I SWEAR —
TOKYU
DROOP
しゅん
I'M SO PATHETIC —
APPARENTLY, IRIE-KUN HAD HIS ARM AROUND ME EXACTLY ACCORDING TO PLAN, BUT...
...I DON'T REMEMBER ANY OF IT!
OH! HOLD ON JUST A SEC — NEXT UP IS...
ゴソ
RUMMAGE
ゴソ
RUMMAGE
SO, WHERE TO NEXT?
ACCORDING TO YOUR ITINERARY..

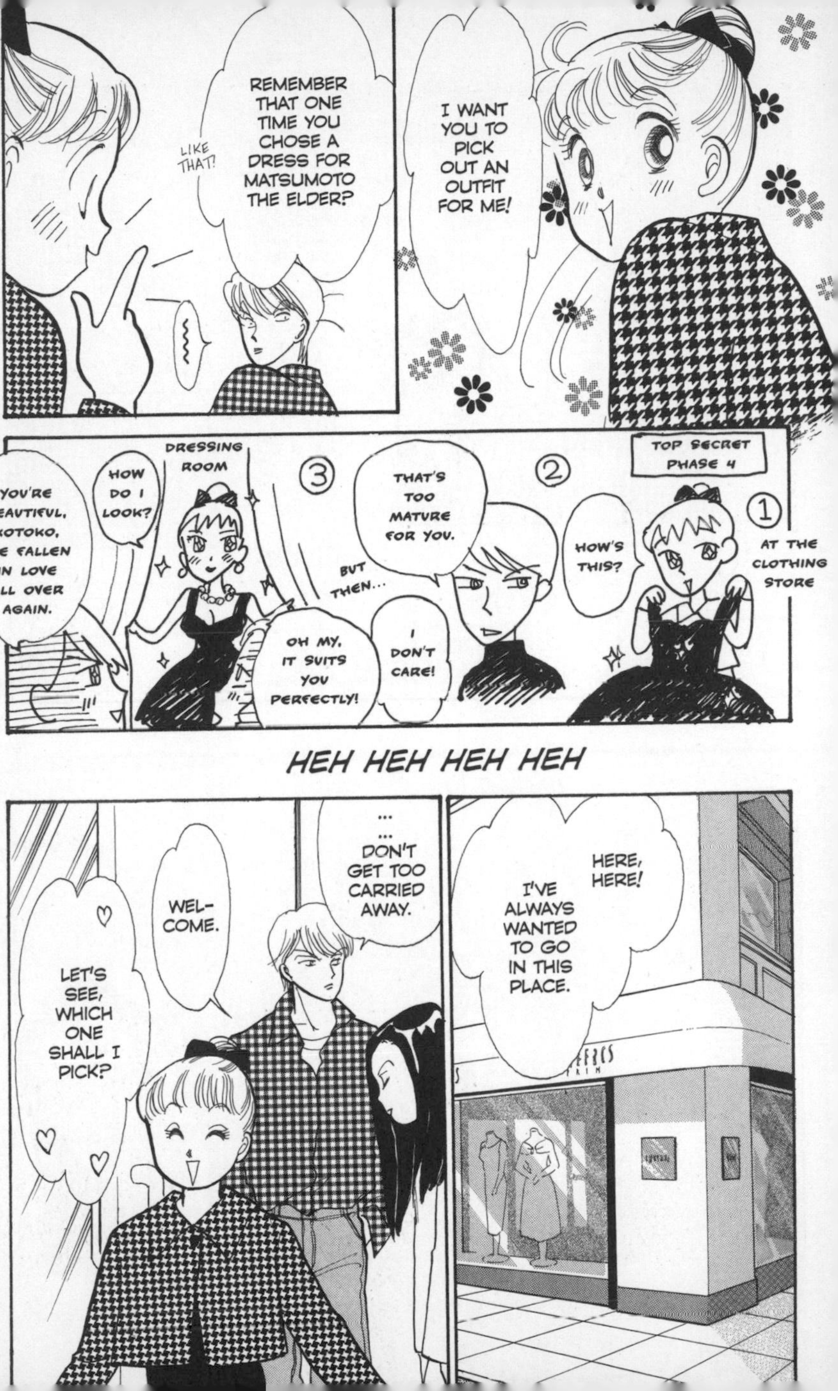
I WANT YOU TO PICK OUT AN OUTFIT FOR ME!
REMEMBER THAT ONE TIME YOU CHOSE A DRESS FOR MATSUMOTO THE ELDER?
LIKE THAT!
TOP SECRET PHASE 4
①
AT THE CLOTHING STORE
HOW'S THIS?
②
THAT'S TOO MATURE FOR YOU.
I DON'T CARE!
BUT THEN...
③
DRESSING ROOM
HOW DO I LOOK?
OH MY, IT SUITS YOU PERFECTLY!
YOU'RE BEAUTIFUL, KOTOKO, I'VE FALLEN IN LOVE ALL OVER AGAIN.
HEH HEH HEH HEH
HERE, HERE!
I'VE ALWAYS WANTED TO GO IN THIS PLACE.
... ... DON'T GET TOO CARRIED AWAY.
WEL-COME.
LET'S SEE, WHICH ONE SHALL I PICK?

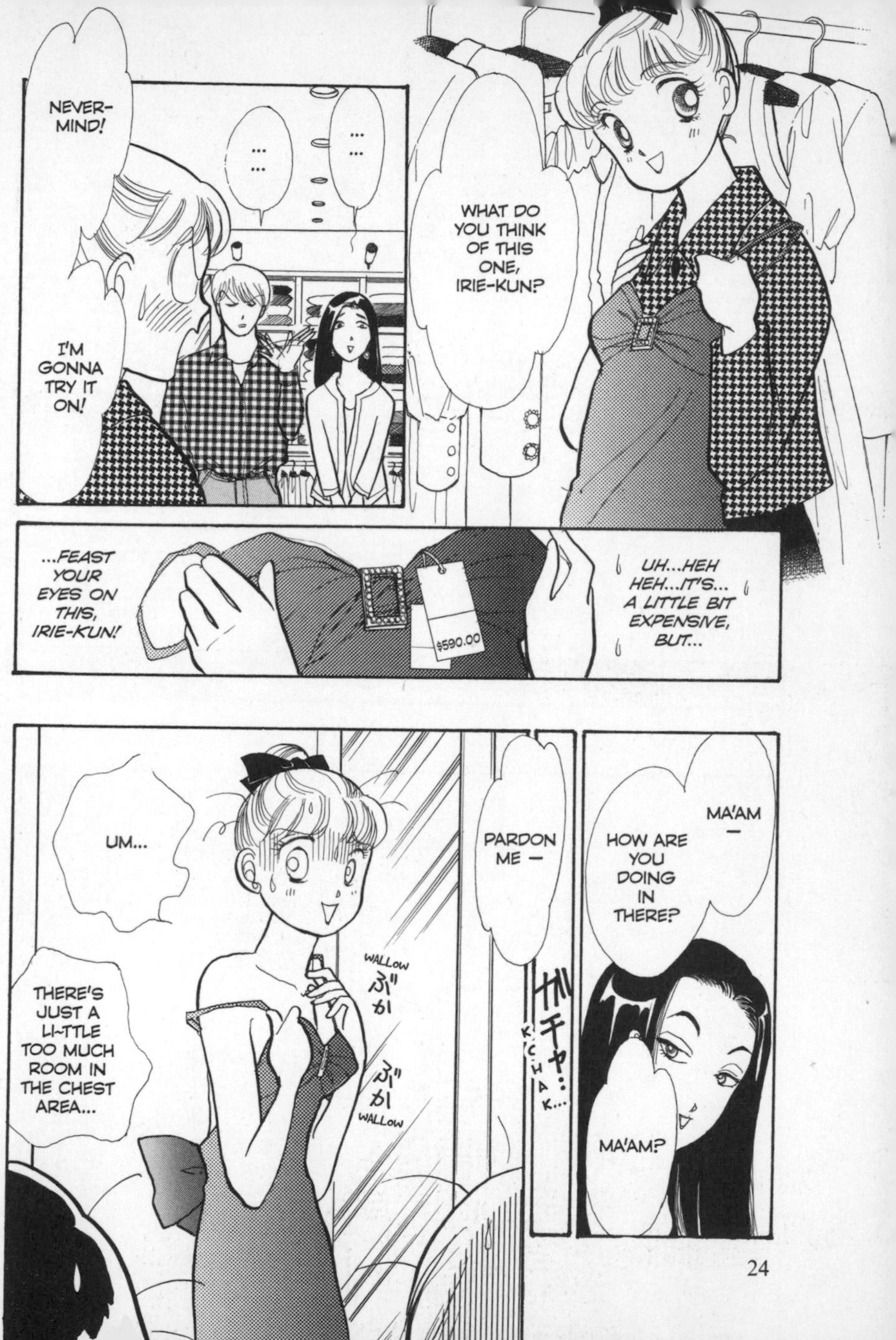
WHAT DO YOU THINK OF THIS ONE, IRIE-KUN?
...
...
...
...
...
NEVER-MIND!
I'M GONNA TRY IT ON!
UH...HEH HEH...IT'S... A LITTLE BIT EXPENSIVE, BUT...
$590.00
...FEAST YOUR EYES ON THIS, IRIE-KUN!
MA'AM —
HOW ARE YOU DOING IN THERE?
ガチャ…
KCHAK...
MA'AM?
PARDON ME —
UM...
ぶか WALLOW
ぶか WALLOW
THERE'S JUST A LI~TTLE TOO MUCH ROOM IN THE CHEST AREA...

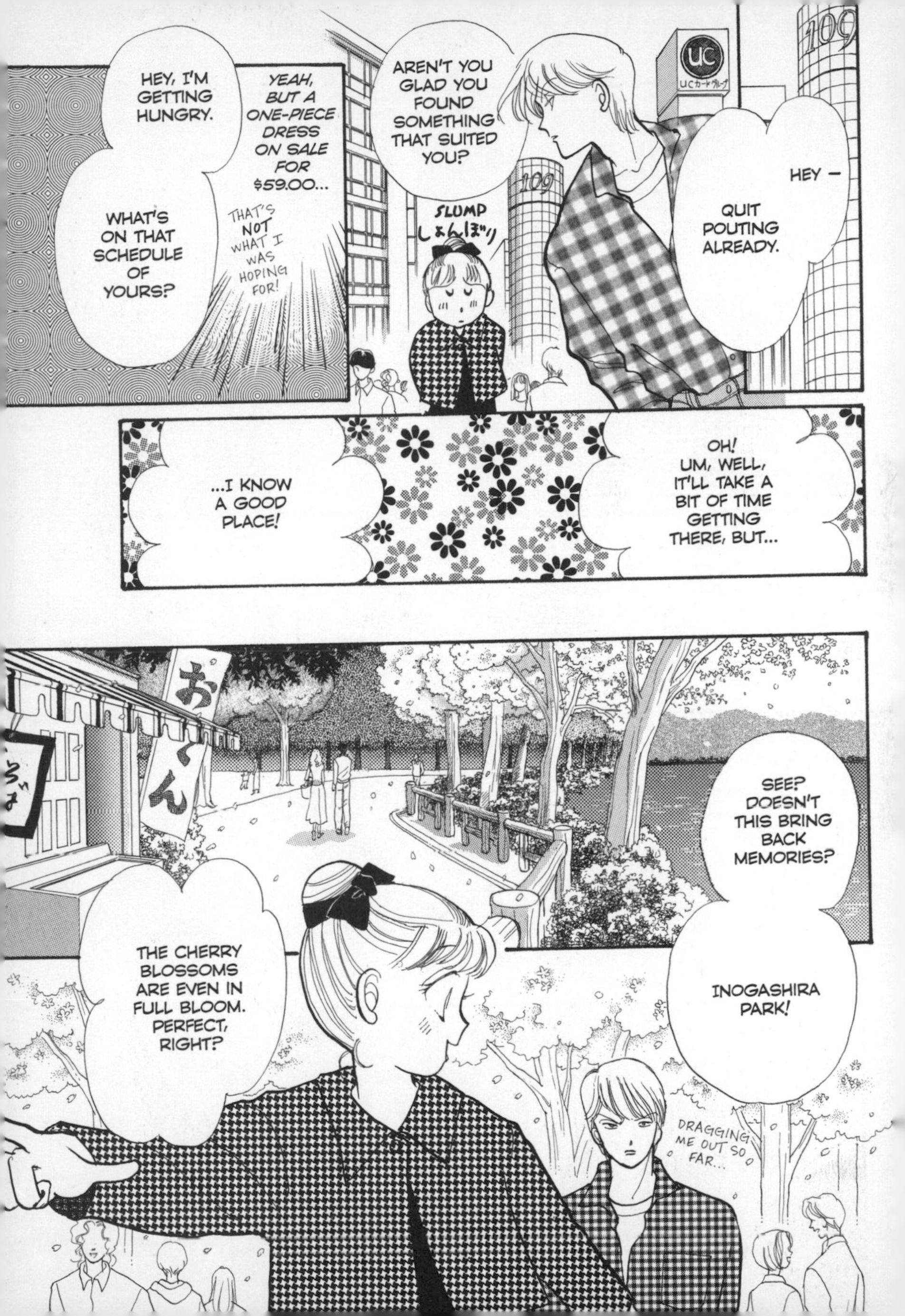

HEY — QUIT POUTING ALREADY.
AREN'T YOU GLAD YOU FOUND SOMETHING THAT SUITED YOU?
SLUMP
しょんぼり
YEAH, BUT A ONE-PIECE DRESS ON SALE FOR $59.00...
THAT'S NOT WHAT I WAS HOPING FOR!
HEY, I'M GETTING HUNGRY.
WHAT'S ON THAT SCHEDULE OF YOURS?
OH! UM, WELL, IT'LL TAKE A BIT OF TIME GETTING THERE, BUT...
...I KNOW A GOOD PLACE!
SEE? DOESN'T THIS BRING BACK MEMORIES?
INOGASHIRA PARK!
THE CHERRY BLOSSOMS ARE EVEN IN FULL BLOOM. PERFECT, RIGHT?
DRAGGING ME OUT SO FAR...

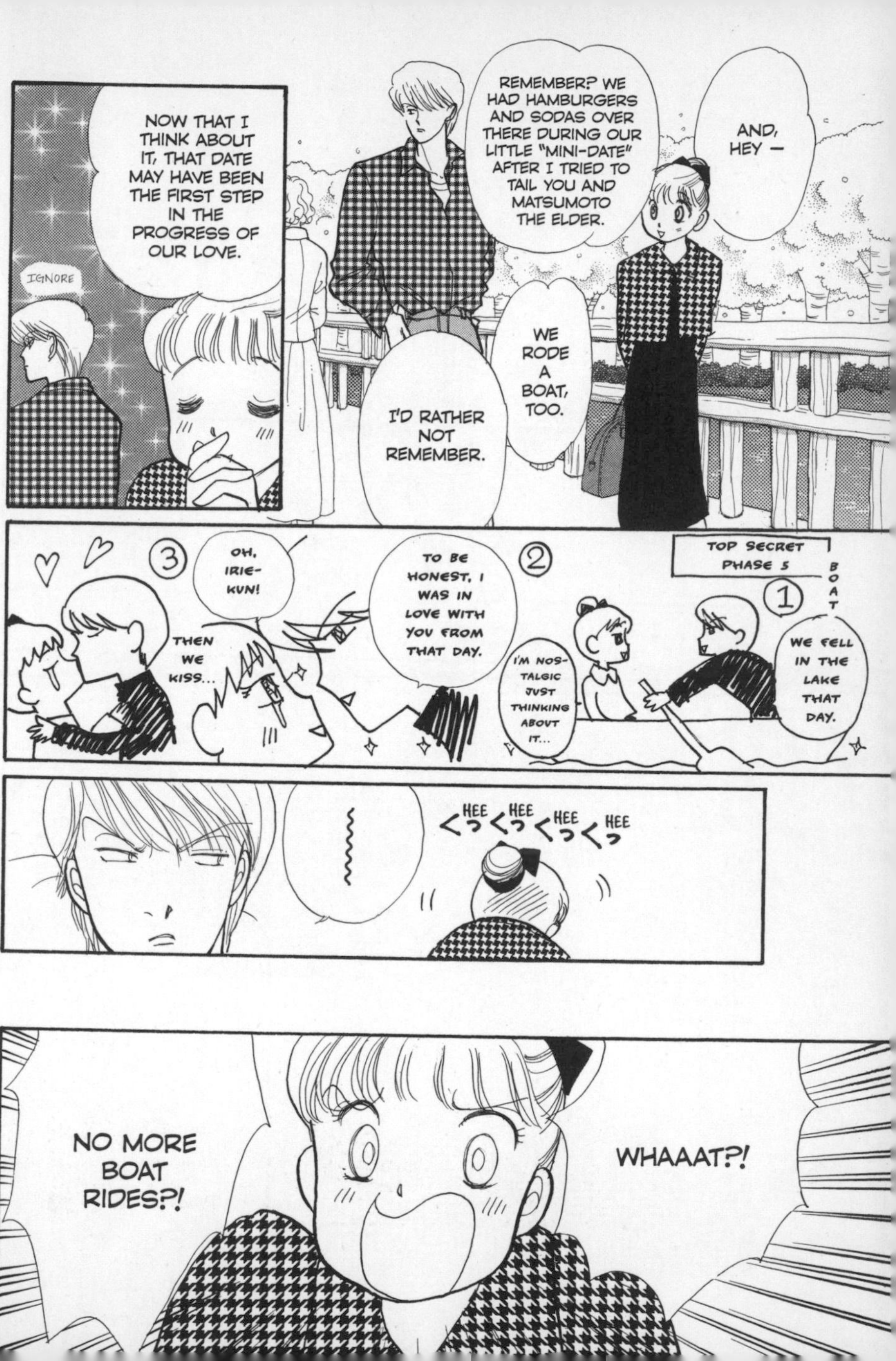
AND, HEY —
REMEMBER? WE HAD HAMBURGERS AND SODAS OVER THERE DURING OUR LITTLE "MINI-DATE" AFTER I TRIED TO TAIL YOU AND MATSUMOTO THE ELDER.
WE RODE A BOAT, TOO.
I'D RATHER NOT REMEMBER.
NOW THAT I THINK ABOUT IT, THAT DATE MAY HAVE BEEN THE FIRST STEP IN THE PROGRESS OF OUR LOVE.
IGNORE
TOP SECRET PHASE 5
BOAT
1
WE FELL IN THE LAKE THAT DAY.
I'M NOSTALGIC JUST THINKING ABOUT IT...
2
TO BE HONEST, I WAS IN LOVE WITH YOU FROM THAT DAY.
3
OH, IRIE-KUN!
THEN WE KISS...
くっくっくっくっ
HEE HEE HEE HEE
WHAAAT?!
NO MORE BOAT RIDES?!

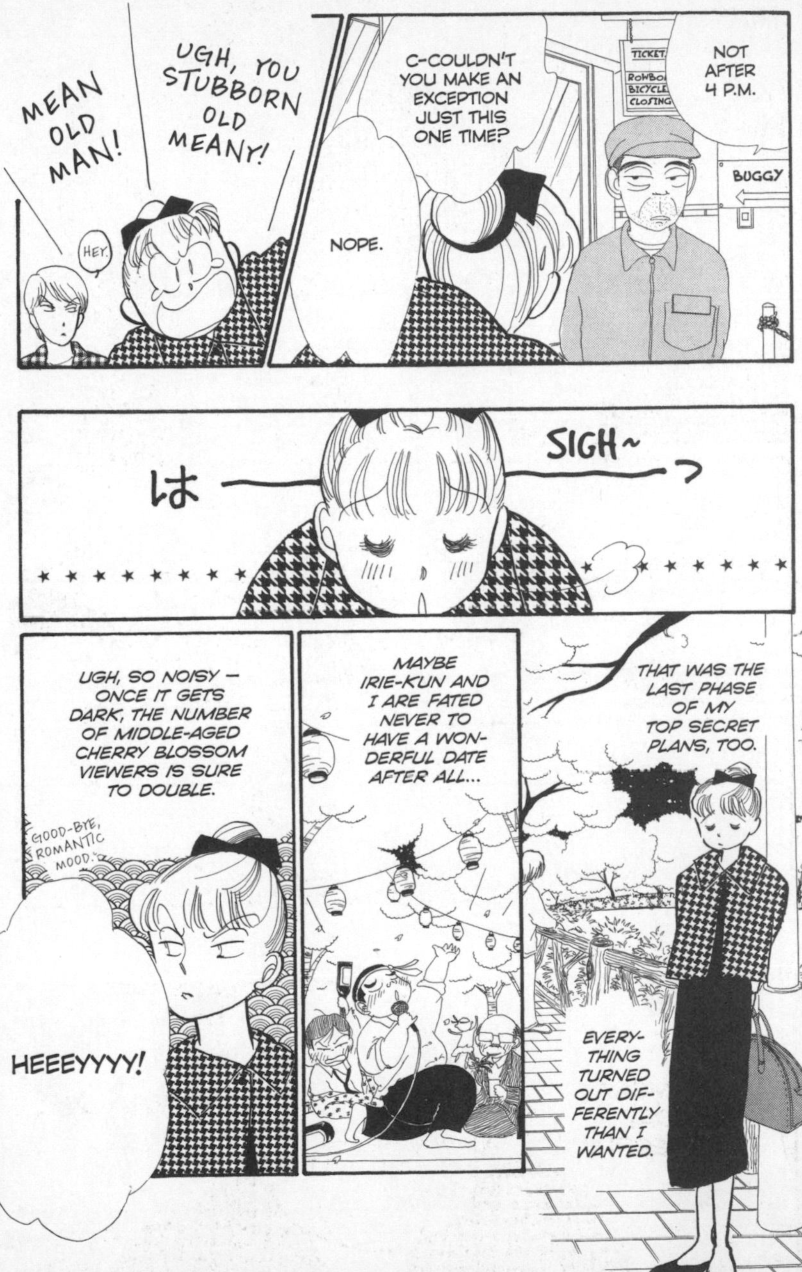
NOT AFTER 4 P.M.
TICKET
ROWBO
BICYCLE
CLOSING
C-COULDN'T YOU MAKE AN EXCEPTION JUST THIS ONE TIME?
BUGGY
NOPE.
UGH, YOU STUBBORN OLD MEANY!
MEAN OLD MAN!
HEY.
SIGH~
は
THAT WAS THE LAST PHASE OF MY TOP SECRET PLANS, TOO.
EVERY-THING TURNED OUT DIF-FERENTLY THAN I WANTED.
MAYBE IRIE-KUN AND I ARE FATED NEVER TO HAVE A WON-DERFUL DATE AFTER ALL...
UGH, SO NOISY — ONCE IT GETS DARK, THE NUMBER OF MIDDLE-AGED CHERRY BLOSSOM VIEWERS IS SURE TO DOUBLE.
GOOD-BYE, ROMANTIC MOOD.
HEEEYYYY!

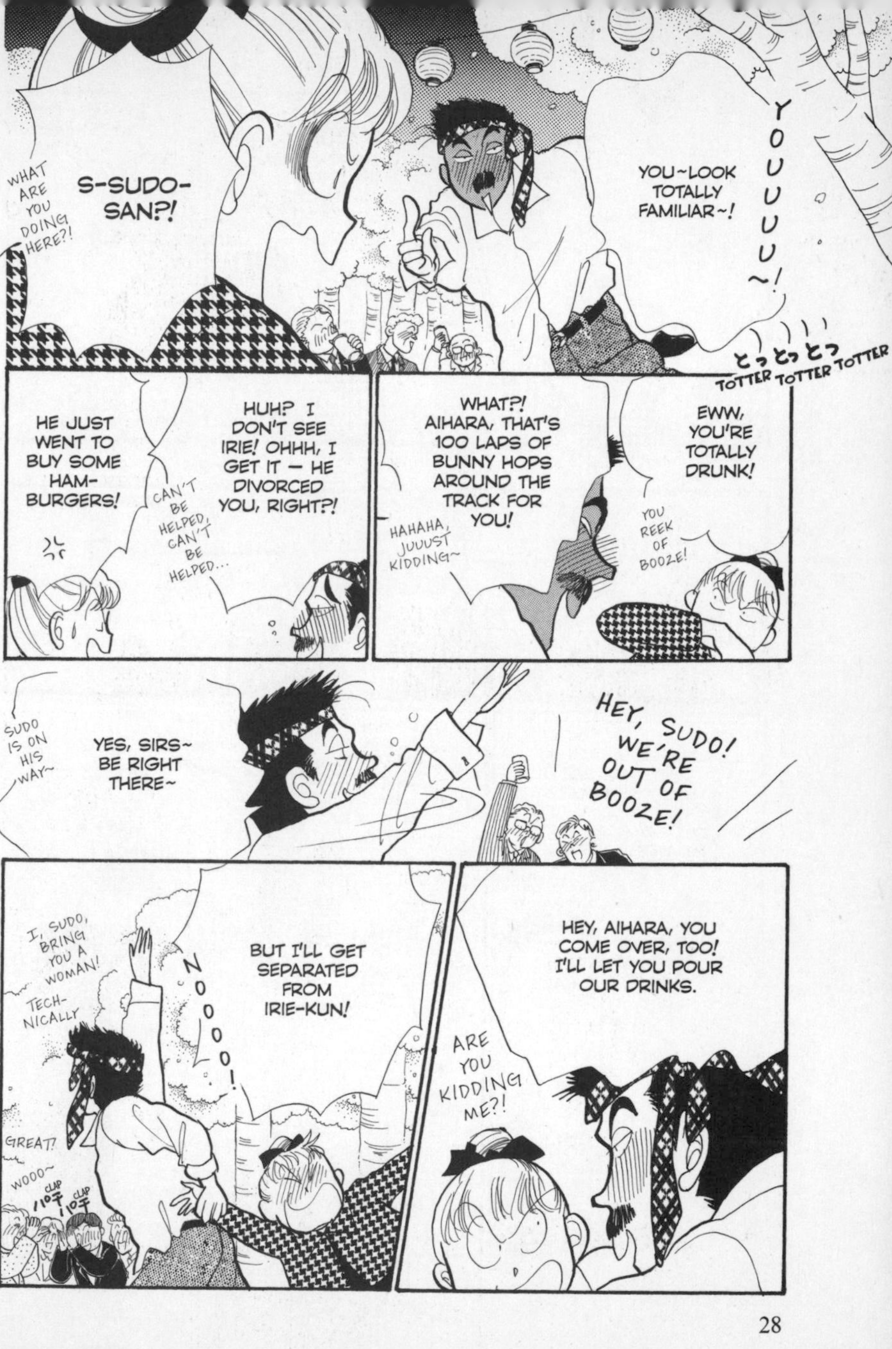
YOUUUUU~!
YOU~LOOK TOTALLY FAMILIAR~!
とっとっとっ
TOTTER TOTTER TOTTER
S-SUDO-SAN?!
WHAT ARE YOU DOING HERE?!
EWW, YOU'RE TOTALLY DRUNK!
YOU REEK OF BOOZE!
WHAT?! AIHARA, THAT'S 100 LAPS OF BUNNY HOPS AROUND THE TRACK FOR YOU!
HAHAHA, JUUUST KIDDING~
HUH? I DON'T SEE IRIE! OHHH, I GET IT — HE DIVORCED YOU, RIGHT?!
CAN'T BE HELPED, CAN'T BE HELPED...
HE JUST WENT TO BUY SOME HAMBURGERS!
HEY, SUDO! WE'RE OUT OF BOOZE!
YES, SIRS~ BE RIGHT THERE~
SUDO IS ON HIS WAY~
HEY, AIHARA, YOU COME OVER, TOO! I'LL LET YOU POUR OUR DRINKS.
ARE YOU KIDDING ME?!
BUT I'LL GET SEPARATED FROM IRIE-KUN!
NOOOOO!
I, SUDO, BRING YOU A WOMAN!
TECHNICALLY
GREAT!
WOOO~
CLAP CLAP

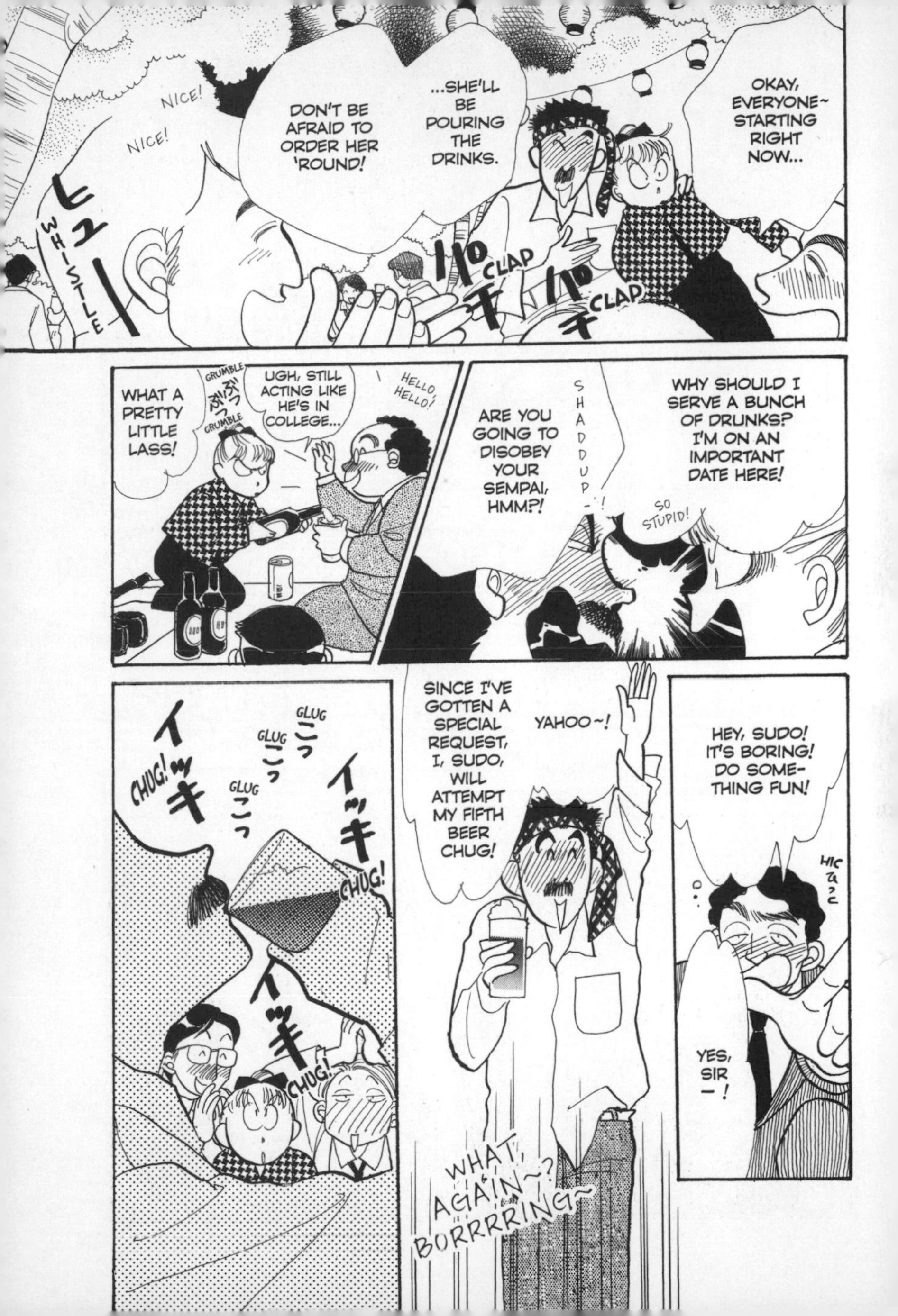
OKAY, EVERYONE~ STARTING RIGHT NOW...
...SHE'LL BE POURING THE DRINKS.
DON'T BE AFRAID TO ORDER HER 'ROUND!
NICE!
NICE!
ヒュー
WHISTLE
パチ
CLAP
パチ
CLAP
WHY SHOULD I SERVE A BUNCH OF DRUNKS? I'M ON AN IMPORTANT DATE HERE!
SO STUPID!
SHADDUP~!
ARE YOU GOING TO DISOBEY YOUR SEMPAI, HMM?!
HELLO, HELLO!
UGH, STILL ACTING LIKE HE'S IN COLLEGE...
GRUMBLE
ぶつぶつ
GRUMBLE
WHAT A PRETTY LITTLE LASS!
HEY, SUDO! IT'S BORING! DO SOME-THING FUN!
HIC
ひっく
YES, SIR—!
YAHOO~!
SINCE I'VE GOTTEN A SPECIAL REQUEST, I, SUDO, WILL ATTEMPT MY FIFTH BEER CHUG!
WHAT, AGAIN~? BORRRRING~
イッキ
CHUG!
GLUG
ごっ
GLUG
ごっ
GLUG
ごっ
イッキ
CHUG!
イッキ
CHUG!
イッキ
CHUG!

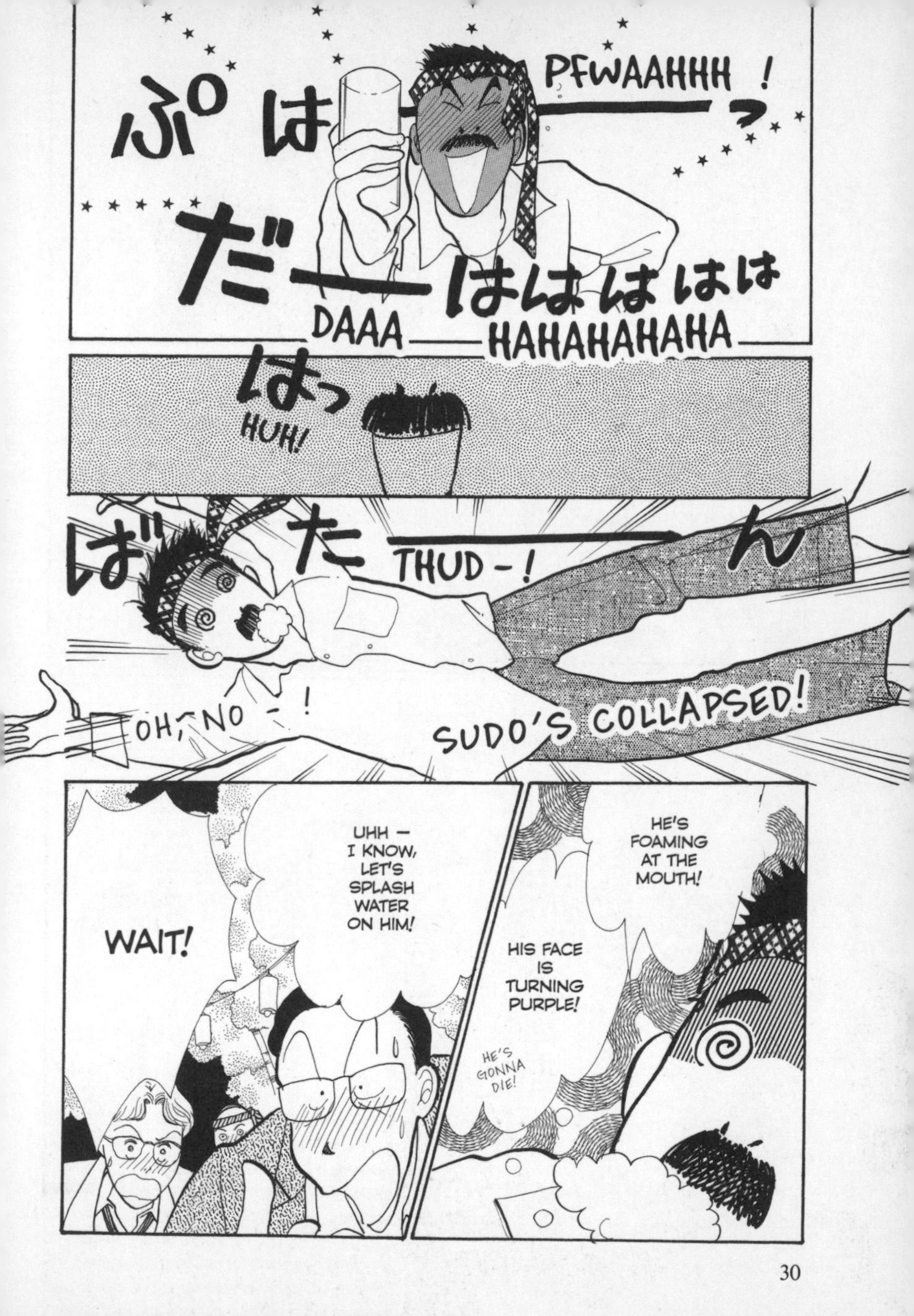
ぷはー
PFWAAHHH!
だーはははははは
DAAA—HAHAHAHAHA
はっ
HUH!
ばたーん
THUD—!
SUDO'S COLLAPSED!
OH, NO—!
HE'S FOAMING AT THE MOUTH!
HIS FACE IS TURNING PURPLE!
HE'S GONNA DIE!
UHH— I KNOW, LET'S SPLASH WATER ON HIM!
WAIT!

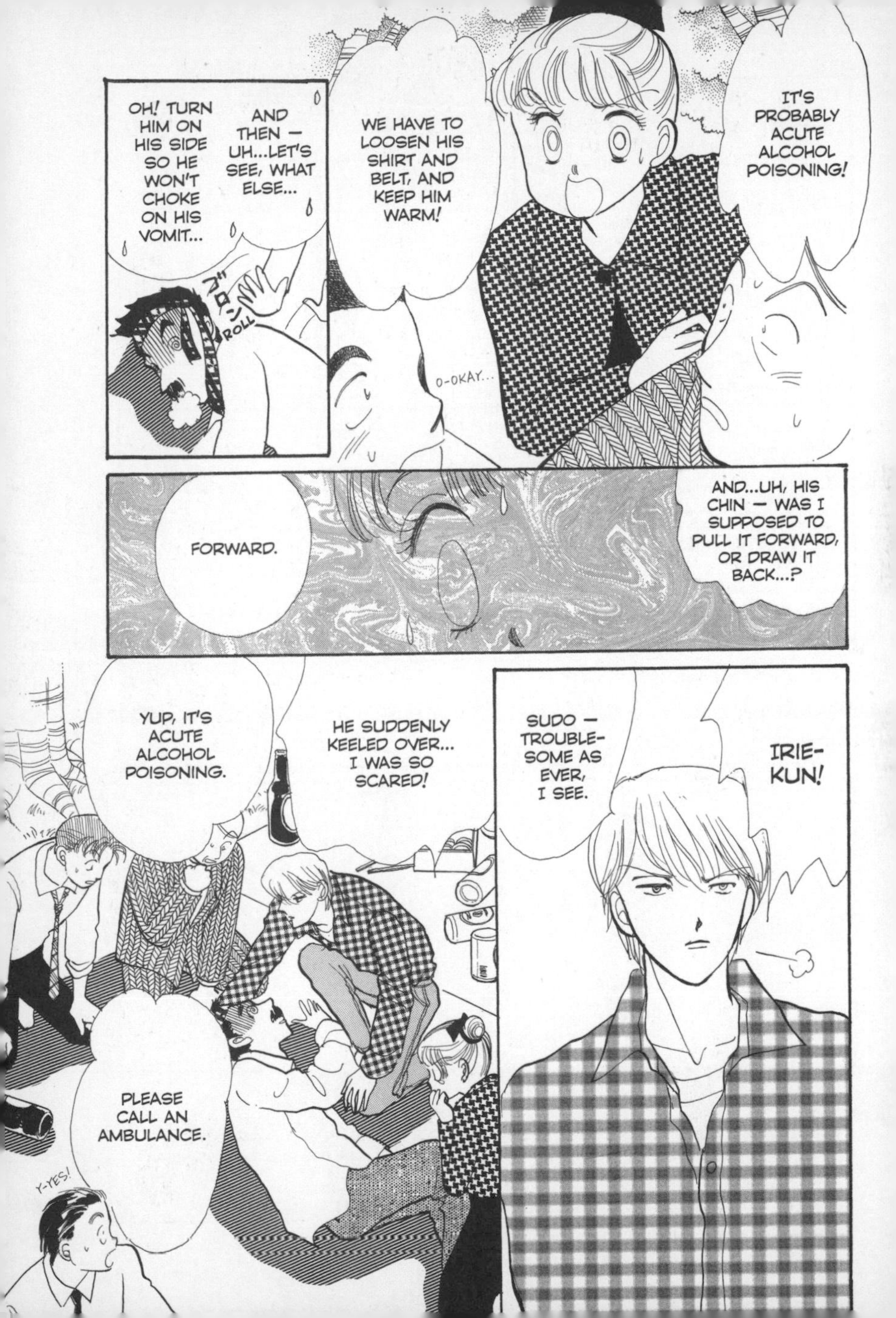
IT'S PROBABLY ACUTE ALCOHOL POISONING!
WE HAVE TO LOOSEN HIS SHIRT AND BELT, AND KEEP HIM WARM!
O-OKAY...
AND THEN — UH...LET'S SEE, WHAT ELSE...
OH! TURN HIM ON HIS SIDE SO HE WON'T CHOKE ON HIS VOMIT...
ゴロン ROLL
AND...UH, HIS CHIN — WAS I SUPPOSED TO PULL IT FORWARD, OR DRAW IT BACK...?
FORWARD.
IRIE-KUN!
SUDO — TROUBLE-SOME AS EVER, I SEE.
HE SUDDENLY KEELED OVER... I WAS SO SCARED!
YUP, IT'S ACUTE ALCOHOL POISONING.
PLEASE CALL AN AMBULANCE.
Y-YES!

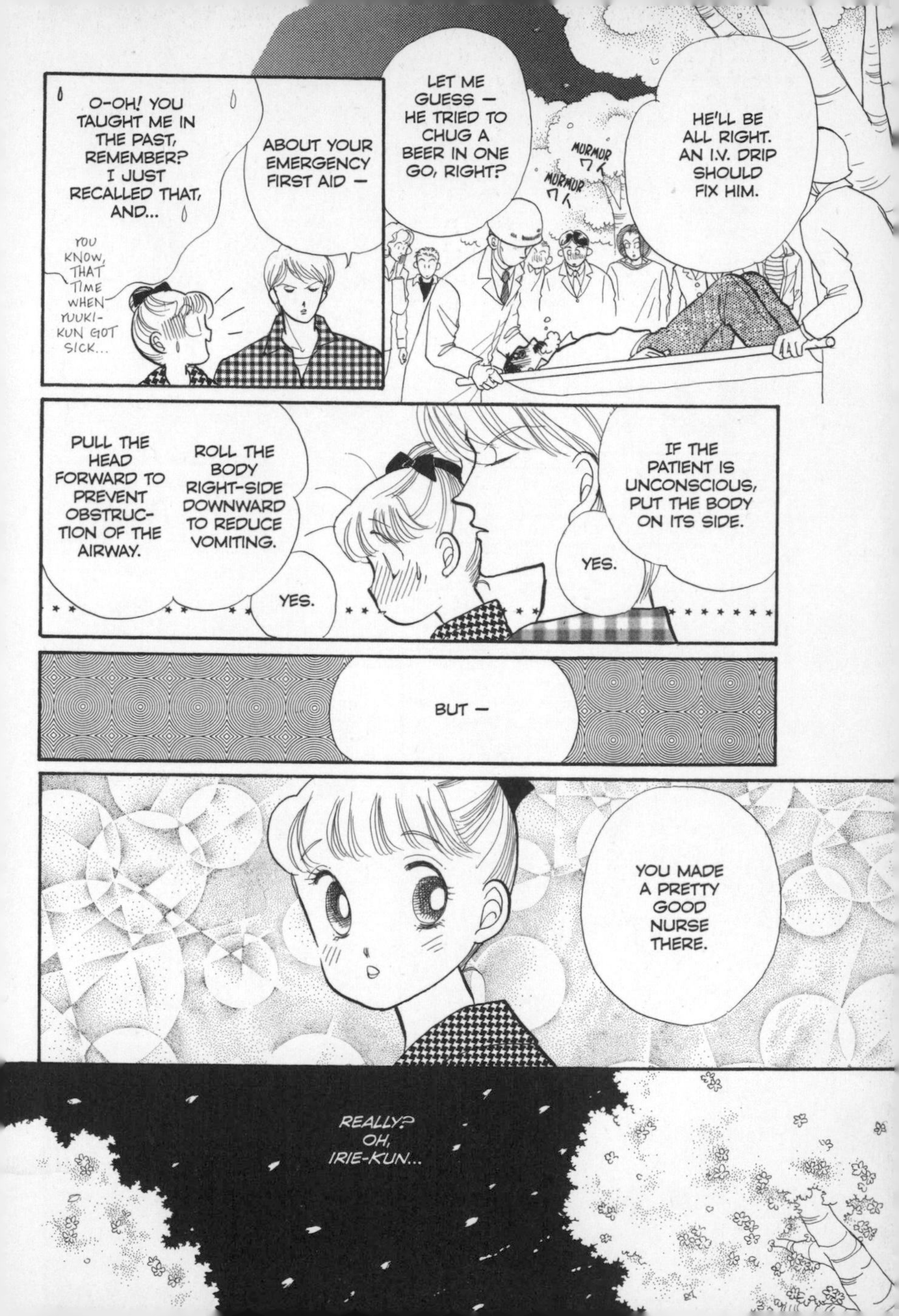
HE'LL BE ALL RIGHT. AN I.V. DRIP SHOULD FIX HIM.
MURMUR
MURMUR
LET ME GUESS — HE TRIED TO CHUG A BEER IN ONE GO, RIGHT?
ABOUT YOUR EMERGENCY FIRST AID —
O-OH! YOU TAUGHT ME IN THE PAST, REMEMBER? I JUST RECALLED THAT, AND...
YOU KNOW, THAT TIME WHEN YUUKI-KUN GOT SICK...
IF THE PATIENT IS UNCONSCIOUS, PUT THE BODY ON ITS SIDE.
YES.
ROLL THE BODY RIGHT-SIDE DOWNWARD TO REDUCE VOMITING.
PULL THE HEAD FORWARD TO PREVENT OBSTRUCTION OF THE AIRWAY.
YES.
BUT —
YOU MADE A PRETTY GOOD NURSE THERE.
REALLY? OH, IRIE-KUN...

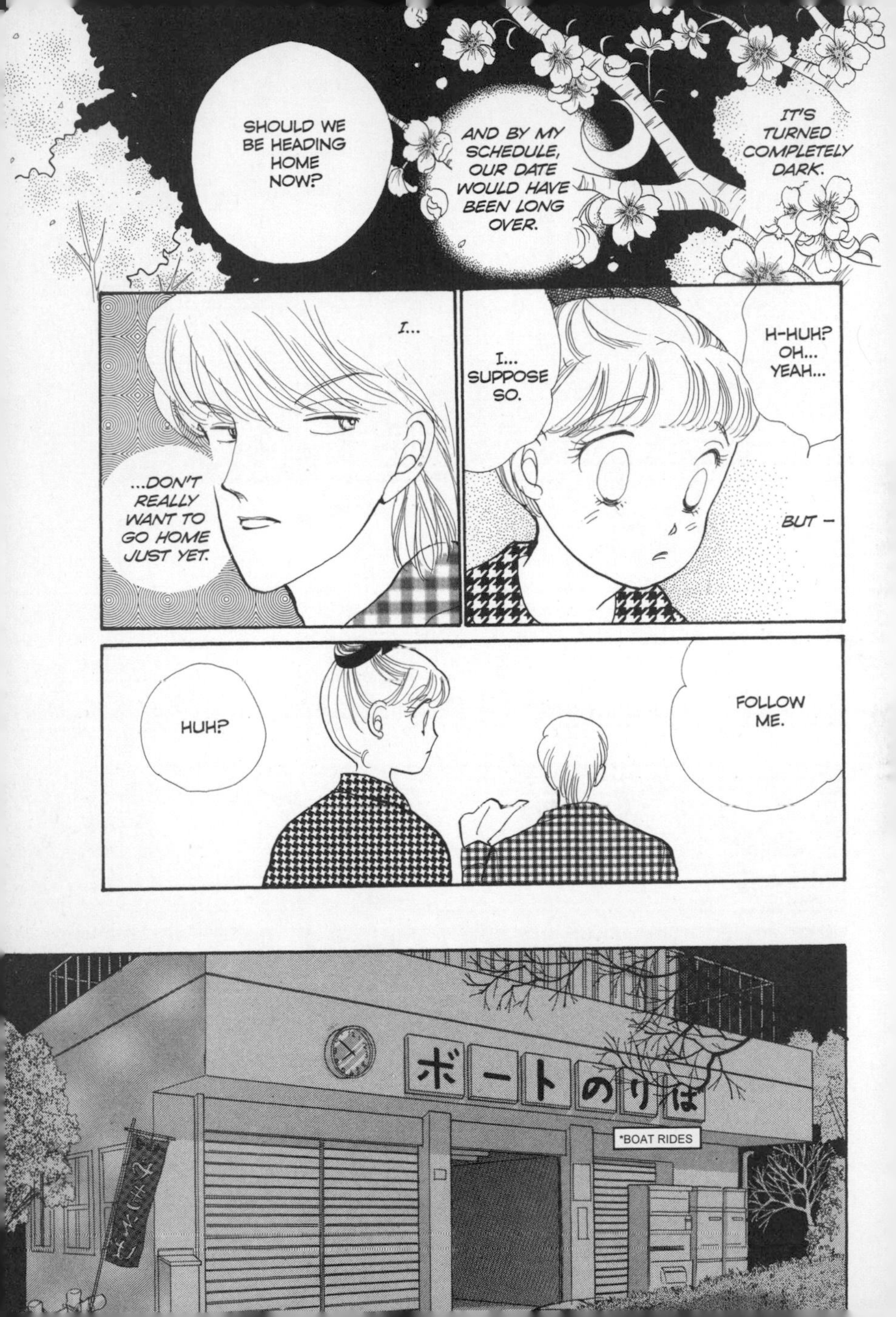
IT'S TURNED COMPLETELY DARK.
AND BY MY SCHEDULE, OUR DATE WOULD HAVE BEEN LONG OVER.
SHOULD WE BE HEADING HOME NOW?
H-HUH? OH... YEAH...
I... SUPPOSE SO.
BUT –
I...
...DON'T REALLY WANT TO GO HOME JUST YET.
FOLLOW ME.
HUH?
ボートのりば
*BOAT RIDES

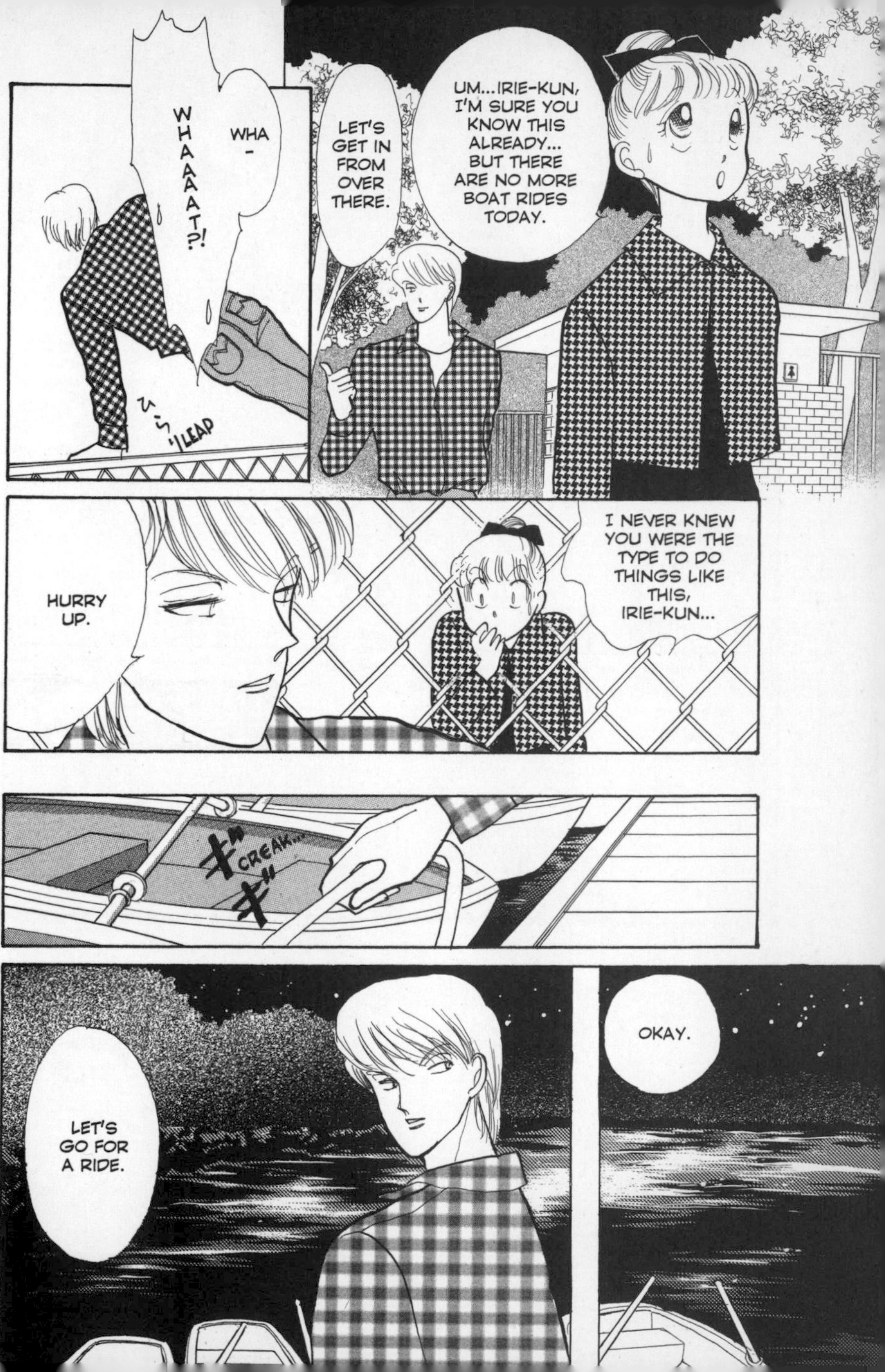
UM...IRIE-KUN, I'M SURE YOU KNOW THIS ALREADY... BUT THERE ARE NO MORE BOAT RIDES TODAY.
LET'S GET IN FROM OVER THERE.
WHA-
WHAAAAAT?!
ひらっ
LEAP
I NEVER KNEW YOU WERE THE TYPE TO DO THINGS LIKE THIS, IRIE-KUN...
HURRY UP.
CREAK...
OKAY.
LET'S GO FOR A RIDE.

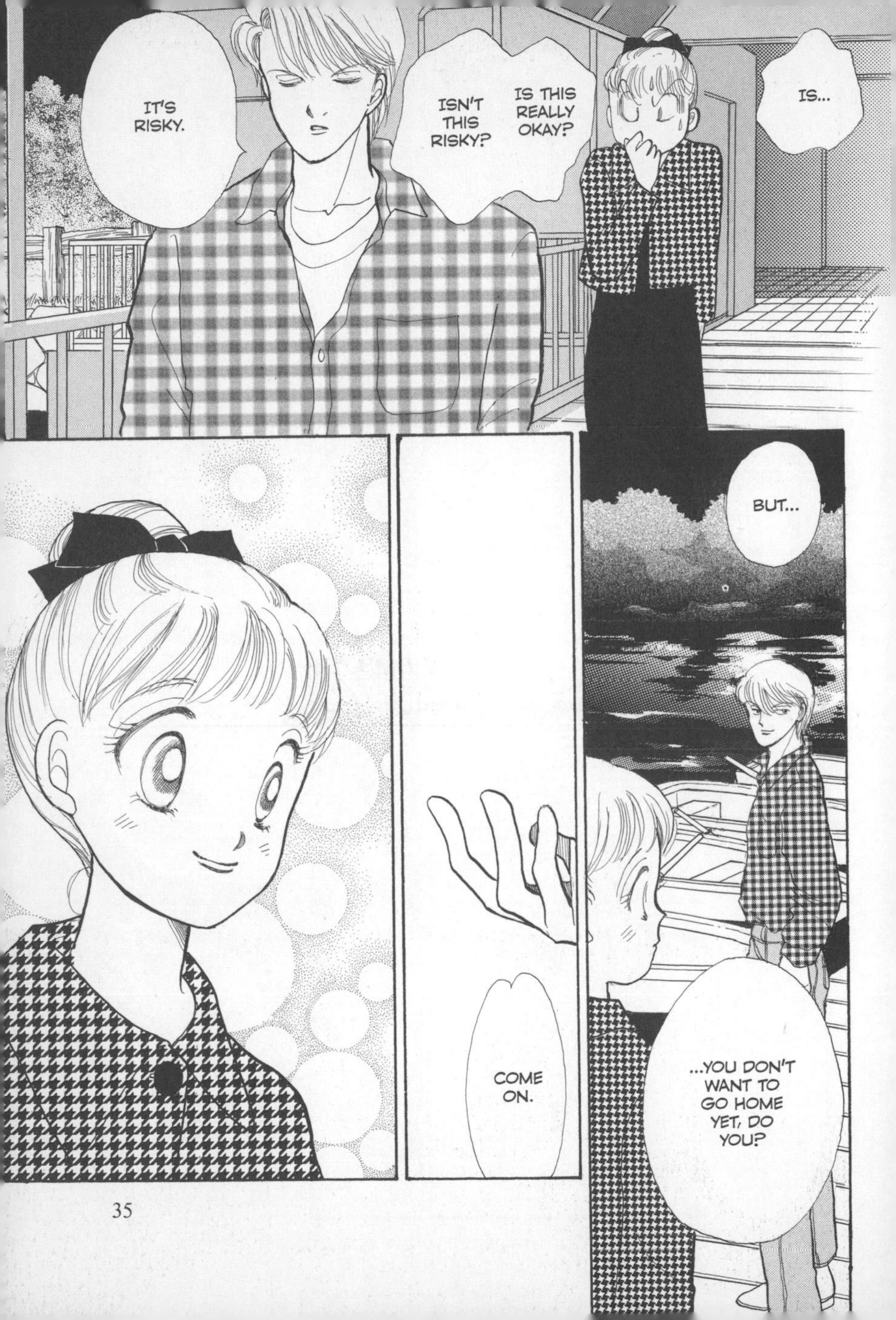
IS...
IS THIS REALLY OKAY?
ISN'T THIS RISKY?
IT'S RISKY.
BUT...
...YOU DON'T WANT TO GO HOME YET, DO YOU?
COME ON.

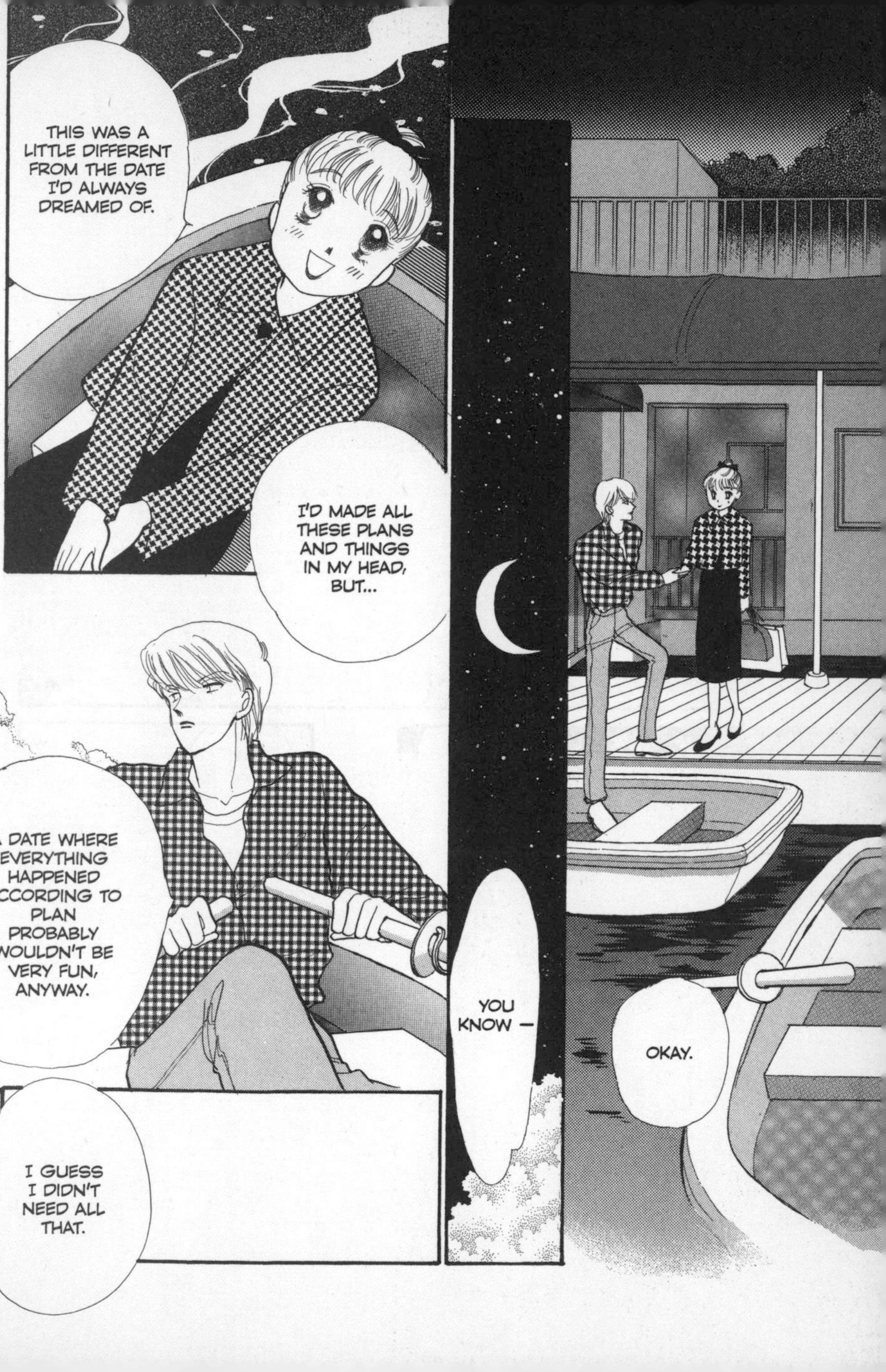
OKAY.
YOU KNOW —
THIS WAS A LITTLE DIFFERENT FROM THE DATE I'D ALWAYS DREAMED OF.
I'D MADE ALL THESE PLANS AND THINGS IN MY HEAD, BUT...
A DATE WHERE EVERYTHING HAPPENED ACCORDING TO PLAN PROBABLY WOULDN'T BE VERY FUN, ANYWAY.
I GUESS I DIDN'T NEED ALL THAT.

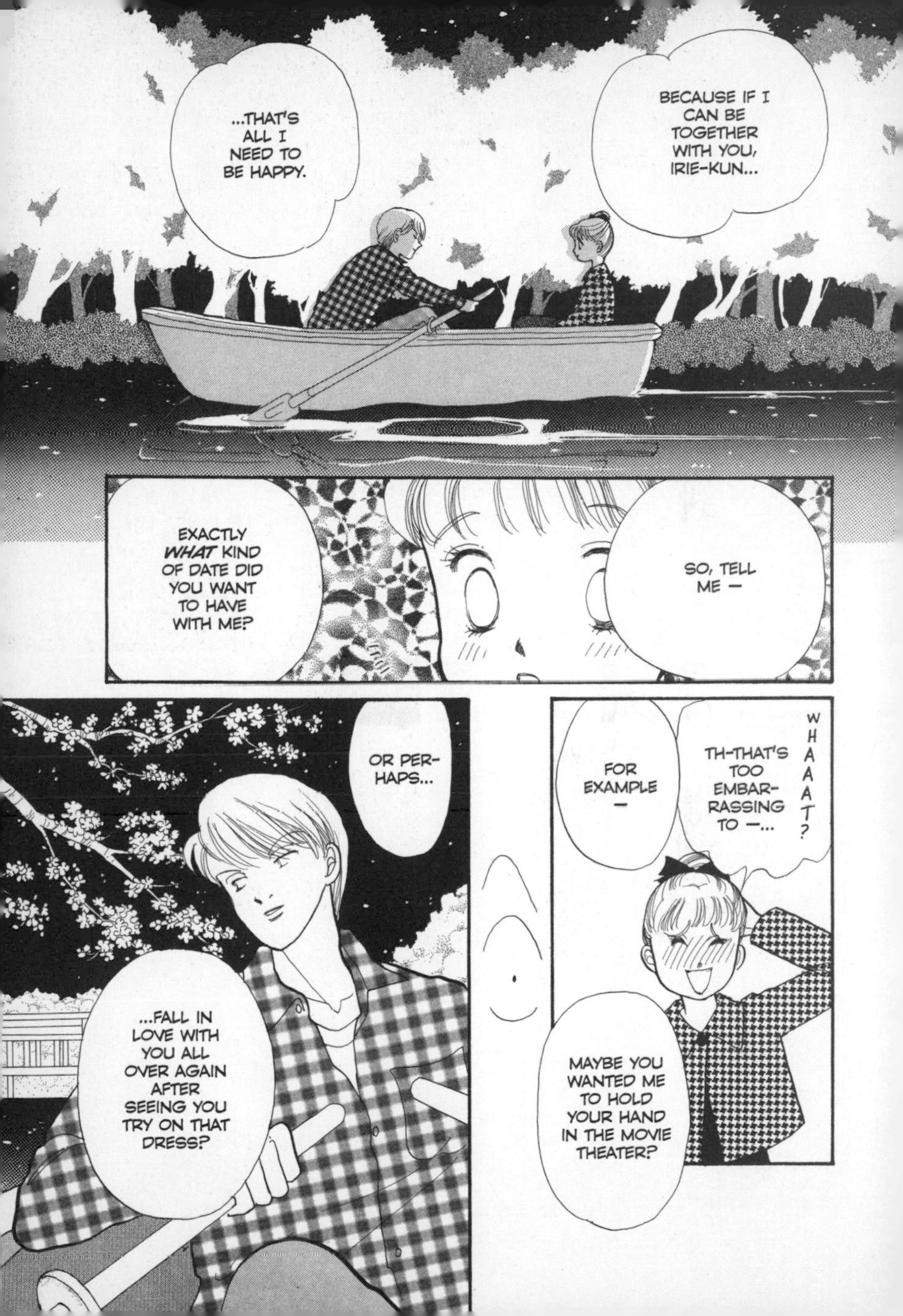
BECAUSE IF I CAN BE TOGETHER WITH YOU, IRIE-KUN...
...THAT'S ALL I NEED TO BE HAPPY.
SO, TELL ME —
EXACTLY *WHAT* KIND OF DATE DID YOU WANT TO HAVE WITH ME?
WHAAAT?
TH-THAT'S TOO EMBAR-RASSING TO —...
FOR EXAMPLE —
MAYBE YOU WANTED ME TO HOLD YOUR HAND IN THE MOVIE THEATER?
OR PER-HAPS...
...FALL IN LOVE WITH YOU ALL OVER AGAIN AFTER SEEING YOU TRY ON THAT DRESS?

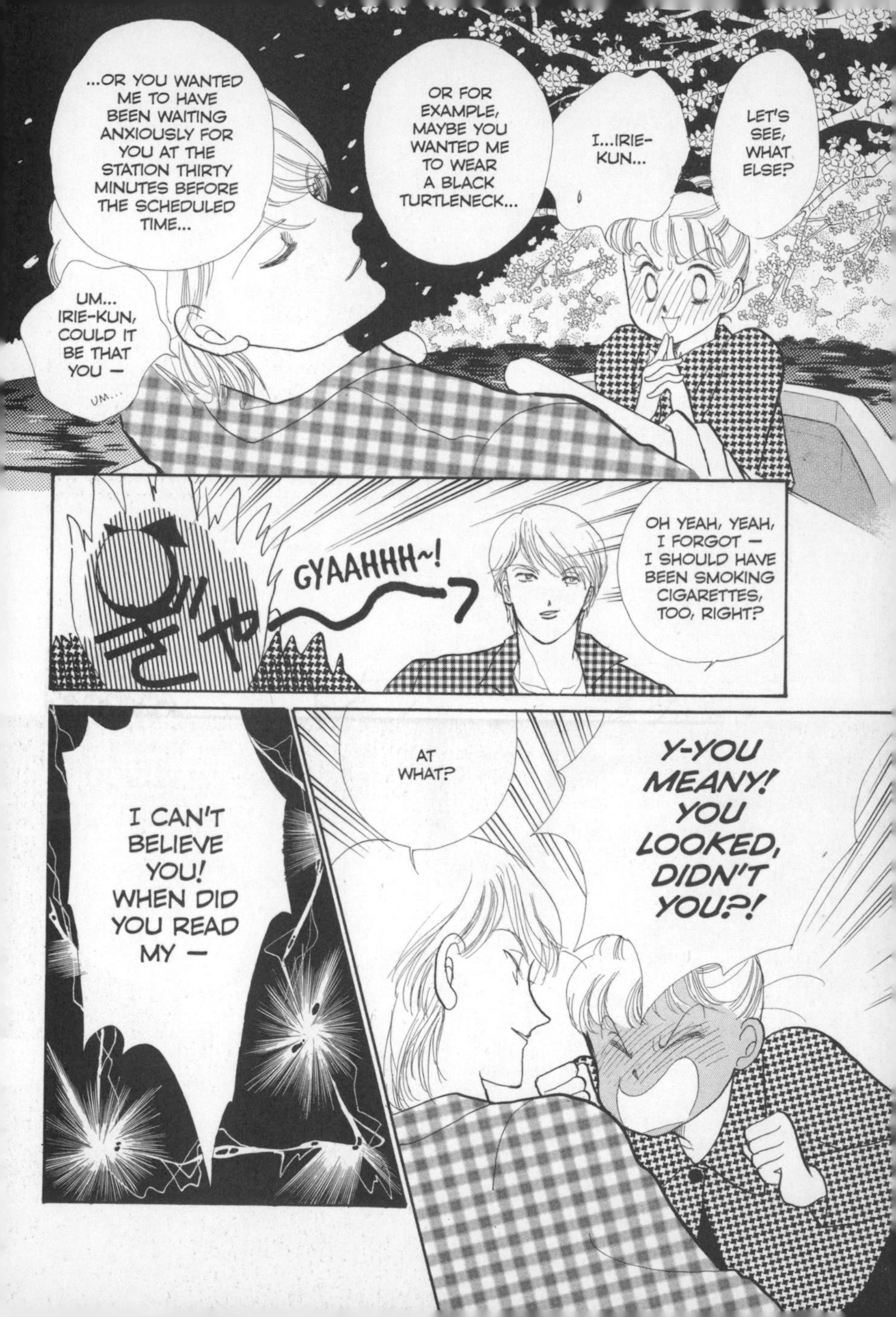
LET'S SEE, WHAT ELSE?
I...IRIE-KUN...
OR FOR EXAMPLE, MAYBE YOU WANTED ME TO WEAR A BLACK TURTLENECK...
...OR YOU WANTED ME TO HAVE BEEN WAITING ANXIOUSLY FOR YOU AT THE STATION THIRTY MINUTES BEFORE THE SCHEDULED TIME...
UM... IRIE-KUN, COULD IT BE THAT YOU —
UM...
OH YEAH, YEAH, I FORGOT — I SHOULD HAVE BEEN SMOKING CIGARETTES, TOO, RIGHT?
GYAAHHH~!
Y-YOU MEANY! YOU LOOKED, DIDN'T YOU?!
AT WHAT?
I CAN'T BELIEVE YOU! WHEN DID YOU READ MY —

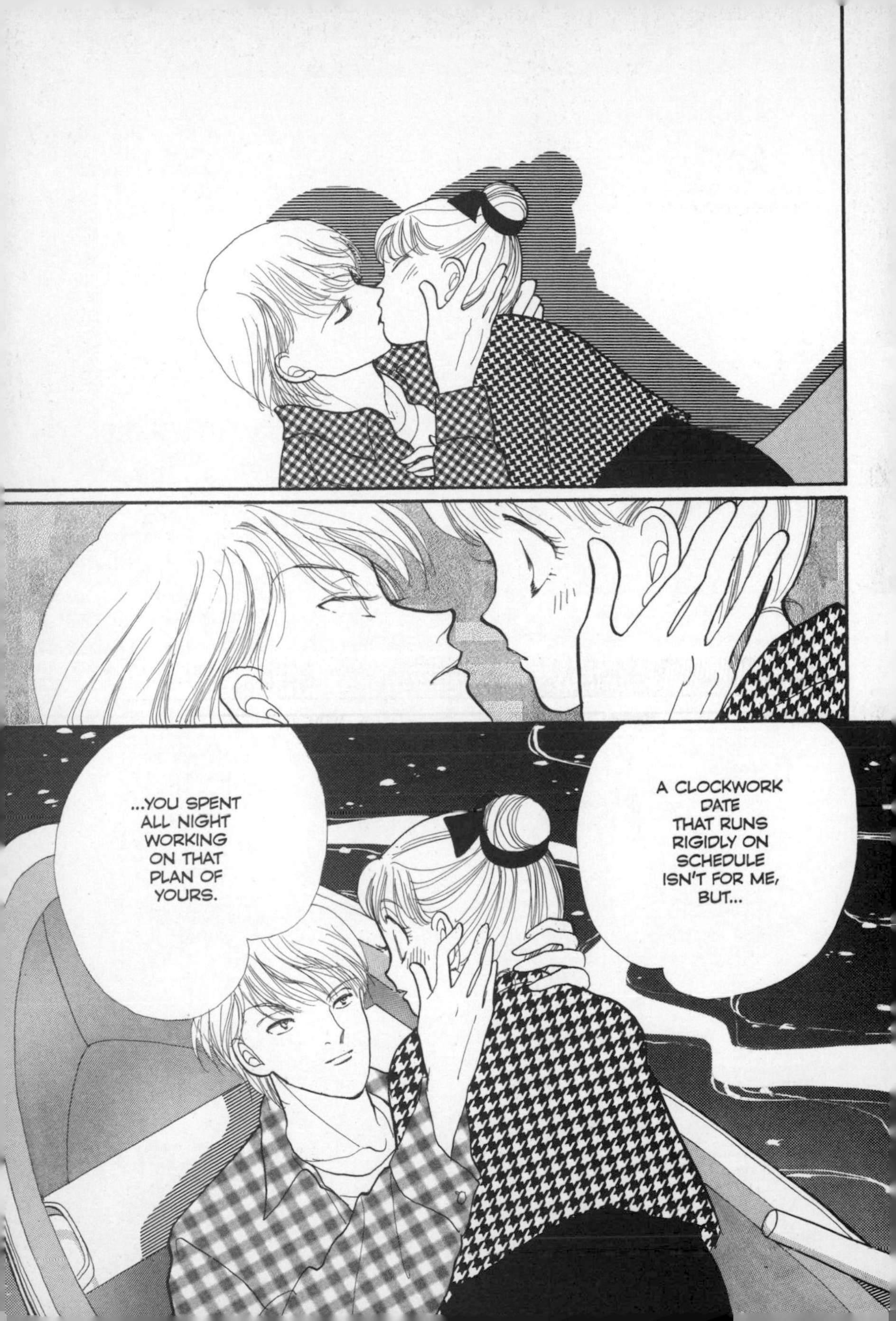
A CLOCKWORK DATE THAT RUNS RIGIDLY ON SCHEDULE ISN'T FOR ME, BUT...
...YOU SPENT ALL NIGHT WORKING ON THAT PLAN OF YOURS.

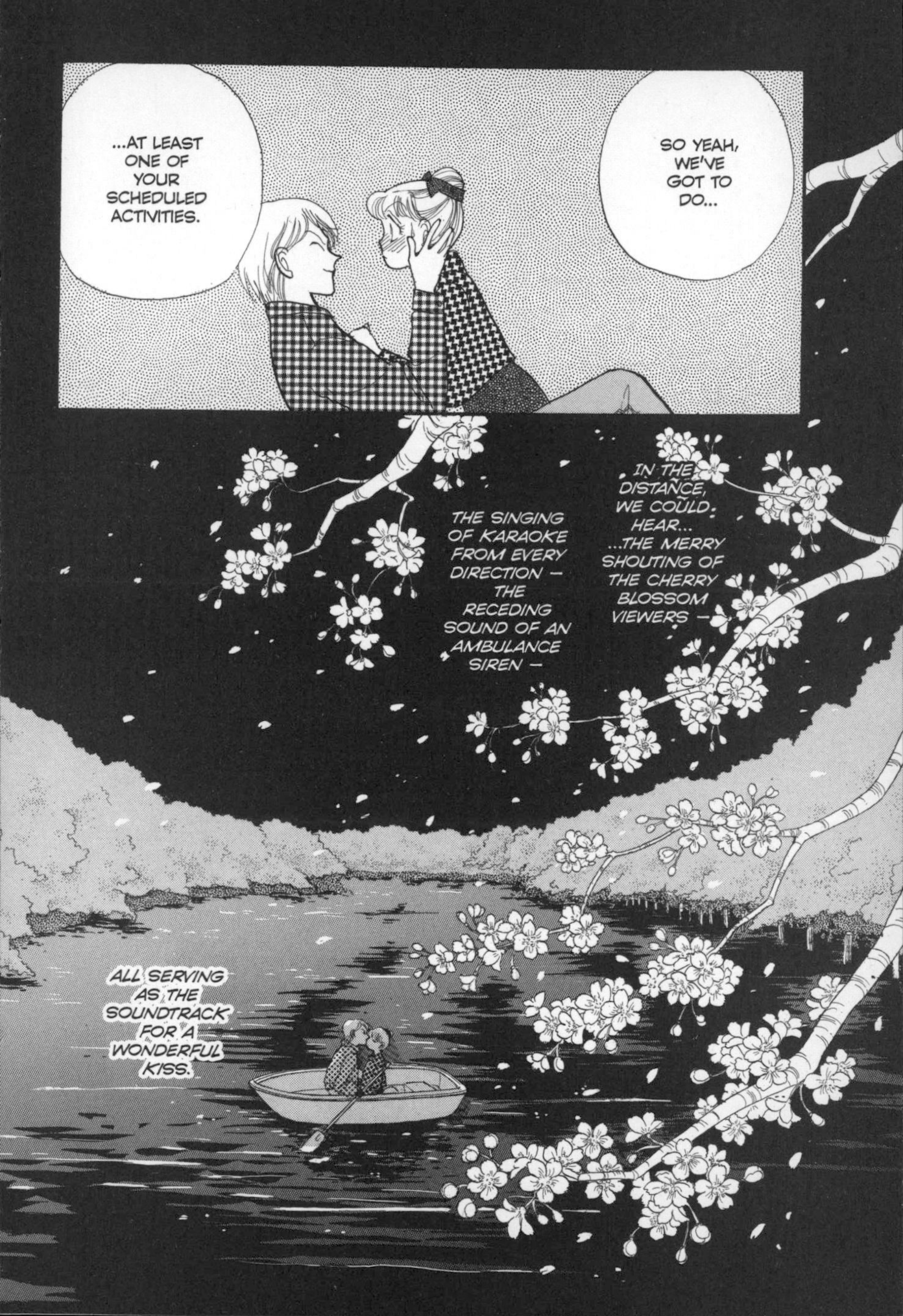
SO YEAH, WE'VE GOT TO DO...
...AT LEAST ONE OF YOUR SCHEDULED ACTIVITIES.
IN THE DISTANCE, WE COULD HEAR...
...THE MERRY SHOUTING OF THE CHERRY BLOSSOM VIEWERS –
THE SINGING OF KARAOKE FROM EVERY DIRECTION – THE RECEDING SOUND OF AN AMBULANCE SIREN –
ALL SERVING AS THE SOUNDTRACK FOR A WONDERFUL KISS.

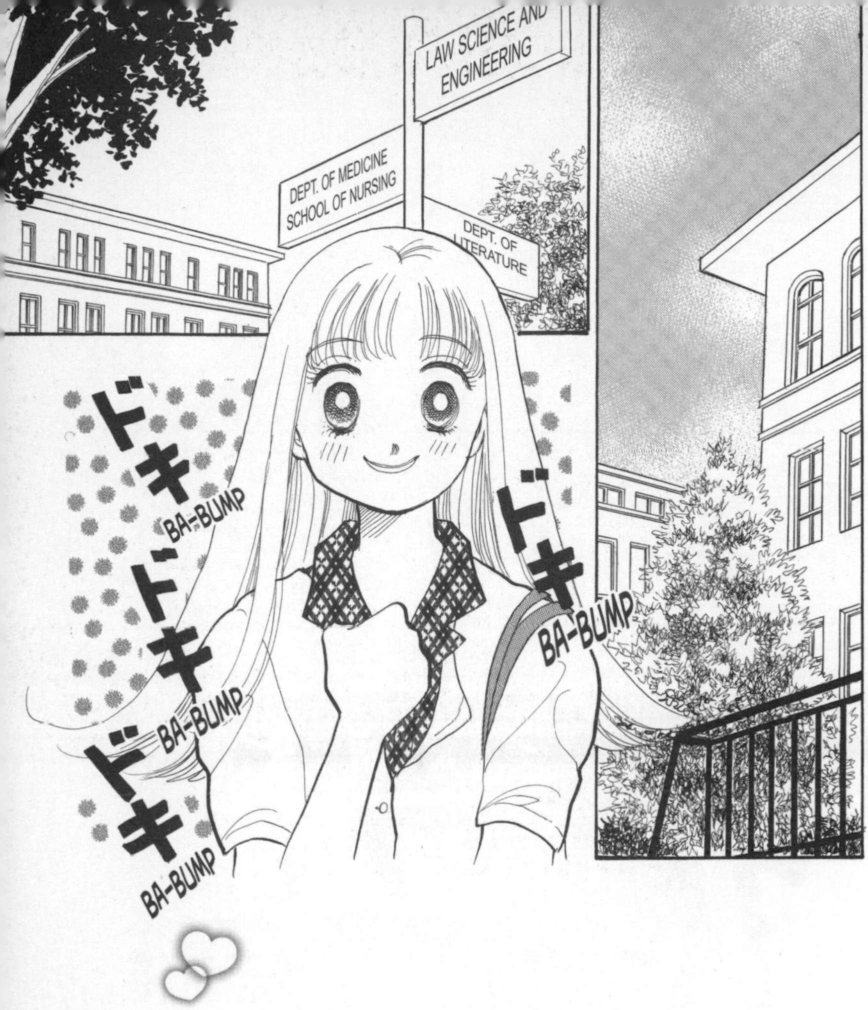
LAW SCIENCE AND ENGINEERING
DEPT. OF MEDICINE SCHOOL OF NURSING
DEPT. OF LITERATURE
ドキ
BA-BUMP
ドキ
BA-BUMP
ドキ
BA-BUMP
ドキ
BA-BUMP

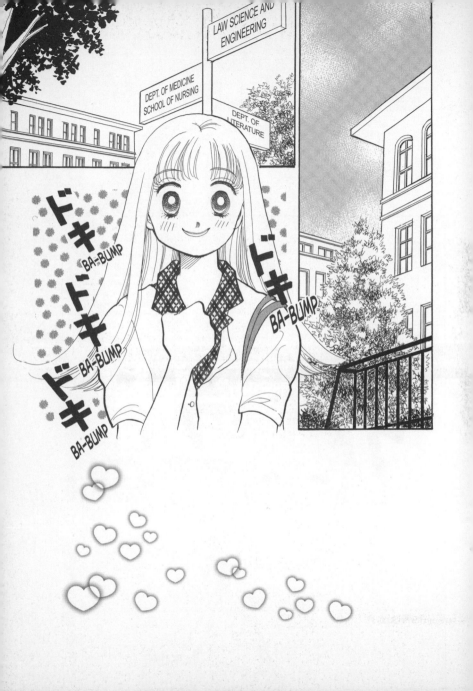

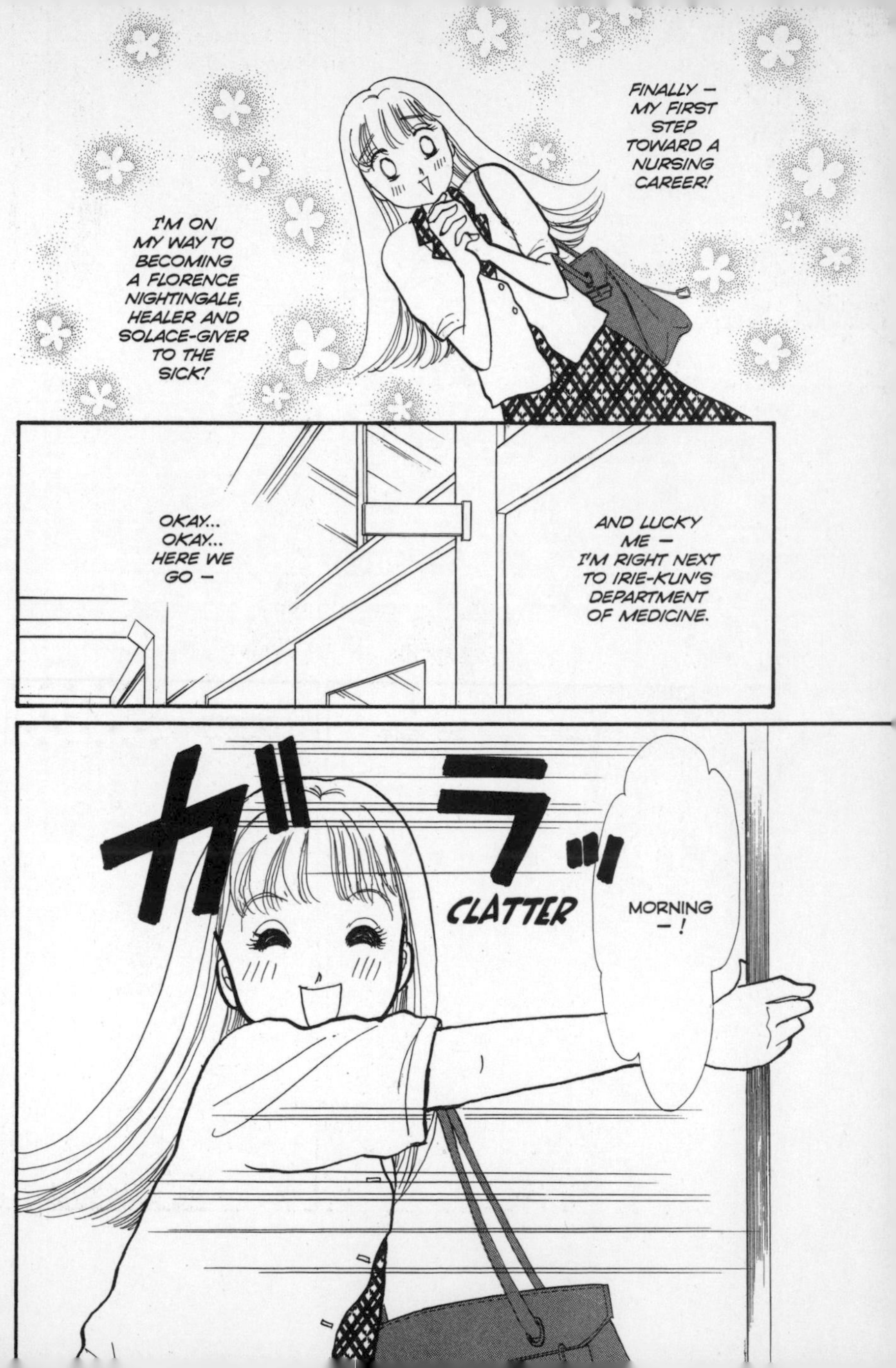
FINALLY — MY FIRST STEP TOWARD A NURSING CAREER!
I'M ON MY WAY TO BECOMING A FLORENCE NIGHTINGALE, HEALER AND SOLACE-GIVER TO THE SICK!
AND LUCKY ME — I'M RIGHT NEXT TO IRIE-KUN'S DEPARTMENT OF MEDICINE.
OKAY... OKAY... HERE WE GO —
MORNING —!
ガラッ
CLATTER

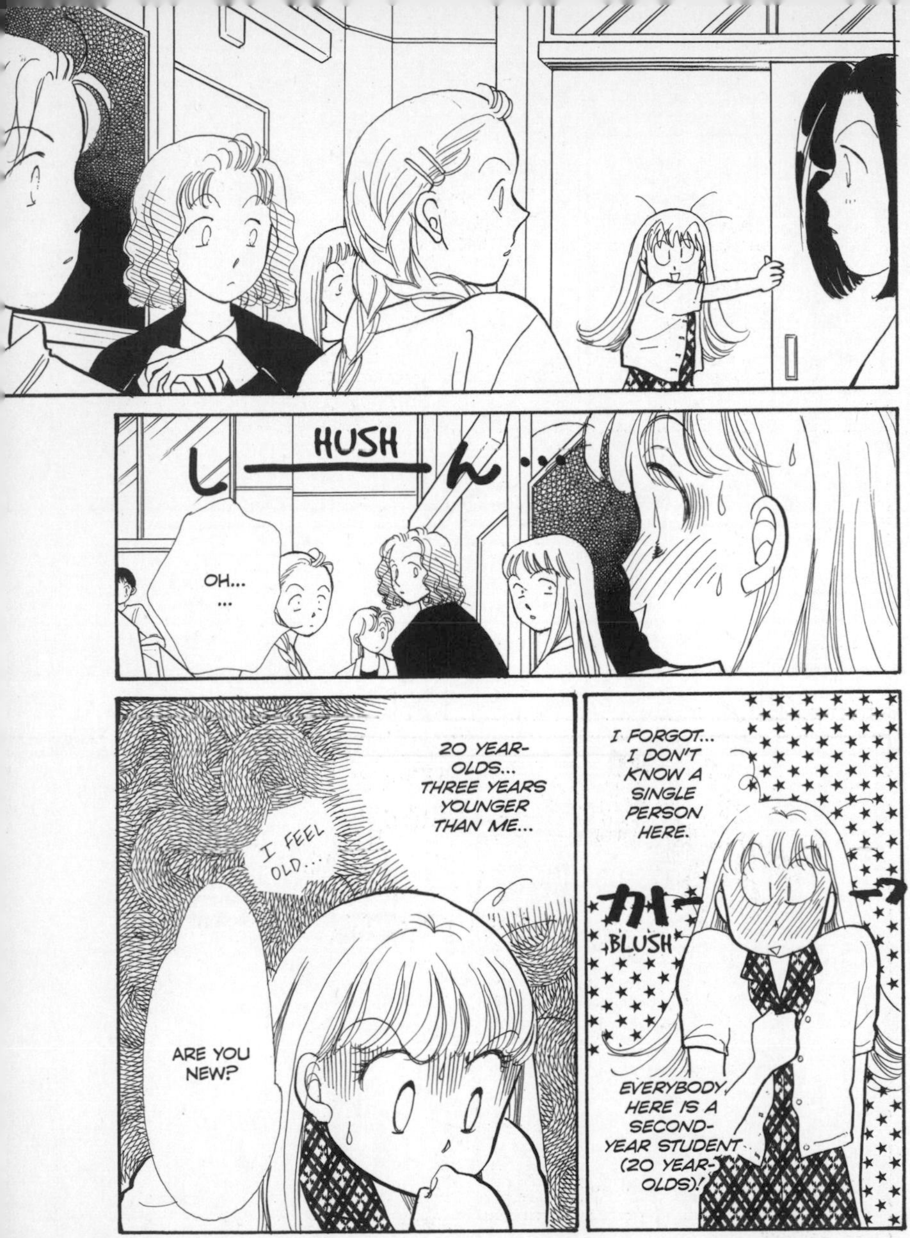
し——ん…
HUSH
OH... ...
I FORGOT... I DON'T KNOW A SINGLE PERSON HERE.
カー—ッ
BLUSH
EVERYBODY HERE IS A SECOND-YEAR STUDENT (20 YEAR-OLDS)!
20 YEAR-OLDS... THREE YEARS YOUNGER THAN ME...
I FEEL OLD...
ARE YOU NEW?

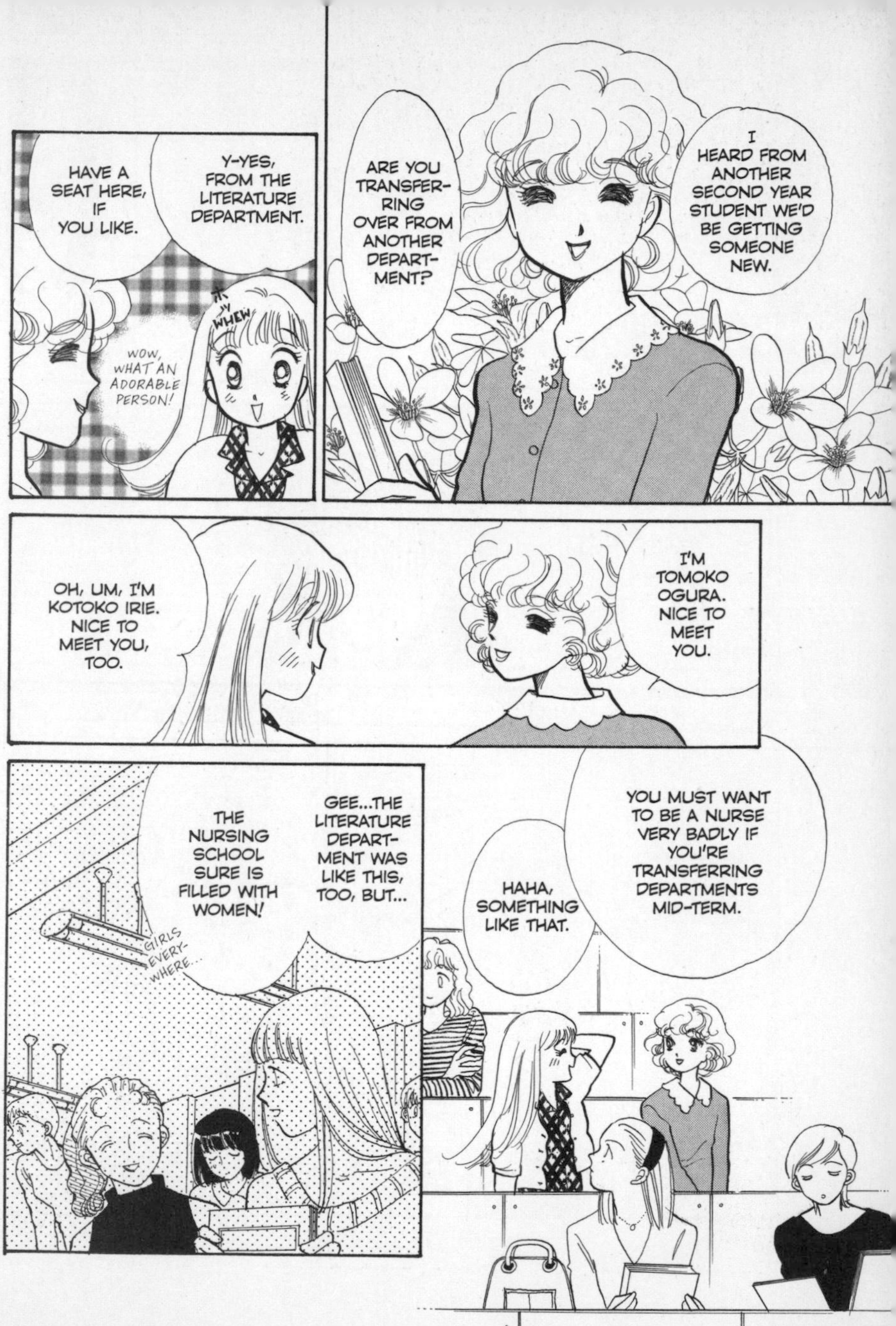
I HEARD FROM ANOTHER SECOND YEAR STUDENT WE'D BE GETTING SOMEONE NEW.
ARE YOU TRANSFERRING OVER FROM ANOTHER DEPARTMENT?
Y-YES, FROM THE LITERATURE DEPARTMENT.
HAVE A SEAT HERE, IF YOU LIKE.
WHEW
WOW, WHAT AN ADORABLE PERSON!
I'M TOMOKO OGURA. NICE TO MEET YOU.
OH, UM, I'M KOTOKO IRIE. NICE TO MEET YOU, TOO.
YOU MUST WANT TO BE A NURSE VERY BADLY IF YOU'RE TRANSFERRING DEPARTMENTS MID-TERM.
HAHA, SOMETHING LIKE THAT.
GEE...THE LITERATURE DEPARTMENT WAS LIKE THIS, TOO, BUT...
THE NURSING SCHOOL SURE IS FILLED WITH WOMEN!
GIRLS EVERYWHERE...

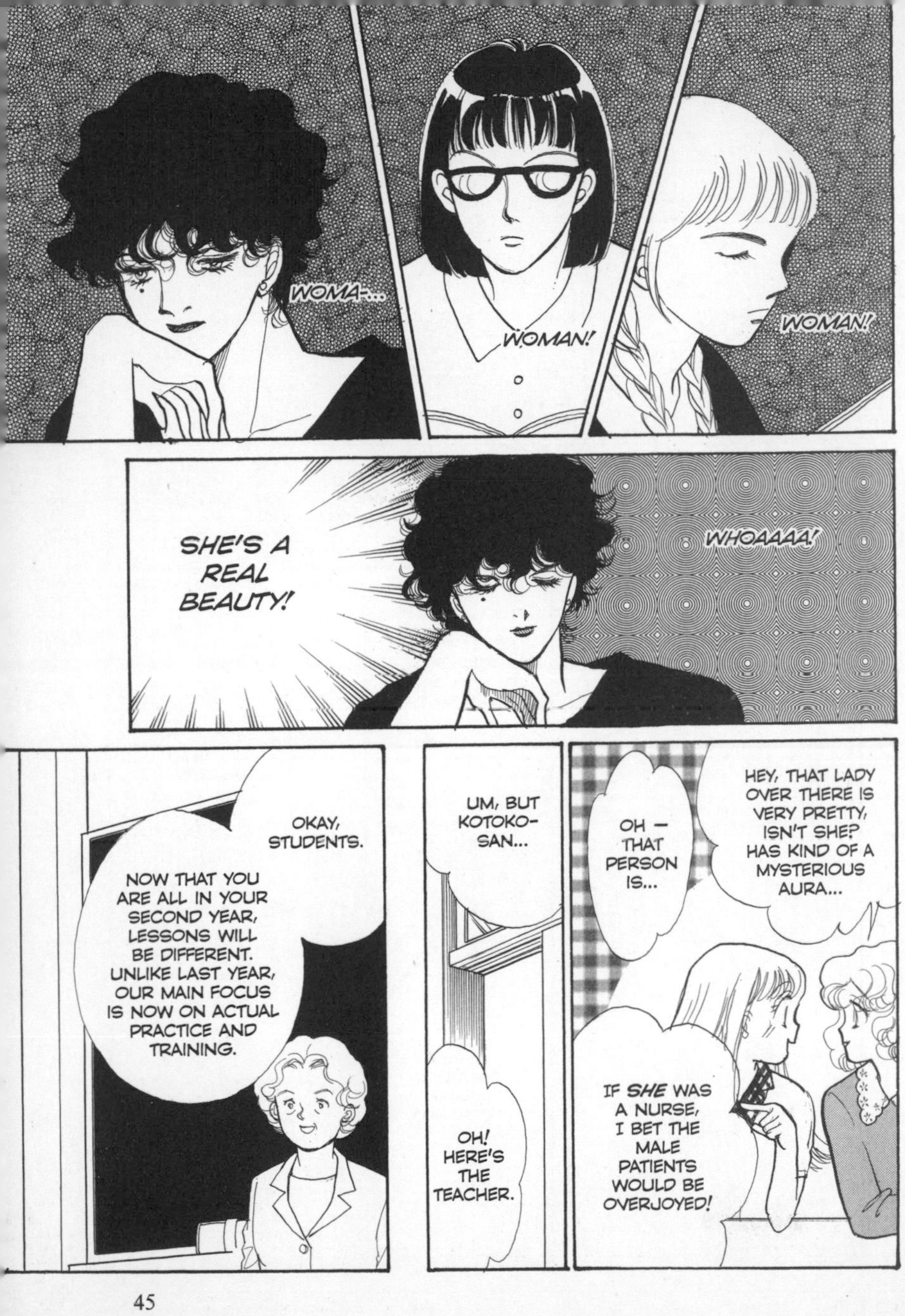
WOMAN!
WOMAN!
WOMA-...
WHOAAAA!
SHE'S A REAL BEAUTY!
HEY, THAT LADY OVER THERE IS VERY PRETTY, ISN'T SHE? HAS KIND OF A MYSTERIOUS AURA...
OH — THAT PERSON IS...
IF *SHE* WAS A NURSE, I BET THE MALE PATIENTS WOULD BE OVERJOYED!
UM, BUT KOTOKO-SAN...
OH! HERE'S THE TEACHER.
OKAY, STUDENTS.
NOW THAT YOU ARE ALL IN YOUR SECOND YEAR, LESSONS WILL BE DIFFERENT. UNLIKE LAST YEAR, OUR MAIN FOCUS IS NOW ON ACTUAL PRACTICE AND TRAINING.

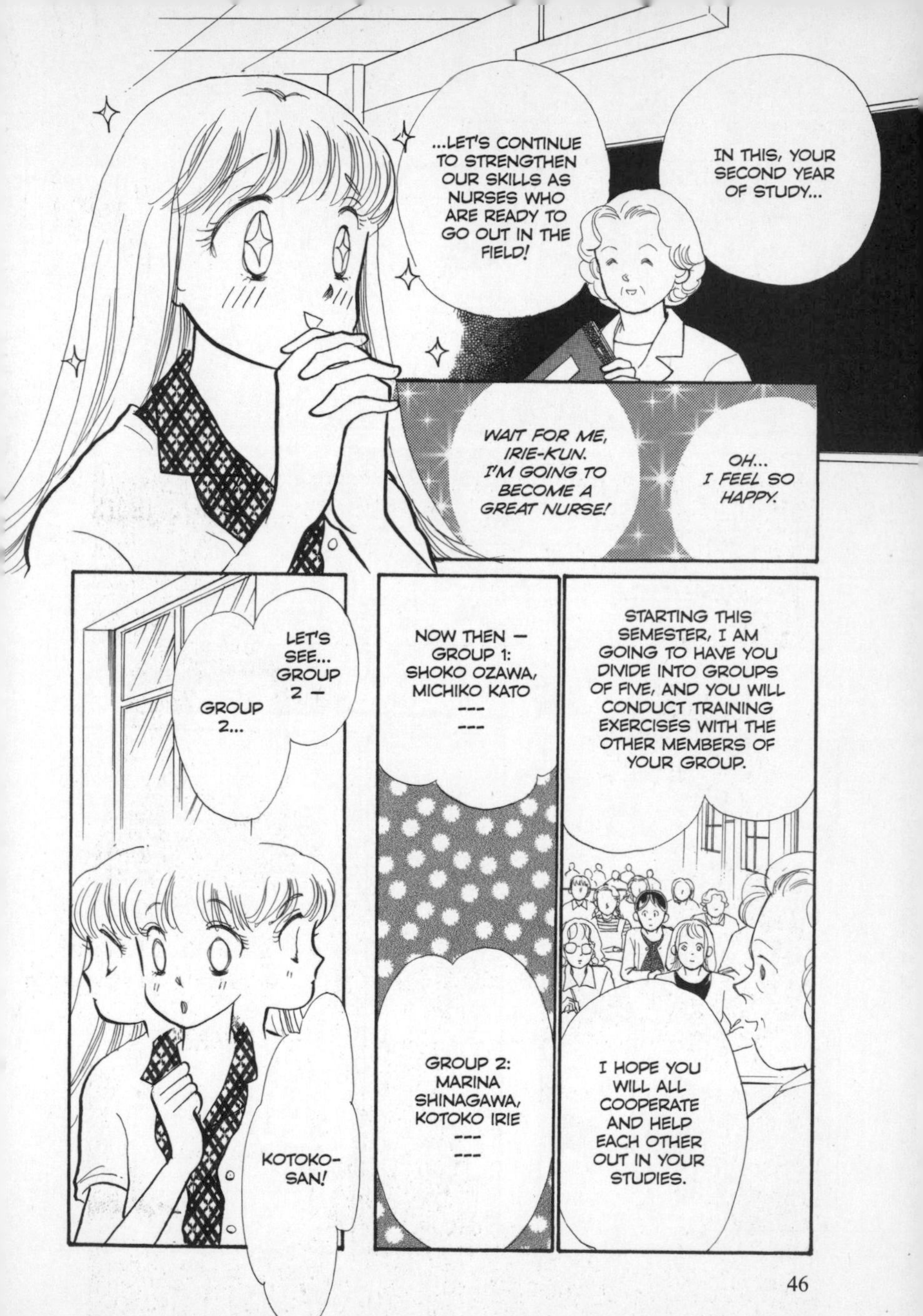
IN THIS, YOUR SECOND YEAR OF STUDY...
...LET'S CONTINUE TO STRENGTHEN OUR SKILLS AS NURSES WHO ARE READY TO GO OUT IN THE FIELD!
OH... I FEEL SO HAPPY.
WAIT FOR ME, IRIE-KUN. I'M GOING TO BECOME A GREAT NURSE!
STARTING THIS SEMESTER, I AM GOING TO HAVE YOU DIVIDE INTO GROUPS OF FIVE, AND YOU WILL CONDUCT TRAINING EXERCISES WITH THE OTHER MEMBERS OF YOUR GROUP.
I HOPE YOU WILL ALL COOPERATE AND HELP EACH OTHER OUT IN YOUR STUDIES.
NOW THEN — GROUP 1: SHOKO OZAWA, MICHIKO KATO --- ---
GROUP 2: MARINA SHINAGAWA, KOTOKO IRIE --- ---
LET'S SEE... GROUP 2 —
GROUP 2...
KOTOKO-SAN!

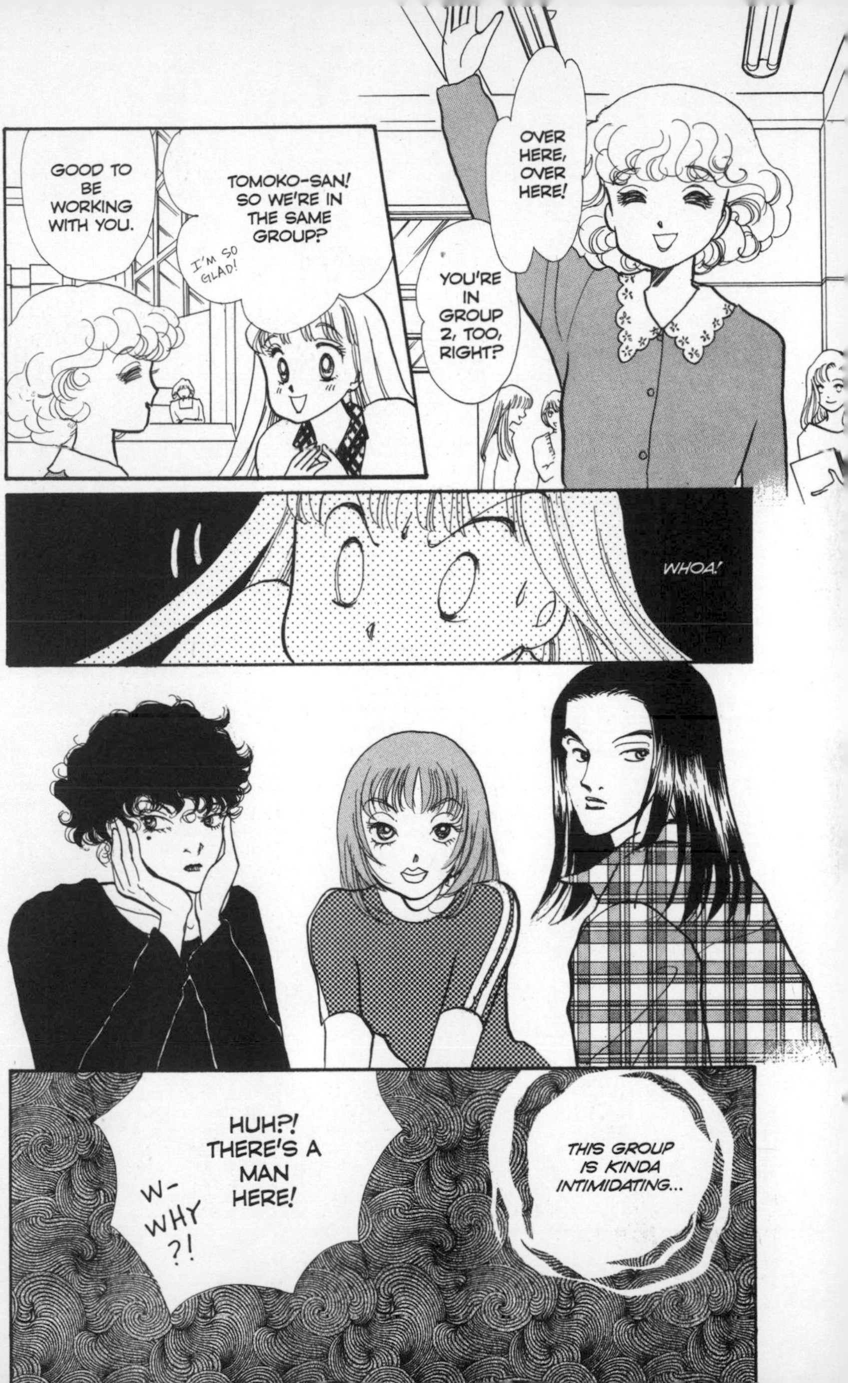
OVER HERE, OVER HERE!
YOU'RE IN GROUP 2, TOO, RIGHT?
TOMOKO-SAN! SO WE'RE IN THE SAME GROUP?
I'M SO GLAD!
GOOD TO BE WORKING WITH YOU.
WHOA!
THIS GROUP IS KINDA INTIMIDATING...
HUH?! THERE'S A MAN HERE!
W-WHY?!

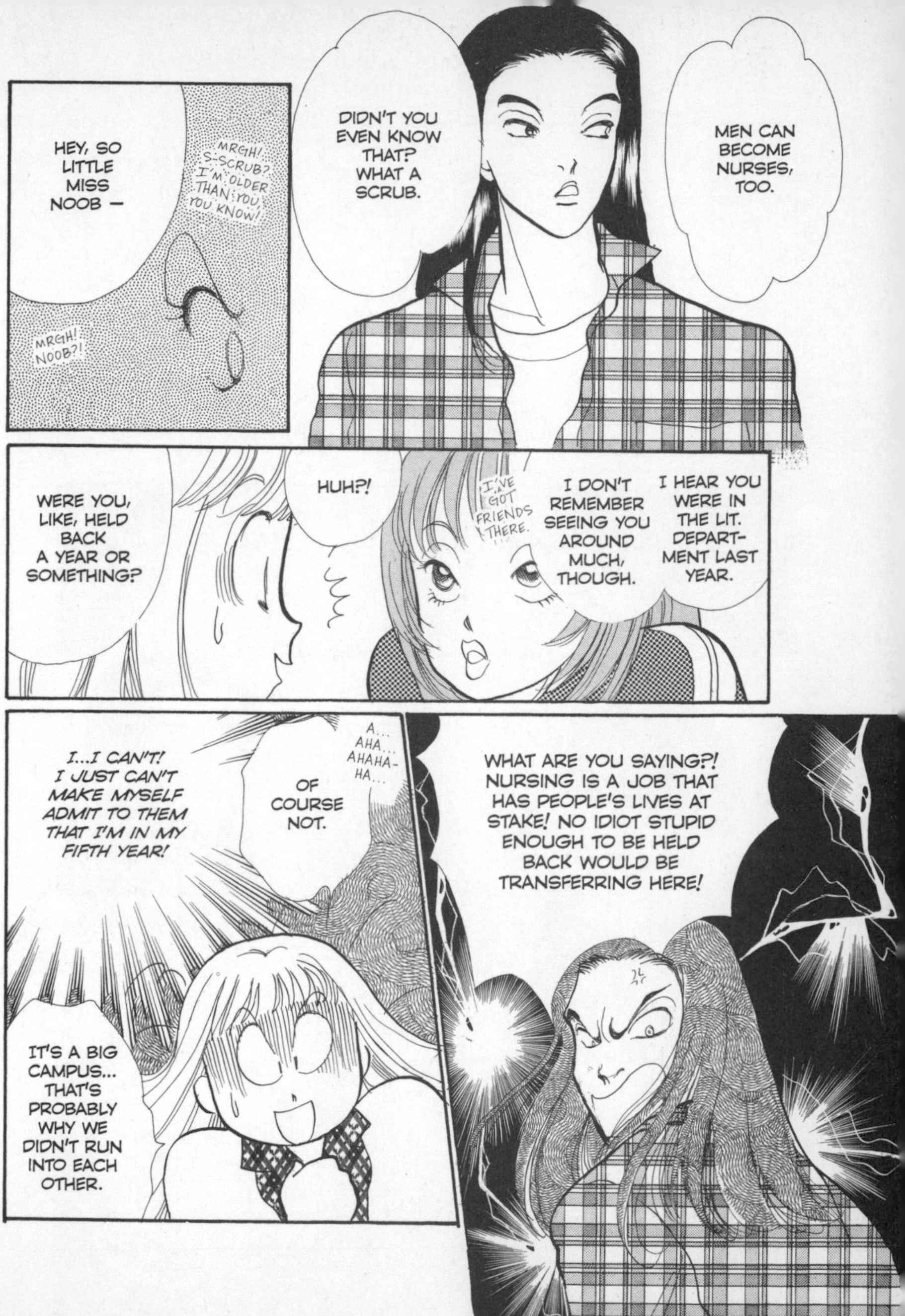
MEN CAN BECOME NURSES, TOO.
DIDN'T YOU EVEN KNOW THAT? WHAT A SCRUB.
MRGH! S-SCRUB? I'M OLDER THAN YOU, YOU KNOW!
HEY, SO LITTLE MISS NOOB —
MRGH! NOOB?!
I HEAR YOU WERE IN THE LIT. DEPART-MENT LAST YEAR.
I DON'T REMEMBER SEEING YOU AROUND MUCH, THOUGH.
I'VE GOT FRIENDS THERE.
HUH?!
WERE YOU, LIKE, HELD BACK A YEAR OR SOMETHING?
WHAT ARE YOU SAYING?! NURSING IS A JOB THAT HAS PEOPLE'S LIVES AT STAKE! NO IDIOT STUPID ENOUGH TO BE HELD BACK WOULD BE TRANSFERRING HERE!
A... AHA... AHAHA-HA...
OF COURSE NOT.
I...I CAN'T! I JUST CAN'T MAKE MYSELF ADMIT TO THEM THAT I'M IN MY FIFTH YEAR!
IT'S A BIG CAMPUS... THAT'S PROBABLY WHY WE DIDN'T RUN INTO EACH OTHER.

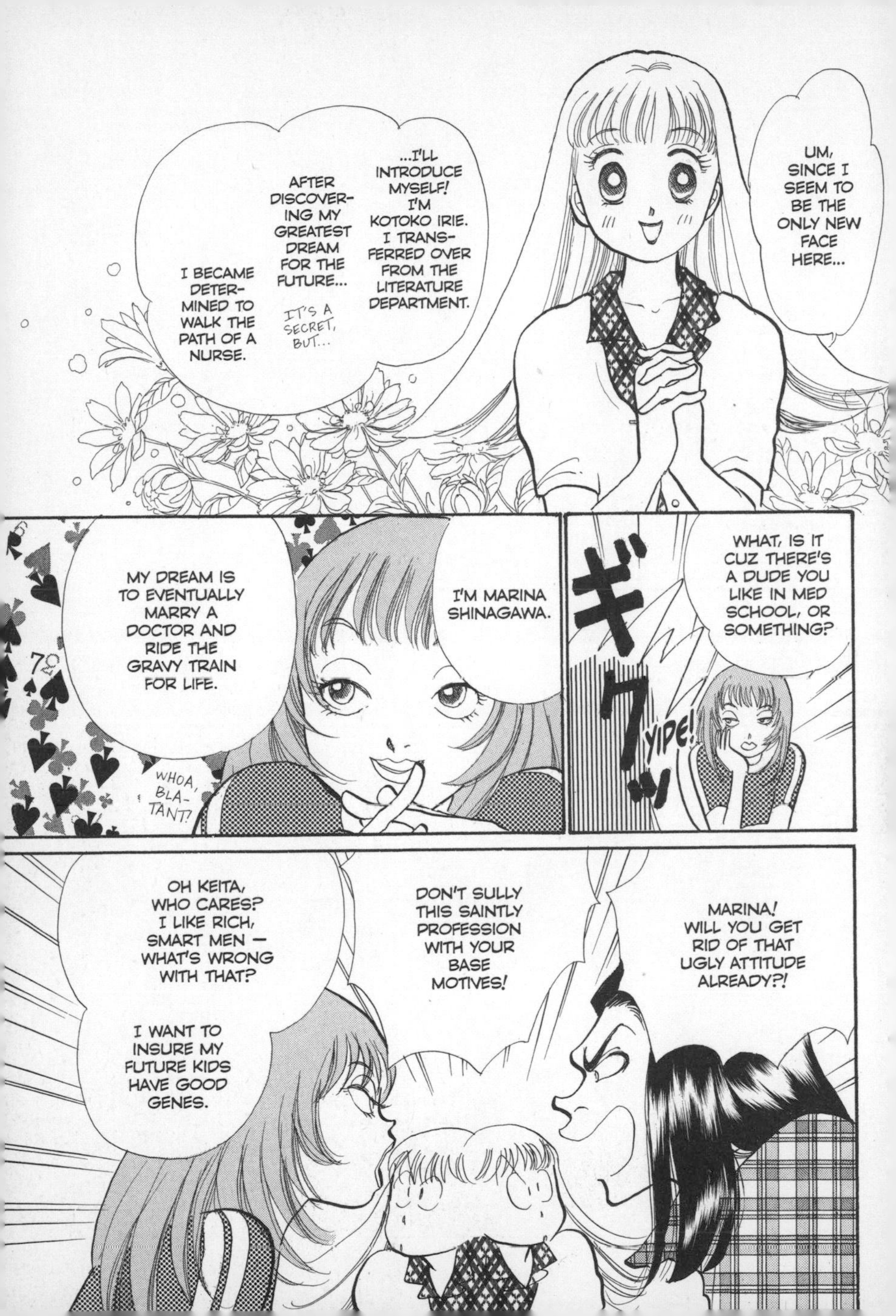
UM, SINCE I SEEM TO BE THE ONLY NEW FACE HERE...
...I'LL INTRODUCE MYSELF! I'M KOTOKO IRIE. I TRANSFERRED OVER FROM THE LITERATURE DEPARTMENT.
AFTER DISCOVERING MY GREATEST DREAM FOR THE FUTURE...
IT'S A SECRET, BUT...
I BECAME DETERMINED TO WALK THE PATH OF A NURSE.
WHAT, IS IT CUZ THERE'S A DUDE YOU LIKE IN MED SCHOOL, OR SOMETHING?
ギクッ
YIPE!
I'M MARINA SHINAGAWA.
MY DREAM IS TO EVENTUALLY MARRY A DOCTOR AND RIDE THE GRAVY TRAIN FOR LIFE.
WHOA, BLATANT!
MARINA! WILL YOU GET RID OF THAT UGLY ATTITUDE ALREADY?!
DON'T SULLY THIS SAINTLY PROFESSION WITH YOUR BASE MOTIVES!
OH KEITA, WHO CARES? I LIKE RICH, SMART MEN — WHAT'S WRONG WITH THAT?
I WANT TO INSURE MY FUTURE KIDS HAVE GOOD GENES.

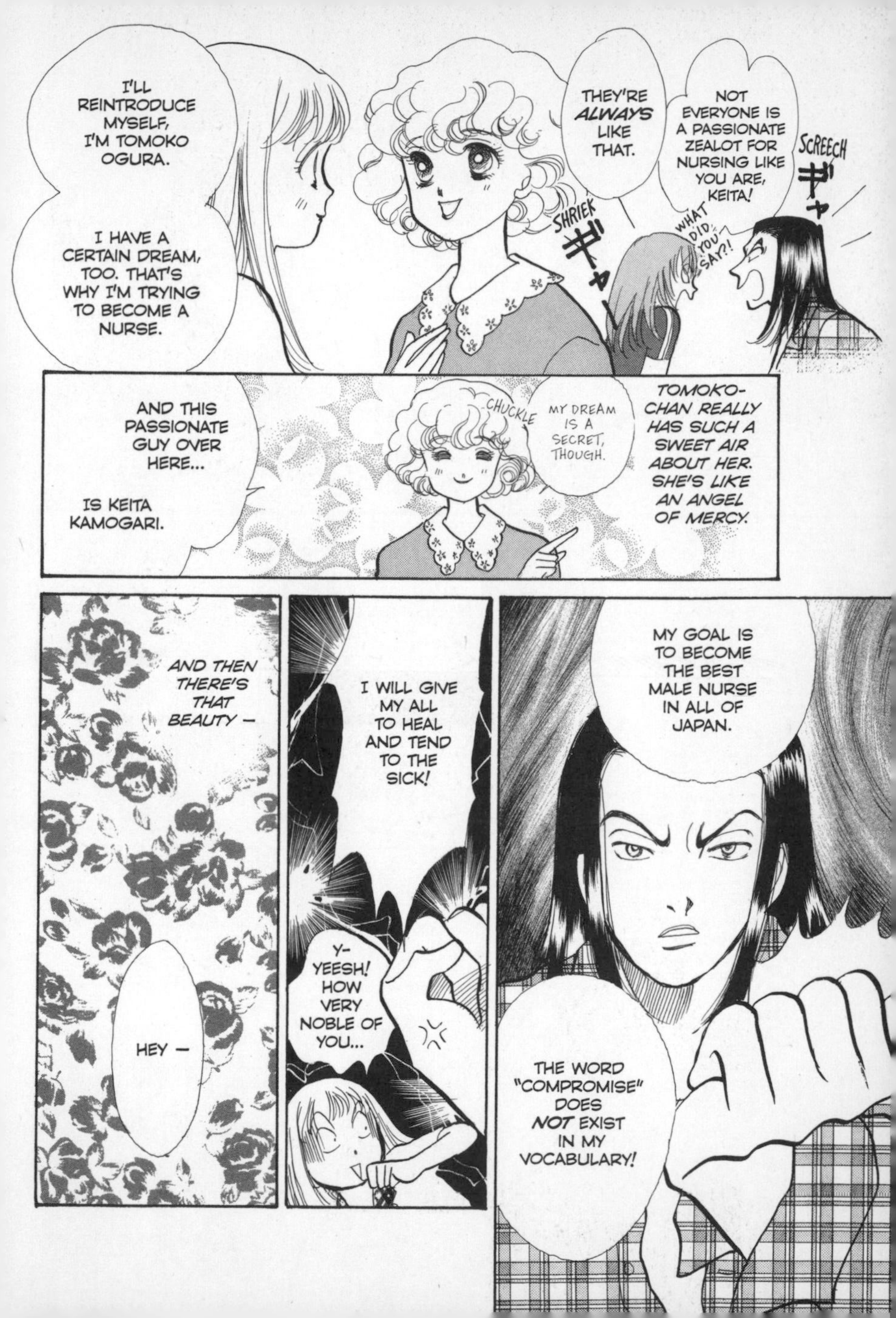
NOT EVERYONE IS A PASSIONATE ZEALOT FOR NURSING LIKE YOU ARE, KEITA!
SCREECH
WHAT DID YOU SAY?!
SHRIEK
THEY'RE *ALWAYS* LIKE THAT.
I'LL REINTRODUCE MYSELF, I'M TOMOKO OGURA.
I HAVE A CERTAIN DREAM, TOO. THAT'S WHY I'M TRYING TO BECOME A NURSE.
TOMOKO-CHAN REALLY HAS SUCH A SWEET AIR ABOUT HER. SHE'S LIKE AN ANGEL OF MERCY.
MY DREAM IS A SECRET, THOUGH.
CHUCKLE
AND THIS PASSIONATE GUY OVER HERE...
IS KEITA KAMOGARI.
MY GOAL IS TO BECOME THE BEST MALE NURSE IN ALL OF JAPAN.
THE WORD "COMPROMISE" DOES **NOT** EXIST IN MY VOCABULARY!
I WILL GIVE MY ALL TO HEAL AND TEND TO THE SICK!
Y-YEESH! HOW VERY NOBLE OF YOU...
AND THEN THERE'S THAT BEAUTY —
HEY —

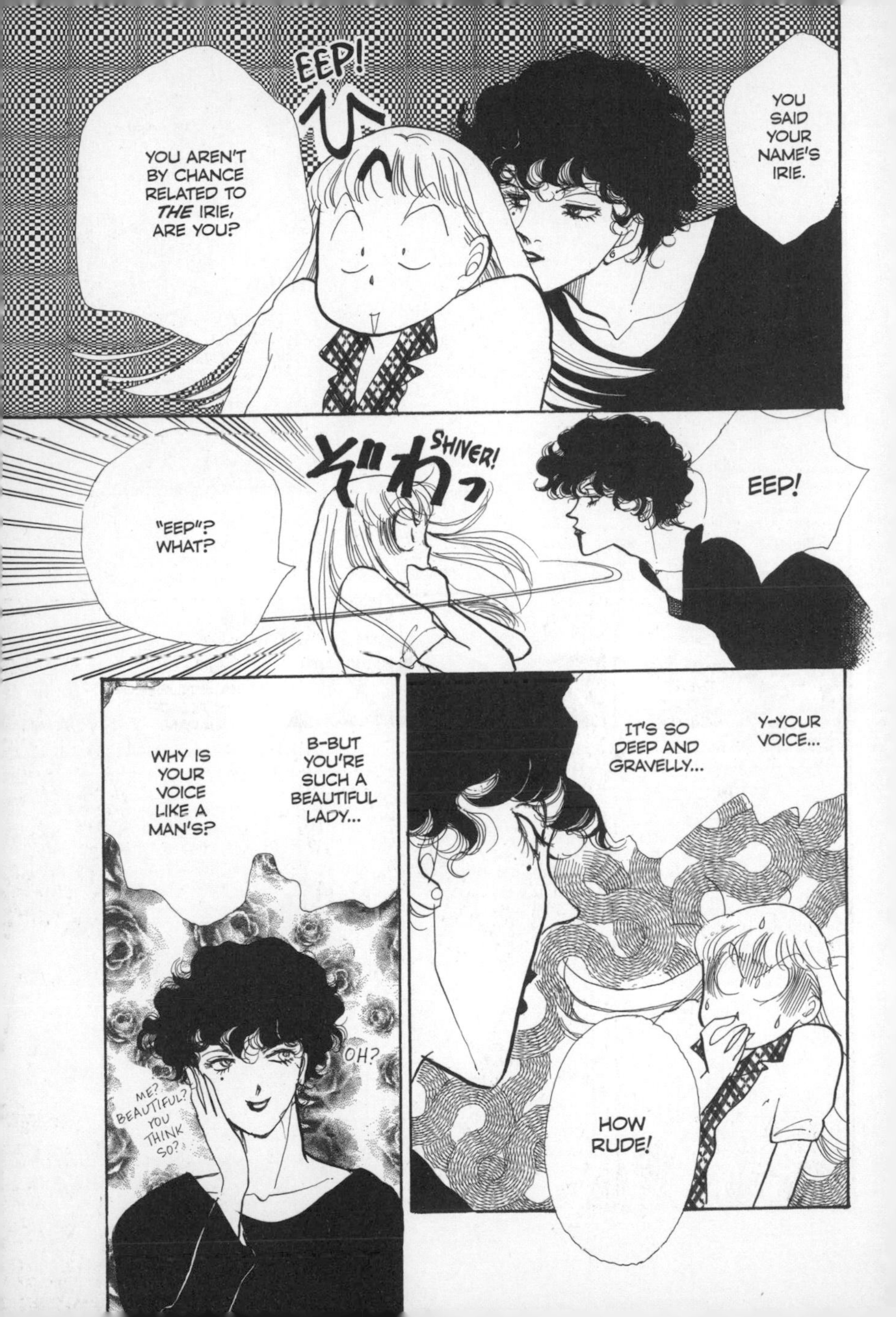
YOU SAID YOUR NAME'S IRIE.
ひ
EEP!
YOU AREN'T BY CHANCE RELATED TO *THE* IRIE, ARE YOU?
EEP!
ぞわっ
SHIVER!
"EEP"? WHAT?
Y-YOUR VOICE...
IT'S SO DEEP AND GRAVELLY...
HOW RUDE!
B-BUT YOU'RE SUCH A BEAUTIFUL LADY...
WHY IS YOUR VOICE LIKE A MAN'S?
OH?
ME? BEAUTIFUL? YOU THINK SO?

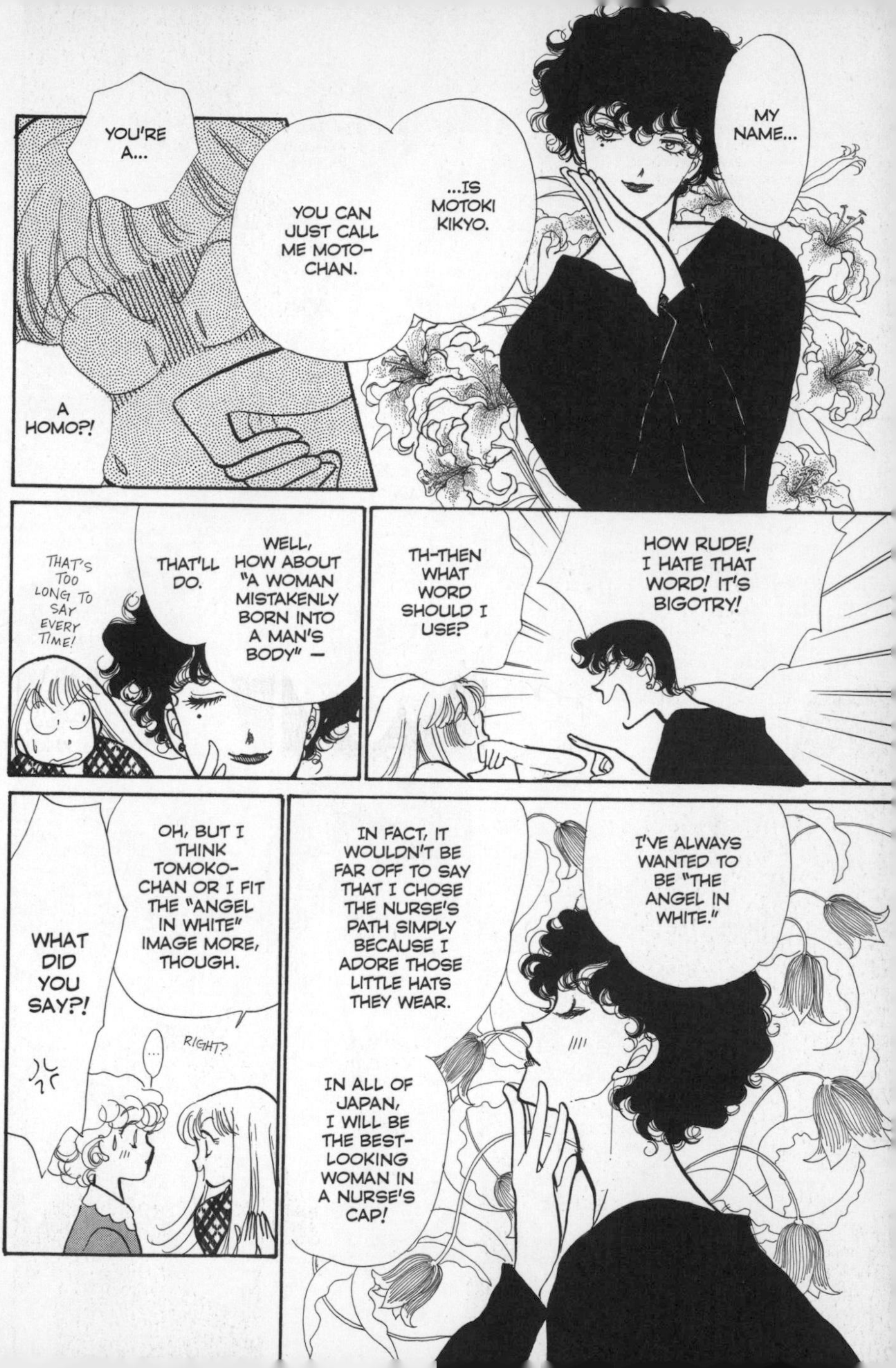
MY NAME...
...IS MOTOKI KIKYO.
YOU CAN JUST CALL ME MOTO-CHAN.
YOU'RE A...
A HOMO?!
HOW RUDE! I HATE THAT WORD! IT'S BIGOTRY!
TH-THEN WHAT WORD SHOULD I USE?
WELL, HOW ABOUT "A WOMAN MISTAKENLY BORN INTO A MAN'S BODY" —
THAT'LL DO.
THAT'S TOO LONG TO SAY EVERY TIME!
I'VE ALWAYS WANTED TO BE "THE ANGEL IN WHITE."
IN FACT, IT WOULDN'T BE FAR OFF TO SAY THAT I CHOSE THE NURSE'S PATH SIMPLY BECAUSE I ADORE THOSE LITTLE HATS THEY WEAR.
IN ALL OF JAPAN, I WILL BE THE BEST-LOOKING WOMAN IN A NURSE'S CAP!
OH, BUT I THINK TOMOKO-CHAN OR I FIT THE "ANGEL IN WHITE" IMAGE MORE, THOUGH.
RIGHT?
...
WHAT DID YOU SAY?!

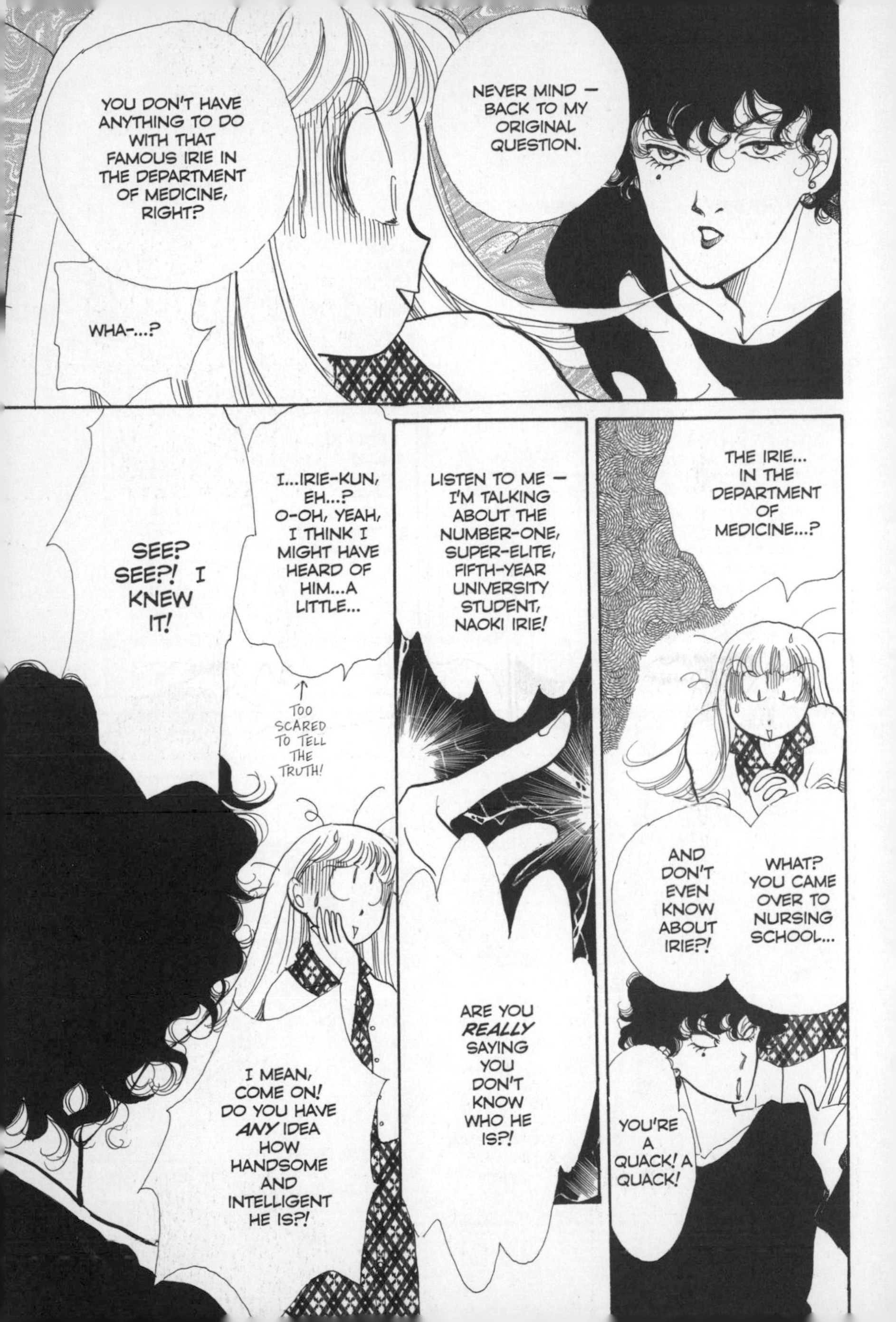
NEVER MIND — BACK TO MY ORIGINAL QUESTION.
YOU DON'T HAVE ANYTHING TO DO WITH THAT FAMOUS IRIE IN THE DEPARTMENT OF MEDICINE, RIGHT?
WHA-...?
THE IRIE... IN THE DEPARTMENT OF MEDICINE...?
WHAT? YOU CAME OVER TO NURSING SCHOOL...
AND DON'T EVEN KNOW ABOUT IRIE?!
YOU'RE A QUACK! A QUACK!
LISTEN TO ME — I'M TALKING ABOUT THE NUMBER-ONE, SUPER-ELITE, FIFTH-YEAR UNIVERSITY STUDENT, NAOKI IRIE!
ARE YOU *REALLY* SAYING YOU DON'T KNOW WHO HE IS?!
I...IRIE-KUN, EH...? O-OH, YEAH, I THINK I MIGHT HAVE HEARD OF HIM...A LITTLE...
TOO SCARED TO TELL THE TRUTH!
SEE? SEE?! I KNEW IT!
I MEAN, COME ON! DO YOU HAVE *ANY* IDEA HOW HANDSOME AND INTELLIGENT HE IS?!

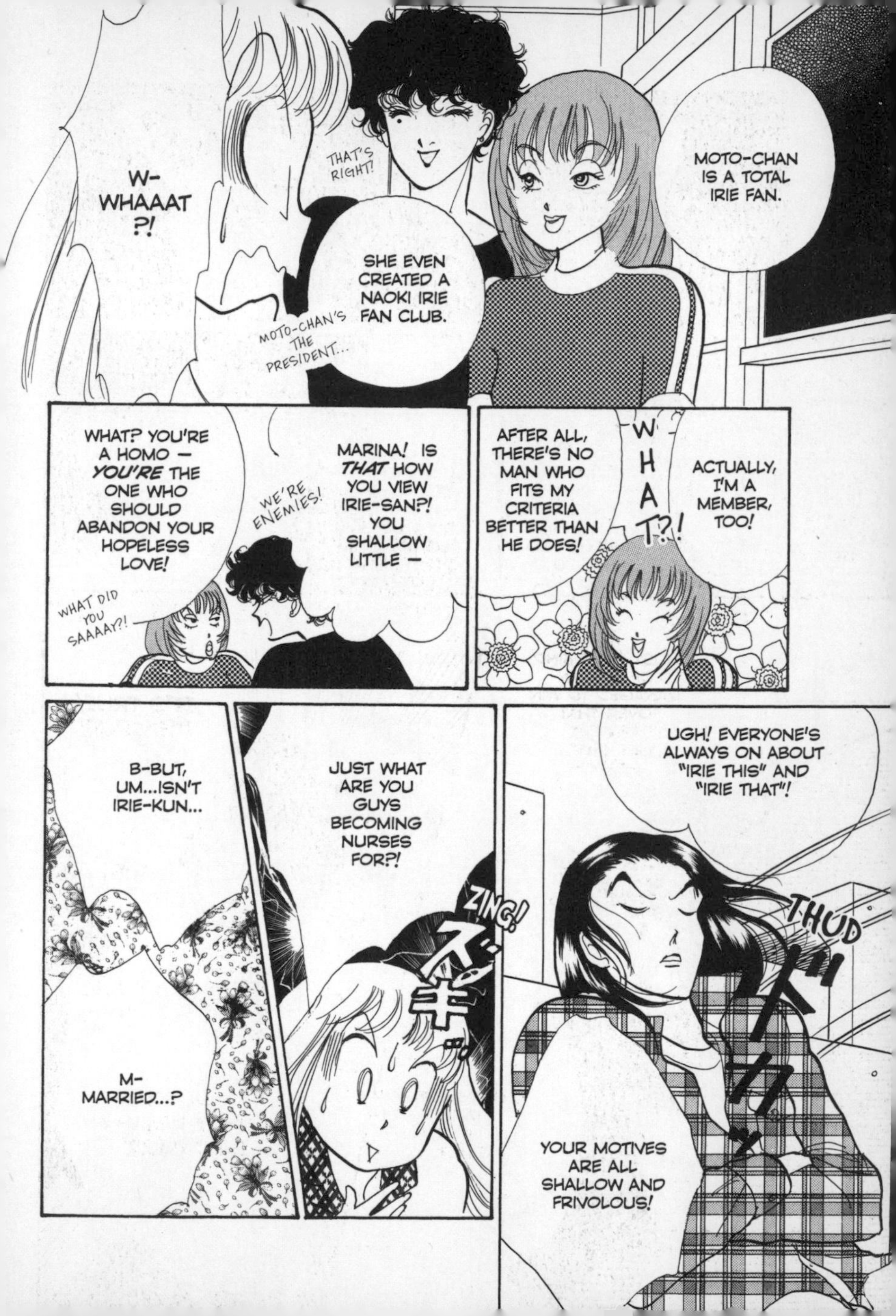
MOTO-CHAN IS A TOTAL IRIE FAN.
THAT'S RIGHT!
SHE EVEN CREATED A NAOKI IRIE FAN CLUB.
MOTO-CHAN'S THE PRESIDENT...
W-WHAAAT?!
ACTUALLY, I'M A MEMBER, TOO!
WHAT?!
AFTER ALL, THERE'S NO MAN WHO FITS MY CRITERIA BETTER THAN HE DOES!
MARINA! IS THAT HOW YOU VIEW IRIE-SAN?! YOU SHALLOW LITTLE —
WE'RE ENEMIES!
WHAT? YOU'RE A HOMO — YOU'RE THE ONE WHO SHOULD ABANDON YOUR HOPELESS LOVE!
WHAT DID YOU SAAAAY?!
UGH! EVERYONE'S ALWAYS ON ABOUT "IRIE THIS" AND "IRIE THAT"!
THUD
YOUR MOTIVES ARE ALL SHALLOW AND FRIVOLOUS!
JUST WHAT ARE YOU GUYS BECOMING NURSES FOR?!
ZING!
B-BUT, UM...ISN'T IRIE-KUN...
M-MARRIED...?

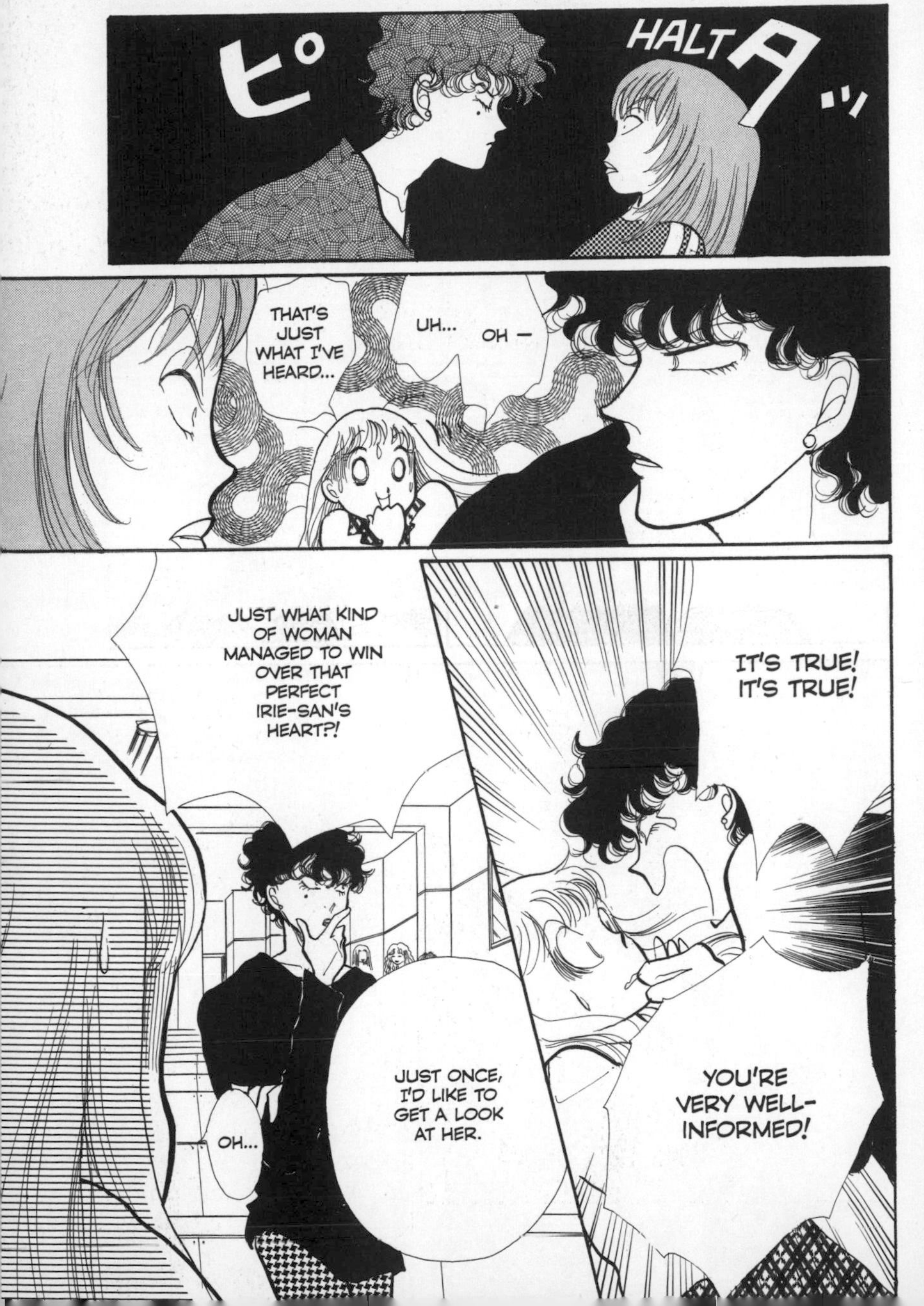
HALT タッ
ピ
OH —
UH...
THAT'S JUST WHAT I'VE HEARD...
IT'S TRUE! IT'S TRUE!
YOU'RE VERY WELL-INFORMED!
JUST WHAT KIND OF WOMAN MANAGED TO WIN OVER THAT PERFECT IRIE-SAN'S HEART?!
JUST ONCE, I'D LIKE TO GET A LOOK AT HER.
OH...

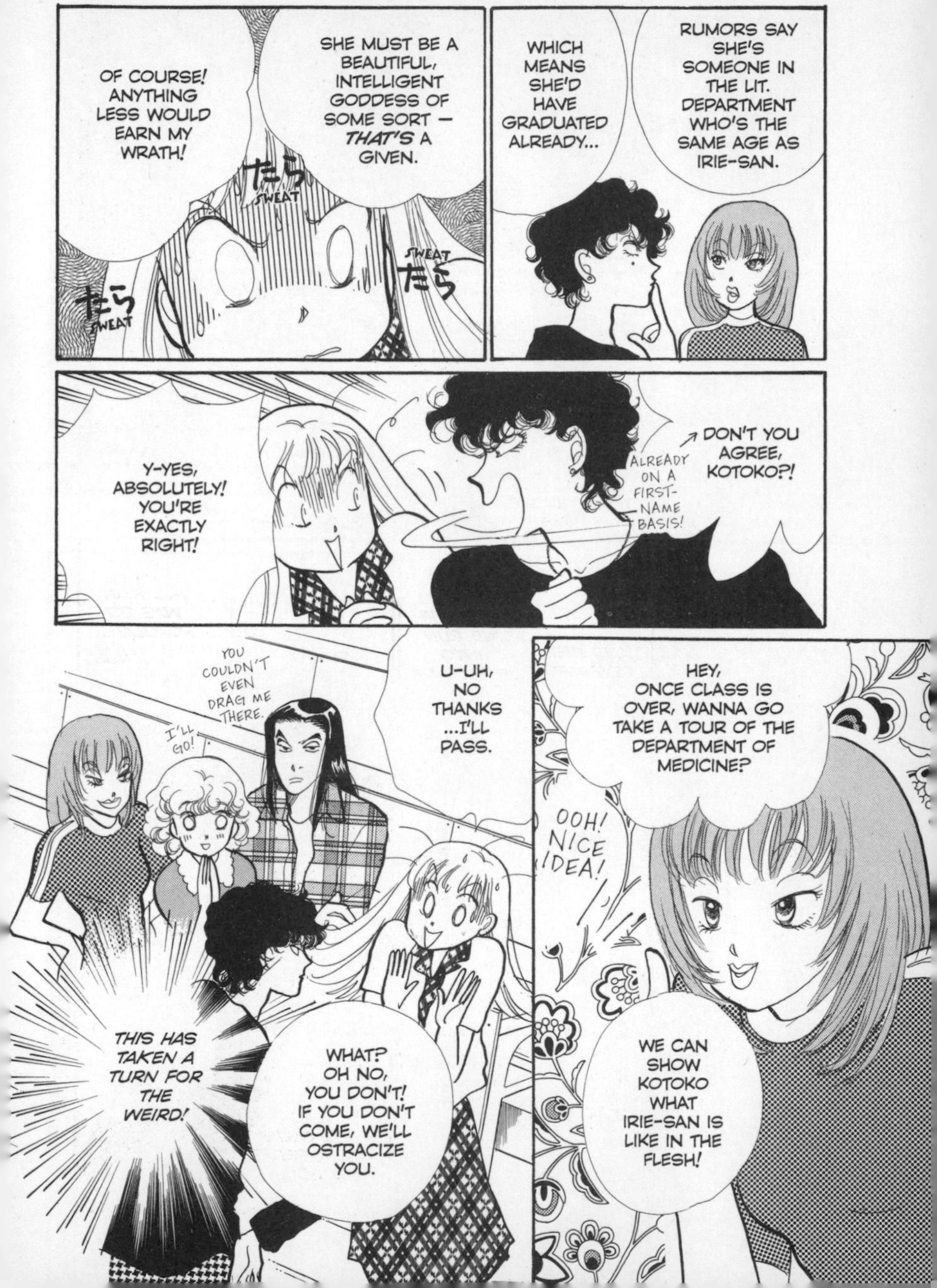
RUMORS SAY SHE'S SOMEONE IN THE LIT. DEPARTMENT WHO'S THE SAME AGE AS IRIE-SAN.
WHICH MEANS SHE'D HAVE GRADUATED ALREADY...
SHE MUST BE A BEAUTIFUL, INTELLIGENT GODDESS OF SOME SORT — *THAT'S* A GIVEN.
OF COURSE! ANYTHING LESS WOULD EARN MY WRATH!
たら SWEAT
たら SWEAT
たら SWEAT
DON'T YOU AGREE, KOTOKO?!
ALREADY ON A FIRST-NAME BASIS!
Y-YES, ABSOLUTELY! YOU'RE EXACTLY RIGHT!
HEY, ONCE CLASS IS OVER, WANNA GO TAKE A TOUR OF THE DEPARTMENT OF MEDICINE?
OOH! NICE IDEA!
WE CAN SHOW KOTOKO WHAT IRIE-SAN IS LIKE IN THE FLESH!
U-UH, NO THANKS ...I'LL PASS.
YOU COULDN'T EVEN DRAG ME THERE.
I'LL GO!
WHAT? OH NO, YOU DON'T! IF YOU DON'T COME, WE'LL OSTRACIZE YOU.
THIS HAS TAKEN A TURN FOR THE WEIRD!

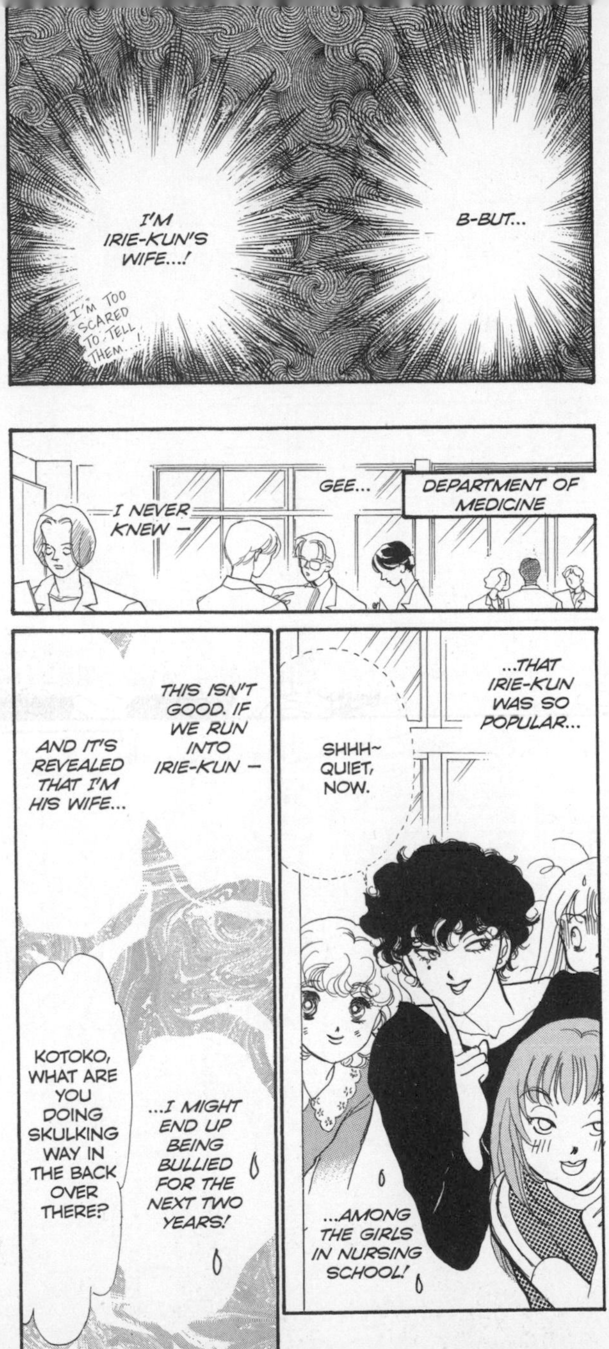
I'M IRIE-KUN'S WIFE...!
B-BUT...
I'M TOO SCARED TO TELL THEM...!
DEPARTMENT OF MEDICINE
GEE...
I NEVER KNEW —
...THAT IRIE-KUN WAS SO POPULAR...
SHHH~ QUIET, NOW.
...AMONG THE GIRLS IN NURSING SCHOOL!
THIS ISN'T GOOD. IF WE RUN INTO IRIE-KUN —
AND IT'S REVEALED THAT I'M HIS WIFE...
...I MIGHT END UP BEING BULLIED FOR THE NEXT TWO YEARS!
KOTOKO, WHAT ARE YOU DOING SKULKING WAY IN THE BACK OVER THERE?

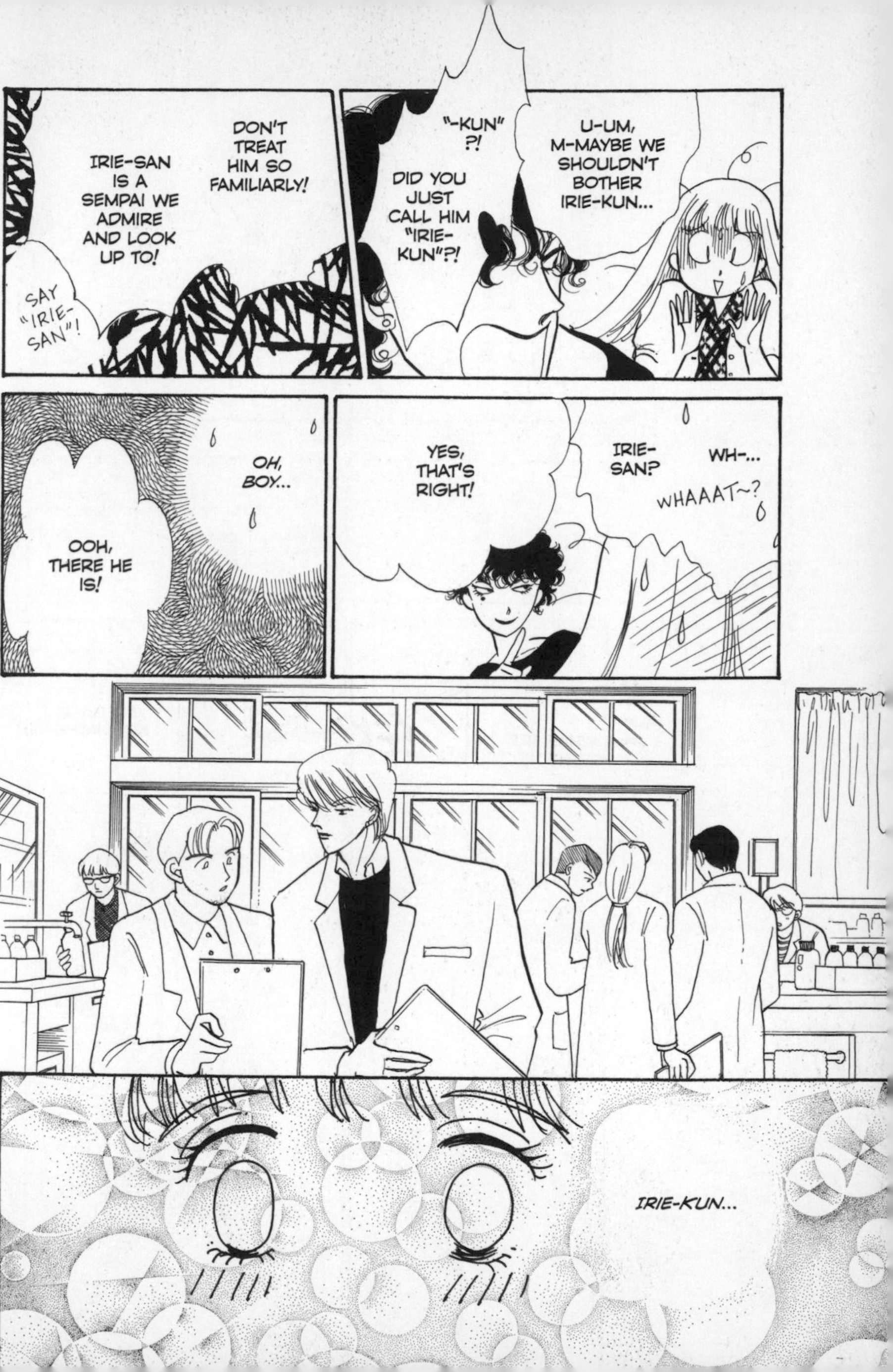
U-UM, M-MAYBE WE SHOULDN'T BOTHER IRIE-KUN...
"-KUN" ?!
DID YOU JUST CALL HIM "IRIE-KUN"?!
DON'T TREAT HIM SO FAMILIARLY!
IRIE-SAN IS A SEMPAI WE ADMIRE AND LOOK UP TO!
SAY "IRIE-SAN"!
WH-...
WHAAAT~?
IRIE-SAN?
YES, THAT'S RIGHT!
OH, BOY...
OOH, THERE HE IS!
IRIE-KUN...

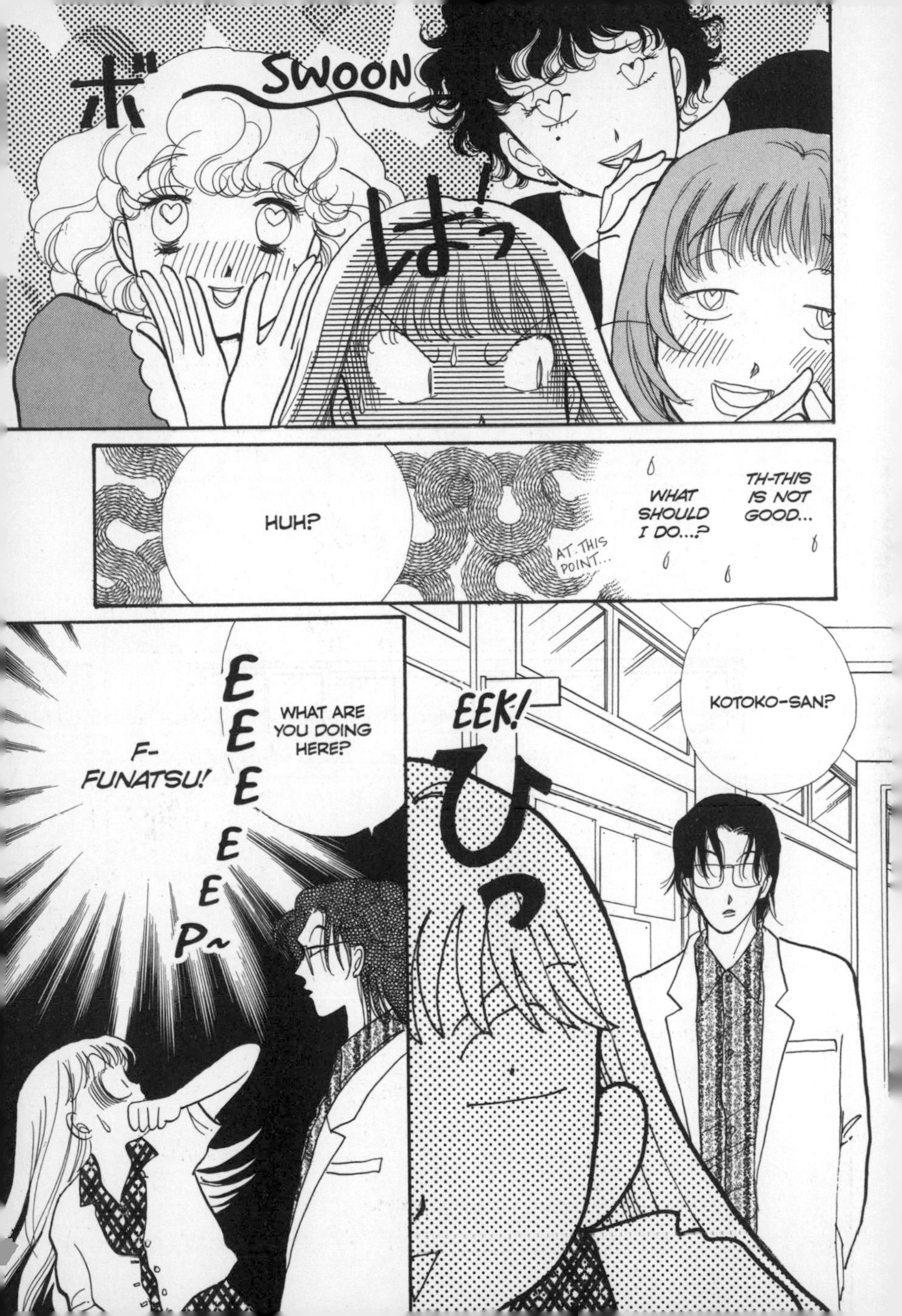
ボ
SWOON
はっ
TH-THIS IS NOT GOOD...
WHAT SHOULD I DO...?
AT THIS POINT...
HUH?
KOTOKO-SAN?
EEK!
ひっ
WHAT ARE YOU DOING HERE?
EEEEEEP~
F- FUNATSU!

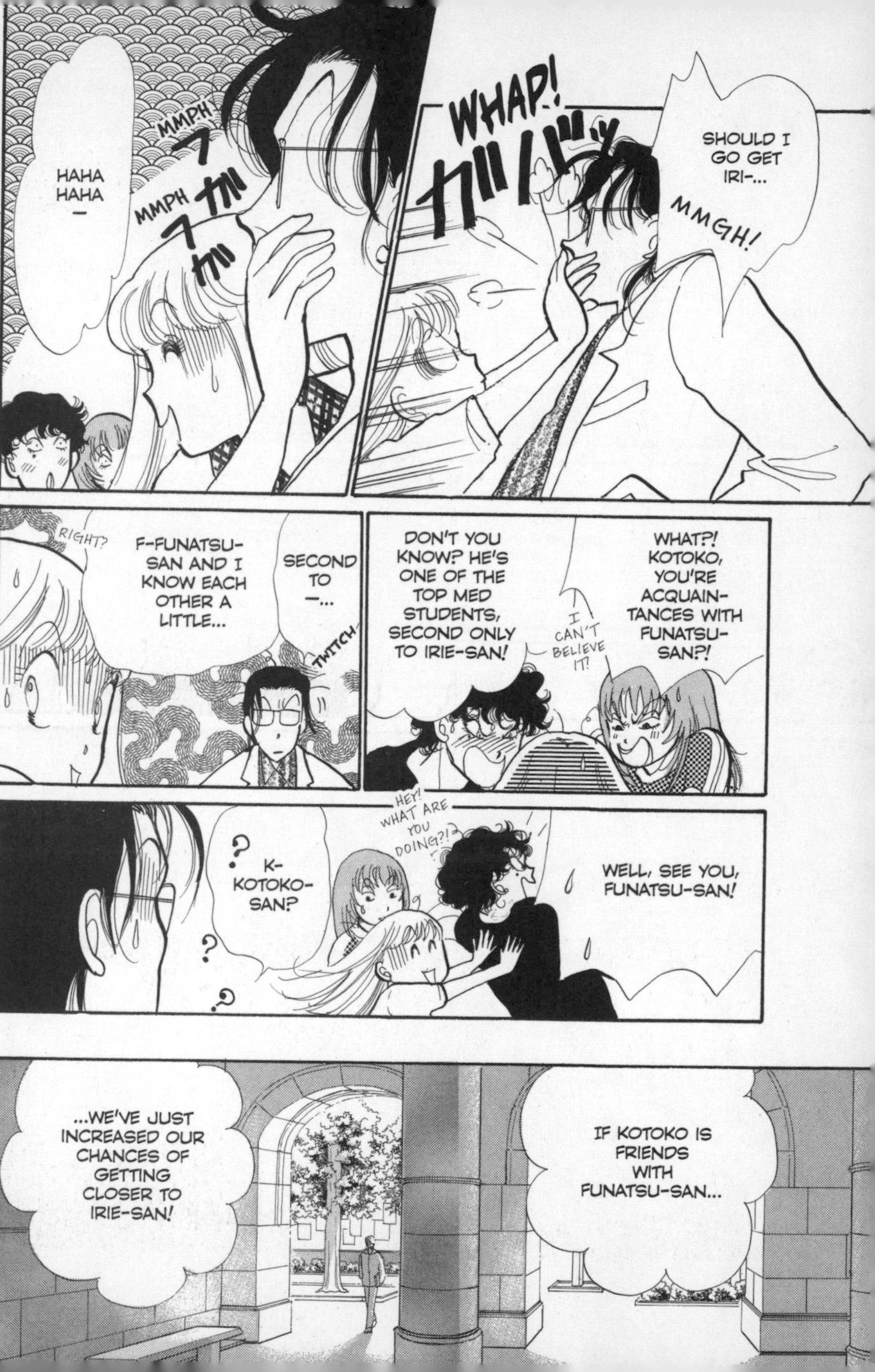
SHOULD I GO GET IRI-...
MMGH!
WHAP!
MMPH
MMPH
HAHA HAHA —
WHAT?! KOTOKO, YOU'RE ACQUAINTANCES WITH FUNATSU-SAN?!
I CAN'T BELIEVE IT!
DON'T YOU KNOW? HE'S ONE OF THE TOP MED STUDENTS, SECOND ONLY TO IRIE-SAN!
SECOND TO —...
TWITCH
F-FUNATSU-SAN AND I KNOW EACH OTHER A LITTLE...
RIGHT?
WELL, SEE YOU, FUNATSU-SAN!
HEY! WHAT ARE YOU DOING?!
K-KOTOKO-SAN?
IF KOTOKO IS FRIENDS WITH FUNATSU-SAN...
...WE'VE JUST INCREASED OUR CHANCES OF GETTING CLOSER TO IRIE-SAN!

STAFF: AKIKO ISHIKAWA, ATSUKO SUGIMOTO, MASAKO KATAGAI THANK YOU VERY MUCH ♡

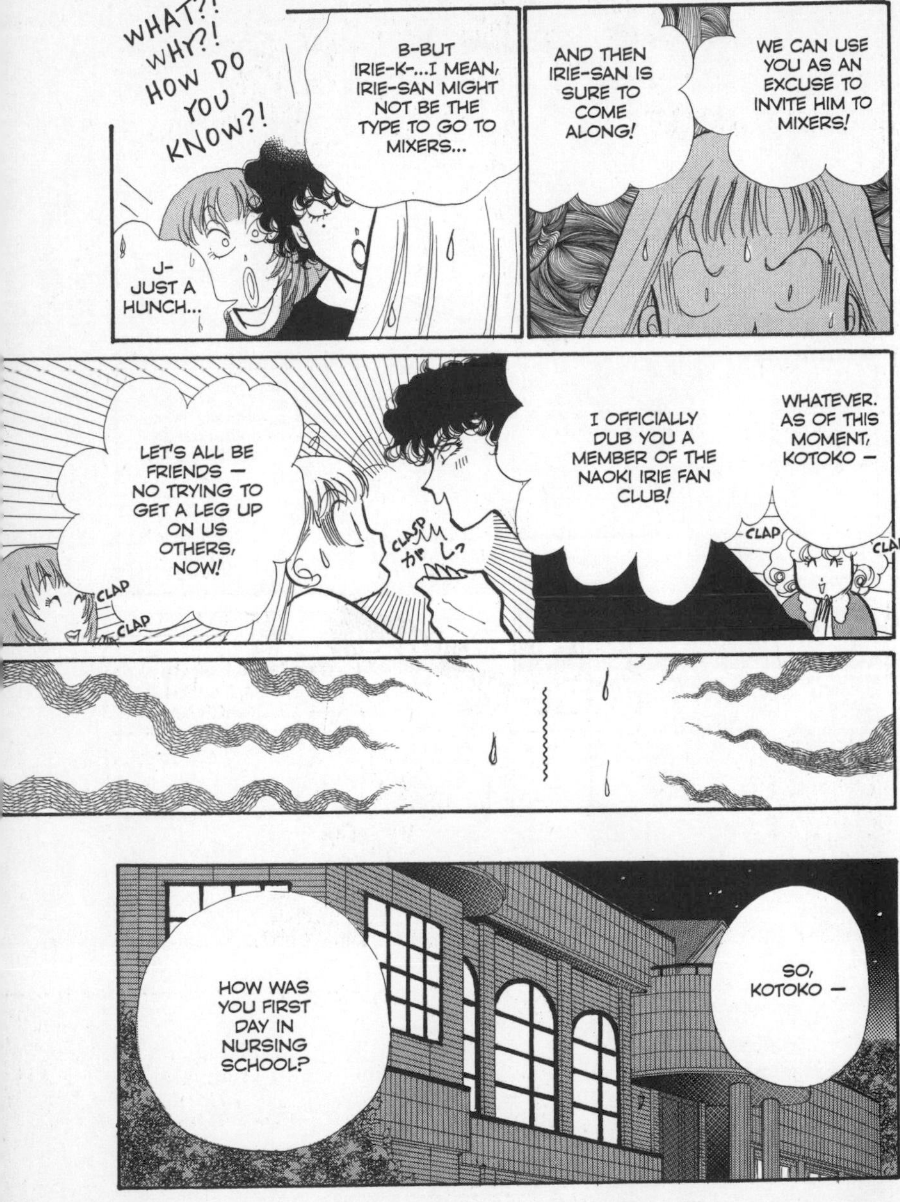
WE CAN USE YOU AS AN EXCUSE TO INVITE HIM TO MIXERS!
AND THEN IRIE-SAN IS SURE TO COME ALONG!
B-BUT IRIE-K-...I MEAN, IRIE-SAN MIGHT NOT BE THE TYPE TO GO TO MIXERS...
WHAT?! WHY?! HOW DO YOU KNOW?!
J- JUST A HUNCH...
WHATEVER. AS OF THIS MOMENT, KOTOKO —
I OFFICIALLY DUB YOU A MEMBER OF THE NAOKI IRIE FAN CLUB!
CLAP
CLAP
CLASP
がしっ
LET'S ALL BE FRIENDS — NO TRYING TO GET A LEG UP ON US OTHERS, NOW!
CLAP
CLAP
SO, KOTOKO —
HOW WAS YOU FIRST DAY IN NURSING SCHOOL?

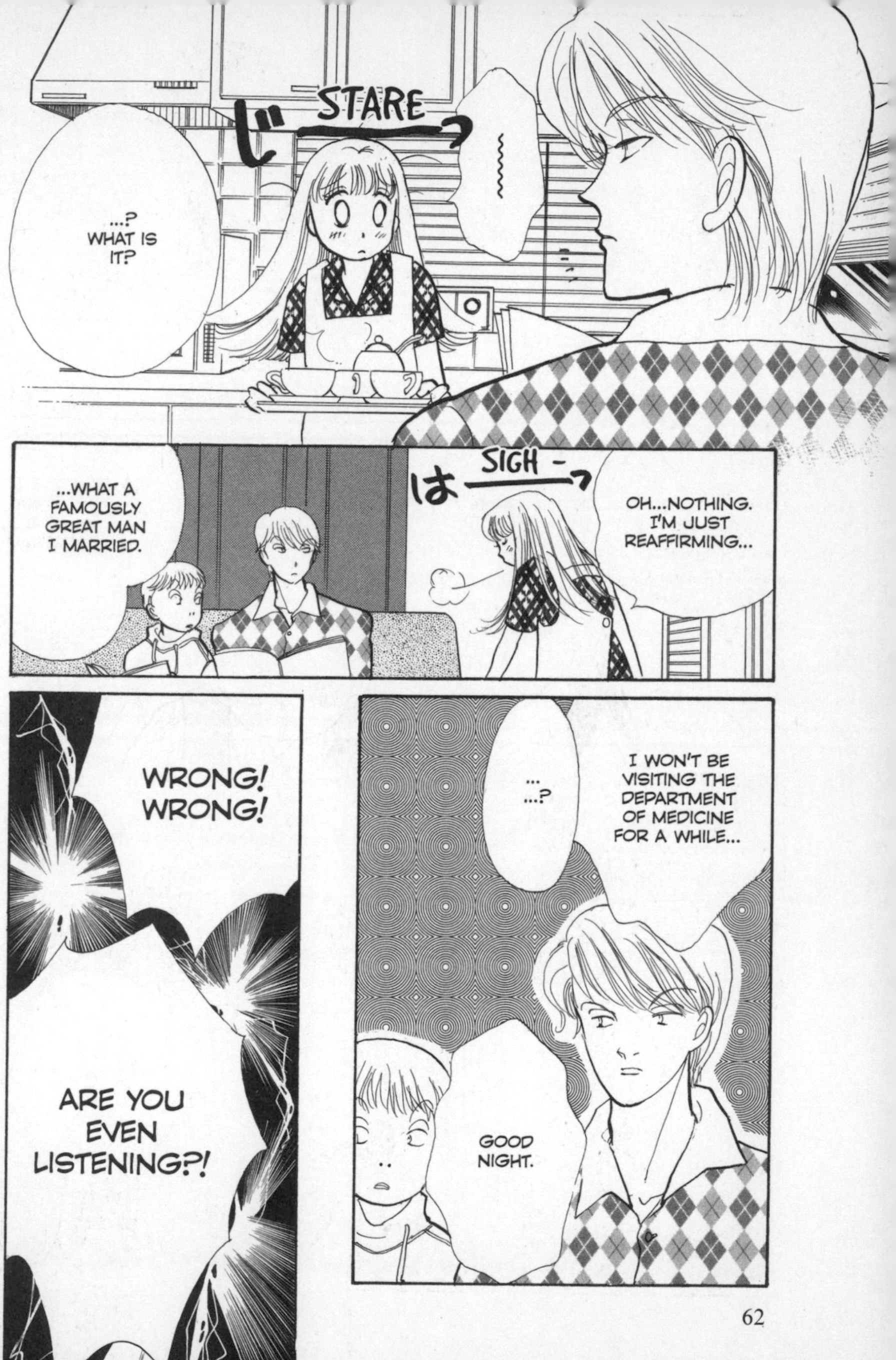
じ STARE
...? WHAT IS IT?
は SIGH
OH...NOTHING. I'M JUST REAFFIRMING...
...WHAT A FAMOUSLY GREAT MAN I MARRIED.
I WON'T BE VISITING THE DEPARTMENT OF MEDICINE FOR A WHILE...
... ...?
GOOD NIGHT.
WRONG! WRONG!
ARE YOU EVEN LISTENING?!

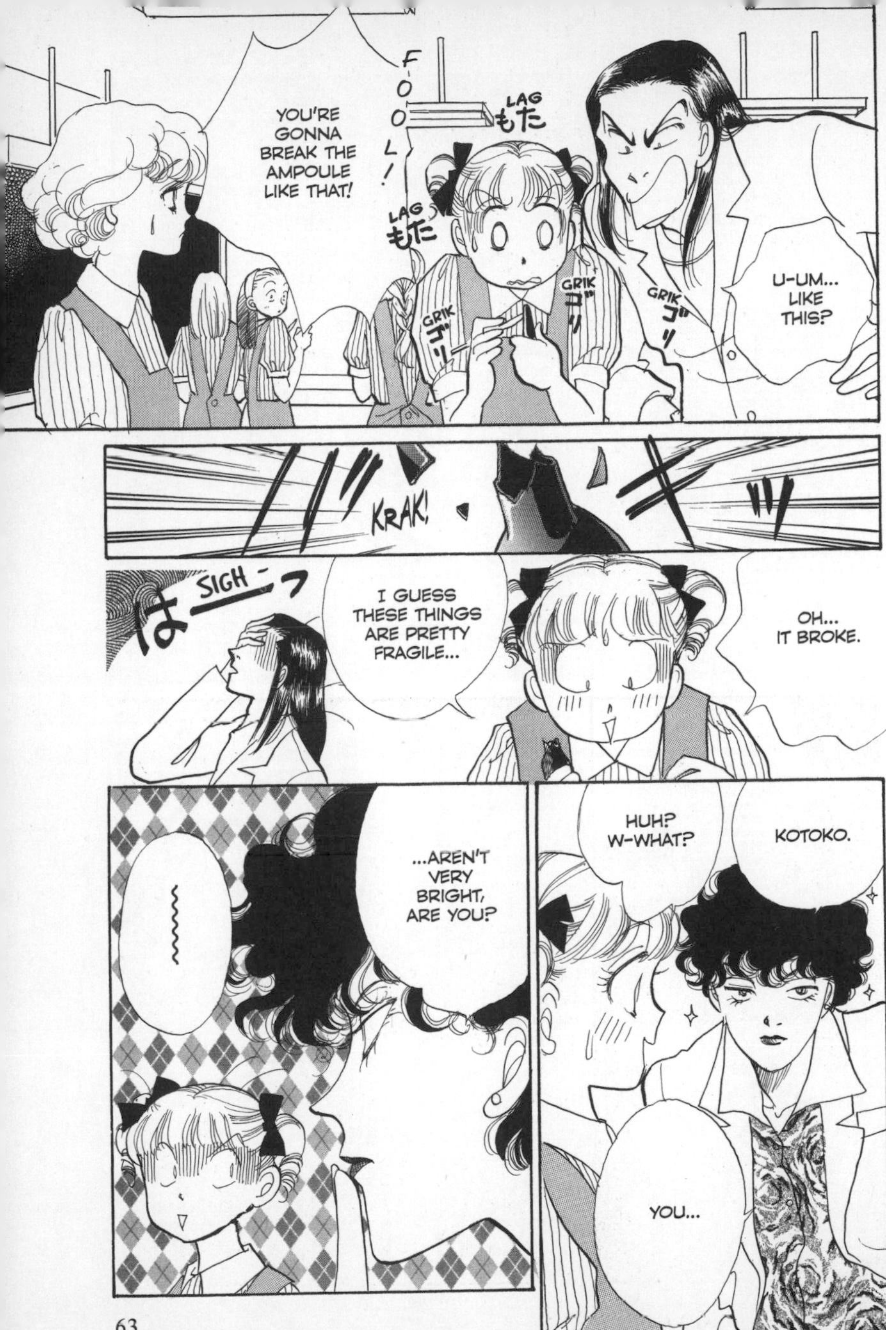
U-UM... LIKE THIS?
GRIK ゴリ
GRIK ゴリ
LAG もた
F-O-O-L!
GRIK ゴリ
LAG もた
YOU'RE GONNA BREAK THE AMPOULE LIKE THAT!
KRAK!
OH... IT BROKE.
I GUESS THESE THINGS ARE PRETTY FRAGILE...
SIGH は一っ
KOTOKO.
HUH? W-WHAT?
YOU...
...AREN'T VERY BRIGHT, ARE YOU?

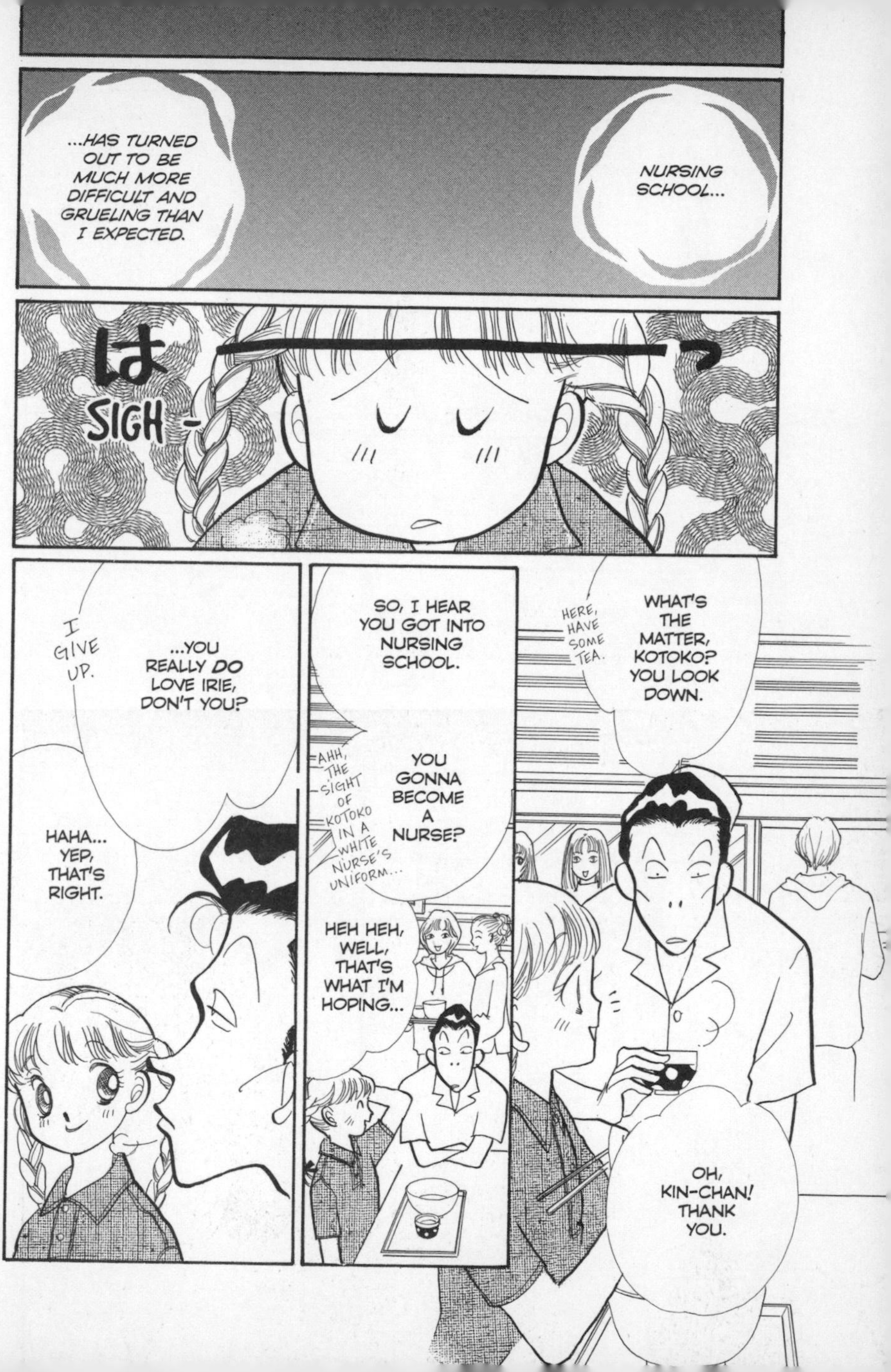
NURSING SCHOOL...
...HAS TURNED OUT TO BE MUCH MORE DIFFICULT AND GRUELING THAN I EXPECTED.
は
SIGH
WHAT'S THE MATTER, KOTOKO? YOU LOOK DOWN.
HERE, HAVE SOME TEA.
OH, KIN-CHAN! THANK YOU.
SO, I HEAR YOU GOT INTO NURSING SCHOOL.
YOU GONNA BECOME A NURSE?
AHH, THE SIGHT OF KOTOKO IN A WHITE NURSE'S UNIFORM...
HEH HEH, WELL, THAT'S WHAT I'M HOPING...
...YOU REALLY *DO* LOVE IRIE, DON'T YOU?
I GIVE UP.
HAHA... YEP, THAT'S RIGHT.

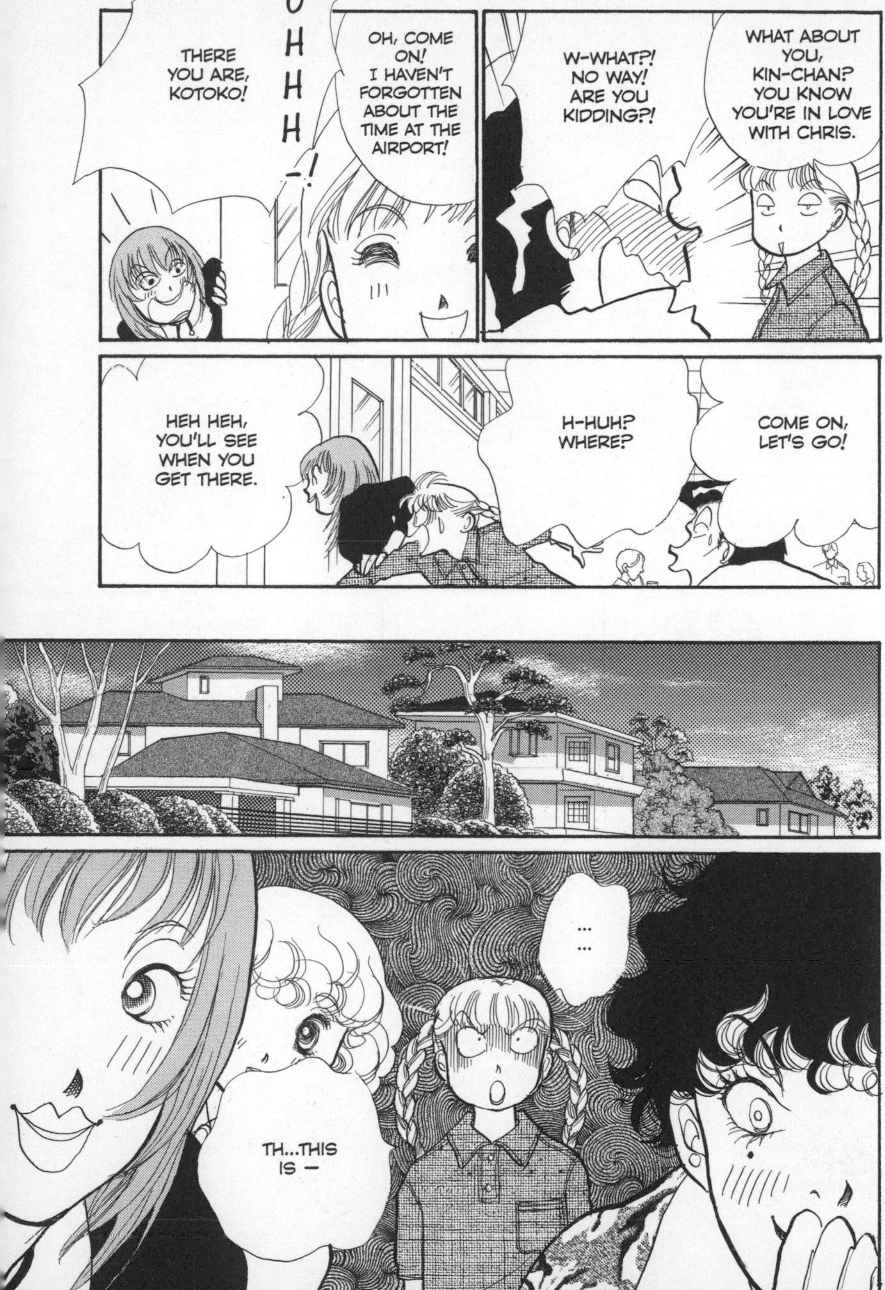
WHAT ABOUT YOU, KIN-CHAN? YOU KNOW YOU'RE IN LOVE WITH CHRIS.
W-WHAT?! NO WAY! ARE YOU KIDDING?!
OH, COME ON! I HAVEN'T FORGOTTEN ABOUT THE TIME AT THE AIRPORT!
OHHH—!
THERE YOU ARE, KOTOKO!
COME ON, LET'S GO!
H-HUH? WHERE?
HEH HEH, YOU'LL SEE WHEN YOU GET THERE.
......
TH...THIS IS —

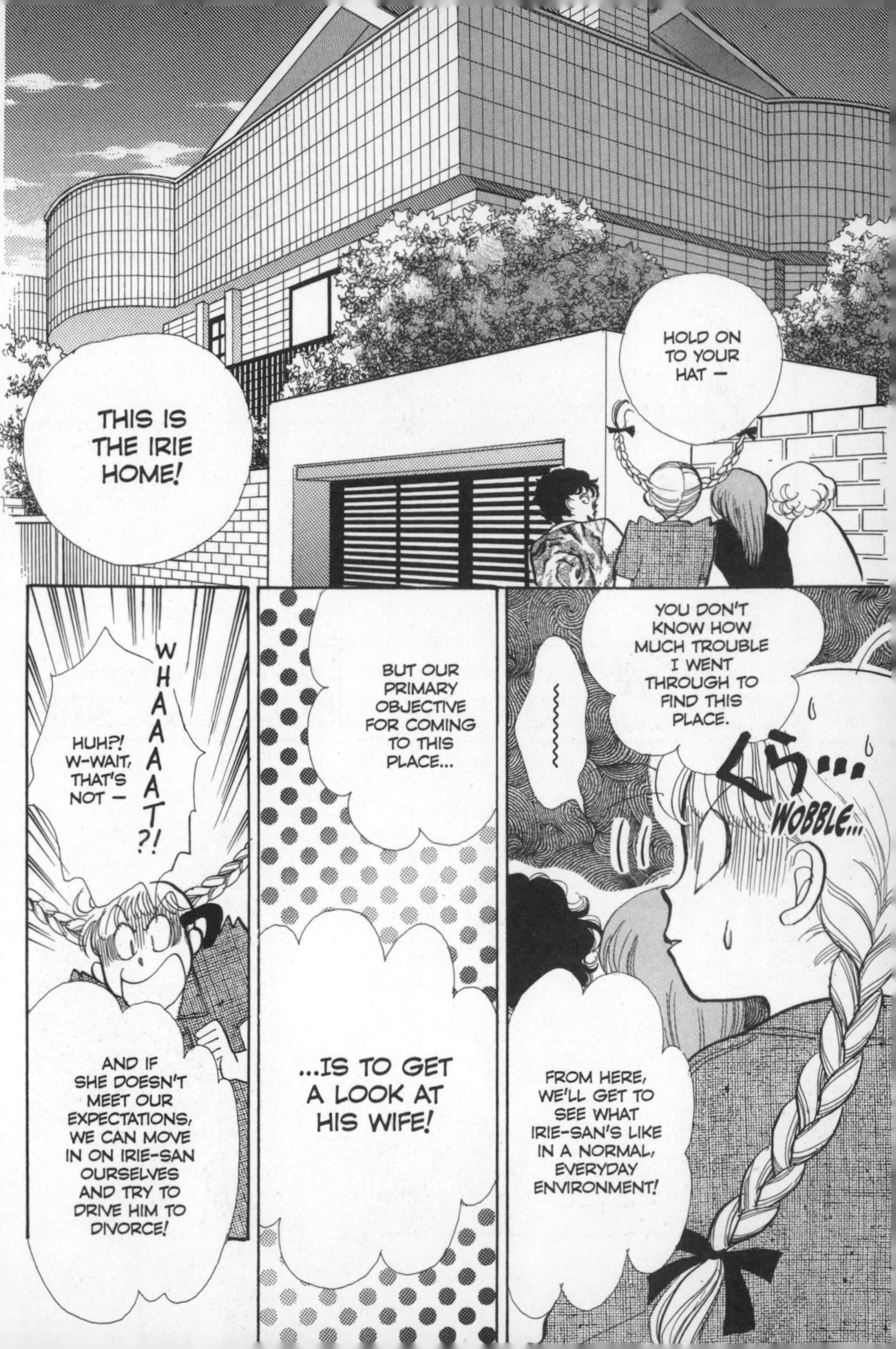
HOLD ON TO YOUR HAT —
THIS IS THE IRIE HOME!
YOU DON'T KNOW HOW MUCH TROUBLE I WENT THROUGH TO FIND THIS PLACE.
くら…
WOBBLE...
FROM HERE, WE'LL GET TO SEE WHAT IRIE-SAN'S LIKE IN A NORMAL, EVERYDAY ENVIRONMENT!
BUT OUR PRIMARY OBJECTIVE FOR COMING TO THIS PLACE...
...IS TO GET A LOOK AT HIS WIFE!
WHAAAAAT?!
HUH?! W-WAIT, THAT'S NOT —
AND IF SHE DOESN'T MEET OUR EXPECTATIONS, WE CAN MOVE IN ON IRIE-SAN OURSELVES AND TRY TO DRIVE HIM TO DIVORCE!

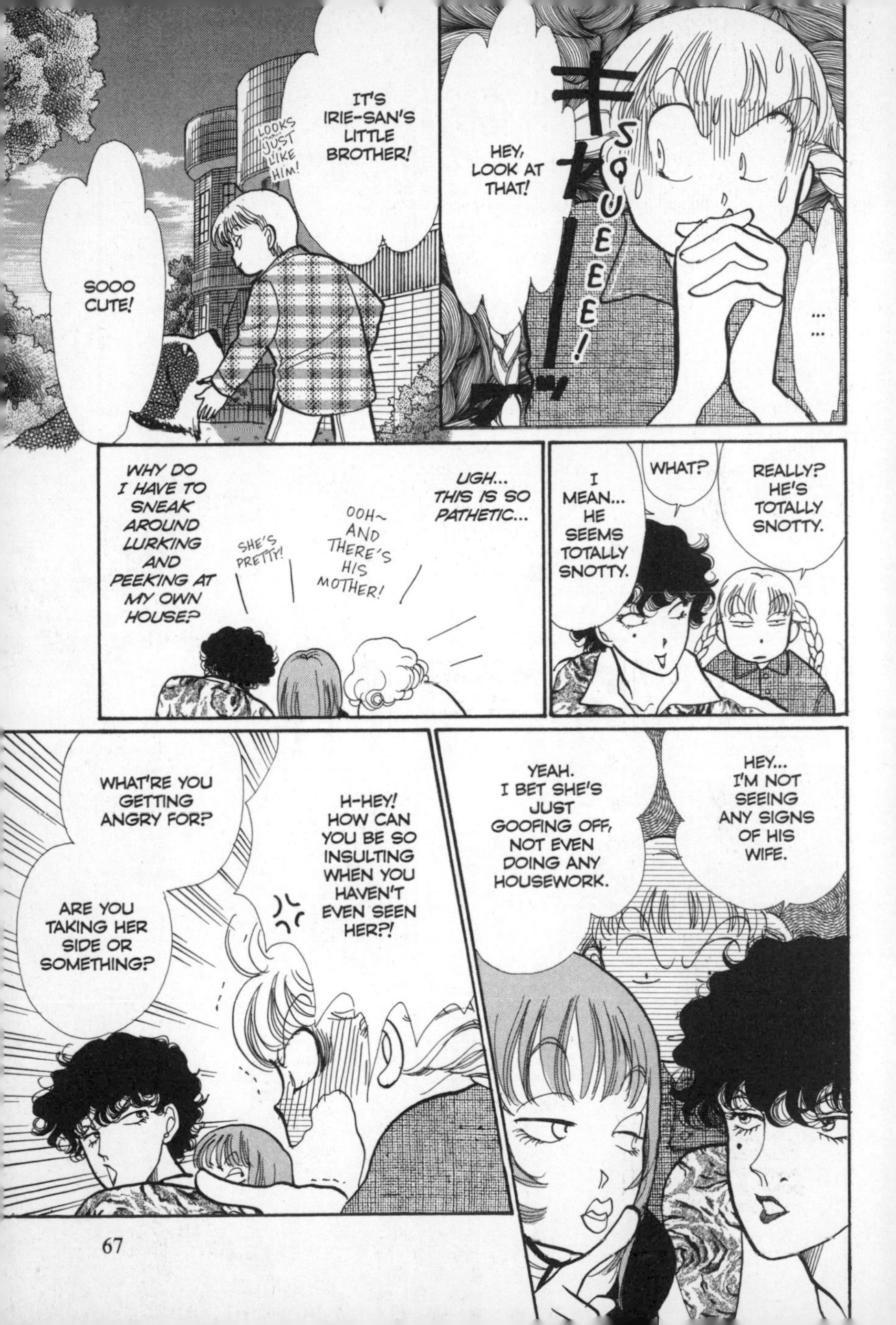
HEY, LOOK AT THAT!
SQUEEE!
......
IT'S IRIE-SAN'S LITTLE BROTHER!
LOOKS JUST LIKE HIM!
SOOO CUTE!
REALLY? HE'S TOTALLY SNOTTY.
WHAT?
I MEAN... HE SEEMS TOTALLY SNOTTY.
UGH... THIS IS SO PATHETIC...
OOH~ AND THERE'S HIS MOTHER!
SHE'S PRETTY!
WHY DO I HAVE TO SNEAK AROUND LURKING AND PEEKING AT MY OWN HOUSE?
HEY... I'M NOT SEEING ANY SIGNS OF HIS WIFE.
YEAH. I BET SHE'S JUST GOOFING OFF, NOT EVEN DOING ANY HOUSEWORK.
H-HEY! HOW CAN YOU BE SO INSULTING WHEN YOU HAVEN'T EVEN SEEN HER?!
WHAT'RE YOU GETTING ANGRY FOR?
ARE YOU TAKING HER SIDE OR SOMETHING?

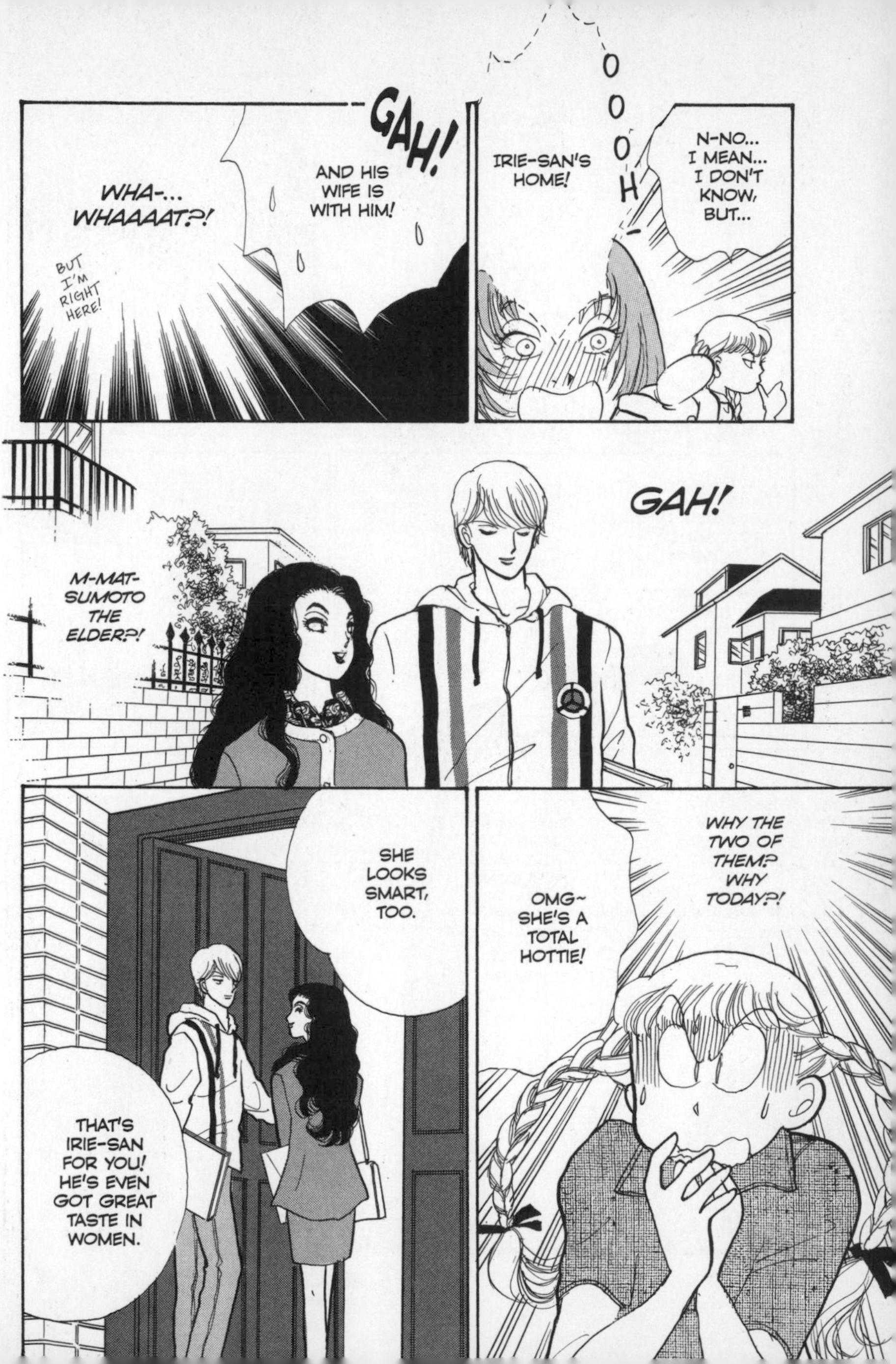
OOOH
N-NO... I MEAN... I DON'T KNOW, BUT...
IRIE-SAN'S HOME!
GAH!
AND HIS WIFE IS WITH HIM!
WHA-... WHAAAAT?!
BUT I'M RIGHT HERE!
GAH!
M-MAT-SUMOTO THE ELDER?!
WHY THE TWO OF THEM? WHY TODAY?!
OMG~ SHE'S A TOTAL HOTTIE!
SHE LOOKS SMART, TOO.
THAT'S IRIE-SAN FOR YOU! HE'S EVEN GOT GREAT TASTE IN WOMEN.

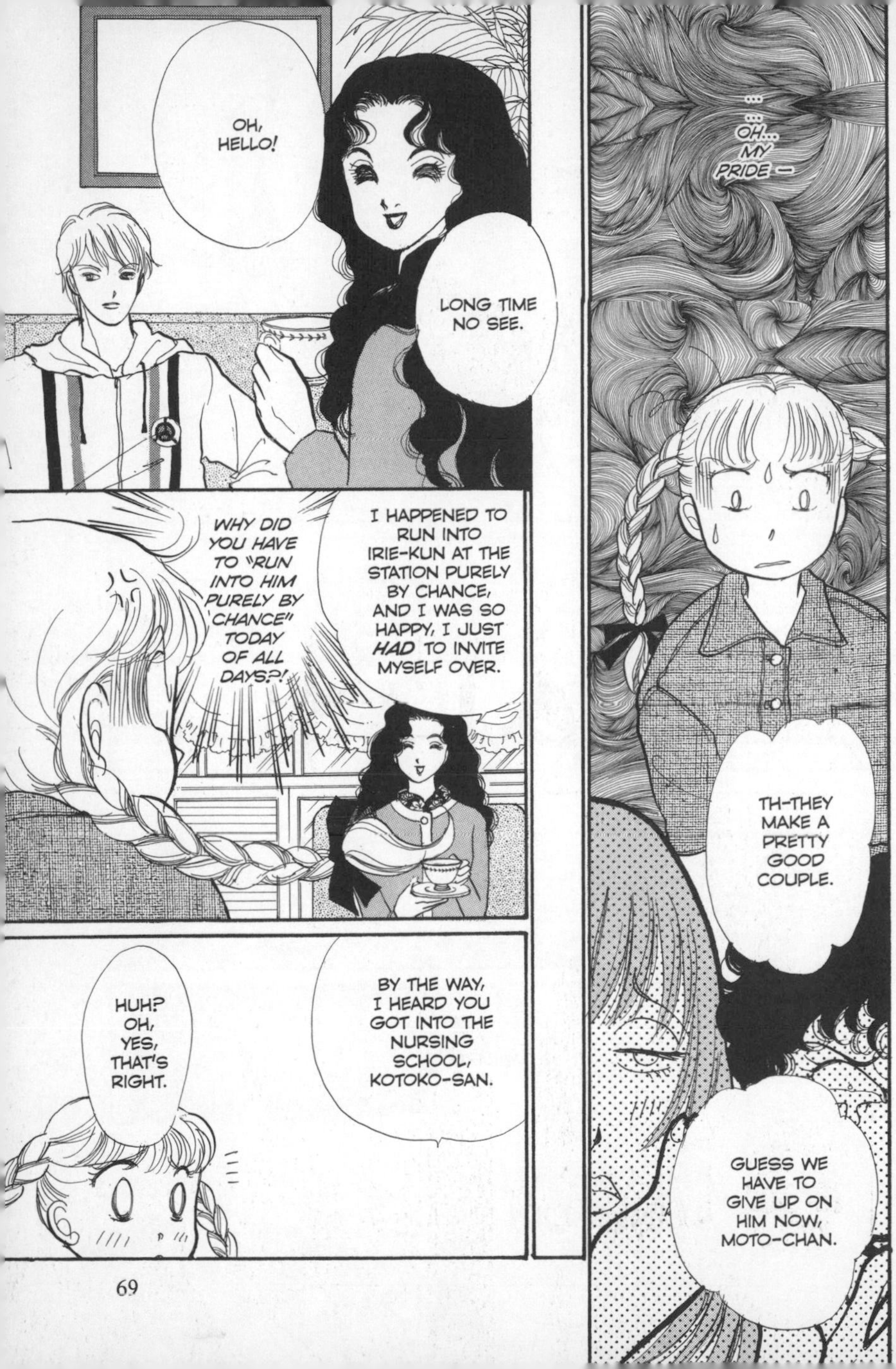
... ... OH... MY PRIDE —
TH-THEY MAKE A PRETTY GOOD COUPLE.
GUESS WE HAVE TO GIVE UP ON HIM NOW, MOTO-CHAN.
OH, HELLO!
LONG TIME NO SEE.
I HAPPENED TO RUN INTO IRIE-KUN AT THE STATION PURELY BY CHANCE, AND I WAS SO HAPPY, I JUST *HAD* TO INVITE MYSELF OVER.
WHY DID YOU HAVE TO "RUN INTO HIM PURELY BY CHANCE" TODAY OF ALL DAYS?!
BY THE WAY, I HEARD YOU GOT INTO THE NURSING SCHOOL, KOTOKO-SAN.
HUH? OH, YES, THAT'S RIGHT.

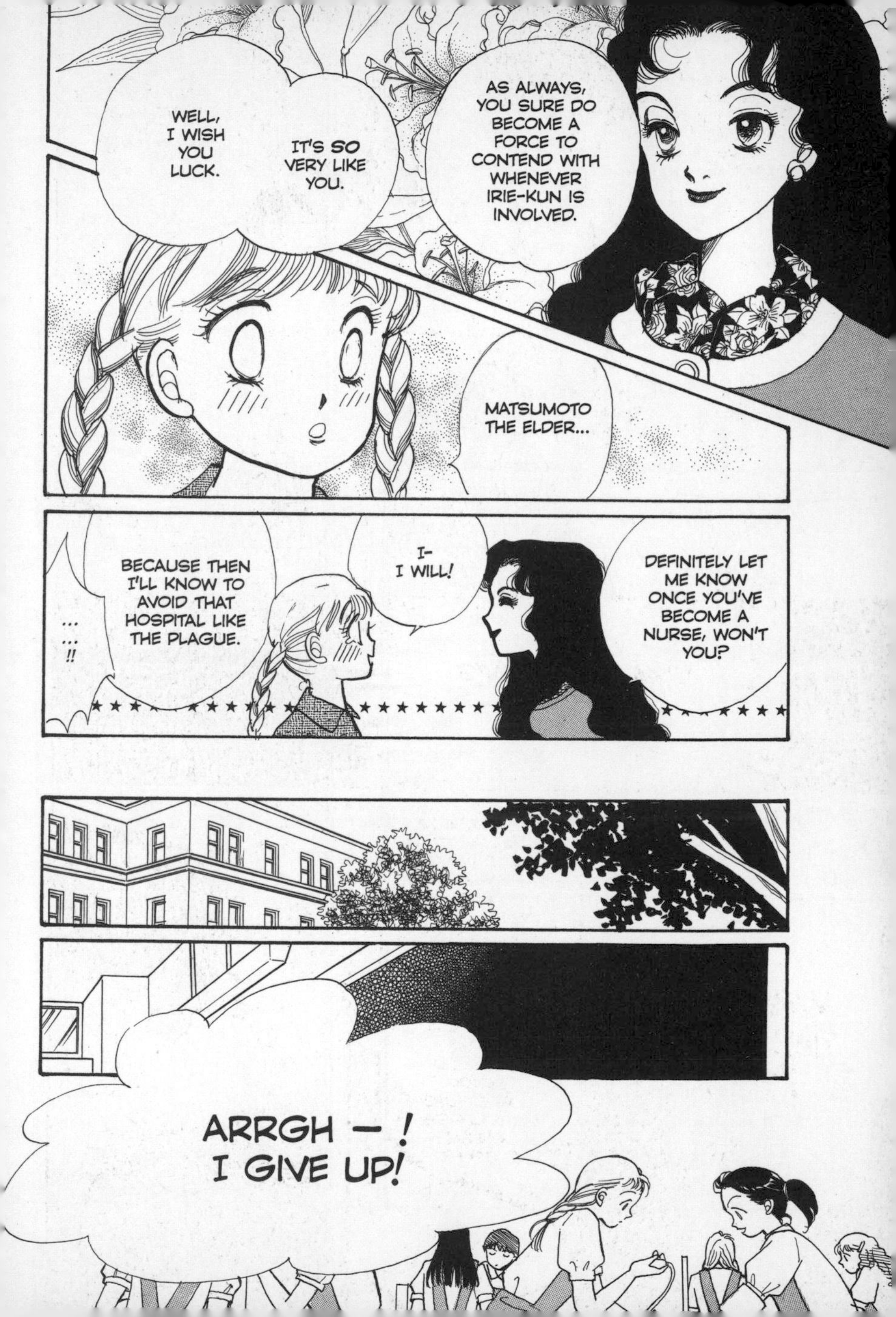
AS ALWAYS, YOU SURE DO BECOME A FORCE TO CONTEND WITH WHENEVER IRIE-KUN IS INVOLVED.
IT'S SO VERY LIKE YOU.
WELL, I WISH YOU LUCK.
MATSUMOTO THE ELDER...
DEFINITELY LET ME KNOW ONCE YOU'VE BECOME A NURSE, WON'T YOU?
I- I WILL!
BECAUSE THEN I'LL KNOW TO AVOID THAT HOSPITAL LIKE THE PLAGUE.
... ... !!
ARRGH — ! I GIVE UP!

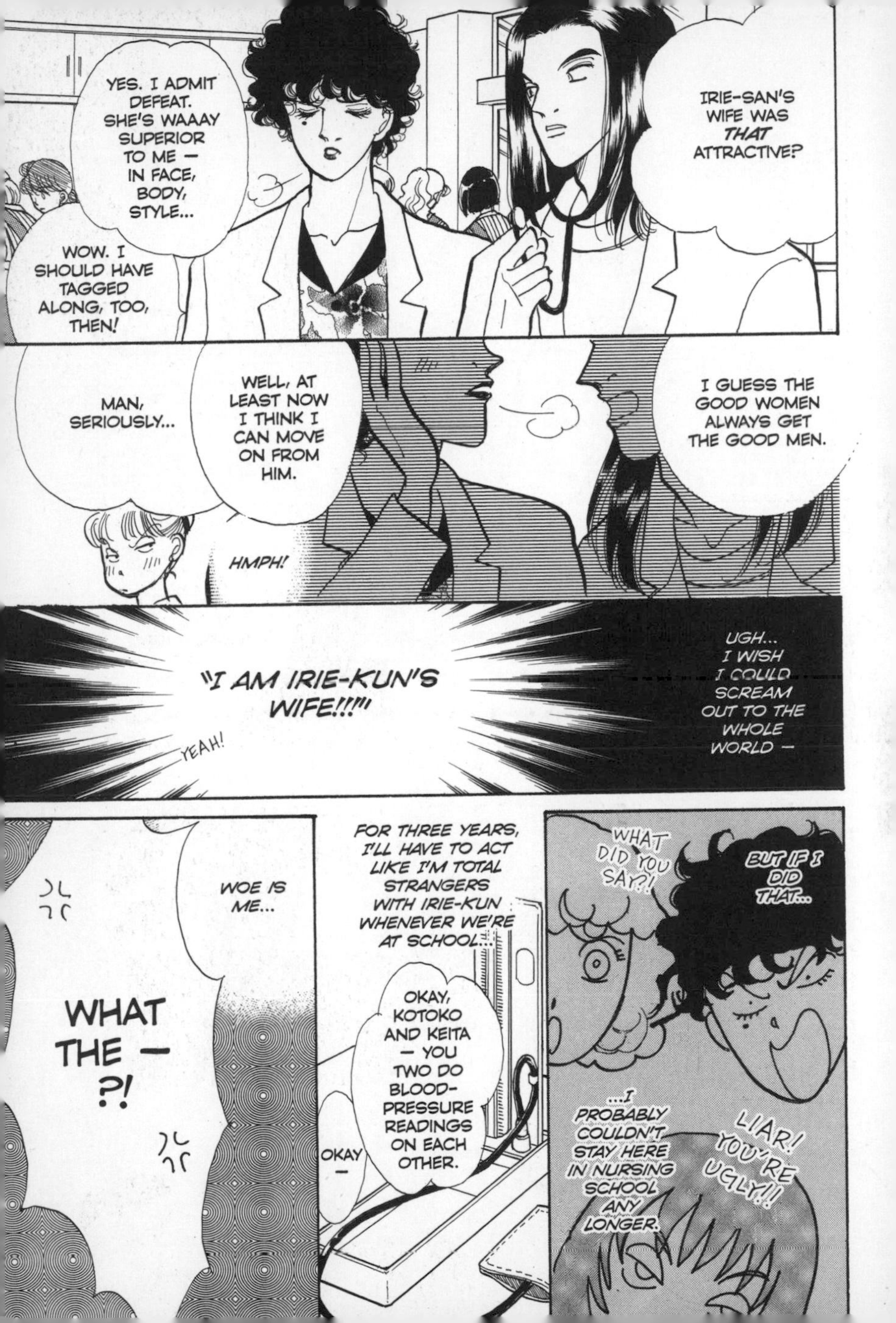
IRIE-SAN'S WIFE WAS *THAT* ATTRACTIVE?
YES. I ADMIT DEFEAT. SHE'S WAAAY SUPERIOR TO ME — IN FACE, BODY, STYLE...
WOW. I SHOULD HAVE TAGGED ALONG, TOO, THEN!
I GUESS THE GOOD WOMEN ALWAYS GET THE GOOD MEN.
WELL, AT LEAST NOW I THINK I CAN MOVE ON FROM HIM.
MAN, SERIOUSLY...
HMPH!
UGH... I WISH I COULD SCREAM OUT TO THE WHOLE WORLD —
"I AM IRIE-KUN'S WIFE!!!"
YEAH!
BUT IF I DID THAT...
WHAT DID YOU SAY?!
...I PROBABLY COULDN'T STAY HERE IN NURSING SCHOOL ANY LONGER.
LIAR! YOU'RE UGLY!!
FOR THREE YEARS, I'LL HAVE TO ACT LIKE I'M TOTAL STRANGERS WITH IRIE-KUN WHENEVER WE'RE AT SCHOOL...
OKAY, KOTOKO AND KEITA — YOU TWO DO BLOOD-PRESSURE READINGS ON EACH OTHER.
OKAY —
WOE IS ME...
WHAT THE — ?!

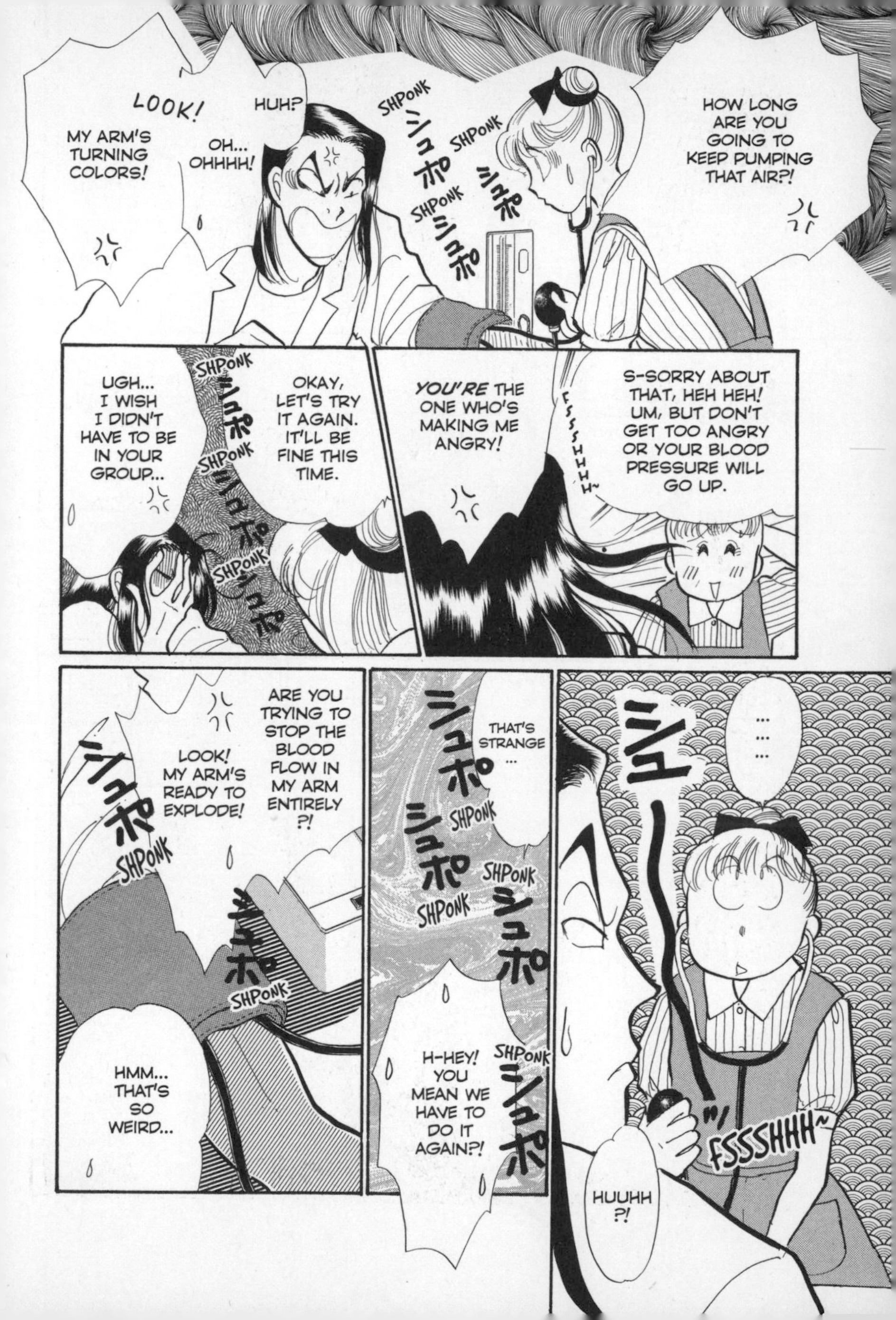
HOW LONG ARE YOU GOING TO KEEP PUMPING THAT AIR?!
SHPONK シュポ SHPONK シュポ SHPONK シュポ シュポ
HUH?
OH... OHHHH!
LOOK!
MY ARM'S TURNING COLORS!
S-SORRY ABOUT THAT, HEH HEH! UM, BUT DON'T GET TOO ANGRY OR YOUR BLOOD PRESSURE WILL GO UP.
FSSSHHHH~
YOU'RE THE ONE WHO'S MAKING ME ANGRY!
OKAY, LET'S TRY IT AGAIN. IT'LL BE FINE THIS TIME.
SHPONK シュポ SHPONK シュポ SHPONK シュポ
UGH... I WISH I DIDN'T HAVE TO BE IN YOUR GROUP...
... ...
シュー
FSSSHHH~
HUUHH ?!
THAT'S STRANGE ...
シュポ SHPONK シュポ SHPONK SHPONK シュポ SHPONK シュポ
H-HEY! YOU MEAN WE HAVE TO DO IT AGAIN?!
ARE YOU TRYING TO STOP THE BLOOD FLOW IN MY ARM ENTIRELY ?!
LOOK! MY ARM'S READY TO EXPLODE!
シュポ SHPONK シュポ SHPONK
HMM... THAT'S SO WEIRD...

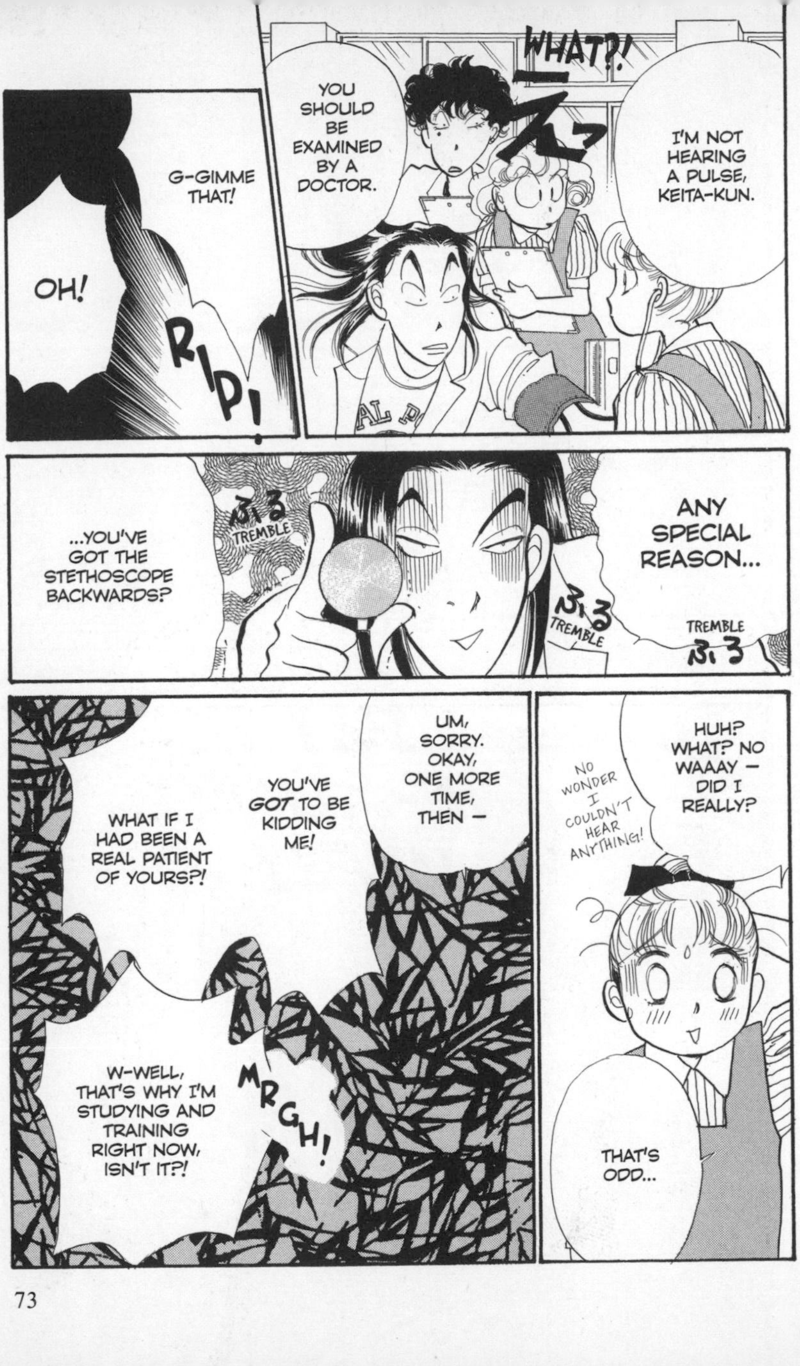
I'M NOT HEARING A PULSE, KEITA-KUN.
WHAT?!
YOU SHOULD BE EXAMINED BY A DOCTOR.
G-GIMME THAT!
OH!
RIP!
ANY SPECIAL REASON...
ふる TREMBLE
ふる TREMBLE
ふる TREMBLE
...YOU'VE GOT THE STETHOSCOPE BACKWARDS?
HUH? WHAT? NO WAAAY — DID I REALLY?
NO WONDER I COULDN'T HEAR ANYTHING!
THAT'S ODD...
UM, SORRY. OKAY, ONE MORE TIME, THEN —
YOU'VE *GOT* TO BE KIDDING ME!
WHAT IF I HAD BEEN A REAL PATIENT OF YOURS?!
MRGH!
W-WELL, THAT'S WHY I'M STUDYING AND TRAINING RIGHT NOW, ISN'T IT?!

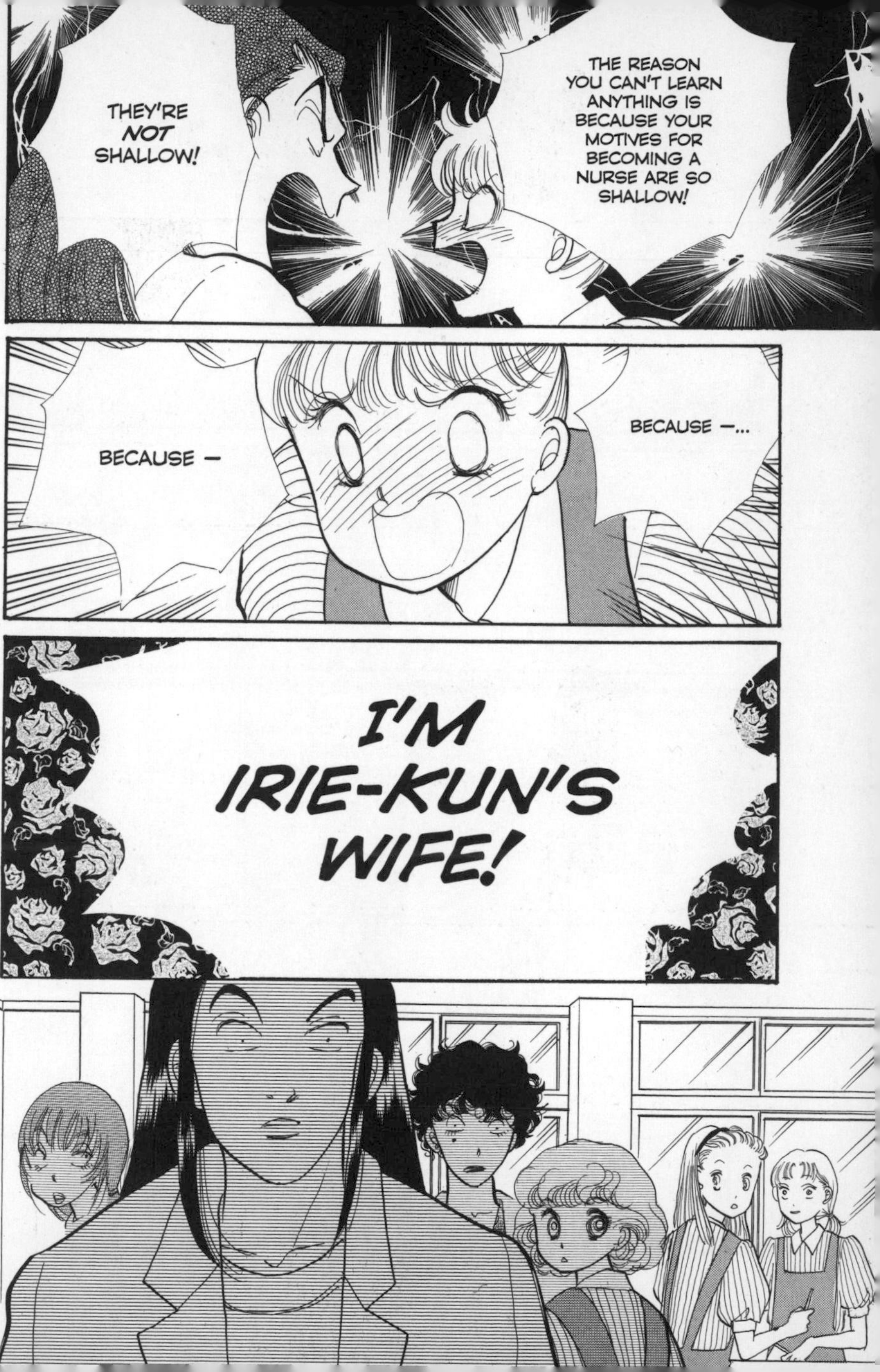
THE REASON YOU CAN'T LEARN ANYTHING IS BECAUSE YOUR MOTIVES FOR BECOMING A NURSE ARE SO SHALLOW!
THEY'RE *NOT* SHALLOW!
BECAUSE —...
BECAUSE —
I'M IRIE-KUN'S WIFE!

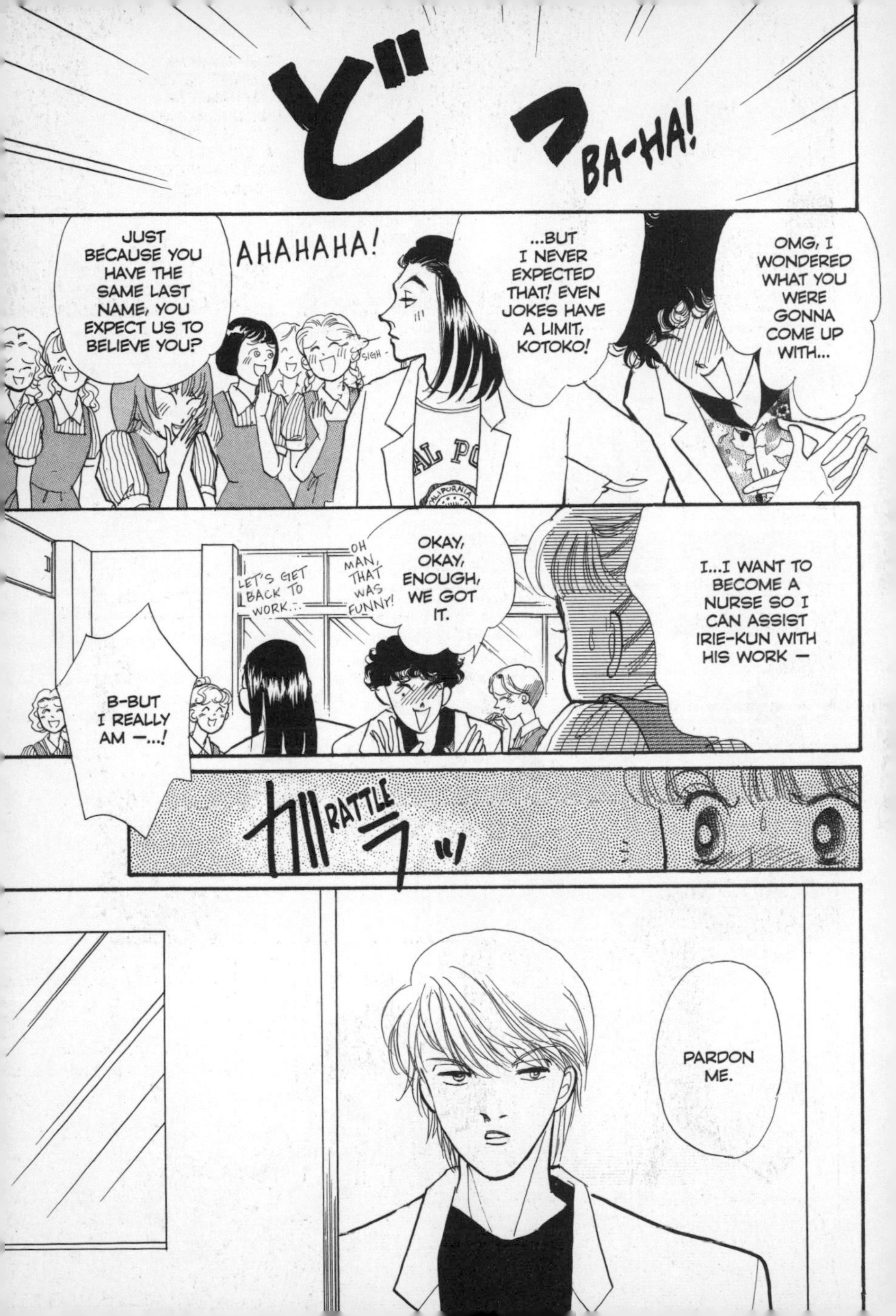
どっ
BA-HA!
OMG, I WONDERED WHAT YOU WERE GONNA COME UP WITH...
...BUT I NEVER EXPECTED THAT! EVEN JOKES HAVE A LIMIT, KOTOKO!
SIGH
AHAHAHA!
JUST BECAUSE YOU HAVE THE SAME LAST NAME, YOU EXPECT US TO BELIEVE YOU?
I...I WANT TO BECOME A NURSE SO I CAN ASSIST IRIE-KUN WITH HIS WORK —
OKAY, OKAY, ENOUGH, WE GOT IT.
OH MAN, THAT WAS FUNNY!
LET'S GET BACK TO WORK...
B-BUT I REALLY AM —...!
カラッ
RATTLE
PARDON ME.

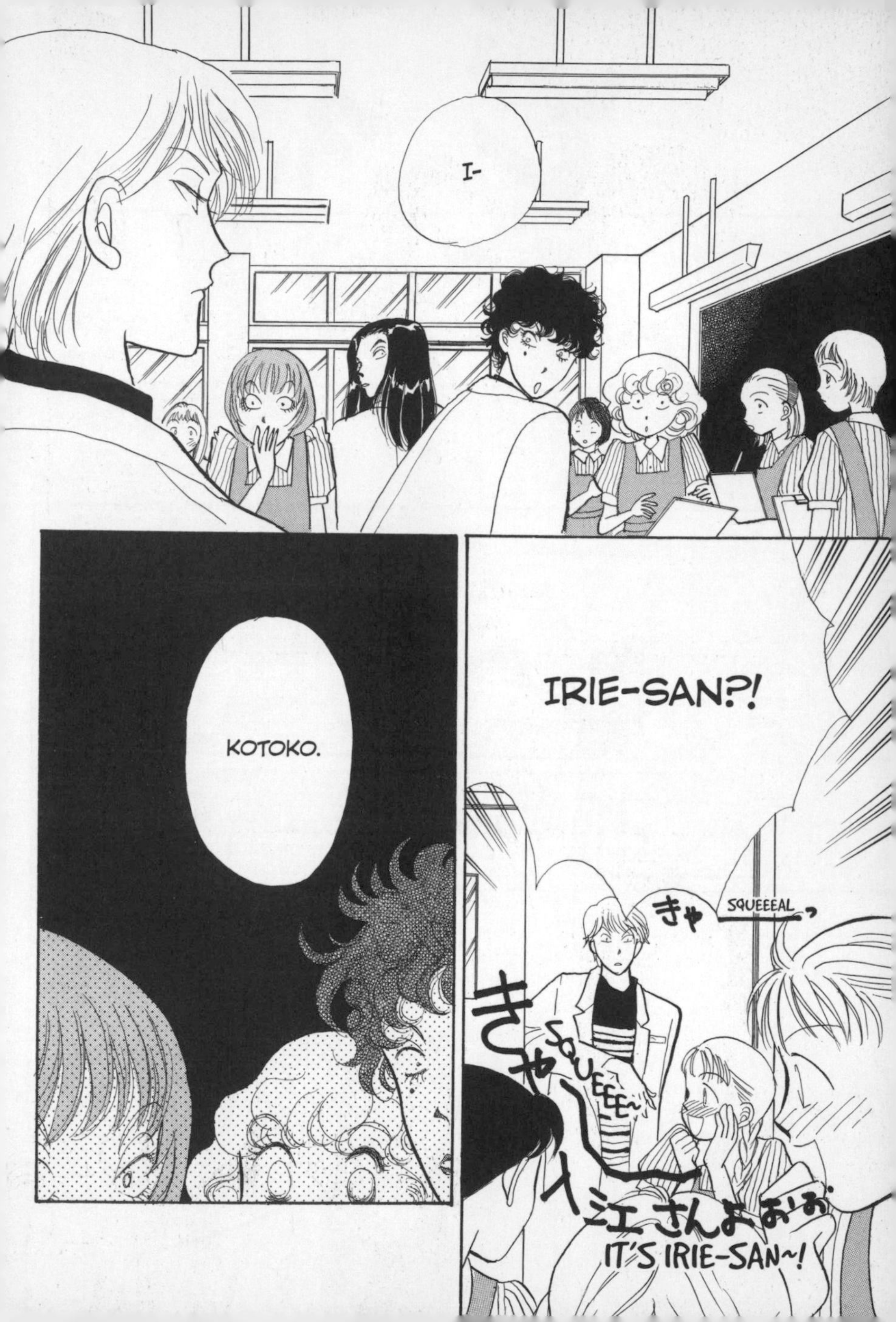
I-
IRIE-SAN?!
きゃ SQUEEEAL
きゃー SQUEEEE~
イ江さんよぉぉ
IT'S IRIE-SAN~!
KOTOKO.

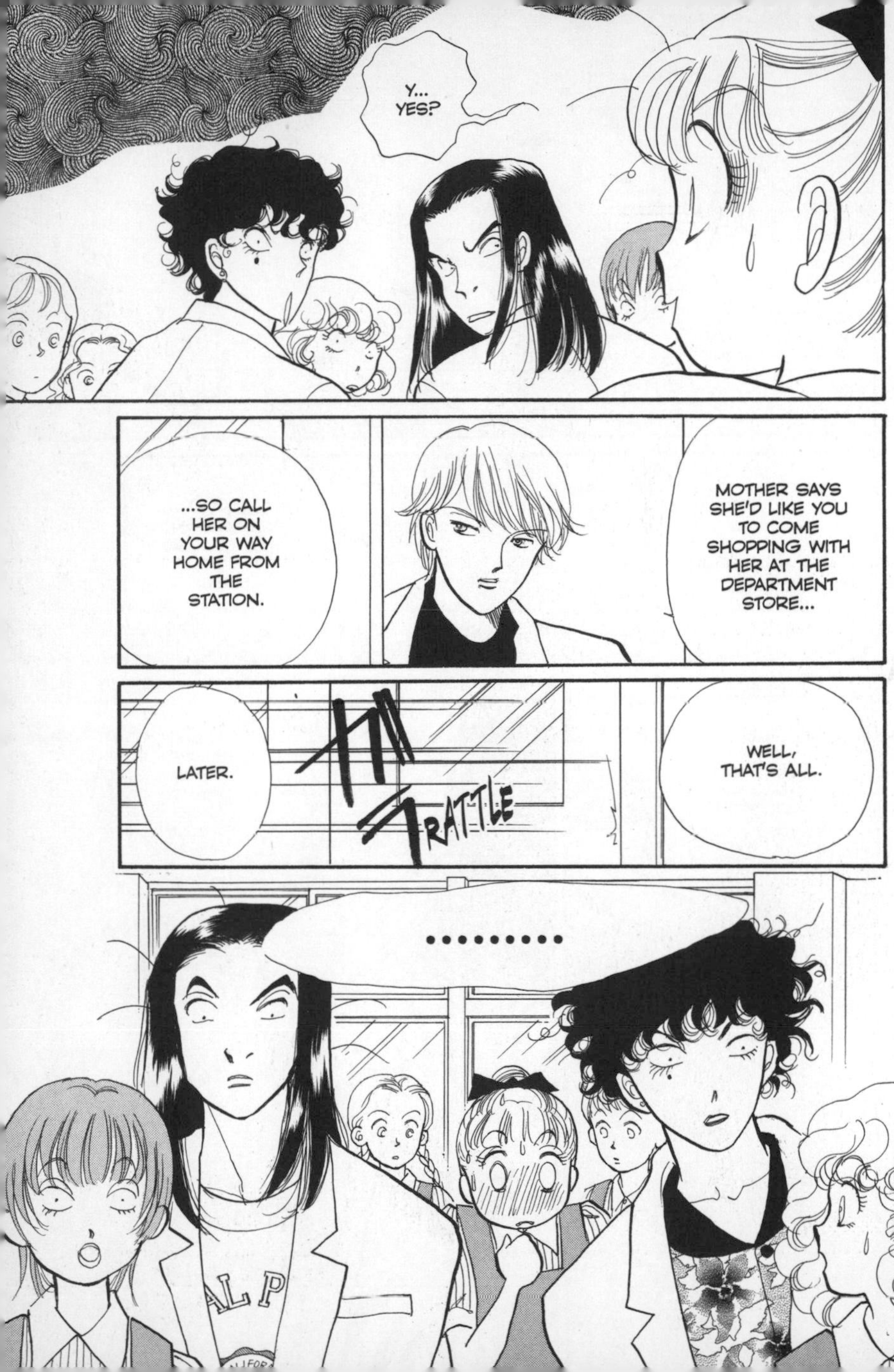
Y... YES?
MOTHER SAYS SHE'D LIKE YOU TO COME SHOPPING WITH HER AT THE DEPARTMENT STORE...
...SO CALL HER ON YOUR WAY HOME FROM THE STATION.
WELL, THAT'S ALL.
RATTLE
LATER.
....

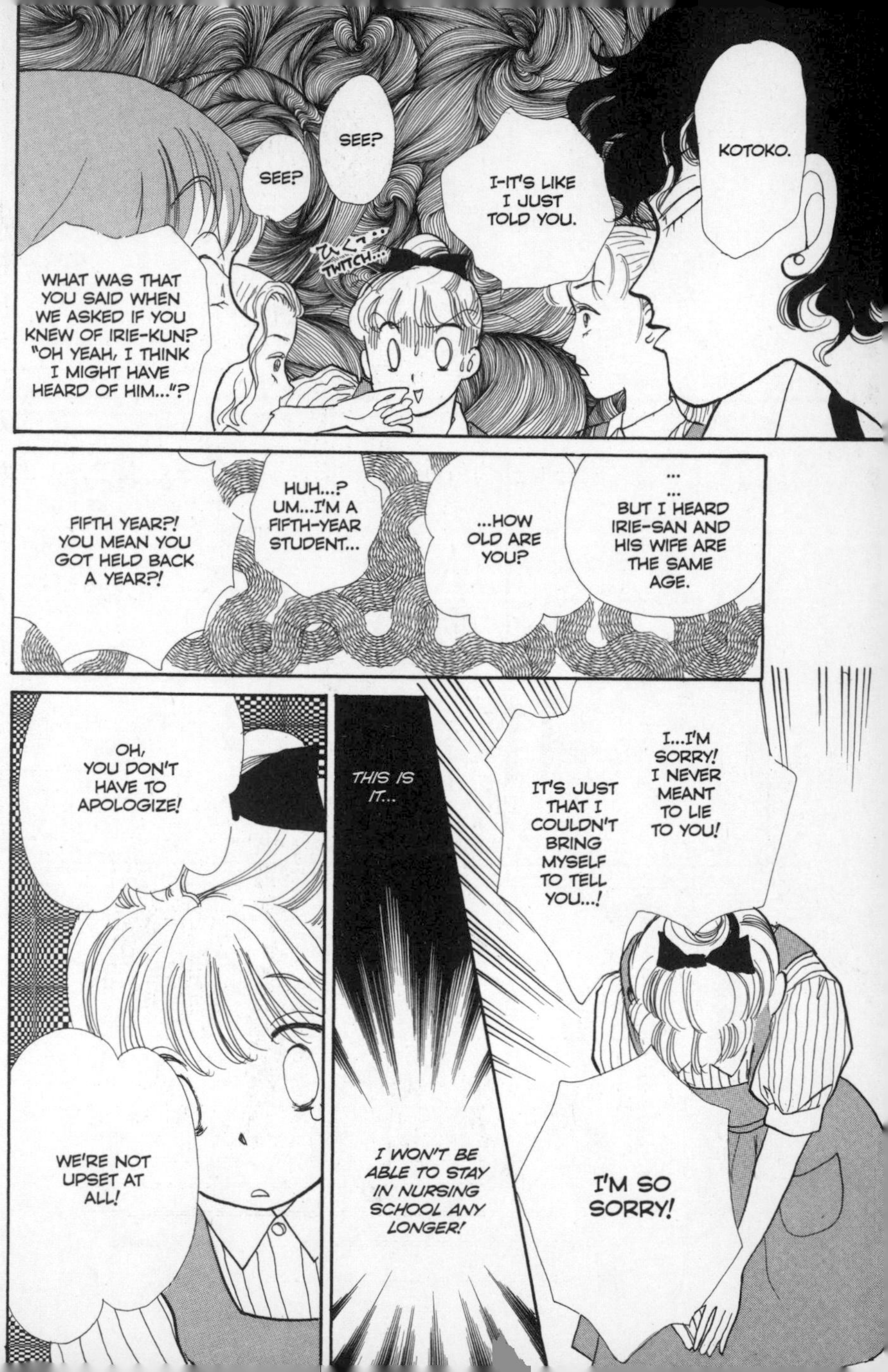
KOTOKO.
I-IT'S LIKE I JUST TOLD YOU.
SEE?
SEE?
ひくっ・・
TWITCH...
WHAT WAS THAT YOU SAID WHEN WE ASKED IF YOU KNEW OF IRIE-KUN? "OH YEAH, I THINK I MIGHT HAVE HEARD OF HIM..."?
... ... BUT I HEARD IRIE-SAN AND HIS WIFE ARE THE SAME AGE.
...HOW OLD ARE YOU?
HUH...? UM...I'M A FIFTH-YEAR STUDENT...
FIFTH YEAR?! YOU MEAN YOU GOT HELD BACK A YEAR?!
I...I'M SORRY! I NEVER MEANT TO LIE TO YOU!
IT'S JUST THAT I COULDN'T BRING MYSELF TO TELL YOU...!
I'M SO SORRY!
THIS IS IT...
I WON'T BE ABLE TO STAY IN NURSING SCHOOL ANY LONGER!
OH, YOU DON'T HAVE TO APOLOGIZE!
WE'RE NOT UPSET AT ALL!

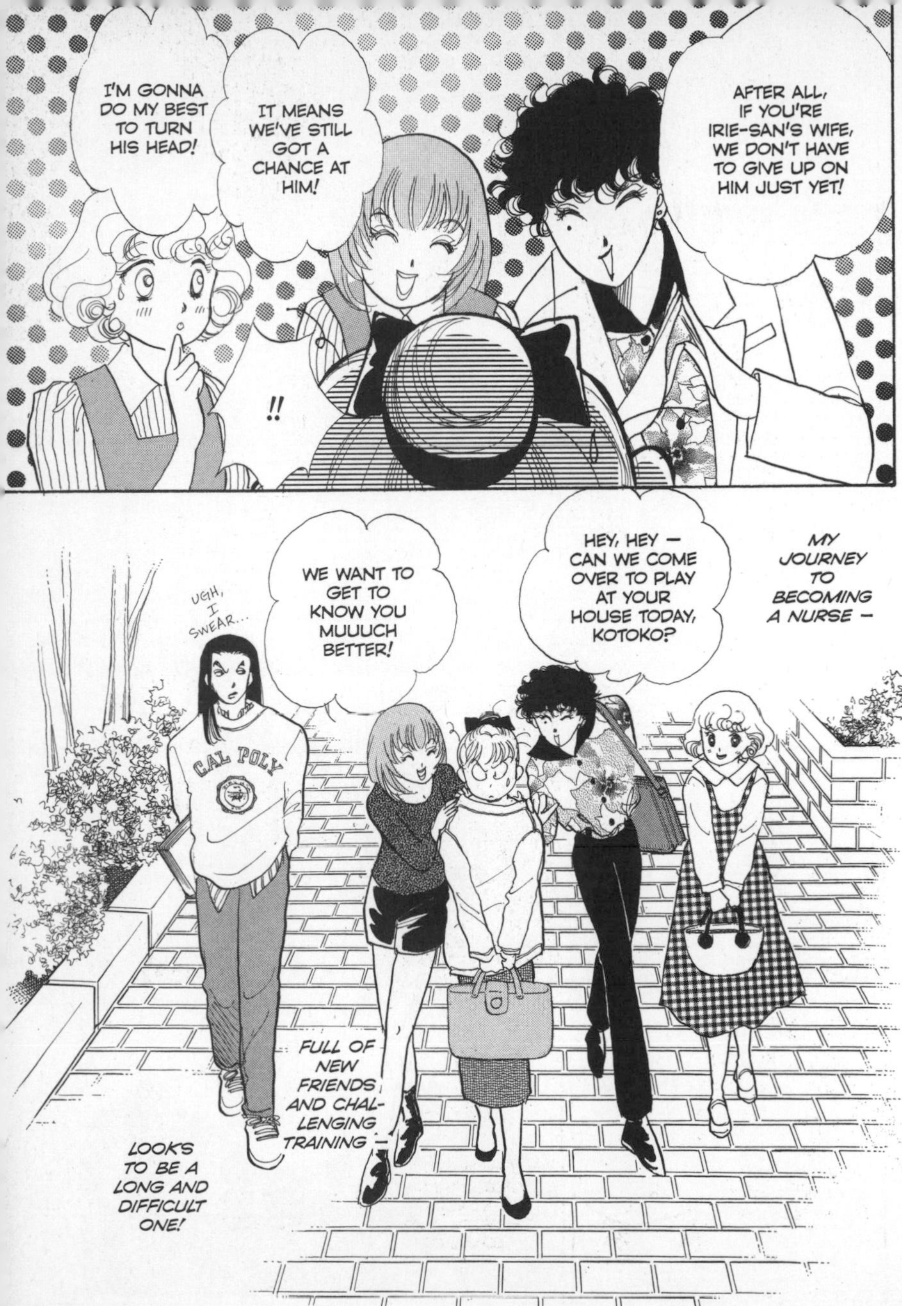
AFTER ALL, IF YOU'RE IRIE-SAN'S WIFE, WE DON'T HAVE TO GIVE UP ON HIM JUST YET!
IT MEANS WE'VE STILL GOT A CHANCE AT HIM!
I'M GONNA DO MY BEST TO TURN HIS HEAD!
!!
MY JOURNEY TO BECOMING A NURSE –
HEY, HEY – CAN WE COME OVER TO PLAY AT YOUR HOUSE TODAY, KOTOKO?
WE WANT TO GET TO KNOW YOU MUUUCH BETTER!
UGH, I SWEAR...
CAL POLY
FULL OF NEW FRIENDS AND CHAL-LENGING TRAINING –
LOOKS TO BE A LONG AND DIFFICULT ONE!

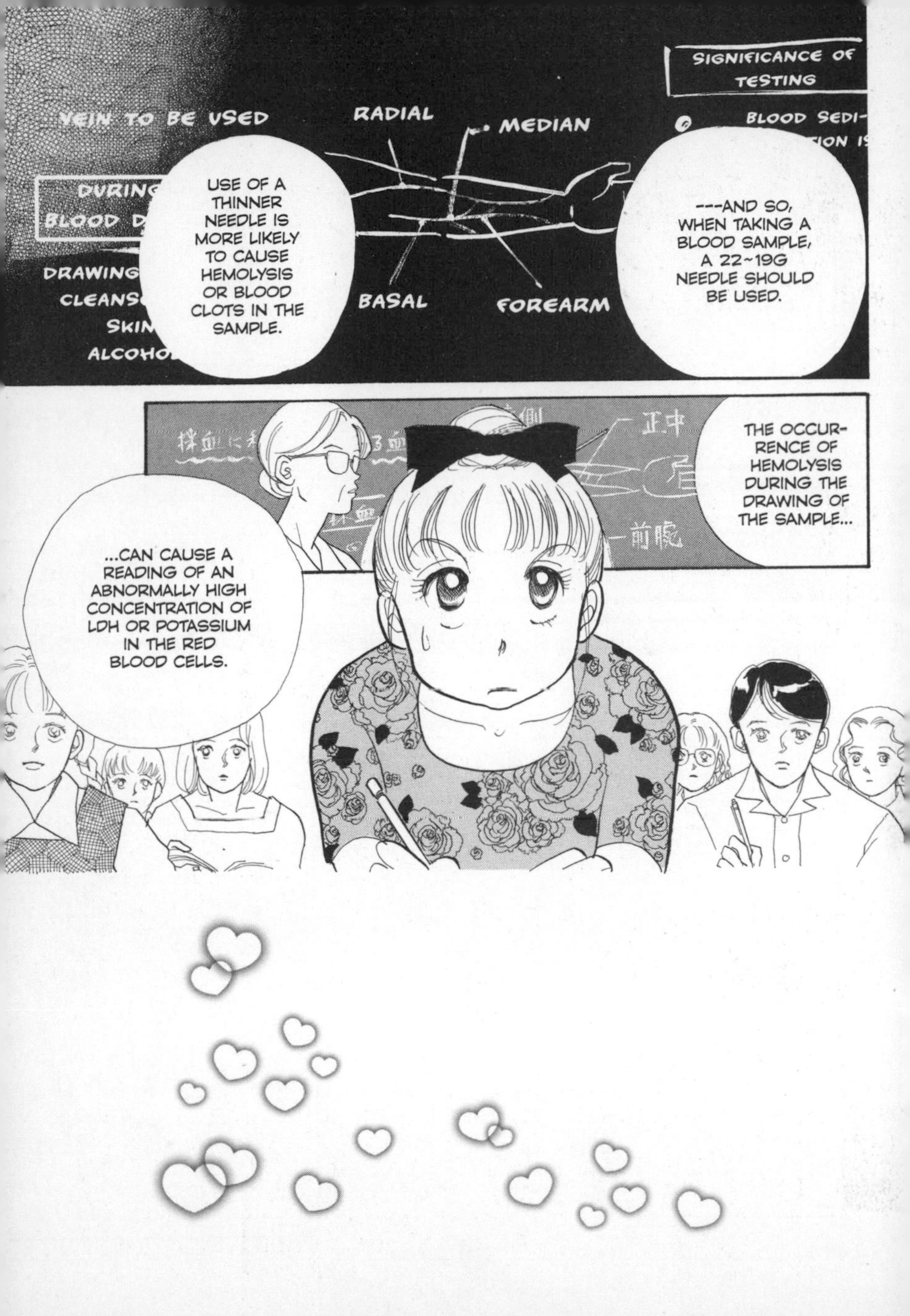
SIGNIFICANCE OF TESTING
VEIN TO BE USED
RADIAL
MEDIAN
BASAL
FOREARM
---AND SO, WHEN TAKING A BLOOD SAMPLE, A 22~19G NEEDLE SHOULD BE USED.
USE OF A THINNER NEEDLE IS MORE LIKELY TO CAUSE HEMOLYSIS OR BLOOD CLOTS IN THE SAMPLE.
正中
前腕
THE OCCURRENCE OF HEMOLYSIS DURING THE DRAWING OF THE SAMPLE...
...CAN CAUSE A READING OF AN ABNORMALLY HIGH CONCENTRATION OF LDH OR POTASSIUM IN THE RED BLOOD CELLS.

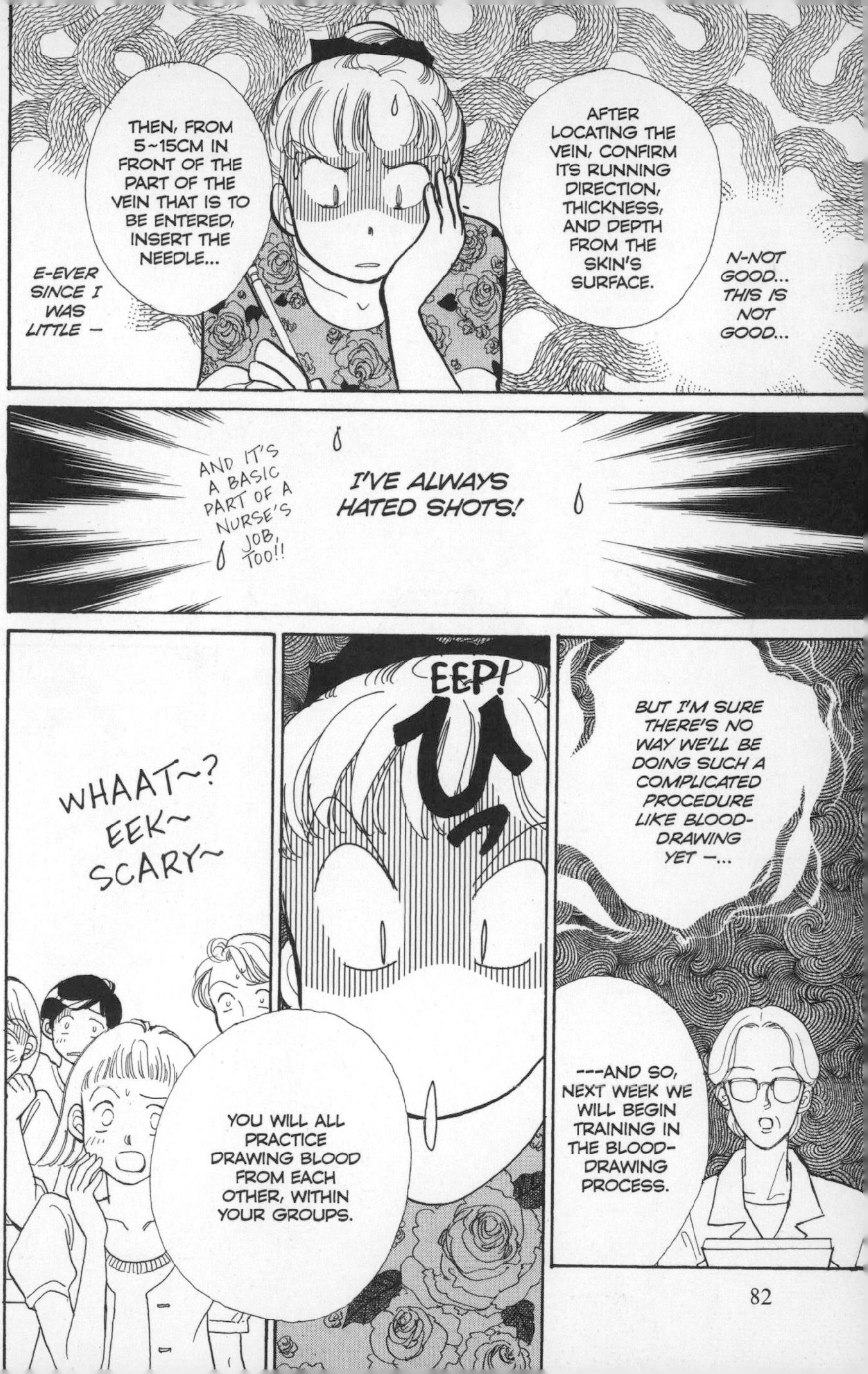

AFTER LOCATING THE VEIN, CONFIRM ITS RUNNING DIRECTION, THICKNESS, AND DEPTH FROM THE SKIN'S SURFACE.
N-NOT GOOD... THIS IS NOT GOOD...
THEN, FROM 5~15CM IN FRONT OF THE PART OF THE VEIN THAT IS TO BE ENTERED, INSERT THE NEEDLE...
E-EVER SINCE I WAS LITTLE —
I'VE ALWAYS HATED SHOTS!
AND IT'S A BASIC PART OF A NURSE'S JOB, TOO!!
BUT I'M SURE THERE'S NO WAY WE'LL BE DOING SUCH A COMPLICATED PROCEDURE LIKE BLOOD-DRAWING YET —...
---AND SO, NEXT WEEK WE WILL BEGIN TRAINING IN THE BLOOD-DRAWING PROCESS.
YOU WILL ALL PRACTICE DRAWING BLOOD FROM EACH OTHER, WITHIN YOUR GROUPS.
EEP!
WHAAT~? EEK~ SCARY~

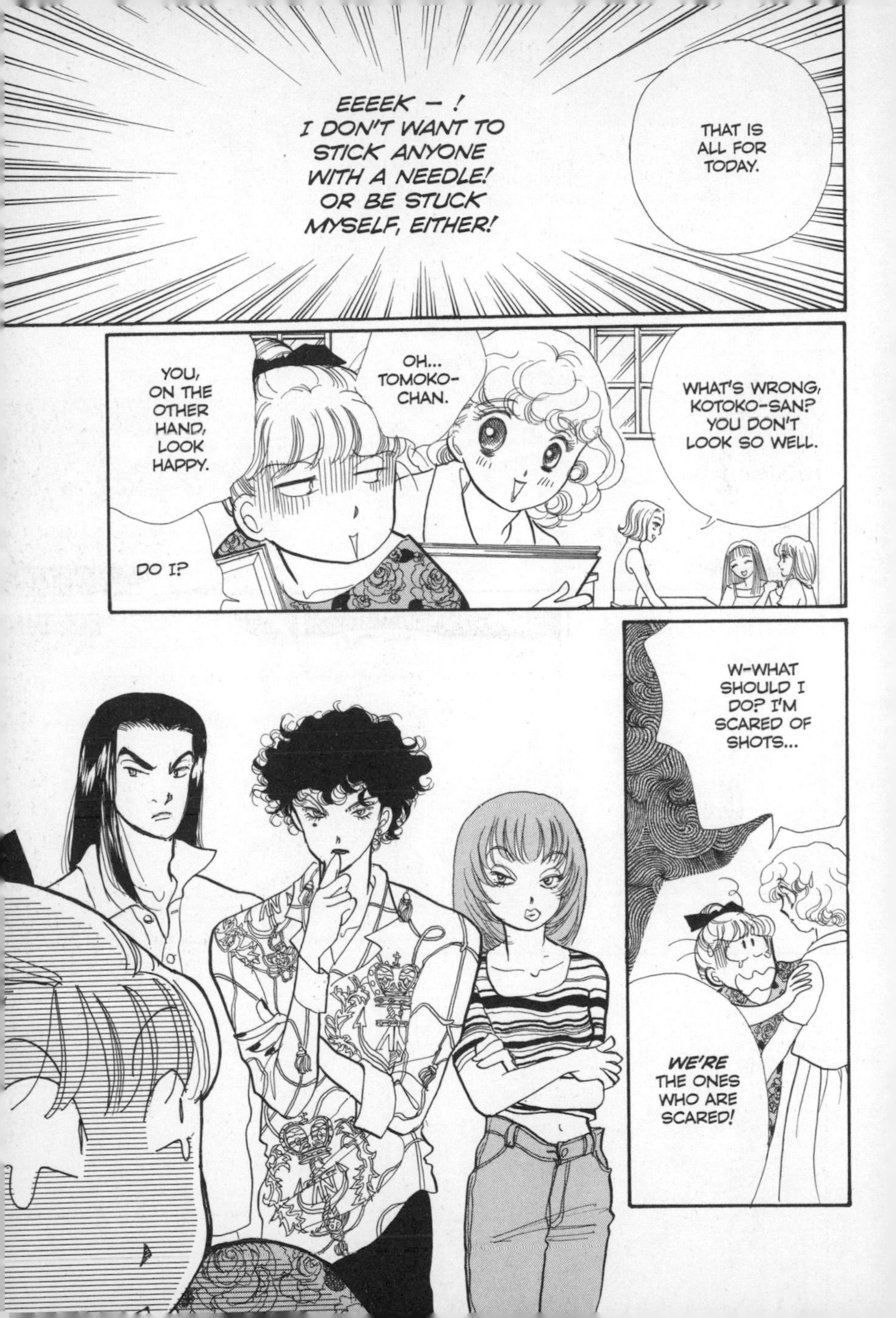
THAT IS ALL FOR TODAY.
EEEEK —! I DON'T WANT TO STICK ANYONE WITH A NEEDLE! OR BE STUCK MYSELF, EITHER!
WHAT'S WRONG, KOTOKO-SAN? YOU DON'T LOOK SO WELL.
OH... TOMOKO-CHAN.
YOU, ON THE OTHER HAND, LOOK HAPPY.
DO I?
W-WHAT SHOULD I DO? I'M SCARED OF SHOTS...
WE'RE THE ONES WHO ARE SCARED!

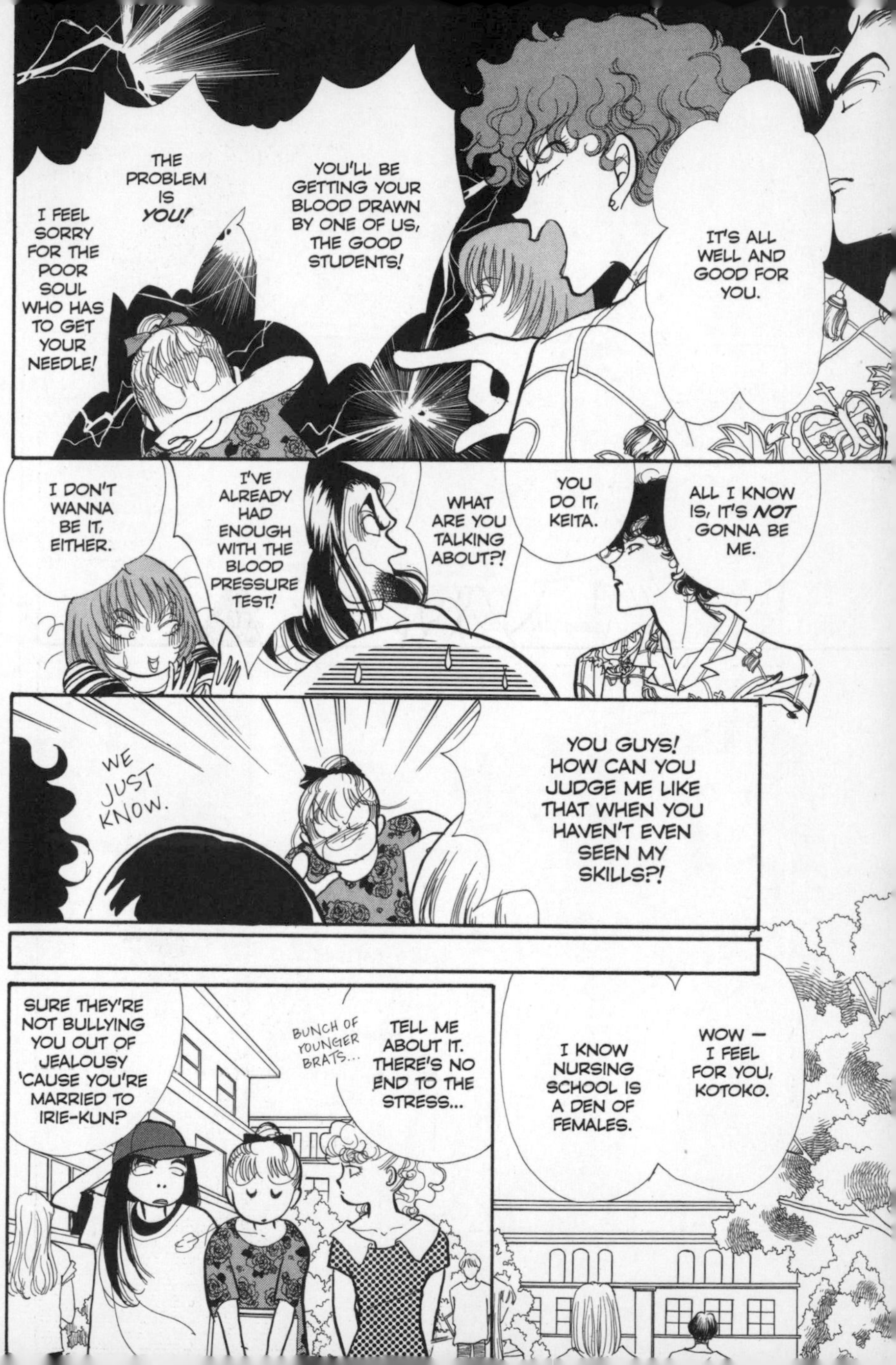
IT'S ALL WELL AND GOOD FOR YOU.
YOU'LL BE GETTING YOUR BLOOD DRAWN BY ONE OF US, THE GOOD STUDENTS!
THE PROBLEM IS *YOU!*
I FEEL SORRY FOR THE POOR SOUL WHO HAS TO GET YOUR NEEDLE!
ALL I KNOW IS, IT'S *NOT* GONNA BE ME.
YOU DO IT, KEITA.
WHAT ARE YOU TALKING ABOUT?!
I'VE ALREADY HAD ENOUGH WITH THE BLOOD PRESSURE TEST!
I DON'T WANNA BE IT, EITHER.
YOU GUYS! HOW CAN YOU JUDGE ME LIKE THAT WHEN YOU HAVEN'T EVEN SEEN MY SKILLS?!
WE JUST KNOW.
WOW — I FEEL FOR YOU, KOTOKO.
I KNOW NURSING SCHOOL IS A DEN OF FEMALES.
TELL ME ABOUT IT. THERE'S NO END TO THE STRESS...
BUNCH OF YOUNGER BRATS...
SURE THEY'RE NOT BULLYING YOU OUT OF JEALOUSY 'CAUSE YOU'RE MARRIED TO IRIE-KUN?

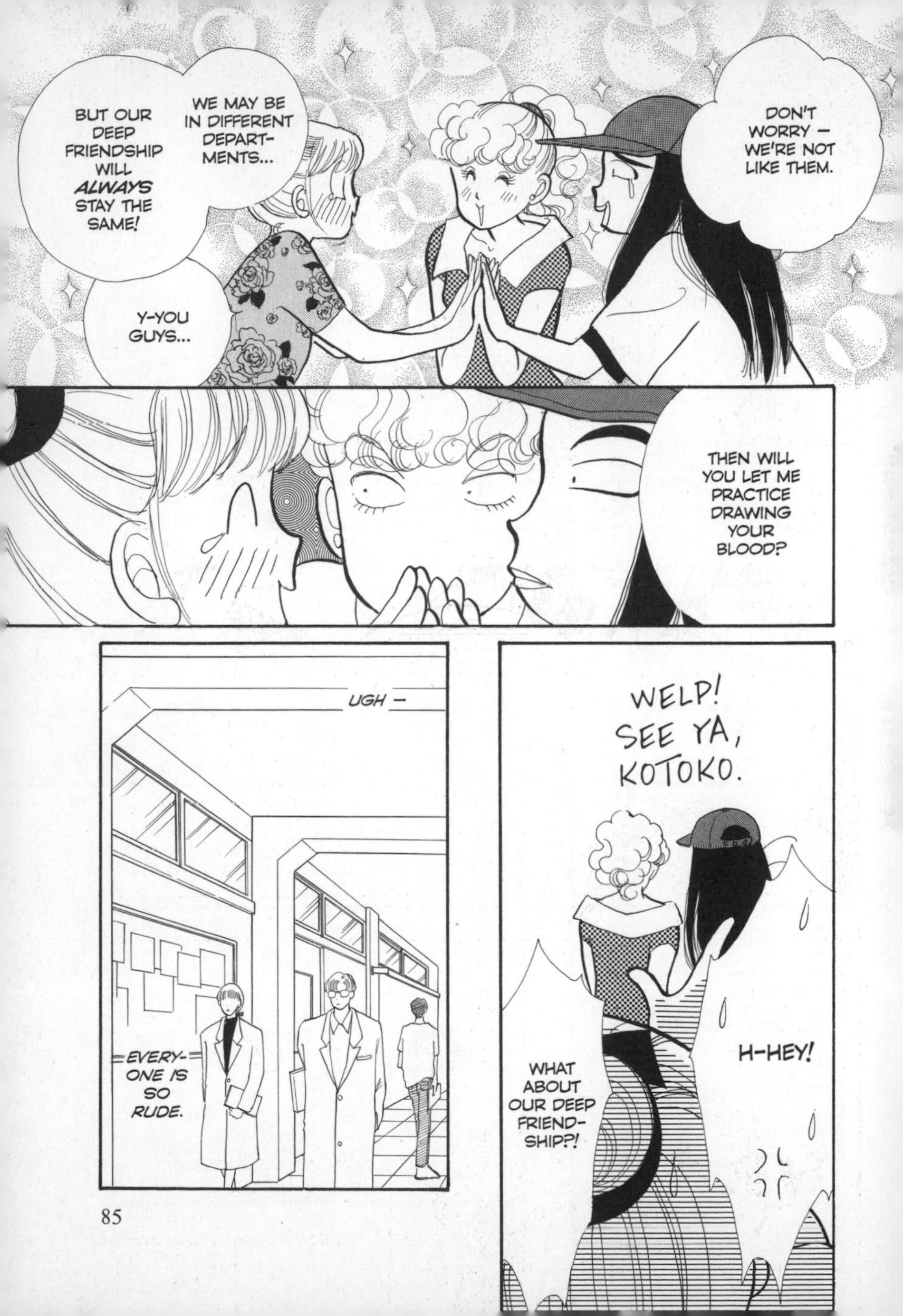
DON'T WORRY — WE'RE NOT LIKE THEM.
WE MAY BE IN DIFFERENT DEPART-MENTS...
BUT OUR DEEP FRIENDSHIP WILL ALWAYS STAY THE SAME!
Y-YOU GUYS...
THEN WILL YOU LET ME PRACTICE DRAWING YOUR BLOOD?
WELP! SEE YA, KOTOKO.
H-HEY!
WHAT ABOUT OUR DEEP FRIEND-SHIP?!
UGH —
EVERY-ONE IS SO RUDE.

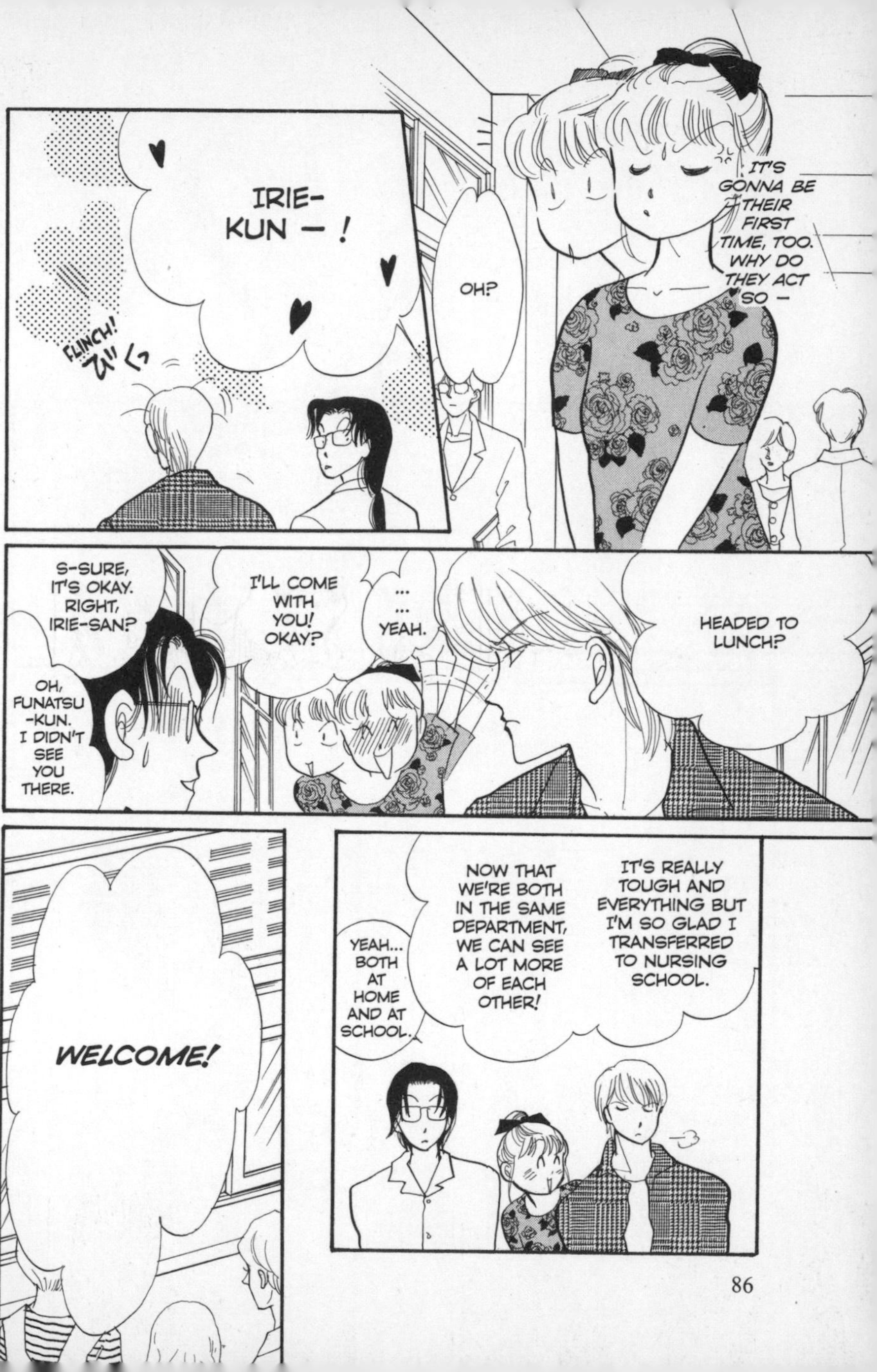
IT'S GONNA BE THEIR FIRST TIME, TOO. WHY DO THEY ACT SO –
OH?
IRIE-KUN – !
FLINCH! びくっ
HEADED TO LUNCH?
... ... YEAH.
I'LL COME WITH YOU! OKAY?
S-SURE, IT'S OKAY. RIGHT, IRIE-SAN?
OH, FUNATSU-KUN. I DIDN'T SEE YOU THERE.
IT'S REALLY TOUGH AND EVERYTHING BUT I'M SO GLAD I TRANSFERRED TO NURSING SCHOOL.
NOW THAT WE'RE BOTH IN THE SAME DEPARTMENT, WE CAN SEE A LOT MORE OF EACH OTHER!
YEAH... BOTH AT HOME AND AT SCHOOL.
WELCOME!

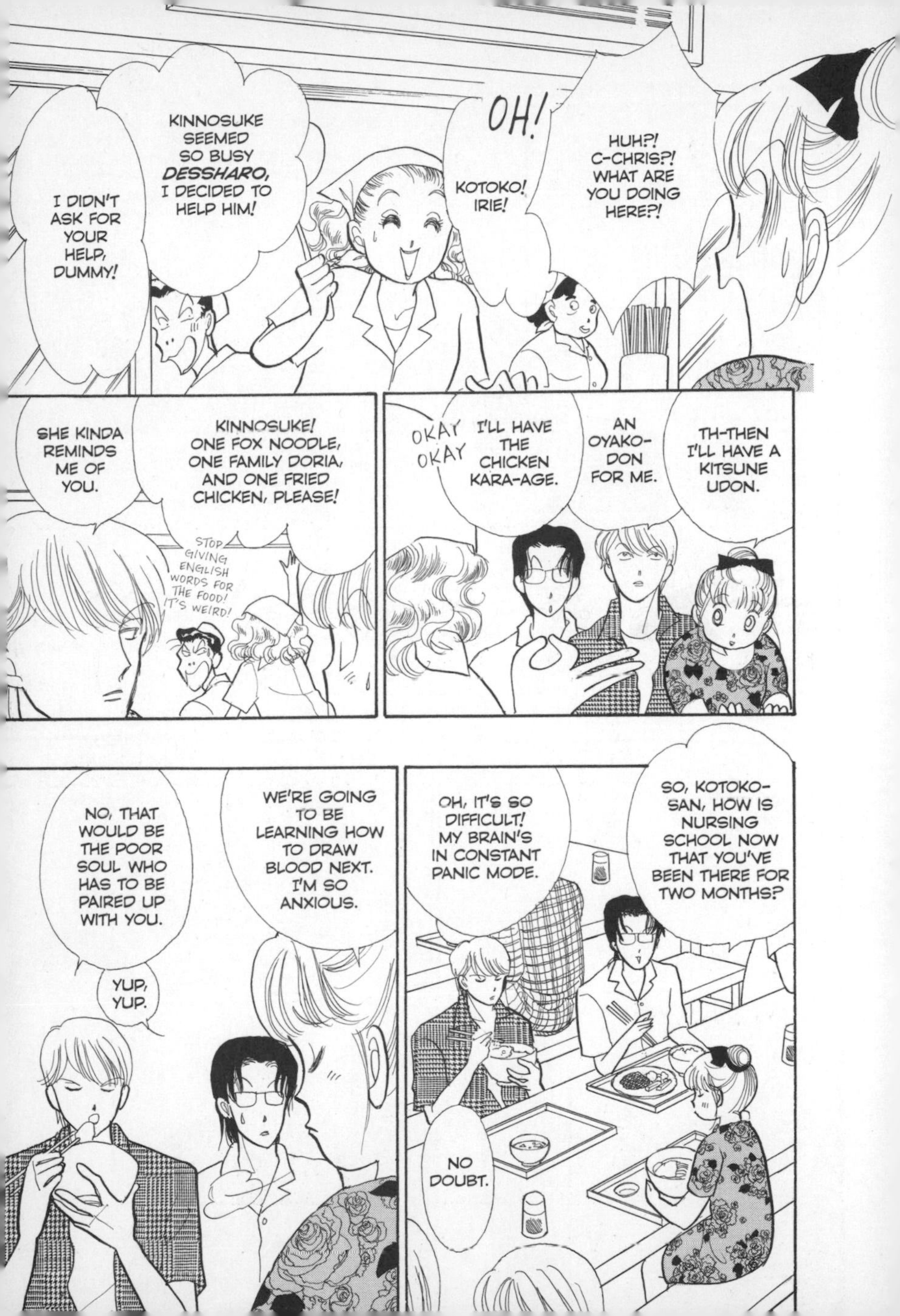
HUH?! C-CHRIS?! WHAT ARE YOU DOING HERE?!
OH!
KOTOKO! IRIE!
KINNOSUKE SEEMED SO BUSY *DESSHARO*, I DECIDED TO HELP HIM!
I DIDN'T ASK FOR YOUR HELP, DUMMY!
TH-THEN I'LL HAVE A KITSUNE UDON.
AN OYAKO-DON FOR ME.
I'LL HAVE THE CHICKEN KARA-AGE.
OKAY OKAY
KINNOSUKE! ONE FOX NOODLE, ONE FAMILY DORIA, AND ONE FRIED CHICKEN, PLEASE!
STOP GIVING ENGLISH WORDS FOR THE FOOD! IT'S WEIRD!
SHE KINDA REMINDS ME OF YOU.
SO, KOTOKO-SAN, HOW IS NURSING SCHOOL NOW THAT YOU'VE BEEN THERE FOR TWO MONTHS?
OH, IT'S SO DIFFICULT! MY BRAIN'S IN CONSTANT PANIC MODE.
NO DOUBT.
WE'RE GOING TO BE LEARNING HOW TO DRAW BLOOD NEXT. I'M SO ANXIOUS.
NO, THAT WOULD BE THE POOR SOUL WHO HAS TO BE PAIRED UP WITH YOU.
YUP, YUP.

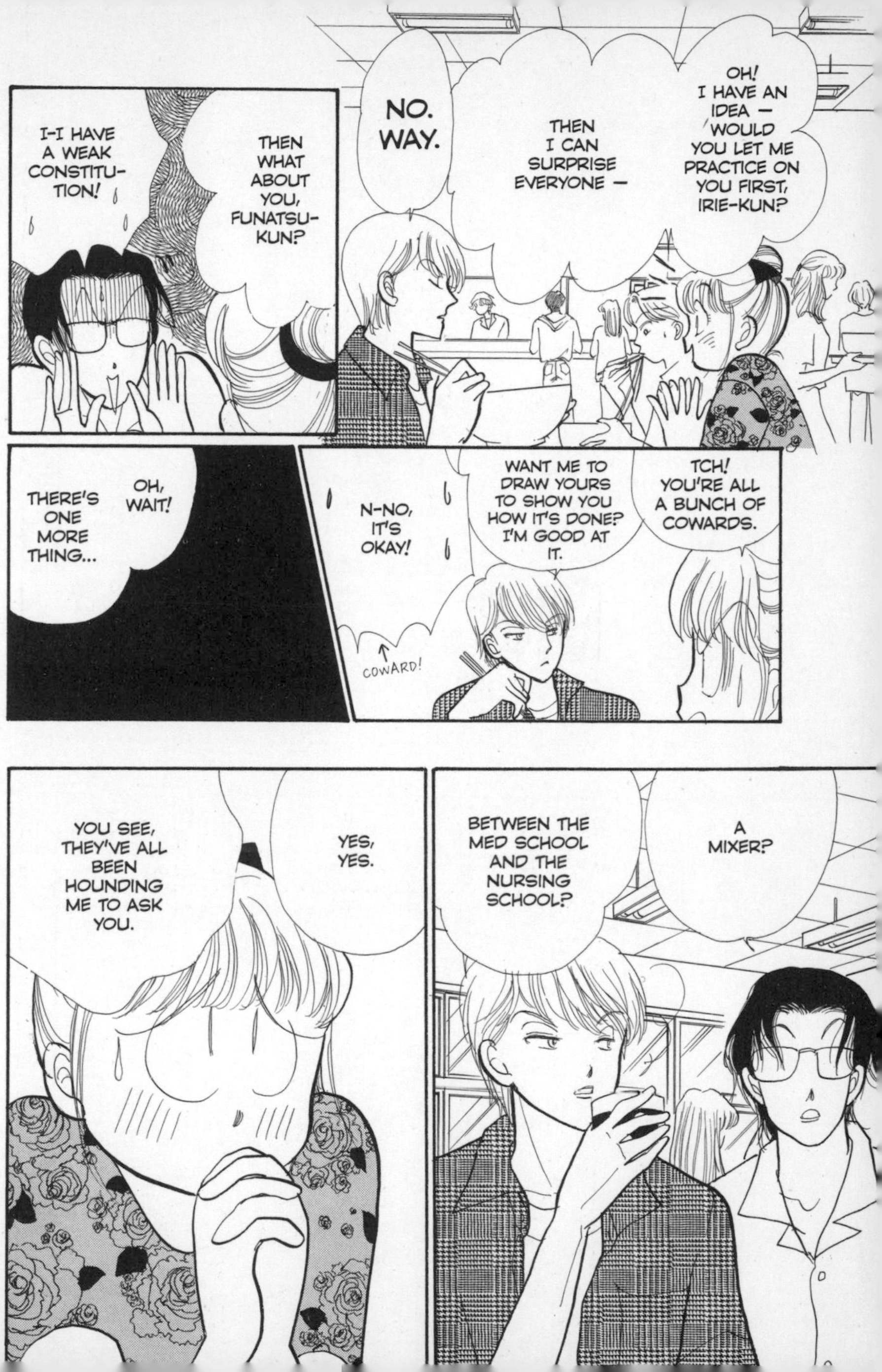

OH! I HAVE AN IDEA — WOULD YOU LET ME PRACTICE ON YOU FIRST, IRIE-KUN?
THEN I CAN SURPRISE EVERYONE —
NO. WAY.
THEN WHAT ABOUT YOU, FUNATSU-KUN?
I-I HAVE A WEAK CONSTITUTION!
TCH! YOU'RE ALL A BUNCH OF COWARDS.
WANT ME TO DRAW YOURS TO SHOW YOU HOW IT'S DONE? I'M GOOD AT IT.
N-NO, IT'S OKAY!
COWARD!
OH, WAIT!
THERE'S ONE MORE THING...
A MIXER?
BETWEEN THE MED SCHOOL AND THE NURSING SCHOOL?
YES, YES.
YOU SEE, THEY'VE ALL BEEN HOUNDING ME TO ASK YOU.

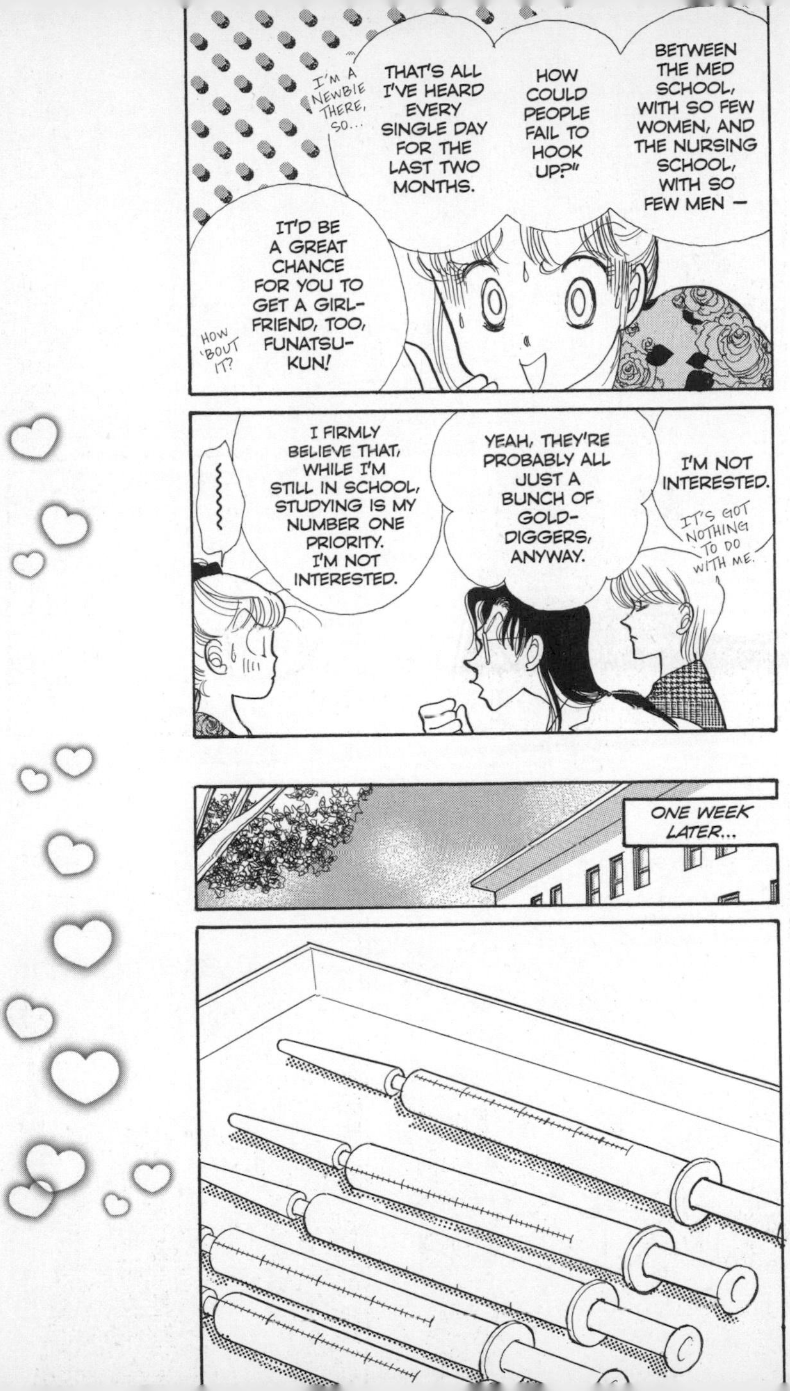
BETWEEN THE MED SCHOOL, WITH SO FEW WOMEN, AND THE NURSING SCHOOL, WITH SO FEW MEN —
HOW COULD PEOPLE FAIL TO HOOK UP?"
THAT'S ALL I'VE HEARD EVERY SINGLE DAY FOR THE LAST TWO MONTHS.
I'M A NEWBIE THERE, SO...
IT'D BE A GREAT CHANCE FOR YOU TO GET A GIRL-FRIEND, TOO, FUNATSU-KUN!
HOW 'BOUT IT?
I'M NOT INTERESTED.
IT'S GOT NOTHING TO DO WITH ME.
YEAH, THEY'RE PROBABLY ALL JUST A BUNCH OF GOLD-DIGGERS, ANYWAY.
I FIRMLY BELIEVE THAT, WHILE I'M STILL IN SCHOOL, STUDYING IS MY NUMBER ONE PRIORITY. I'M NOT INTERESTED.
ONE WEEK LATER...

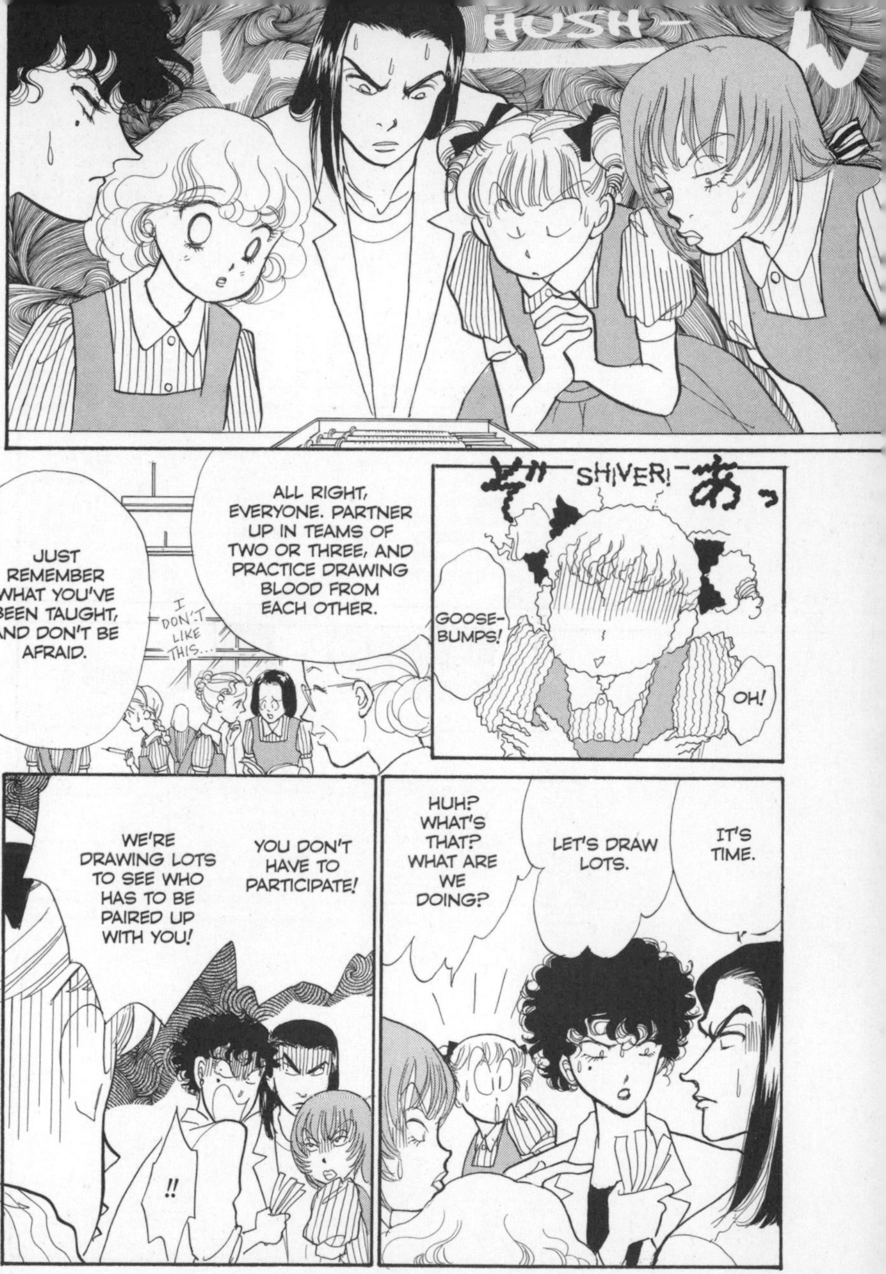
HUSH
ぞっ
SHIVER!
あっ
GOOSE-BUMPS!
OH!
ALL RIGHT, EVERYONE. PARTNER UP IN TEAMS OF TWO OR THREE, AND PRACTICE DRAWING BLOOD FROM EACH OTHER.
JUST REMEMBER WHAT YOU'VE BEEN TAUGHT, AND DON'T BE AFRAID.
I DON'T LIKE THIS...
IT'S TIME.
LET'S DRAW LOTS.
HUH? WHAT'S THAT? WHAT ARE WE DOING?
YOU DON'T HAVE TO PARTICIPATE!
WE'RE DRAWING LOTS TO SEE WHO HAS TO BE PAIRED UP WITH YOU!
!!

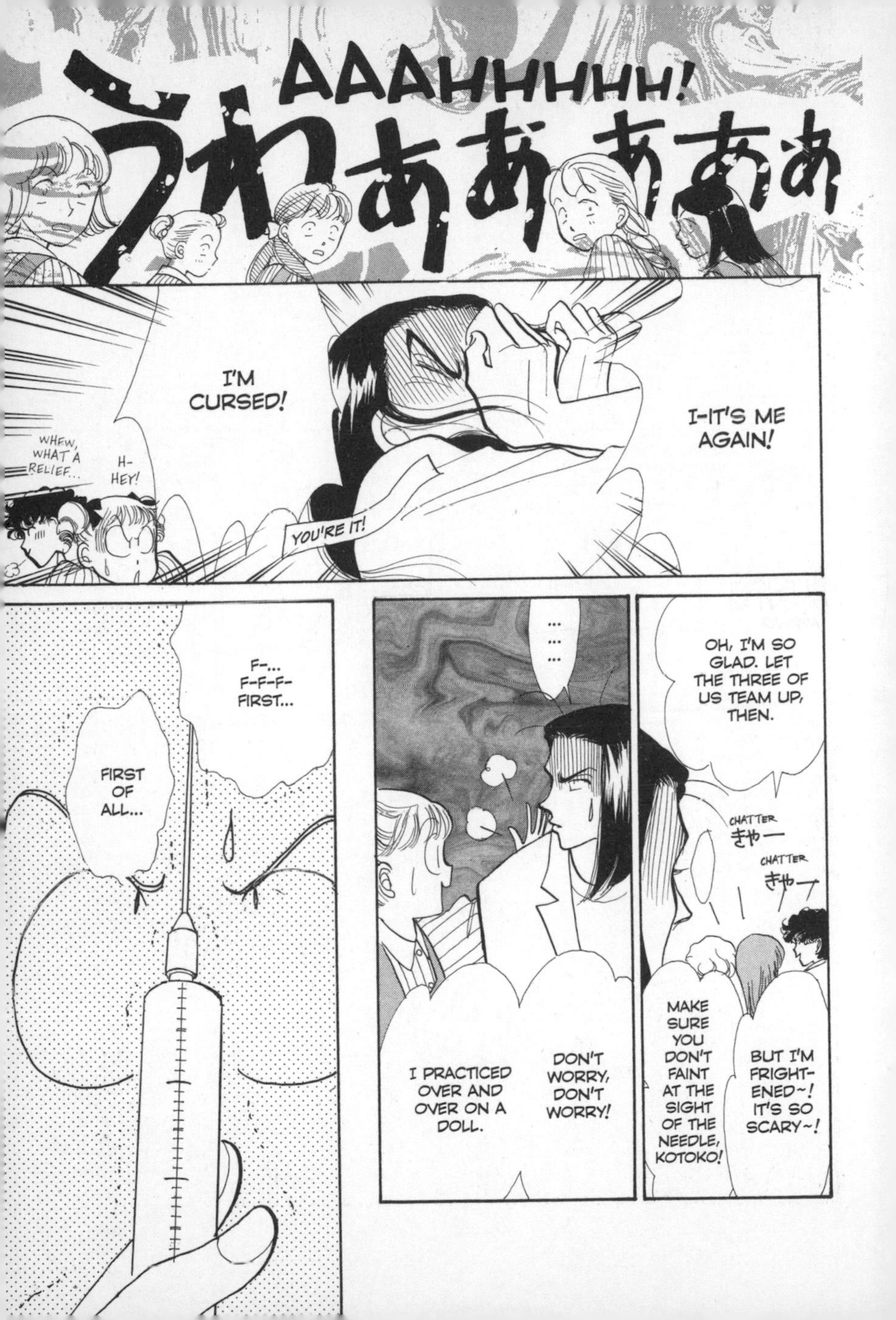
AAAHHHHH!
うわあああああ
I-IT'S ME AGAIN!
YOU'RE IT!
I'M CURSED!
H-HEY!
WHEW, WHAT A RELIEF...
OH, I'M SO GLAD. LET THE THREE OF US TEAM UP, THEN.
CHATTER きゃー
CHATTER きゃー
BUT I'M FRIGHT-ENED~! IT'S SO SCARY~!
MAKE SURE YOU DON'T FAINT AT THE SIGHT OF THE NEEDLE, KOTOKO!
... ...
DON'T WORRY, DON'T WORRY!
I PRACTICED OVER AND OVER ON A DOLL.
F-... F-F-F-FIRST...
FIRST OF ALL...

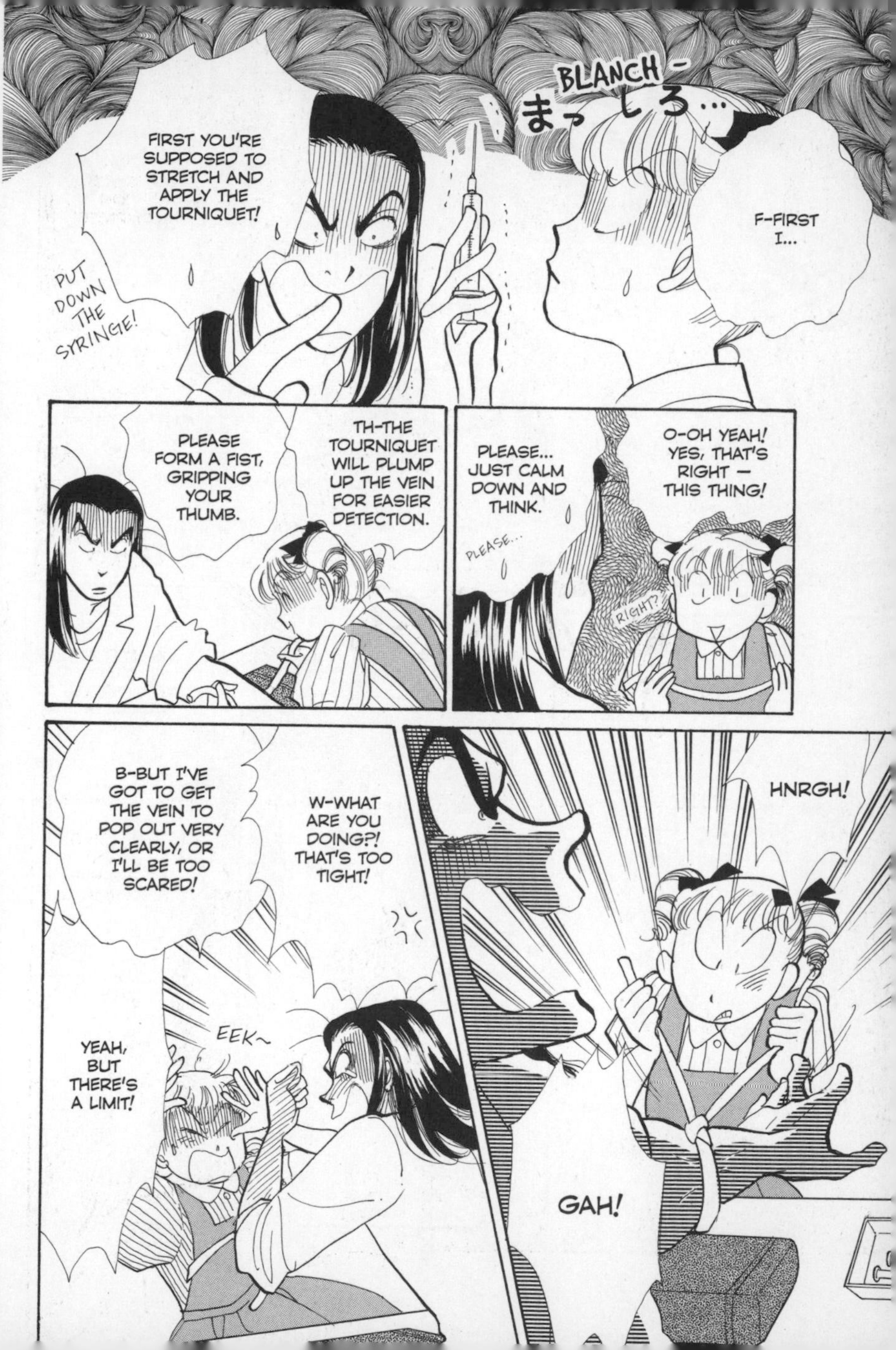
F-FIRST I...
BLANCH -
まっしろ…
FIRST YOU'RE SUPPOSED TO STRETCH AND APPLY THE TOURNIQUET!
PUT DOWN THE SYRINGE!
O-OH YEAH! YES, THAT'S RIGHT — THIS THING!
PLEASE... JUST CALM DOWN AND THINK.
PLEASE...
RIGHT?
TH-THE TOURNIQUET WILL PLUMP UP THE VEIN FOR EASIER DETECTION.
PLEASE FORM A FIST, GRIPPING YOUR THUMB.
HNRGH!
GAH!
W-WHAT ARE YOU DOING?! THAT'S TOO TIGHT!
B-BUT I'VE GOT TO GET THE VEIN TO POP OUT VERY CLEARLY, OR I'LL BE TOO SCARED!
EEK~
YEAH, BUT THERE'S A LIMIT!

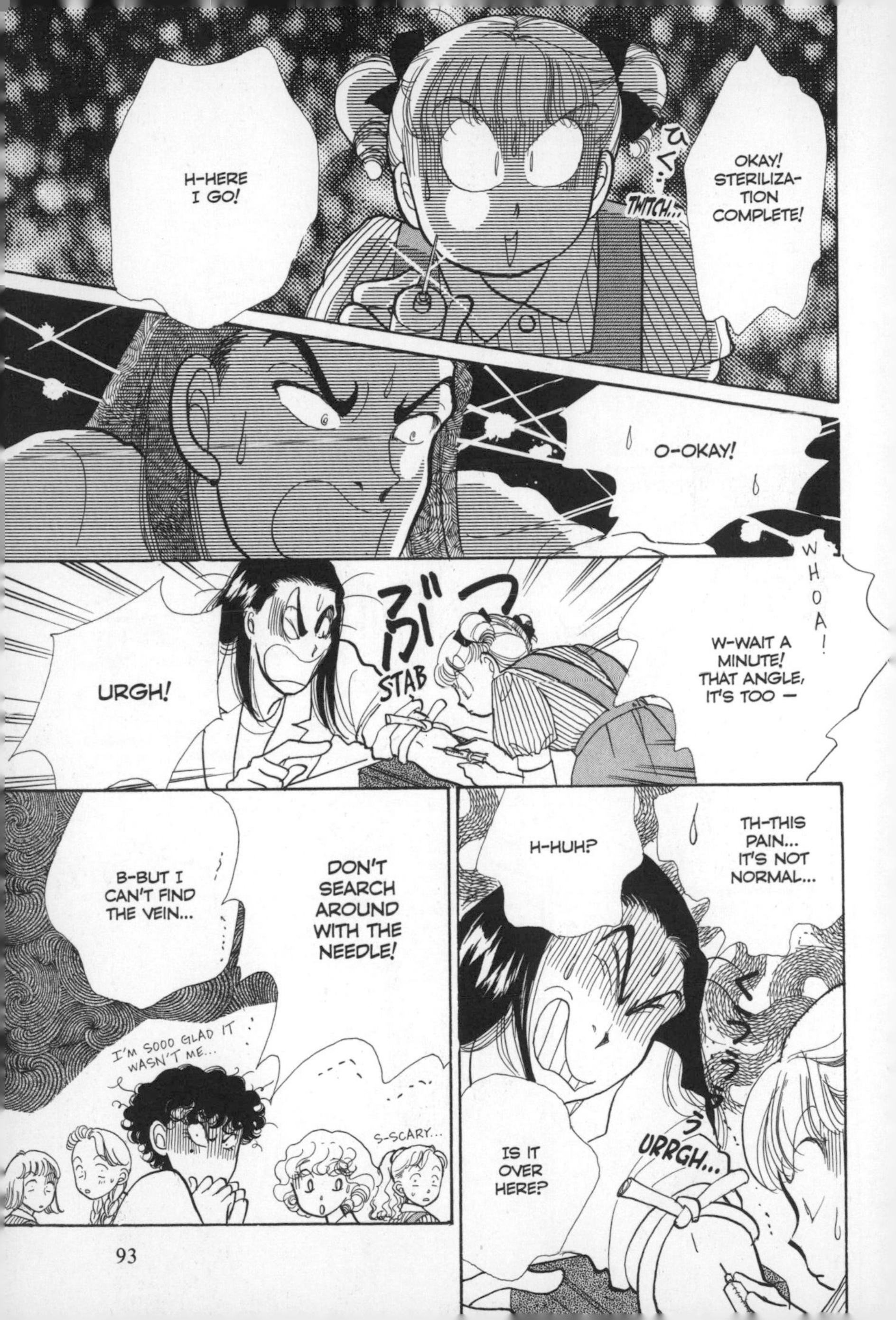
OKAY! STERILIZA-TION COMPLETE!
ひく…
TWITCH...
H-HERE I GO!
O-OKAY!
W-WAIT A MINUTE! THAT ANGLE, IT'S TOO —
WHOA!
ぶっ
STAB
URGH!
TH-THIS PAIN... IT'S NOT NORMAL...
H-HUH?
URRGH...
IS IT OVER HERE?
DON'T SEARCH AROUND WITH THE NEEDLE!
B-BUT I CAN'T FIND THE VEIN...
I'M SOOO GLAD IT WASN'T ME...
S-SCARY...

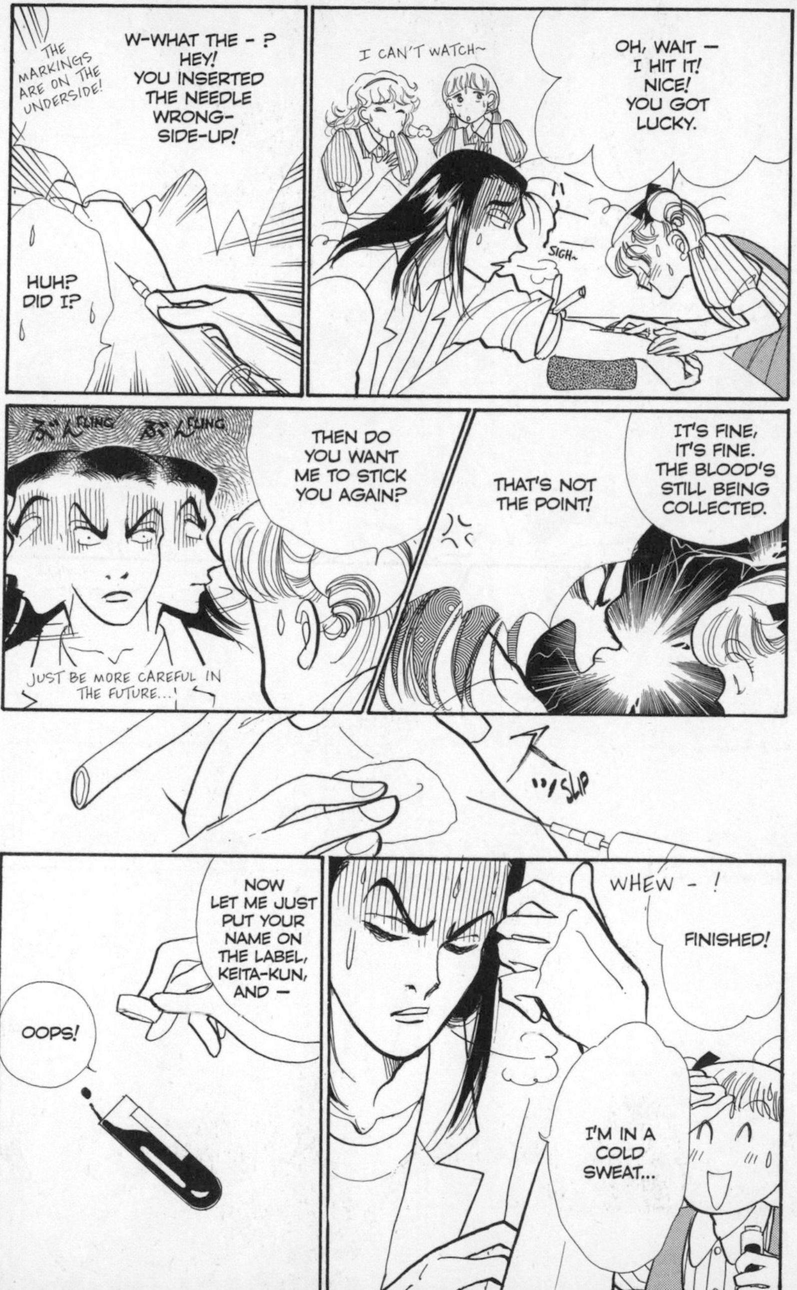
OH, WAIT — I HIT IT! NICE! YOU GOT LUCKY.
I CAN'T WATCH~
SIGH~
W-WHAT THE - ? HEY! YOU INSERTED THE NEEDLE WRONG-SIDE-UP!
THE MARKINGS ARE ON THE UNDERSIDE!
HUH? DID I?
IT'S FINE, IT'S FINE. THE BLOOD'S STILL BEING COLLECTED.
THAT'S NOT THE POINT!
ぶん FLING
ぶん FLING
THEN DO YOU WANT ME TO STICK YOU AGAIN?
JUST BE MORE CAREFUL IN THE FUTURE...!
SLIP
WHEW - !
FINISHED!
I'M IN A COLD SWEAT...
NOW LET ME JUST PUT YOUR NAME ON THE LABEL, KEITA-KUN, AND —
OOPS!

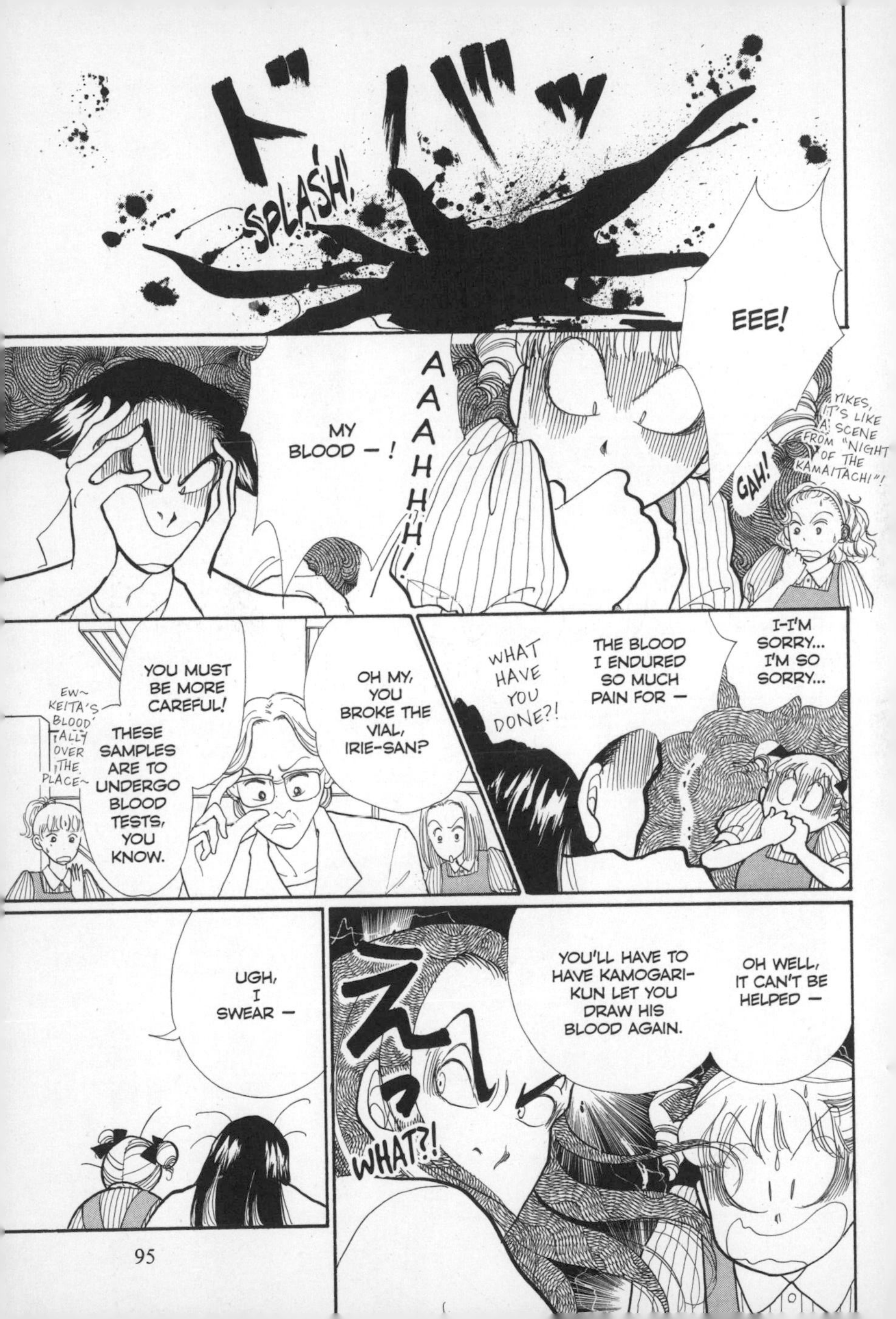
SPLASH!
EEE!
YIKES, IT'S LIKE A SCENE FROM "NIGHT OF THE KAMAITACHI"!
GAH!
AAAHHHH!
MY BLOOD —!
I-I'M SORRY... I'M SO SORRY...
THE BLOOD I ENDURED SO MUCH PAIN FOR —
WHAT HAVE YOU DONE?!
OH MY, YOU BROKE THE VIAL, IRIE-SAN?
YOU MUST BE MORE CAREFUL!
THESE SAMPLES ARE TO UNDERGO BLOOD TESTS, YOU KNOW.
EW~ KEITA'S BLOOD' ALL OVER THE PLACE~
OH WELL, IT CAN'T BE HELPED —
YOU'LL HAVE TO HAVE KAMOGARI-KUN LET YOU DRAW HIS BLOOD AGAIN.
WHAT?!
UGH, I SWEAR —

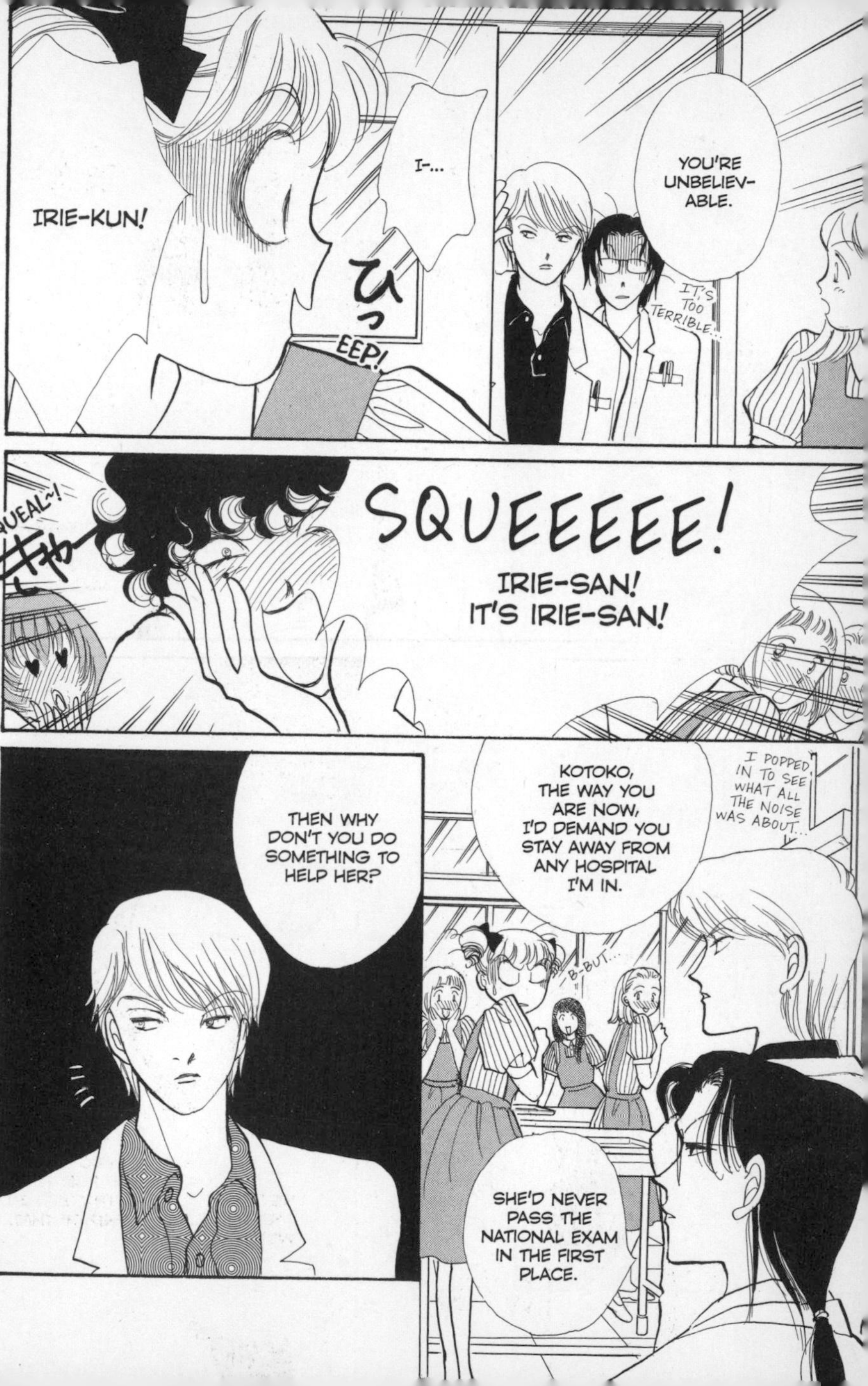
YOU'RE UNBELIEVABLE.
IT'S TOO TERRIBLE...
I-...
IRIE-KUN!
ひっ
EEP!
SQUEEEEEE!
IRIE-SAN! IT'S IRIE-SAN!
SQUEAL~!
きゃー
I POPPED IN TO SEE WHAT ALL THE NOISE WAS ABOUT...
KOTOKO, THE WAY YOU ARE NOW, I'D DEMAND YOU STAY AWAY FROM ANY HOSPITAL I'M IN.
B-BUT...
SHE'D NEVER PASS THE NATIONAL EXAM IN THE FIRST PLACE.
THEN WHY DON'T YOU DO SOMETHING TO HELP HER?

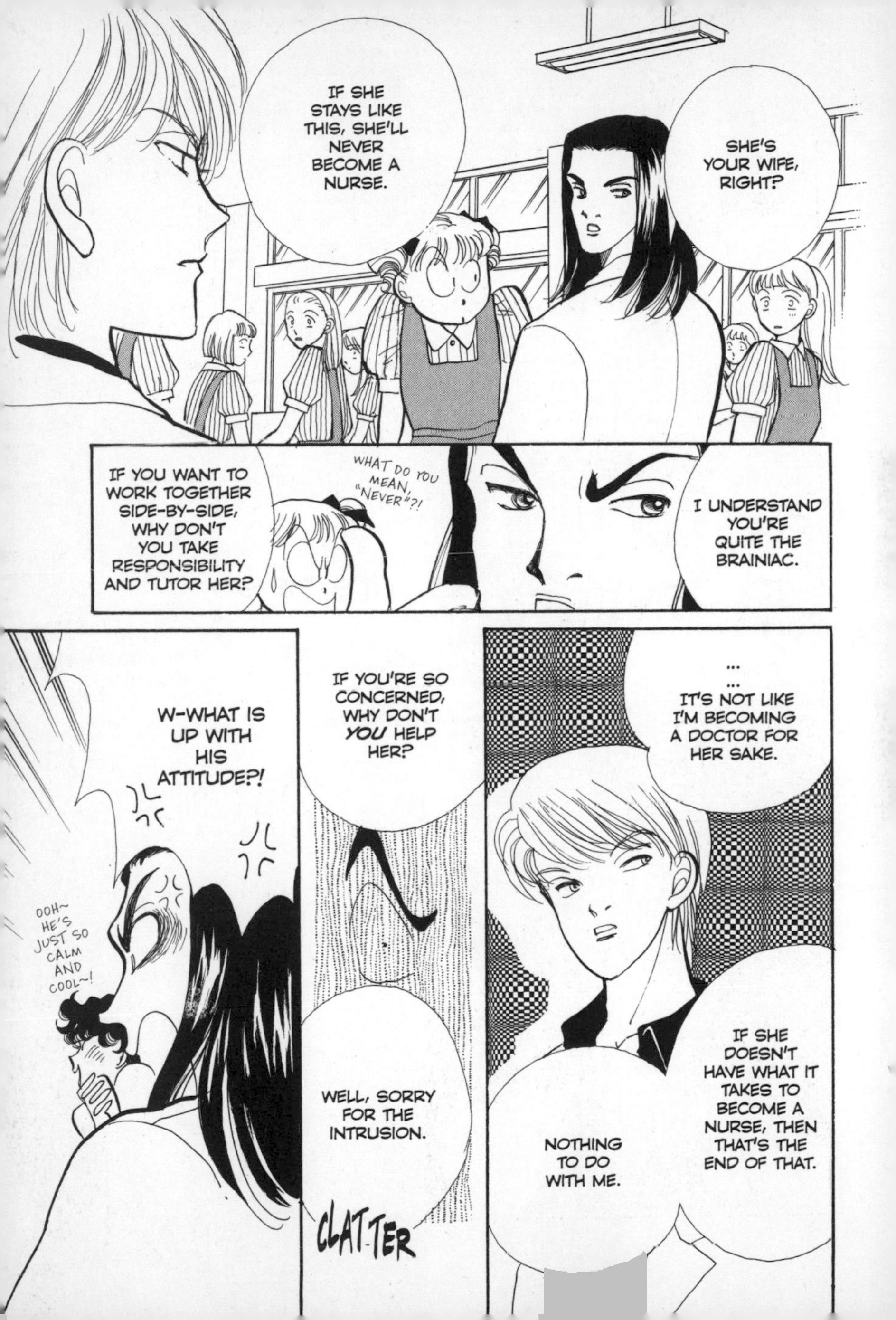
SHE'S YOUR WIFE, RIGHT?
IF SHE STAYS LIKE THIS, SHE'LL NEVER BECOME A NURSE.
I UNDERSTAND YOU'RE QUITE THE BRAINIAC.
WHAT DO YOU MEAN, "NEVER"?!
IF YOU WANT TO WORK TOGETHER SIDE-BY-SIDE, WHY DON'T YOU TAKE RESPONSIBILITY AND TUTOR HER?
... ... IT'S NOT LIKE I'M BECOMING A DOCTOR FOR HER SAKE.
IF SHE DOESN'T HAVE WHAT IT TAKES TO BECOME A NURSE, THEN THAT'S THE END OF THAT.
NOTHING TO DO WITH ME.
IF YOU'RE SO CONCERNED, WHY DON'T *YOU* HELP HER?
WELL, SORRY FOR THE INTRUSION.
CLAT-TER
W-WHAT IS UP WITH HIS ATTITUDE?!
OOH~ HE'S JUST SO CALM AND COOL~!

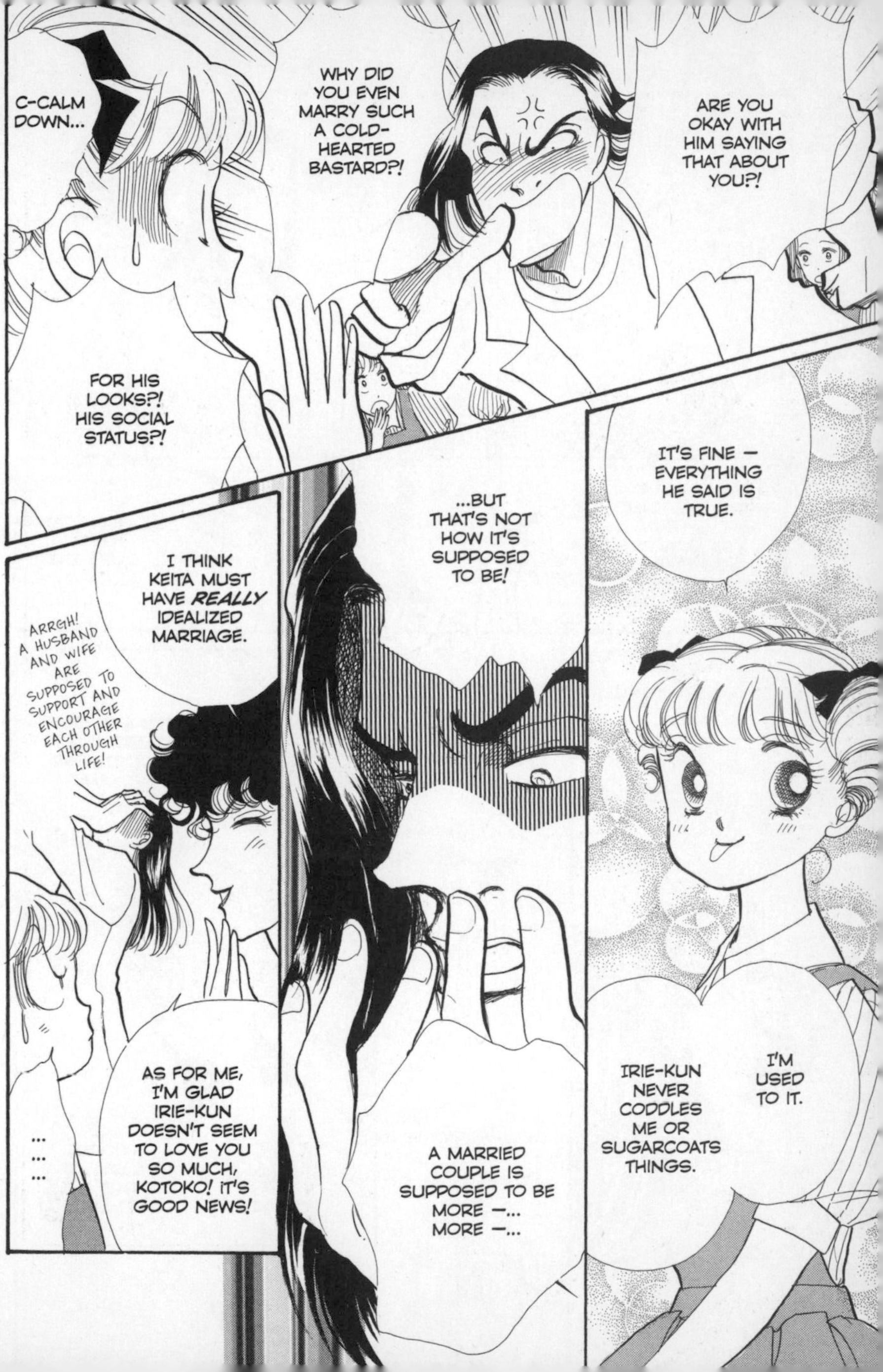
ARE YOU OKAY WITH HIM SAYING THAT ABOUT YOU?!
WHY DID YOU EVEN MARRY SUCH A COLD-HEARTED BASTARD?!
C-CALM DOWN...
FOR HIS LOOKS?! HIS SOCIAL STATUS?!
IT'S FINE — EVERYTHING HE SAID IS TRUE.
I'M USED TO IT.
IRIE-KUN NEVER CODDLES ME OR SUGARCOATS THINGS.
...BUT THAT'S NOT HOW IT'S SUPPOSED TO BE!
A MARRIED COUPLE IS SUPPOSED TO BE MORE —... MORE —...
I THINK KEITA MUST HAVE *REALLY* IDEALIZED MARRIAGE.
ARRGH! A HUSBAND AND WIFE ARE SUPPOSED TO SUPPORT AND ENCOURAGE EACH OTHER THROUGH LIFE!
AS FOR ME, I'M GLAD IRIE-KUN DOESN'T SEEM TO LOVE YOU SO MUCH, KOTOKO! IT'S GOOD NEWS!
... ...

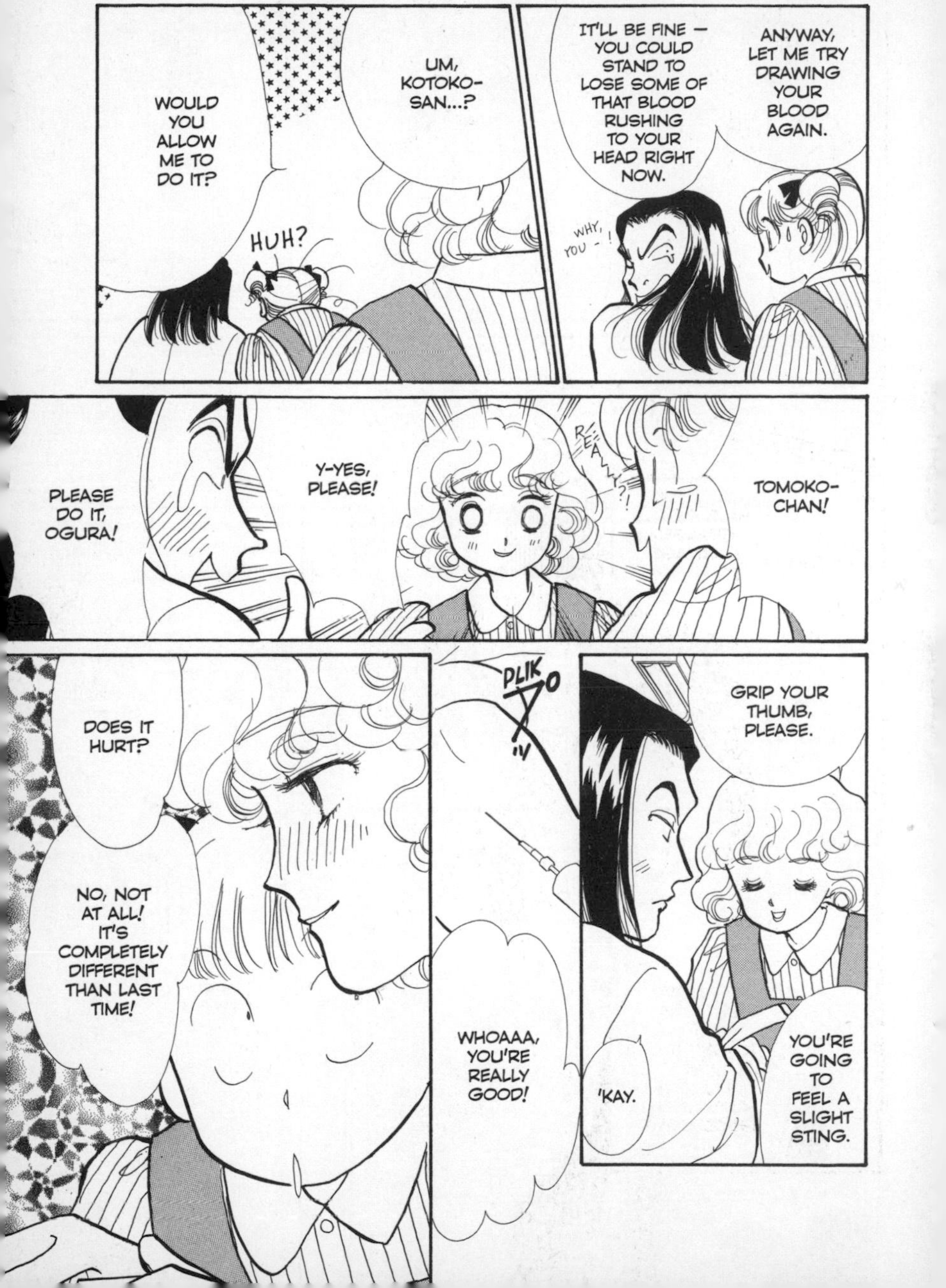
ANYWAY, LET ME TRY DRAWING YOUR BLOOD AGAIN.
IT'LL BE FINE — YOU COULD STAND TO LOSE SOME OF THAT BLOOD RUSHING TO YOUR HEAD RIGHT NOW.
WHY, YOU—!
UM, KOTOKO-SAN...?
WOULD YOU ALLOW ME TO DO IT?
HUH?
TOMOKO-CHAN!
REALLY?!
Y-YES, PLEASE!
PLEASE DO IT, OGURA!
GRIP YOUR THUMB, PLEASE.
YOU'RE GOING TO FEEL A SLIGHT STING.
'KAY.
PLIK
WHOAAA, YOU'RE REALLY GOOD!
DOES IT HURT?
NO, NOT AT ALL! IT'S COMPLETELY DIFFERENT THAN LAST TIME!

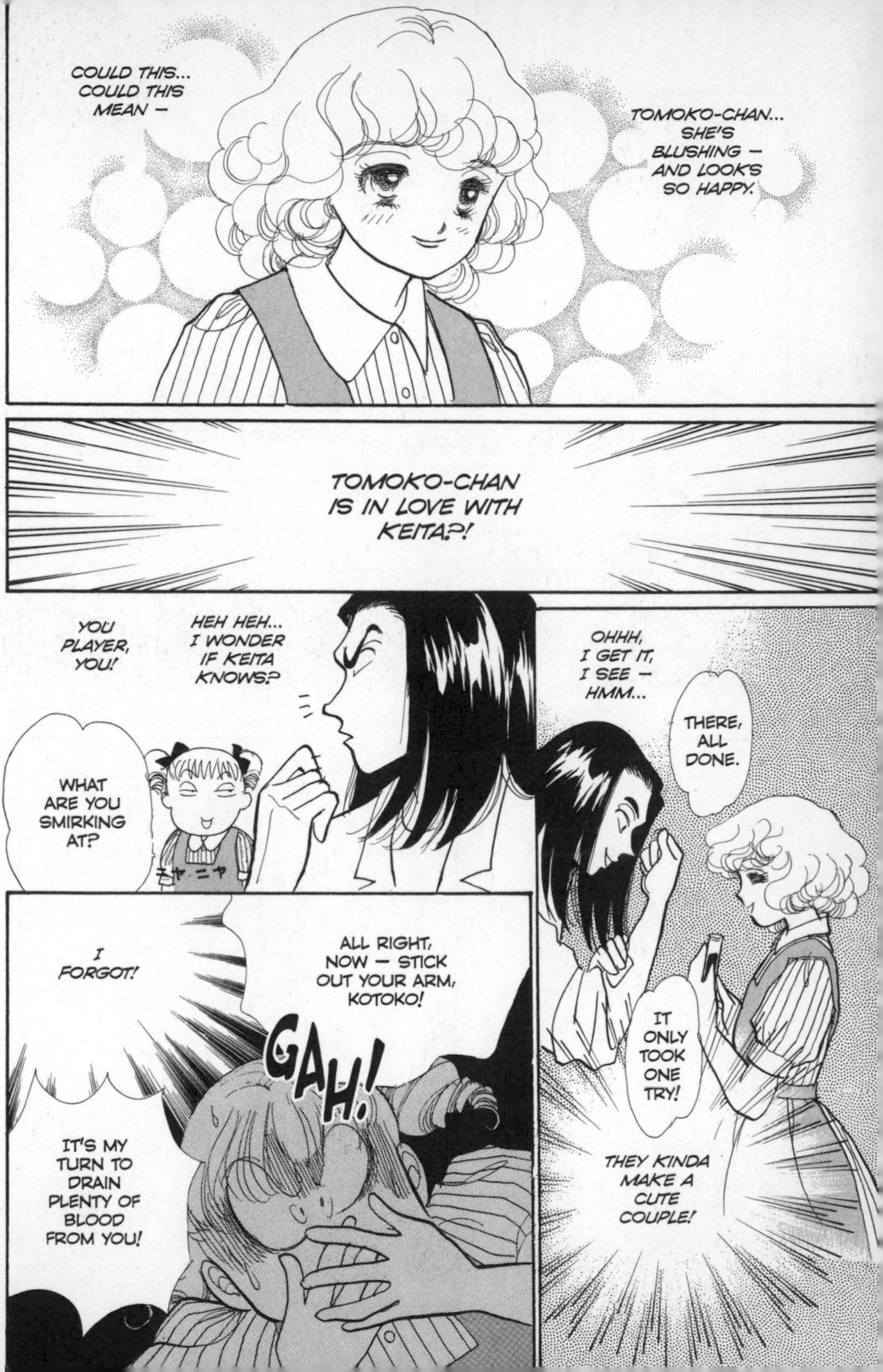
TOMOKO-CHAN... SHE'S BLUSHING – AND LOOKS SO HAPPY.
COULD THIS... COULD THIS MEAN –
TOMOKO-CHAN IS IN LOVE WITH KEITA?!
OHHH, I GET IT, I SEE – HMM...
THERE, ALL DONE.
IT ONLY TOOK ONE TRY!
THEY KINDA MAKE A CUTE COUPLE!
HEH HEH... I WONDER IF KEITA KNOWS?
YOU PLAYER, YOU!
WHAT ARE YOU SMIRKING AT?
ニヤ ニヤ
ALL RIGHT, NOW – STICK OUT YOUR ARM, KOTOKO!
I FORGOT!
GAH!
IT'S MY TURN TO DRAIN PLENTY OF BLOOD FROM YOU!

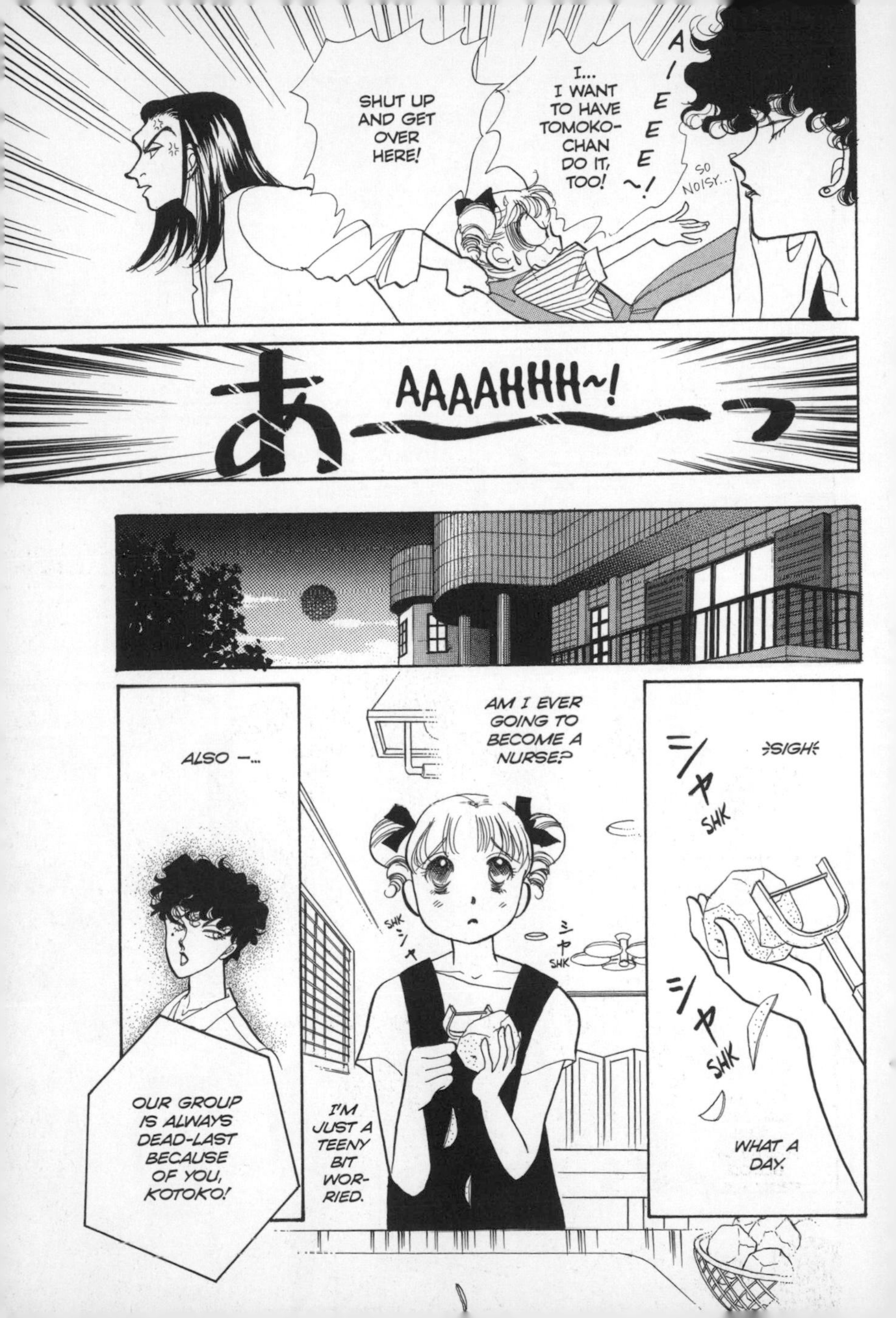
AIEEEE~!
SO NOISY...
I... I WANT TO HAVE TOMOKO-CHAN DO IT, TOO!
SHUT UP AND GET OVER HERE!
あーっ
AAAAHHH~!
シャ SHK
SIGH
シャ SHK
WHAT A DAY.
AM I EVER GOING TO BECOME A NURSE?
シャ SHK
シャ SHK
I'M JUST A TEENY BIT WOR-RIED.
ALSO —...
OUR GROUP IS ALWAYS DEAD-LAST BECAUSE OF YOU, KOTOKO!

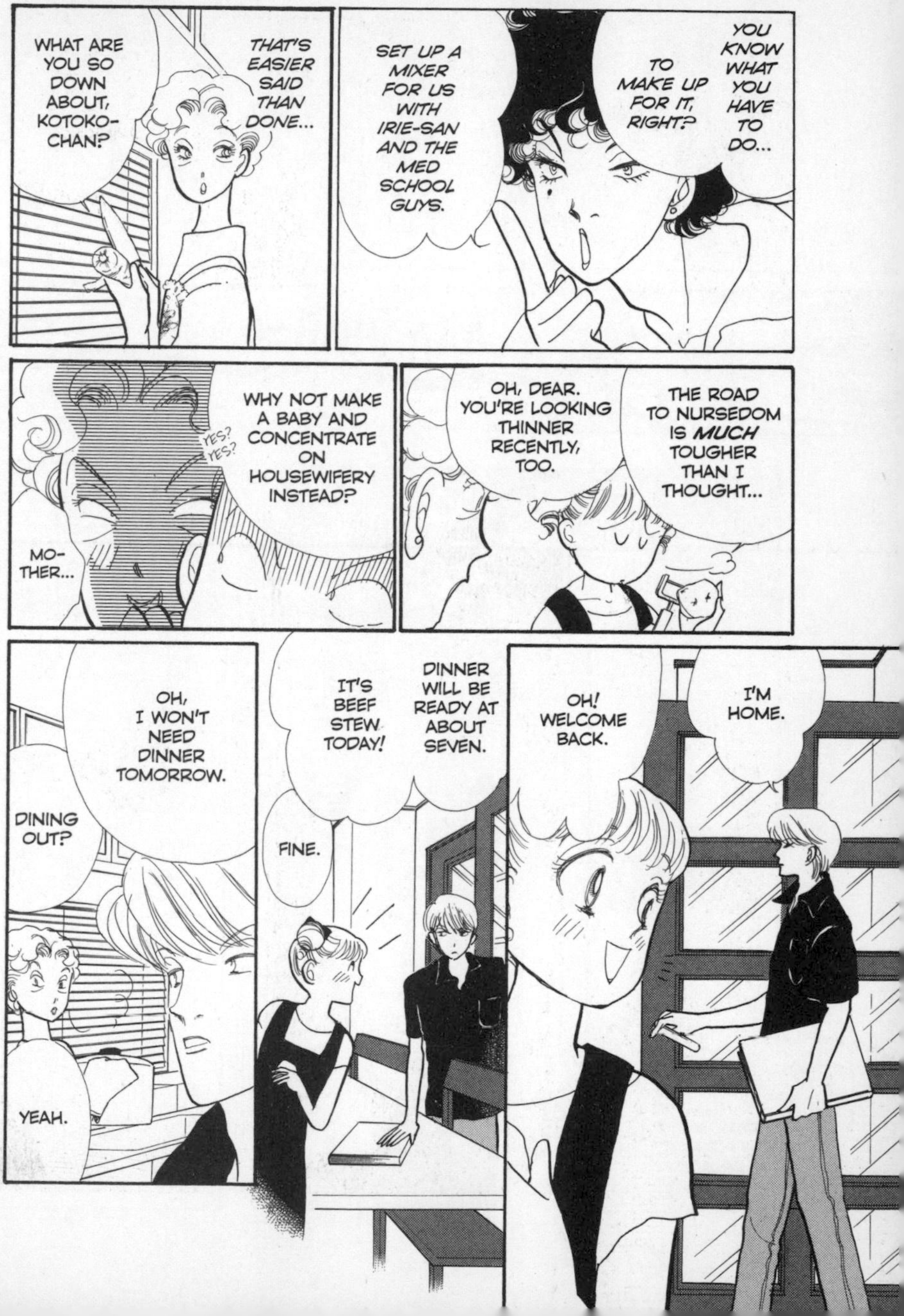
YOU KNOW WHAT YOU HAVE TO DO...
TO MAKE UP FOR IT, RIGHT?
SET UP A MIXER FOR US WITH IRIE-SAN AND THE MED SCHOOL GUYS.
THAT'S EASIER SAID THAN DONE...
WHAT ARE YOU SO DOWN ABOUT, KOTOKO-CHAN?
THE ROAD TO NURSEDOM IS *MUCH* TOUGHER THAN I THOUGHT...
OH, DEAR. YOU'RE LOOKING THINNER RECENTLY, TOO.
WHY NOT MAKE A BABY AND CONCENTRATE ON HOUSEWIFERY INSTEAD?
YES? YES?
MO-THER...
I'M HOME.
OH! WELCOME BACK.
DINNER WILL BE READY AT ABOUT SEVEN.
IT'S BEEF STEW TODAY!
FINE.
OH, I WON'T NEED DINNER TOMORROW.
DINING OUT?
YEAH.

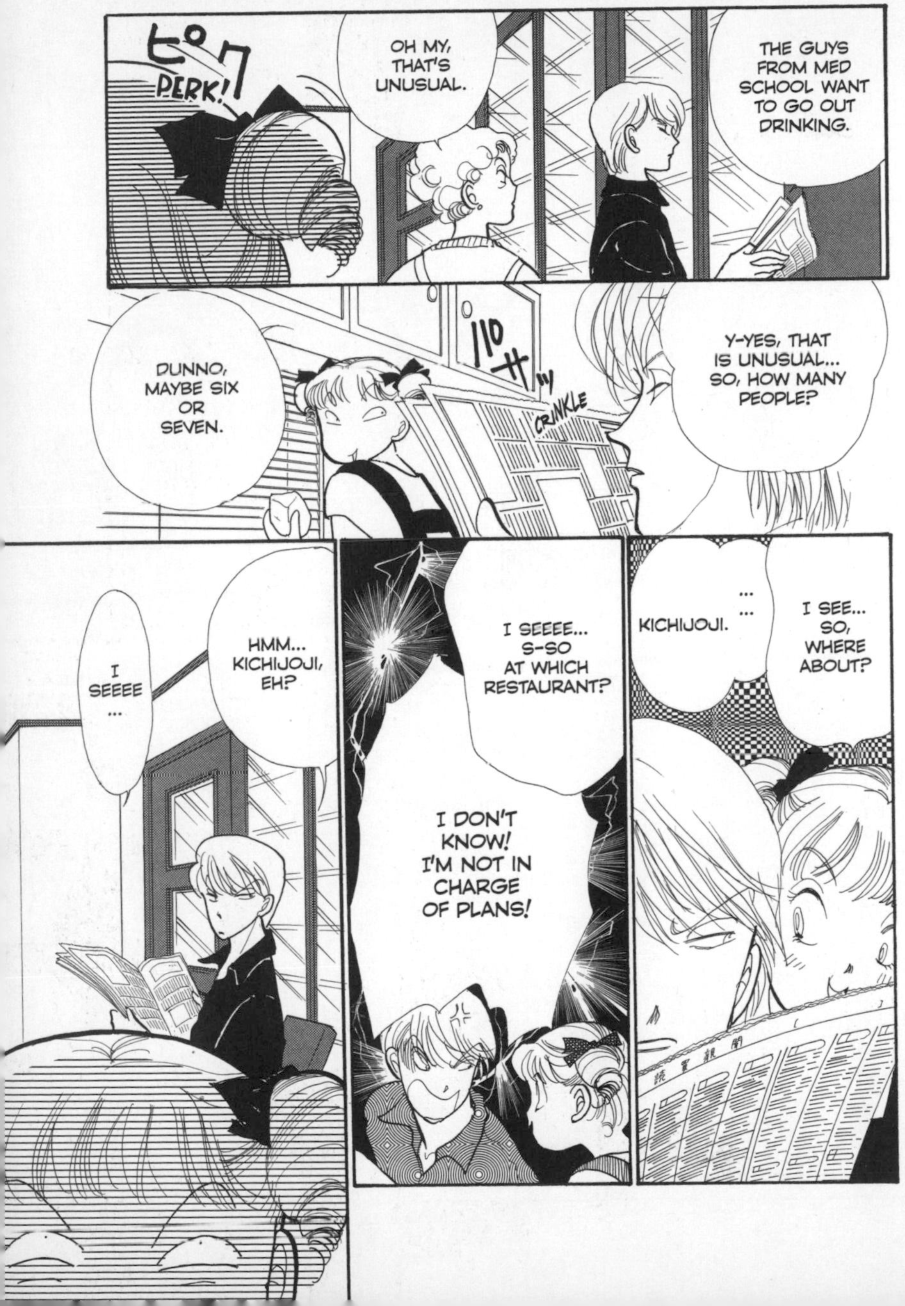
THE GUYS FROM MED SCHOOL WANT TO GO OUT DRINKING.
OH MY, THAT'S UNUSUAL.
ピク
PERK!
Y-YES, THAT IS UNUSUAL... SO, HOW MANY PEOPLE?
バサッ
CRINKLE
DUNNO, MAYBE SIX OR SEVEN.
I SEE... SO, WHERE ABOUT?
... ...
KICHIJOJI.
I SEEEE... S-SO AT WHICH RESTAURANT?
I DON'T KNOW! I'M NOT IN CHARGE OF PLANS!
HMM... KICHIJOJI, EH?
I SEEEE ...

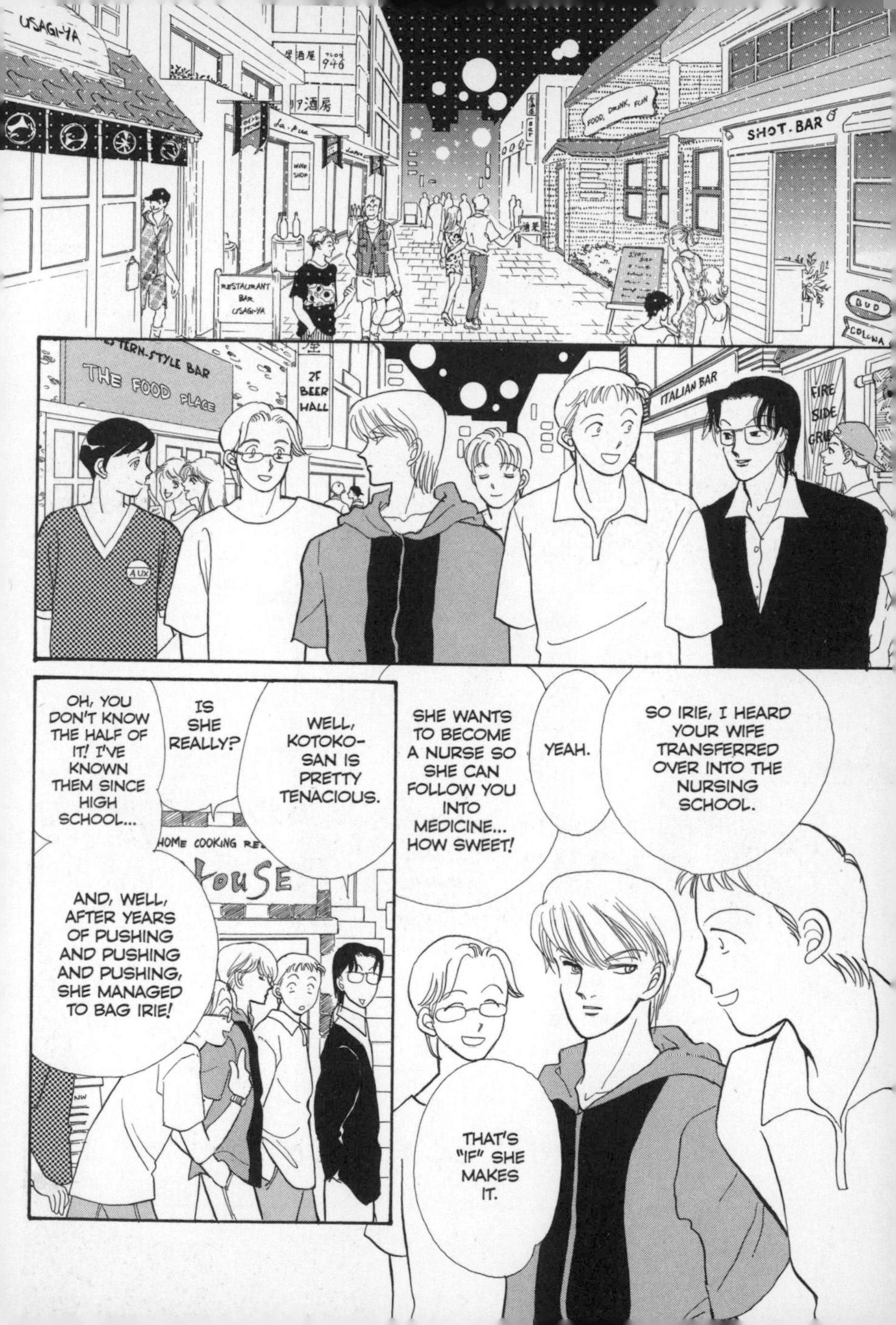
SHOT-BAR
FOOD, DRINK, FUN
BUD
USAGI-YA
RESTAURANT BAR USAGI-YA
WINE SHOP
ITALIAN BAR
2F BEER HALL
THE FOOD PLACE
SO IRIE, I HEARD YOUR WIFE TRANSFERRED OVER INTO THE NURSING SCHOOL.
YEAH.
SHE WANTS TO BECOME A NURSE SO SHE CAN FOLLOW YOU INTO MEDICINE... HOW SWEET!
THAT'S "IF" SHE MAKES IT.
WELL, KOTOKO-SAN IS PRETTY TENACIOUS.
IS SHE REALLY?
OH, YOU DON'T KNOW THE HALF OF IT! I'VE KNOWN THEM SINCE HIGH SCHOOL...
AND, WELL, AFTER YEARS OF PUSHING AND PUSHING AND PUSHING, SHE MANAGED TO BAG IRIE!

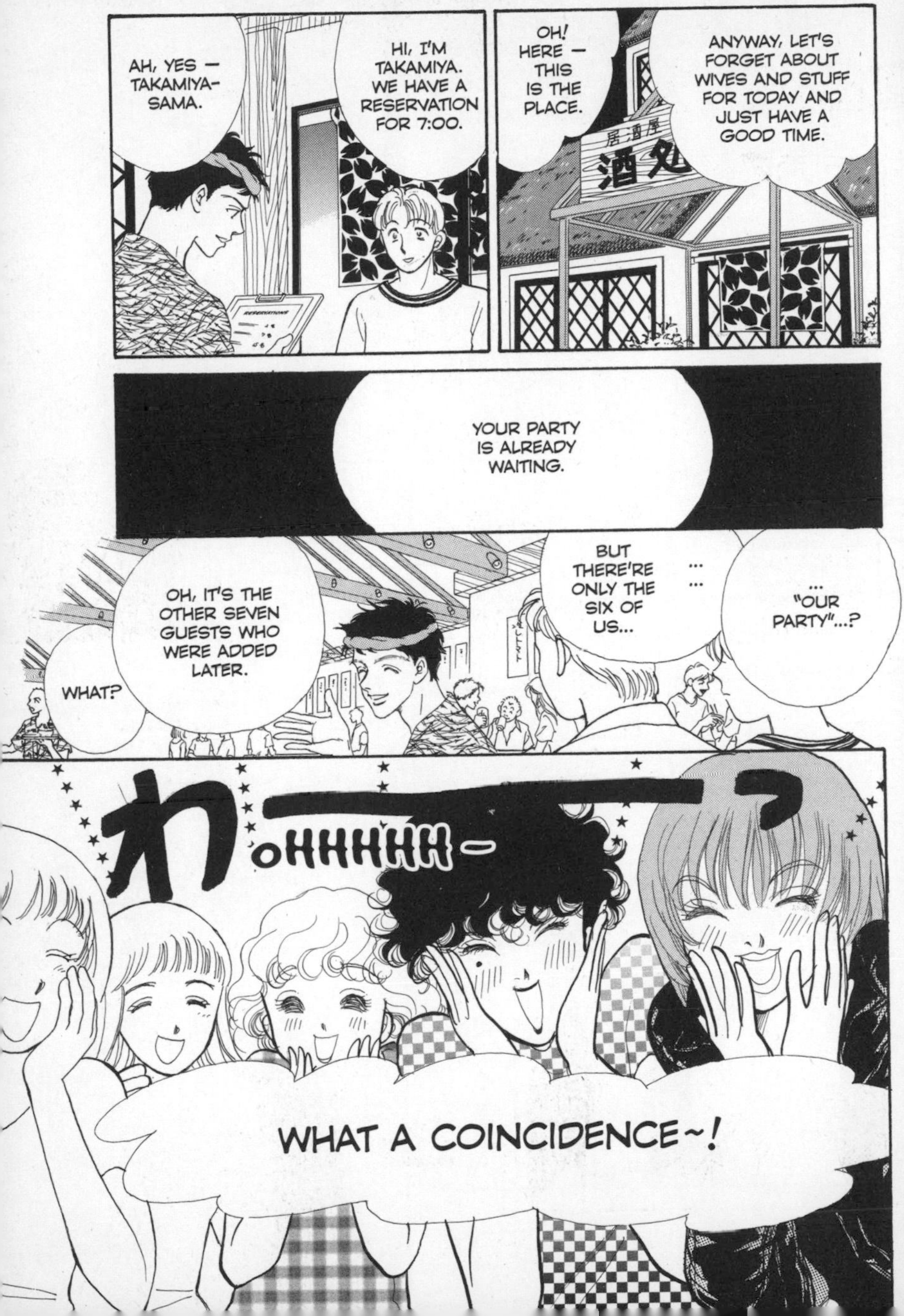
ANYWAY, LET'S FORGET ABOUT WIVES AND STUFF FOR TODAY AND JUST HAVE A GOOD TIME.
OH! HERE — THIS IS THE PLACE.
HI, I'M TAKAMIYA. WE HAVE A RESERVATION FOR 7:00.
AH, YES — TAKAMIYA-SAMA.
YOUR PARTY IS ALREADY WAITING.
... "OUR PARTY"...?
... ...
BUT THERE'RE ONLY THE SIX OF US...
OH, IT'S THE OTHER SEVEN GUESTS WHO WERE ADDED LATER.
WHAT?
わーーっ
OHHHHH-
WHAT A COINCIDENCE~!

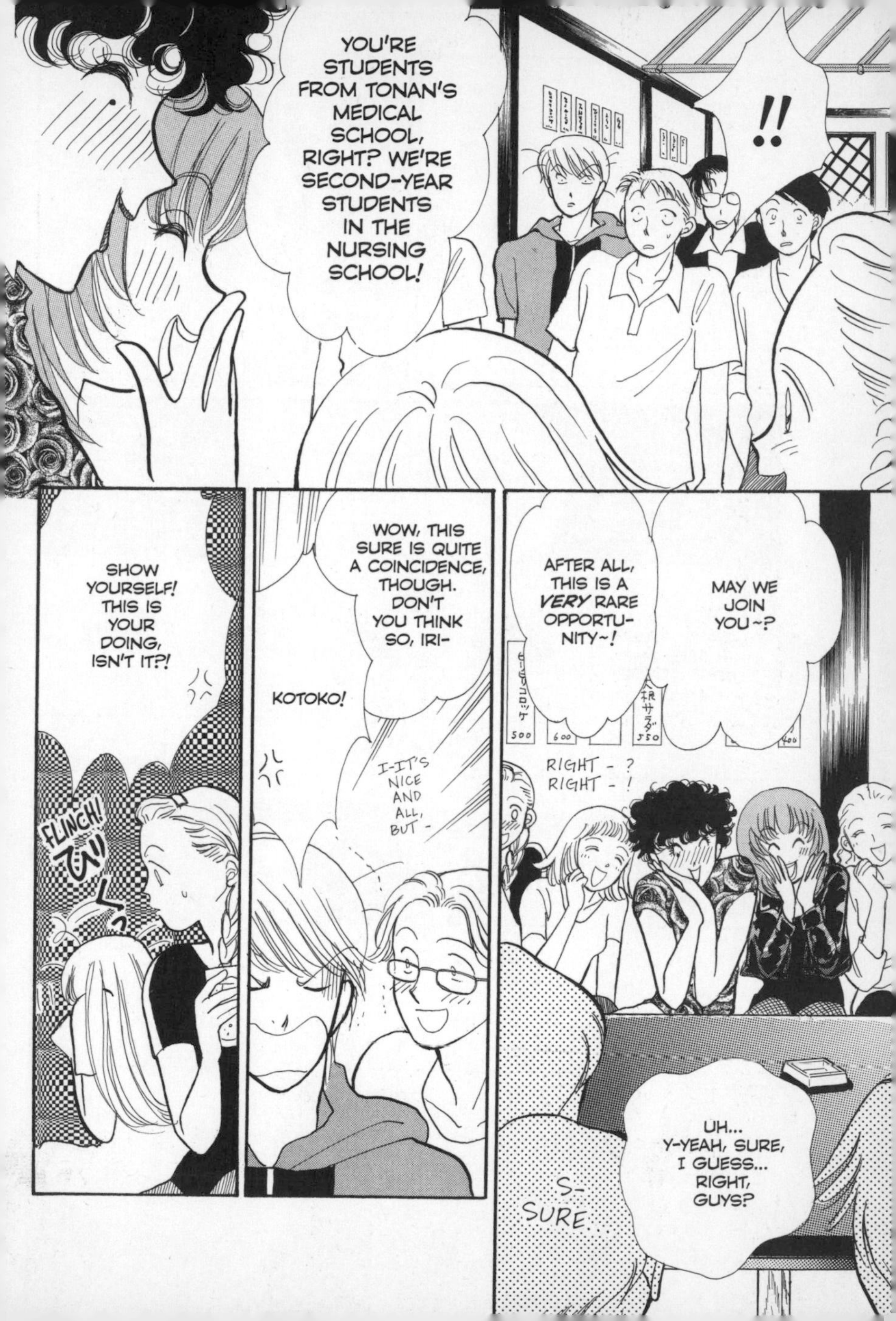
!!
YOU'RE STUDENTS FROM TONAN'S MEDICAL SCHOOL, RIGHT? WE'RE SECOND-YEAR STUDENTS IN THE NURSING SCHOOL!
MAY WE JOIN YOU~?
AFTER ALL, THIS IS A *VERY* RARE OPPORTUNITY~!
RIGHT-? RIGHT-!
UH... Y-YEAH, SURE, I GUESS... RIGHT, GUYS?
S-SURE.
WOW, THIS SURE IS QUITE A COINCIDENCE, THOUGH. DON'T YOU THINK SO, IRI-
KOTOKO!
I-IT'S NICE AND ALL, BUT-
SHOW YOURSELF! THIS IS YOUR DOING, ISN'T IT?!
FLINCH!

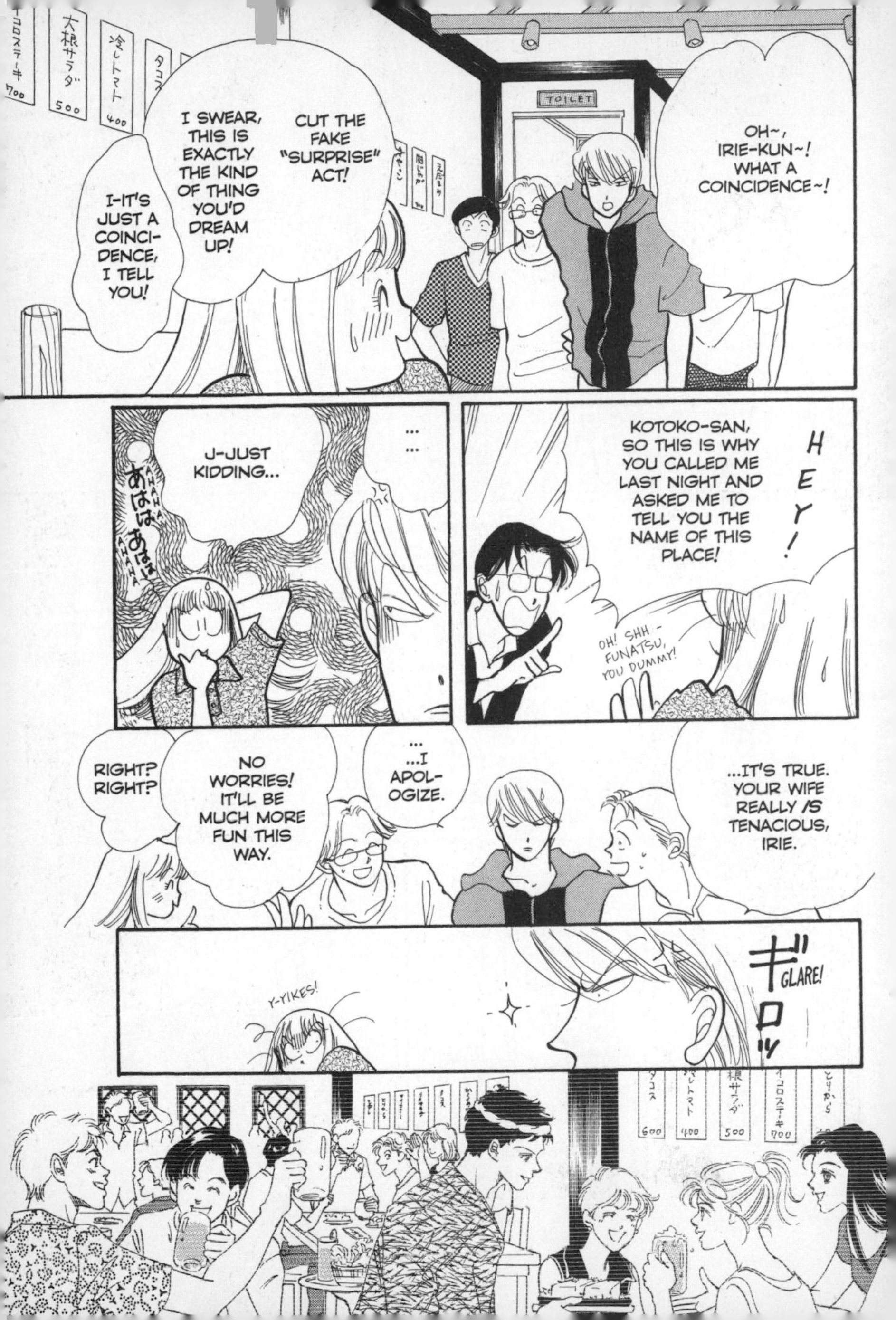
OH~, IRIE-KUN~! WHAT A COINCIDENCE~!
CUT THE FAKE "SURPRISE" ACT!
I SWEAR, THIS IS EXACTLY THE KIND OF THING YOU'D DREAM UP!
I-IT'S JUST A COINCIDENCE, I TELL YOU!
TOILET
KOTOKO-SAN, SO THIS IS WHY YOU CALLED ME LAST NIGHT AND ASKED ME TO TELL YOU THE NAME OF THIS PLACE!
HEY!
OH! SHH- FUNATSU, YOU DUMMY!
... ...
J-JUST KIDDING...
あはは AHAHA あはは AHAHA
...IT'S TRUE. YOUR WIFE REALLY IS TENACIOUS, IRIE.
... ...I APOLOGIZE.
NO WORRIES! IT'LL BE MUCH MORE FUN THIS WAY.
RIGHT? RIGHT?
ギロッ GLARE!
Y-YIKES!

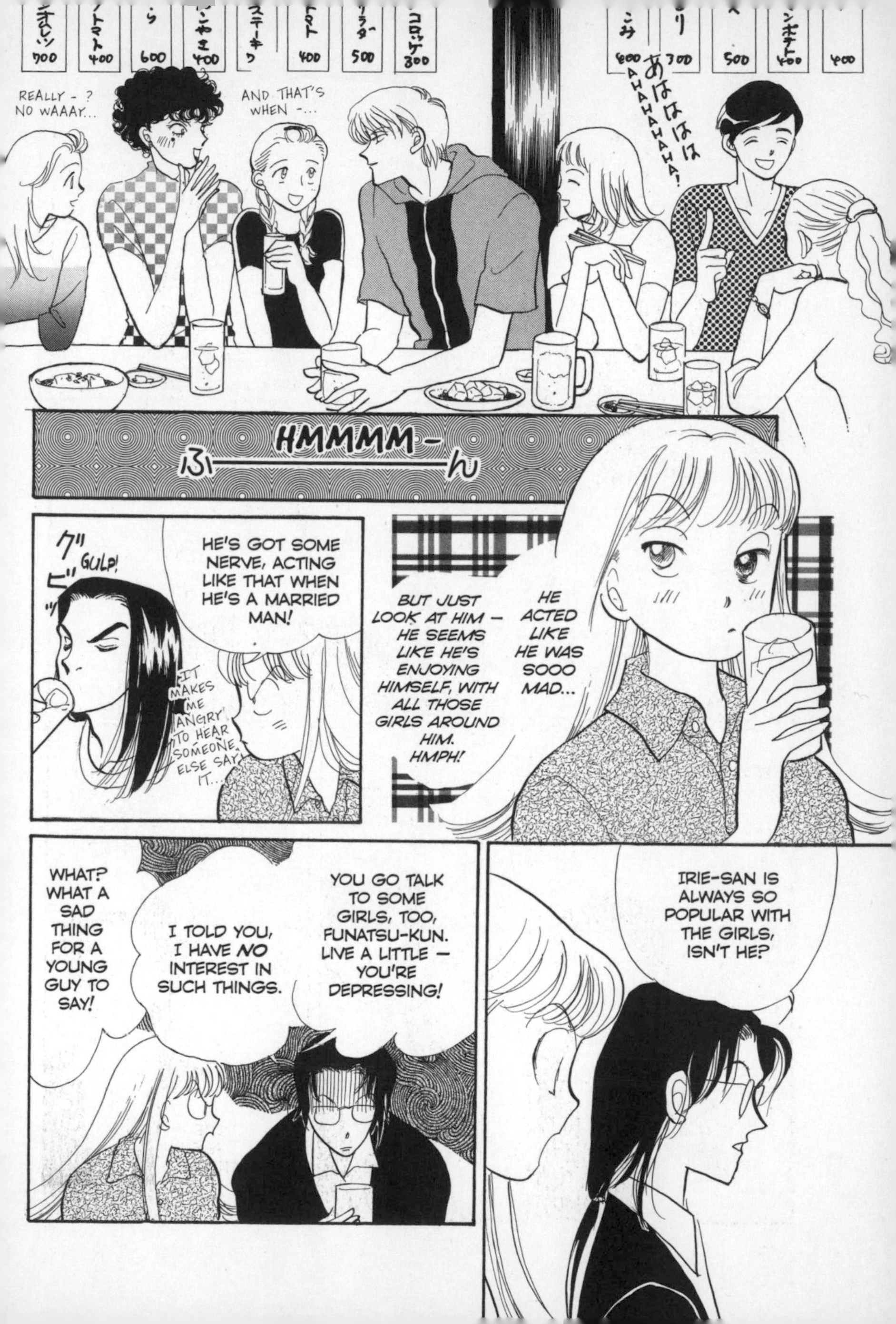
あはははは AHAHAHAHA!
AND THAT'S WHEN -...
REALLY - ? NO WAAAY...
HMMMM- ふーーん
HE ACTED LIKE HE WAS SOOO MAD...
BUT JUST LOOK AT HIM — HE SEEMS LIKE HE'S ENJOYING HIMSELF, WITH ALL THOSE GIRLS AROUND HIM. HMPH!
HE'S GOT SOME NERVE, ACTING LIKE THAT WHEN HE'S A MARRIED MAN!
IT MAKES ME ANGRY TO HEAR SOMEONE ELSE SAY IT...
グビッ GULP!
IRIE-SAN IS ALWAYS SO POPULAR WITH THE GIRLS, ISN'T HE?
YOU GO TALK TO SOME GIRLS, TOO, FUNATSU-KUN. LIVE A LITTLE — YOU'RE DEPRESSING!
I TOLD YOU, I HAVE NO INTEREST IN SUCH THINGS.
WHAT? WHAT A SAD THING FOR A YOUNG GUY TO SAY!

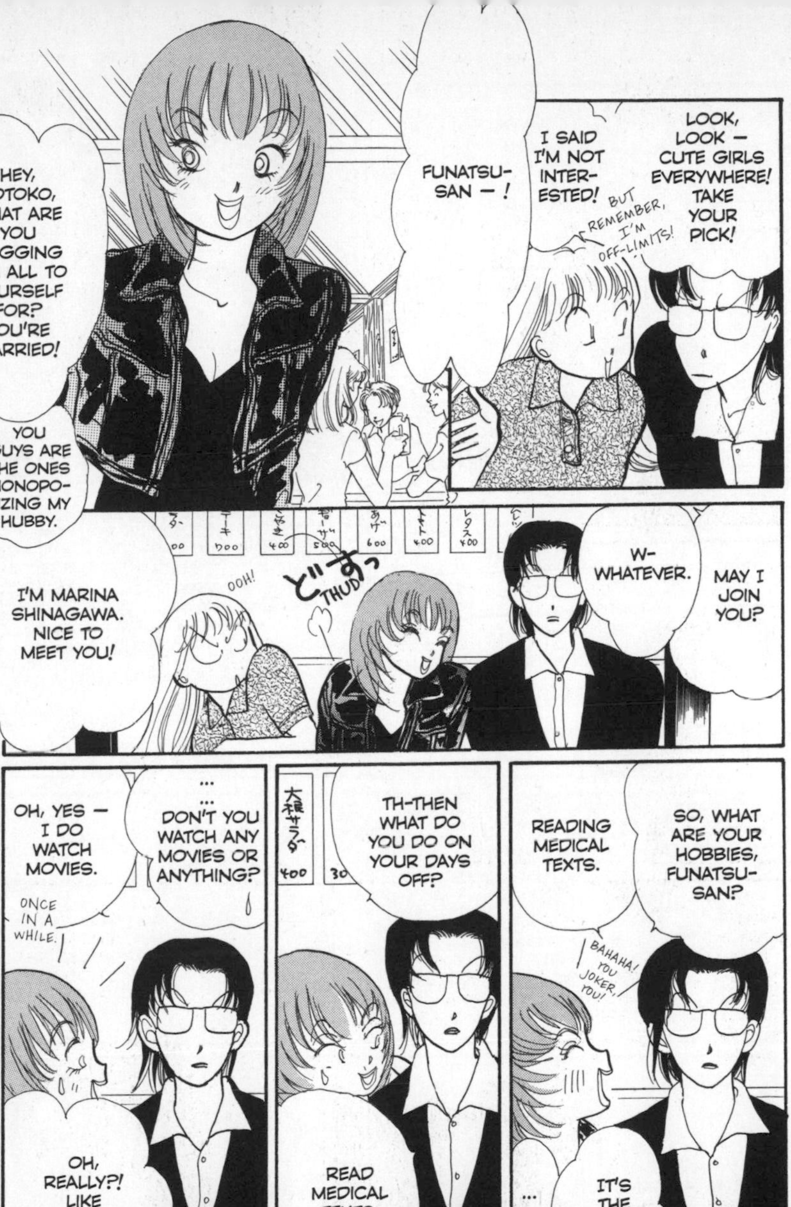
LOOK, LOOK — CUTE GIRLS EVERYWHERE! TAKE YOUR PICK!
I SAID I'M NOT INTERESTED!
BUT REMEMBER, I'M OFF-LIMITS!
FUNATSU-SAN —!
HEY, KOTOKO, WHAT ARE YOU HOGGING HIM ALL TO YOURSELF FOR? YOU'RE MARRIED!
YOU GUYS ARE THE ONES MONOPOLIZING MY HUBBY.
MAY I JOIN YOU?
W-WHATEVER.
どすっ
THUD
OOH!
I'M MARINA SHINAGAWA. NICE TO MEET YOU!
SO, WHAT ARE YOUR HOBBIES, FUNATSU-SAN?
READING MEDICAL TEXTS.
BAHAHA! YOU JOKER, YOU!
IT'S THE TRUTH.
... ...
TH-THEN WHAT DO YOU DO ON YOUR DAYS OFF?
大根サラダ
400
READ MEDICAL TEXTS.
... ... DON'T YOU WATCH ANY MOVIES OR ANYTHING?
OH, YES — I DO WATCH MOVIES.
ONCE IN A WHILE.
OH, REALLY?! LIKE WHAT?

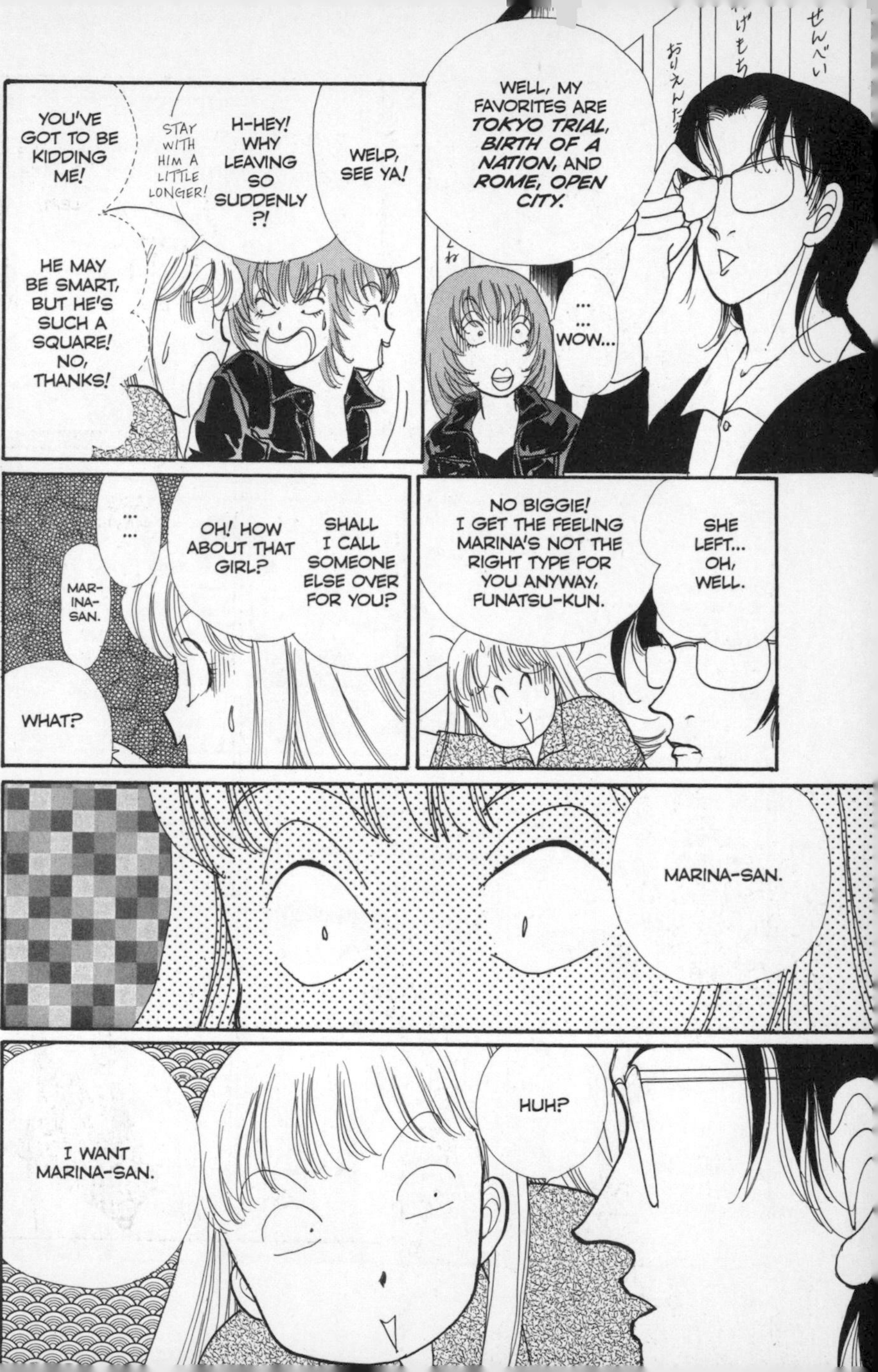
せんべい
WELL, MY FAVORITES ARE *TOKYO TRIAL, BIRTH OF A NATION,* AND *ROME, OPEN CITY.*
... ... WOW...
WELP, SEE YA!
H-HEY! WHY LEAVING SO SUDDENLY?!
STAY WITH HIM A LITTLE LONGER!
YOU'VE GOT TO BE KIDDING ME!
HE MAY BE SMART, BUT HE'S SUCH A SQUARE! NO, THANKS!
SHE LEFT... OH, WELL.
NO BIGGIE! I GET THE FEELING MARINA'S NOT THE RIGHT TYPE FOR YOU ANYWAY, FUNATSU-KUN.
SHALL I CALL SOMEONE ELSE OVER FOR YOU?
OH! HOW ABOUT THAT GIRL?
... ...
MARINA-SAN.
WHAT?
MARINA-SAN.
HUH?
I WANT MARINA-SAN.

STAFF: AKIKO ISHIKAWA, MASAKO KATAGAI, SHUKO AZUNA, ATSUKO SUGIMOTO, JET AKATAMAGO, SHIZUKO KOIKE...THANK YOU♥

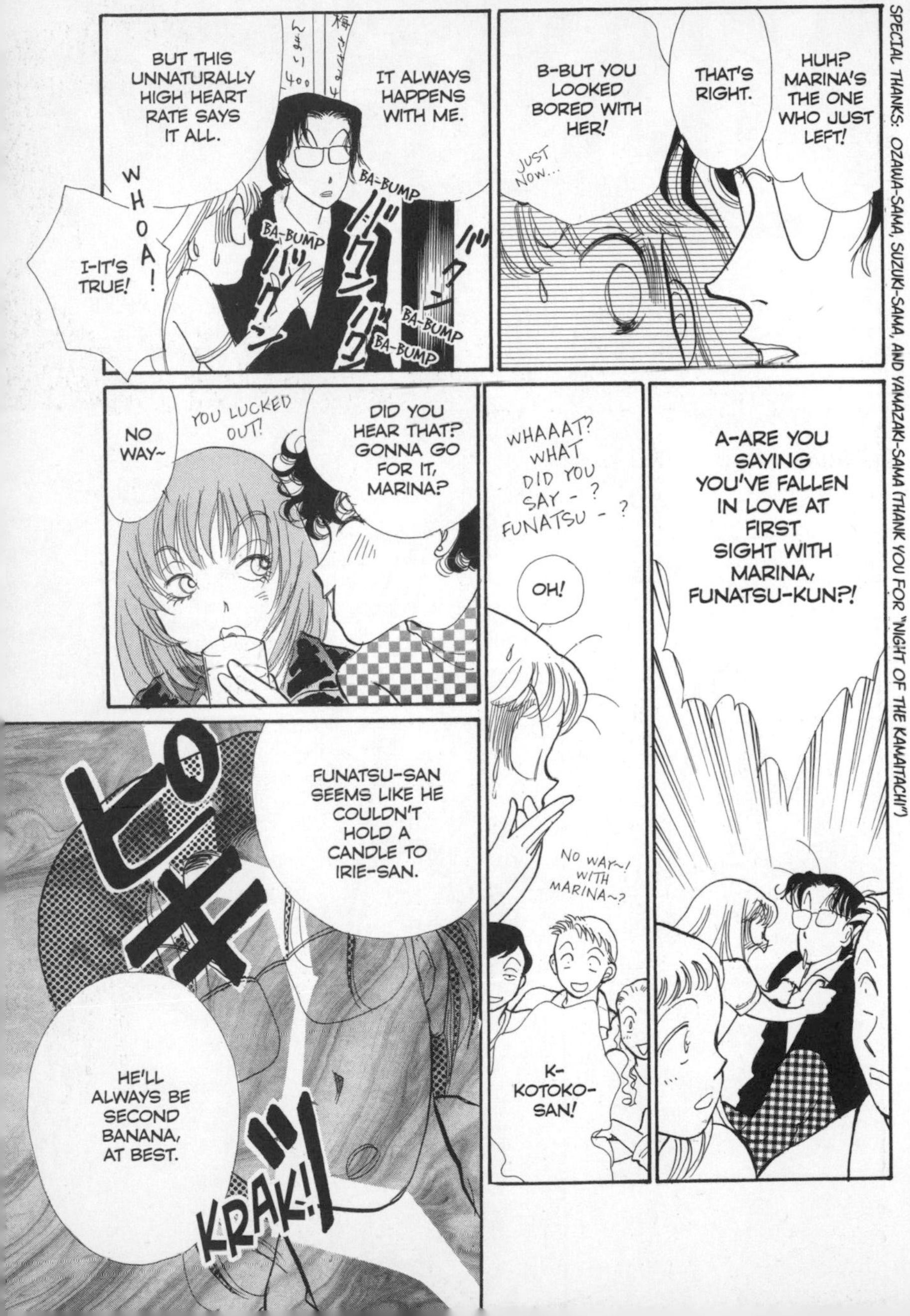
HUH? MARINA'S THE ONE WHO JUST LEFT!
THAT'S RIGHT.
B-BUT YOU LOOKED BORED WITH HER!
JUST NOW...
IT ALWAYS HAPPENS WITH ME.
BUT THIS UNNATURALLY HIGH HEART RATE SAYS IT ALL.
BA-BUMP
BA-BUMP
BA-BUMP
BA-BUMP
WHOA!
I-IT'S TRUE!
A-ARE YOU SAYING YOU'VE FALLEN IN LOVE AT FIRST SIGHT WITH MARINA, FUNATSU-KUN?!
WHAAAT? WHAT DID YOU SAY - ? FUNATSU - ?
OH!
NO WAY~! WITH MARINA~?
K-KOTOKO-SAN!
DID YOU HEAR THAT? GONNA GO FOR IT, MARINA?
YOU LUCKED OUT!
NO WAY~
FUNATSU-SAN SEEMS LIKE HE COULDN'T HOLD A CANDLE TO IRIE-SAN.
HE'LL ALWAYS BE SECOND BANANA, AT BEST.
KRAK!!

SPECIAL THANKS: OZAWA-SAMA, SUZUKI-SAMA, AND YAMAZAKI-SAMA (THANK YOU FOR "NIGHT OF THE KAMAITACHI")

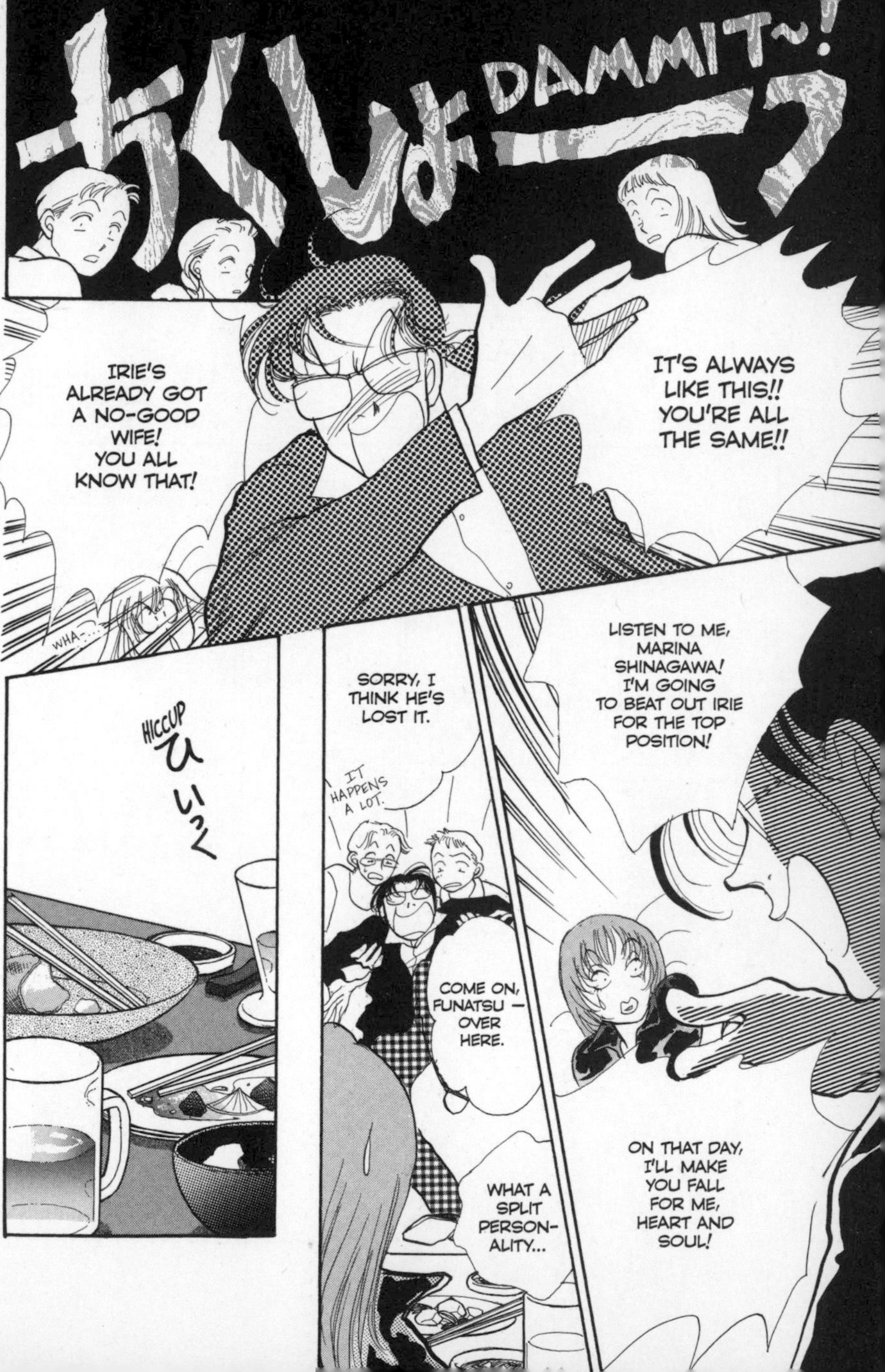
DAMMIT~!
IT'S ALWAYS LIKE THIS!! YOU'RE ALL THE SAME!!
IRIE'S ALREADY GOT A NO-GOOD WIFE! YOU ALL KNOW THAT!
WHA-...
LISTEN TO ME, MARINA SHINAGAWA! I'M GOING TO BEAT OUT IRIE FOR THE TOP POSITION!
ON THAT DAY, I'LL MAKE YOU FALL FOR ME, HEART AND SOUL!
SORRY, I THINK HE'S LOST IT.
IT HAPPENS A LOT.
COME ON, FUNATSU — OVER HERE.
WHAT A SPLIT PERSONALITY...
HICCUP
ひいっく

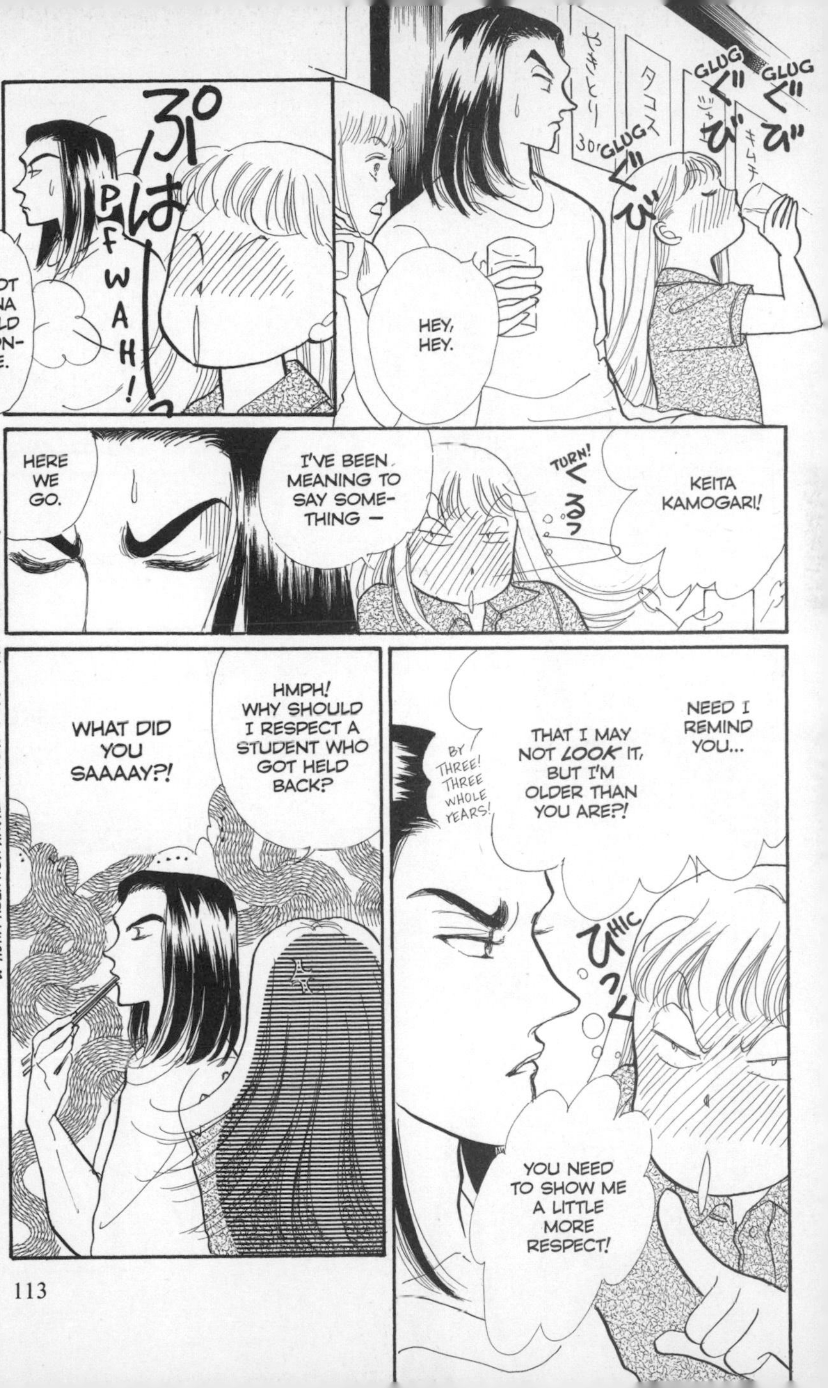

GLUG
GLUG
GLUG
やきとり
タコス
キムチ
HEY, HEY.
PFWAH!
I'M NOT GONNA BE HELD RESPONSIBLE.
TURN!
KEITA KAMOGARI!
I'VE BEEN MEANING TO SAY SOMETHING —
HERE WE GO.
NEED I REMIND YOU...
THAT I MAY NOT *LOOK* IT, BUT I'M OLDER THAN YOU ARE?!
BY THREE! THREE WHOLE YEARS!
HIC
YOU NEED TO SHOW ME A LITTLE MORE RESPECT!
HMPH! WHY SHOULD I RESPECT A STUDENT WHO GOT HELD BACK?
WHAT DID YOU SAAAAY?!

*KANAMI-CHAN, UKKY OSARU, TAORU THANK YOU VERY MUCH

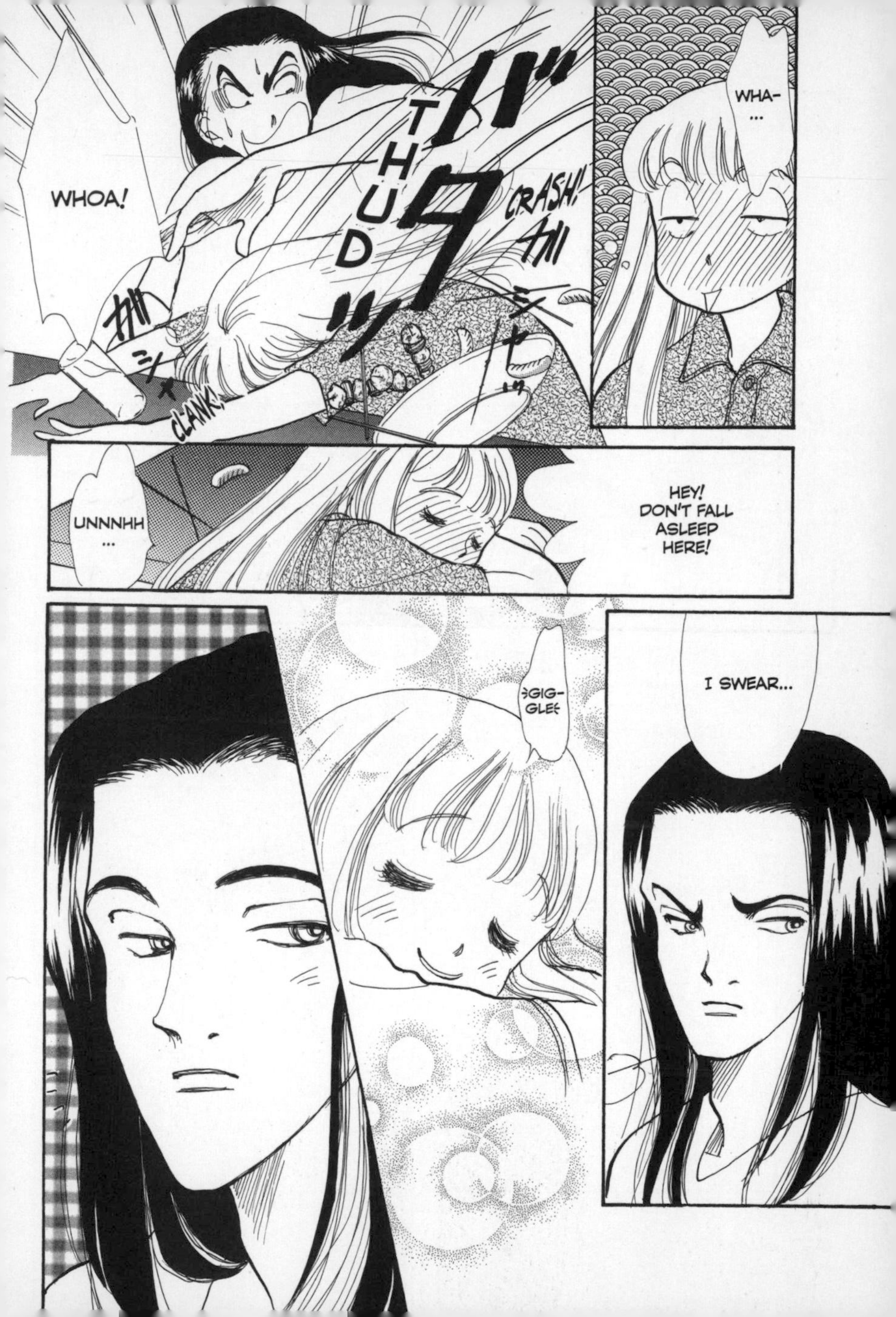
WHA- ...
WHOA!
THUD
CRASH!
CLANK!
HEY! DON'T FALL ASLEEP HERE!
UNNNHH ...
I SWEAR...
GIGGLE

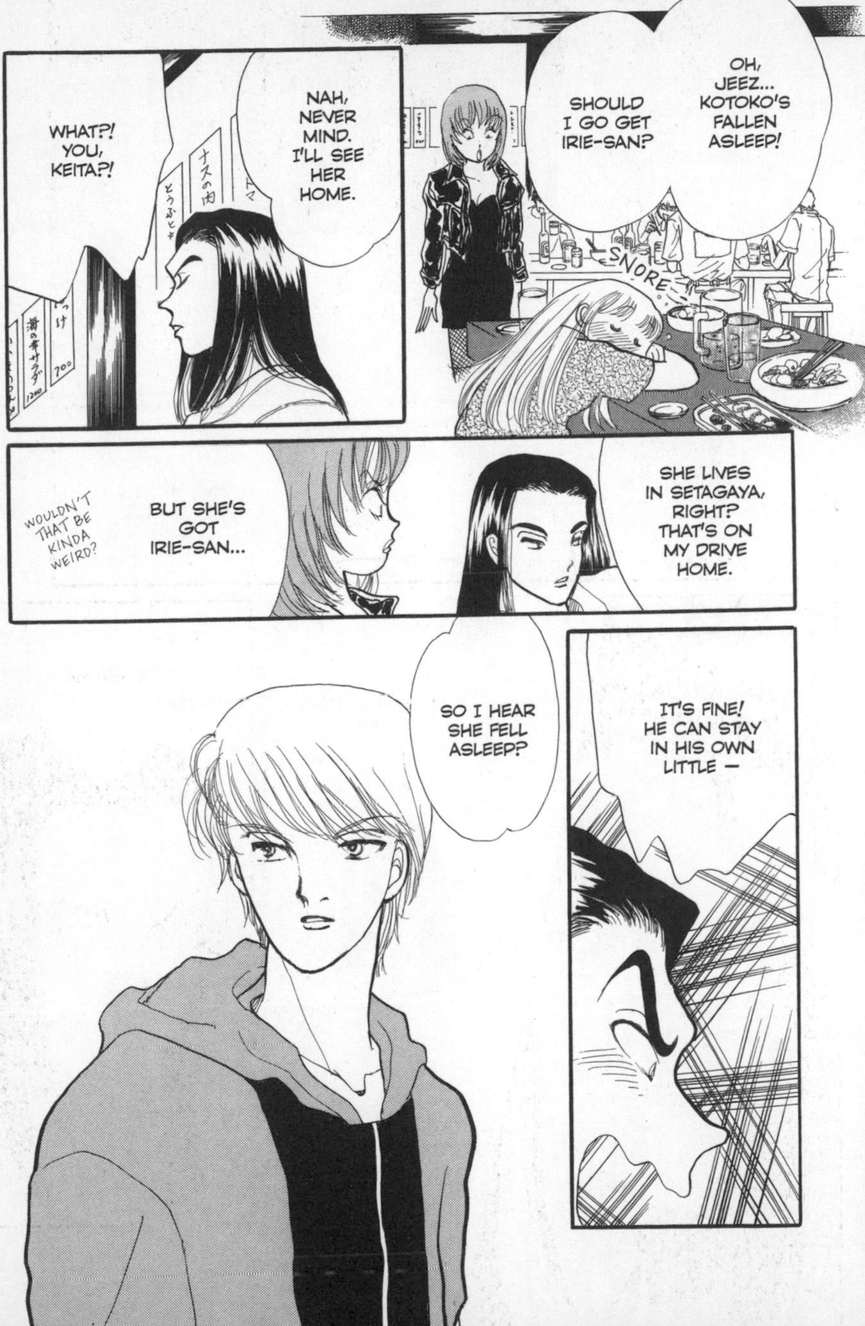
OH, JEEZ... KOTOKO'S FALLEN ASLEEP!
SHOULD I GO GET IRIE-SAN?
SNORE
NAH, NEVER MIND. I'LL SEE HER HOME.
WHAT?! YOU, KEITA?!
SHE LIVES IN SETAGAYA, RIGHT? THAT'S ON MY DRIVE HOME.
BUT SHE'S GOT IRIE-SAN...
WOULDN'T THAT BE KINDA WEIRD?
IT'S FINE! HE CAN STAY IN HIS OWN LITTLE —
SO I HEAR SHE FELL ASLEEP?

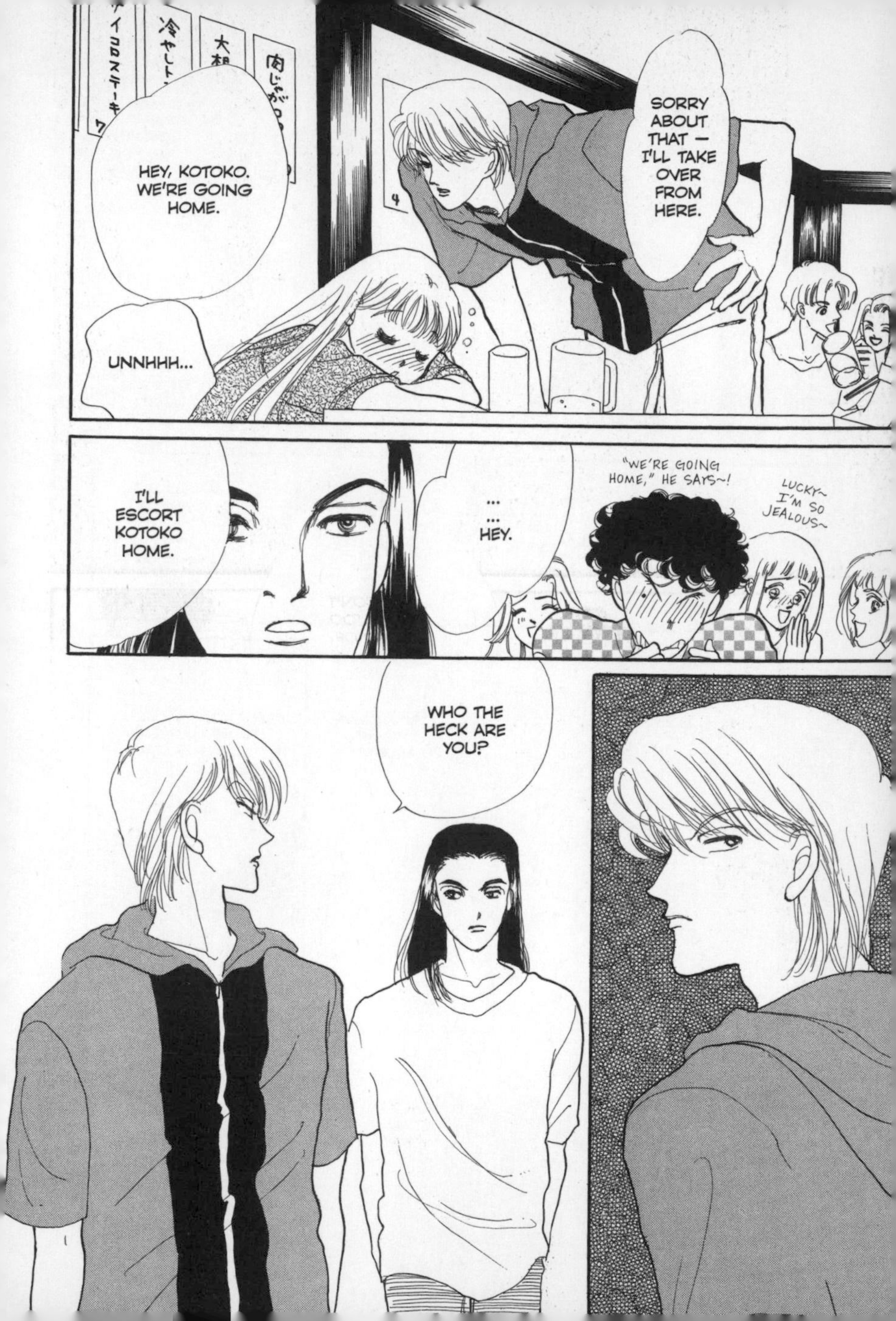
SORRY ABOUT THAT — I'LL TAKE OVER FROM HERE.
HEY, KOTOKO. WE'RE GOING HOME.
UNNHHH...
"WE'RE GOING HOME," HE SAYS~!
LUCKY~ I'M SO JEALOUS~
... ... HEY.
I'LL ESCORT KOTOKO HOME.
WHO THE HECK ARE YOU?

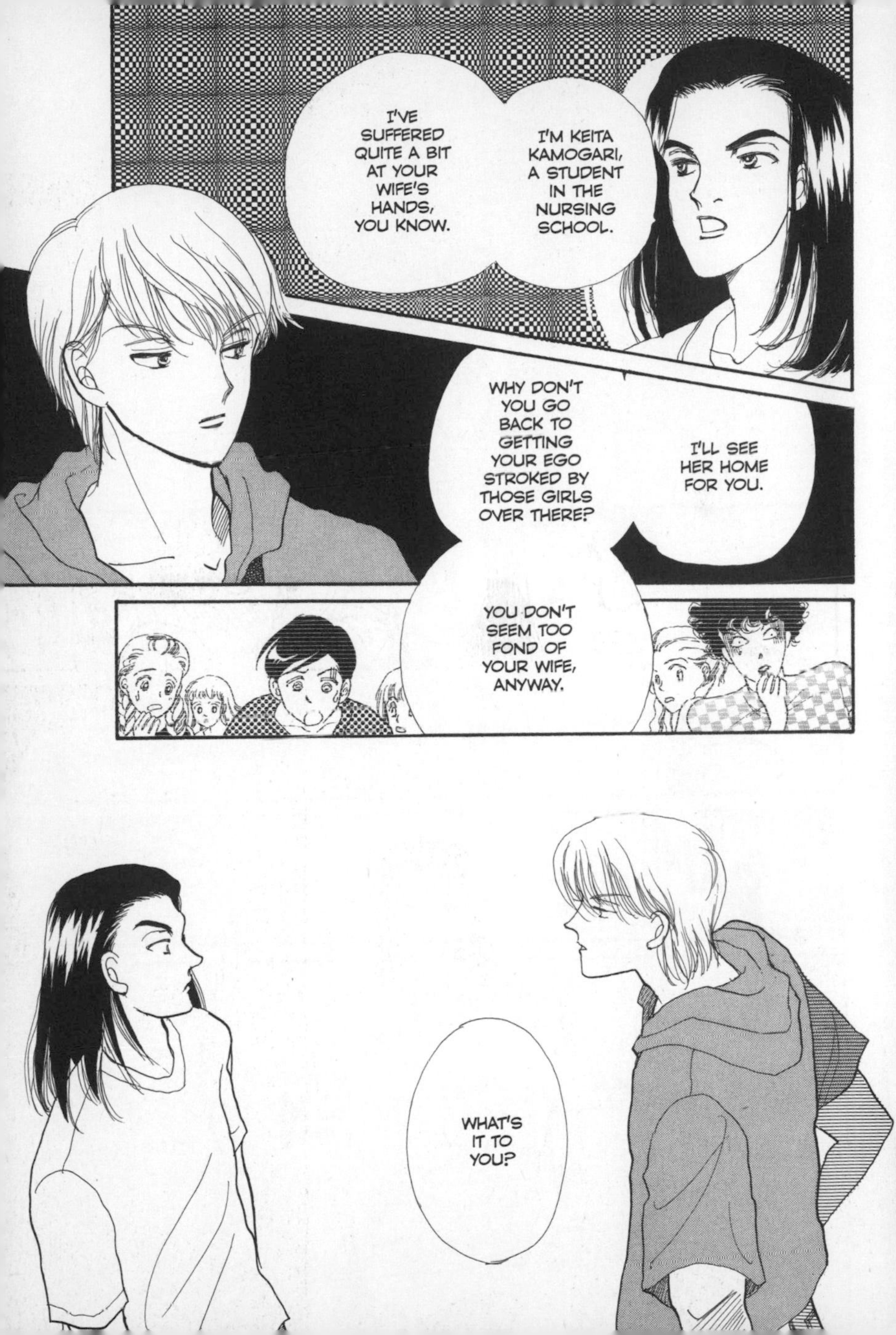
I'M KEITA KAMOGARI, A STUDENT IN THE NURSING SCHOOL.
I'VE SUFFERED QUITE A BIT AT YOUR WIFE'S HANDS, YOU KNOW.
I'LL SEE HER HOME FOR YOU.
WHY DON'T YOU GO BACK TO GETTING YOUR EGO STROKED BY THOSE GIRLS OVER THERE?
YOU DON'T SEEM TOO FOND OF YOUR WIFE, ANYWAY.
WHAT'S IT TO YOU?

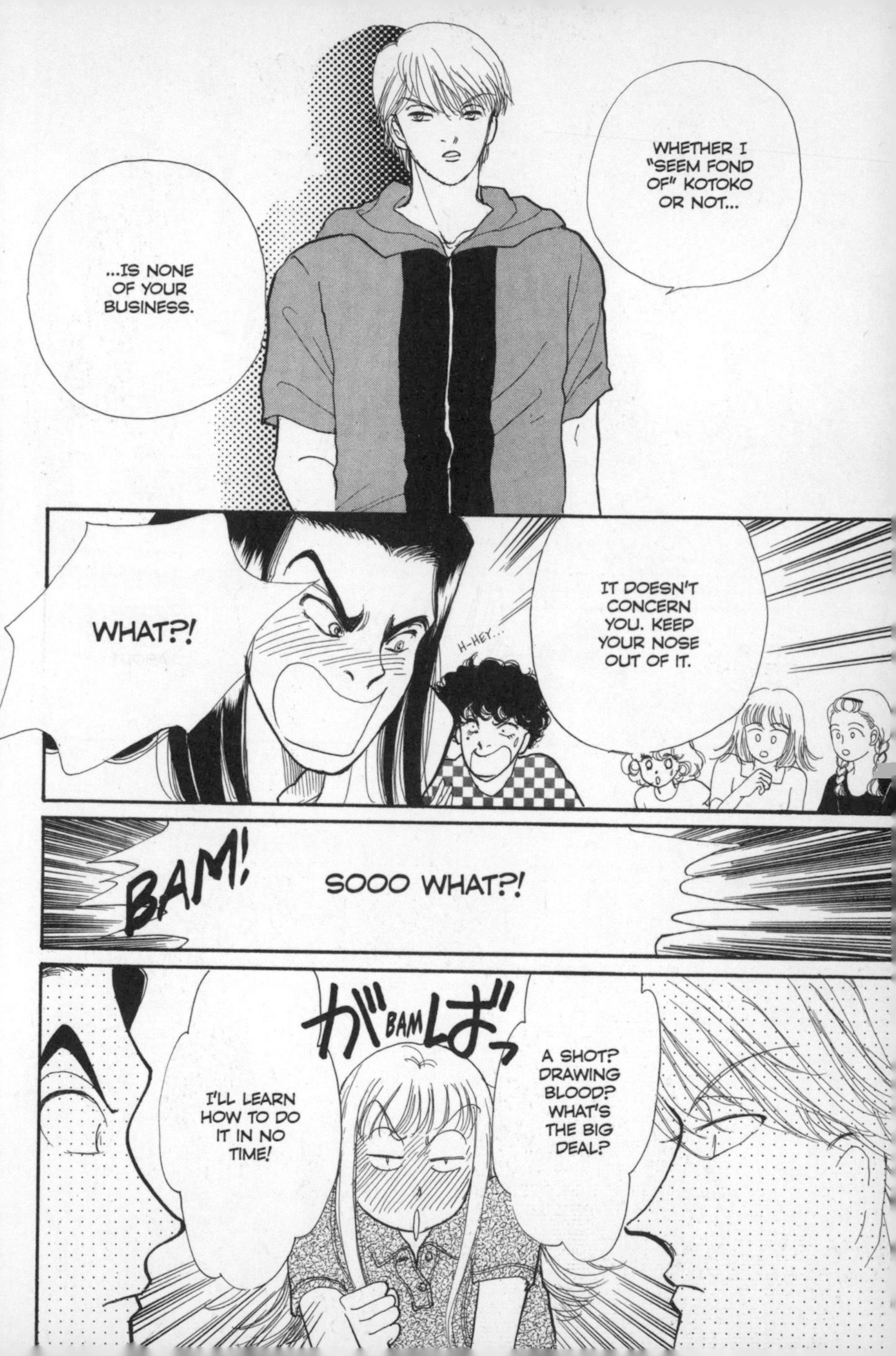
WHETHER I "SEEM FOND OF" KOTOKO OR NOT...
...IS NONE OF YOUR BUSINESS.
IT DOESN'T CONCERN YOU. KEEP YOUR NOSE OUT OF IT.
H-HEY...
WHAT?!
SOOO WHAT?!
BAM!
A SHOT? DRAWING BLOOD? WHAT'S THE BIG DEAL?
が BAM ばっ
I'LL LEARN HOW TO DO IT IN NO TIME!

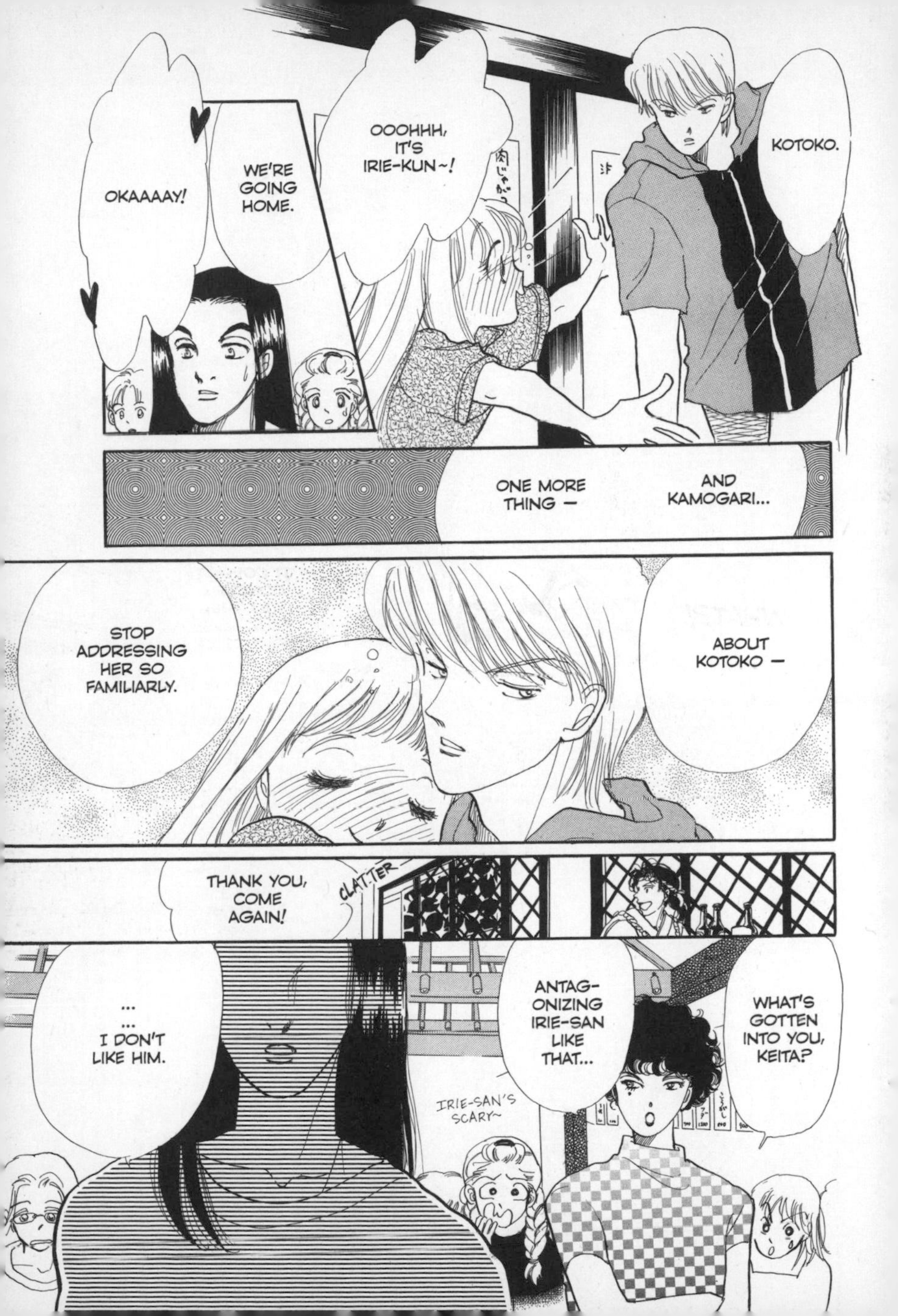
KOTOKO.
OOOHHH, IT'S IRIE-KUN~!
WE'RE GOING HOME.
OKAAAAY!
AND KAMOGARI...
ONE MORE THING –
ABOUT KOTOKO –
STOP ADDRESSING HER SO FAMILIARLY.
CLATTER
THANK YOU, COME AGAIN!
WHAT'S GOTTEN INTO YOU, KEITA?
ANTAG-ONIZING IRIE-SAN LIKE THAT...
IRIE-SAN'S SCARY~
... ... I DON'T LIKE HIM.

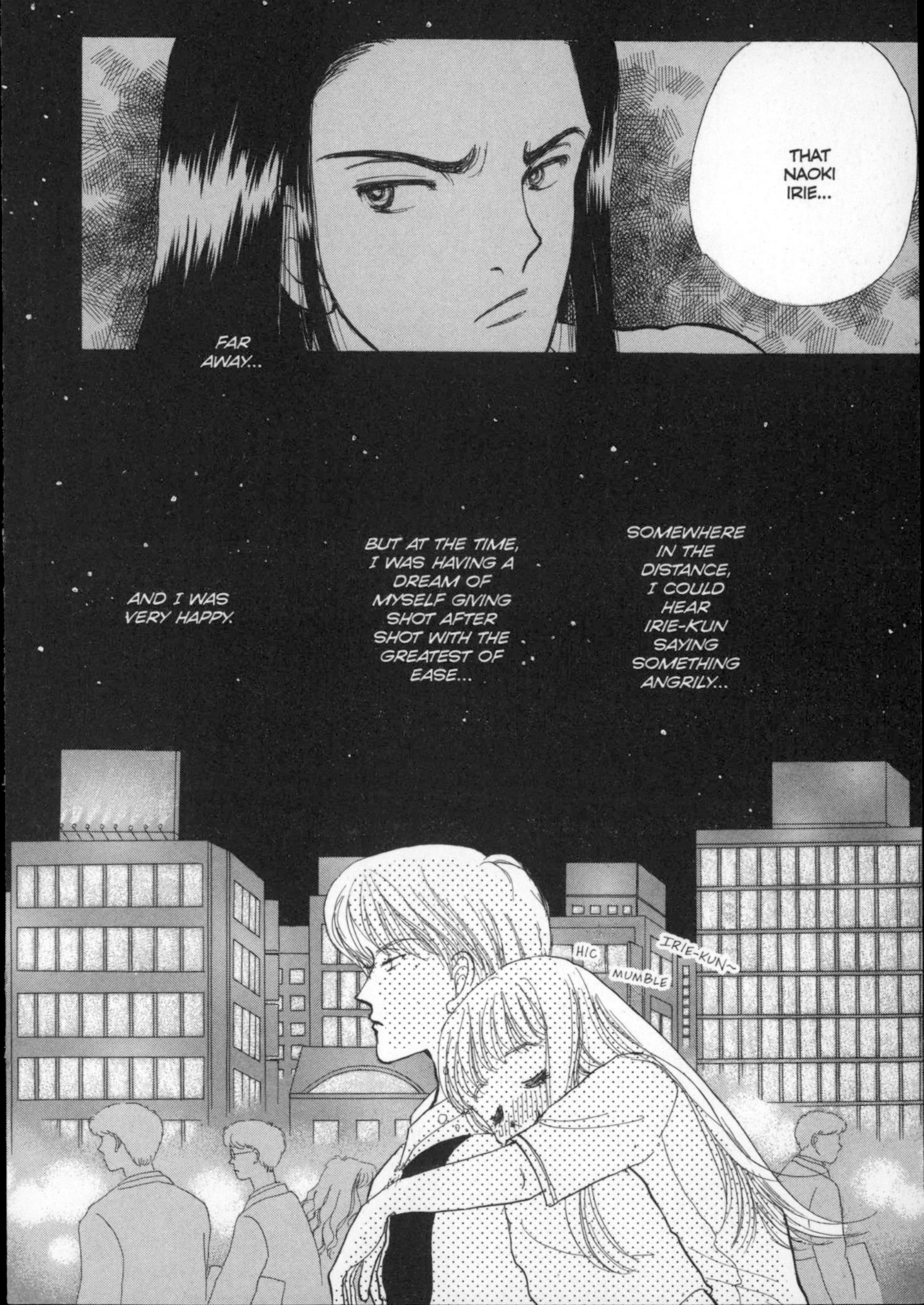
THAT NAOKI IRIE...
FAR AWAY...
SOMEWHERE IN THE DISTANCE, I COULD HEAR IRIE-KUN SAYING SOMETHING ANGRILY...
BUT AT THE TIME, I WAS HAVING A DREAM OF MYSELF GIVING SHOT AFTER SHOT WITH THE GREATEST OF EASE...
AND I WAS VERY HAPPY.
IRIE-KUN~
HIC
MUMBLE

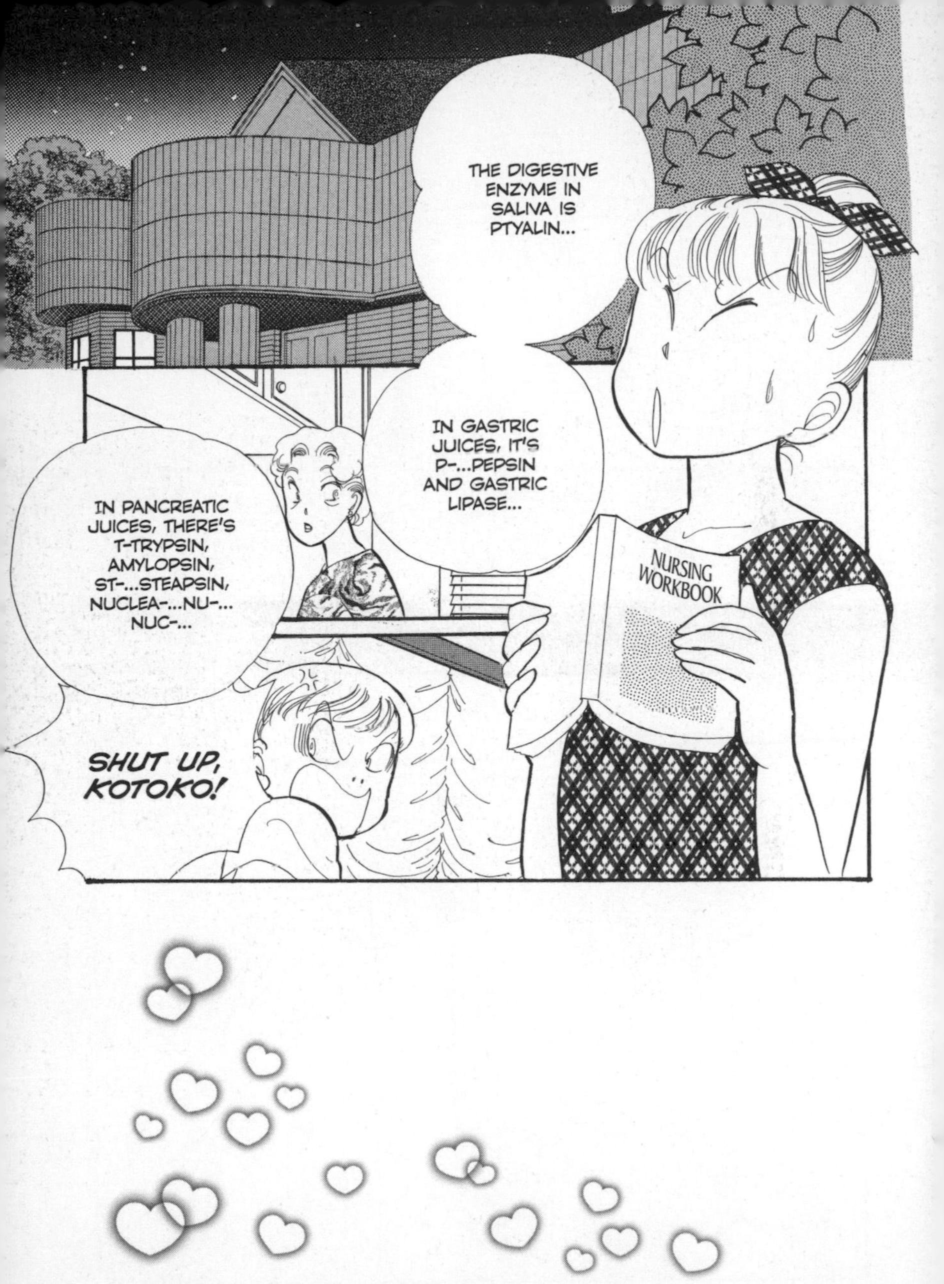
THE DIGESTIVE ENZYME IN SALIVA IS PTYALIN...
IN GASTRIC JUICES, IT'S P-...PEPSIN AND GASTRIC LIPASE...
NURSING WORKBOOK
IN PANCREATIC JUICES, THERE'S T-TRYPSIN, AMYLOPSIN, ST-...STEAPSIN, NUCLEA-...NU-... NUC-...
SHUT UP, KOTOKO!

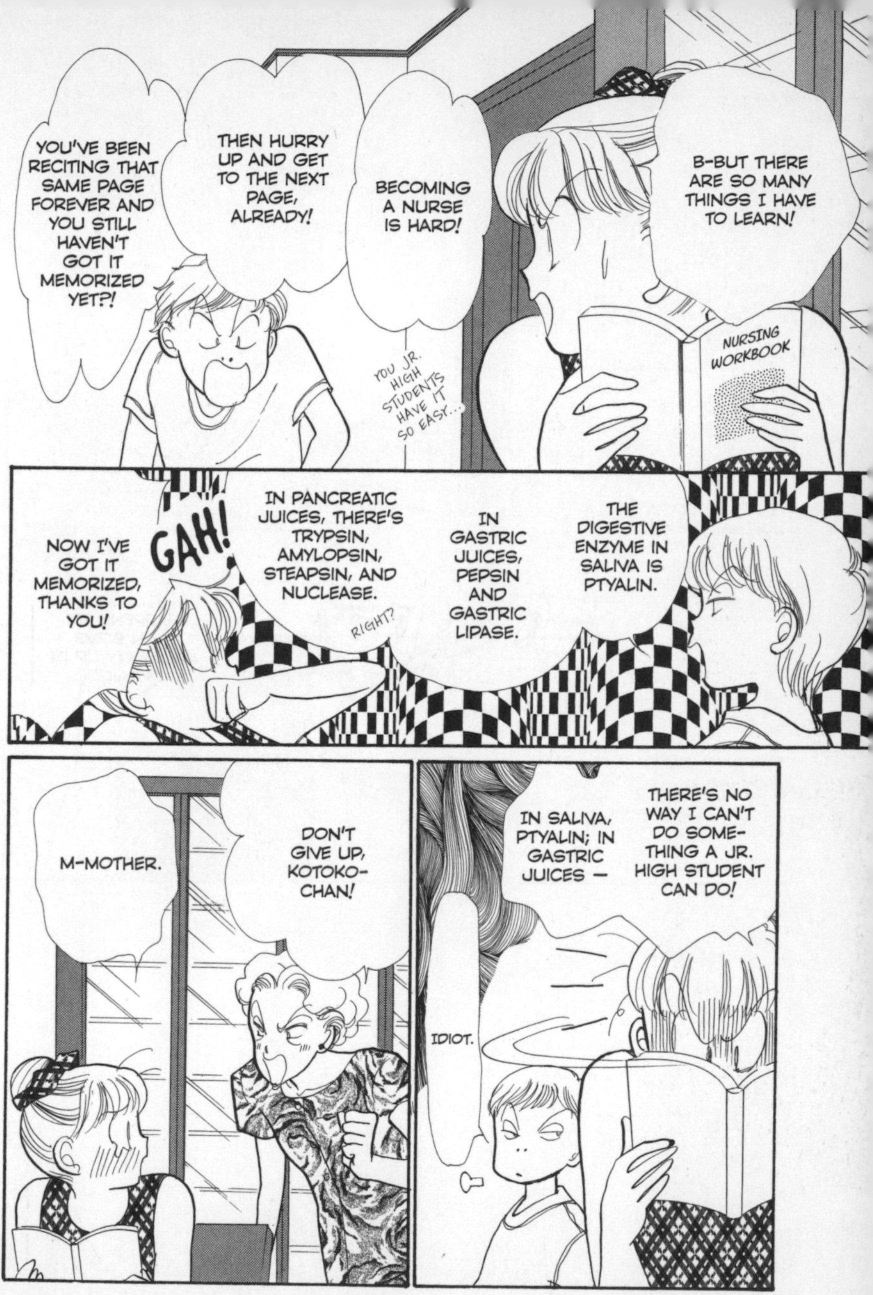
B-BUT THERE ARE SO MANY THINGS I HAVE TO LEARN!
NURSING WORKBOOK
BECOMING A NURSE IS HARD!
YOU JR. HIGH STUDENTS HAVE IT SO EASY...
THEN HURRY UP AND GET TO THE NEXT PAGE, ALREADY!
YOU'VE BEEN RECITING THAT SAME PAGE FOREVER AND YOU STILL HAVEN'T GOT IT MEMORIZED YET?!
THE DIGESTIVE ENZYME IN SALIVA IS PTYALIN.
IN GASTRIC JUICES, PEPSIN AND GASTRIC LIPASE.
IN PANCREATIC JUICES, THERE'S TRYPSIN, AMYLOPSIN, STEAPSIN, AND NUCLEASE.
RIGHT?
GAH!
NOW I'VE GOT IT MEMORIZED, THANKS TO YOU!
THERE'S NO WAY I CAN'T DO SOME-THING A JR. HIGH STUDENT CAN DO!
IN SALIVA, PTYALIN; IN GASTRIC JUICES —
IDIOT.
DON'T GIVE UP, KOTOKO-CHAN!
M-MOTHER.

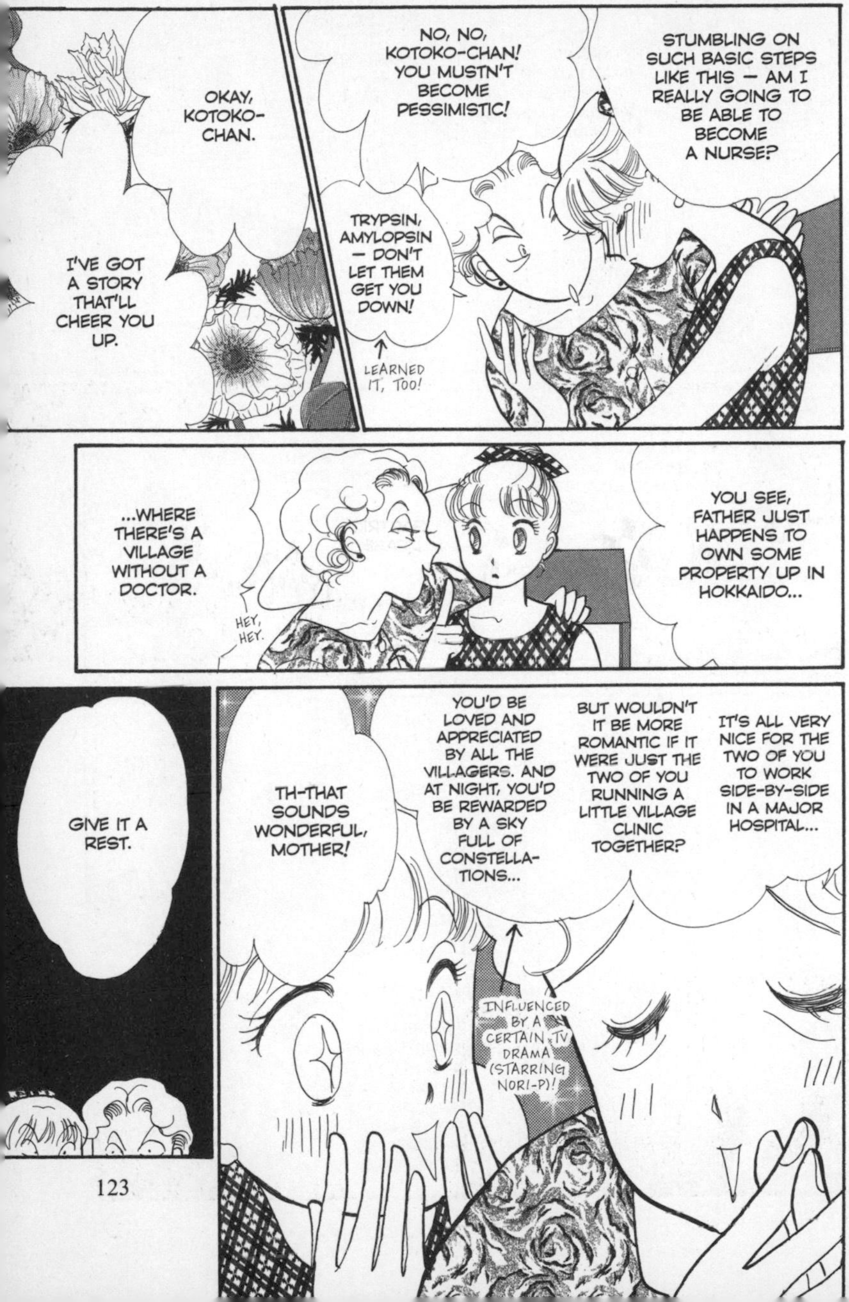
STUMBLING ON SUCH BASIC STEPS LIKE THIS — AM I REALLY GOING TO BE ABLE TO BECOME A NURSE?
NO, NO, KOTOKO-CHAN! YOU MUSTN'T BECOME PESSIMISTIC!
TRYPSIN, AMYLOPSIN — DON'T LET THEM GET YOU DOWN!
LEARNED IT, TOO!
OKAY, KOTOKO-CHAN.
I'VE GOT A STORY THAT'LL CHEER YOU UP.
YOU SEE, FATHER JUST HAPPENS TO OWN SOME PROPERTY UP IN HOKKAIDO...
...WHERE THERE'S A VILLAGE WITHOUT A DOCTOR.
HEY, HEY.
IT'S ALL VERY NICE FOR THE TWO OF YOU TO WORK SIDE-BY-SIDE IN A MAJOR HOSPITAL...
BUT WOULDN'T IT BE MORE ROMANTIC IF IT WERE JUST THE TWO OF YOU RUNNING A LITTLE VILLAGE CLINIC TOGETHER?
YOU'D BE LOVED AND APPRECIATED BY ALL THE VILLAGERS. AND AT NIGHT, YOU'D BE REWARDED BY A SKY FULL OF CONSTELLA-TIONS...
TH-THAT SOUNDS WONDERFUL, MOTHER!
INFLUENCED BY A CERTAIN TV DRAMA (STARRING NORI-P)!
GIVE IT A REST.

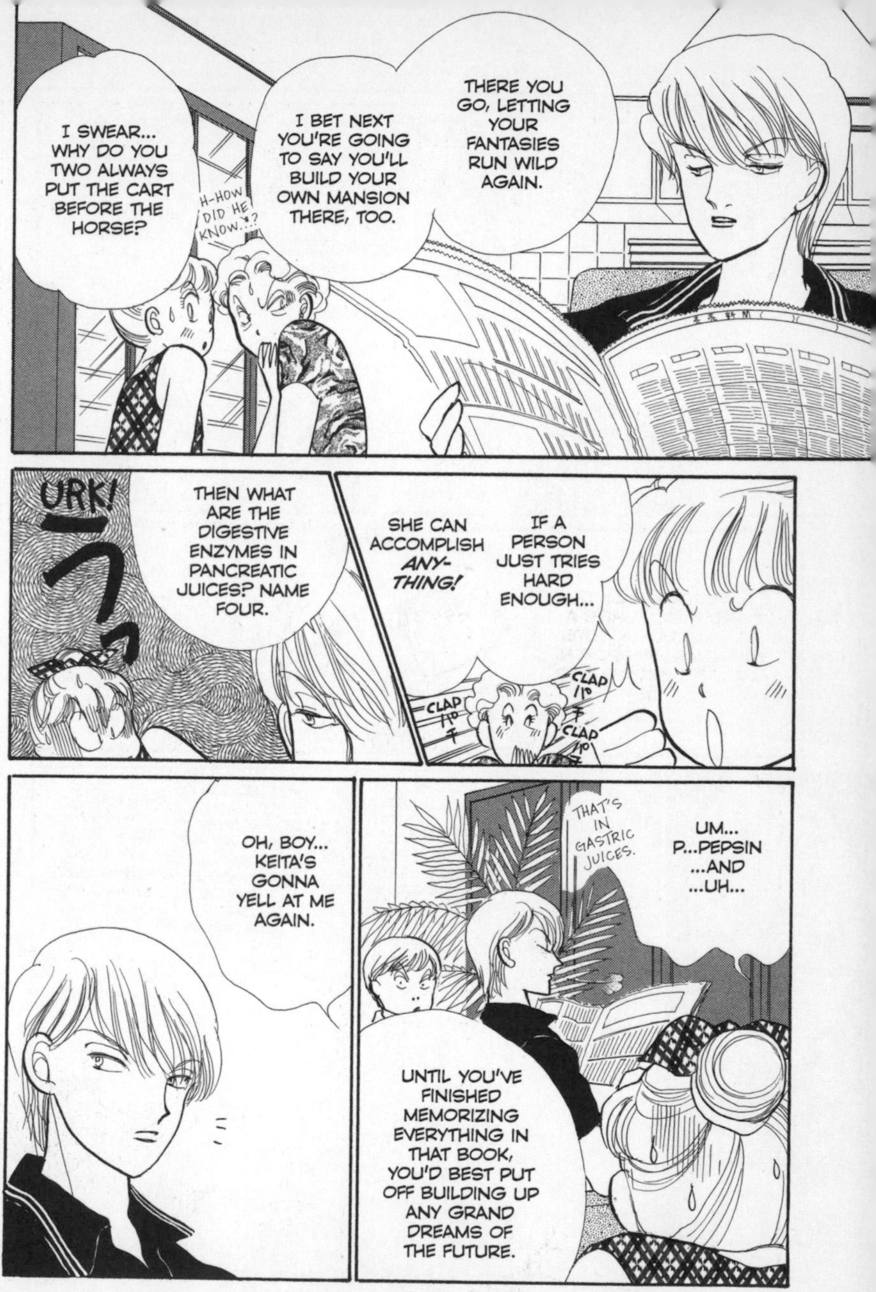
THERE YOU GO, LETTING YOUR FANTASIES RUN WILD AGAIN.
I BET NEXT YOU'RE GOING TO SAY YOU'LL BUILD YOUR OWN MANSION THERE, TOO.
H-HOW DID HE KNOW...?
I SWEAR... WHY DO YOU TWO ALWAYS PUT THE CART BEFORE THE HORSE?
IF A PERSON JUST TRIES HARD ENOUGH...
SHE CAN ACCOMPLISH *ANYTHING!*
CLAP
CLAP
CLAP
THEN WHAT ARE THE DIGESTIVE ENZYMES IN PANCREATIC JUICES? NAME FOUR.
URK!
UM... P...PEPSIN ...AND ...UH...
THAT'S IN GASTRIC JUICES.
UNTIL YOU'VE FINISHED MEMORIZING EVERYTHING IN THAT BOOK, YOU'D BEST PUT OFF BUILDING UP ANY GRAND DREAMS OF THE FUTURE.
OH, BOY... KEITA'S GONNA YELL AT ME AGAIN.

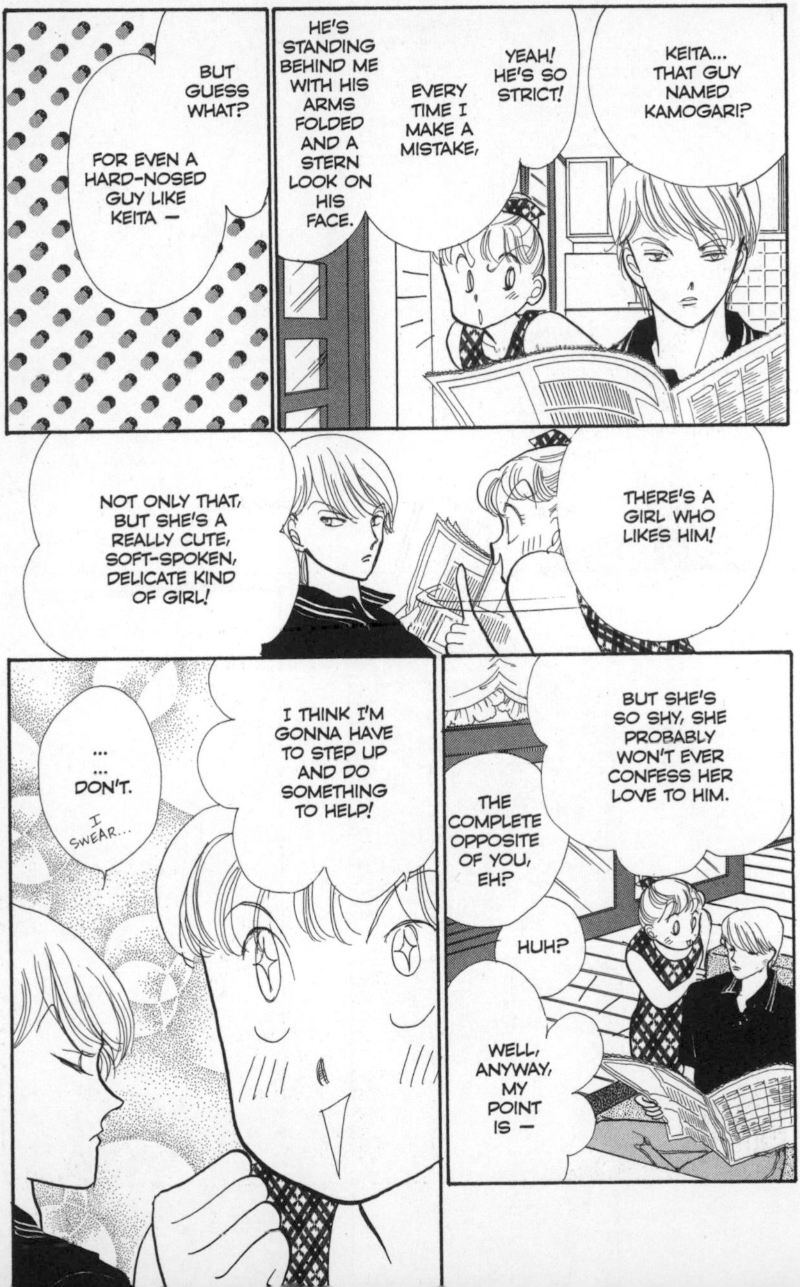
KEITA... THAT GUY NAMED KAMOGARI?
YEAH! HE'S SO STRICT!
EVERY TIME I MAKE A MISTAKE,
HE'S STANDING BEHIND ME WITH HIS ARMS FOLDED AND A STERN LOOK ON HIS FACE.
BUT GUESS WHAT?
FOR EVEN A HARD-NOSED GUY LIKE KEITA —
THERE'S A GIRL WHO LIKES HIM!
NOT ONLY THAT, BUT SHE'S A REALLY CUTE, SOFT-SPOKEN, DELICATE KIND OF GIRL!
BUT SHE'S SO SHY, SHE PROBABLY WON'T EVER CONFESS HER LOVE TO HIM.
THE COMPLETE OPPOSITE OF YOU, EH?
HUH?
WELL, ANYWAY, MY POINT IS —
I THINK I'M GONNA HAVE TO STEP UP AND DO SOMETHING TO HELP!
... ... DON'T.
I SWEAR...

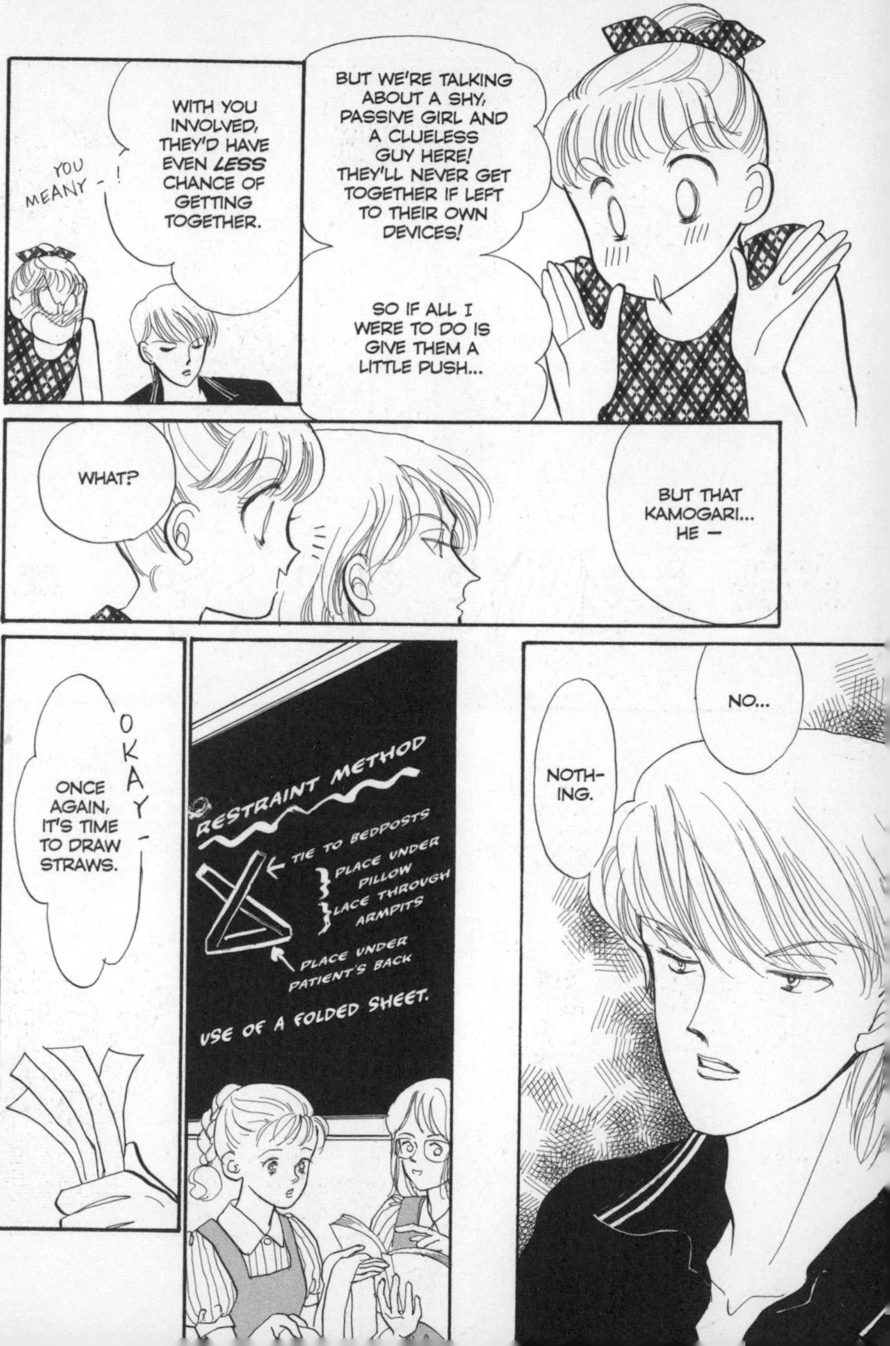
BUT WE'RE TALKING ABOUT A SHY, PASSIVE GIRL AND A CLUELESS GUY HERE! THEY'LL NEVER GET TOGETHER IF LEFT TO THEIR OWN DEVICES!
SO IF ALL I WERE TO DO IS GIVE THEM A LITTLE PUSH...
WITH YOU INVOLVED, THEY'D HAVE EVEN *LESS* CHANCE OF GETTING TOGETHER.
YOU MEANY—!
BUT THAT KAMOGARI... HE —
WHAT?
NO...
NOTH-ING.
RESTRAINT METHOD
TIE TO BEDPOSTS
PLACE UNDER PILLOW
LACE THROUGH ARMPITS
PLACE UNDER PATIENT'S BACK
USE OF A FOLDED SHEET.
ONCE AGAIN, IT'S TIME TO DRAW STRAWS.
OKAY—

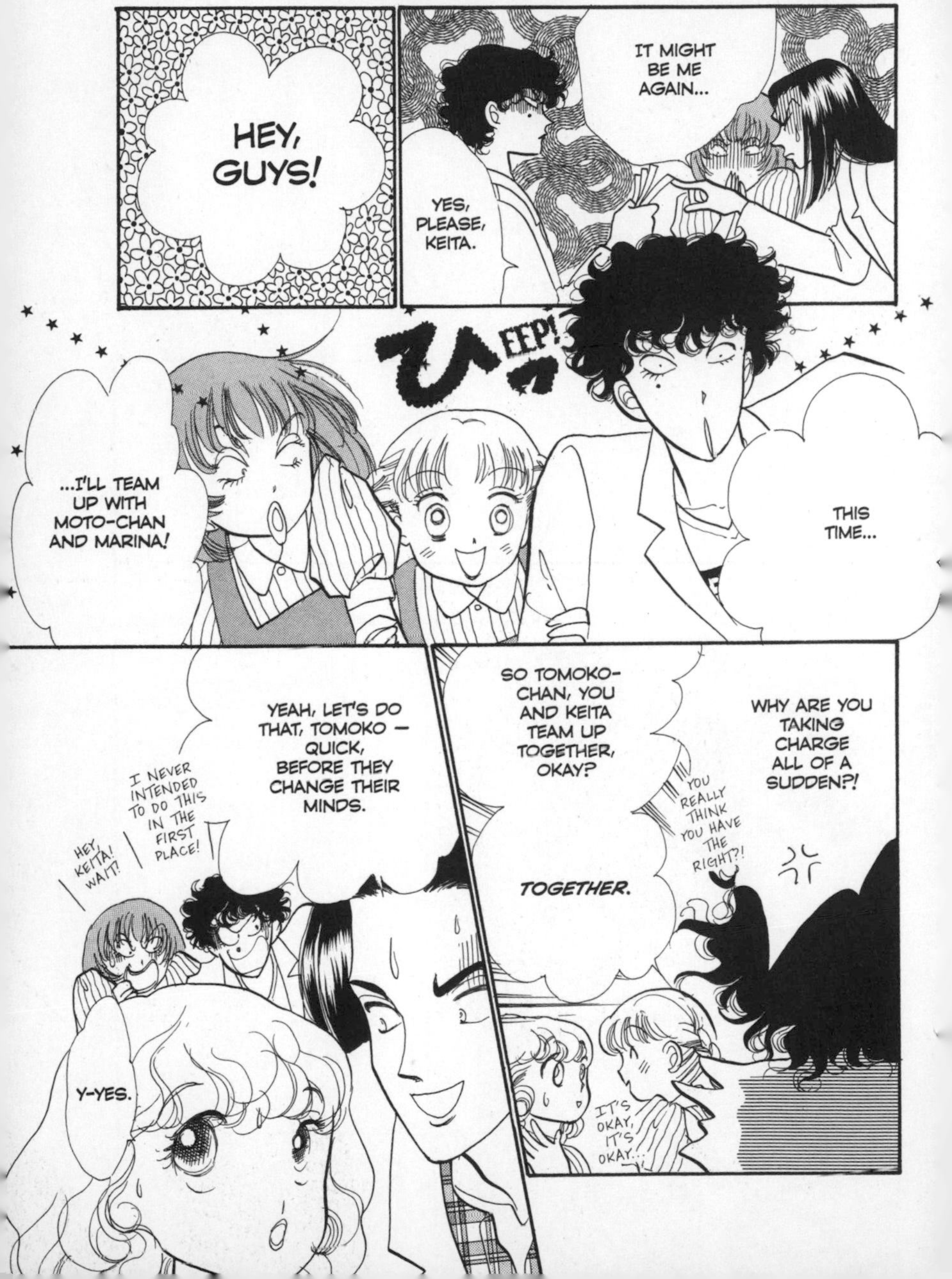
IT MIGHT BE ME AGAIN...
YES, PLEASE, KEITA.
HEY, GUYS!
ひEEP!
THIS TIME...
...I'LL TEAM UP WITH MOTO-CHAN AND MARINA!
WHY ARE YOU TAKING CHARGE ALL OF A SUDDEN?!
SO TOMOKO-CHAN, YOU AND KEITA TEAM UP TOGETHER, OKAY?
YOU REALLY THINK YOU HAVE THE RIGHT?!
TOGETHER.
IT'S OKAY, IT'S OKAY...
YEAH, LET'S DO THAT, TOMOKO — QUICK, BEFORE THEY CHANGE THEIR MINDS.
I NEVER INTENDED TO DO THIS IN THE FIRST PLACE!
HEY, KEITA! WAIT!
Y-YES.

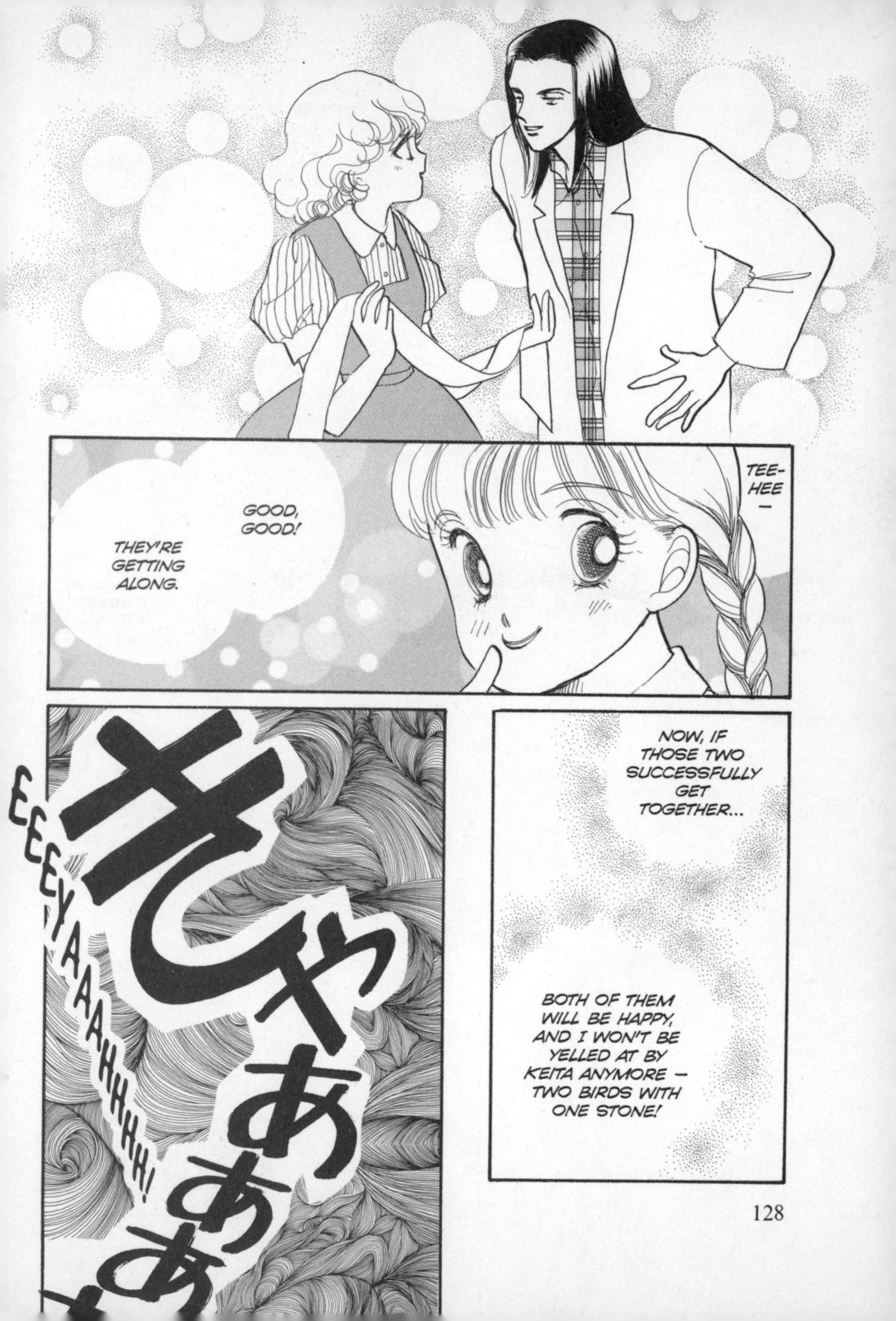
TEE-HEE —
GOOD, GOOD!
THEY'RE GETTING ALONG.
NOW, IF THOSE TWO SUCCESSFULLY GET TOGETHER...
BOTH OF THEM WILL BE HAPPY, AND I WON'T BE YELLED AT BY KEITA ANYMORE — TWO BIRDS WITH ONE STONE!
きゃああ
EEEYAAAAHHHHH!

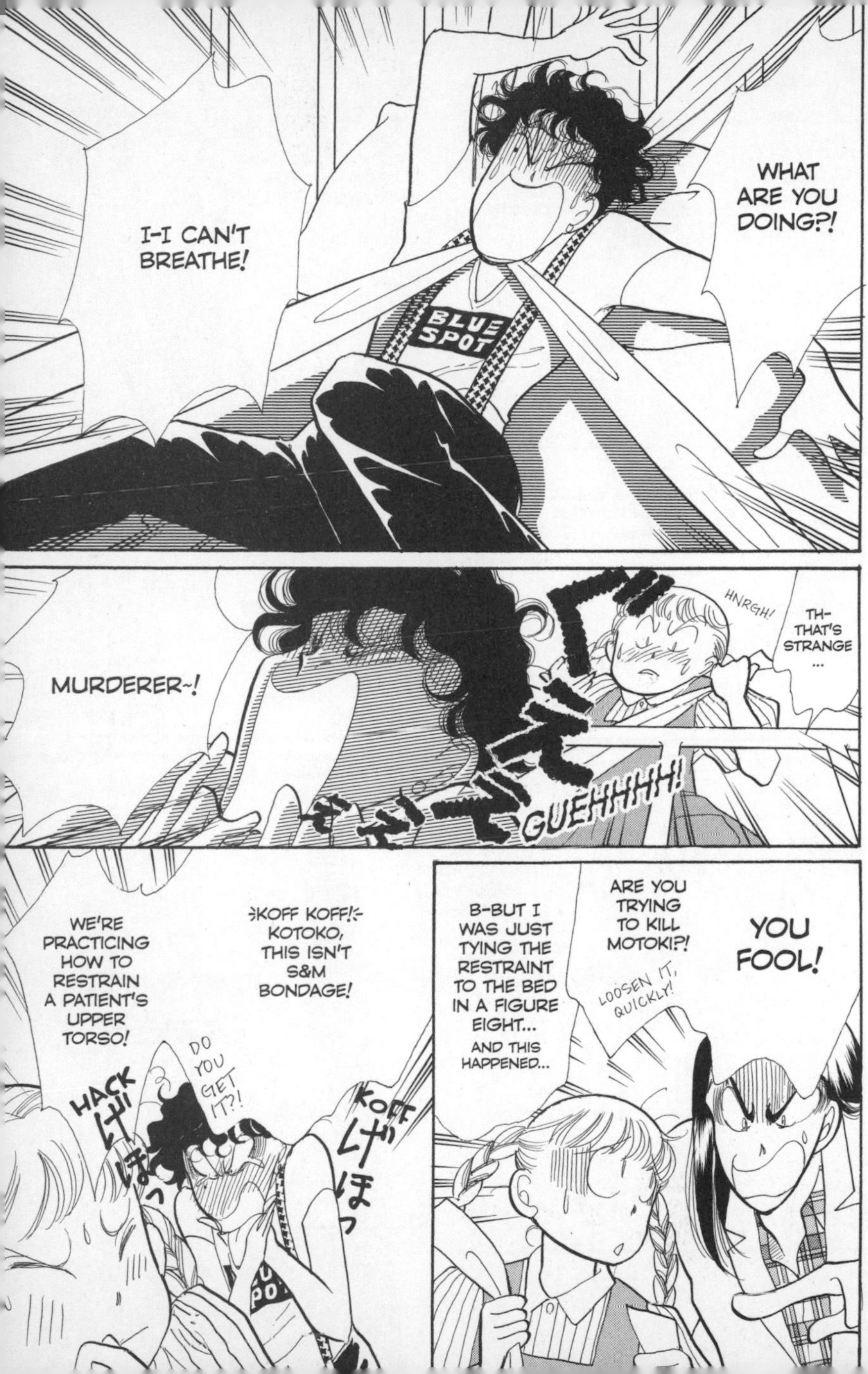
WHAT ARE YOU DOING?!
I-I CAN'T BREATHE!
BLUE SPOT
TH-THAT'S STRANGE ...
HNRGH!
GUEHHHH!
MURDERER~!
YOU FOOL!
ARE YOU TRYING TO KILL MOTOKI?!
LOOSEN IT, QUICKLY!
B-BUT I WAS JUST TYING THE RESTRAINT TO THE BED IN A FIGURE EIGHT...
AND THIS HAPPENED...
KOFF KOFF! KOTOKO, THIS ISN'T S&M BONDAGE!
WE'RE PRACTICING HOW TO RESTRAIN A PATIENT'S UPPER TORSO!
KOFF げほっ
DO YOU GET IT?!
HACK げほっ

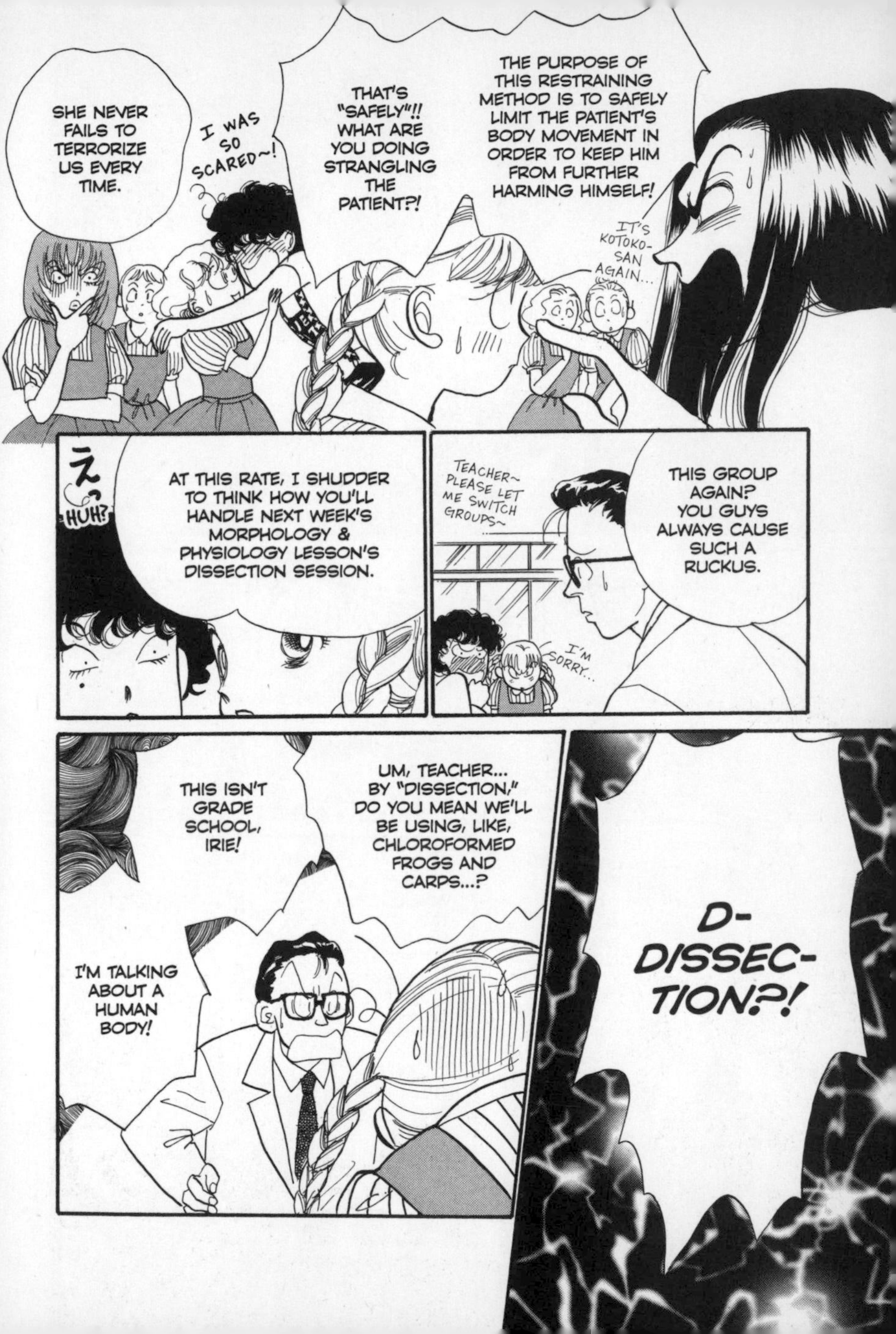
THE PURPOSE OF THIS RESTRAINING METHOD IS TO SAFELY LIMIT THE PATIENT'S BODY MOVEMENT IN ORDER TO KEEP HIM FROM FURTHER HARMING HIMSELF!
IT'S KOTOKO-SAN AGAIN...
THAT'S "SAFELY"!! WHAT ARE YOU DOING STRANGLING THE PATIENT?!
I WAS SO SCARED~!
SHE NEVER FAILS TO TERRORIZE US EVERY TIME.
THIS GROUP AGAIN? YOU GUYS ALWAYS CAUSE SUCH A RUCKUS.
TEACHER~ PLEASE LET ME SWITCH GROUPS~
I'M SORRY...
え HUH?
AT THIS RATE, I SHUDDER TO THINK HOW YOU'LL HANDLE NEXT WEEK'S MORPHOLOGY & PHYSIOLOGY LESSON'S DISSECTION SESSION.
D-DISSECTION?!
UM, TEACHER... BY "DISSECTION," DO YOU MEAN WE'LL BE USING, LIKE, CHLOROFORMED FROGS AND CARPS...?
THIS ISN'T GRADE SCHOOL, IRIE!
I'M TALKING ABOUT A HUMAN BODY!

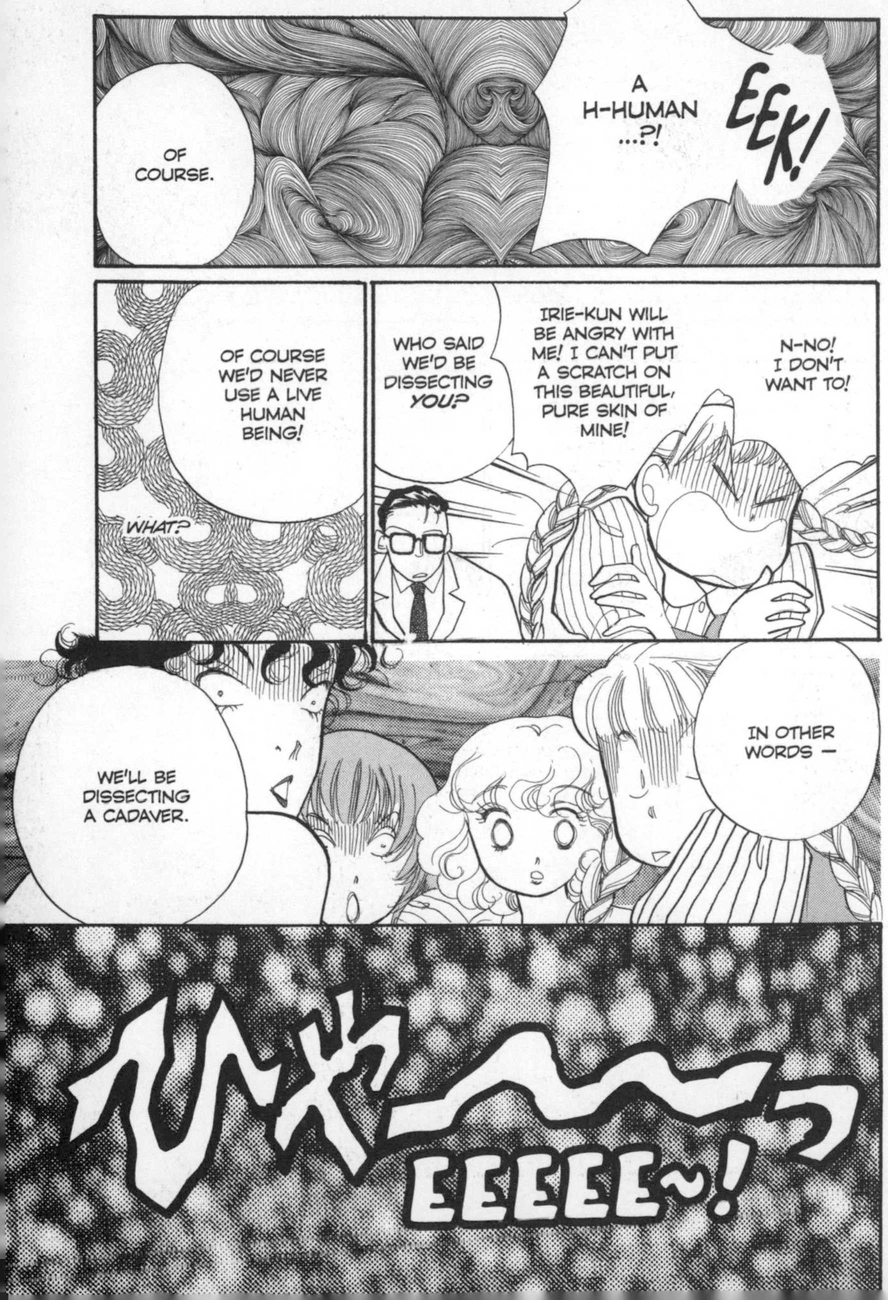
EEK!
A H-HUMAN ...?!
OF COURSE.
N-NO! I DON'T WANT TO!
IRIE-KUN WILL BE ANGRY WITH ME! I CAN'T PUT A SCRATCH ON THIS BEAUTIFUL, PURE SKIN OF MINE!
WHO SAID WE'D BE DISSECTING *YOU?*
OF COURSE WE'D NEVER USE A LIVE HUMAN BEING!
WHAT?
IN OTHER WORDS —
WE'LL BE DISSECTING A CADAVER.
EEEEE~!

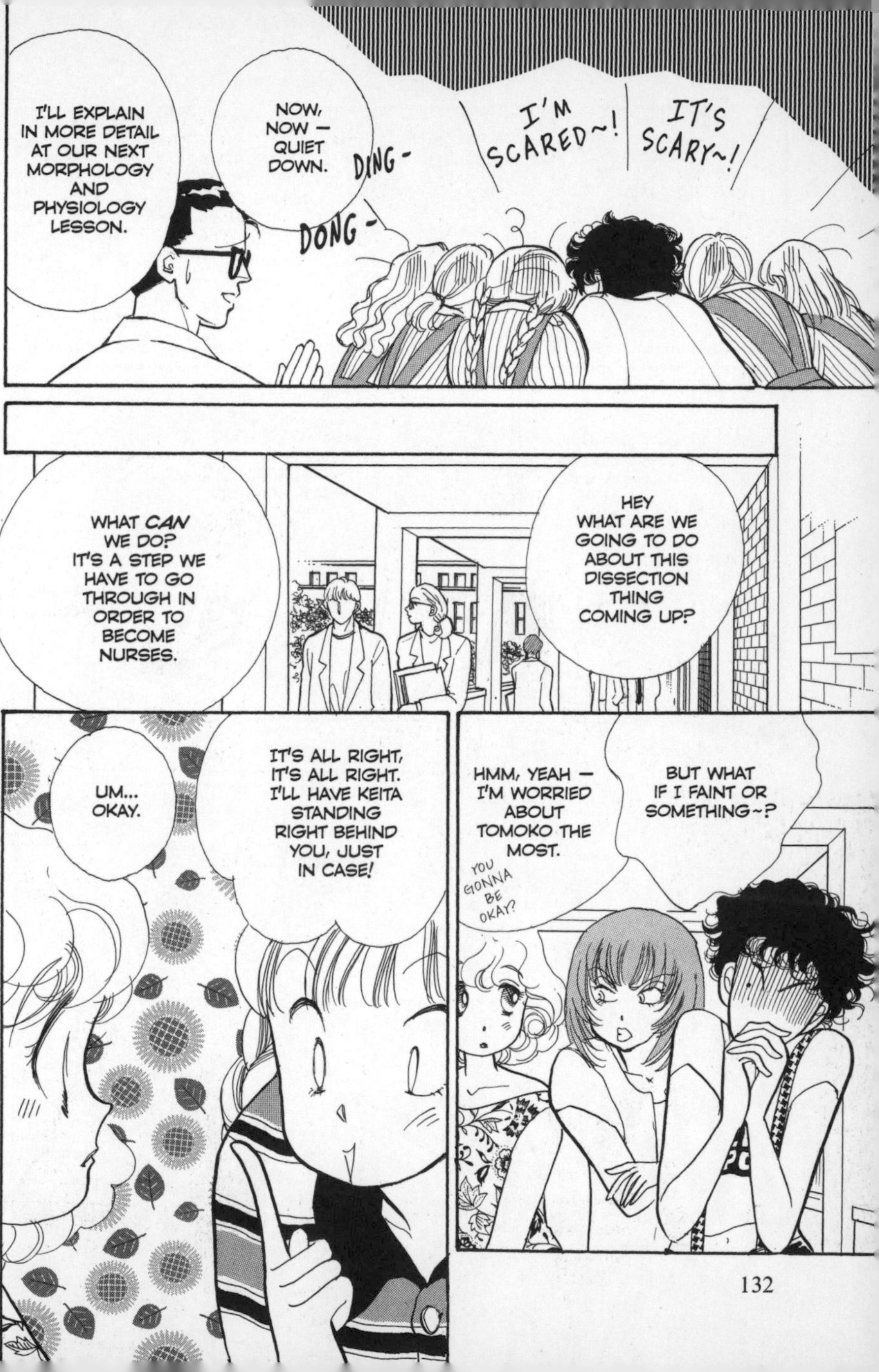
IT'S SCARY~!
I'M SCARED~!
DING-
DONG-
NOW, NOW — QUIET DOWN.
I'LL EXPLAIN IN MORE DETAIL AT OUR NEXT MORPHOLOGY AND PHYSIOLOGY LESSON.
HEY WHAT ARE WE GOING TO DO ABOUT THIS DISSECTION THING COMING UP?
WHAT CAN WE DO? IT'S A STEP WE HAVE TO GO THROUGH IN ORDER TO BECOME NURSES.
BUT WHAT IF I FAINT OR SOMETHING~?
HMM, YEAH — I'M WORRIED ABOUT TOMOKO THE MOST.
YOU GONNA BE OKAY?
IT'S ALL RIGHT, IT'S ALL RIGHT. I'LL HAVE KEITA STANDING RIGHT BEHIND YOU, JUST IN CASE!
UM... OKAY.

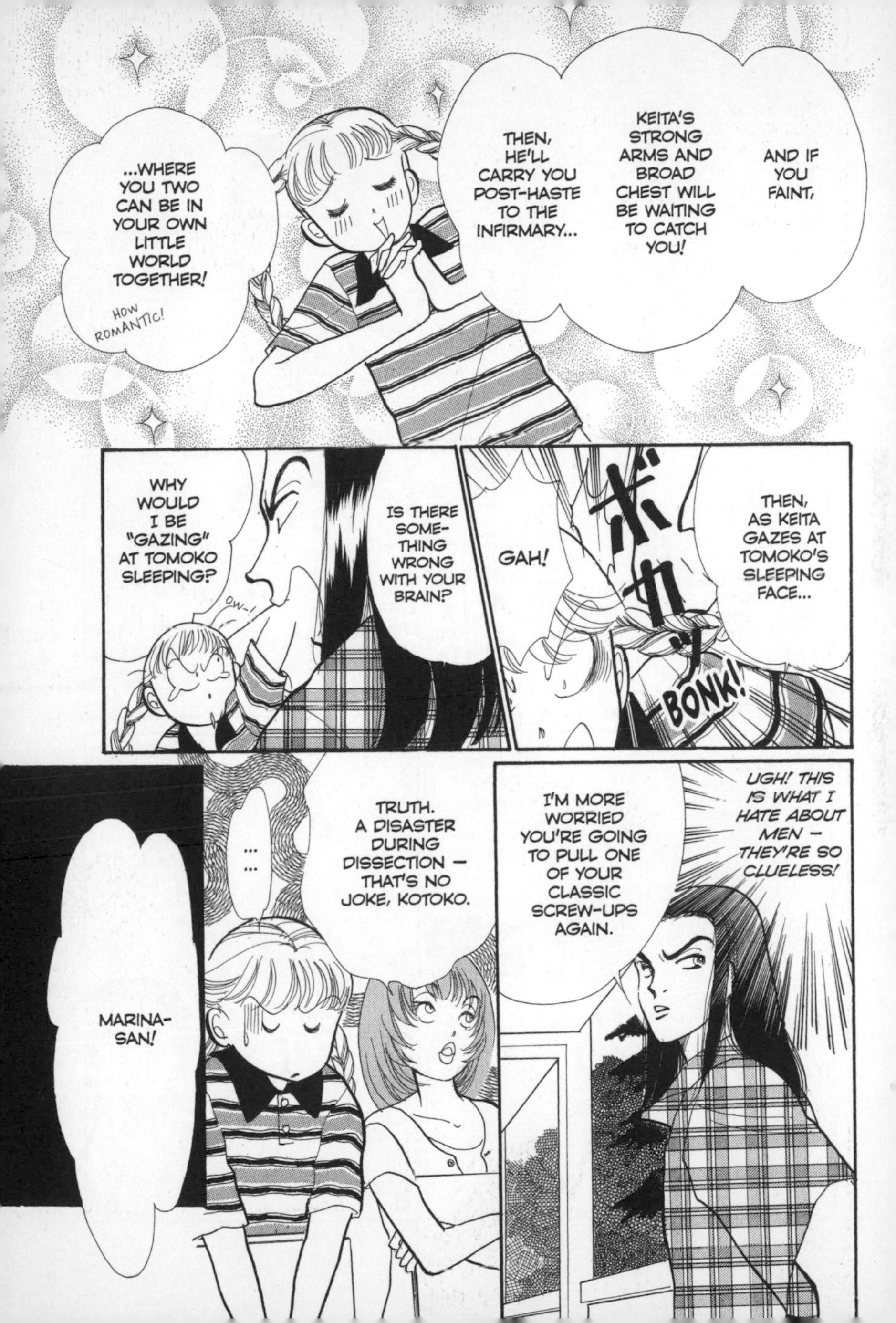
AND IF YOU FAINT,
KEITA'S STRONG ARMS AND BROAD CHEST WILL BE WAITING TO CATCH YOU!
THEN, HE'LL CARRY YOU POST-HASTE TO THE INFIRMARY...
...WHERE YOU TWO CAN BE IN YOUR OWN LITTLE WORLD TOGETHER!
HOW ROMANTIC!
THEN, AS KEITA GAZES AT TOMOKO'S SLEEPING FACE...
ボカッ
BONK!
GAH!
IS THERE SOMETHING WRONG WITH YOUR BRAIN?
WHY WOULD I BE "GAZING" AT TOMOKO SLEEPING?
OW-!
UGH! THIS IS WHAT I HATE ABOUT MEN — THEY'RE SO CLUELESS!
I'M MORE WORRIED YOU'RE GOING TO PULL ONE OF YOUR CLASSIC SCREW-UPS AGAIN.
TRUTH. A DISASTER DURING DISSECTION — THAT'S NO JOKE, KOTOKO.
... ...
MARINA-SAN!

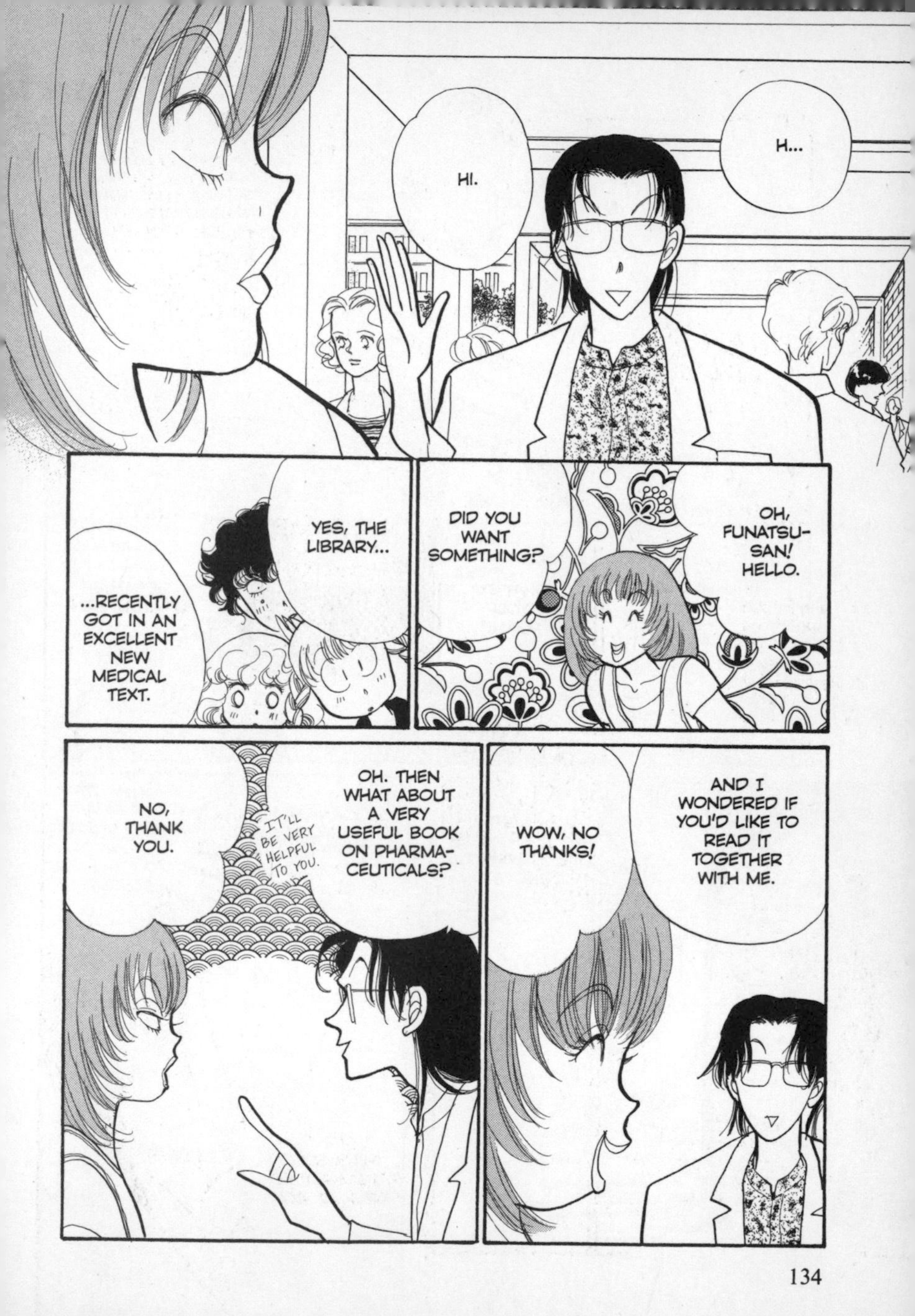
H...
HI.
OH, FUNATSU-SAN! HELLO.
DID YOU WANT SOMETHING?
YES, THE LIBRARY...
...RECENTLY GOT IN AN EXCELLENT NEW MEDICAL TEXT.
AND I WONDERED IF YOU'D LIKE TO READ IT TOGETHER WITH ME.
WOW, NO THANKS!
OH. THEN WHAT ABOUT A VERY USEFUL BOOK ON PHARMA-CEUTICALS?
IT'LL BE VERY HELPFUL TO YOU.
NO, THANK YOU.

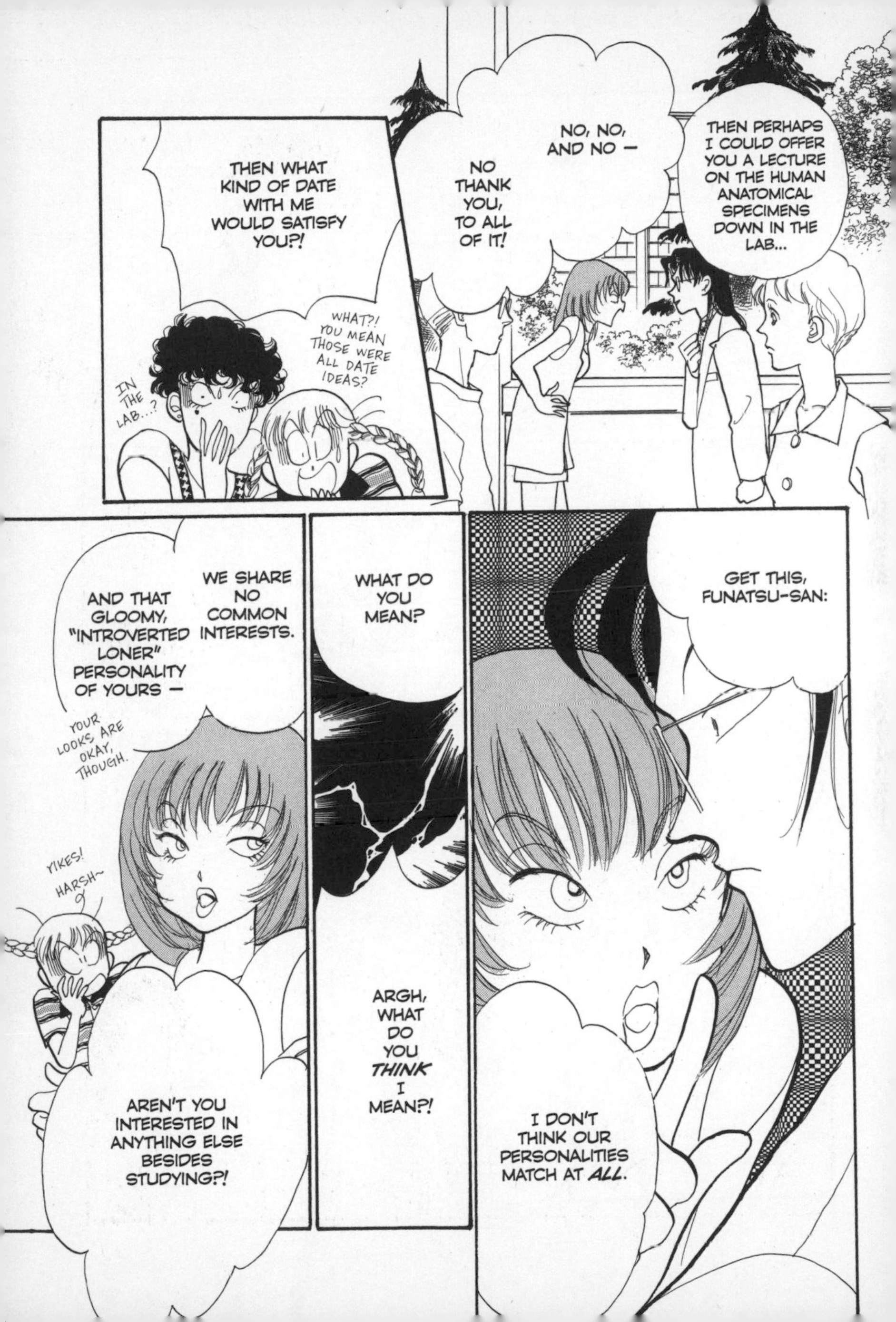
THEN PERHAPS I COULD OFFER YOU A LECTURE ON THE HUMAN ANATOMICAL SPECIMENS DOWN IN THE LAB...
NO, NO, AND NO —
NO THANK YOU, TO ALL OF IT!
THEN WHAT KIND OF DATE WITH ME WOULD SATISFY YOU?!
WHAT?! YOU MEAN THOSE WERE ALL DATE IDEAS?
IN THE LAB...?
GET THIS, FUNATSU-SAN:
I DON'T THINK OUR PERSONALITIES MATCH AT *ALL*.
WHAT DO YOU MEAN?
ARGH, WHAT DO YOU *THINK* I MEAN?!
WE SHARE NO COMMON INTERESTS.
AND THAT GLOOMY, "INTROVERTED LONER" PERSONALITY OF YOURS —
YOUR LOOKS ARE OKAY, THOUGH.
YIKES! HARSH~
AREN'T YOU INTERESTED IN ANYTHING ELSE BESIDES STUDYING?!

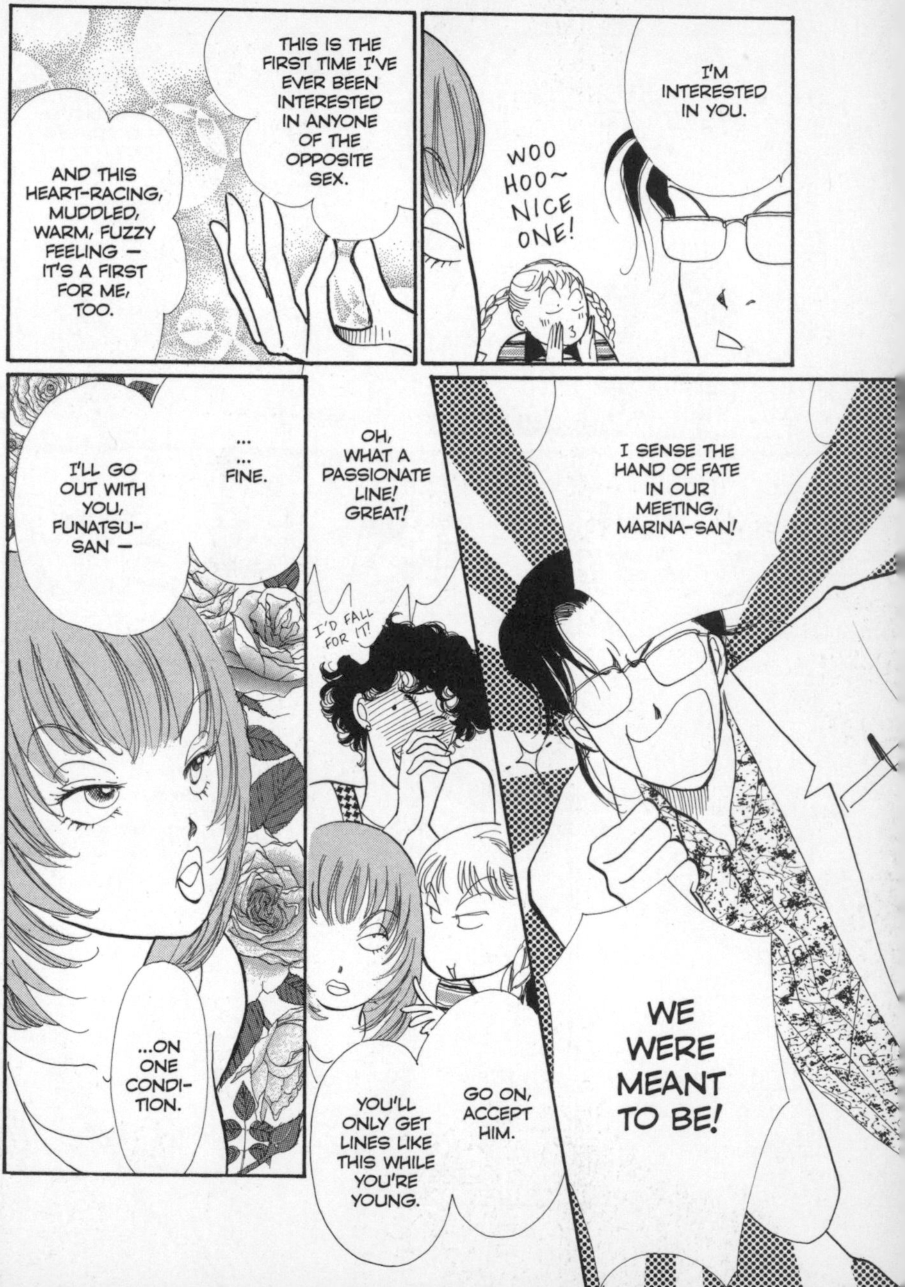
I'M INTERESTED IN YOU.
WOO HOO~ NICE ONE!
THIS IS THE FIRST TIME I'VE EVER BEEN INTERESTED IN ANYONE OF THE OPPOSITE SEX.
AND THIS HEART-RACING, MUDDLED, WARM, FUZZY FEELING — IT'S A FIRST FOR ME, TOO.
I SENSE THE HAND OF FATE IN OUR MEETING, MARINA-SAN!
WE WERE MEANT TO BE!
OH, WHAT A PASSIONATE LINE! GREAT!
I'D FALL FOR IT!
GO ON, ACCEPT HIM.
YOU'LL ONLY GET LINES LIKE THIS WHILE YOU'RE YOUNG.
... ... FINE.
I'LL GO OUT WITH YOU, FUNATSU-SAN —
...ON ONE CONDITION.

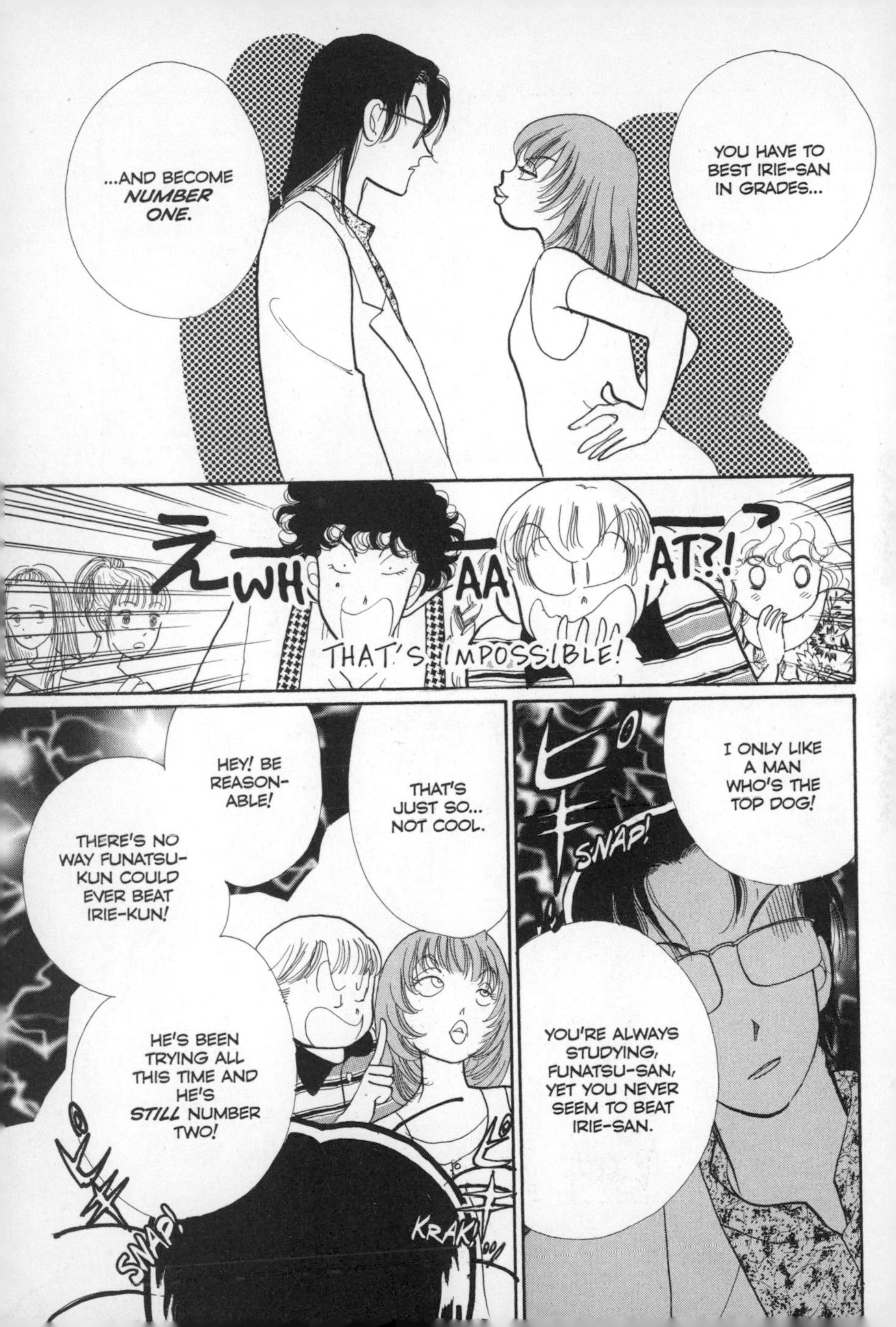
YOU HAVE TO BEST IRIE-SAN IN GRADES...
...AND BECOME *NUMBER ONE.*
WHAAAT?!
THAT'S IMPOSSIBLE!
I ONLY LIKE A MAN WHO'S THE TOP DOG!
SNAP!
YOU'RE ALWAYS STUDYING, FUNATSU-SAN, YET YOU NEVER SEEM TO BEAT IRIE-SAN.
THAT'S JUST SO... NOT COOL.
HEY! BE REASONABLE!
THERE'S NO WAY FUNATSU-KUN COULD EVER BEAT IRIE-KUN!
HE'S BEEN TRYING ALL THIS TIME AND HE'S *STILL* NUMBER TWO!
KRAK!
SNAP!

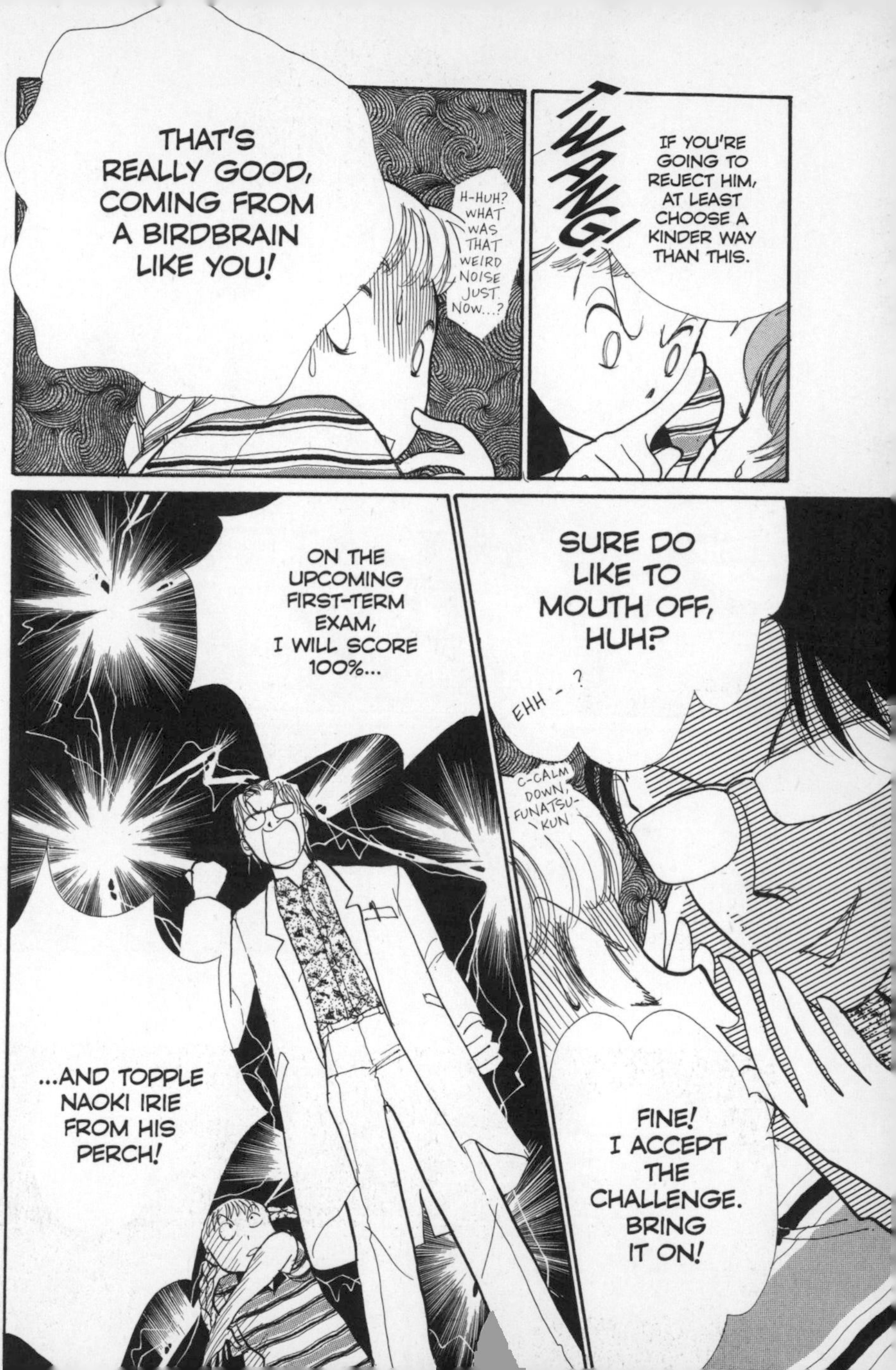
TWANG!
IF YOU'RE GOING TO REJECT HIM, AT LEAST CHOOSE A KINDER WAY THAN THIS.
THAT'S REALLY GOOD, COMING FROM A BIRDBRAIN LIKE YOU!
H-HUH? WHAT WAS THAT WEIRD NOISE JUST NOW...?
SURE DO LIKE TO MOUTH OFF, HUH?
EHH--?
C-CALM DOWN, FUNATSU-KUN
FINE! I ACCEPT THE CHALLENGE. BRING IT ON!
ON THE UPCOMING FIRST-TERM EXAM, I WILL SCORE 100%...
...AND TOPPLE NAOKI IRIE FROM HIS PERCH!

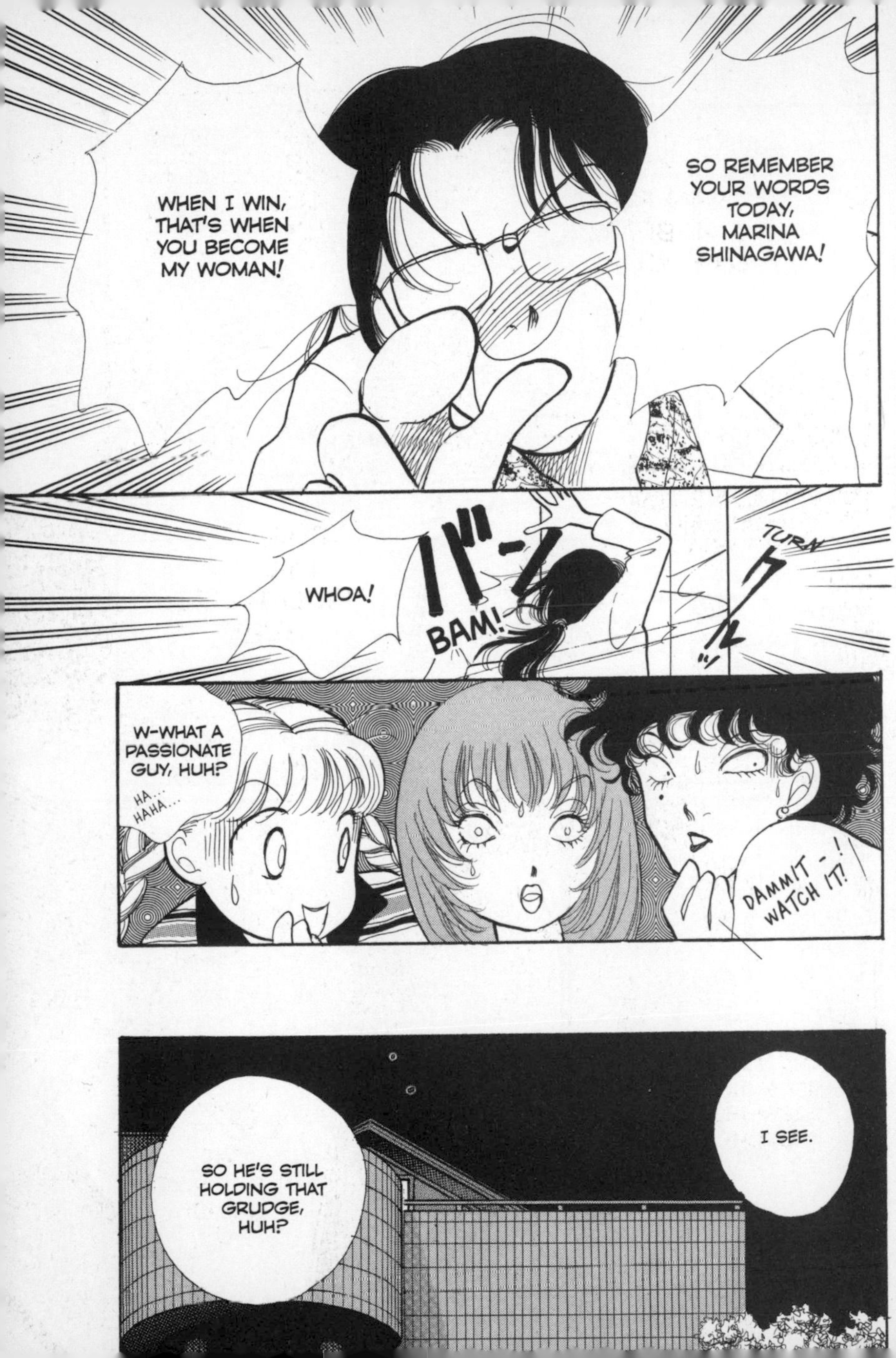
SO REMEMBER YOUR WORDS TODAY, MARINA SHINAGAWA!
WHEN I WIN, THAT'S WHEN YOU BECOME MY WOMAN!
TURN
BAM!
WHOA!
DAMMIT- WATCH IT!
W-WHAT A PASSIONATE GUY, HUH?
HA... HAHA...
I SEE.
SO HE'S STILL HOLDING THAT GRUDGE, HUH?

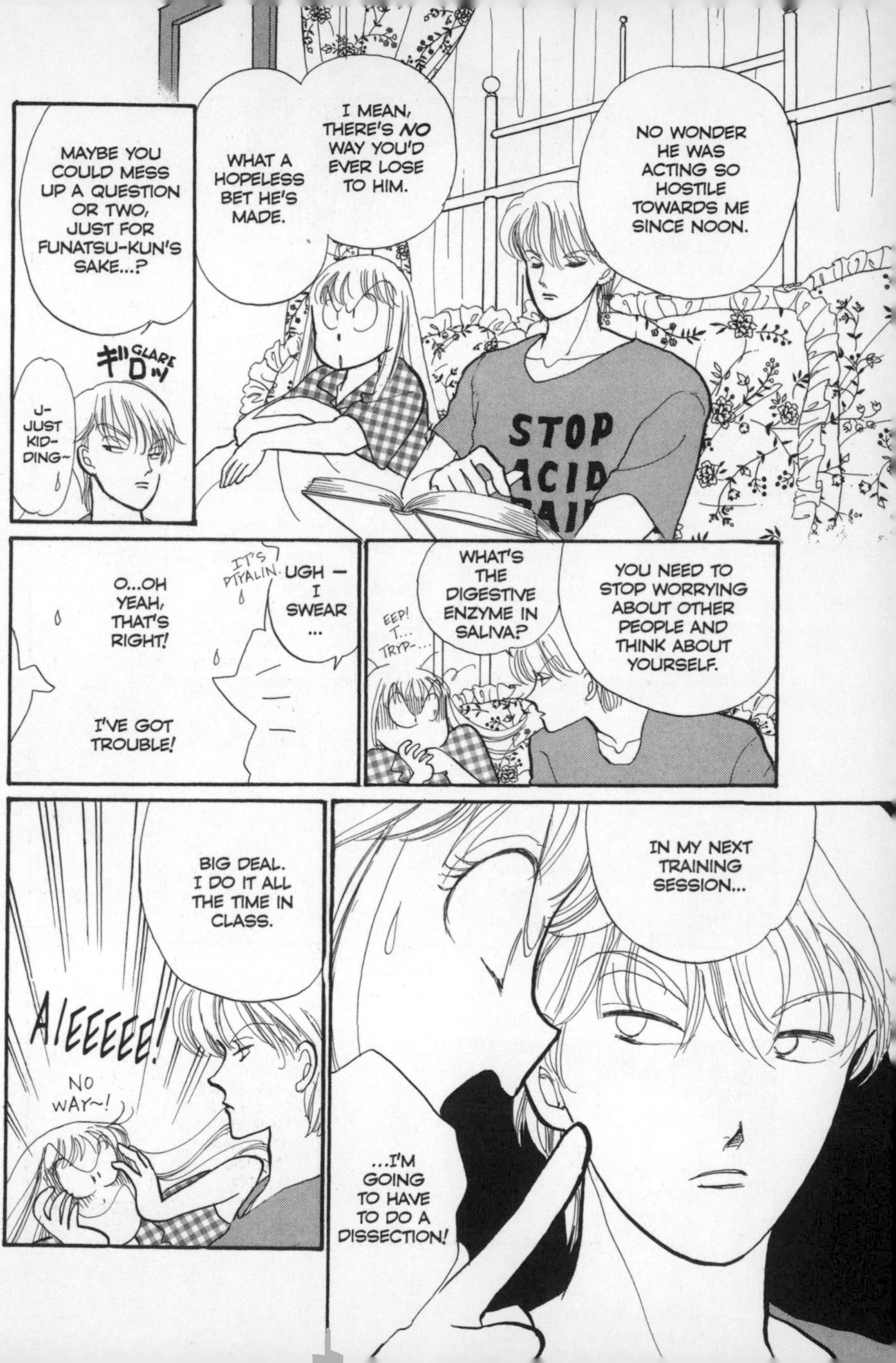
NO WONDER HE WAS ACTING SO HOSTILE TOWARDS ME SINCE NOON.
I MEAN, THERE'S **NO** WAY YOU'D EVER LOSE TO HIM.
WHAT A HOPELESS BET HE'S MADE.
STOP ACID
MAYBE YOU COULD MESS UP A QUESTION OR TWO, JUST FOR FUNATSU-KUN'S SAKE...?
GLARE
J-JUST KIDDING~
YOU NEED TO STOP WORRYING ABOUT OTHER PEOPLE AND THINK ABOUT YOURSELF.
WHAT'S THE DIGESTIVE ENZYME IN SALIVA?
EEP! T... TRYP-...
UGH — I SWEAR ...
IT'S PTYALIN.
O...OH YEAH, THAT'S RIGHT!
I'VE GOT TROUBLE!
IN MY NEXT TRAINING SESSION...
...I'M GOING TO HAVE TO DO A DISSECTION!
BIG DEAL. I DO IT ALL THE TIME IN CLASS.
AIEEEEEE!
NO WAY~!

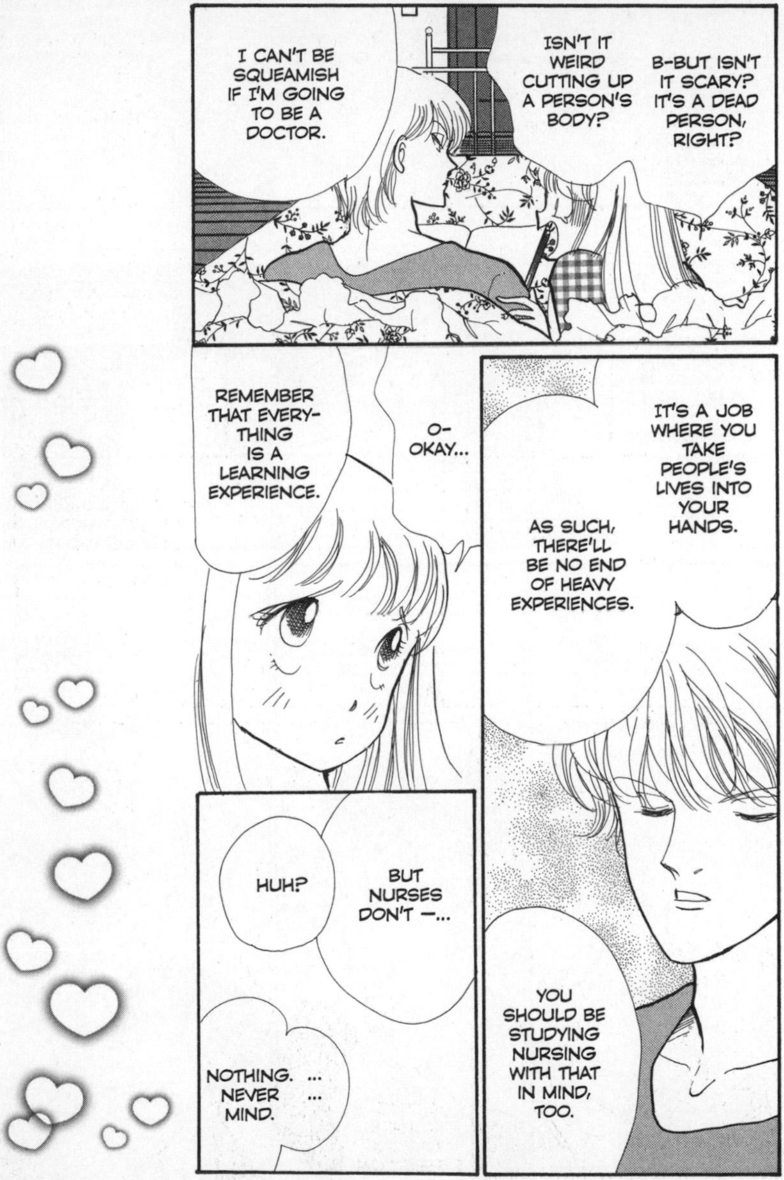
B-BUT ISN'T IT SCARY? IT'S A DEAD PERSON, RIGHT?
ISN'T IT WEIRD CUTTING UP A PERSON'S BODY?
I CAN'T BE SQUEAMISH IF I'M GOING TO BE A DOCTOR.
IT'S A JOB WHERE YOU TAKE PEOPLE'S LIVES INTO YOUR HANDS.
AS SUCH, THERE'LL BE NO END OF HEAVY EXPERIENCES.
YOU SHOULD BE STUDYING NURSING WITH THAT IN MIND, TOO.
REMEMBER THAT EVERY-THING IS A LEARNING EXPERIENCE.
O-OKAY...
BUT NURSES DON'T —...
HUH?
NOTHING. ... NEVER ... MIND.

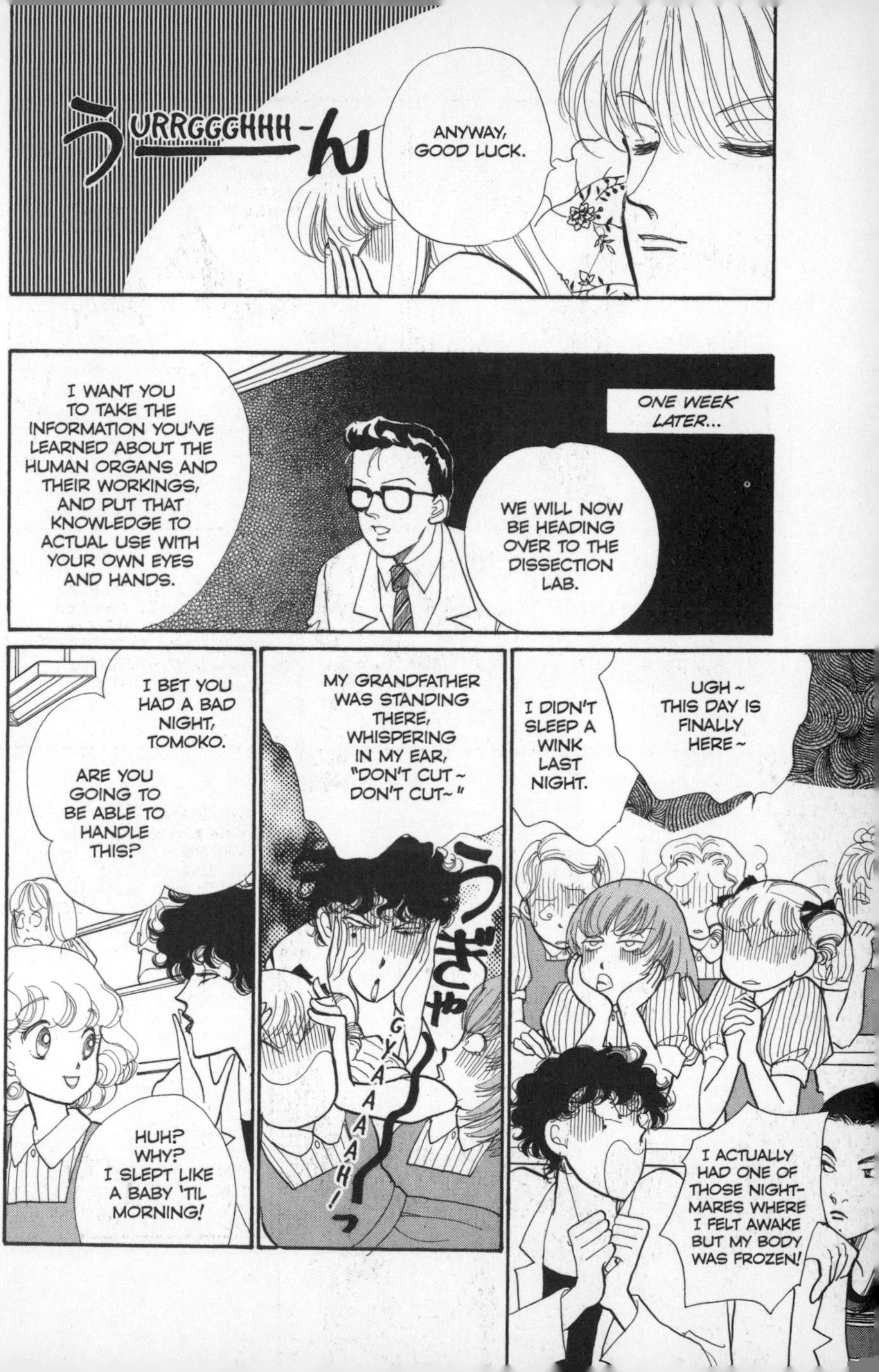
ANYWAY, GOOD LUCK.
うURRGGGHHH-ん
ONE WEEK LATER...
WE WILL NOW BE HEADING OVER TO THE DISSECTION LAB.
I WANT YOU TO TAKE THE INFORMATION YOU'VE LEARNED ABOUT THE HUMAN ORGANS AND THEIR WORKINGS, AND PUT THAT KNOWLEDGE TO ACTUAL USE WITH YOUR OWN EYES AND HANDS.
UGH~ THIS DAY IS FINALLY HERE~
I DIDN'T SLEEP A WINK LAST NIGHT.
I ACTUALLY HAD ONE OF THOSE NIGHTMARES WHERE I FELT AWAKE BUT MY BODY WAS FROZEN!
MY GRANDFATHER WAS STANDING THERE, WHISPERING IN MY EAR, "DON'T CUT~ DON'T CUT~"
うぎゃ
GYAAAAAH!
I BET YOU HAD A BAD NIGHT, TOMOKO.
ARE YOU GOING TO BE ABLE TO HANDLE THIS?
HUH? WHY? I SLEPT LIKE A BABY 'TIL MORNING!

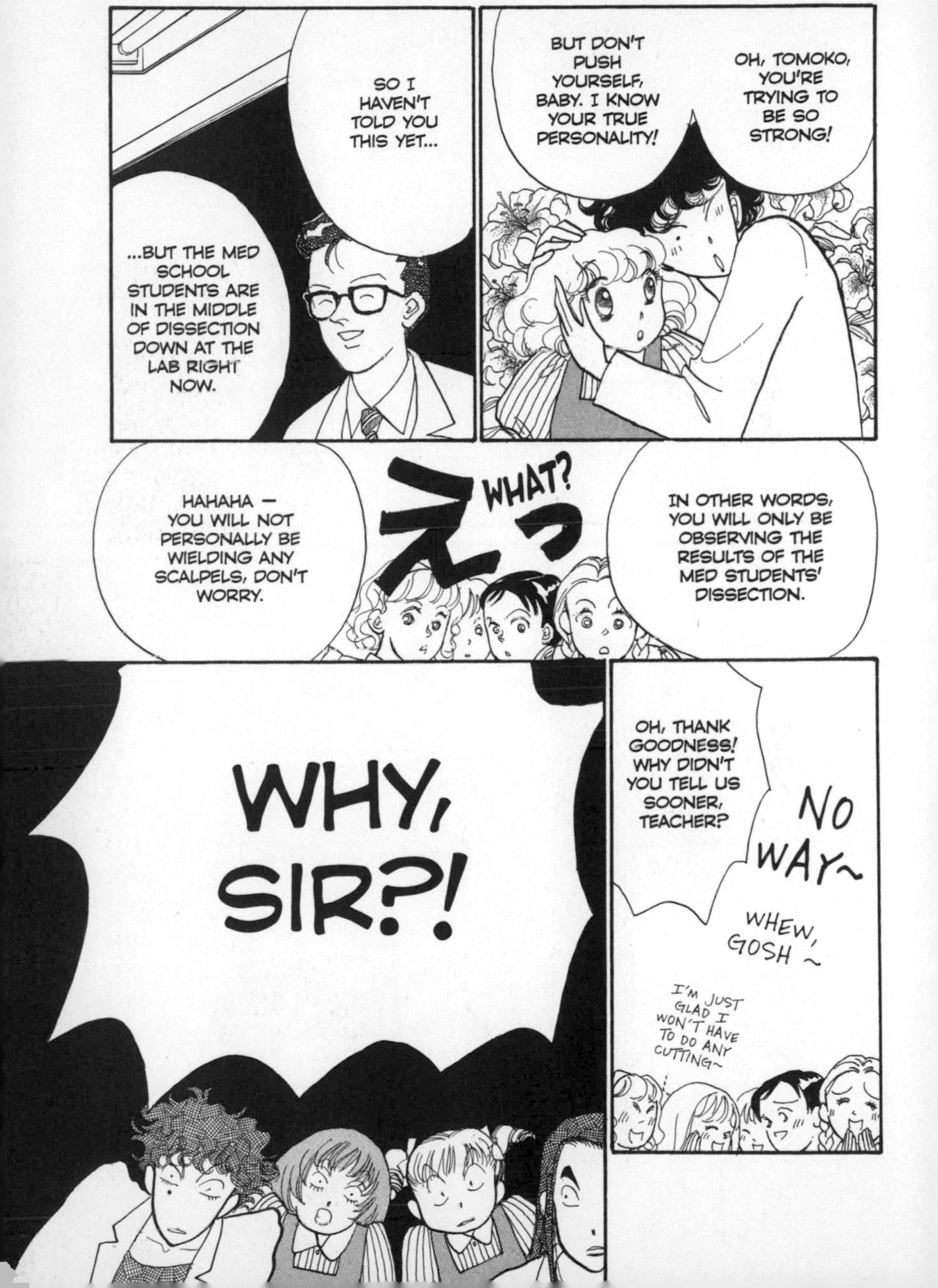
OH, TOMOKO, YOU'RE TRYING TO BE SO STRONG!
BUT DON'T PUSH YOURSELF, BABY. I KNOW YOUR TRUE PERSONALITY!
SO I HAVEN'T TOLD YOU THIS YET...
...BUT THE MED SCHOOL STUDENTS ARE IN THE MIDDLE OF DISSECTION DOWN AT THE LAB RIGHT NOW.
IN OTHER WORDS, YOU WILL ONLY BE OBSERVING THE RESULTS OF THE MED STUDENTS' DISSECTION.
えっ
WHAT?
HAHAHA — YOU WILL NOT PERSONALLY BE WIELDING ANY SCALPELS, DON'T WORRY.
OH, THANK GOODNESS! WHY DIDN'T YOU TELL US SOONER, TEACHER?
NO WAY~
WHEW, GOSH ~
I'M JUST GLAD I WON'T HAVE TO DO ANY CUTTING~
WHY, SIR?!

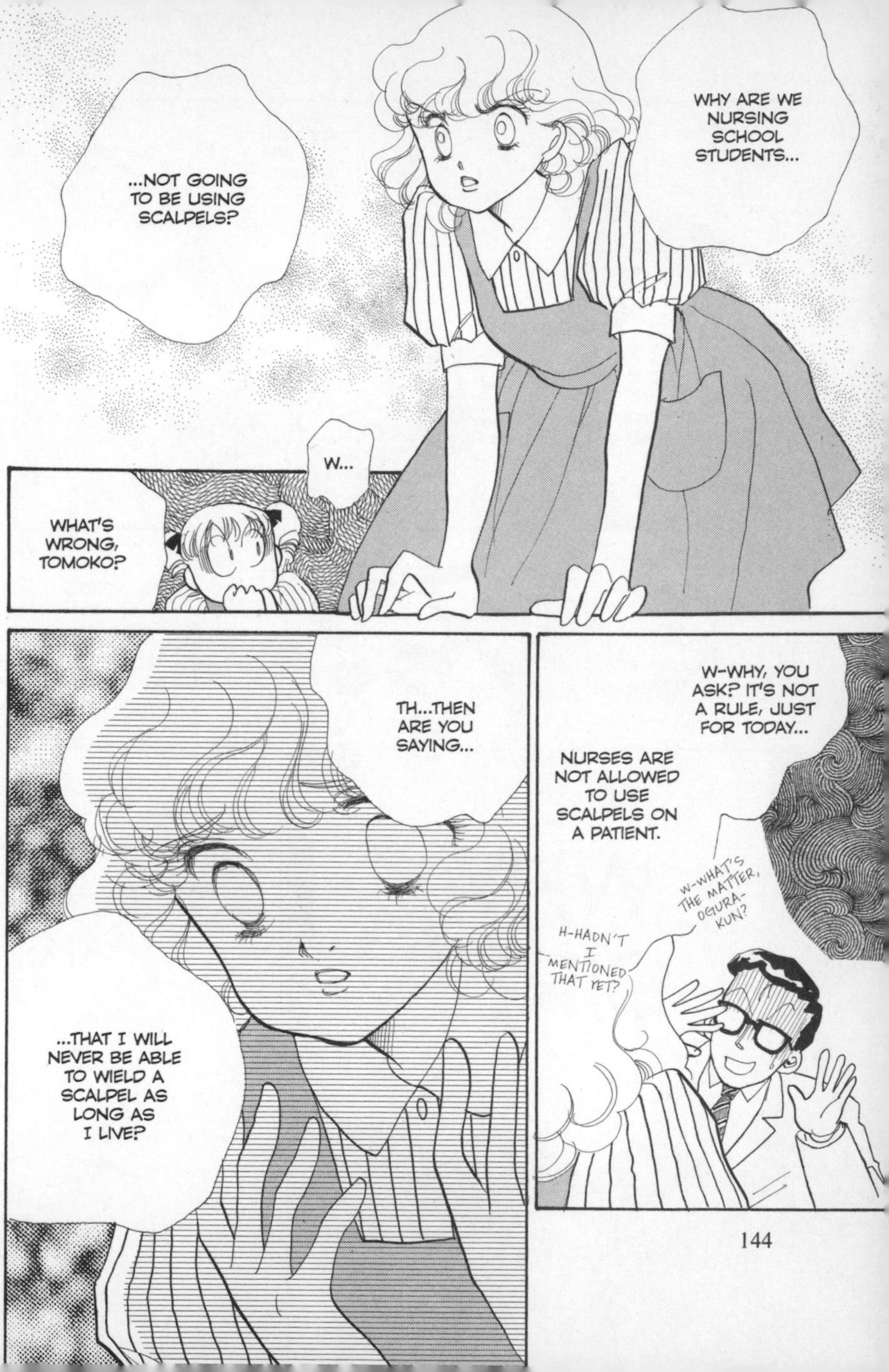

WHY ARE WE NURSING SCHOOL STUDENTS...
...NOT GOING TO BE USING SCALPELS?
W...
WHAT'S WRONG, TOMOKO?
W-WHY, YOU ASK? IT'S NOT A RULE, JUST FOR TODAY...
NURSES ARE NOT ALLOWED TO USE SCALPELS ON A PATIENT.
W-WHAT'S THE MATTER, OGURA-KUN?
H-HADN'T I MENTIONED THAT YET?
TH...THEN ARE YOU SAYING...
...THAT I WILL NEVER BE ABLE TO WIELD A SCALPEL AS LONG AS I LIVE?

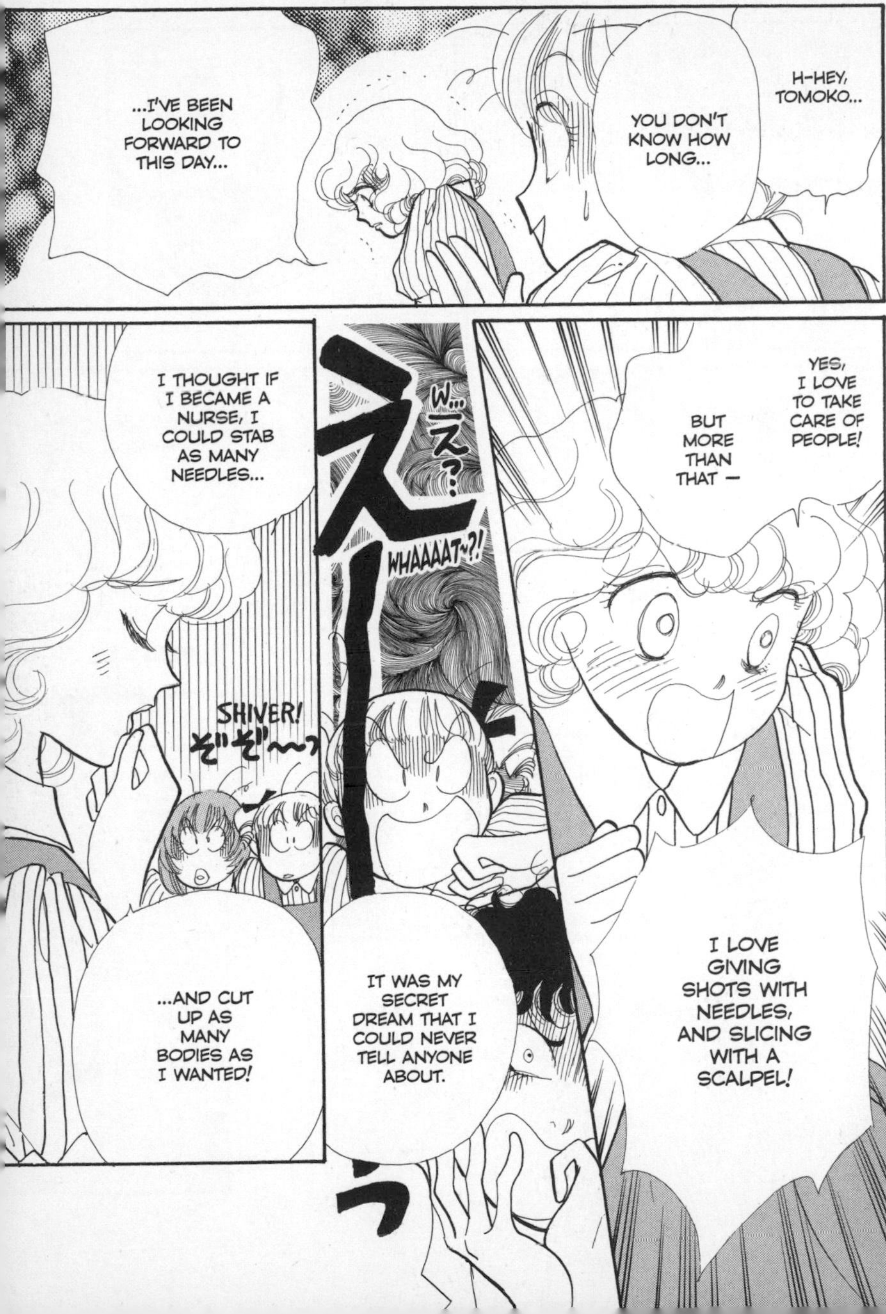
H-HEY, TOMOKO...
YOU DON'T KNOW HOW LONG...
...I'VE BEEN LOOKING FORWARD TO THIS DAY...
YES, I LOVE TO TAKE CARE OF PEOPLE!
BUT MORE THAN THAT —
I LOVE GIVING SHOTS WITH NEEDLES, AND SLICING WITH A SCALPEL!
W...
WHAAAAT~?!
IT WAS MY SECRET DREAM THAT I COULD NEVER TELL ANYONE ABOUT.
I THOUGHT IF I BECAME A NURSE, I COULD STAB AS MANY NEEDLES...
SHIVER!
...AND CUT UP AS MANY BODIES AS I WANTED!

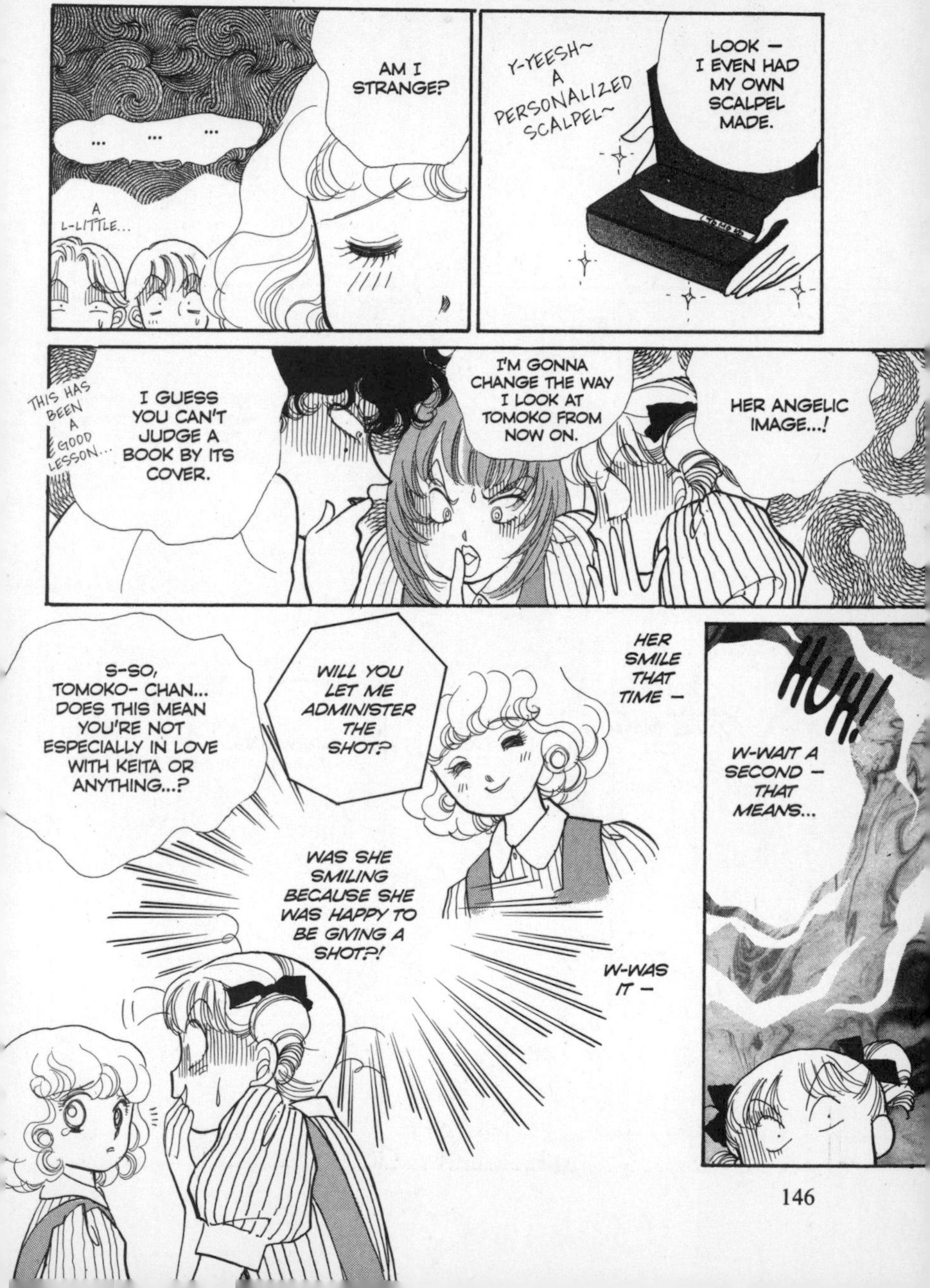
LOOK — I EVEN HAD MY OWN SCALPEL MADE.
Y-YEESH~ A PERSONALIZED SCALPEL~
AM I STRANGE?
... ...
A L-LITTLE...
HER ANGELIC IMAGE...!
I'M GONNA CHANGE THE WAY I LOOK AT TOMOKO FROM NOW ON.
I GUESS YOU CAN'T JUDGE A BOOK BY ITS COVER.
THIS HAS BEEN A GOOD LESSON...
HUH!
W-WAIT A SECOND — THAT MEANS...
HER SMILE THAT TIME —
W-WAS IT —
WAS SHE SMILING BECAUSE SHE WAS HAPPY TO BE GIVING A SHOT?!
WILL YOU LET ME ADMINISTER THE SHOT?
S-SO, TOMOKO-CHAN... DOES THIS MEAN YOU'RE NOT ESPECIALLY IN LOVE WITH KEITA OR ANYTHING...?

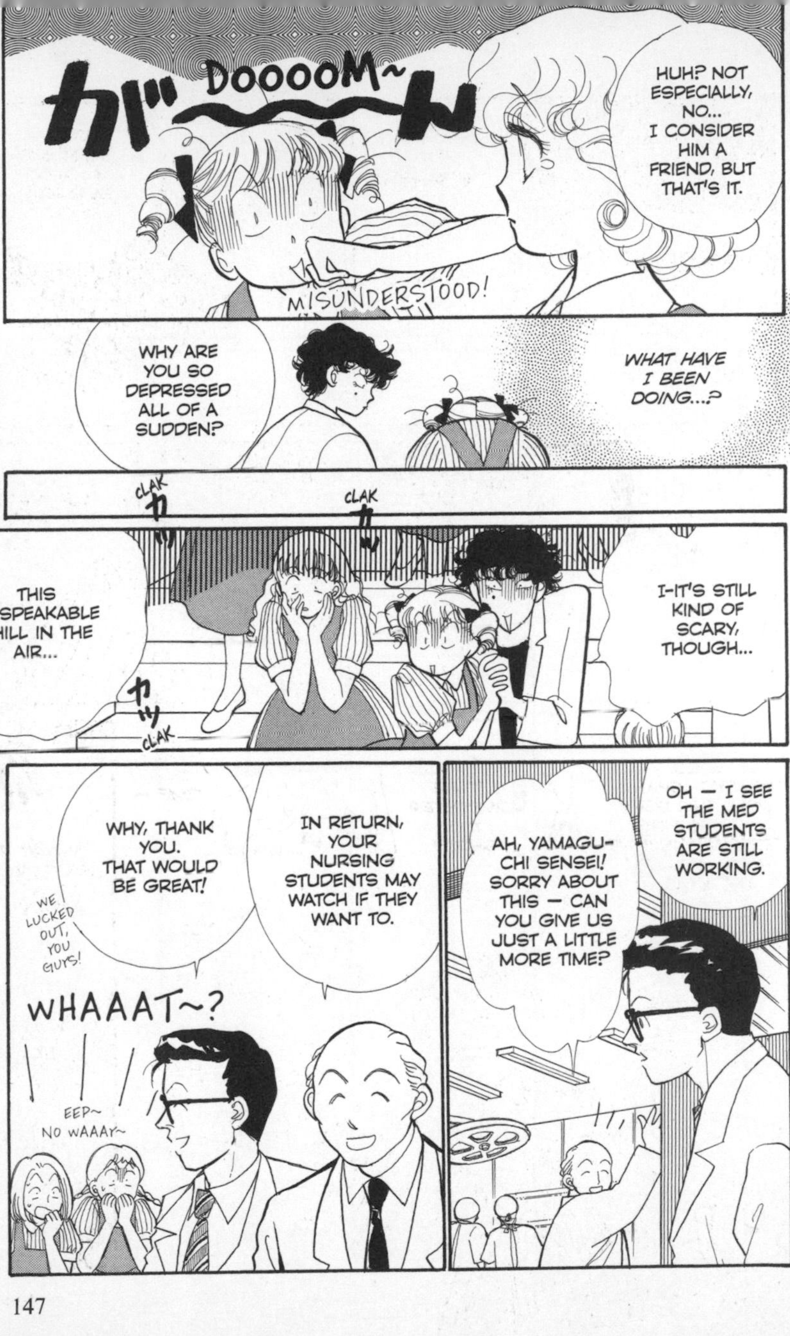
HUH? NOT ESPECIALLY, NO... I CONSIDER HIM A FRIEND, BUT THAT'S IT.
DOOOOM~
MISUNDERSTOOD!
WHAT HAVE I BEEN DOING...?
WHY ARE YOU SO DEPRESSED ALL OF A SUDDEN?
CLAK
CLAK
I-IT'S STILL KIND OF SCARY, THOUGH...
THIS UNSPEAKABLE CHILL IN THE AIR...
CLAK
OH — I SEE THE MED STUDENTS ARE STILL WORKING.
AH, YAMAGU-CHI SENSEI! SORRY ABOUT THIS — CAN YOU GIVE US JUST A LITTLE MORE TIME?
IN RETURN, YOUR NURSING STUDENTS MAY WATCH IF THEY WANT TO.
WHY, THANK YOU. THAT WOULD BE GREAT!
WE LUCKED OUT, YOU GUYS!
WHAAAT~?
EEP~ NO WAAAY~

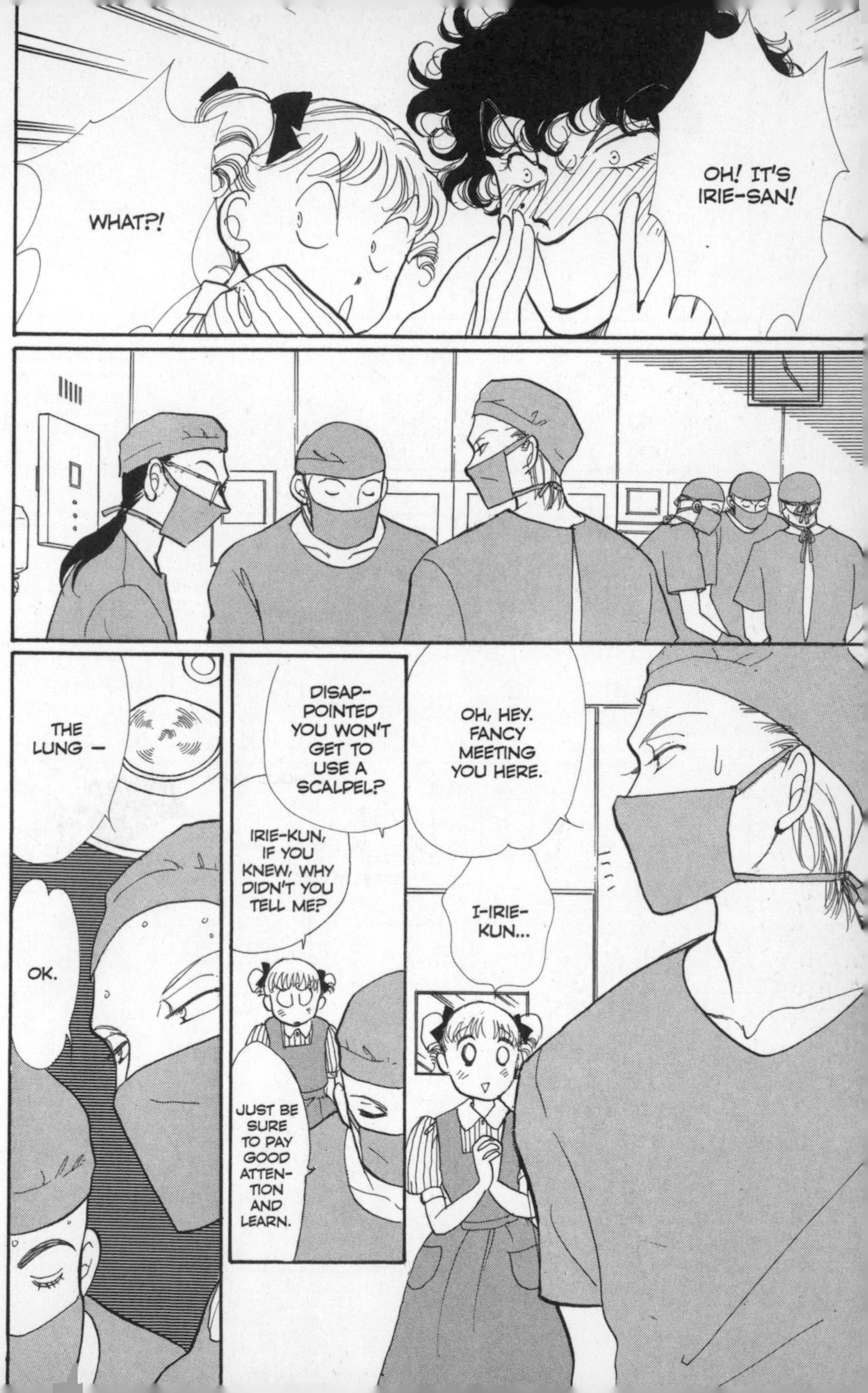
OH! IT'S IRIE-SAN!
WHAT?!
OH, HEY. FANCY MEETING YOU HERE.
I-IRIE-KUN...
DISAP-POINTED YOU WON'T GET TO USE A SCALPEL?
IRIE-KUN, IF YOU KNEW, WHY DIDN'T YOU TELL ME?
JUST BE SURE TO PAY GOOD ATTEN-TION AND LEARN.
THE LUNG —
OK.

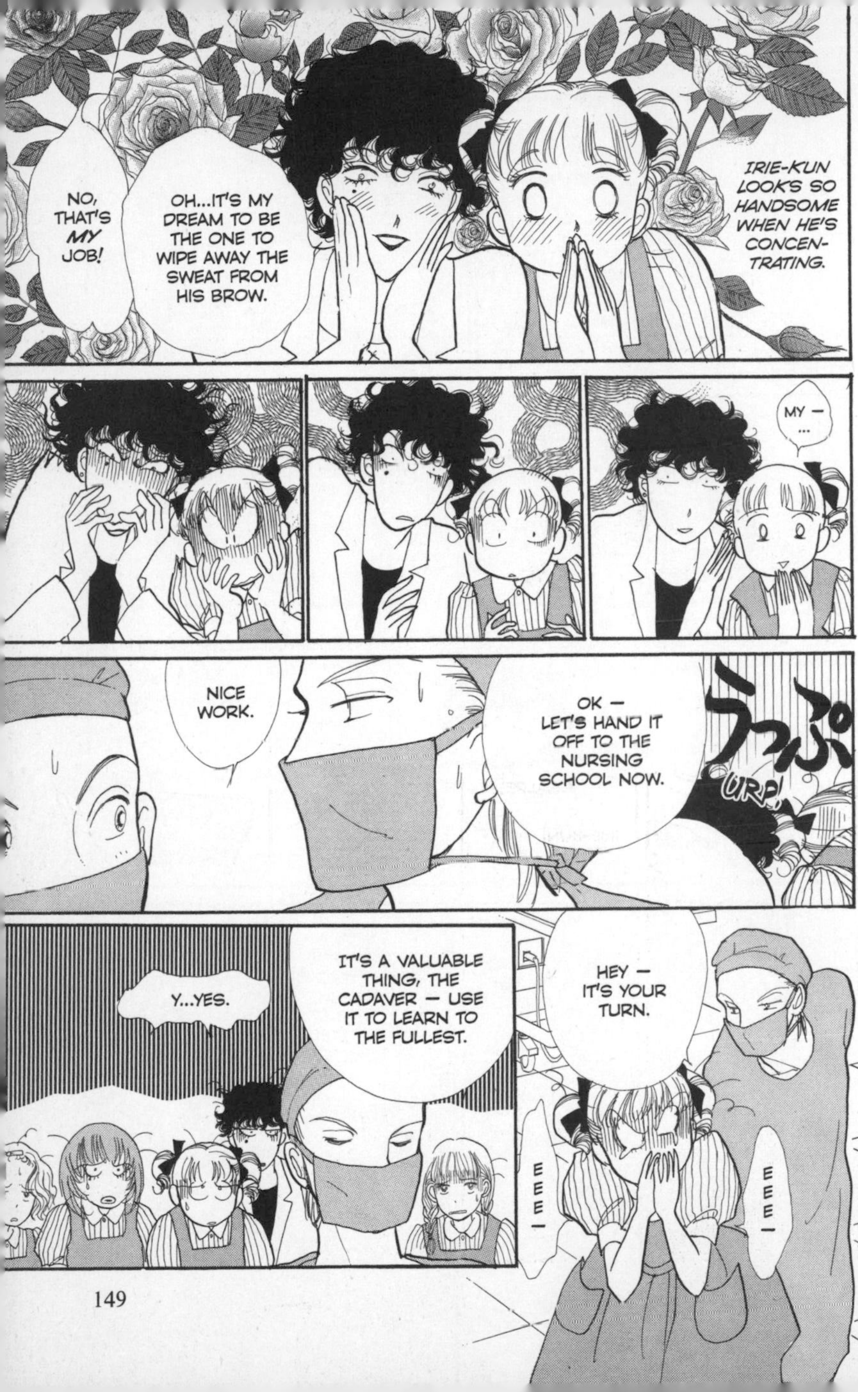
IRIE-KUN LOOKS SO HANDSOME WHEN HE'S CONCEN-TRATING.
OH...IT'S MY DREAM TO BE THE ONE TO WIPE AWAY THE SWEAT FROM HIS BROW.
NO, THAT'S *MY* JOB!
MY — ...
うっぷ
URP!
OK — LET'S HAND IT OFF TO THE NURSING SCHOOL NOW.
NICE WORK.
EEE—
HEY — IT'S YOUR TURN.
EEE—
IT'S A VALUABLE THING, THE CADAVER — USE IT TO LEARN TO THE FULLEST.
Y...YES.

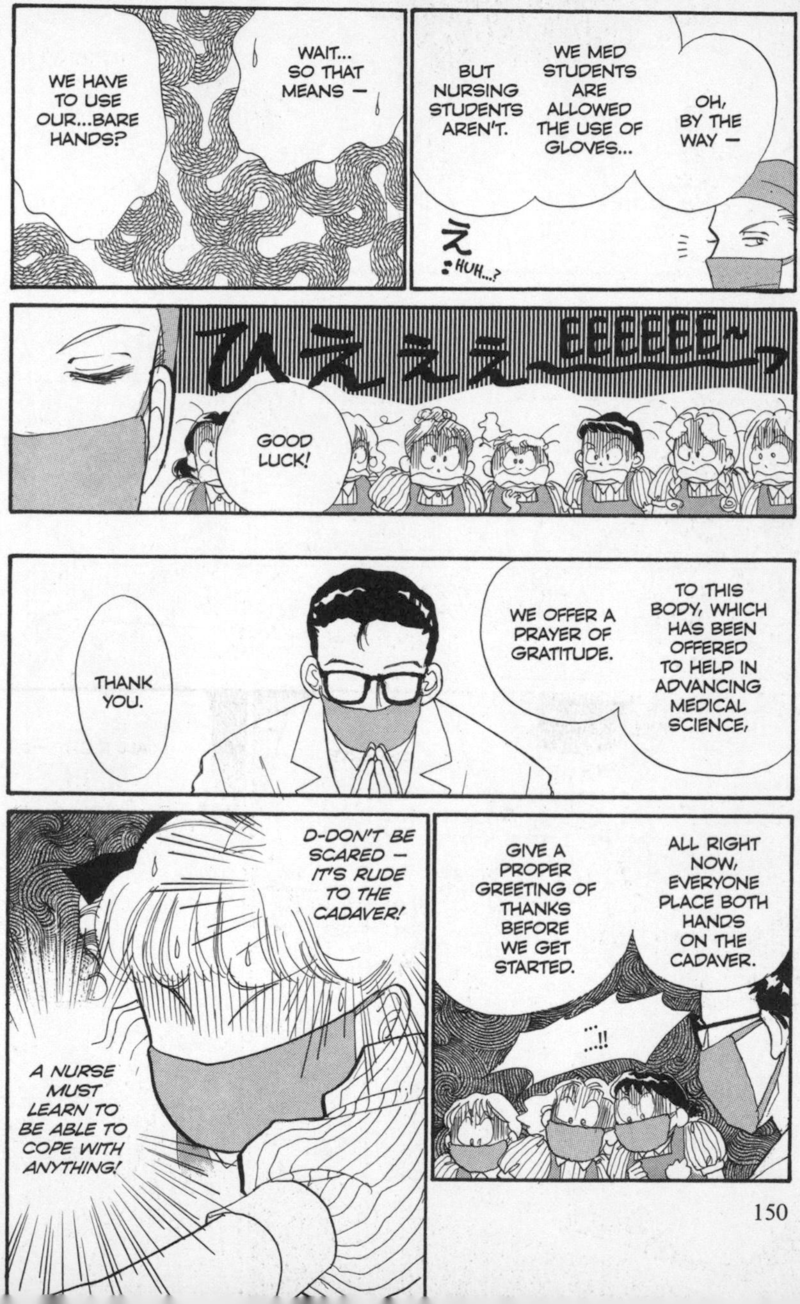
OH, BY THE WAY —
WE MED STUDENTS ARE ALLOWED THE USE OF GLOVES...
BUT NURSING STUDENTS AREN'T.
え: HUH...?
WAIT... SO THAT MEANS —
WE HAVE TO USE OUR...BARE HANDS?
ひえええ~EEEEEE~っ
GOOD LUCK!
TO THIS BODY, WHICH HAS BEEN OFFERED TO HELP IN ADVANCING MEDICAL SCIENCE,
WE OFFER A PRAYER OF GRATITUDE.
THANK YOU.
ALL RIGHT NOW, EVERYONE PLACE BOTH HANDS ON THE CADAVER.
GIVE A PROPER GREETING OF THANKS BEFORE WE GET STARTED.
...!!
D-DON'T BE SCARED — IT'S RUDE TO THE CADAVER!
A NURSE MUST LEARN TO BE ABLE TO COPE WITH ANYTHING!

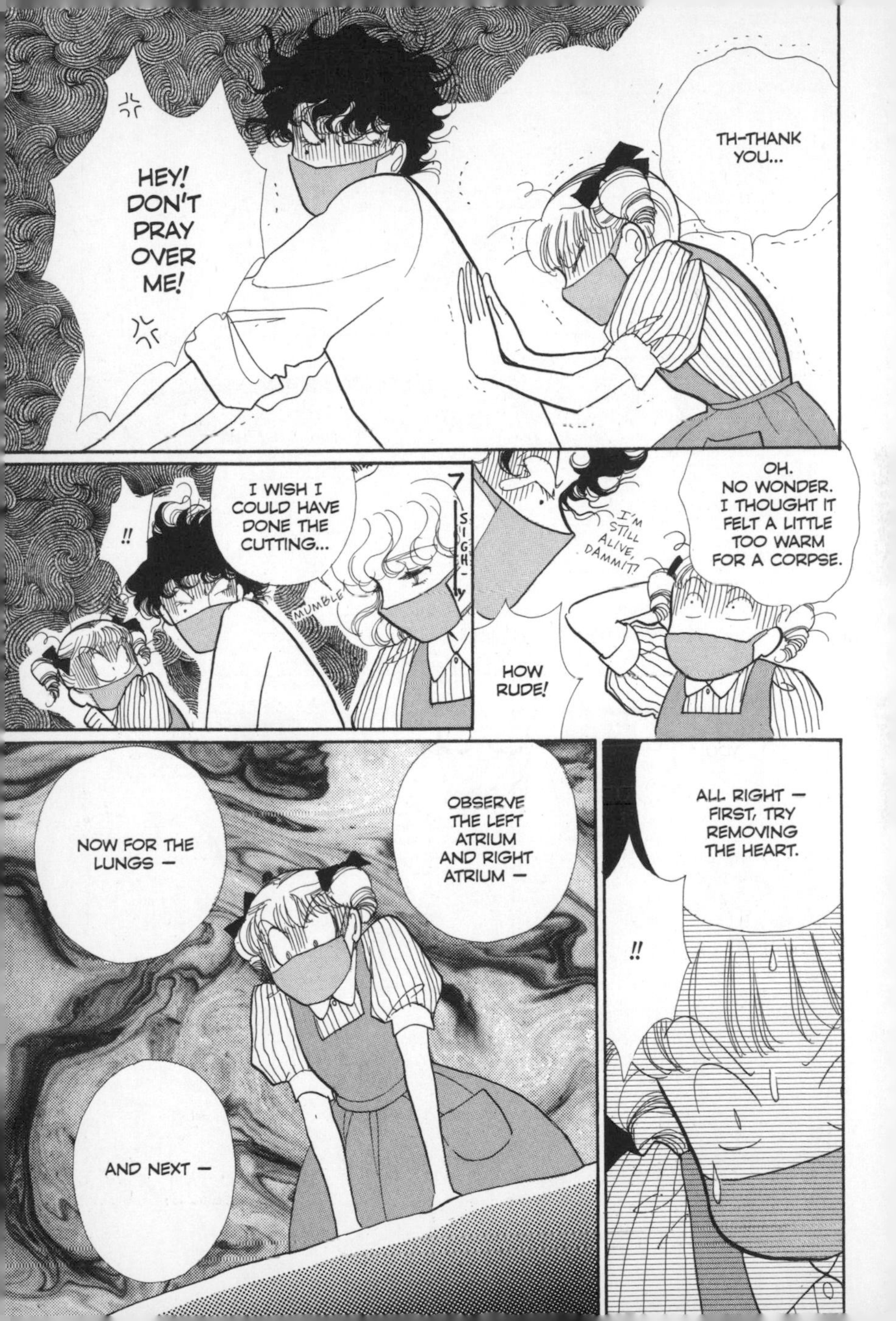
TH-THANK YOU...
HEY! DON'T PRAY OVER ME!
OH. NO WONDER. I THOUGHT IT FELT A LITTLE TOO WARM FOR A CORPSE.
I'M STILL ALIVE, DAMMIT!
HOW RUDE!
SIGH-Y
I WISH I COULD HAVE DONE THE CUTTING...
MUMBLE
!!
ALL RIGHT — FIRST, TRY REMOVING THE HEART.
!!
OBSERVE THE LEFT ATRIUM AND RIGHT ATRIUM —
NOW FOR THE LUNGS —
AND NEXT —

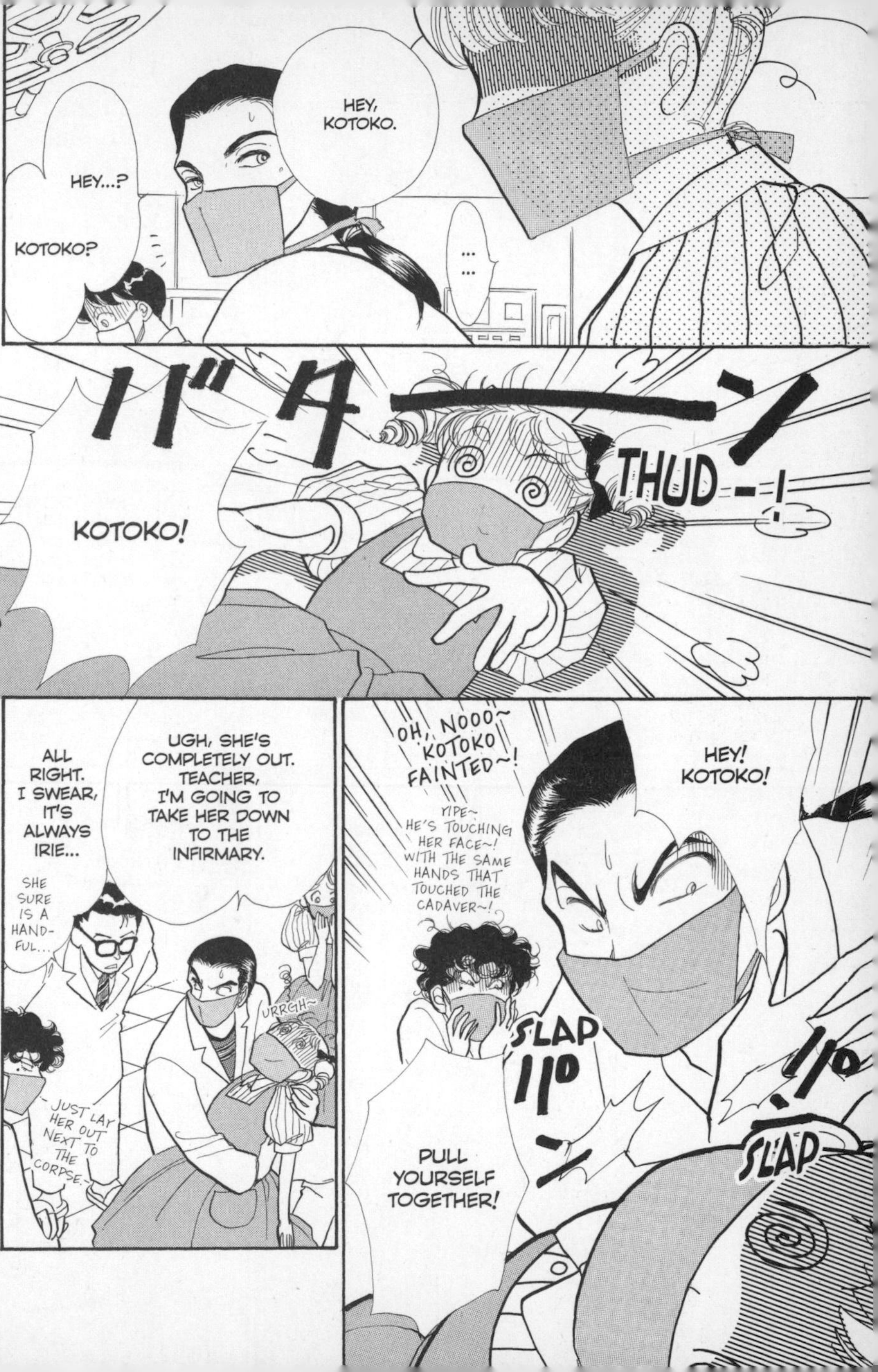
HEY, KOTOKO.
...
...
HEY...?
KOTOKO?
バタ——ン
THUD--!
KOTOKO!
HEY! KOTOKO!
OH, NOOO~ KOTOKO FAINTED~!
YIPE~ HE'S TOUCHING HER FACE~! WITH THE SAME HANDS THAT TOUCHED THE CADAVER~!
SLAP
SLAP
PULL YOURSELF TOGETHER!
UGH, SHE'S COMPLETELY OUT. TEACHER, I'M GOING TO TAKE HER DOWN TO THE INFIRMARY.
ALL RIGHT. I SWEAR, IT'S ALWAYS IRIE...
SHE SURE IS A HAND-FUL...
URRGH~
JUST LAY HER OUT NEXT TO THE CORPSE.

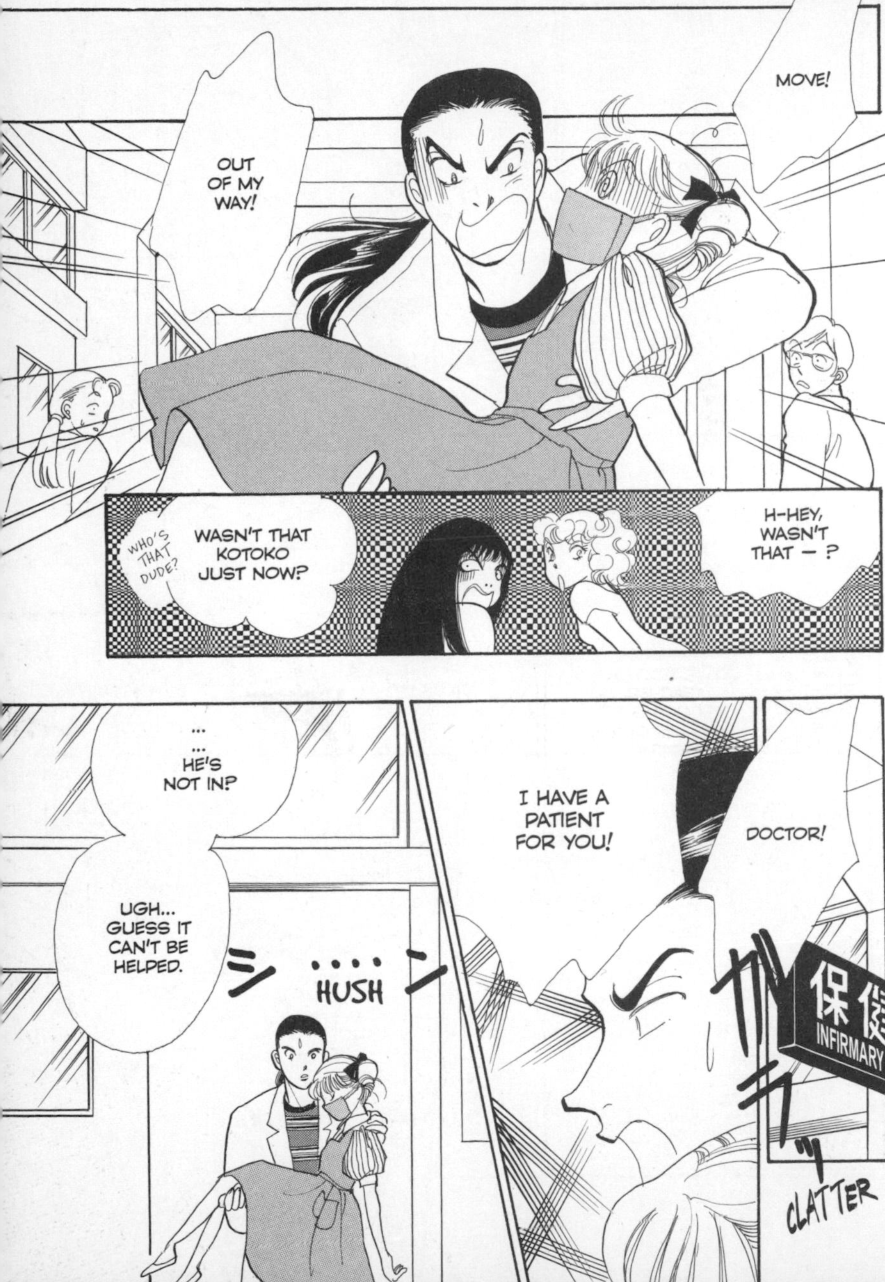
MOVE!
OUT OF MY WAY!
H-HEY, WASN'T THAT — ?
WASN'T THAT KOTOKO JUST NOW?
WHO'S THAT DUDE?
DOCTOR!
I HAVE A PATIENT FOR YOU!
保健
INFIRMARY
CLATTER
... ... HE'S NOT IN?
UGH... GUESS IT CAN'T BE HELPED.
.... HUSH

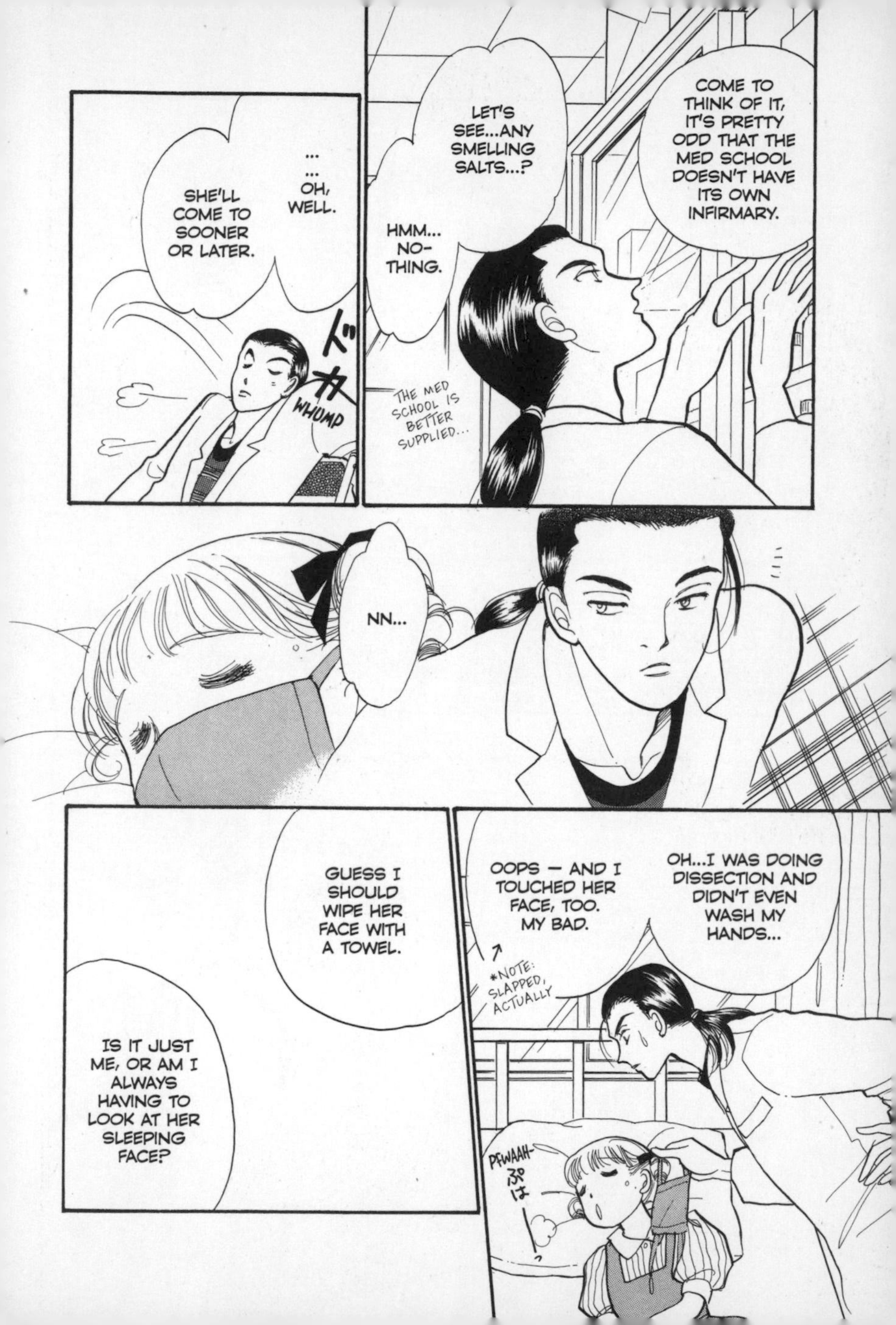
COME TO THINK OF IT, IT'S PRETTY ODD THAT THE MED SCHOOL DOESN'T HAVE ITS OWN INFIRMARY.
LET'S SEE...ANY SMELLING SALTS...?
HMM... NO-THING.
THE MED SCHOOL IS BETTER SUPPLIED...
... ... OH, WELL.
SHE'LL COME TO SOONER OR LATER.
ドカ
WHUMP
NN...
OH...I WAS DOING DISSECTION AND DIDN'T EVEN WASH MY HANDS...
OOPS — AND I TOUCHED HER FACE, TOO. MY BAD.
*NOTE: SLAPPED, ACTUALLY
PFWAAH-
ぷはー
GUESS I SHOULD WIPE HER FACE WITH A TOWEL.
IS IT JUST ME, OR AM I ALWAYS HAVING TO LOOK AT HER SLEEPING FACE?

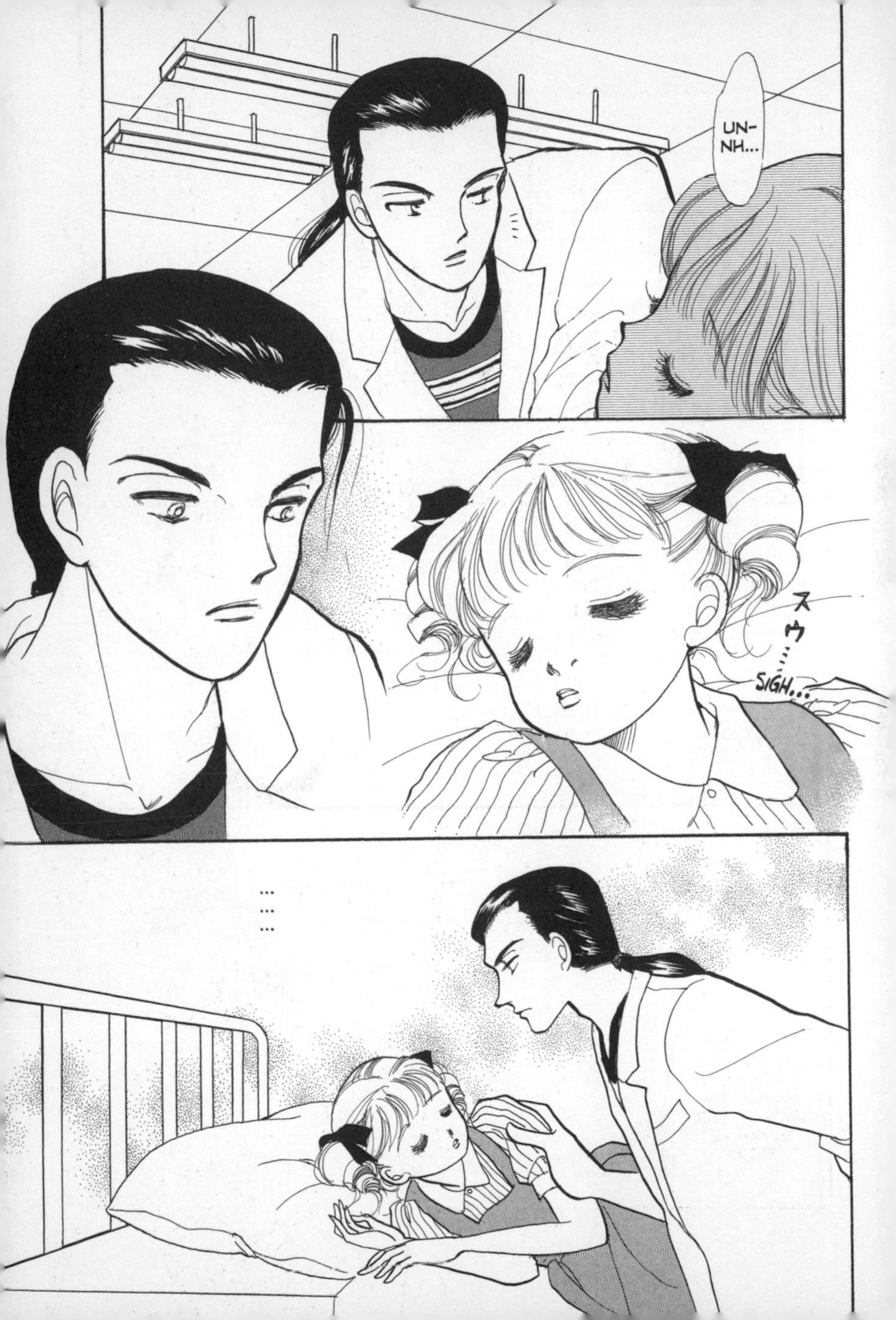
UN-NH...
スゥ…
SIGH...
...
...
...

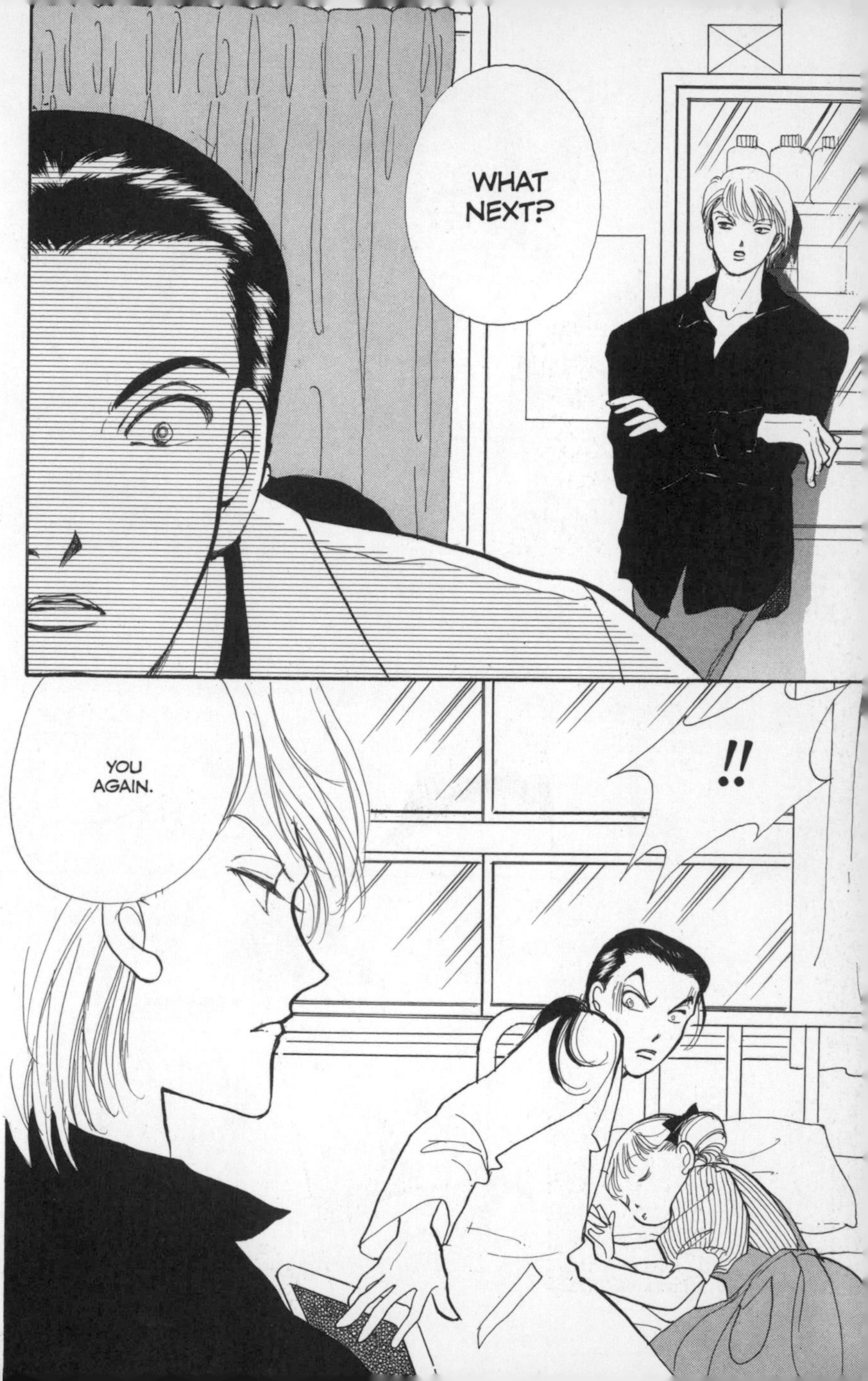
WHAT NEXT?
YOU AGAIN.
!!

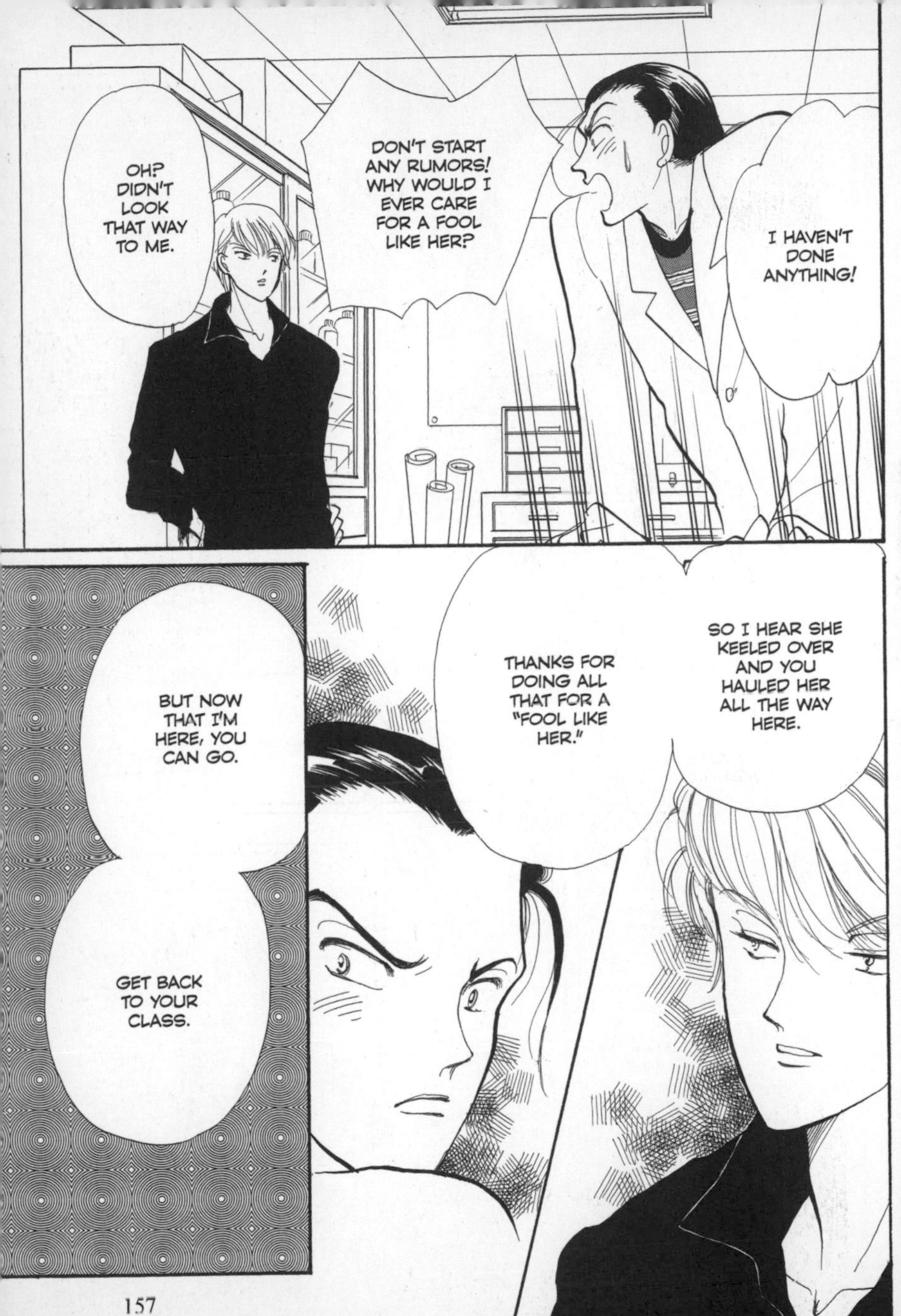
I HAVEN'T DONE ANYTHING!
DON'T START ANY RUMORS! WHY WOULD I EVER CARE FOR A FOOL LIKE HER?
OH? DIDN'T LOOK THAT WAY TO ME.
SO I HEAR SHE KEELED OVER AND YOU HAULED HER ALL THE WAY HERE.
THANKS FOR DOING ALL THAT FOR A "FOOL LIKE HER."
BUT NOW THAT I'M HERE, YOU CAN GO.
GET BACK TO YOUR CLASS.

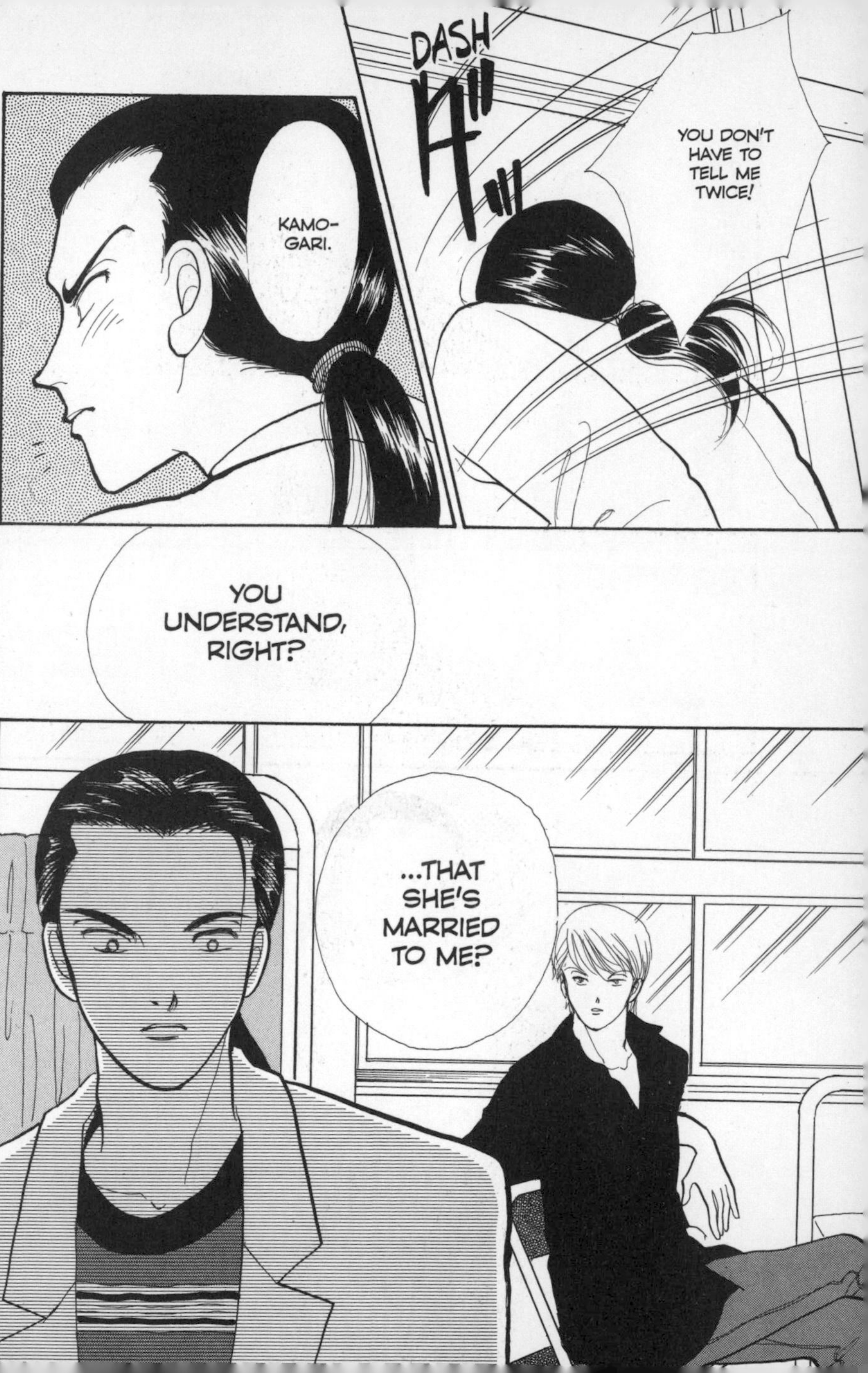
DASH
YOU DON'T HAVE TO TELL ME TWICE!
KAMO-GARI.
YOU UNDERSTAND, RIGHT?
...THAT SHE'S MARRIED TO ME?

STAFF: AKIKO ISHIKAWA, MASAKO KATAGAI, ATSUKO SUGIMOTO, KANAMI SUDÔ THANK YOU VERY MUCH ♡

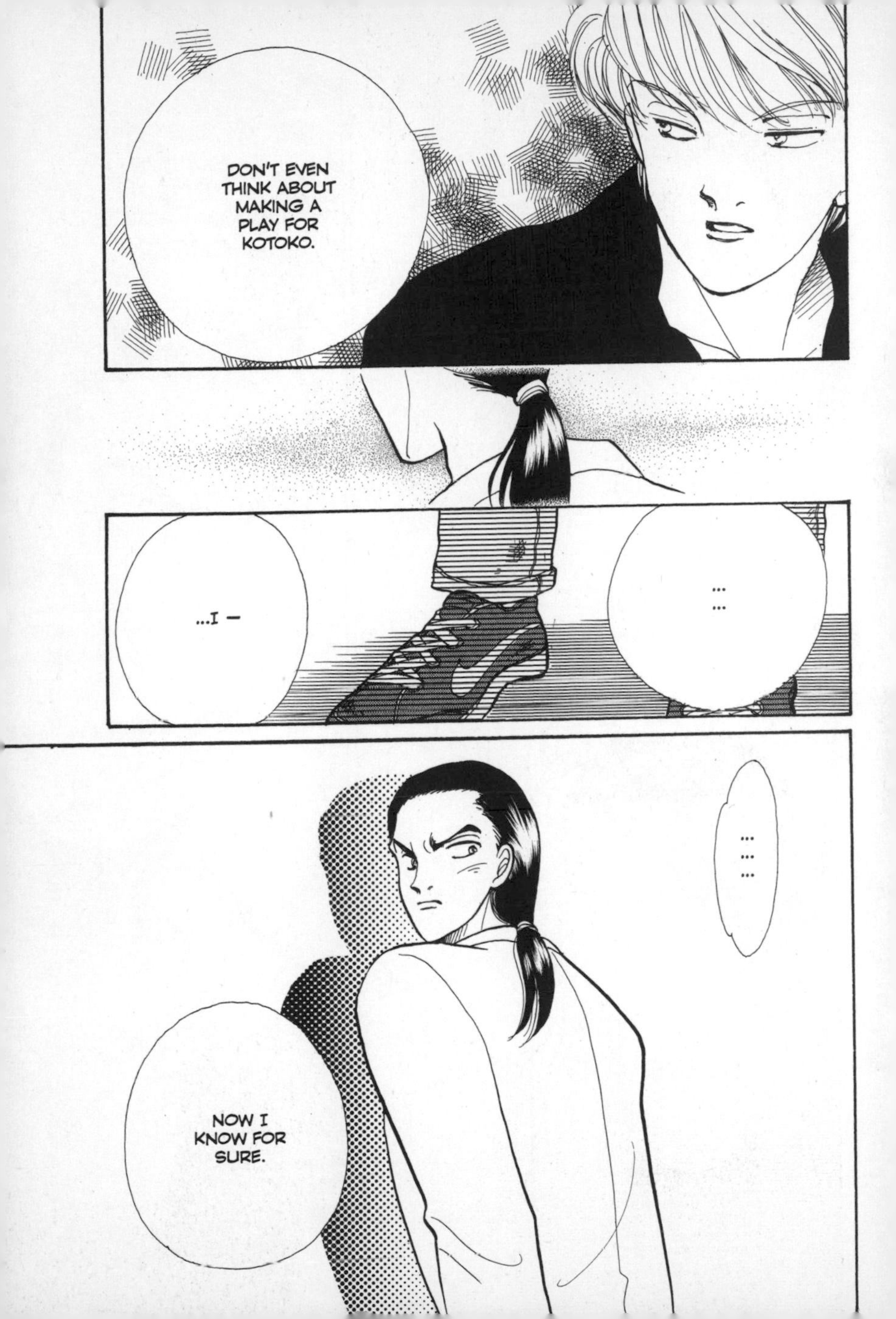
DON'T EVEN THINK ABOUT MAKING A PLAY FOR KOTOKO.
... ...
...I —
... ...
NOW I KNOW FOR SURE.

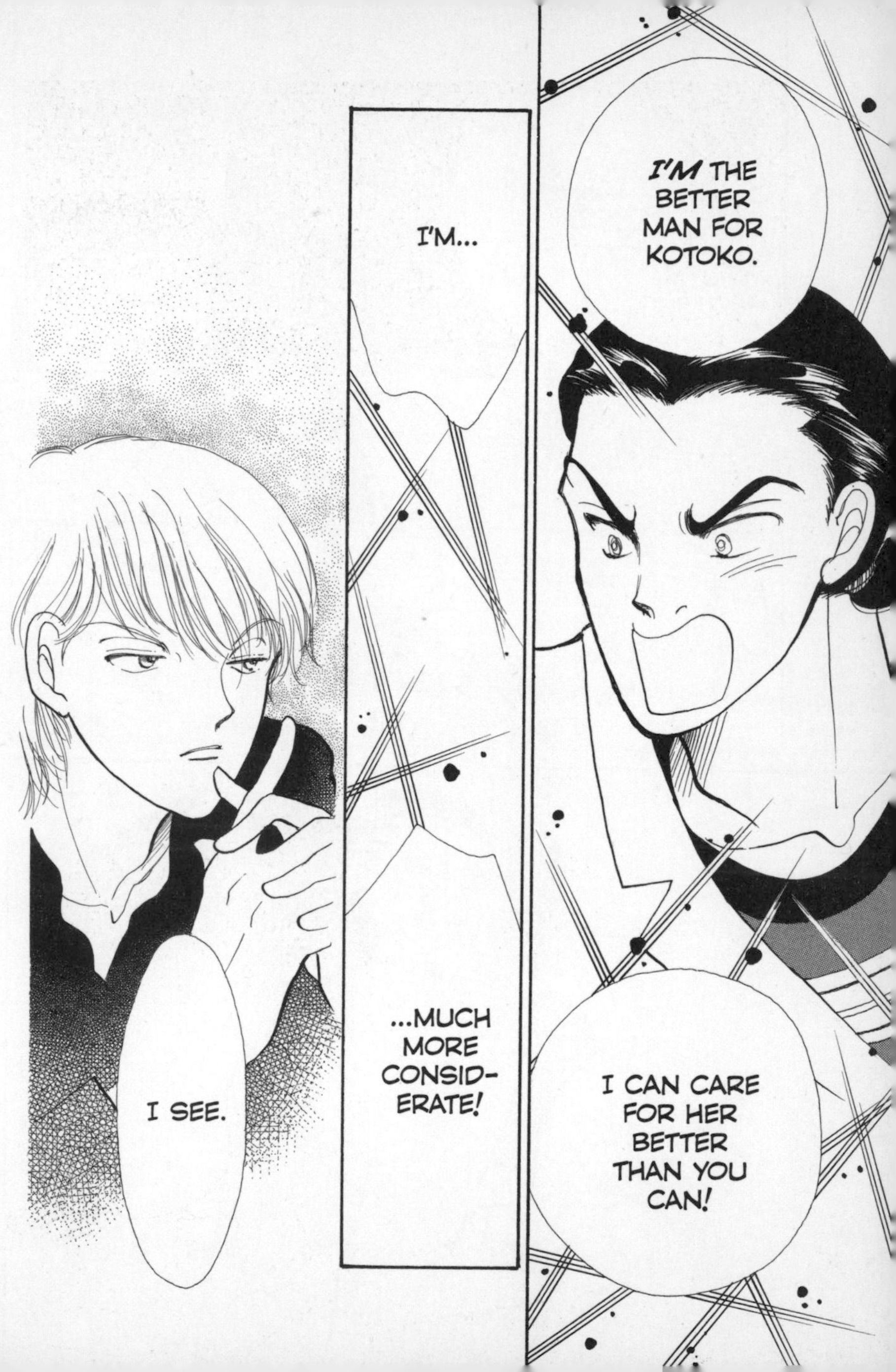
I'M THE BETTER MAN FOR KOTOKO.
I CAN CARE FOR HER BETTER THAN YOU CAN!
I'M...
...MUCH MORE CONSID-ERATE!
I SEE.

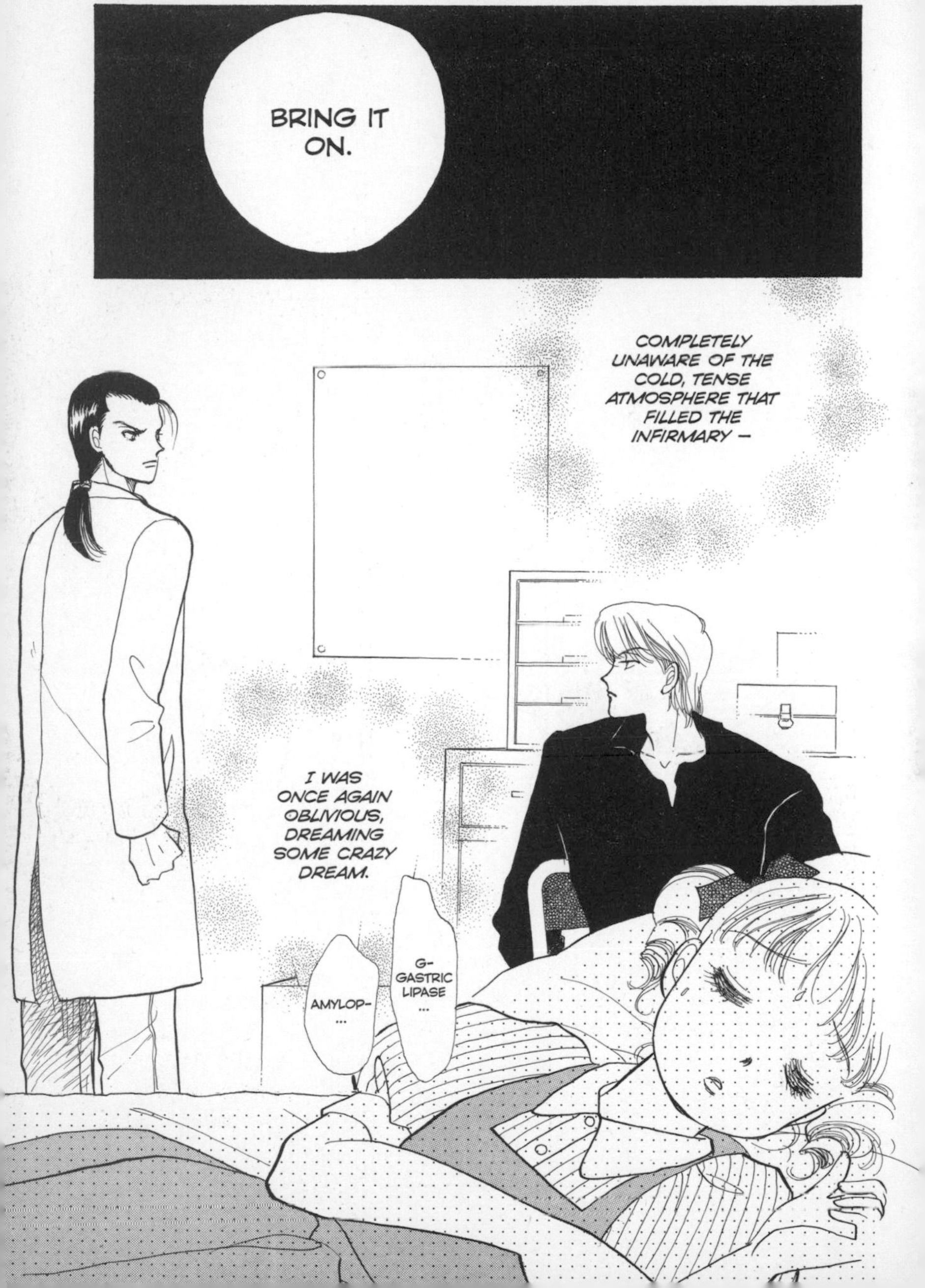
BRING IT ON.
COMPLETELY UNAWARE OF THE COLD, TENSE ATMOSPHERE THAT FILLED THE INFIRMARY –
I WAS ONCE AGAIN OBLIVIOUS, DREAMING SOME CRAZY DREAM.
G-GASTRIC LIPASE ...
AMYLOP- ...

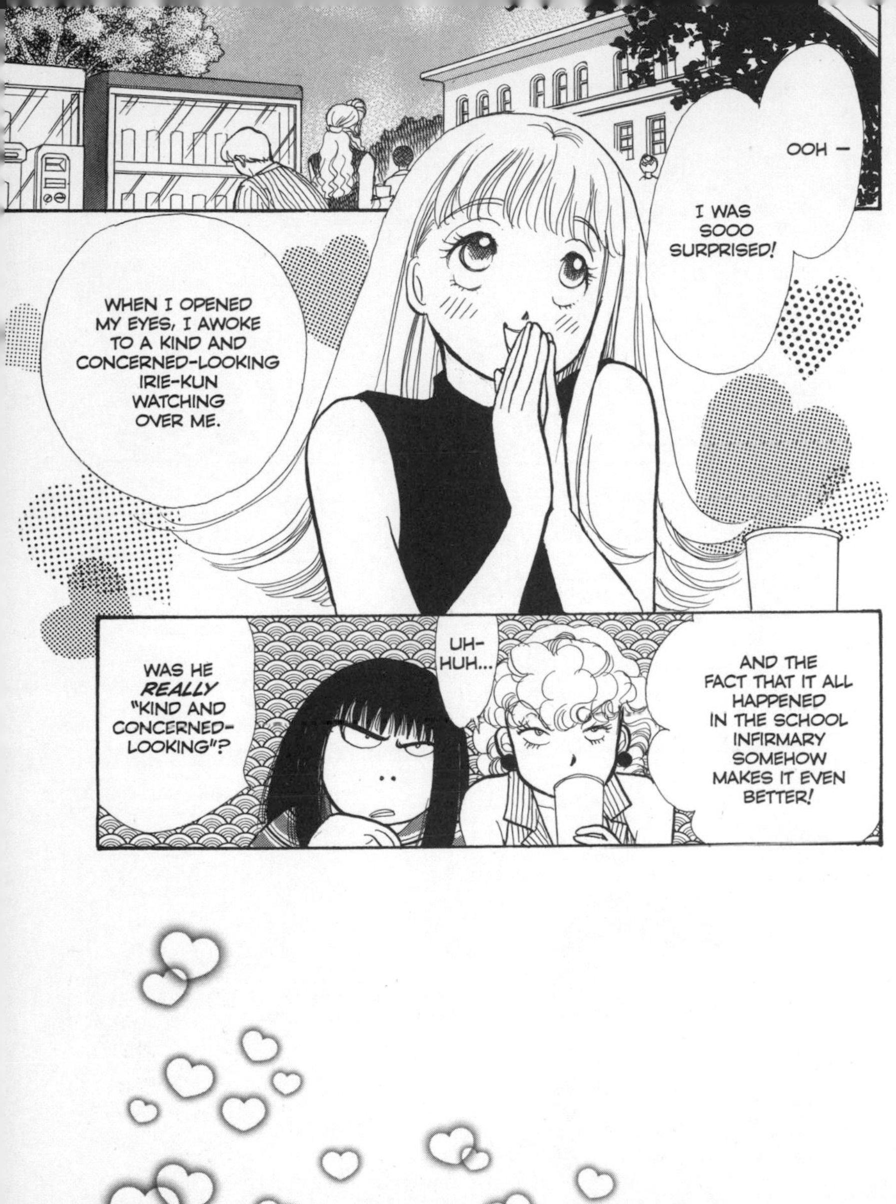
OOH — I WAS SOOO SURPRISED!
WHEN I OPENED MY EYES, I AWOKE TO A KIND AND CONCERNED-LOOKING IRIE-KUN WATCHING OVER ME.
AND THE FACT THAT IT ALL HAPPENED IN THE SCHOOL INFIRMARY SOMEHOW MAKES IT EVEN BETTER!
UH-HUH...
WAS HE REALLY "KIND AND CONCERNED-LOOKING"?

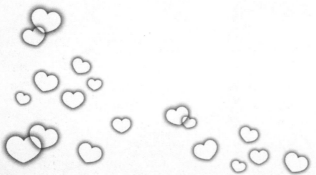

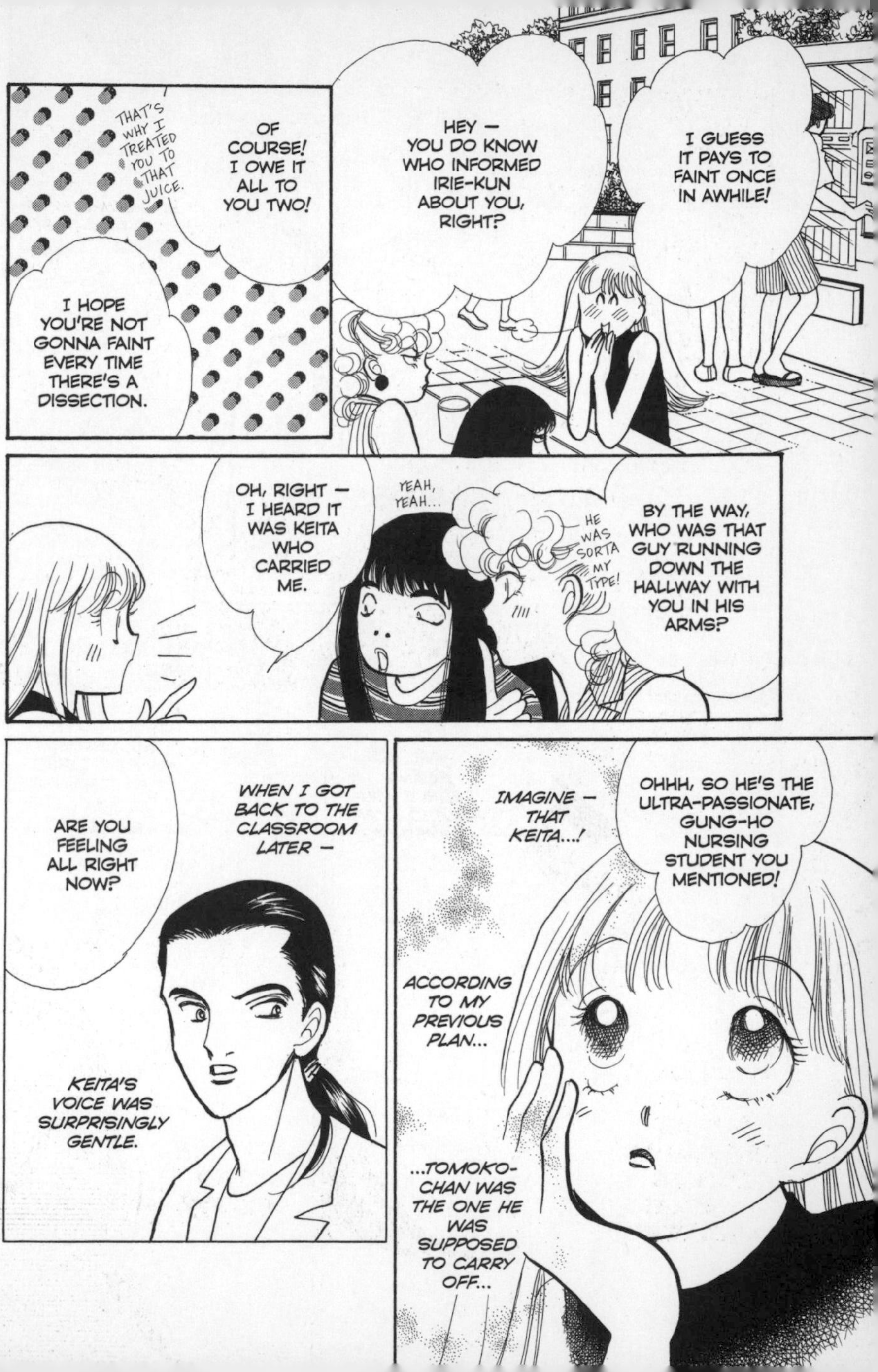
I GUESS IT PAYS TO FAINT ONCE IN AWHILE!
HEY — YOU DO KNOW WHO INFORMED IRIE-KUN ABOUT YOU, RIGHT?
OF COURSE! I OWE IT ALL TO YOU TWO!
THAT'S WHY I TREATED YOU TO THAT JUICE.
I HOPE YOU'RE NOT GONNA FAINT EVERY TIME THERE'S A DISSECTION.
BY THE WAY, WHO WAS THAT GUY RUNNING DOWN THE HALLWAY WITH YOU IN HIS ARMS?
HE WAS SORTA MY TYPE!
YEAH, YEAH...
OH, RIGHT — I HEARD IT WAS KEITA WHO CARRIED ME.
OHHH, SO HE'S THE ULTRA-PASSIONATE, GUNG-HO NURSING STUDENT YOU MENTIONED!
IMAGINE — THAT KEITA...!
ACCORDING TO MY PREVIOUS PLAN...
...TOMOKO-CHAN WAS THE ONE HE WAS SUPPOSED TO CARRY OFF...
WHEN I GOT BACK TO THE CLASSROOM LATER —
ARE YOU FEELING ALL RIGHT NOW?
KEITA'S VOICE WAS SURPRISINGLY GENTLE.

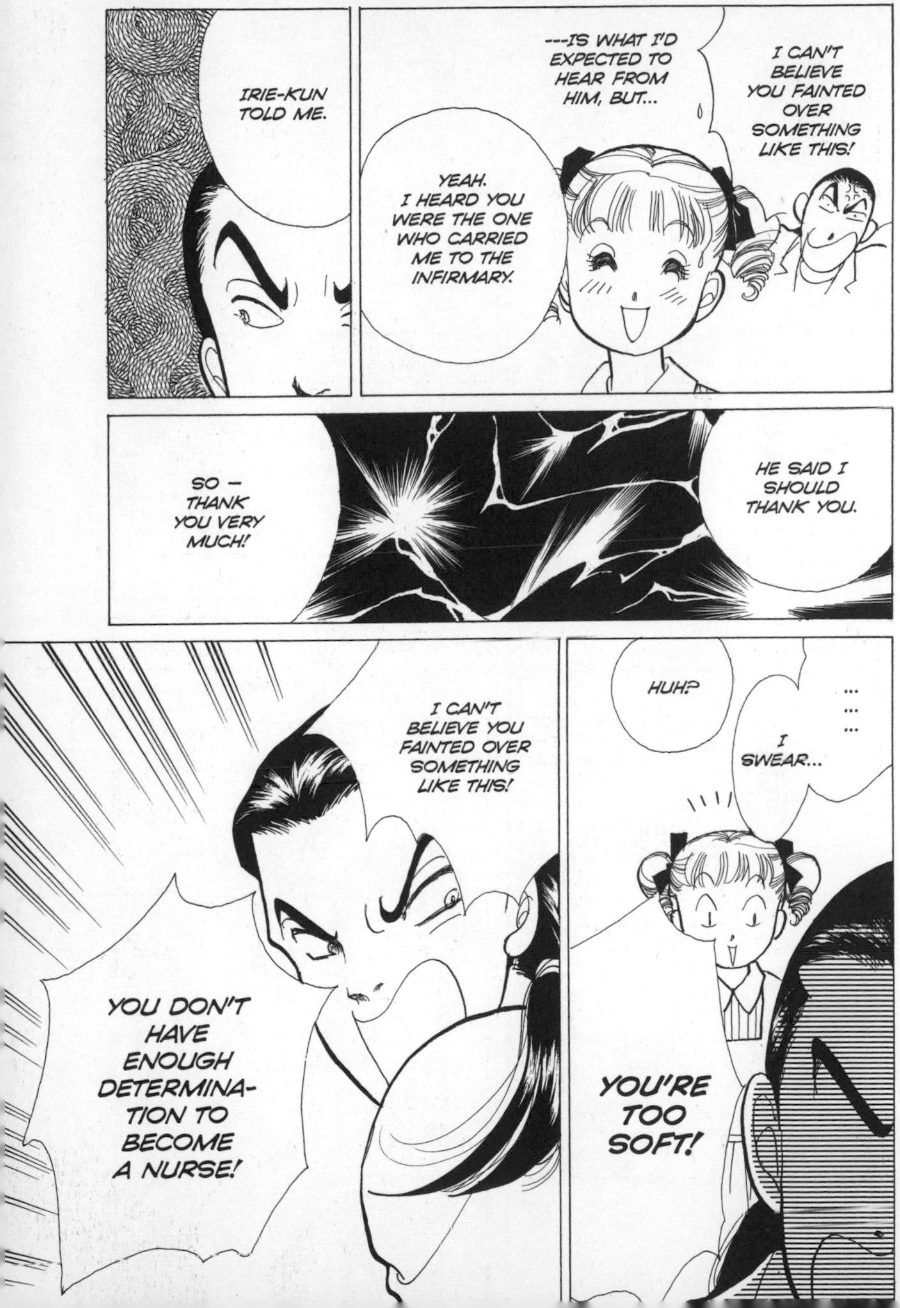
I CAN'T BELIEVE YOU FAINTED OVER SOMETHING LIKE THIS!
---IS WHAT I'D EXPECTED TO HEAR FROM HIM, BUT...
YEAH. I HEARD YOU WERE THE ONE WHO CARRIED ME TO THE INFIRMARY.
IRIE-KUN TOLD ME.
HE SAID I SHOULD THANK YOU.
SO — THANK YOU VERY MUCH!
HUH?
...
...
...
I SWEAR...
YOU'RE TOO SOFT!
I CAN'T BELIEVE YOU FAINTED OVER SOMETHING LIKE THIS!
YOU DON'T HAVE ENOUGH DETERMINA-TION TO BECOME A NURSE!

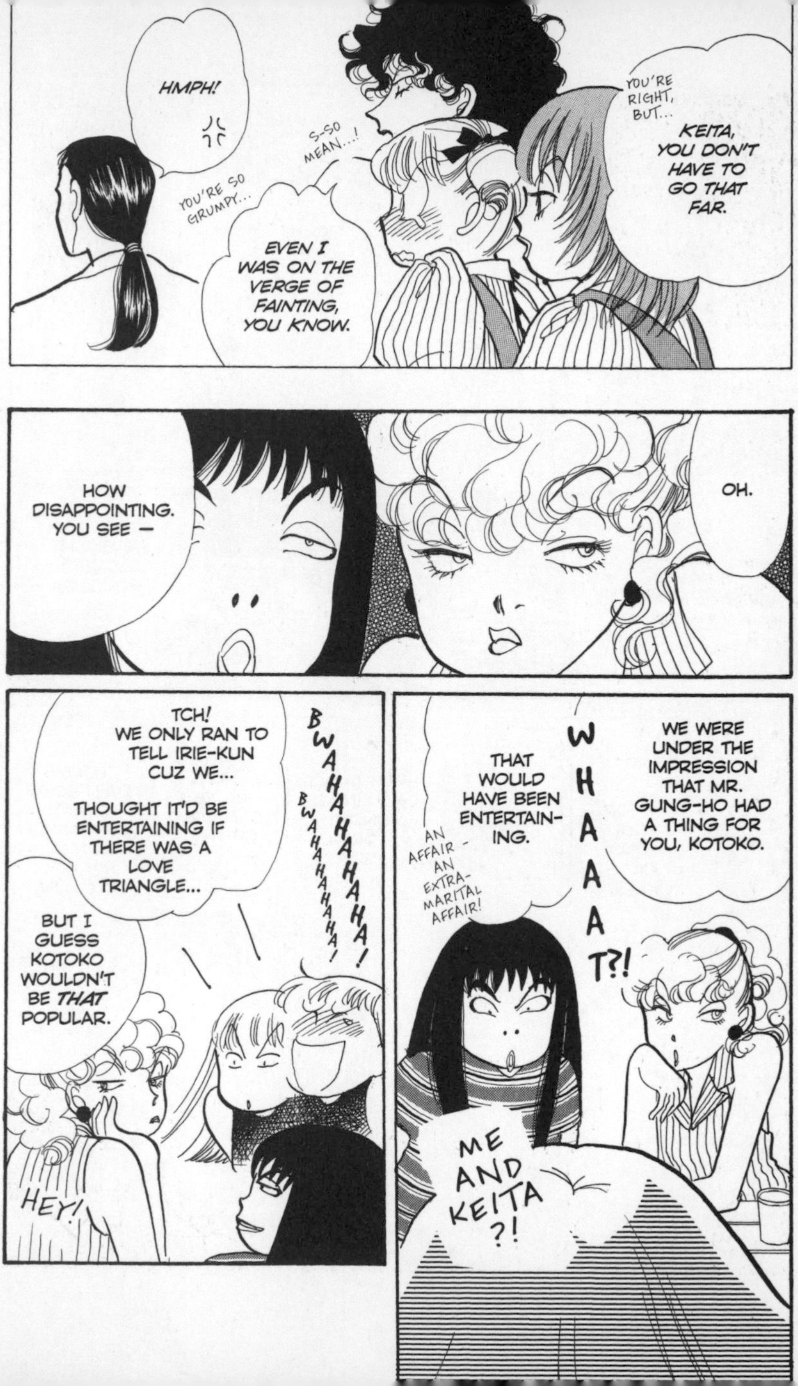
YOU'RE RIGHT, BUT...
KEITA, YOU DON'T HAVE TO GO THAT FAR.
S-SO MEAN...!
EVEN I WAS ON THE VERGE OF FAINTING, YOU KNOW.
YOU'RE SO GRUMPY...
HMPH!
OH.
HOW DISAPPOINTING. YOU SEE —
WE WERE UNDER THE IMPRESSION THAT MR. GUNG-HO HAD A THING FOR YOU, KOTOKO.
WHAAAT?!
THAT WOULD HAVE BEEN ENTERTAIN-ING.
AN AFFAIR - AN EXTRA-MARITAL AFFAIR!
ME AND KEITA?!
BWAHAHAHAHA!
BWAHAHAHAHA!
TCH! WE ONLY RAN TO TELL IRIE-KUN CUZ WE...
THOUGHT IT'D BE ENTERTAINING IF THERE WAS A LOVE TRIANGLE...
BUT I GUESS KOTOKO WOULDN'T BE *THAT* POPULAR.
HEY!

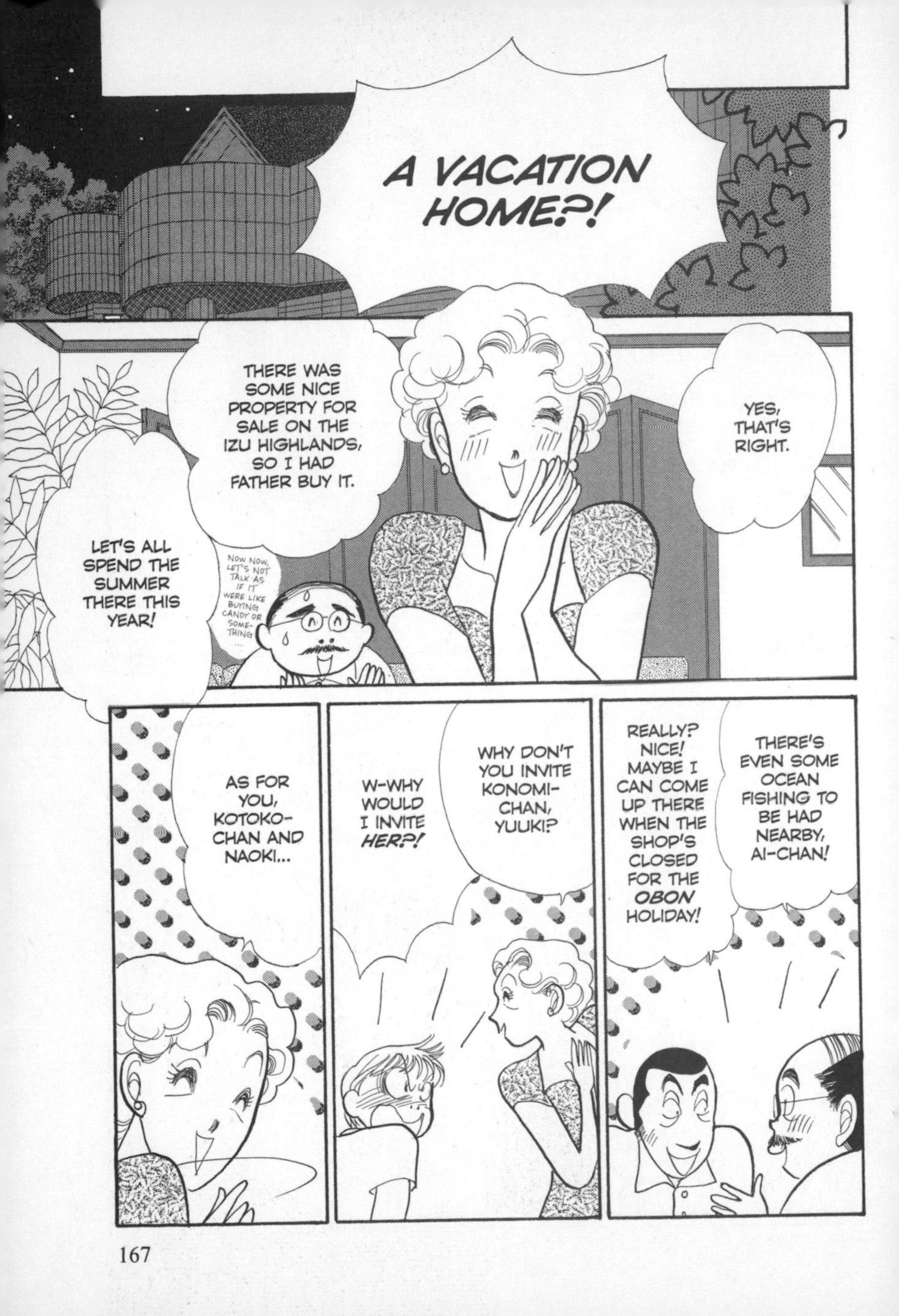
A VACATION HOME?!
YES, THAT'S RIGHT.
THERE WAS SOME NICE PROPERTY FOR SALE ON THE IZU HIGHLANDS, SO I HAD FATHER BUY IT.
LET'S ALL SPEND THE SUMMER THERE THIS YEAR!
NOW NOW, LET'S NOT TALK AS IF IT WERE LIKE BUYING CANDY OR SOMETHING...
THERE'S EVEN SOME OCEAN FISHING TO BE HAD NEARBY, AI-CHAN!
REALLY? NICE! MAYBE I CAN COME UP THERE WHEN THE SHOP'S CLOSED FOR THE *OBON* HOLIDAY!
WHY DON'T YOU INVITE KONOMI-CHAN, YUUKI?
W-WHY WOULD I INVITE *HER?!*
AS FOR YOU, KOTOKO-CHAN AND NAOKI...

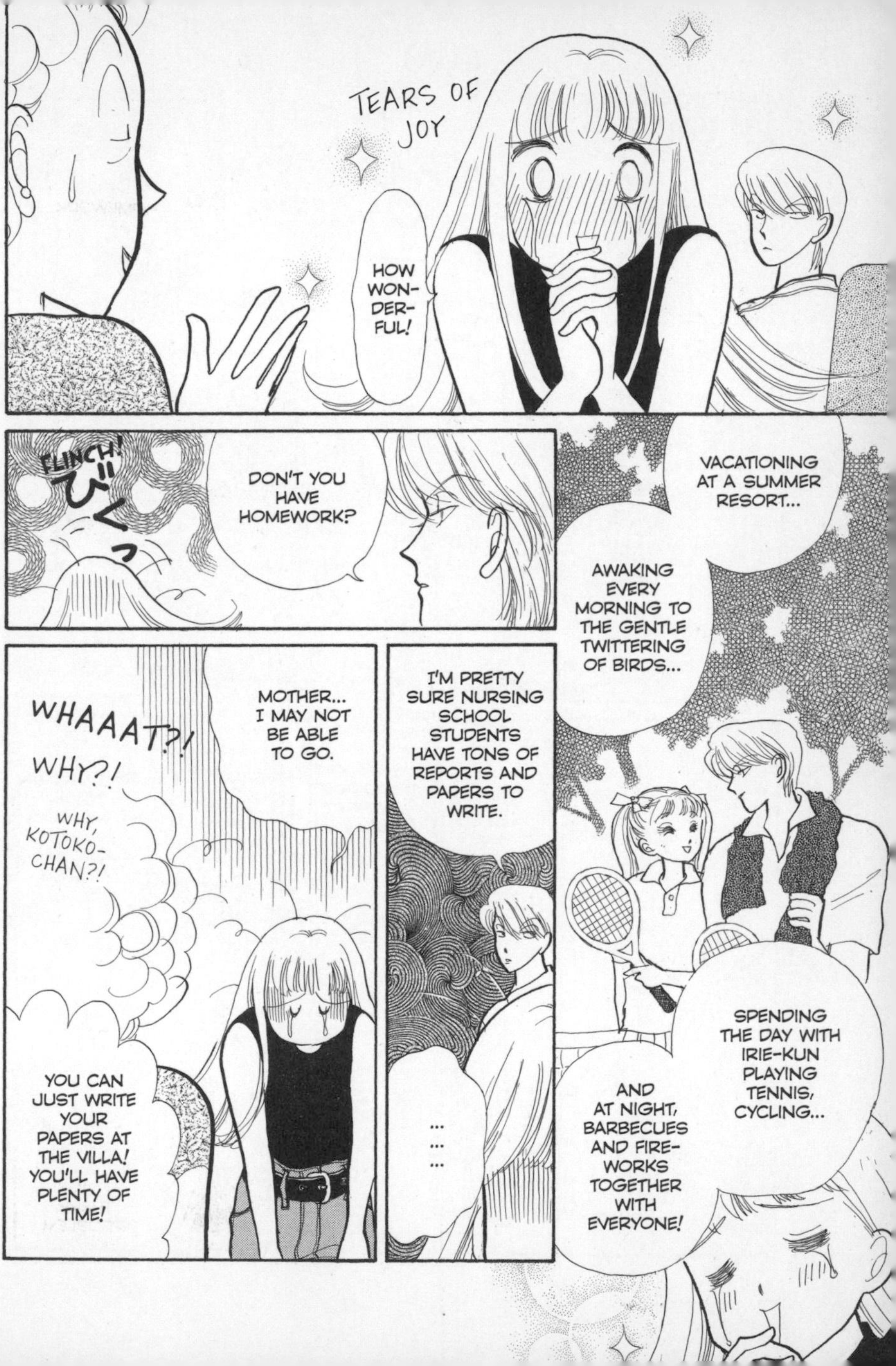
TEARS OF JOY
HOW WON-DER-FUL!
VACATIONING AT A SUMMER RESORT...
AWAKING EVERY MORNING TO THE GENTLE TWITTERING OF BIRDS...
SPENDING THE DAY WITH IRIE-KUN PLAYING TENNIS, CYCLING...
AND AT NIGHT, BARBECUES AND FIRE-WORKS TOGETHER WITH EVERYONE!
DON'T YOU HAVE HOMEWORK?
FLINCH! びくっ
I'M PRETTY SURE NURSING SCHOOL STUDENTS HAVE TONS OF REPORTS AND PAPERS TO WRITE.
....
MOTHER... I MAY NOT BE ABLE TO GO.
WHAAAT?!
WHY?!
WHY, KOTOKO-CHAN?!
YOU CAN JUST WRITE YOUR PAPERS AT THE VILLA! YOU'LL HAVE PLENTY OF TIME!

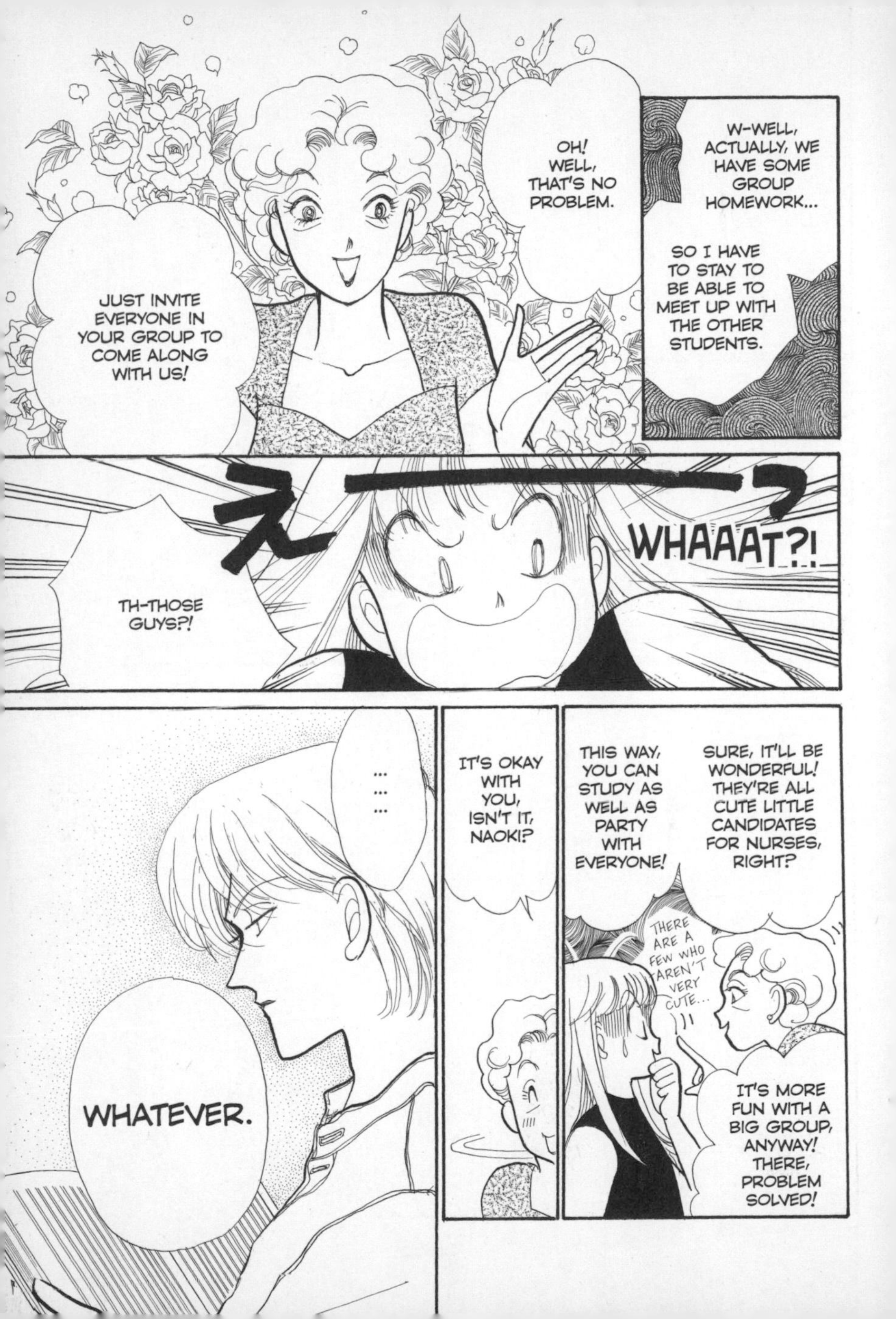

W-WELL, ACTUALLY, WE HAVE SOME GROUP HOMEWORK...
SO I HAVE TO STAY TO BE ABLE TO MEET UP WITH THE OTHER STUDENTS.
OH! WELL, THAT'S NO PROBLEM.
JUST INVITE EVERYONE IN YOUR GROUP TO COME ALONG WITH US!
えーっ
WHAAAT?!
TH-THOSE GUYS?!
SURE, IT'LL BE WONDERFUL! THEY'RE ALL CUTE LITTLE CANDIDATES FOR NURSES, RIGHT?
THIS WAY, YOU CAN STUDY AS WELL AS PARTY WITH EVERYONE!
THERE ARE A FEW WHO AREN'T VERY CUTE...
IT'S MORE FUN WITH A BIG GROUP, ANYWAY! THERE, PROBLEM SOLVED!
IT'S OKAY WITH YOU, ISN'T IT, NAOKI?
... ...
WHATEVER.

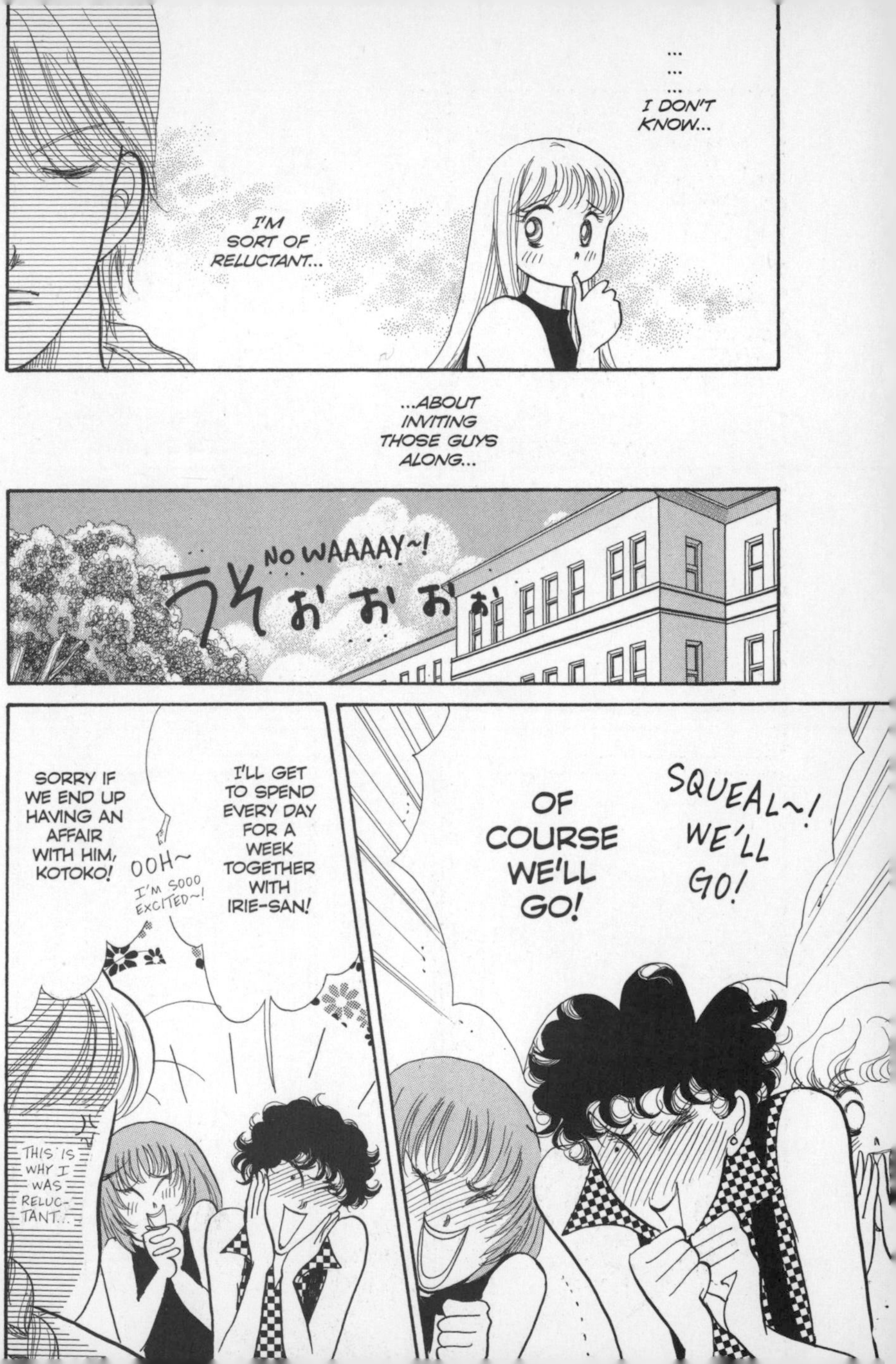
...
...
...
I DON'T KNOW...
I'M SORT OF RELUCTANT...
...ABOUT INVITING THOSE GUYS ALONG...
うそおおおお
No WAAAAY~!
SQUEAL~! WE'LL GO!
OF COURSE WE'LL GO!
I'LL GET TO SPEND EVERY DAY FOR A WEEK TOGETHER WITH IRIE-SAN!
OOH~ I'M SOOO EXCITED~!
SORRY IF WE END UP HAVING AN AFFAIR WITH HIM, KOTOKO!
THIS IS WHY I WAS RELUC-TANT...

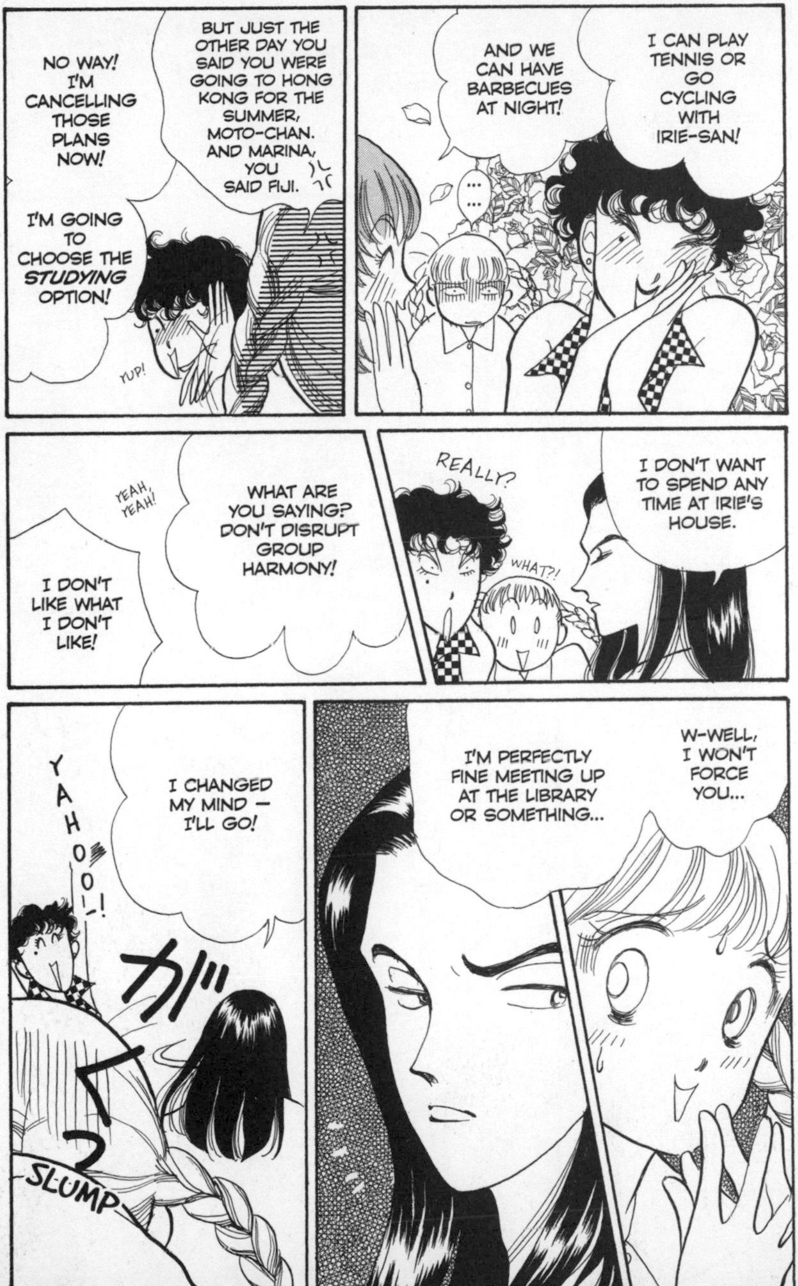
I CAN PLAY TENNIS OR GO CYCLING WITH IRIE-SAN!
AND WE CAN HAVE BARBECUES AT NIGHT!
... ...
BUT JUST THE OTHER DAY YOU SAID YOU WERE GOING TO HONG KONG FOR THE SUMMER, MOTO-CHAN. AND MARINA, YOU SAID FIJI.
NO WAY! I'M CANCELLING THOSE PLANS NOW!
I'M GOING TO CHOOSE THE *STUDYING* OPTION!
YUP!
I DON'T WANT TO SPEND ANY TIME AT IRIE'S HOUSE.
REALLY?
WHAT?!
WHAT ARE YOU SAYING? DON'T DISRUPT GROUP HARMONY!
YEAH, YEAH!
I DON'T LIKE WHAT I DON'T LIKE!
W-WELL, I WON'T FORCE YOU...
I'M PERFECTLY FINE MEETING UP AT THE LIBRARY OR SOMETHING...
I CHANGED MY MIND — I'LL GO!
YAHOOO!
ガ
くっ
SLUMP

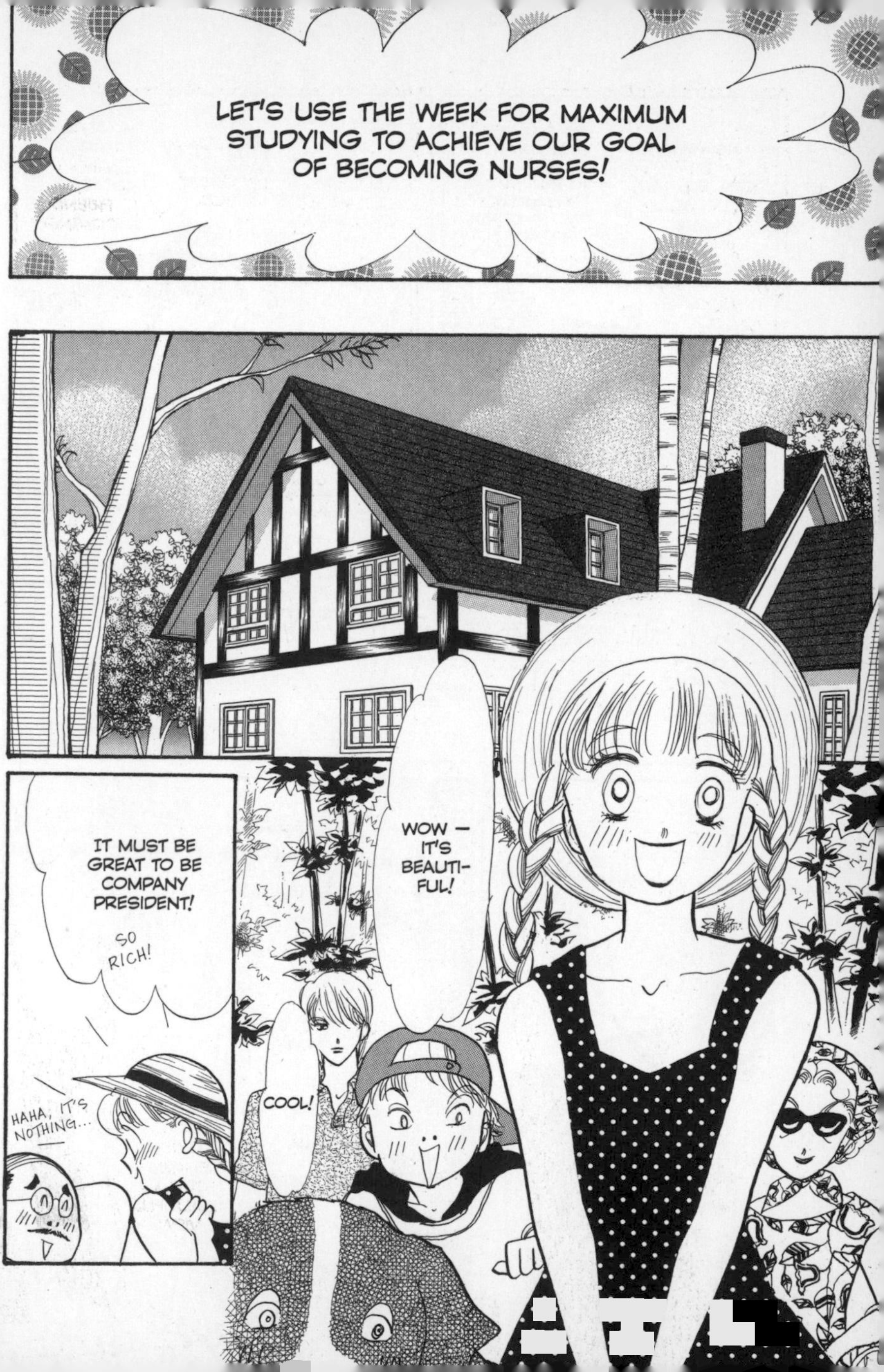
LET'S USE THE WEEK FOR MAXIMUM STUDYING TO ACHIEVE OUR GOAL OF BECOMING NURSES!
WOW — IT'S BEAUTI-FUL!
COOL!
IT MUST BE GREAT TO BE COMPANY PRESIDENT!
SO RICH!
HAHA, IT'S NOTHING...

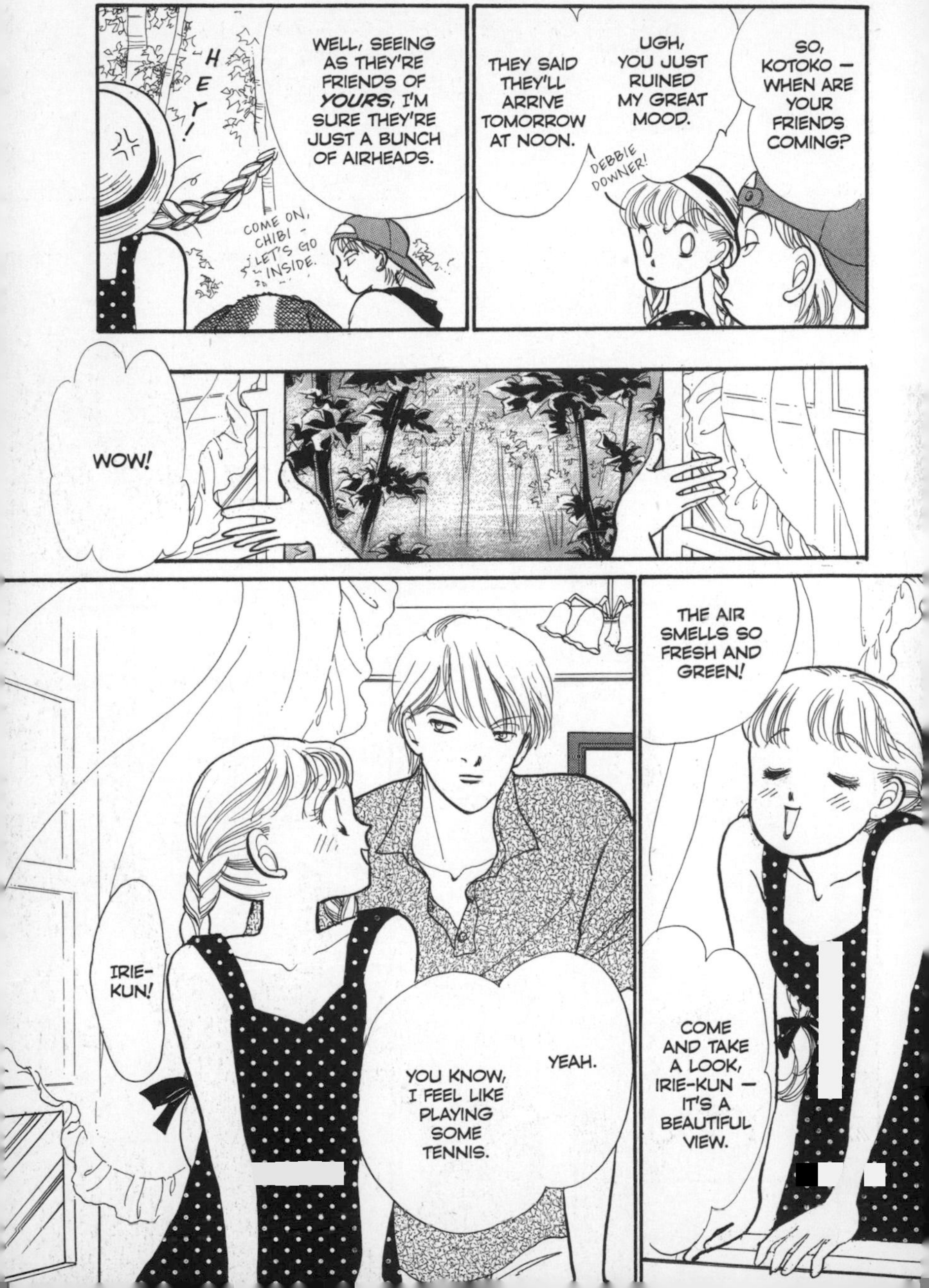
SO, KOTOKO — WHEN ARE YOUR FRIENDS COMING?
UGH, YOU JUST RUINED MY GREAT MOOD.
DEBBIE DOWNER!
THEY SAID THEY'LL ARRIVE TOMORROW AT NOON.
WELL, SEEING AS THEY'RE FRIENDS OF *YOURS*, I'M SURE THEY'RE JUST A BUNCH OF AIRHEADS.
HEY!
COME ON, CHIBI — LET'S GO INSIDE.
WOW!
THE AIR SMELLS SO FRESH AND GREEN!
COME AND TAKE A LOOK, IRIE-KUN — IT'S A BEAUTIFUL VIEW.
IRIE-KUN!
YEAH.
YOU KNOW, I FEEL LIKE PLAYING SOME TENNIS.

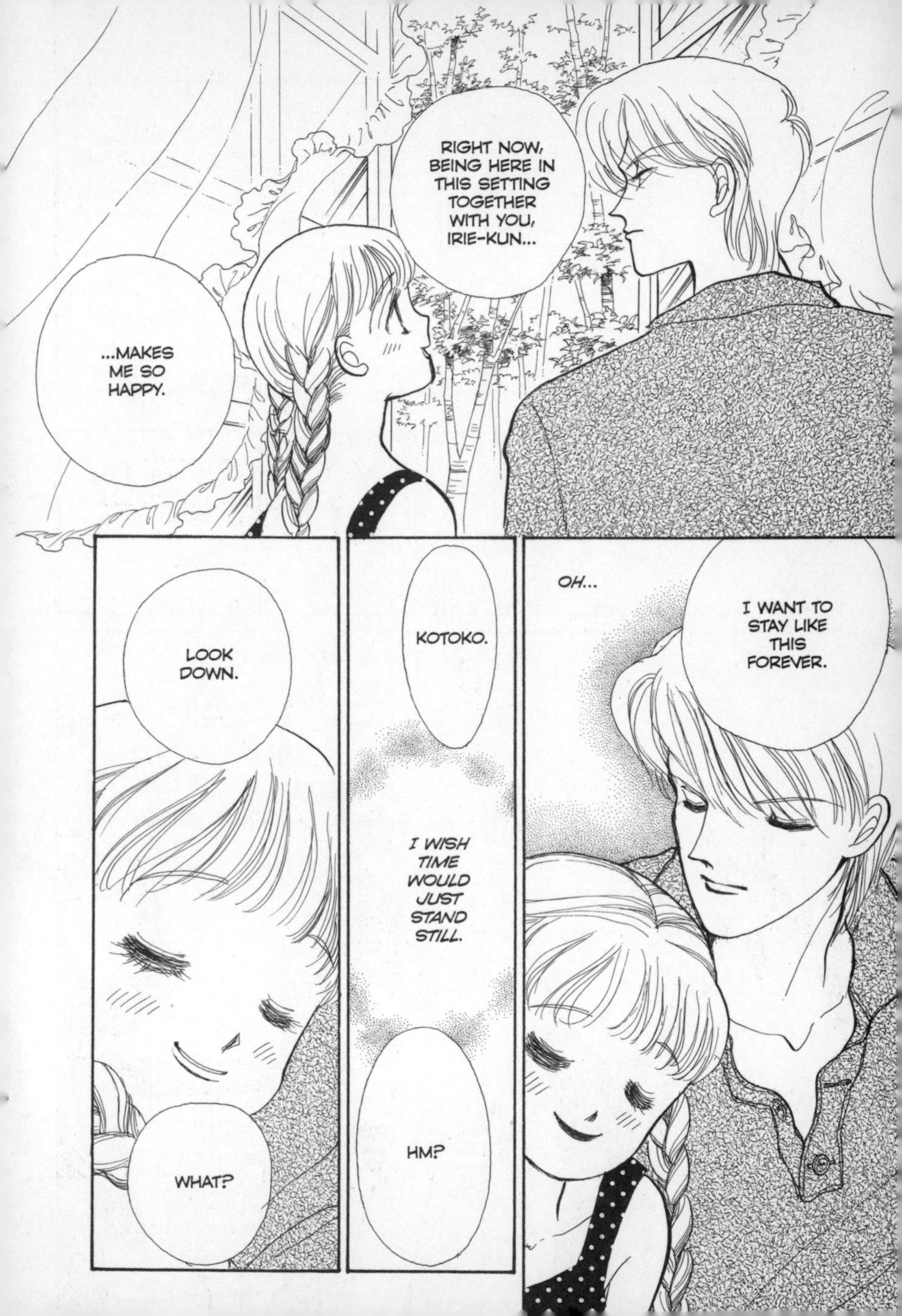
RIGHT NOW, BEING HERE IN THIS SETTING TOGETHER WITH YOU, IRIE-KUN...
...MAKES ME SO HAPPY.
I WANT TO STAY LIKE THIS FOREVER.
OH...
KOTOKO.
I WISH TIME WOULD JUST STAND STILL.
HM?
LOOK DOWN.
WHAT?

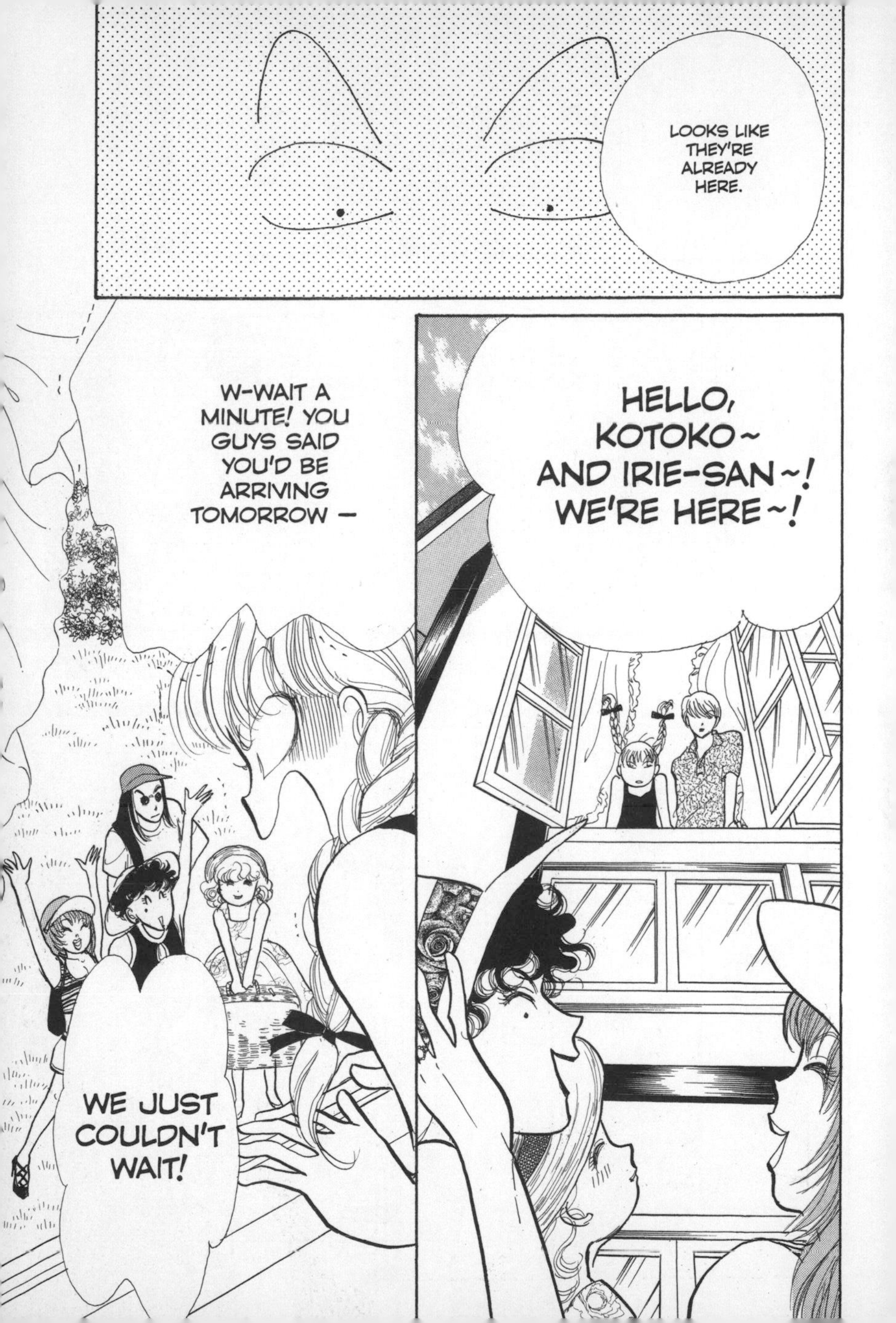
LOOKS LIKE THEY'RE ALREADY HERE.
HELLO, KOTOKO~ AND IRIE-SAN~! WE'RE HERE~!
W-WAIT A MINUTE! YOU GUYS SAID YOU'D BE ARRIVING TOMORROW -
WE JUST COULDN'T WAIT!

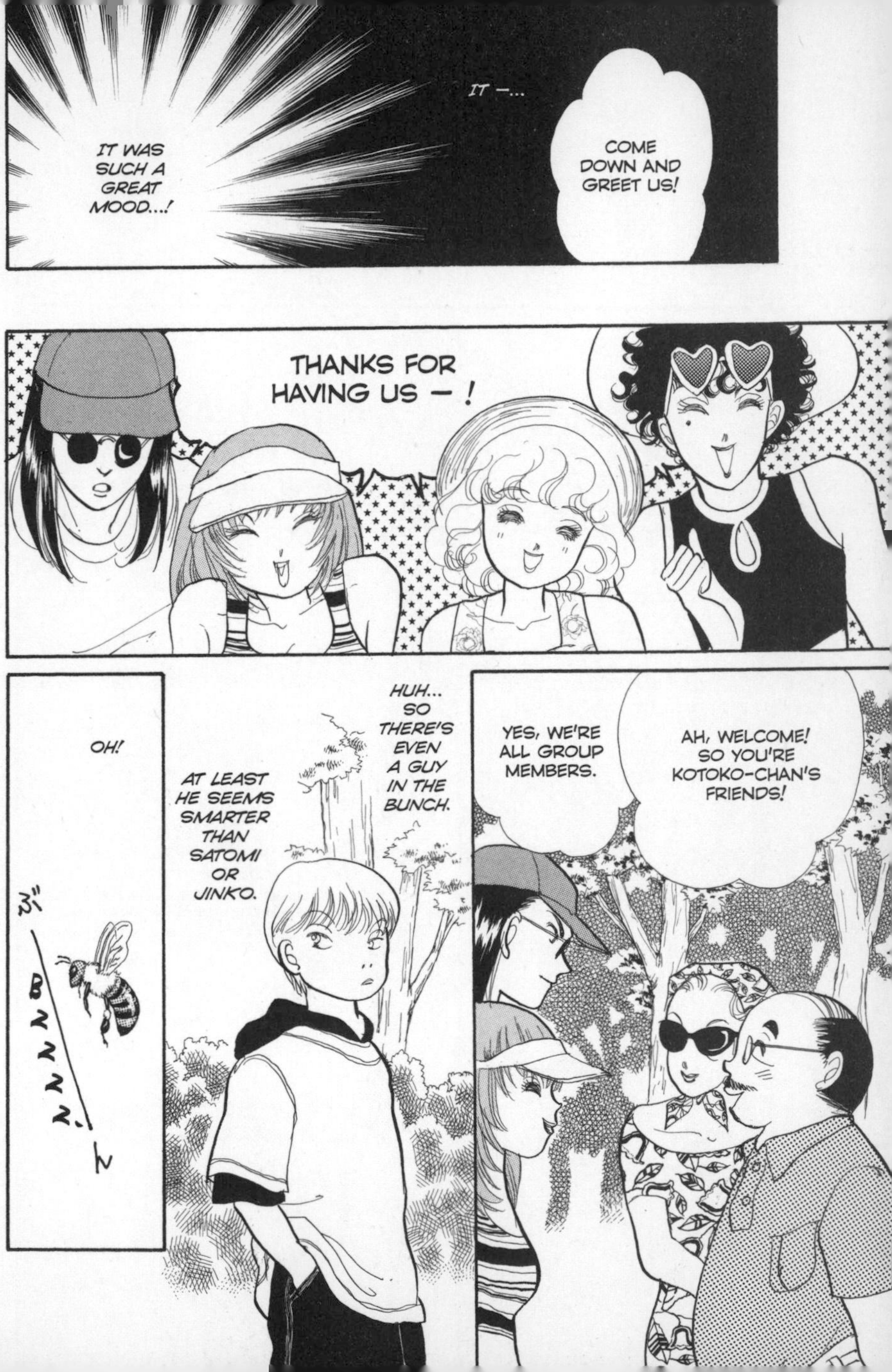
COME DOWN AND GREET US!
IT —...
IT WAS SUCH A GREAT MOOD...!
THANKS FOR HAVING US —!
AH, WELCOME! SO YOU'RE KOTOKO-CHAN'S FRIENDS!
YES, WE'RE ALL GROUP MEMBERS.
HUH... SO THERE'S EVEN A GUY IN THE BUNCH.
AT LEAST HE SEEMS SMARTER THAN SATOMI OR JINKO.
OH!
ぶ
BNNNN...N

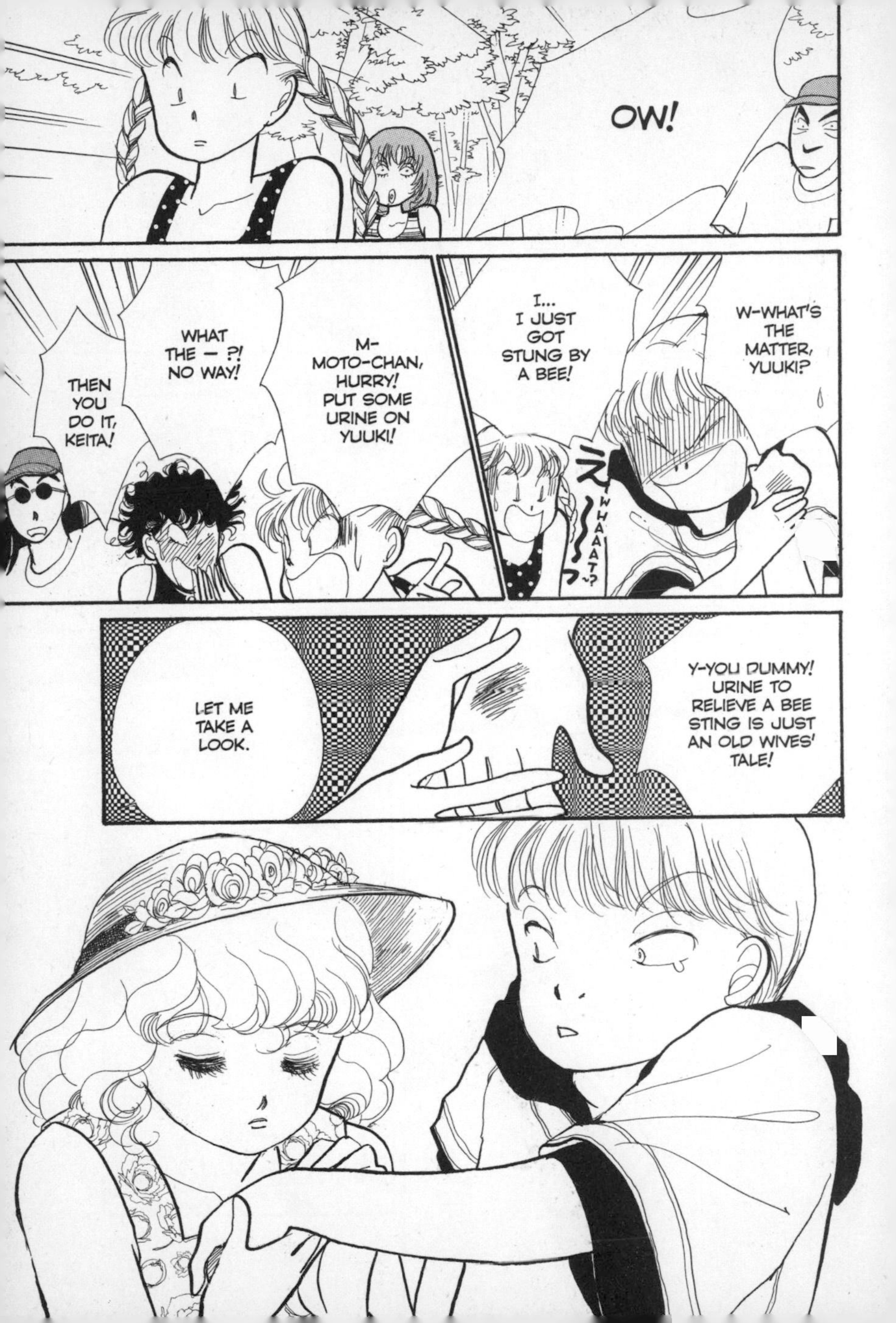

OW!
W-WHAT'S THE MATTER, YUUKI?
I... I JUST GOT STUNG BY A BEE!
え〜〜っ
WHAAAT~?
M-MOTO-CHAN, HURRY! PUT SOME URINE ON YUUKI!
WHAT THE — ?! NO WAY!
THEN YOU DO IT, KEITA!
Y-YOU DUMMY! URINE TO RELIEVE A BEE STING IS JUST AN OLD WIVES' TALE!
LET ME TAKE A LOOK.

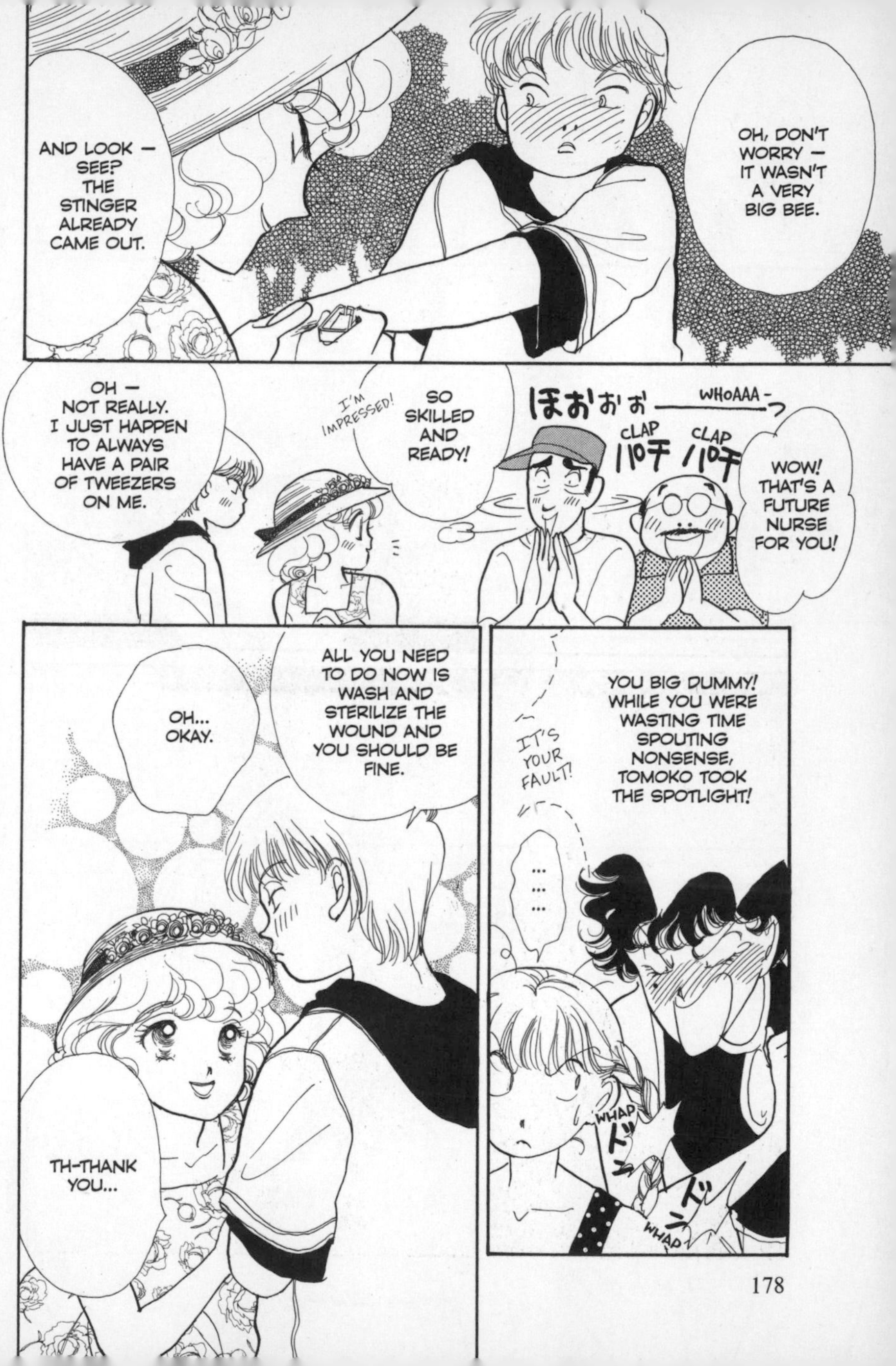
OH, DON'T WORRY — IT WASN'T A VERY BIG BEE.
AND LOOK — SEE? THE STINGER ALREADY CAME OUT.
ほおおぉ — WHOAAA—っ
CLAP パチ CLAP パチ
WOW! THAT'S A FUTURE NURSE FOR YOU!
SO SKILLED AND READY!
I'M IMPRESSED!
OH — NOT REALLY. I JUST HAPPEN TO ALWAYS HAVE A PAIR OF TWEEZERS ON ME.
YOU BIG DUMMY! WHILE YOU WERE WASTING TIME SPOUTING NONSENSE, TOMOKO TOOK THE SPOTLIGHT!
IT'S YOUR FAULT!
... ...
WHAP
WHAP
ALL YOU NEED TO DO NOW IS WASH AND STERILIZE THE WOUND AND YOU SHOULD BE FINE.
OH... OKAY.
TH-THANK YOU...

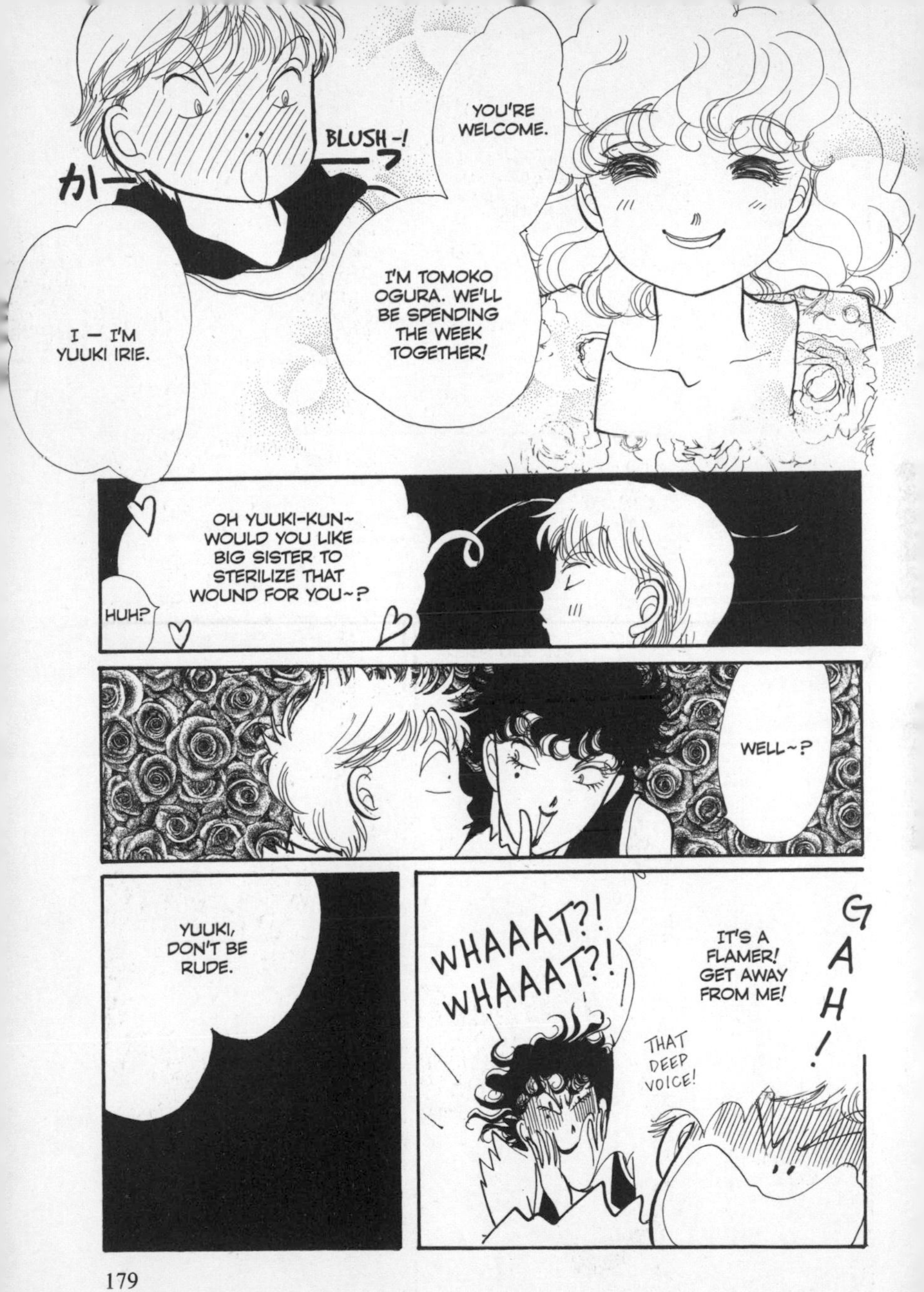
YOU'RE WELCOME.
I'M TOMOKO OGURA. WE'LL BE SPENDING THE WEEK TOGETHER!
BLUSH -!
カー
I — I'M YUUKI IRIE.
OH YUUKI-KUN~ WOULD YOU LIKE BIG SISTER TO STERILIZE THAT WOUND FOR YOU~?
HUH?
WELL~?
GAH!
IT'S A FLAMER! GET AWAY FROM ME!
THAT DEEP VOICE!
WHAAAT?! WHAAAT?!
YUUKI, DON'T BE RUDE.

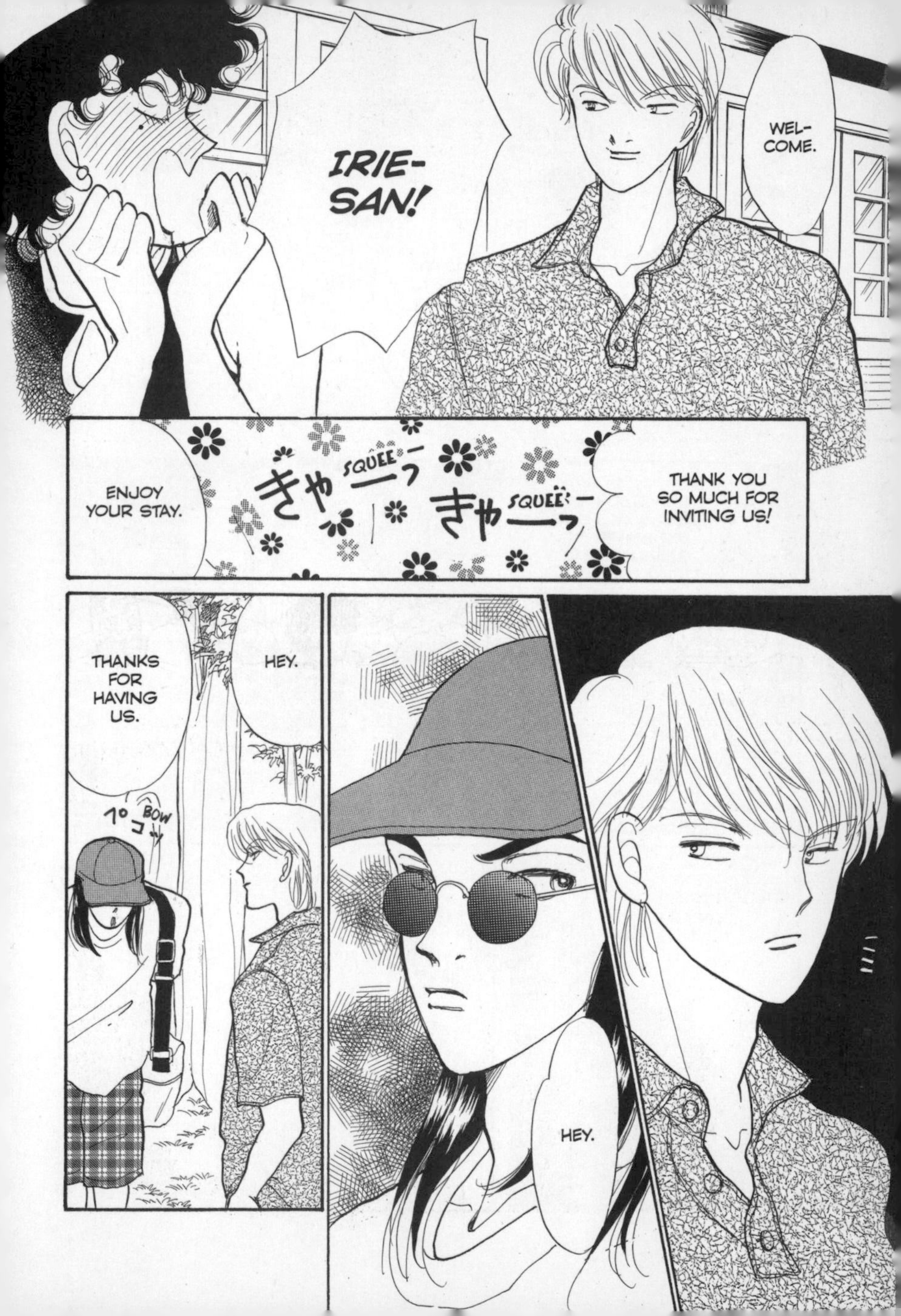
WEL-
COME.
IRIE-
SAN!
THANK YOU SO MUCH FOR INVITING US!
きゃーっ SQUEEE
きゃーっ SQUEEE
ENJOY YOUR STAY.
HEY.
HEY.
THANKS FOR HAVING US.
ペコッ BOW

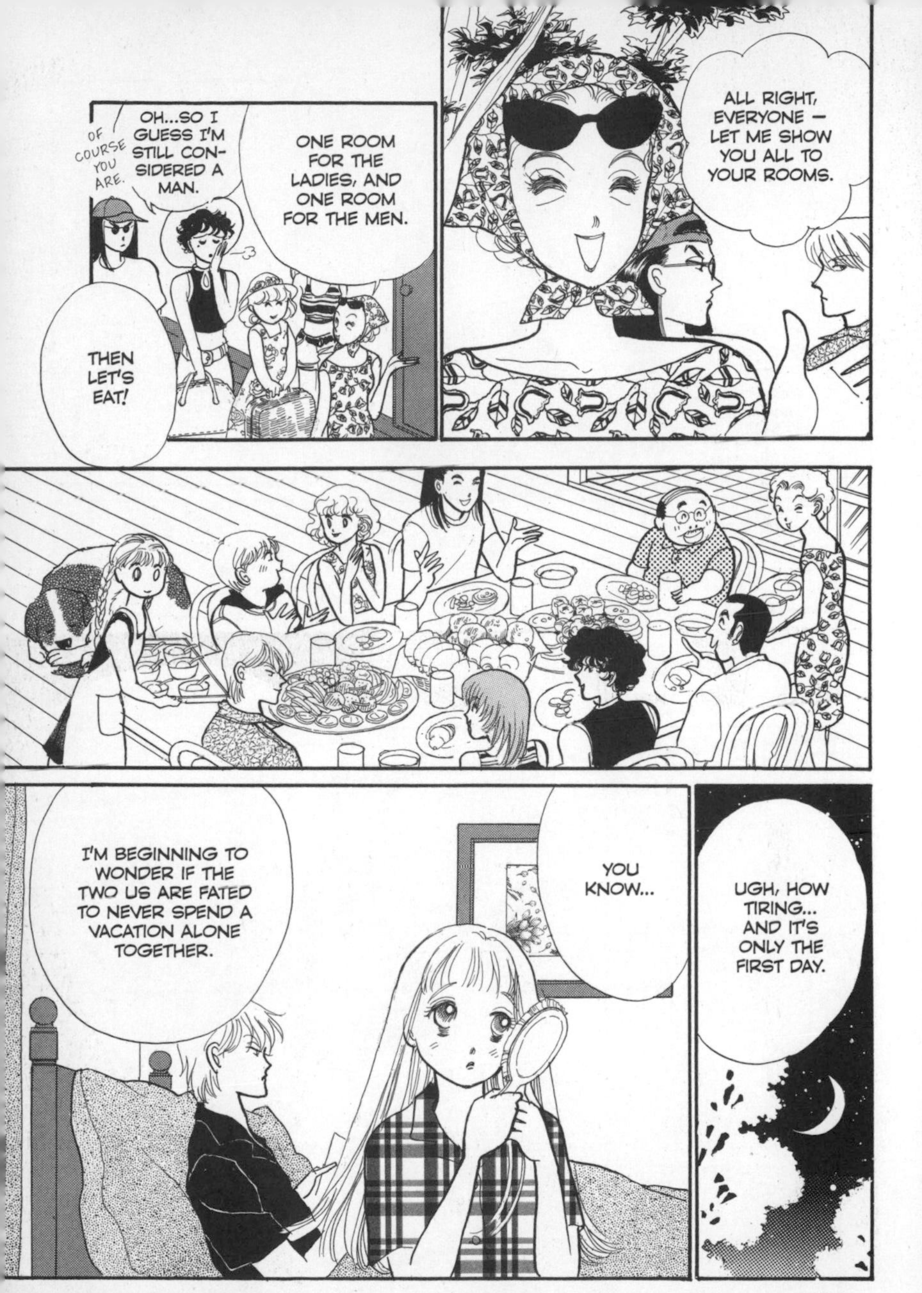
ALL RIGHT, EVERYONE — LET ME SHOW YOU ALL TO YOUR ROOMS.
ONE ROOM FOR THE LADIES, AND ONE ROOM FOR THE MEN.
OH...SO I GUESS I'M STILL CON-SIDERED A MAN.
OF COURSE YOU ARE.
THEN LET'S EAT!
UGH, HOW TIRING... AND IT'S ONLY THE FIRST DAY.
YOU KNOW...
I'M BEGINNING TO WONDER IF THE TWO US ARE FATED TO NEVER SPEND A VACATION ALONE TOGETHER.

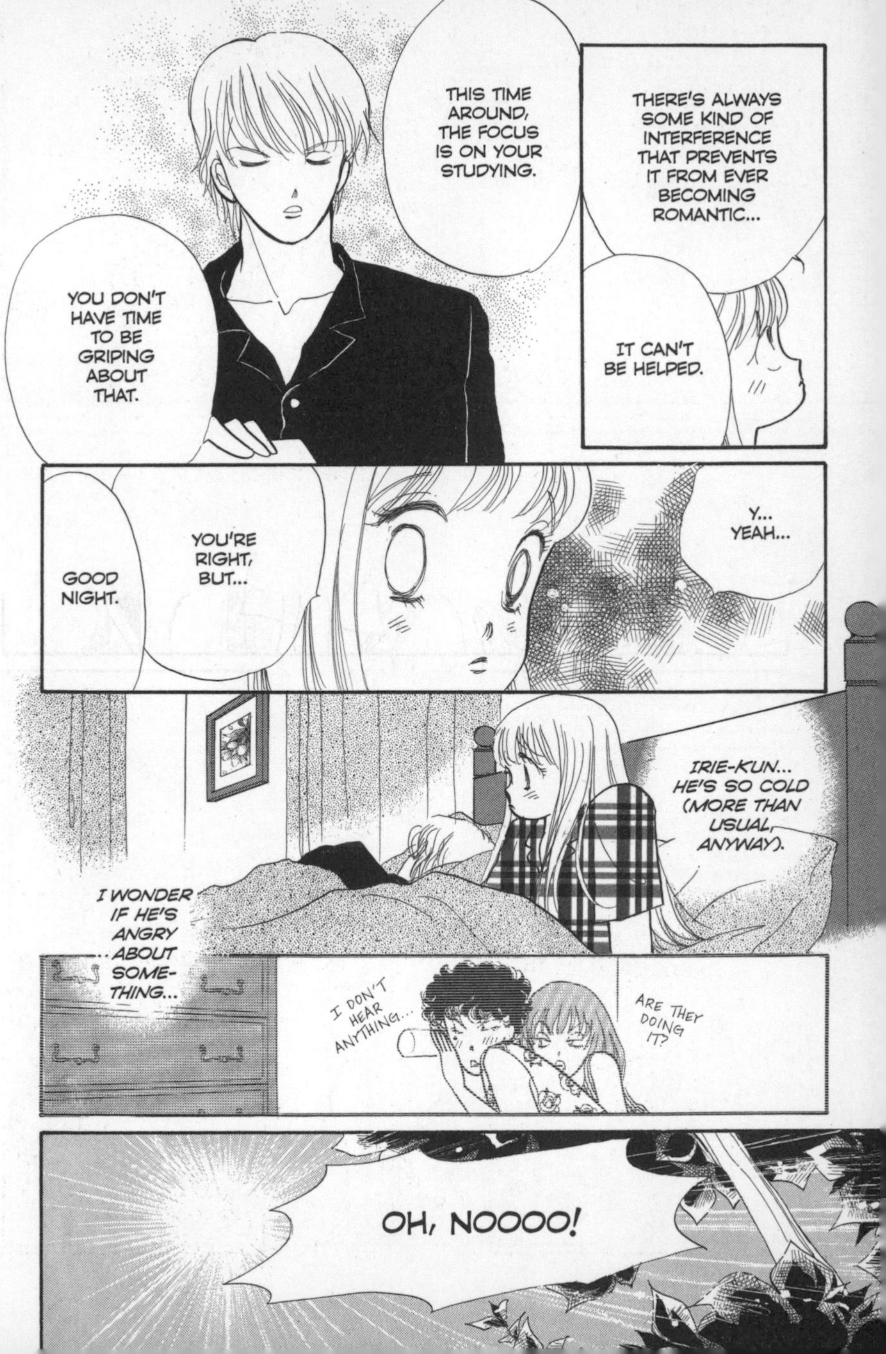
THERE'S ALWAYS SOME KIND OF INTERFERENCE THAT PREVENTS IT FROM EVER BECOMING ROMANTIC...
IT CAN'T BE HELPED.
THIS TIME AROUND, THE FOCUS IS ON YOUR STUDYING.
YOU DON'T HAVE TIME TO BE GRIPING ABOUT THAT.
Y... YEAH...
YOU'RE RIGHT, BUT...
GOOD NIGHT.
IRIE-KUN... HE'S SO COLD (MORE THAN USUAL, ANYWAY).
I WONDER IF HE'S ANGRY ABOUT SOME-THING...
ARE THEY DOING IT?
I DON'T HEAR ANYTHING...
OH, NOOOO!

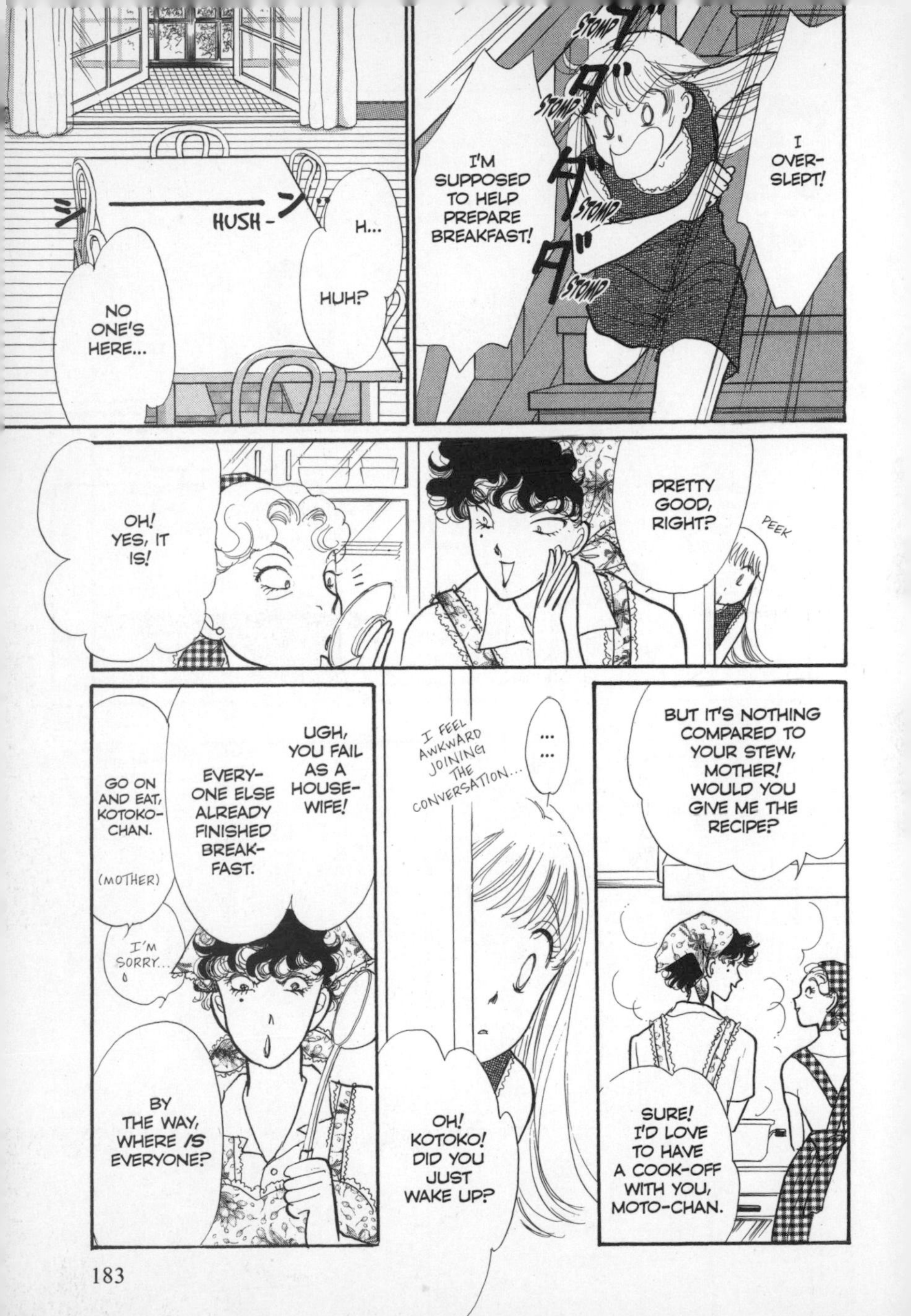
I OVER-SLEPT!
STOMP STOMP STOMP STOMP
I'M SUPPOSED TO HELP PREPARE BREAKFAST!
HUSH-
H...
HUH?
NO ONE'S HERE...
PRETTY GOOD, RIGHT?
PEEK
OH! YES, IT IS!
BUT IT'S NOTHING COMPARED TO YOUR STEW, MOTHER! WOULD YOU GIVE ME THE RECIPE?
SURE! I'D LOVE TO HAVE A COOK-OFF WITH YOU, MOTO-CHAN.
... ...
I FEEL AWKWARD JOINING THE CONVERSATION...
OH! KOTOKO! DID YOU JUST WAKE UP?
UGH, YOU FAIL AS A HOUSE-WIFE!
EVERY-ONE ELSE ALREADY FINISHED BREAK-FAST.
GO ON AND EAT, KOTOKO-CHAN.
(MOTHER)
I'M SORRY...
BY THE WAY, WHERE IS EVERYONE?

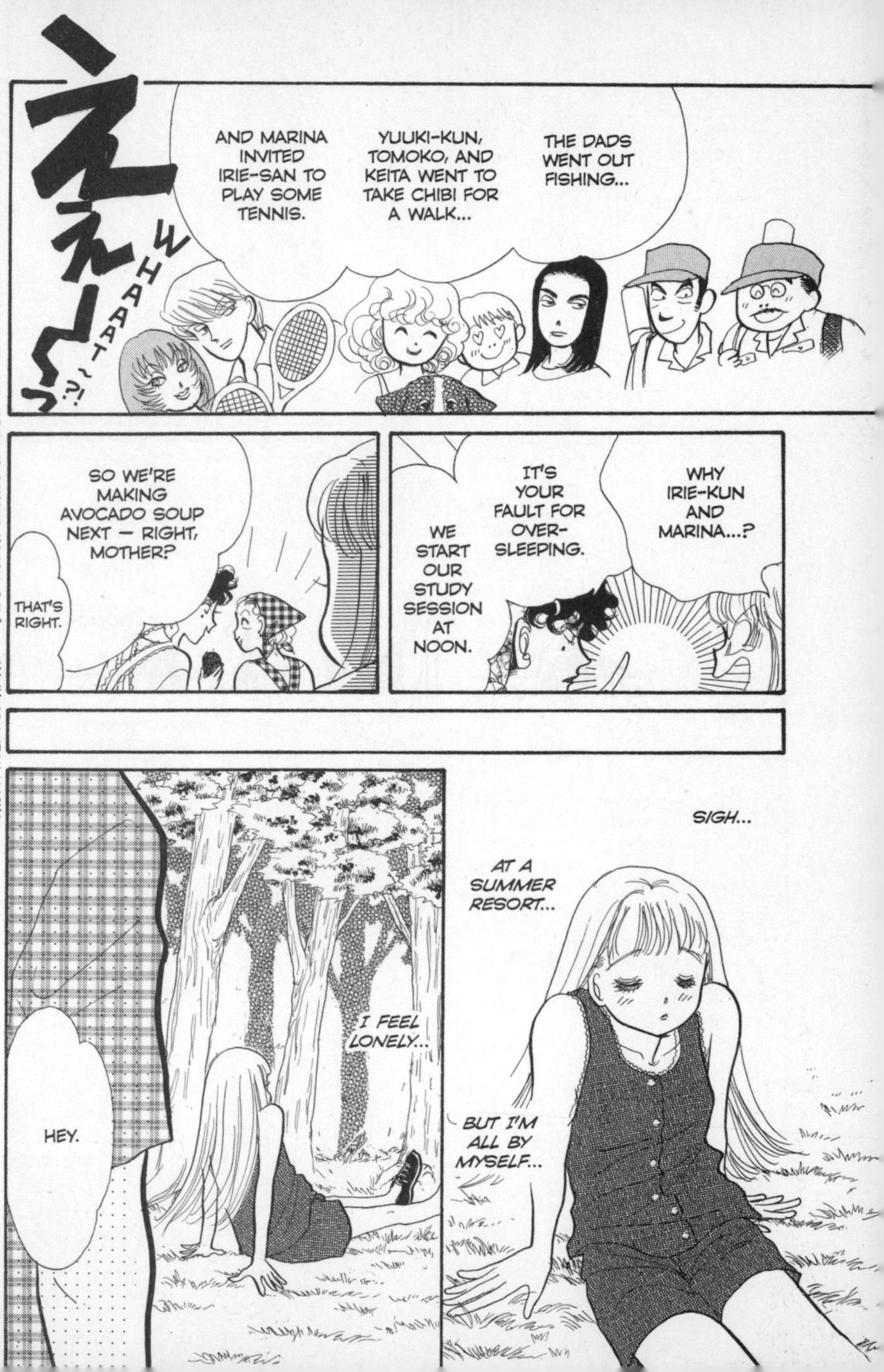
THE DADS WENT OUT FISHING...
YUUKI-KUN, TOMOKO, AND KEITA WENT TO TAKE CHIBI FOR A WALK...
AND MARINA INVITED IRIE-SAN TO PLAY SOME TENNIS.
ええ～っ
WHAAAT~?!
WHY IRIE-KUN AND MARINA...?
IT'S YOUR FAULT FOR OVER-SLEEPING.
WE START OUR STUDY SESSION AT NOON.
SO WE'RE MAKING AVOCADO SOUP NEXT — RIGHT, MOTHER?
THAT'S RIGHT.
SIGH...
AT A SUMMER RESORT...
I FEEL LONELY...
BUT I'M ALL BY MYSELF...
HEY.

STAFF: AKIKO ISHIKAWA, ATSUKO SUGIMOTO, FŪKO KUSAKABE, KANAMI SUDŌ THANK YOU VERY MUCH ♡

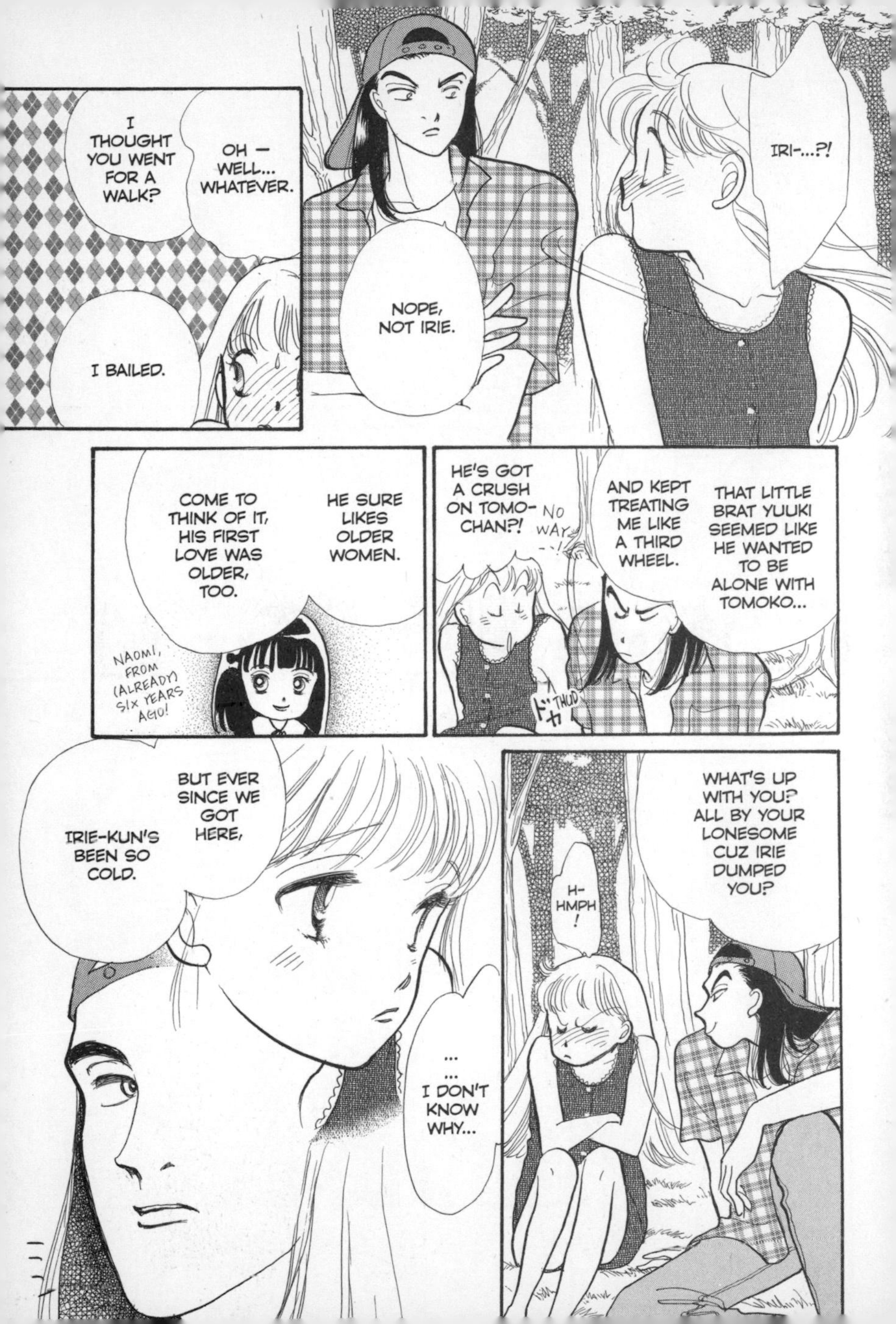
IRI-...?!
NOPE, NOT IRIE.
OH — WELL... WHATEVER.
I THOUGHT YOU WENT FOR A WALK?
I BAILED.
THAT LITTLE BRAT YUUKI SEEMED LIKE HE WANTED TO BE ALONE WITH TOMOKO...
AND KEPT TREATING ME LIKE A THIRD WHEEL.
HE'S GOT A CRUSH ON TOMO-CHAN?!
NO WAY--!
THUD
HE SURE LIKES OLDER WOMEN.
COME TO THINK OF IT, HIS FIRST LOVE WAS OLDER, TOO.
NAOMI, FROM (ALREADY) SIX YEARS AGO!
WHAT'S UP WITH YOU? ALL BY YOUR LONESOME CUZ IRIE DUMPED YOU?
H-HMPH!
BUT EVER SINCE WE GOT HERE,
IRIE-KUN'S BEEN SO COLD.
... ... I DON'T KNOW WHY...

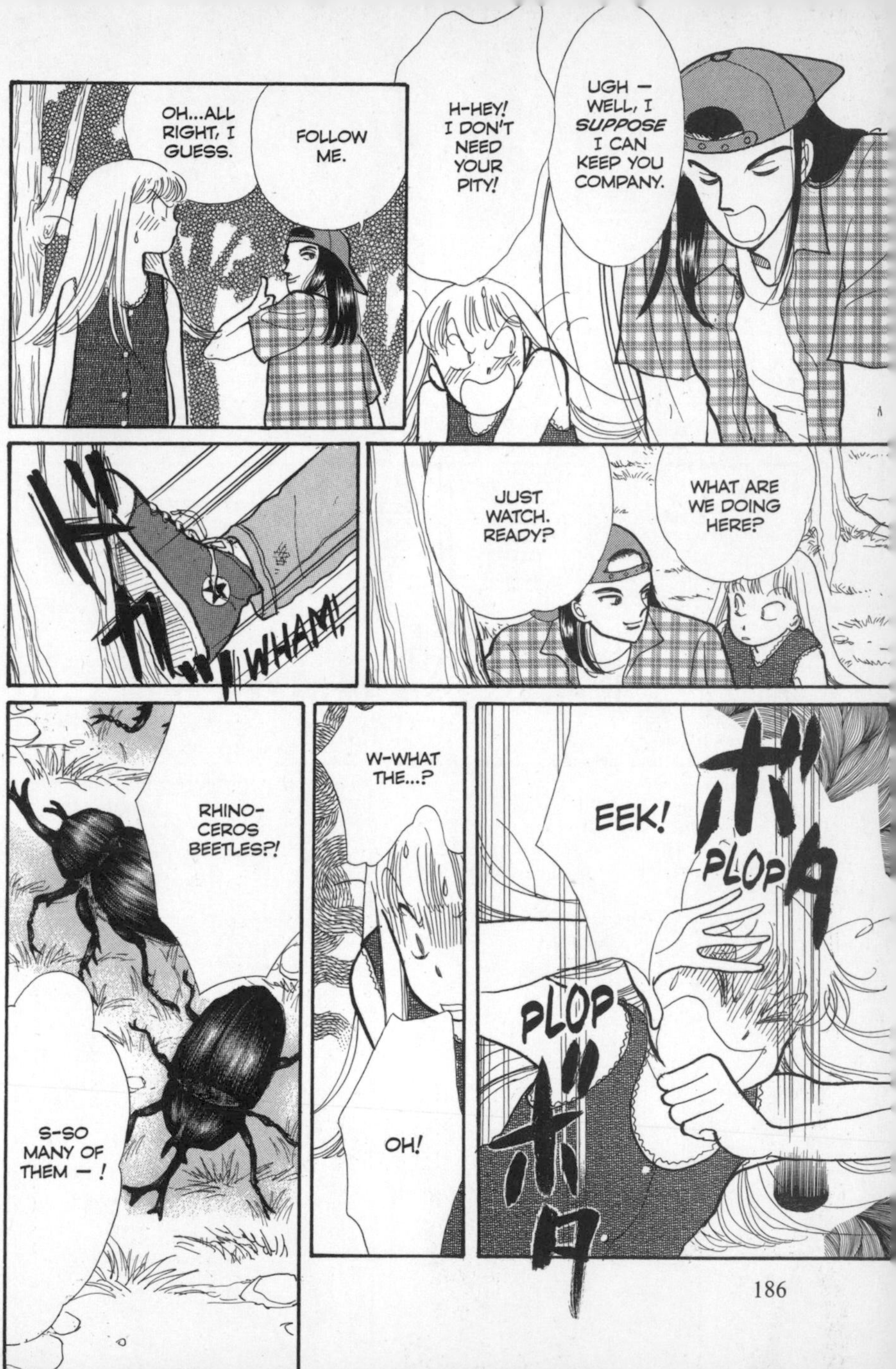
UGH — WELL, I *SUPPOSE* I CAN KEEP YOU COMPANY.
H-HEY! I DON'T NEED YOUR PITY!
FOLLOW ME.
OH...ALL RIGHT, I GUESS.
WHAT ARE WE DOING HERE?
JUST WATCH. READY?
WHAM!
EEK!
PLOP
PLOP
W-WHAT THE...?
OH!
RHINO-CEROS BEETLES?!
S-SO MANY OF THEM — !

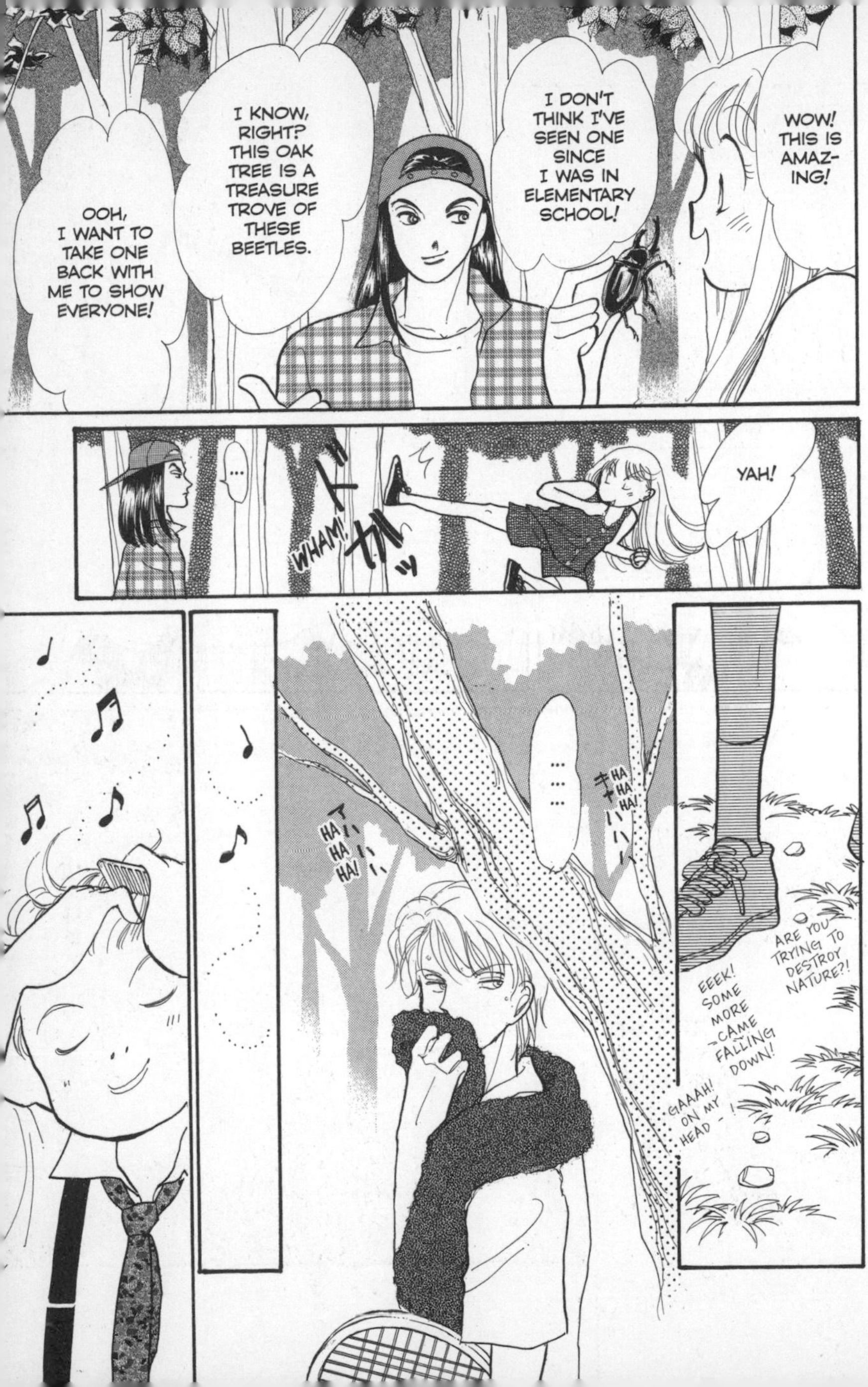
WOW! THIS IS AMAZ-ING!
I DON'T THINK I'VE SEEN ONE SINCE I WAS IN ELEMENTARY SCHOOL!
I KNOW, RIGHT? THIS OAK TREE IS A TREASURE TROVE OF THESE BEETLES.
OOH, I WANT TO TAKE ONE BACK WITH ME TO SHOW EVERYONE!
YAH!
WHAM!
...
ARE YOU TRYING TO DESTROY NATURE?!
EEEK! SOME MORE CAME FALLING DOWN!
GAAAH! ON MY HEAD -!
HA HA HA!
...
...
...
HA HA HA!

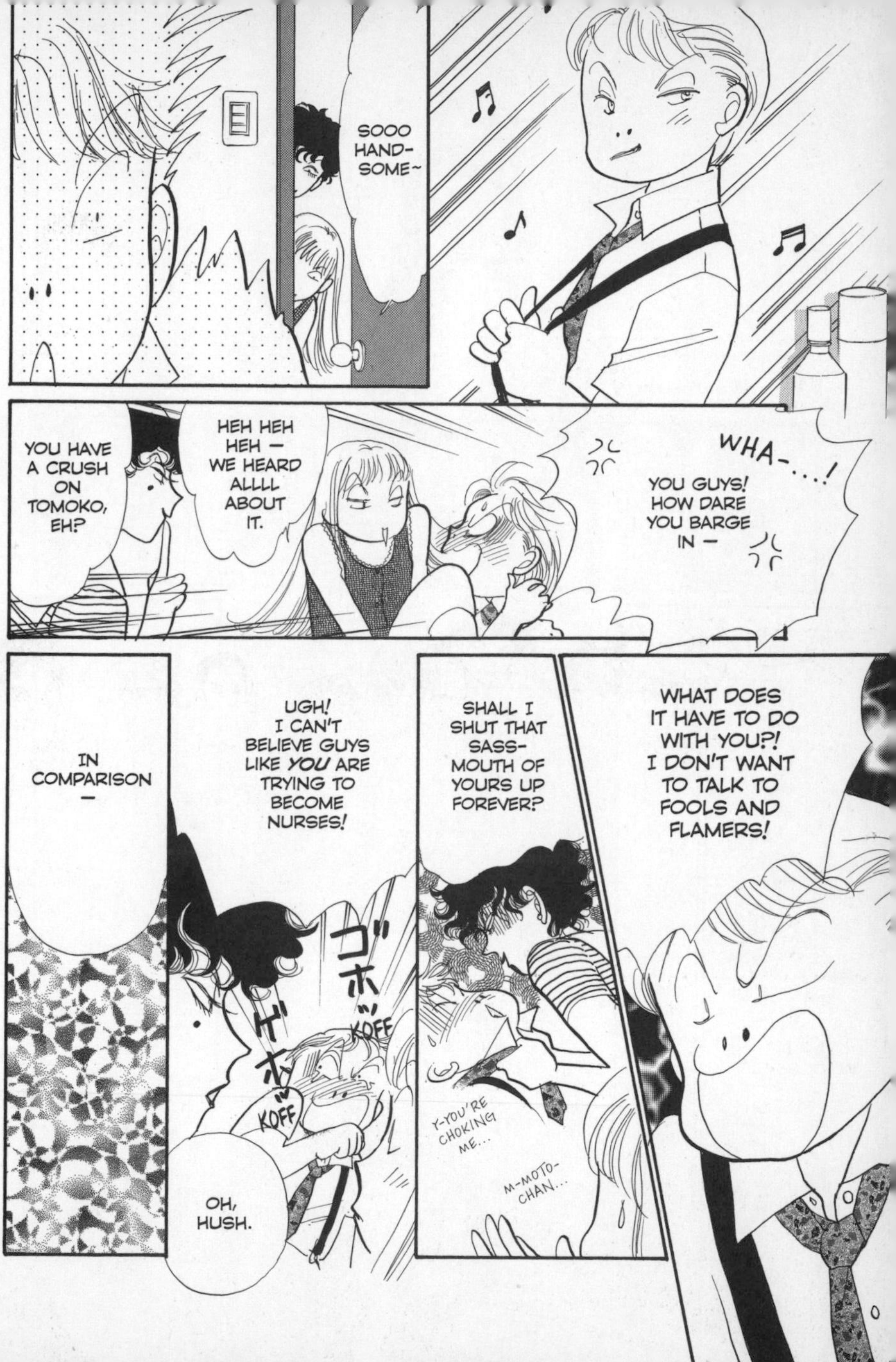
SOOO HAND-SOME~
WHA-...!
YOU GUYS! HOW DARE YOU BARGE IN —
HEH HEH HEH — WE HEARD ALLLL ABOUT IT.
YOU HAVE A CRUSH ON TOMOKO, EH?
WHAT DOES IT HAVE TO DO WITH YOU?! I DON'T WANT TO TALK TO FOOLS AND FLAMERS!
SHALL I SHUT THAT SASS-MOUTH OF YOURS UP FOREVER?
Y-YOU'RE CHOKING ME...
M-MOTO-CHAN...
UGH! I CAN'T BELIEVE GUYS LIKE *YOU* ARE TRYING TO BECOME NURSES!
IN COMPARISON —
ゴホッ KOFF
ゲホッ KOFF
OH, HUSH.

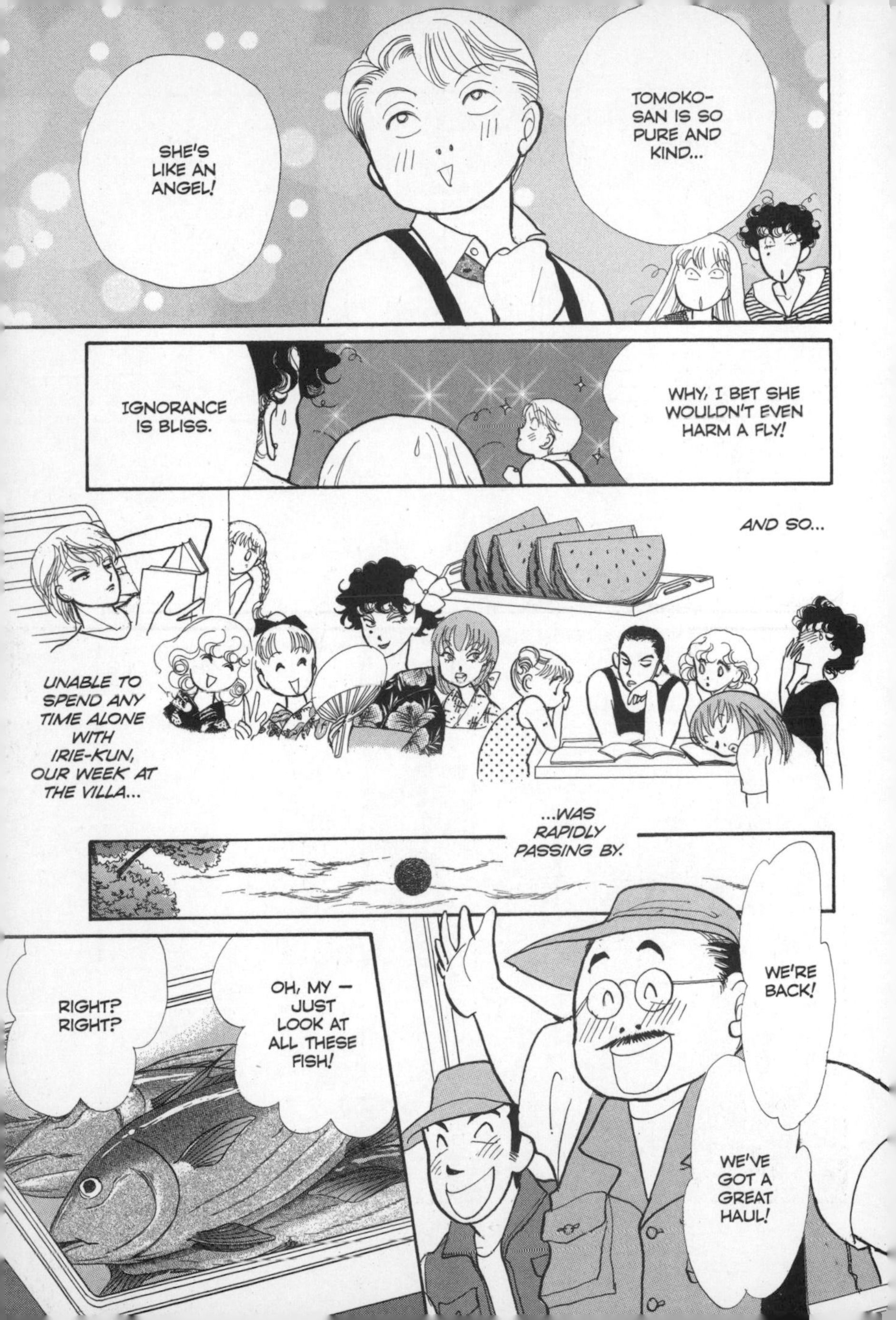
TOMOKO-SAN IS SO PURE AND KIND...
SHE'S LIKE AN ANGEL!
WHY, I BET SHE WOULDN'T EVEN HARM A FLY!
IGNORANCE IS BLISS.
AND SO...
UNABLE TO SPEND ANY TIME ALONE WITH IRIE-KUN, OUR WEEK AT THE VILLA...
...WAS RAPIDLY PASSING BY.
WE'RE BACK!
WE'VE GOT A GREAT HAUL!
OH, MY — JUST LOOK AT ALL THESE FISH!
RIGHT? RIGHT?

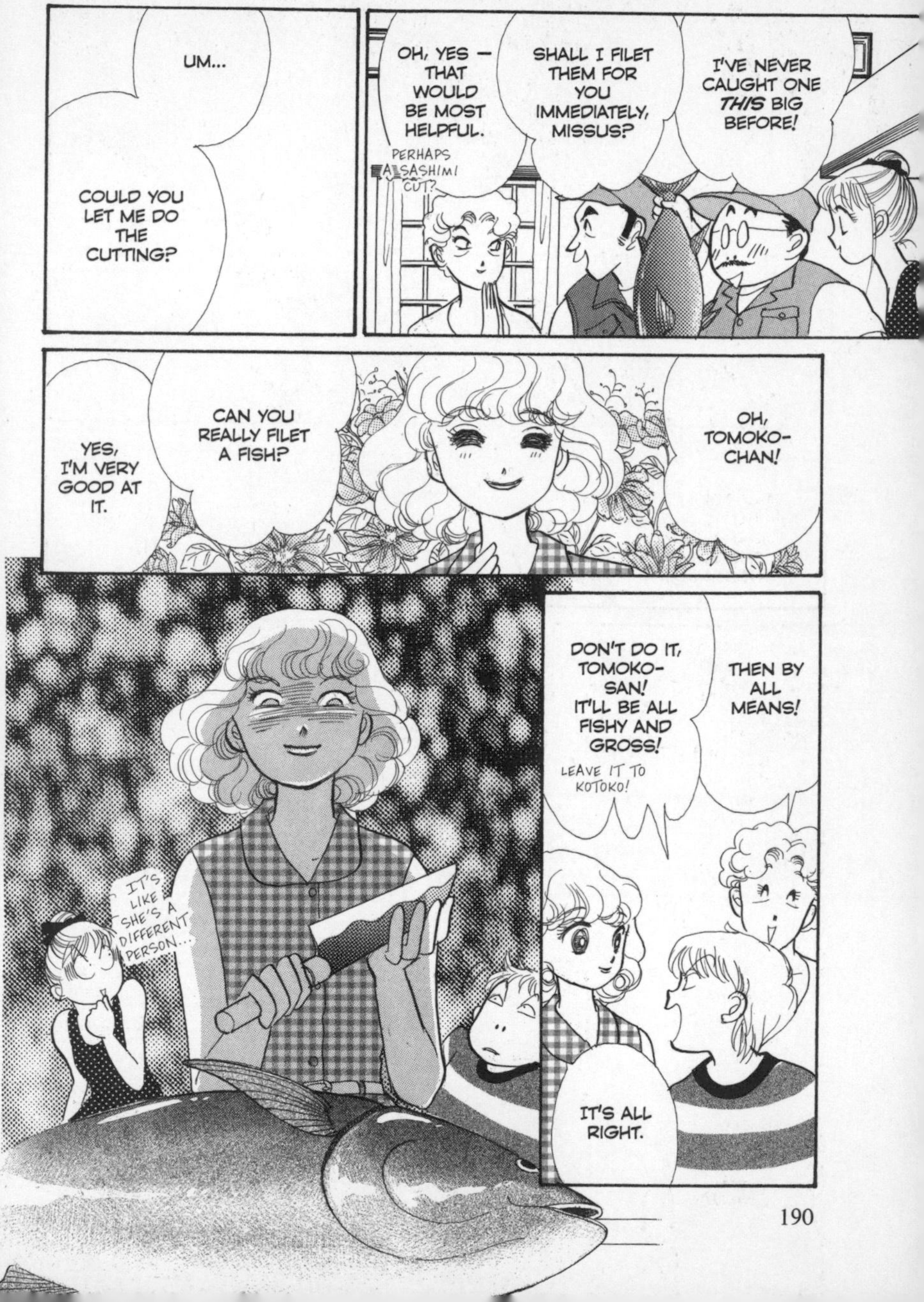
I'VE NEVER CAUGHT ONE *THIS* BIG BEFORE!
SHALL I FILET THEM FOR YOU IMMEDIATELY, MISSUS?
OH, YES — THAT WOULD BE MOST HELPFUL.
PERHAPS A SASHIMI CUT?
UM...
COULD YOU LET ME DO THE CUTTING?
OH, TOMOKO-CHAN!
CAN YOU REALLY FILET A FISH?
YES, I'M VERY GOOD AT IT.
THEN BY ALL MEANS!
DON'T DO IT, TOMOKO-SAN! IT'LL BE ALL FISHY AND GROSS!
LEAVE IT TO KOTOKO!
IT'S ALL RIGHT.
IT'S LIKE SHE'S A DIFFERENT PERSON...

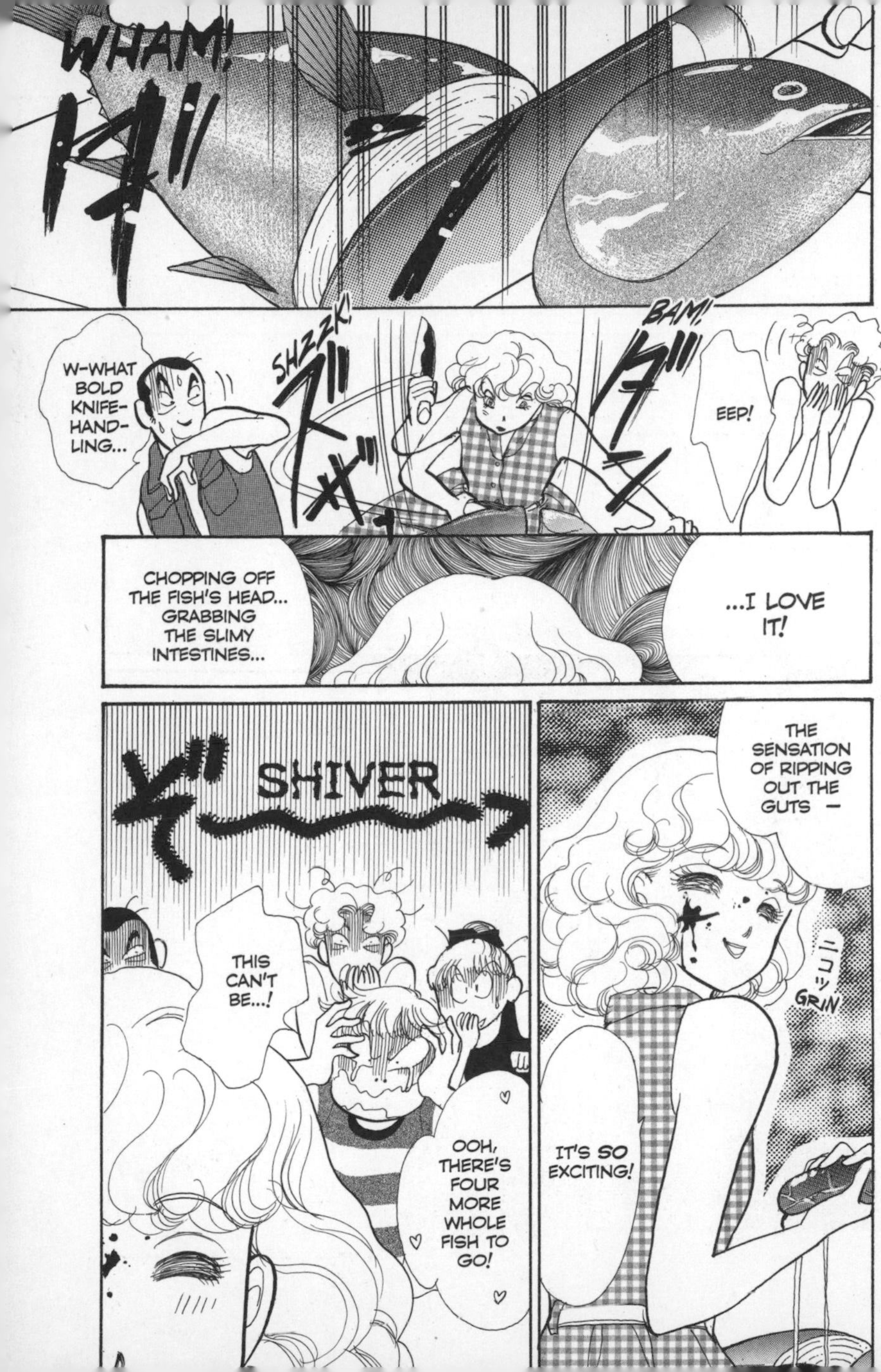
WHAM!
EEP!
BAM!
SHZZK!
W-WHAT BOLD KNIFE-HANDLING...
...I LOVE IT!
CHOPPING OFF THE FISH'S HEAD... GRABBING THE SLIMY INTESTINES...
THE SENSATION OF RIPPING OUT THE GUTS —
ニコッ
GRIN
IT'S SO EXCITING!
SHIVER
THIS CAN'T BE...!
OOH, THERE'S FOUR MORE WHOLE FISH TO GO!

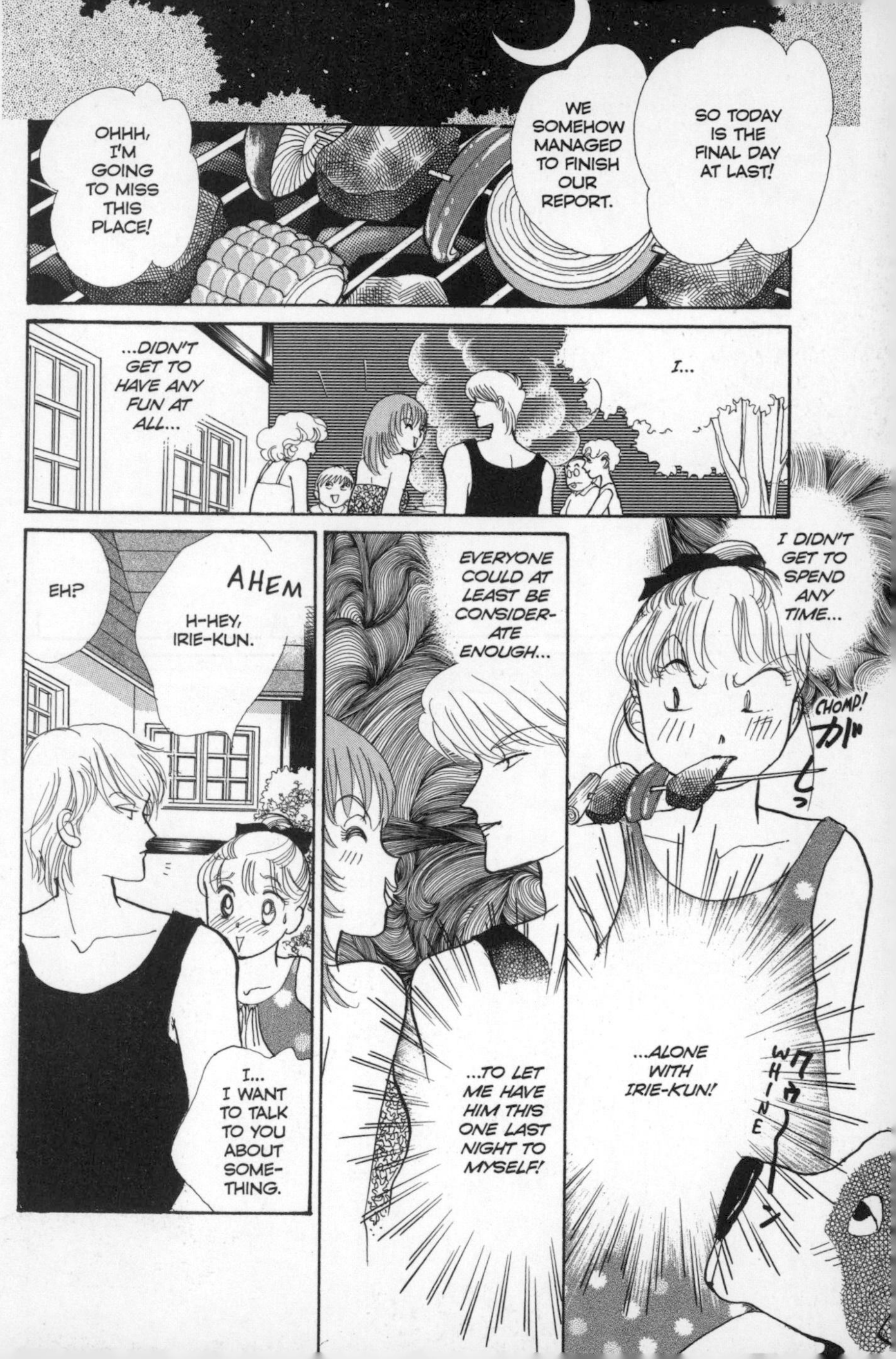
SO TODAY IS THE FINAL DAY AT LAST!
WE SOMEHOW MANAGED TO FINISH OUR REPORT.
OHHH, I'M GOING TO MISS THIS PLACE!
I...
...DIDN'T GET TO HAVE ANY FUN AT ALL...
I DIDN'T GET TO SPEND ANY TIME...
CHOMP!
...ALONE WITH IRIE-KUN!
WHINE
EVERYONE COULD AT LEAST BE CONSIDER-ATE ENOUGH...
...TO LET ME HAVE HIM THIS ONE LAST NIGHT TO MYSELF!
AHEM
H-HEY, IRIE-KUN.
EH?
I... I WANT TO TALK TO YOU ABOUT SOME-THING.

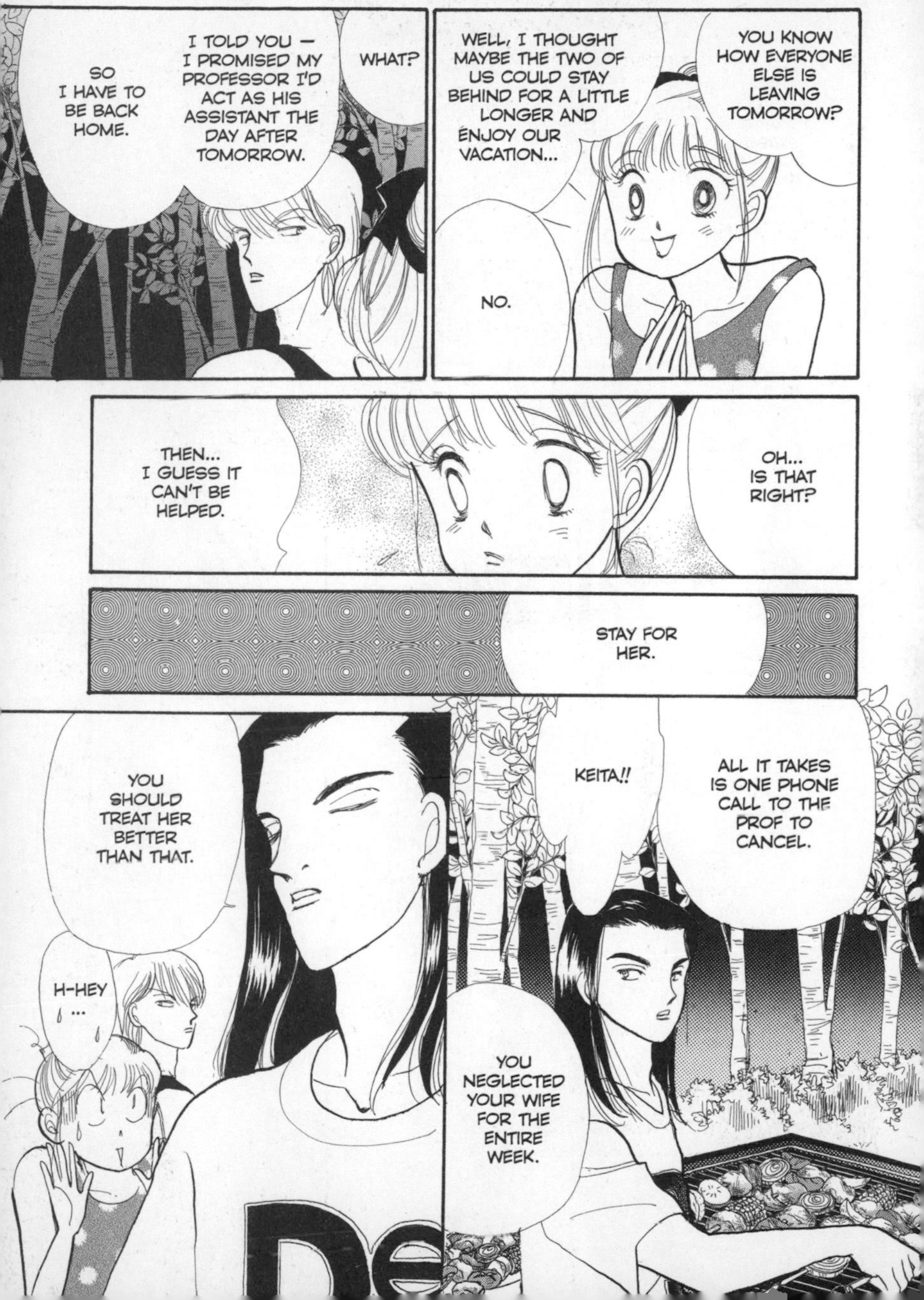

YOU KNOW HOW EVERYONE ELSE IS LEAVING TOMORROW?
WELL, I THOUGHT MAYBE THE TWO OF US COULD STAY BEHIND FOR A LITTLE LONGER AND ENJOY OUR VACATION...
NO.
WHAT?
I TOLD YOU — I PROMISED MY PROFESSOR I'D ACT AS HIS ASSISTANT THE DAY AFTER TOMORROW.
SO I HAVE TO BE BACK HOME.
OH... IS THAT RIGHT?
THEN... I GUESS IT CAN'T BE HELPED.
STAY FOR HER.
ALL IT TAKES IS ONE PHONE CALL TO THE PROF TO CANCEL.
KEITA!!
YOU NEGLECTED YOUR WIFE FOR THE ENTIRE WEEK.
YOU SHOULD TREAT HER BETTER THAN THAT.
H-HEY...

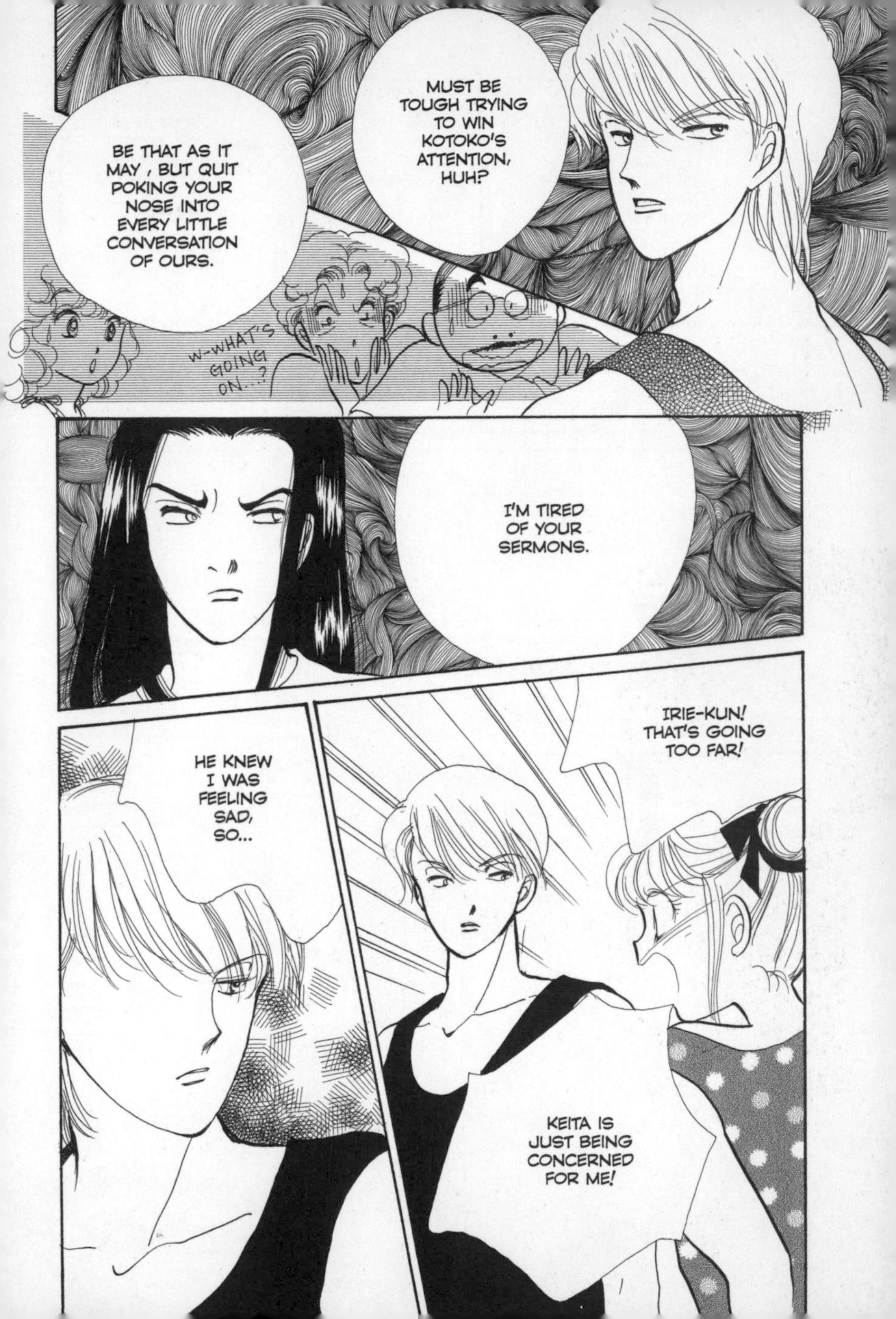
MUST BE TOUGH TRYING TO WIN KOTOKO'S ATTENTION, HUH?
BE THAT AS IT MAY , BUT QUIT POKING YOUR NOSE INTO EVERY LITTLE CONVERSATION OF OURS.
W-WHAT'S GOING ON...?
I'M TIRED OF YOUR SERMONS.
IRIE-KUN! THAT'S GOING TOO FAR!
KEITA IS JUST BEING CONCERNED FOR ME!
HE KNEW I WAS FEELING SAD, SO...

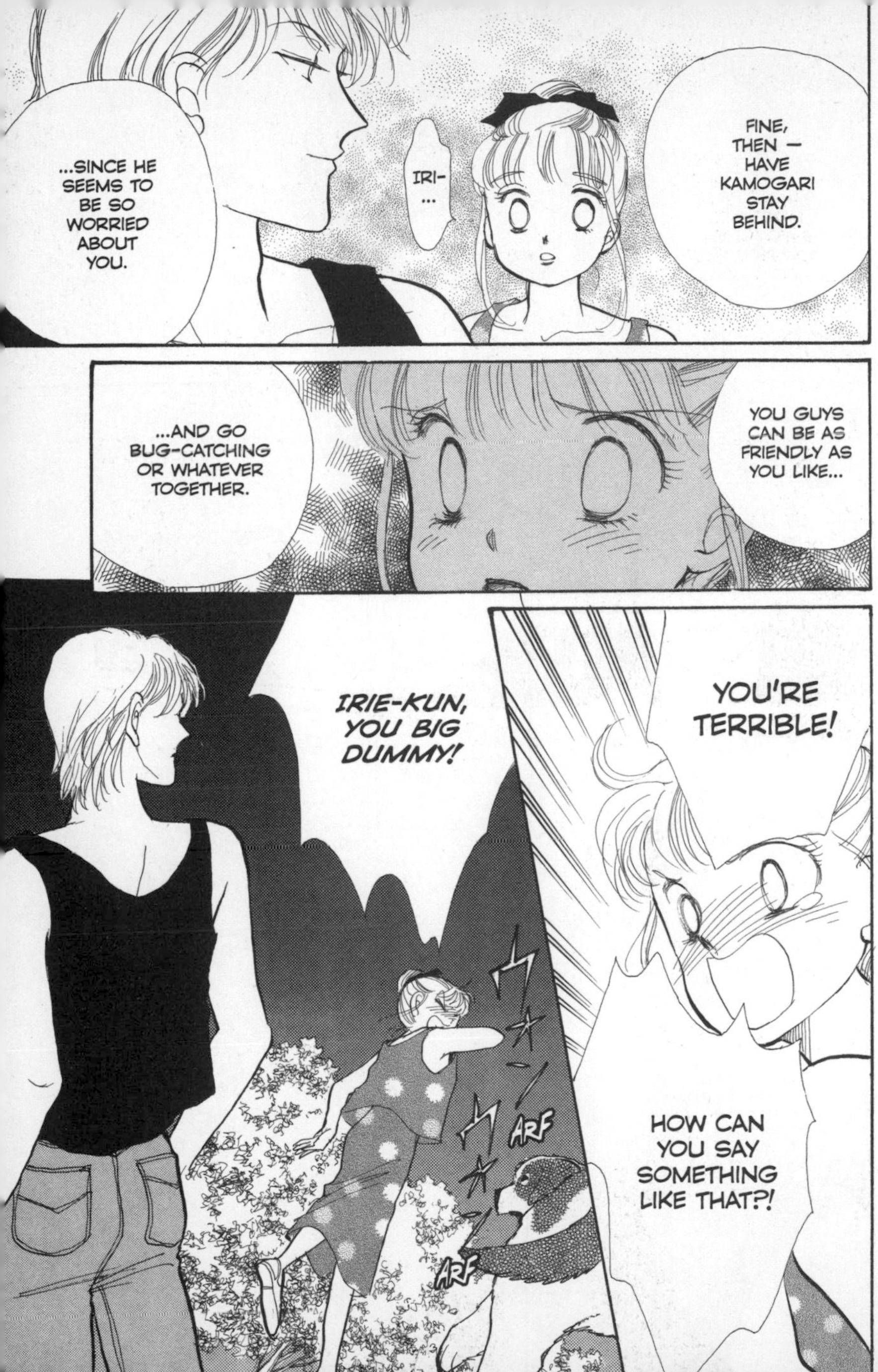
FINE, THEN — HAVE KAMOGARI STAY BEHIND.
IRI- ...
...SINCE HE SEEMS TO BE SO WORRIED ABOUT YOU.
YOU GUYS CAN BE AS FRIENDLY AS YOU LIKE...
...AND GO BUG-CATCHING OR WHATEVER TOGETHER.
YOU'RE TERRIBLE!
HOW CAN YOU SAY SOMETHING LIKE THAT?!
IRIE-KUN, YOU BIG DUMMY!
ARF
ARF

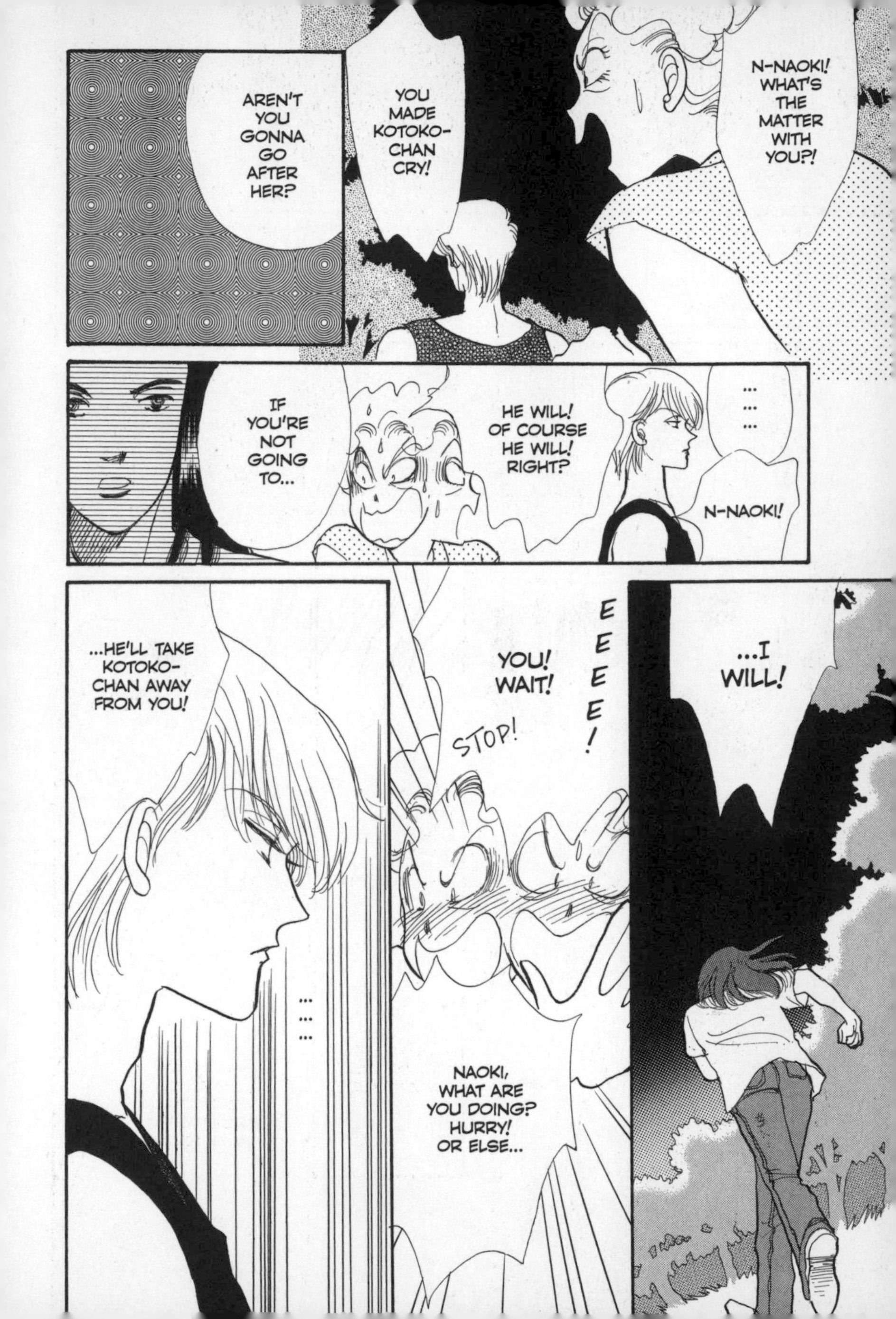

N-NAOKI! WHAT'S THE MATTER WITH YOU?!
YOU MADE KOTOKO-CHAN CRY!
AREN'T YOU GONNA GO AFTER HER?
......
N-NAOKI!
HE WILL! OF COURSE HE WILL! RIGHT?
IF YOU'RE NOT GOING TO...
...I WILL!
EEEEE!
YOU! WAIT!
STOP!
NAOKI, WHAT ARE YOU DOING? HURRY! OR ELSE...
...HE'LL TAKE KOTOKO-CHAN AWAY FROM YOU!
......

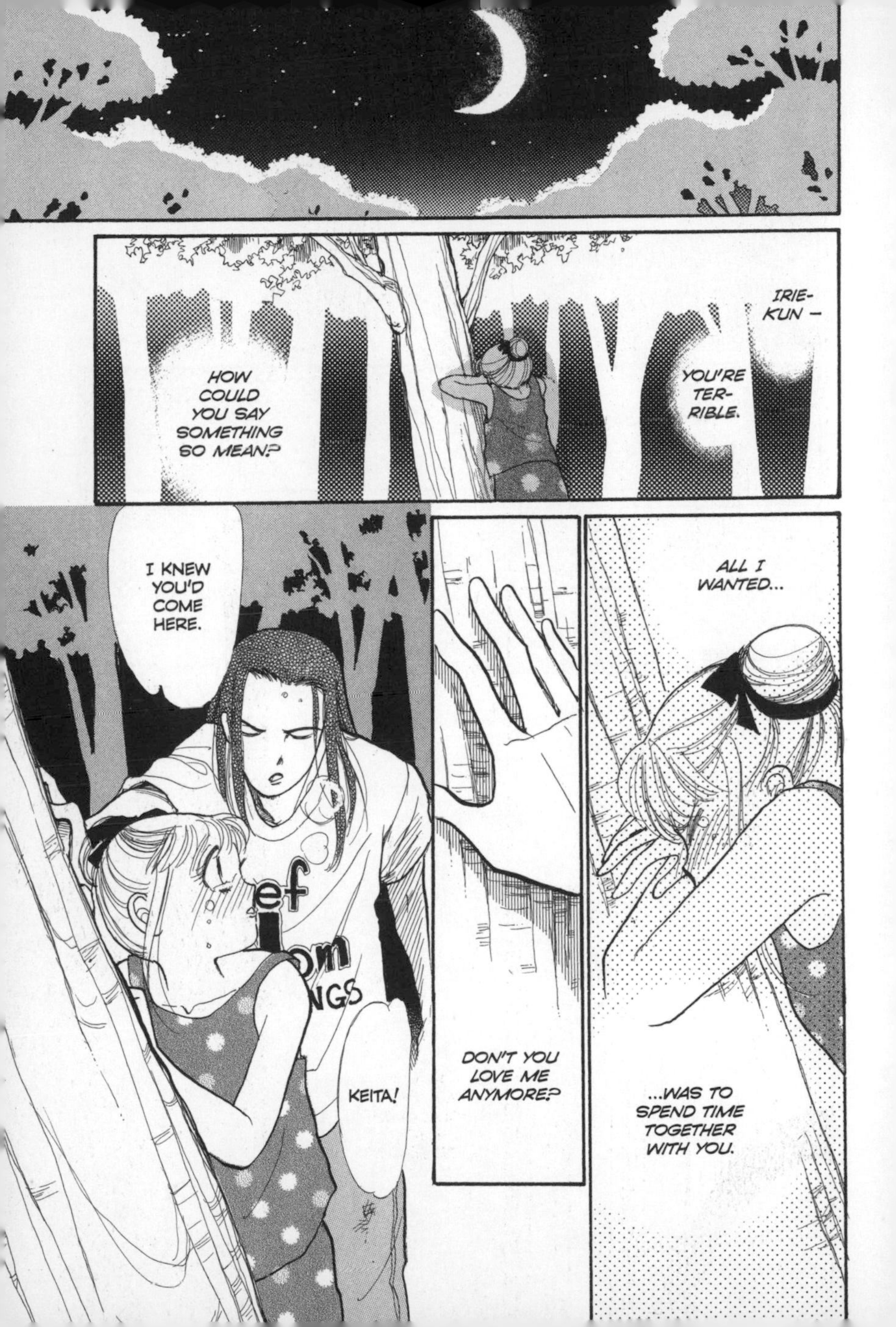
IRIE-KUN —
YOU'RE TER-RIBLE.
HOW COULD YOU SAY SOMETHING SO MEAN?
ALL I WANTED...
...WAS TO SPEND TIME TOGETHER WITH YOU.
DON'T YOU LOVE ME ANYMORE?
I KNEW YOU'D COME HERE.
KEITA!

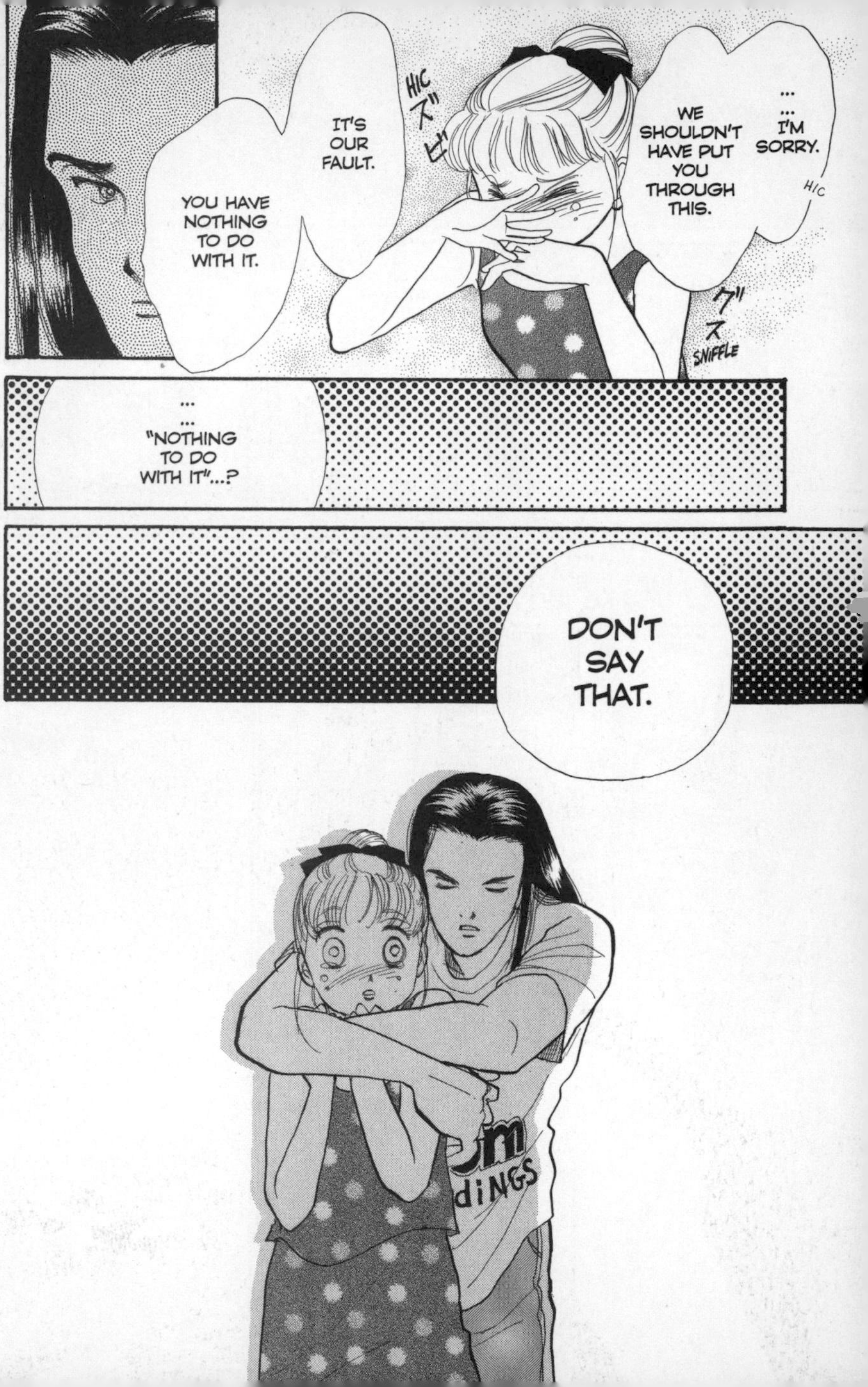
... ... I'M SORRY.
HIC
WE SHOULDN'T HAVE PUT YOU THROUGH THIS.
グス
SNIFFLE
HIC
ズビ
IT'S OUR FAULT.
YOU HAVE NOTHING TO DO WITH IT.
... ... "NOTHING TO DO WITH IT"...?
DON'T SAY THAT.

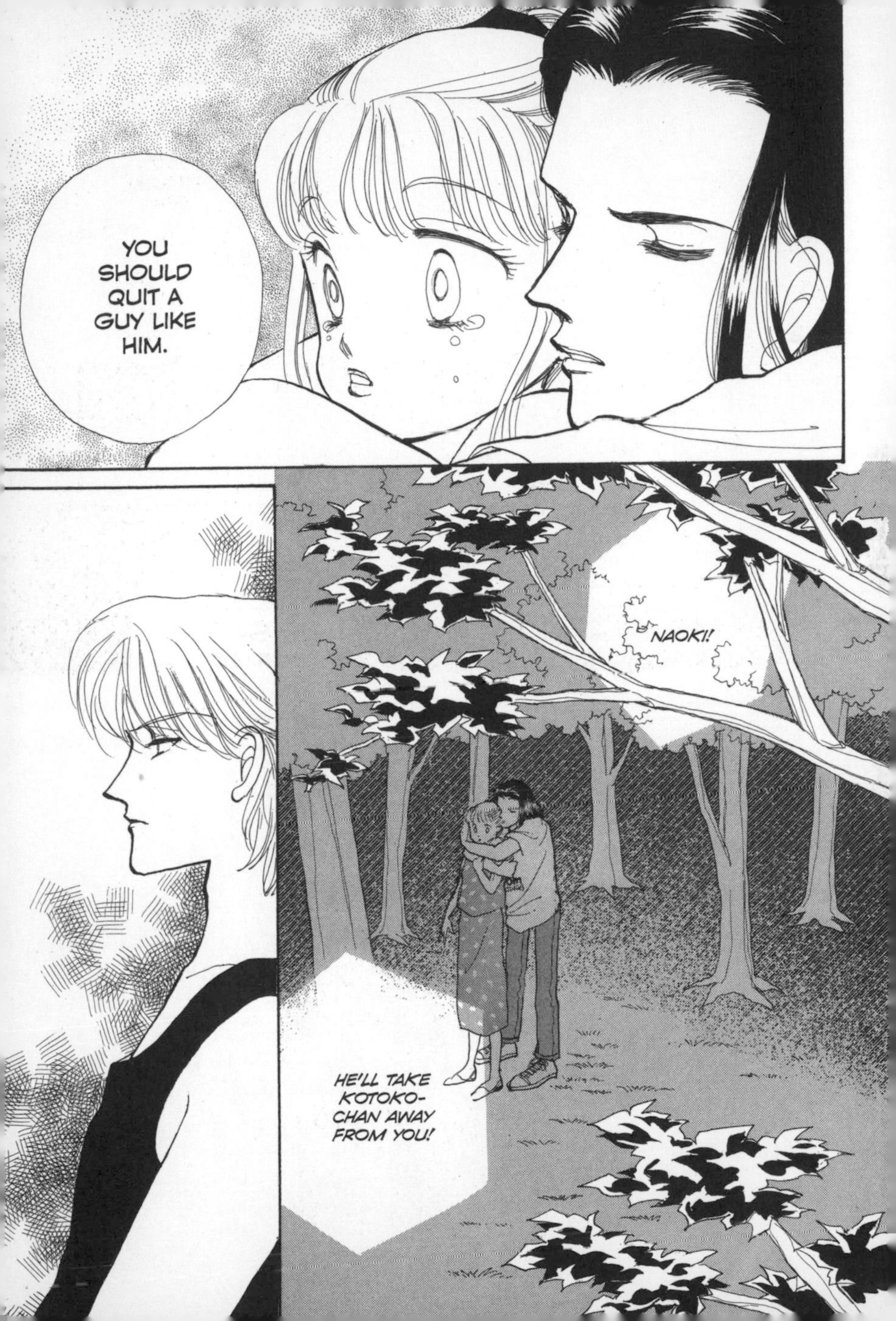
YOU SHOULD QUIT A GUY LIKE HIM.
NAOKI!
HE'LL TAKE KOTOKO-CHAN AWAY FROM YOU!

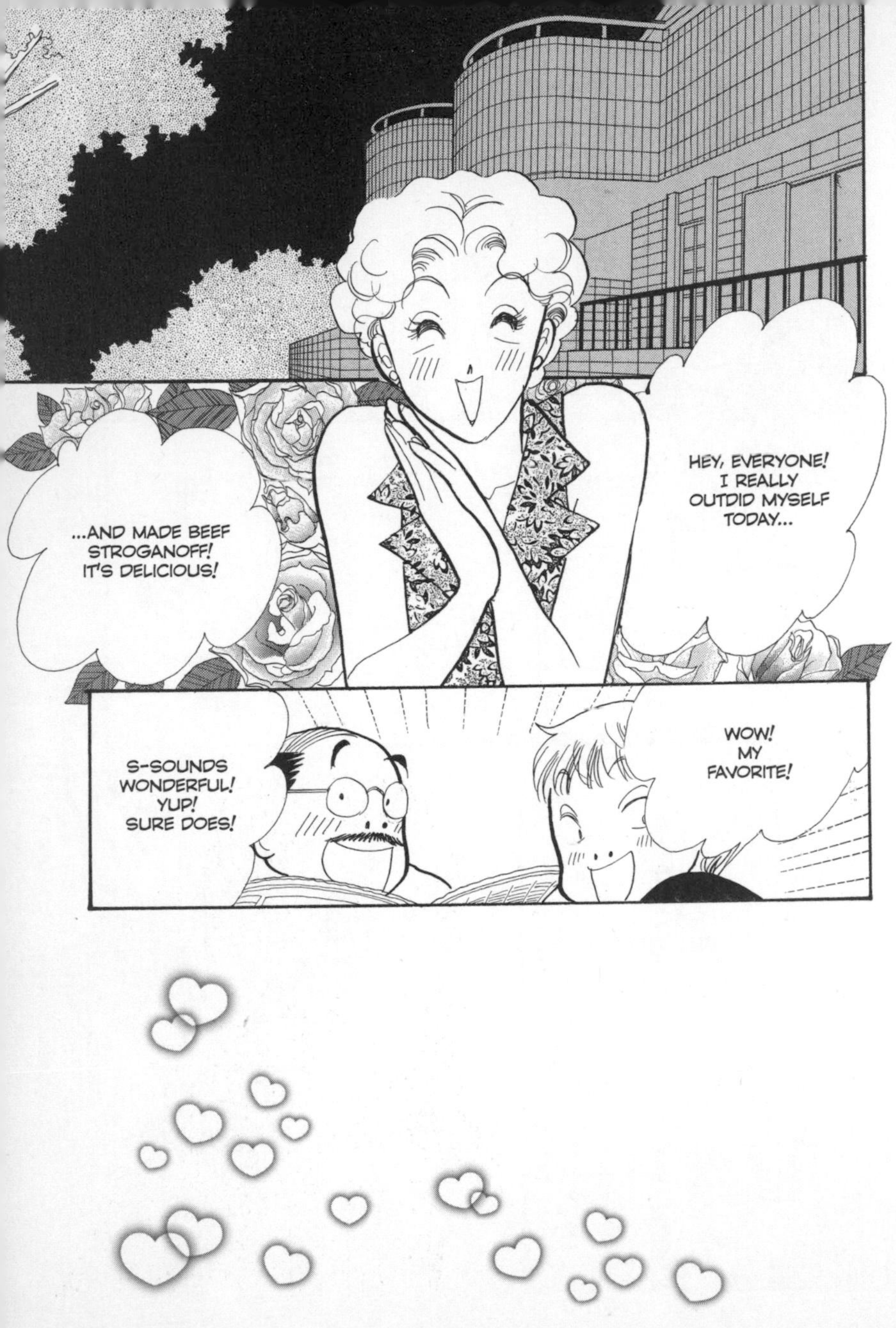

HEY, EVERYONE! I REALLY OUTDID MYSELF TODAY...
...AND MADE BEEF STROGANOFF! IT'S DELICIOUS!
WOW! MY FAVORITE!
S-SOUNDS WONDERFUL! YUP! SURE DOES!

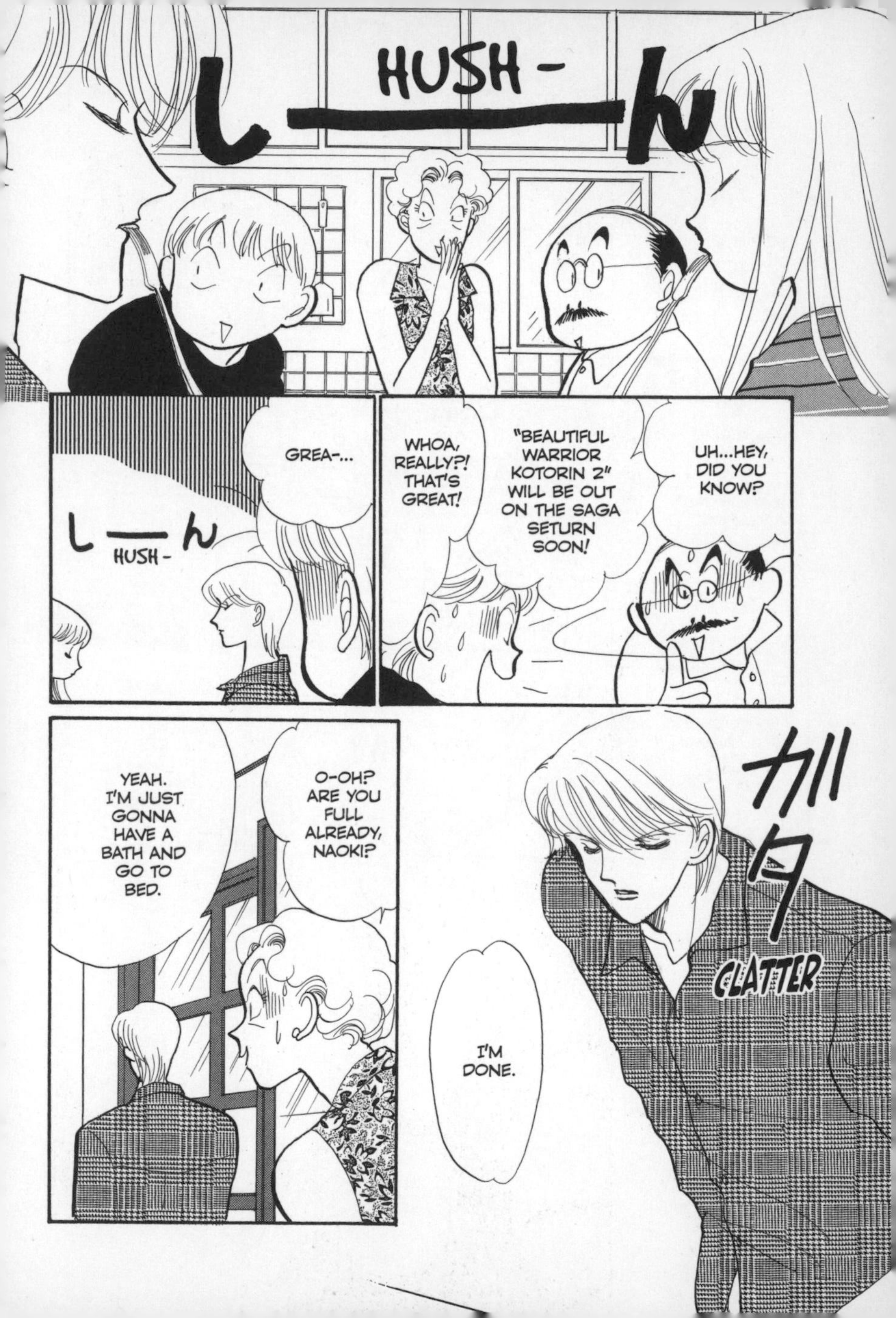
し——ん
HUSH-
UH...HEY, DID YOU KNOW?
"BEAUTIFUL WARRIOR KOTORIN 2" WILL BE OUT ON THE SAGA SETURN SOON!
WHOA, REALLY?! THAT'S GREAT!
GREA-...
し—ん
HUSH-
ガタ
CLATTER
I'M DONE.
O-OH? ARE YOU FULL ALREADY, NAOKI?
YEAH. I'M JUST GONNA HAVE A BATH AND GO TO BED.

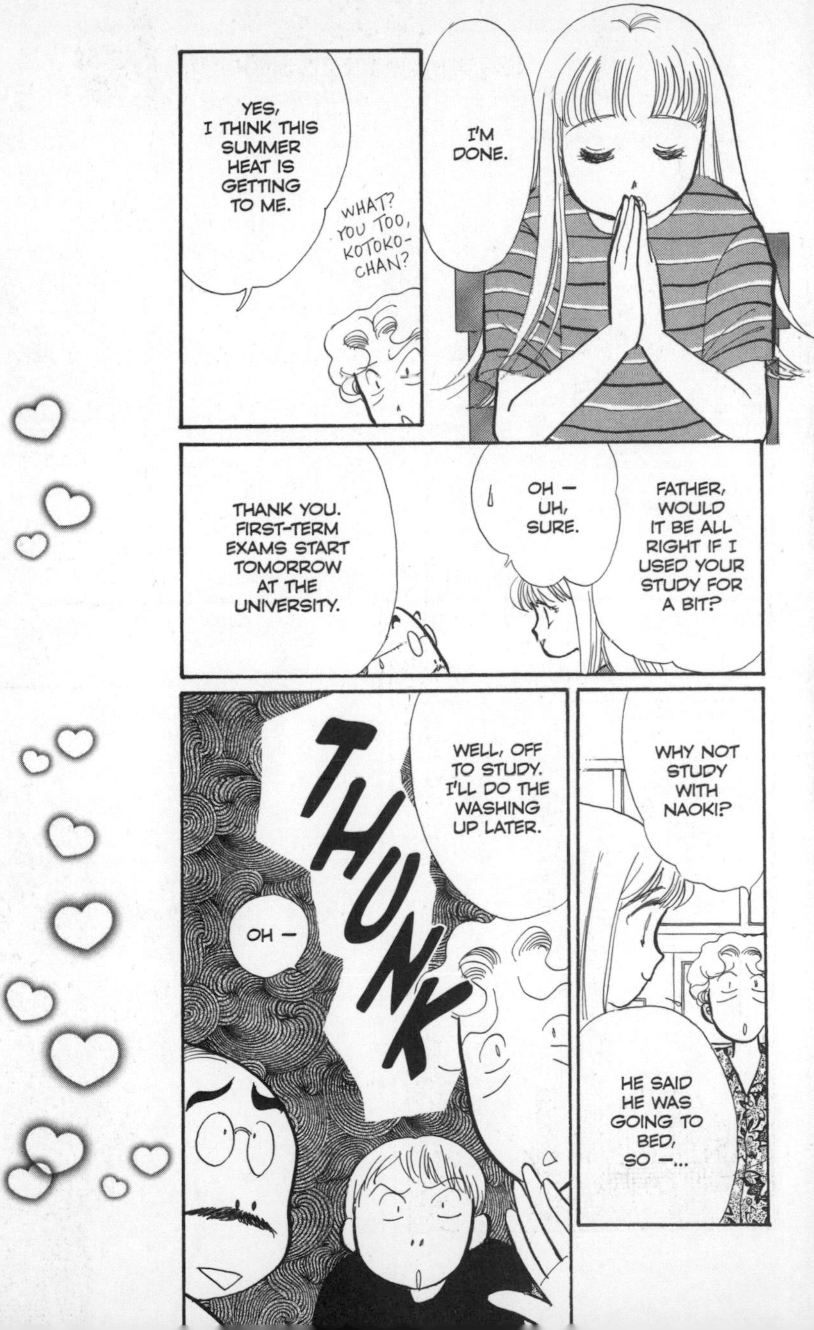
I'M DONE.
WHAT? YOU TOO, KOTOKO-CHAN?
YES, I THINK THIS SUMMER HEAT IS GETTING TO ME.
FATHER, WOULD IT BE ALL RIGHT IF I USED YOUR STUDY FOR A BIT?
OH — UH, SURE.
THANK YOU. FIRST-TERM EXAMS START TOMORROW AT THE UNIVERSITY.
WHY NOT STUDY WITH NAOKI?
HE SAID HE WAS GOING TO BED, SO —...
WELL, OFF TO STUDY. I'LL DO THE WASHING UP LATER.
THUNK
OH —

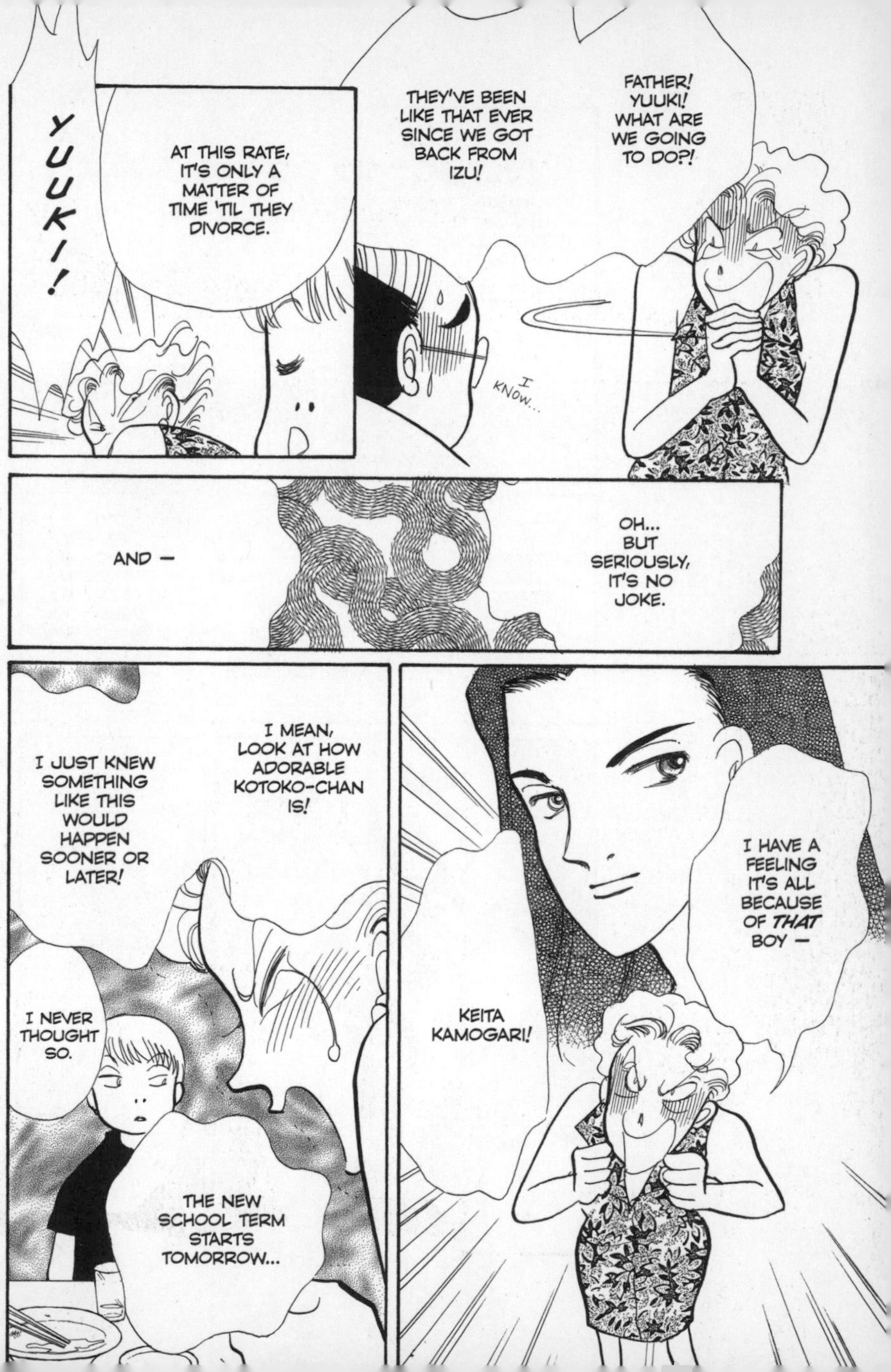
FATHER! YUUKI! WHAT ARE WE GOING TO DO?!
THEY'VE BEEN LIKE THAT EVER SINCE WE GOT BACK FROM IZU!
I KNOW...
AT THIS RATE, IT'S ONLY A MATTER OF TIME 'TIL THEY DIVORCE.
YUUKI!
OH... BUT SERIOUSLY, IT'S NO JOKE.
AND —
I HAVE A FEELING IT'S ALL BECAUSE OF *THAT* BOY —
KEITA KAMOGARI!
I MEAN, LOOK AT HOW ADORABLE KOTOKO-CHAN IS!
I JUST KNEW SOMETHING LIKE THIS WOULD HAPPEN SOONER OR LATER!
I NEVER THOUGHT SO.
THE NEW SCHOOL TERM STARTS TOMORROW...

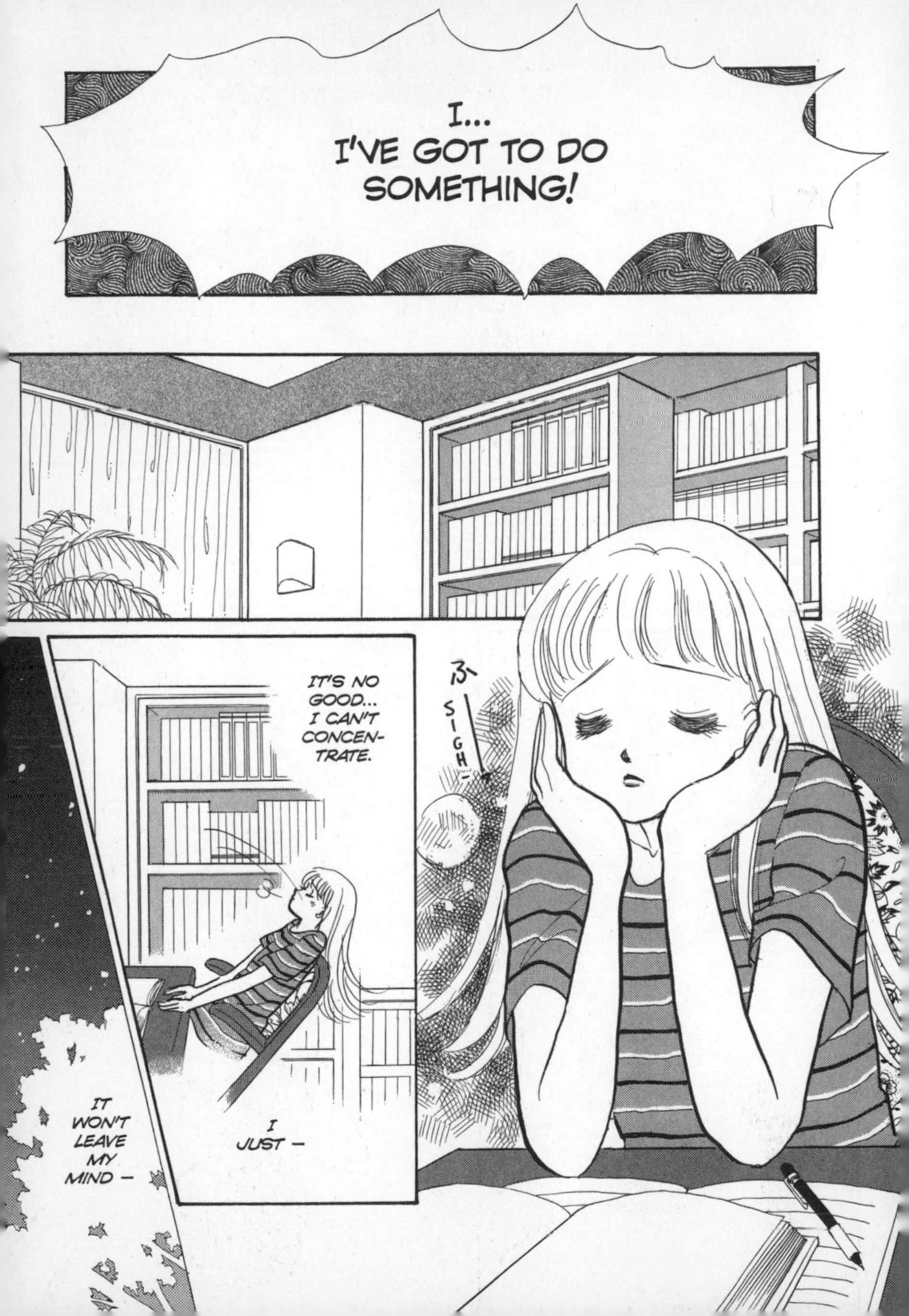
I... I'VE GOT TO DO SOMETHING!
ふ
SIGH
IT'S NO GOOD... I CAN'T CONCENTRATE.
I JUST –
IT WON'T LEAVE MY MIND –

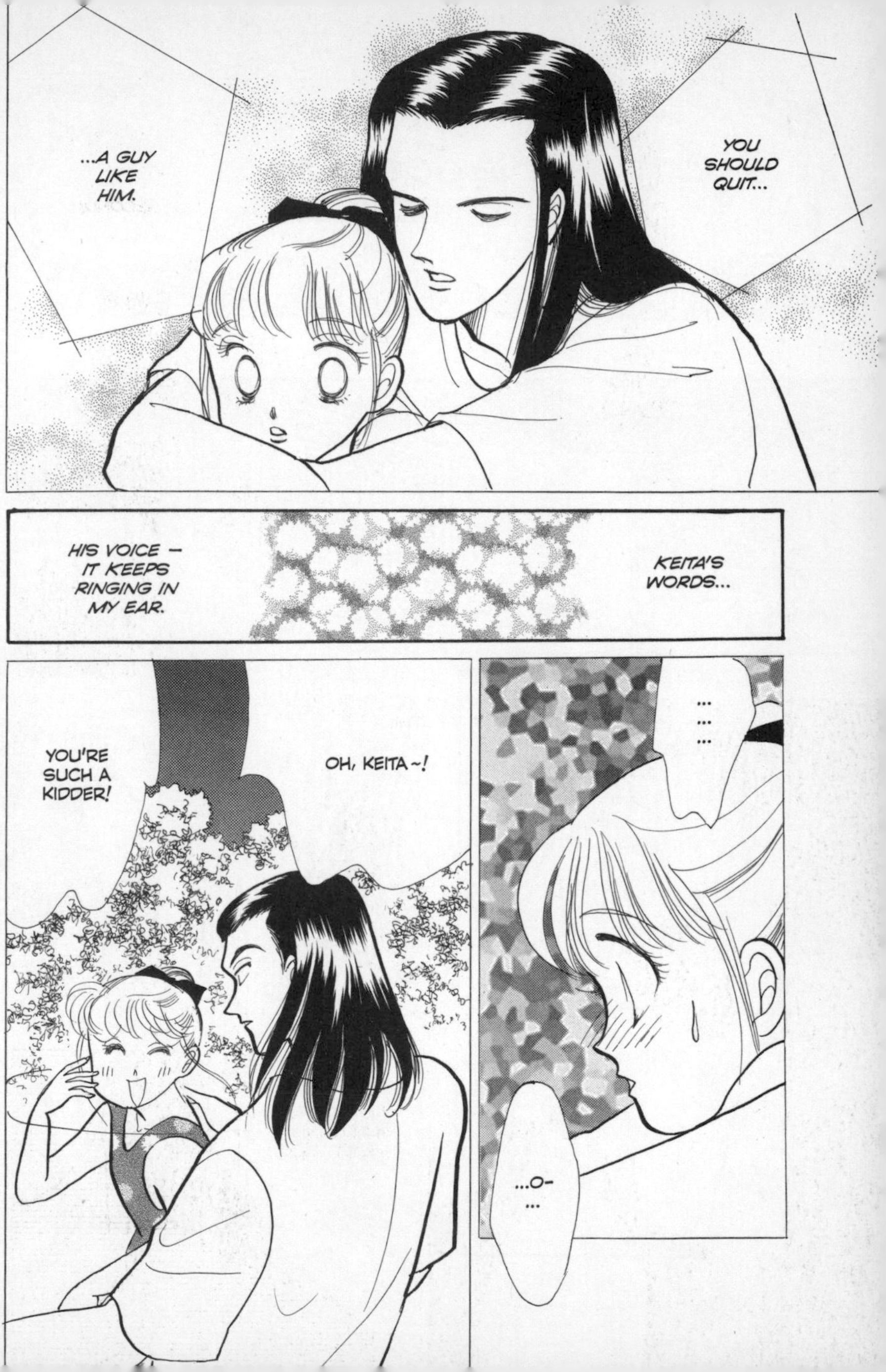
YOU SHOULD QUIT...
...A GUY LIKE HIM.
KEITA'S WORDS...
HIS VOICE — IT KEEPS RINGING IN MY EAR.
... ...
...O- ...
OH, KEITA~!
YOU'RE SUCH A KIDDER!

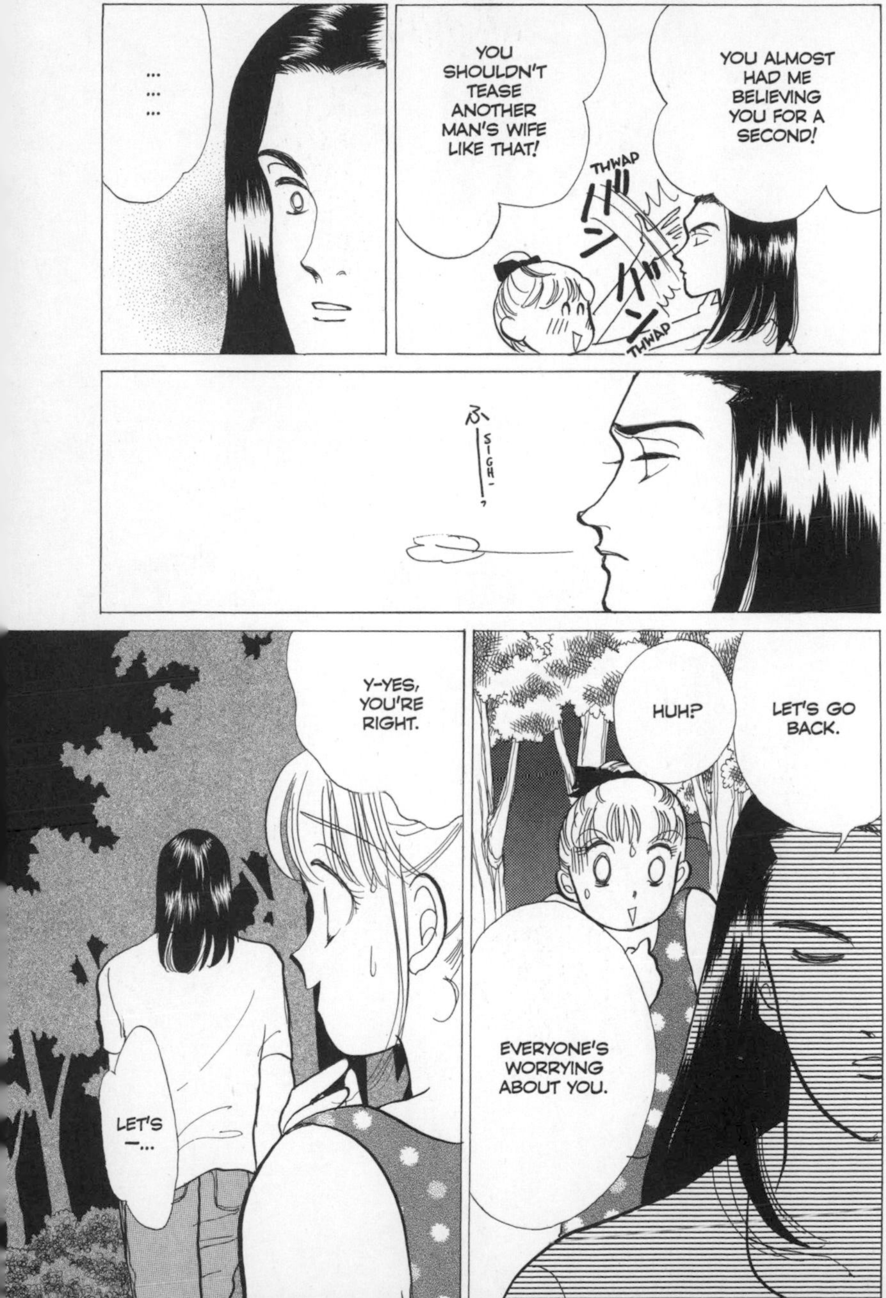
YOU ALMOST HAD ME BELIEVING YOU FOR A SECOND!
YOU SHOULDN'T TEASE ANOTHER MAN'S WIFE LIKE THAT!
THWAP
THWAP
...
...
...
ふ
SIGH
LET'S GO BACK.
HUH?
EVERYONE'S WORRYING ABOUT YOU.
Y-YES, YOU'RE RIGHT.
LET'S —...

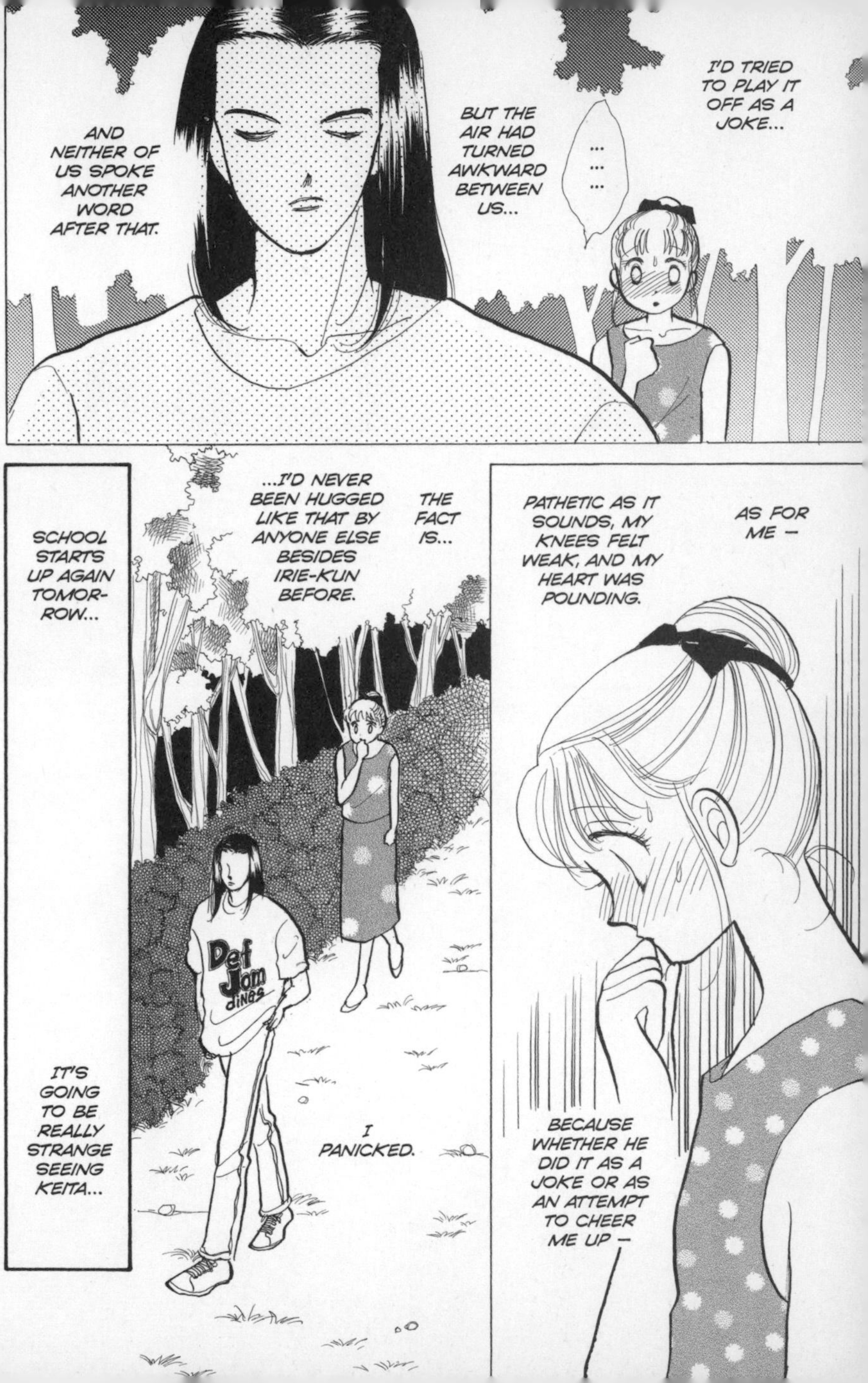
I'D TRIED TO PLAY IT OFF AS A JOKE...
... ...
BUT THE AIR HAD TURNED AWKWARD BETWEEN US...
AND NEITHER OF US SPOKE ANOTHER WORD AFTER THAT.
AS FOR ME —
PATHETIC AS IT SOUNDS, MY KNEES FELT WEAK, AND MY HEART WAS POUNDING.
BECAUSE WHETHER HE DID IT AS A JOKE OR AS AN ATTEMPT TO CHEER ME UP —
THE FACT IS...
...I'D NEVER BEEN HUGGED LIKE THAT BY ANYONE ELSE BESIDES IRIE-KUN BEFORE.
Def Jam
I PANICKED.
SCHOOL STARTS UP AGAIN TOMOR-ROW...
IT'S GOING TO BE REALLY STRANGE SEEING KEITA...

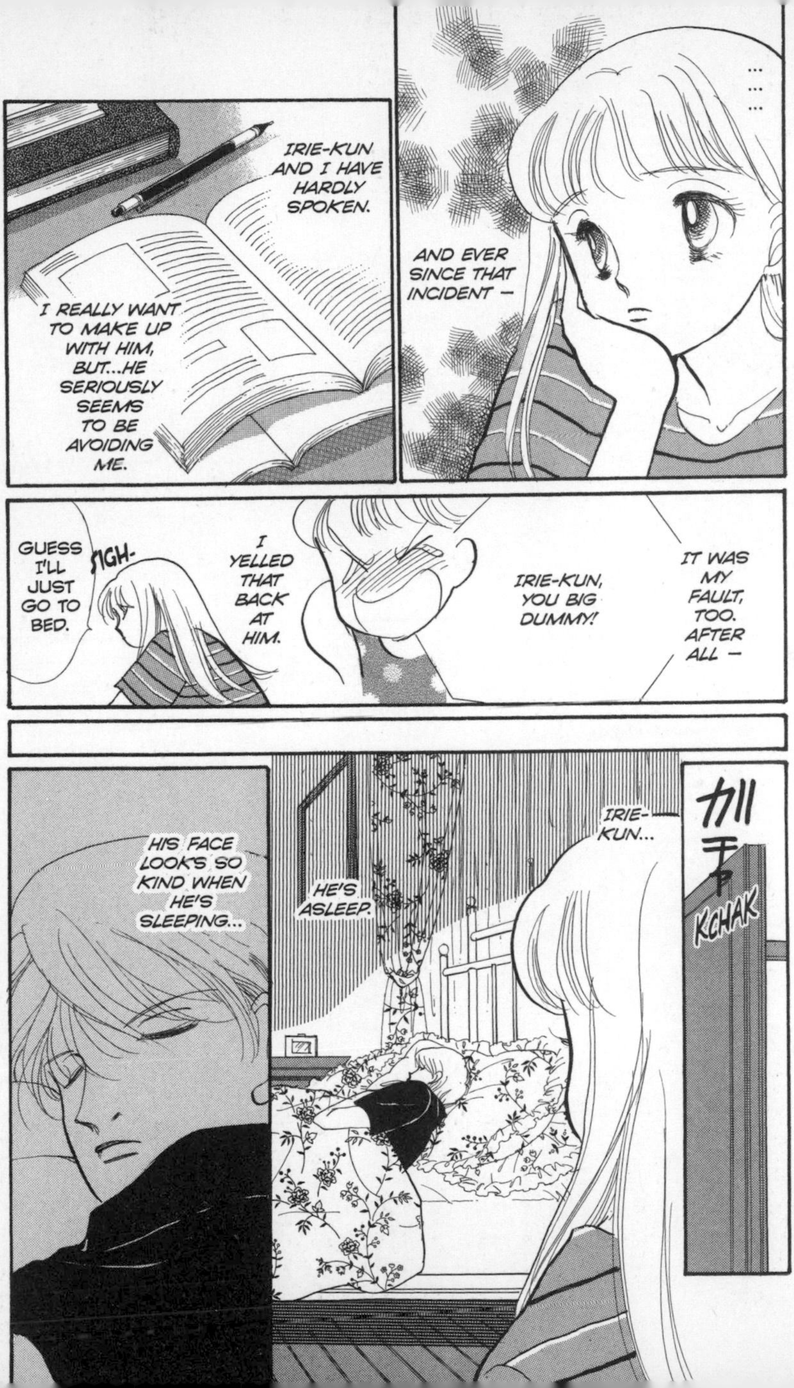
...
...
...
AND EVER SINCE THAT INCIDENT –
IRIE-KUN AND I HAVE HARDLY SPOKEN.
I REALLY WANT TO MAKE UP WITH HIM, BUT...HE SERIOUSLY SEEMS TO BE AVOIDING ME.
IT WAS MY FAULT, TOO. AFTER ALL –
IRIE-KUN, YOU BIG DUMMY!
I YELLED THAT BACK AT HIM.
SIGH-
GUESS I'LL JUST GO TO BED.
ガチャ
KCHAK
IRIE-KUN...
HE'S ASLEEP.
HIS FACE LOOKS SO KIND WHEN HE'S SLEEPING...

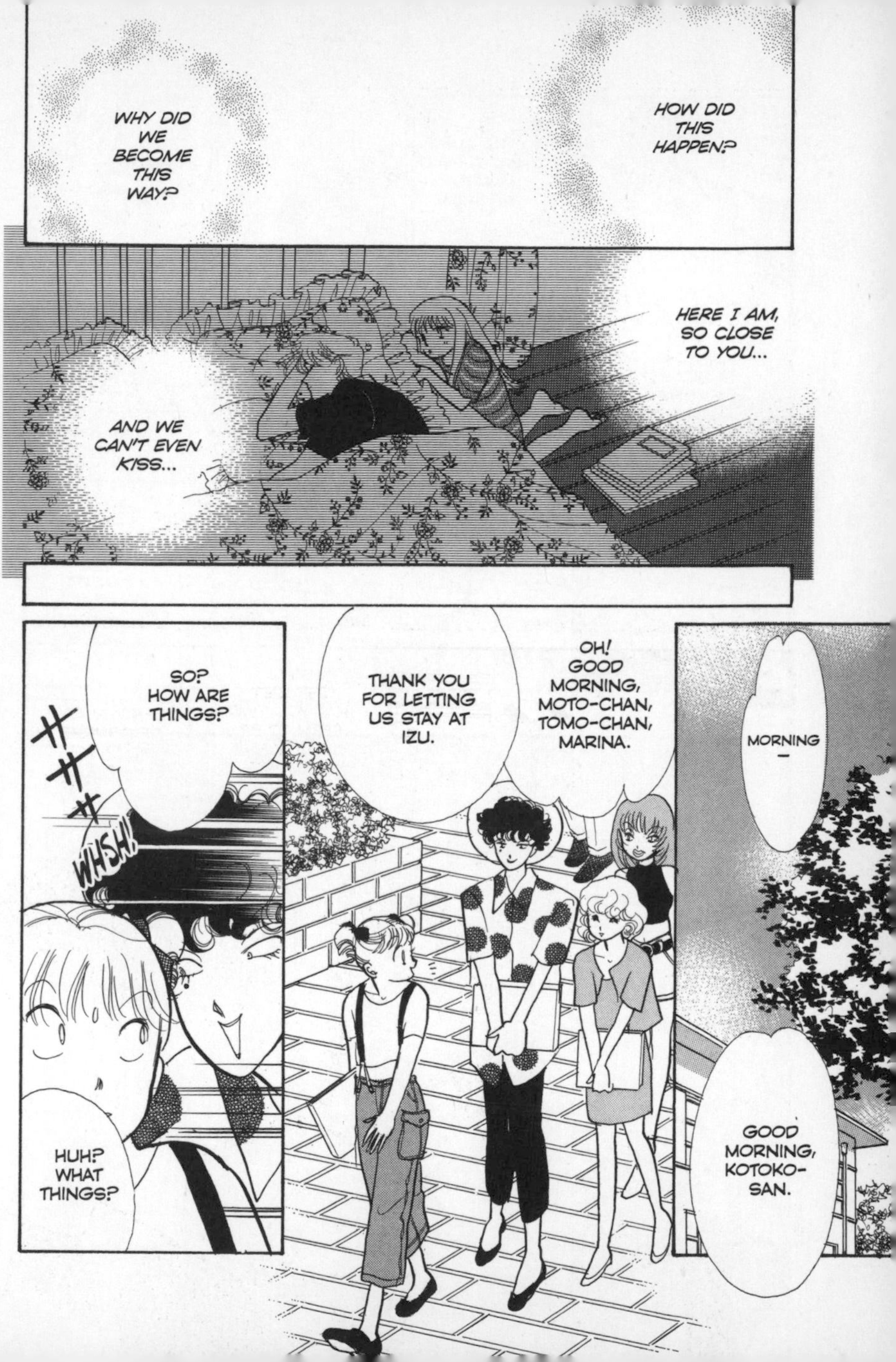
HOW DID THIS HAPPEN?
WHY DID WE BECOME THIS WAY?
HERE I AM, SO CLOSE TO YOU...
AND WE CAN'T EVEN KISS...
MORNING—
GOOD MORNING, KOTOKO-SAN.
OH! GOOD MORNING, MOTO-CHAN, TOMO-CHAN, MARINA.
THANK YOU FOR LETTING US STAY AT IZU.
SO? HOW ARE THINGS?
WHSH!
HUH? WHAT THINGS?

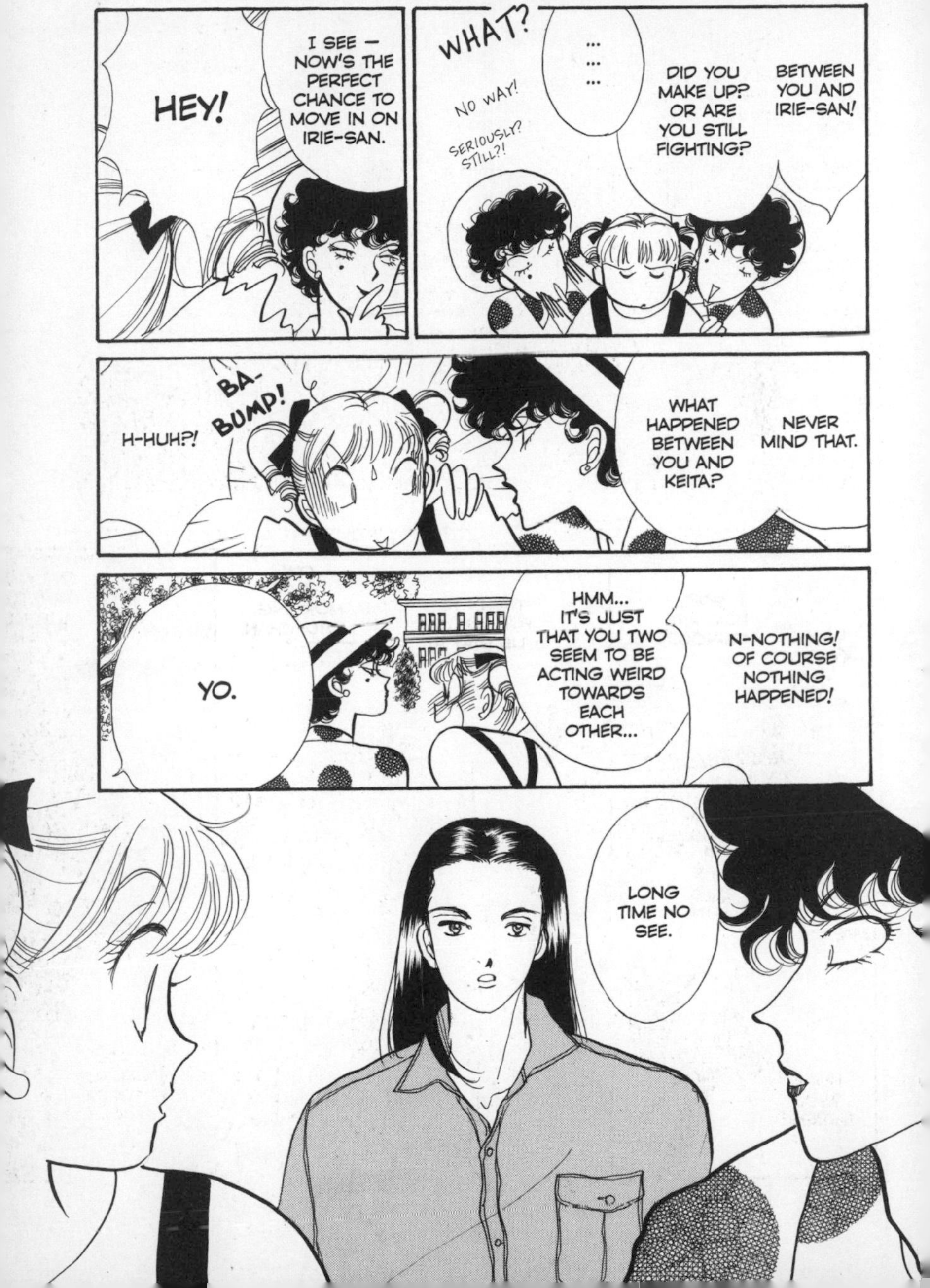
BETWEEN YOU AND IRIE-SAN!
DID YOU MAKE UP? OR ARE YOU STILL FIGHTING?
... ...
WHAT?
NO WAY!
SERIOUSLY? STILL?!
I SEE — NOW'S THE PERFECT CHANCE TO MOVE IN ON IRIE-SAN.
HEY!
NEVER MIND THAT.
WHAT HAPPENED BETWEEN YOU AND KEITA?
BA-BUMP!
H-HUH?!
N-NOTHING! OF COURSE NOTHING HAPPENED!
HMM... IT'S JUST THAT YOU TWO SEEM TO BE ACTING WEIRD TOWARDS EACH OTHER...
YO.
LONG TIME NO SEE.

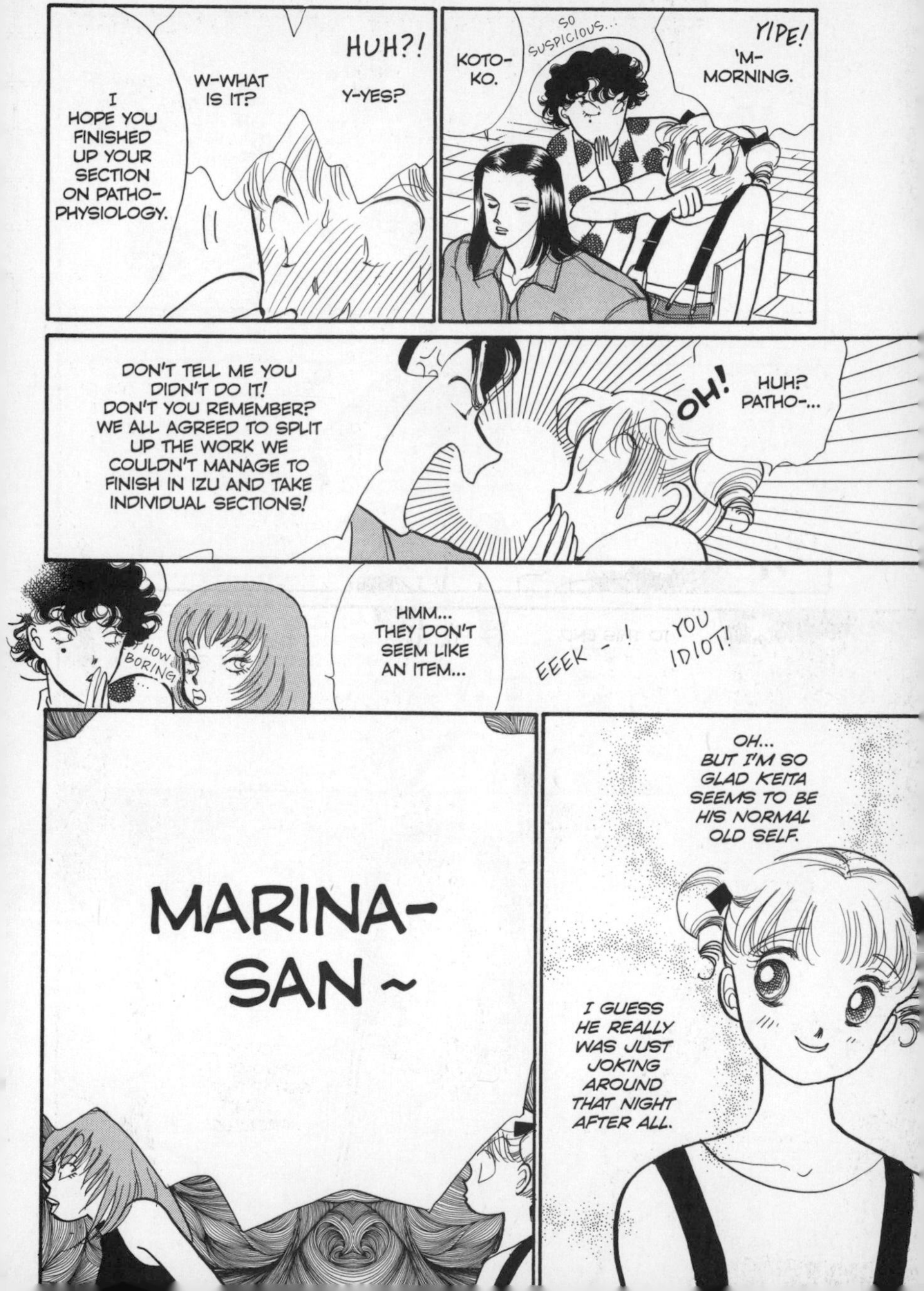
YIPE!
'M-MORNING.
SO SUSPICIOUS...
KOTO-KO.
HUH?!
Y-YES?
W-WHAT IS IT?
I HOPE YOU FINISHED UP YOUR SECTION ON PATHO-PHYSIOLOGY.
HUH? PATHO-...
OH!
DON'T TELL ME YOU DIDN'T DO IT! DON'T YOU REMEMBER? WE ALL AGREED TO SPLIT UP THE WORK WE COULDN'T MANAGE TO FINISH IN IZU AND TAKE INDIVIDUAL SECTIONS!
YOU IDIOT!
EEEK -!
HMM... THEY DON'T SEEM LIKE AN ITEM...
HOW BORING...
OH... BUT I'M SO GLAD KEITA SEEMS TO BE HIS NORMAL OLD SELF.
I GUESS HE REALLY WAS JUST JOKING AROUND THAT NIGHT AFTER ALL.
MARINA-SAN ~

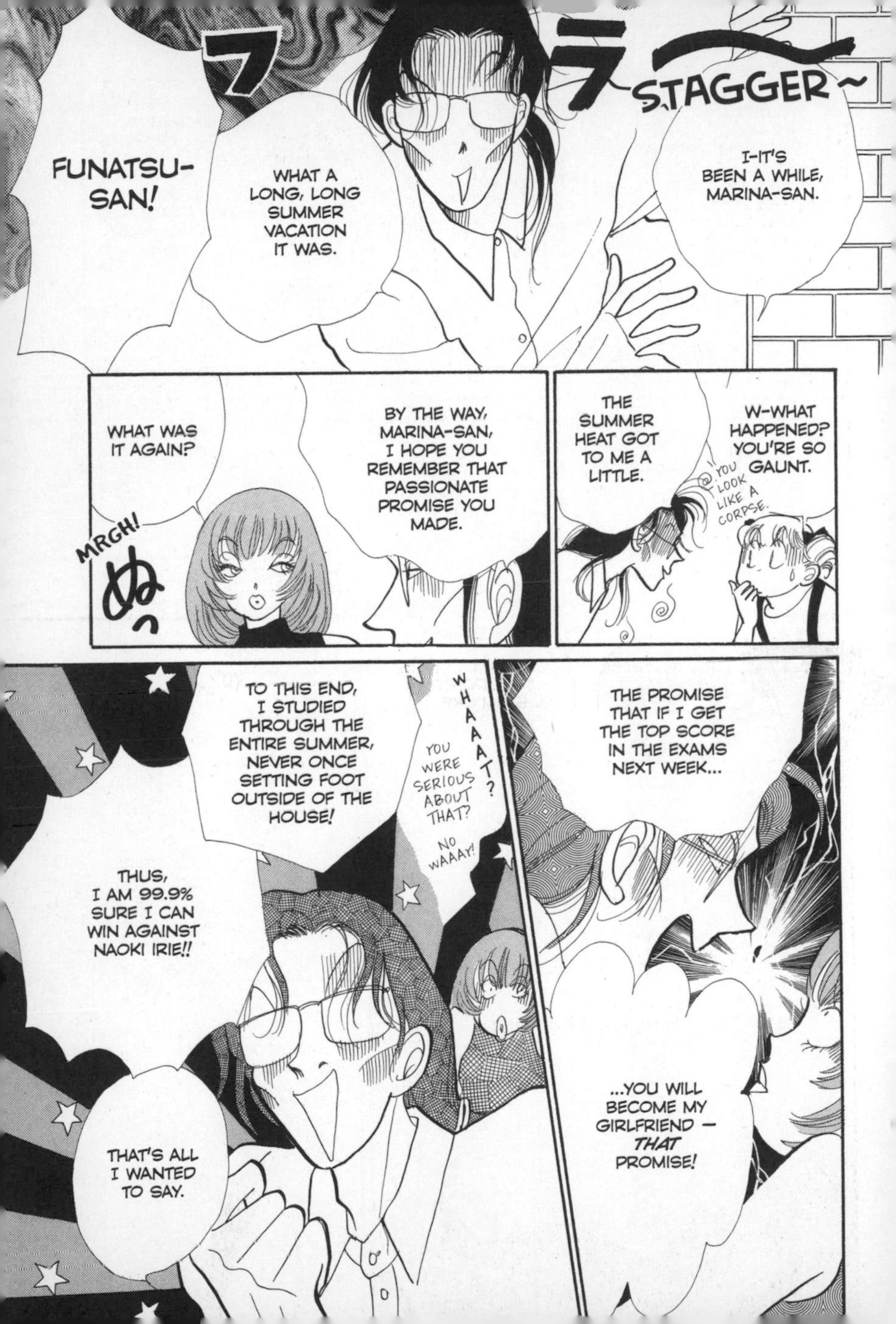
フラ〜
STAGGER~
I-IT'S BEEN A WHILE, MARINA-SAN.
WHAT A LONG, LONG SUMMER VACATION IT WAS.
FUNATSU-SAN!
W-WHAT HAPPENED? YOU'RE SO GAUNT.
YOU LOOK LIKE A CORPSE.
THE SUMMER HEAT GOT TO ME A LITTLE.
BY THE WAY, MARINA-SAN, I HOPE YOU REMEMBER THAT PASSIONATE PROMISE YOU MADE.
WHAT WAS IT AGAIN?
MRGH!
ぬっ
THE PROMISE THAT IF I GET THE TOP SCORE IN THE EXAMS NEXT WEEK...
...YOU WILL BECOME MY GIRLFRIEND — *THAT* PROMISE!
TO THIS END, I STUDIED THROUGH THE ENTIRE SUMMER, NEVER ONCE SETTING FOOT OUTSIDE OF THE HOUSE!
WHAAAAT?
YOU WERE SERIOUS ABOUT THAT?
NO WAAAY!
THUS, I AM 99.9% SURE I CAN WIN AGAINST NAOKI IRIE!!
THAT'S ALL I WANTED TO SAY.

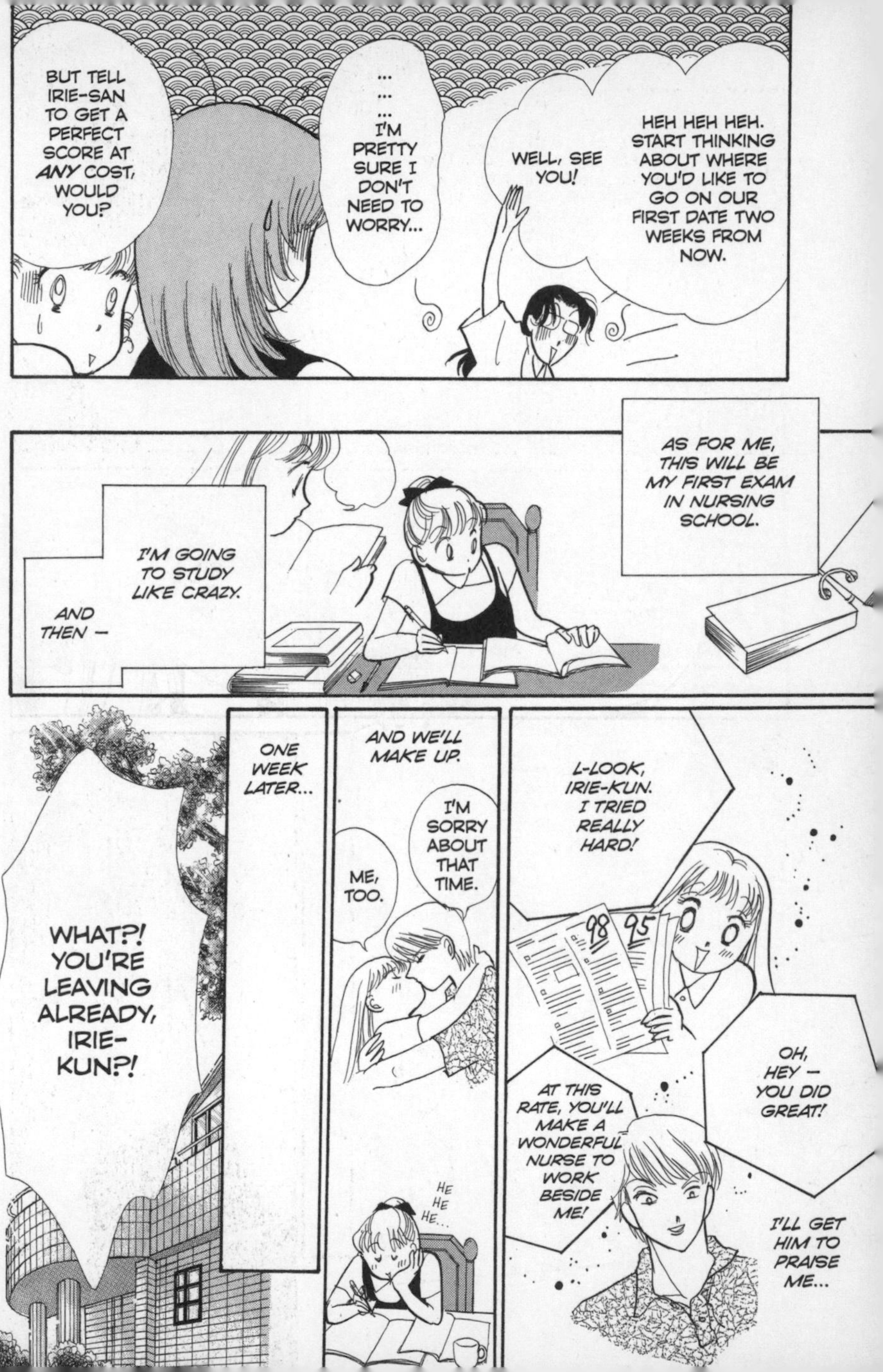
HEH HEH HEH. START THINKING ABOUT WHERE YOU'D LIKE TO GO ON OUR FIRST DATE TWO WEEKS FROM NOW.
WELL, SEE YOU!
... ... I'M PRETTY SURE I DON'T NEED TO WORRY...
BUT TELL IRIE-SAN TO GET A PERFECT SCORE AT ANY COST, WOULD YOU?
AS FOR ME, THIS WILL BE MY FIRST EXAM IN NURSING SCHOOL.
I'M GOING TO STUDY LIKE CRAZY.
AND THEN —
L-LOOK, IRIE-KUN. I TRIED REALLY HARD!
98
95
OH, HEY — YOU DID GREAT!
AT THIS RATE, YOU'LL MAKE A WONDERFUL NURSE TO WORK BESIDE ME!
I'LL GET HIM TO PRAISE ME...
AND WE'LL MAKE UP.
I'M SORRY ABOUT THAT TIME.
ME, TOO.
HE HE HE...
ONE WEEK LATER...
WHAT?! YOU'RE LEAVING ALREADY, IRIE-KUN?!

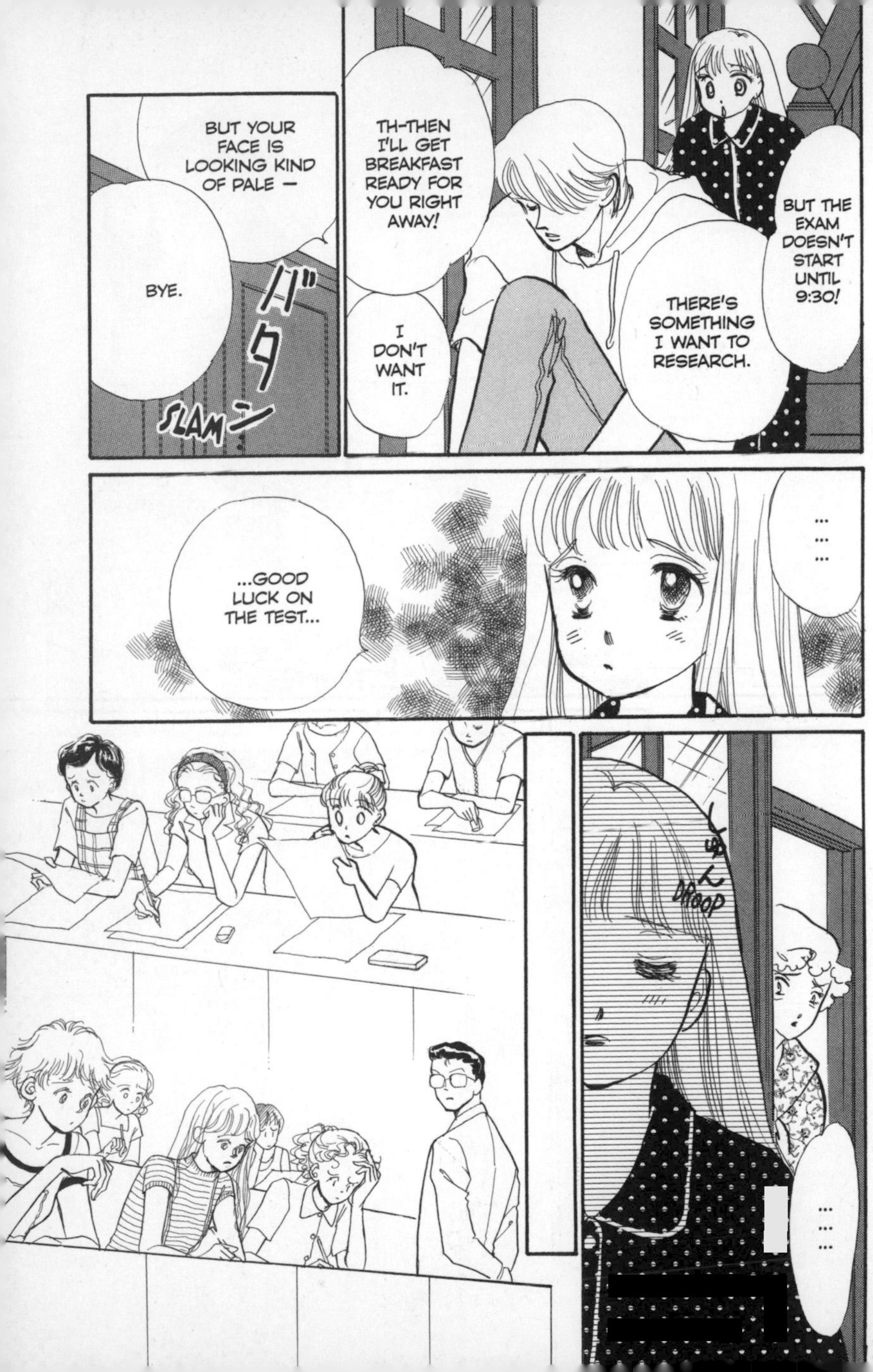
BUT THE EXAM DOESN'T START UNTIL 9:30!
THERE'S SOMETHING I WANT TO RESEARCH.
TH-THEN I'LL GET BREAKFAST READY FOR YOU RIGHT AWAY!
I DON'T WANT IT.
BUT YOUR FACE IS LOOKING KIND OF PALE —
BYE.
バタン
SLAM
...
...
...
...GOOD LUCK ON THE TEST...
しゅん
DROOP
...
...
...
[redacted]

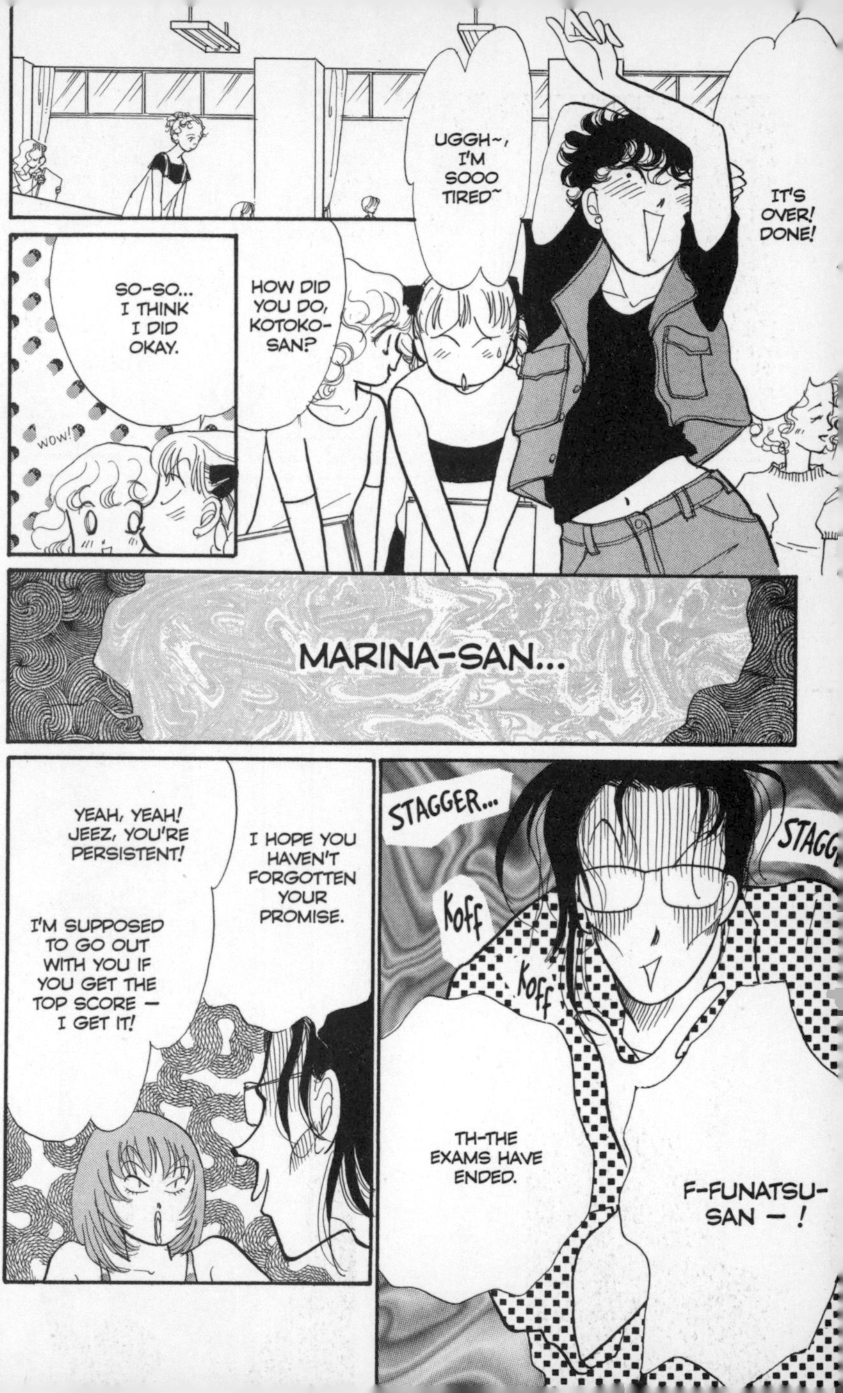
IT'S OVER! DONE!
UGGH~, I'M SOOO TIRED~
HOW DID YOU DO, KOTOKO-SAN?
SO-SO... I THINK I DID OKAY.
WOW!
MARINA-SAN...
STAGGER...
STAGG
KOFF
KOFF
F-FUNATSU-SAN — !
TH-THE EXAMS HAVE ENDED.
I HOPE YOU HAVEN'T FORGOTTEN YOUR PROMISE.
YEAH, YEAH! JEEZ, YOU'RE PERSISTENT!
I'M SUPPOSED TO GO OUT WITH YOU IF YOU GET THE TOP SCORE — I GET IT!

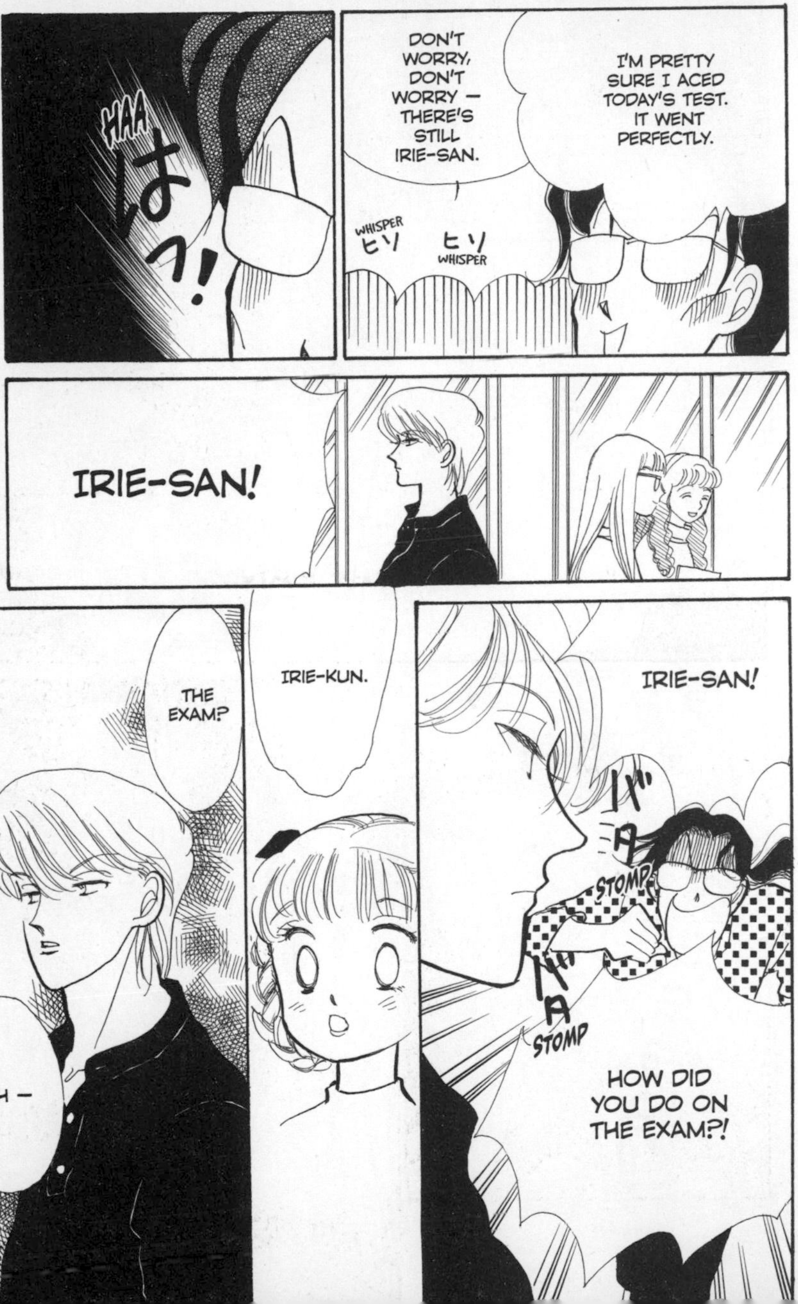
I'M PRETTY SURE I ACED TODAY'S TEST. IT WENT PERFECTLY.
DON'T WORRY, DON'T WORRY — THERE'S STILL IRIE-SAN.
ヒソ WHISPER
ヒソ WHISPER
はっ!
HAA
IRIE-SAN!
IRIE-SAN!
バタ STOMP
バタ STOMP
HOW DID YOU DO ON THE EXAM?!
IRIE-KUN.
THE EXAM?
OH —

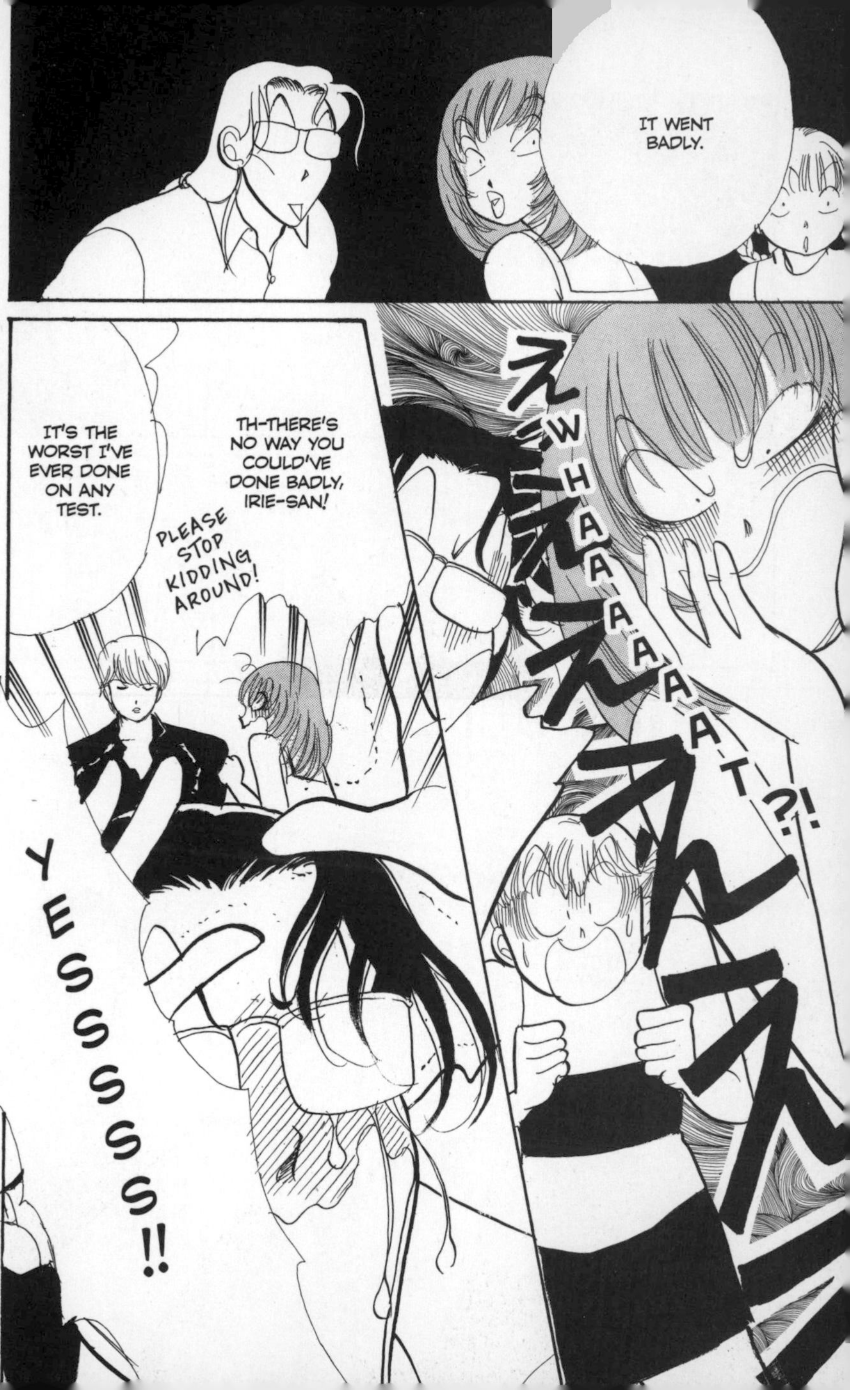
IT WENT BADLY.
WHAAAAAAAT?!
TH-THERE'S NO WAY YOU COULD'VE DONE BADLY, IRIE-SAN!
PLEASE STOP KIDDING AROUND!
IT'S THE WORST I'VE EVER DONE ON ANY TEST.
YESSSSSS!!

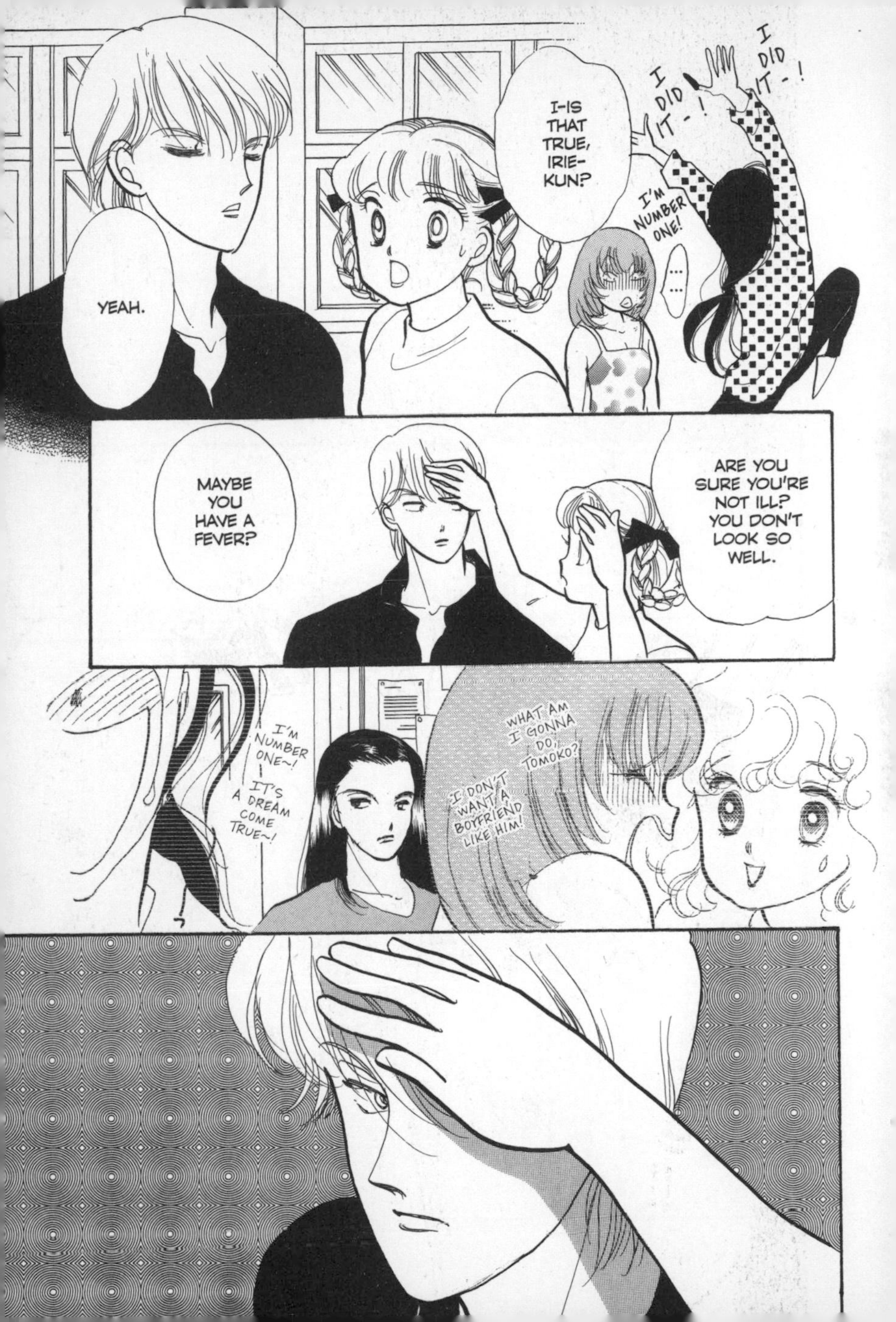
I DID IT-!
I DID IT-!
I-IS THAT TRUE, IRIE-KUN?
I'M NUMBER ONE!
...
YEAH.
ARE YOU SURE YOU'RE NOT ILL? YOU DON'T LOOK SO WELL.
MAYBE YOU HAVE A FEVER?
WHAT AM I GONNA DO, TOMOKO?
I DON'T WANT A BOYFRIEND LIKE HIM!
I'M NUMBER ONE~!
IT'S A DREAM COME TRUE~!

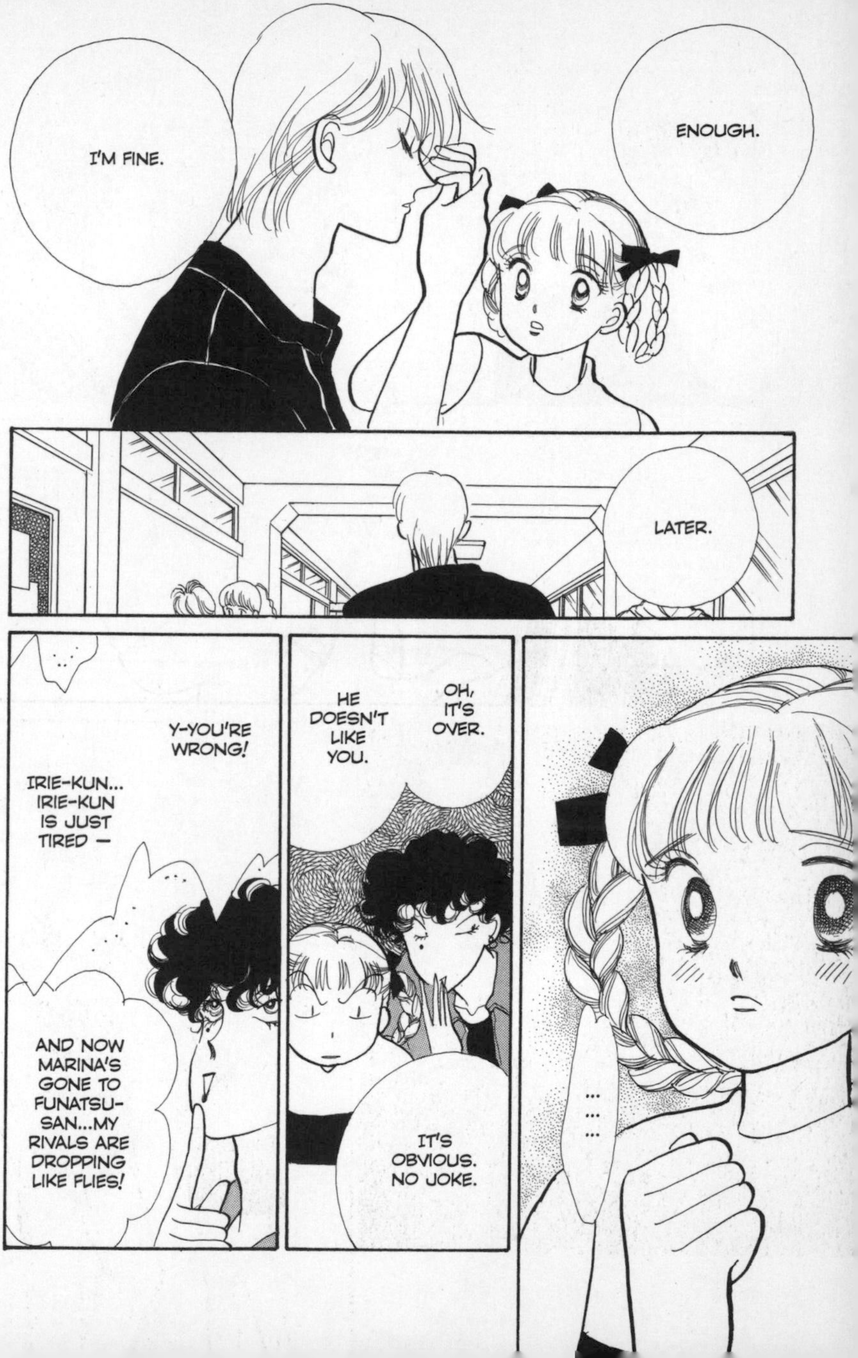
ENOUGH.
I'M FINE.
LATER.
...
...
...
OH, IT'S OVER.
HE DOESN'T LIKE YOU.
IT'S OBVIOUS. NO JOKE.
...
Y-YOU'RE WRONG!
IRIE-KUN... IRIE-KUN IS JUST TIRED —
...
AND NOW MARINA'S GONE TO FUNATSU-SAN...MY RIVALS ARE DROPPING LIKE FLIES!

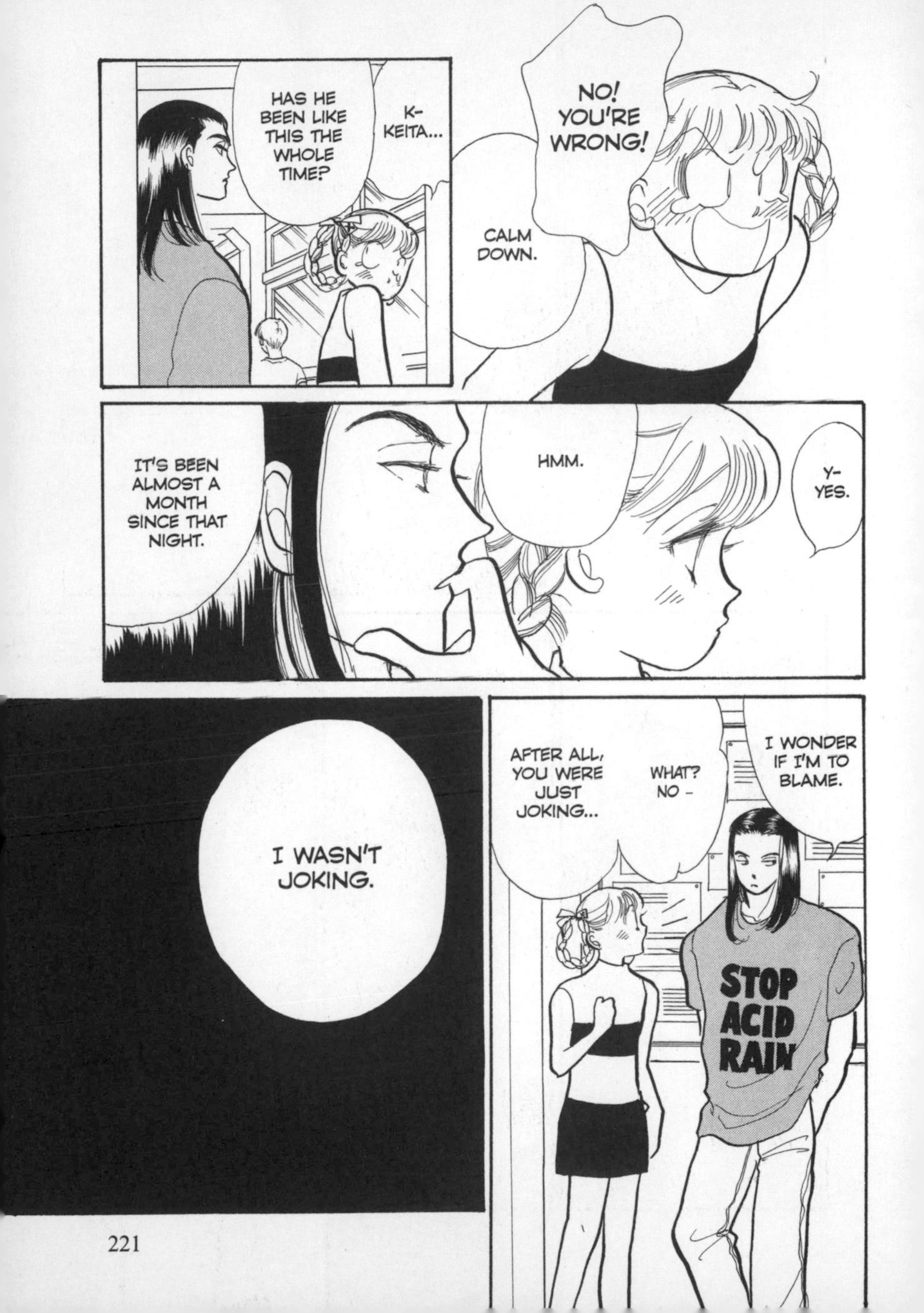
NO! YOU'RE WRONG!
CALM DOWN.
K-KEITA...
HAS HE BEEN LIKE THIS THE WHOLE TIME?
Y-YES.
HMM.
IT'S BEEN ALMOST A MONTH SINCE THAT NIGHT.
I WONDER IF I'M TO BLAME.
WHAT? NO -
AFTER ALL, YOU WERE JUST JOKING...
STOP ACID RAIN
I WASN'T JOKING.

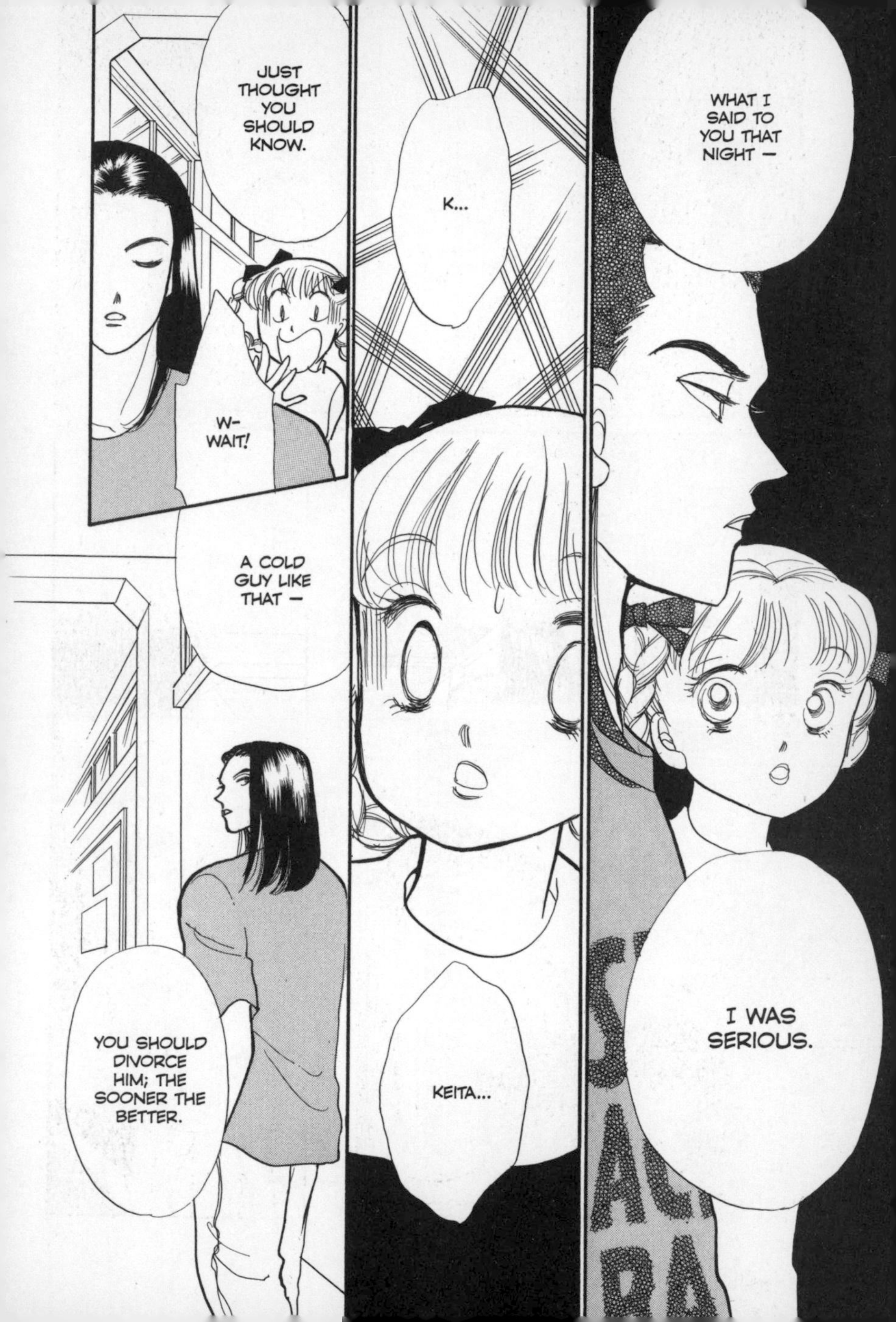
WHAT I SAID TO YOU THAT NIGHT —
I WAS SERIOUS.
K...
KEITA...
JUST THOUGHT YOU SHOULD KNOW.
W- WAIT!
A COLD GUY LIKE THAT —
YOU SHOULD DIVORCE HIM; THE SOONER THE BETTER.

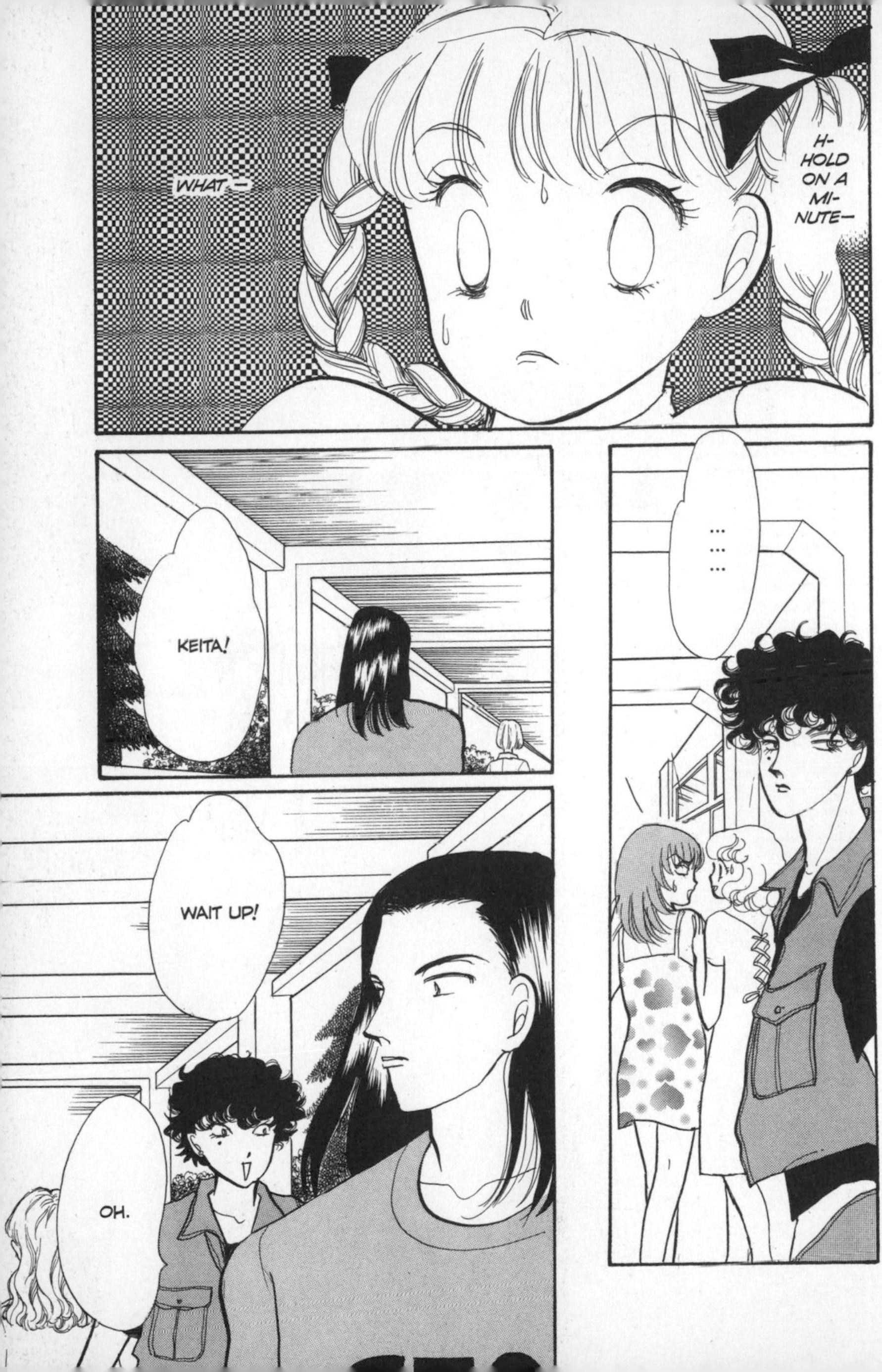
H-HOLD ON A MI-NUTE—
WHAT—
……
KEITA!
WAIT UP!
OH.

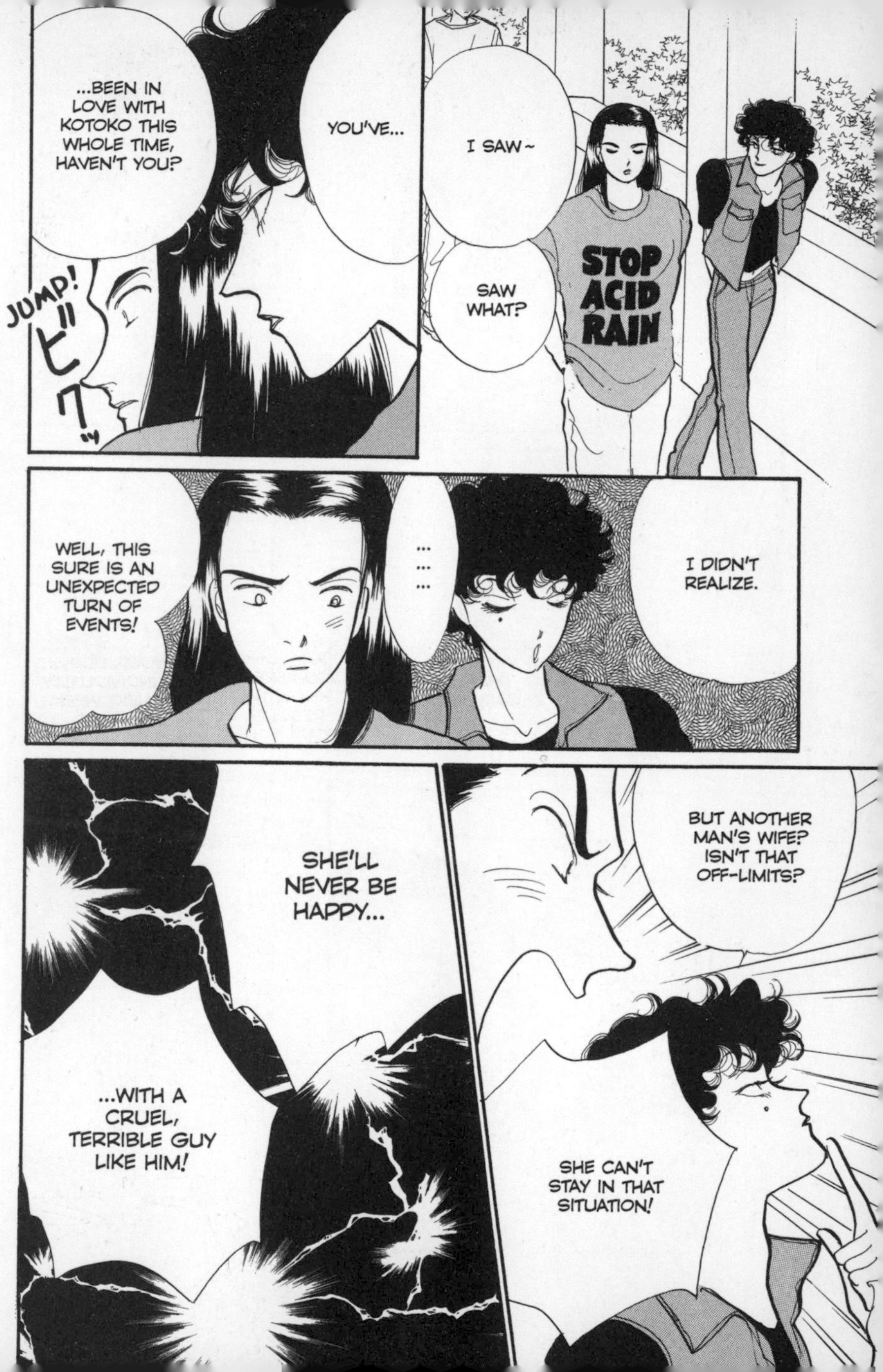
I SAW~
SAW WHAT?
STOP ACID RAIN
YOU'VE...
...BEEN IN LOVE WITH KOTOKO THIS WHOLE TIME, HAVEN'T YOU?
JUMP! ビクッ
I DIDN'T REALIZE.
......
WELL, THIS SURE IS AN UNEXPECTED TURN OF EVENTS!
BUT ANOTHER MAN'S WIFE? ISN'T THAT OFF-LIMITS?
SHE CAN'T STAY IN THAT SITUATION!
SHE'LL NEVER BE HAPPY...
...WITH A CRUEL, TERRIBLE GUY LIKE HIM!

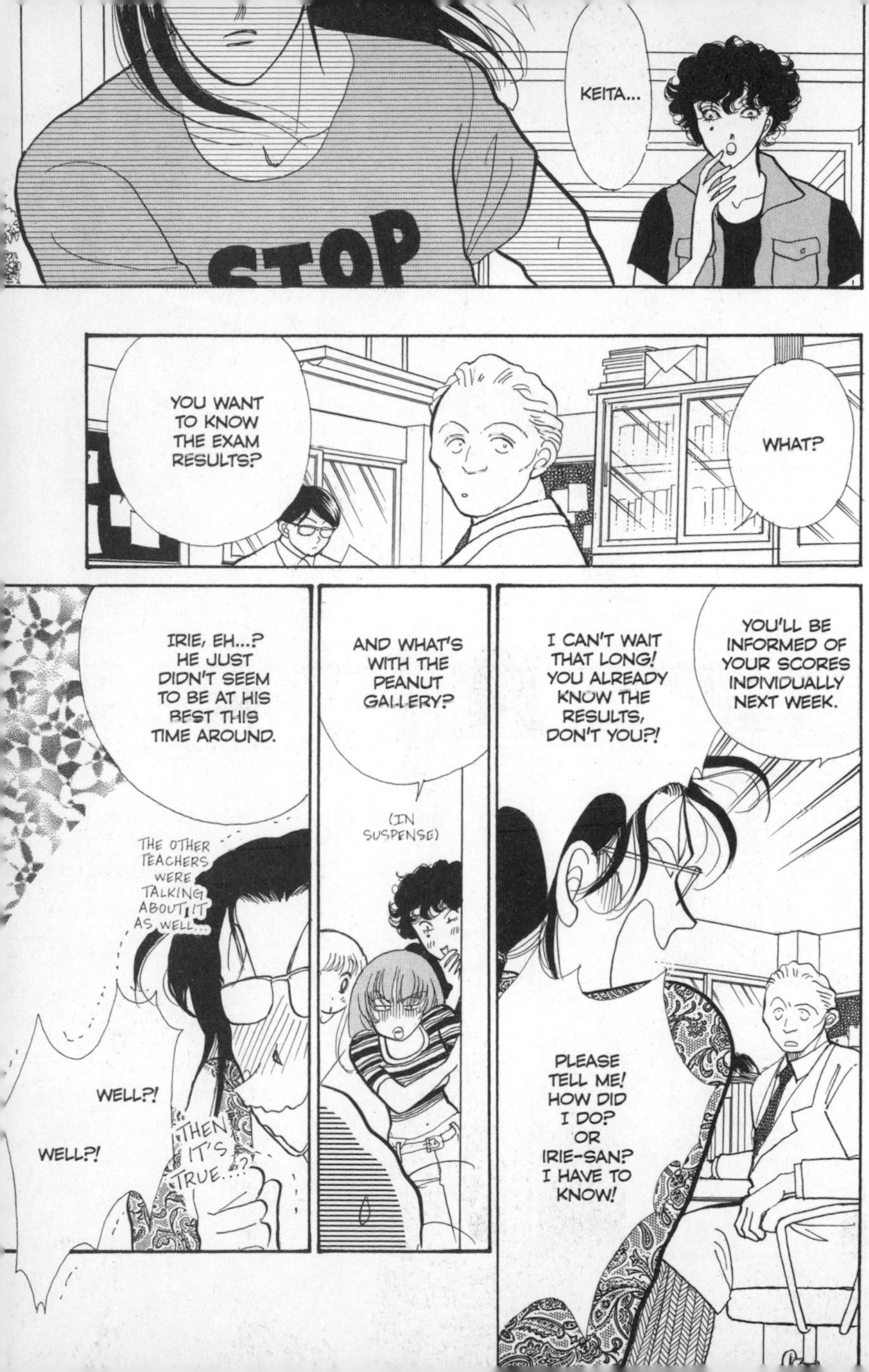
KEITA...
STOP
WHAT?
YOU WANT TO KNOW THE EXAM RESULTS?
YOU'LL BE INFORMED OF YOUR SCORES INDIVIDUALLY NEXT WEEK.
I CAN'T WAIT THAT LONG! YOU ALREADY KNOW THE RESULTS, DON'T YOU?!
PLEASE TELL ME! HOW DID I DO? OR IRIE-SAN? I HAVE TO KNOW!
AND WHAT'S WITH THE PEANUT GALLERY?
(IN SUSPENSE)
IRIE, EH...? HE JUST DIDN'T SEEM TO BE AT HIS BEST THIS TIME AROUND.
THE OTHER TEACHERS WERE TALKING ABOUT IT AS WELL...
WELL?!
THEN IT'S TRUE...?
WELL?!

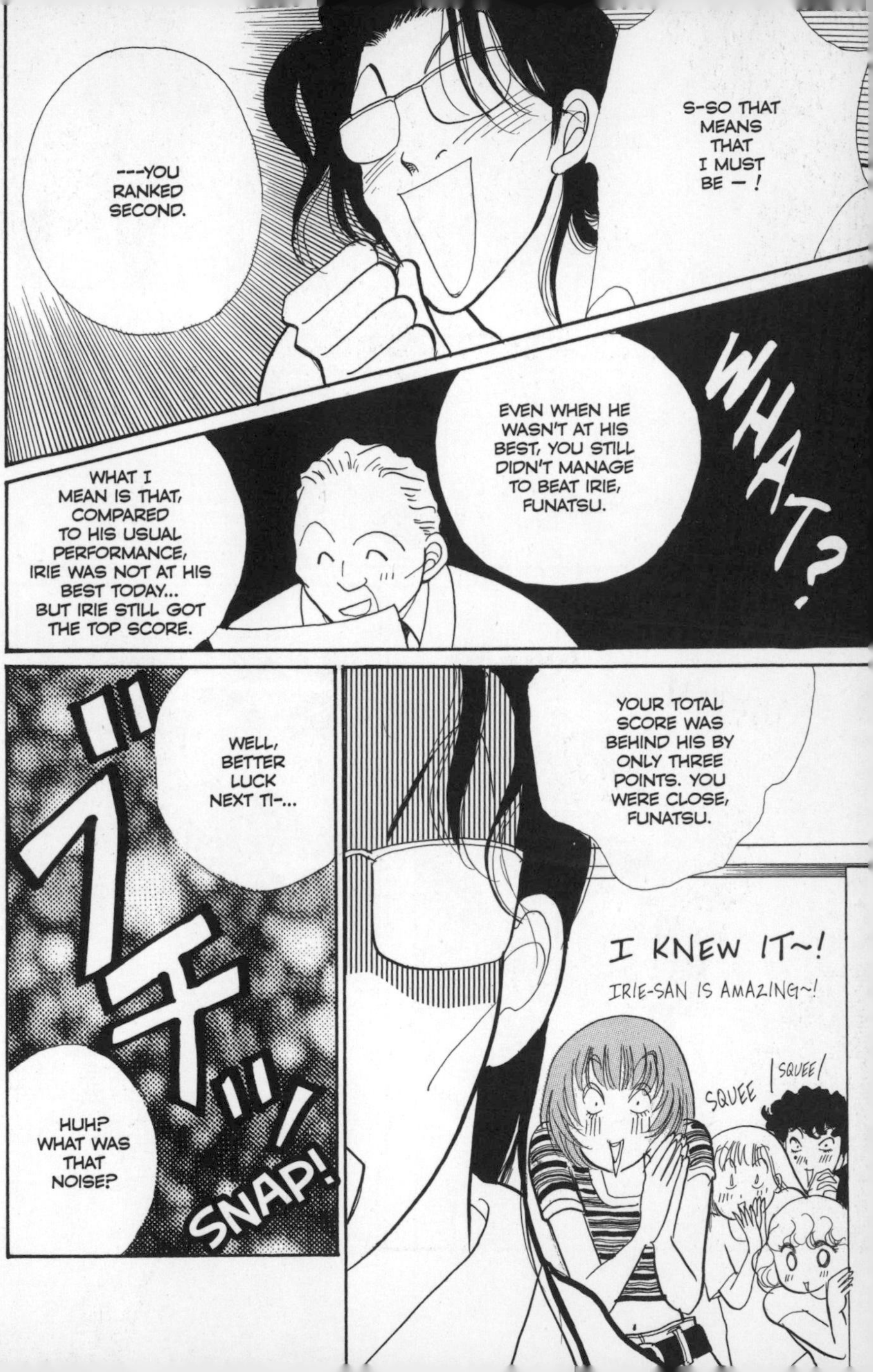
S-SO THAT MEANS THAT I MUST BE —!
---YOU RANKED SECOND.
WHAT?
EVEN WHEN HE WASN'T AT HIS BEST, YOU STILL DIDN'T MANAGE TO BEAT IRIE, FUNATSU.
WHAT I MEAN IS THAT, COMPARED TO HIS USUAL PERFORMANCE, IRIE WAS NOT AT HIS BEST TODAY... BUT IRIE STILL GOT THE TOP SCORE.
YOUR TOTAL SCORE WAS BEHIND HIS BY ONLY THREE POINTS. YOU WERE CLOSE, FUNATSU.
I KNEW IT~!
IRIE-SAN IS AMAZING~!
SQUEE
SQUEE
WELL, BETTER LUCK NEXT TI-...
ブチッ
SNAP!
HUH? WHAT WAS THAT NOISE?

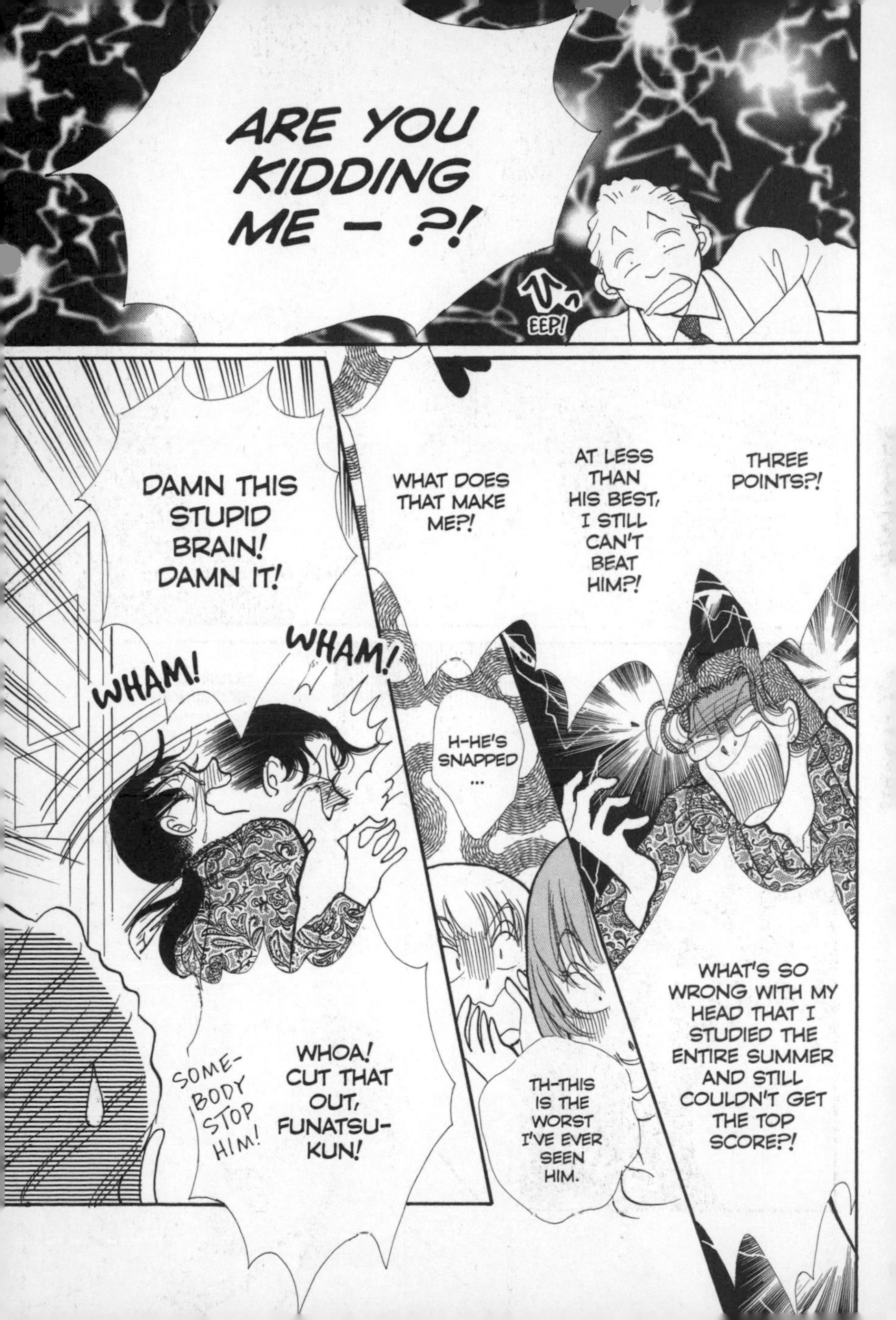
ARE YOU KIDDING ME – ?!
EEP!
THREE POINTS?!
AT LESS THAN HIS BEST, I STILL CAN'T BEAT HIM?!
WHAT DOES THAT MAKE ME?!
H-HE'S SNAPPED ...
WHAT'S SO WRONG WITH MY HEAD THAT I STUDIED THE ENTIRE SUMMER AND STILL COULDN'T GET THE TOP SCORE?!
TH-THIS IS THE WORST I'VE EVER SEEN HIM.
DAMN THIS STUPID BRAIN! DAMN IT!
WHAM!
WHAM!
WHOA! CUT THAT OUT, FUNATSU-KUN!
SOME-BODY STOP HIM!

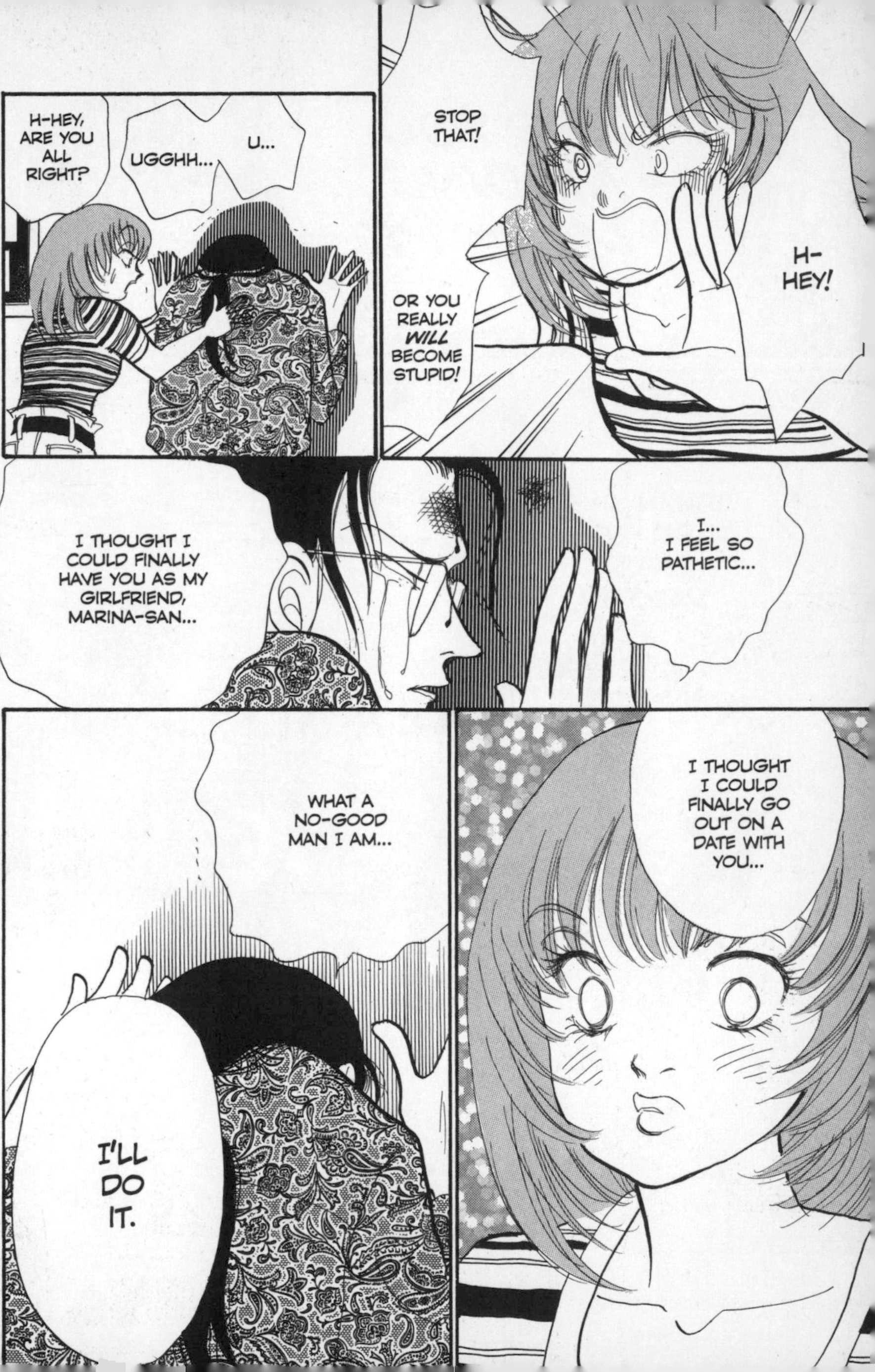
H-HEY!
STOP THAT!
OR YOU REALLY *WILL* BECOME STUPID!
U...
UGGHH...
H-HEY, ARE YOU ALL RIGHT?
I... I FEEL SO PATHETIC...
I THOUGHT I COULD FINALLY HAVE YOU AS MY GIRLFRIEND, MARINA-SAN...
I THOUGHT I COULD FINALLY GO OUT ON A DATE WITH YOU...
WHAT A NO-GOOD MAN I AM...
I'LL DO IT.

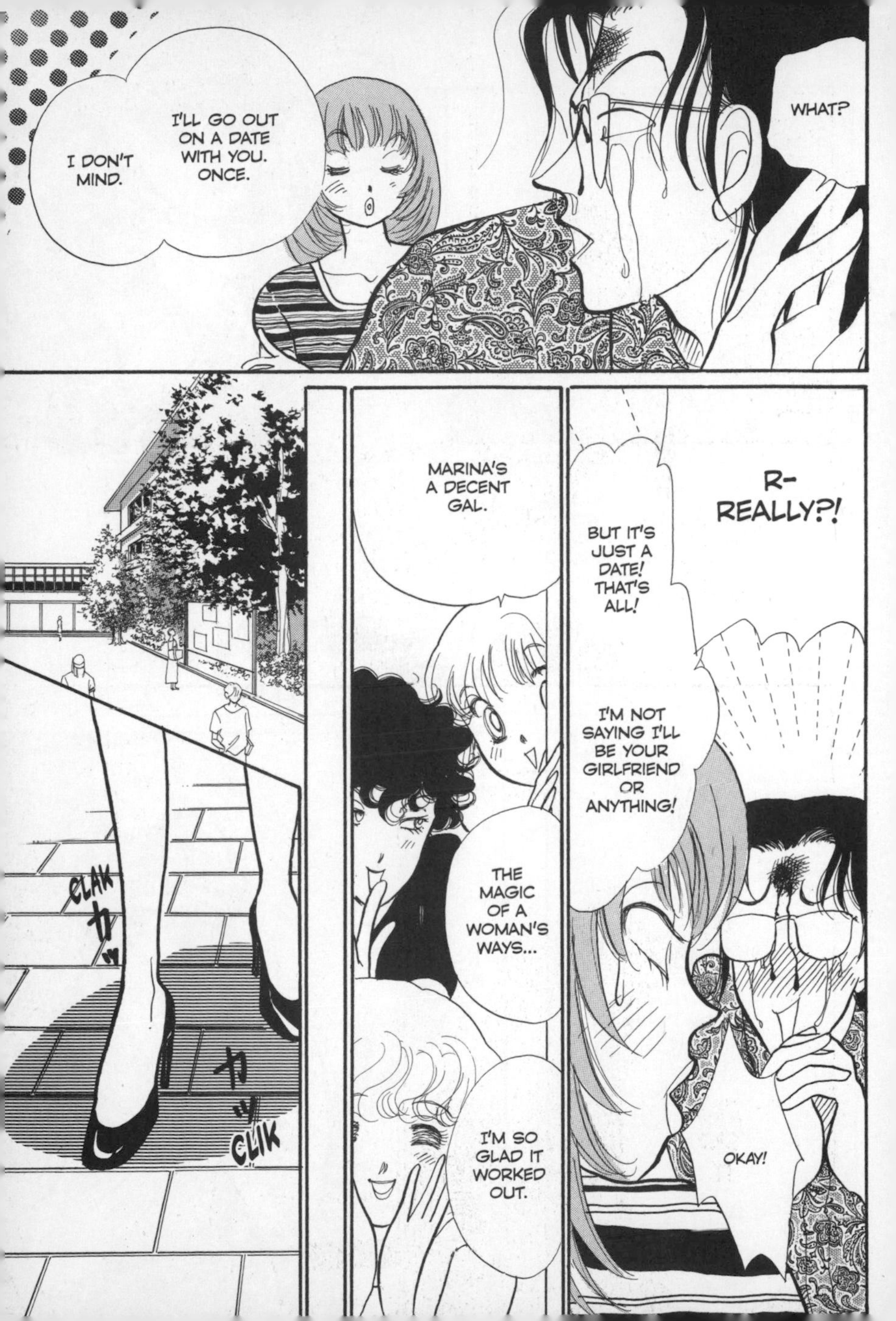
WHAT?
I DON'T MIND. I'LL GO OUT ON A DATE WITH YOU. ONCE.
R-REALLY?!
BUT IT'S JUST A DATE! THAT'S ALL!
I'M NOT SAYING I'LL BE YOUR GIRLFRIEND OR ANYTHING!
OKAY!
MARINA'S A DECENT GAL.
THE MAGIC OF A WOMAN'S WAYS...
I'M SO GLAD IT WORKED OUT.
CLAK
CLIK

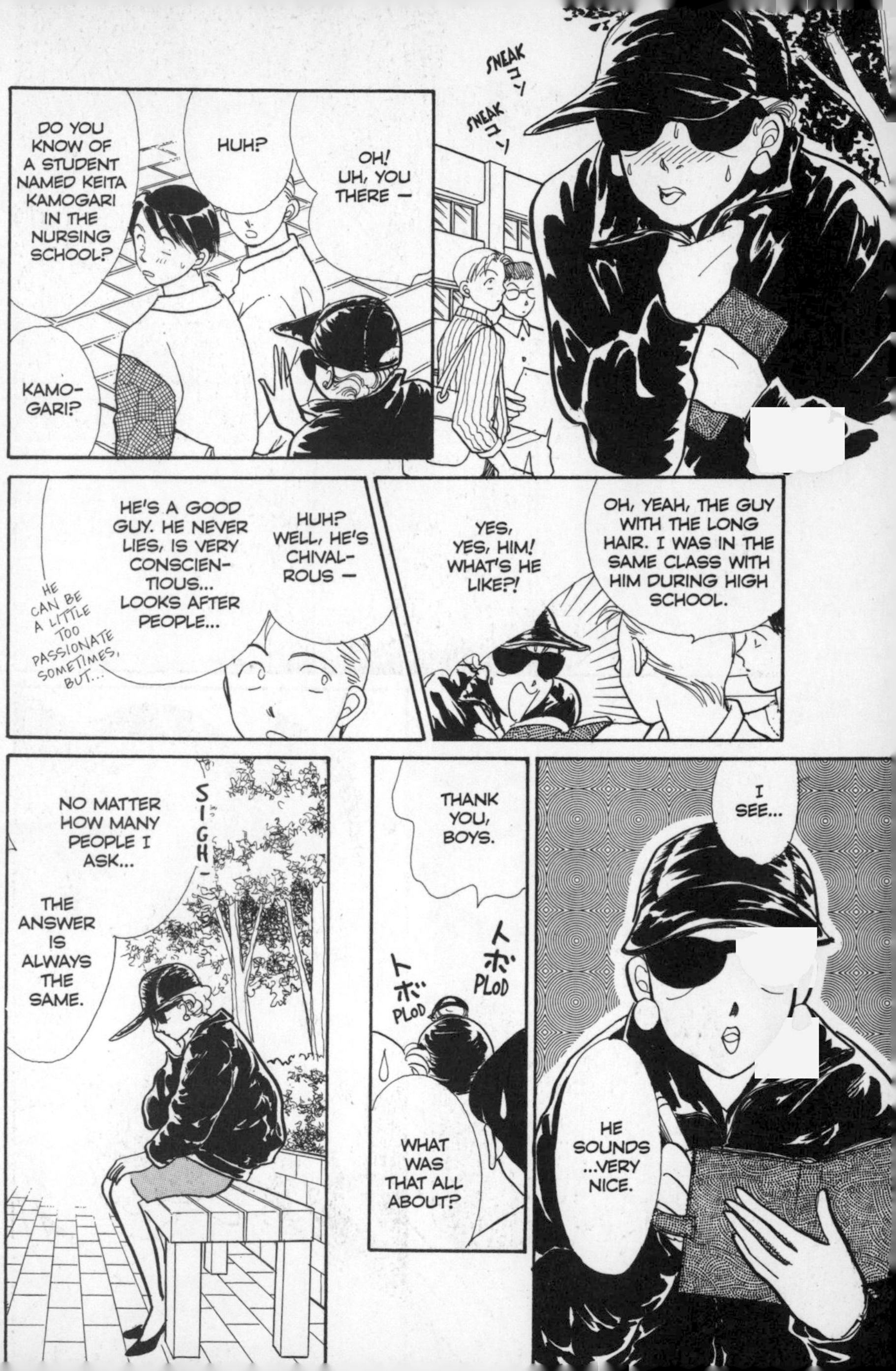
SNEAK コソ
SNEAK コソ
OH! UH, YOU THERE —
HUH?
DO YOU KNOW OF A STUDENT NAMED KEITA KAMOGARI IN THE NURSING SCHOOL?
KAMOGARI?
OH, YEAH, THE GUY WITH THE LONG HAIR. I WAS IN THE SAME CLASS WITH HIM DURING HIGH SCHOOL.
YES, YES, HIM! WHAT'S HE LIKE?!
HUH? WELL, HE'S CHIVALROUS —
HE'S A GOOD GUY. HE NEVER LIES, IS VERY CONSCIENTIOUS... LOOKS AFTER PEOPLE...
HE CAN BE A LITTLE TOO PASSIONATE SOMETIMES, BUT...
I SEE...
HE SOUNDS ...VERY NICE.
THANK YOU, BOYS.
トボ PLOD
トボ PLOD
WHAT WAS THAT ALL ABOUT?
NO MATTER HOW MANY PEOPLE I ASK...
SIGH—
THE ANSWER IS ALWAYS THE SAME.

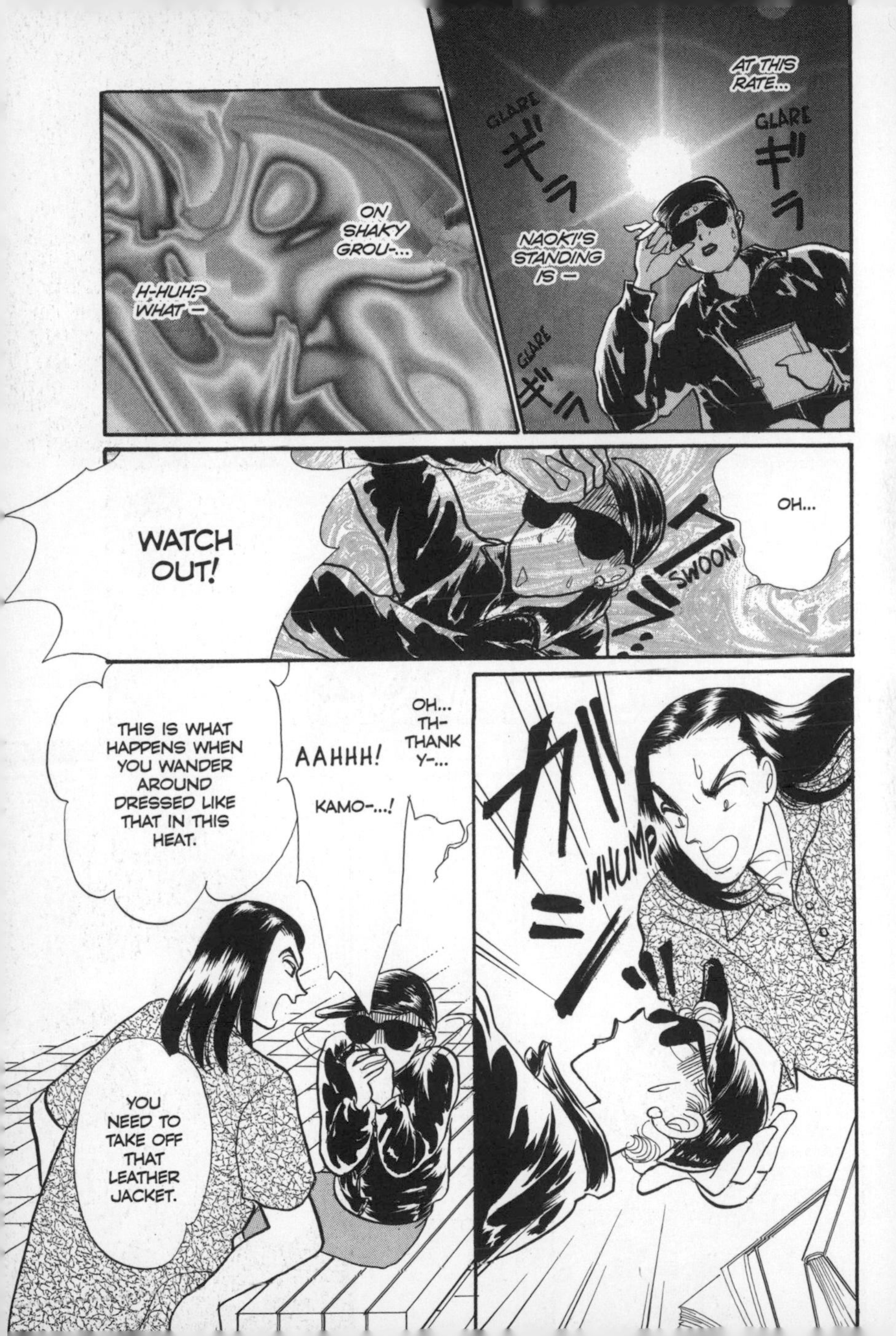
AT THIS RATE...
GLARE
GLARE
NAOKI'S STANDING IS –
GLARE
ON SHAKY GROU-...
H-HUH? WHAT –
OH...
SWOON
WATCH OUT!
WHUMP
OH... TH-THANK Y-...
AAHHH!
KAMO-...!
THIS IS WHAT HAPPENS WHEN YOU WANDER AROUND DRESSED LIKE THAT IN THIS HEAT.
YOU NEED TO TAKE OFF THAT LEATHER JACKET.

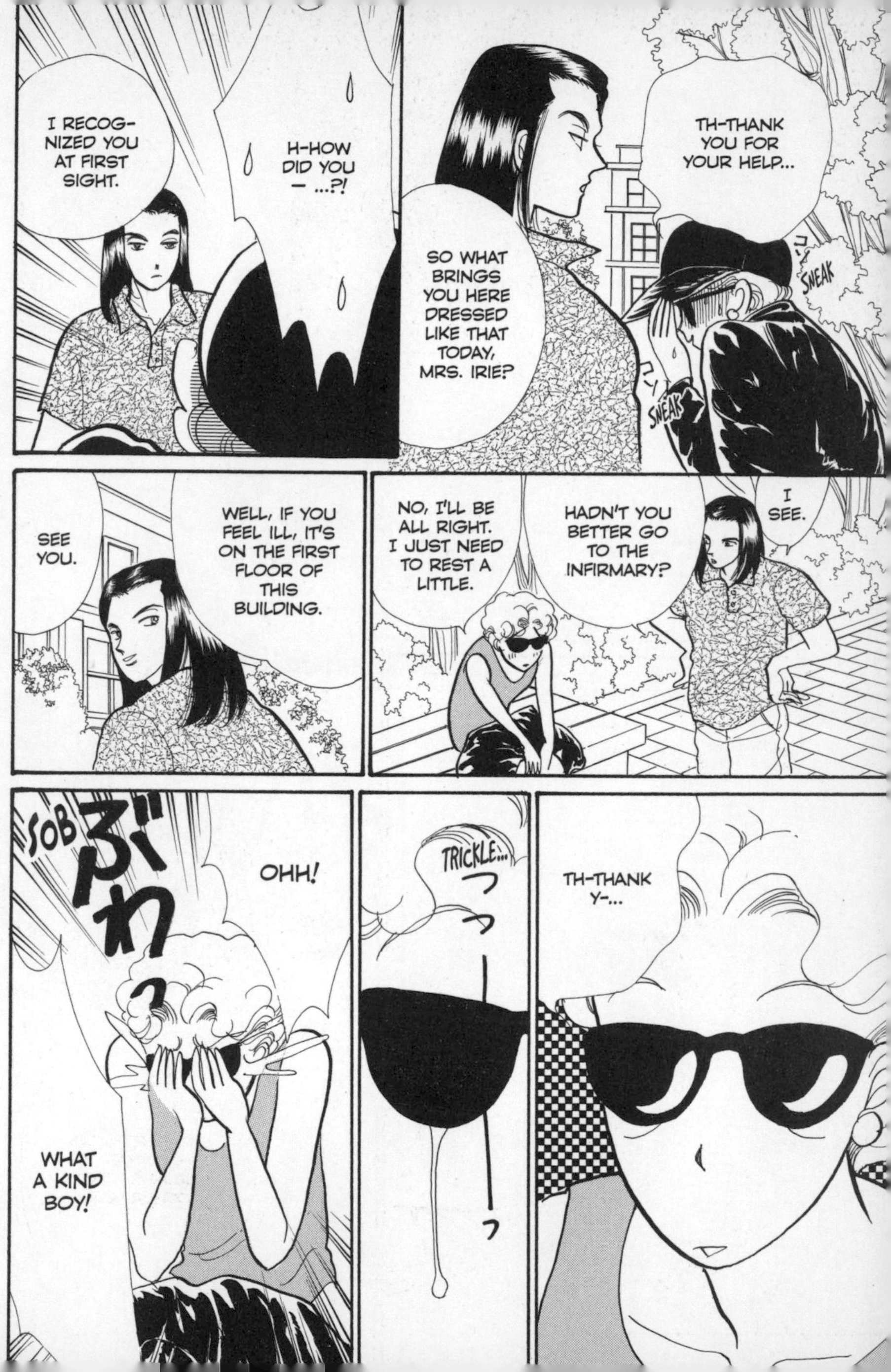
TH-THANK YOU FOR YOUR HELP...
SNEAK
SNEAK
SO WHAT BRINGS YOU HERE DRESSED LIKE THAT TODAY, MRS. IRIE?
H-HOW DID YOU — ...?!
I RECOGNIZED YOU AT FIRST SIGHT.
I SEE.
HADN'T YOU BETTER GO TO THE INFIRMARY?
NO, I'LL BE ALL RIGHT. I JUST NEED TO REST A LITTLE.
WELL, IF YOU FEEL ILL, IT'S ON THE FIRST FLOOR OF THIS BUILDING.
SEE YOU.
TH-THANK Y-...
TRICKLE...
SOB
ぶわっ
OHH!
WHAT A KIND BOY!

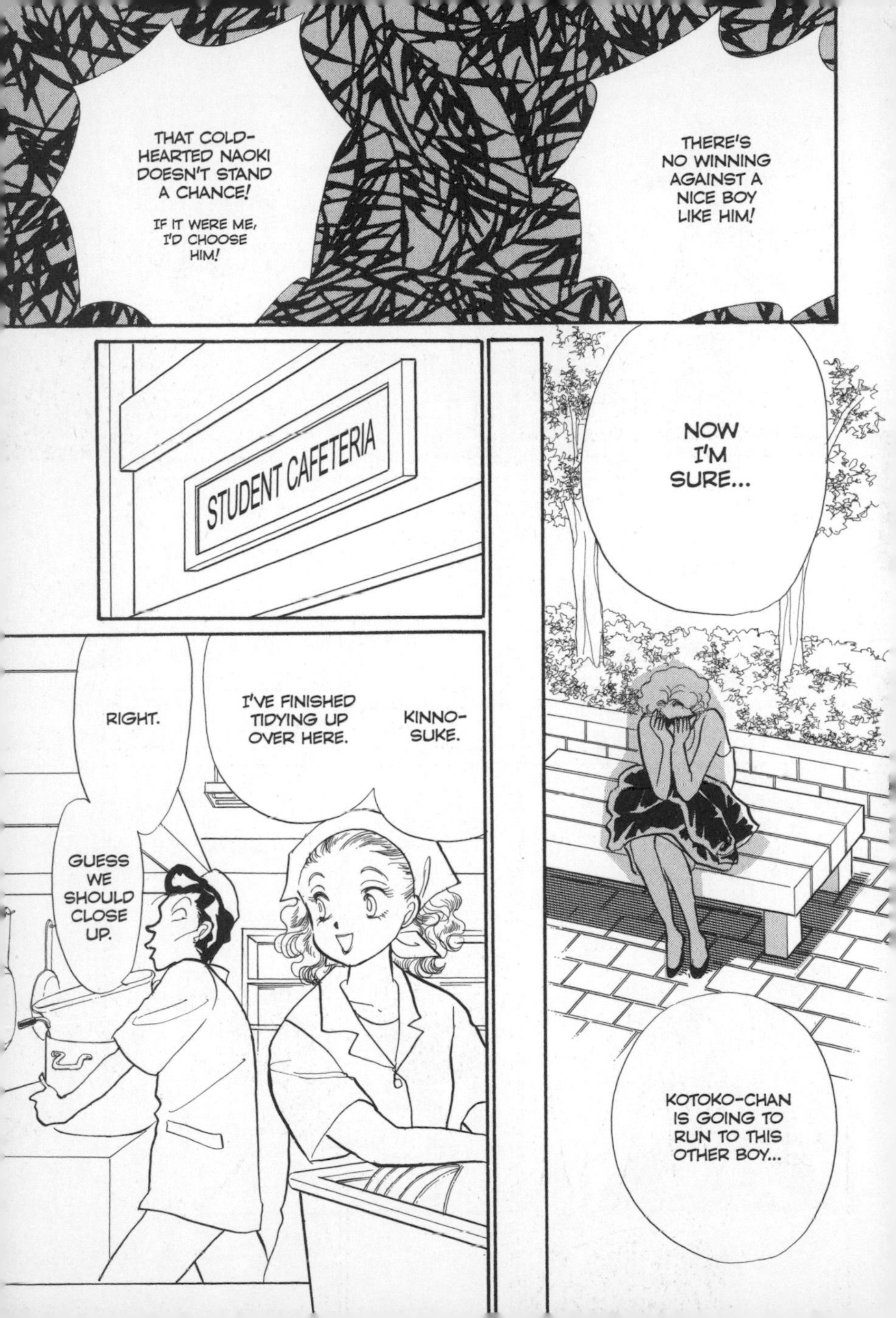
THERE'S NO WINNING AGAINST A NICE BOY LIKE HIM!
THAT COLD-HEARTED NAOKI DOESN'T STAND A CHANCE!
IF IT WERE ME, I'D CHOOSE HIM!
NOW I'M SURE...
KOTOKO-CHAN IS GOING TO RUN TO THIS OTHER BOY...
STUDENT CAFETERIA
KINNO-SUKE.
I'VE FINISHED TIDYING UP OVER HERE.
RIGHT.
GUESS WE SHOULD CLOSE UP.

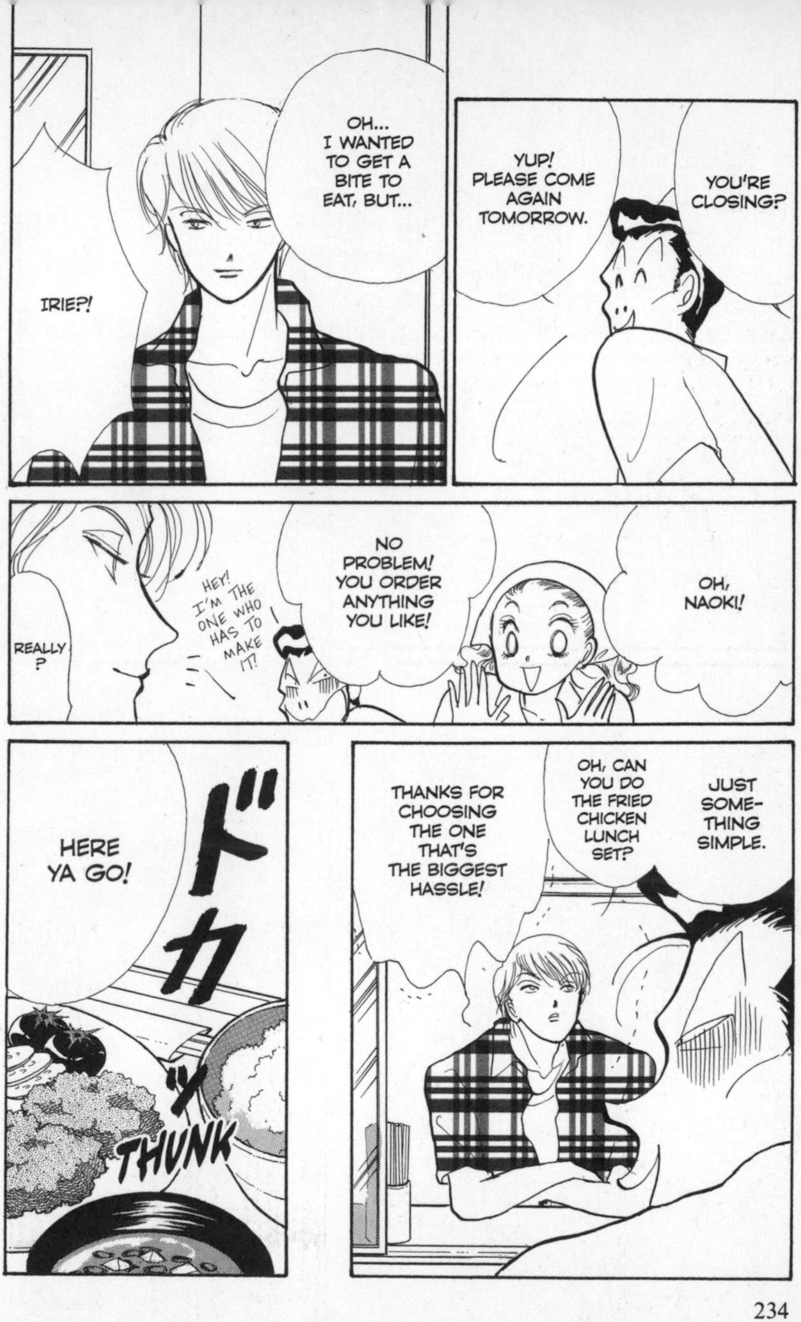
YOU'RE CLOSING?
YUP! PLEASE COME AGAIN TOMORROW.
OH... I WANTED TO GET A BITE TO EAT, BUT...
IRIE?!
OH, NAOKI!
NO PROBLEM! YOU ORDER ANYTHING YOU LIKE!
HEY! I'M THE ONE WHO HAS TO MAKE IT!
REALLY?
JUST SOMETHING SIMPLE.
OH, CAN YOU DO THE FRIED CHICKEN LUNCH SET?
THANKS FOR CHOOSING THE ONE THAT'S THE BIGGEST HASSLE!
HERE YA GO!
ドカッ
THUNK

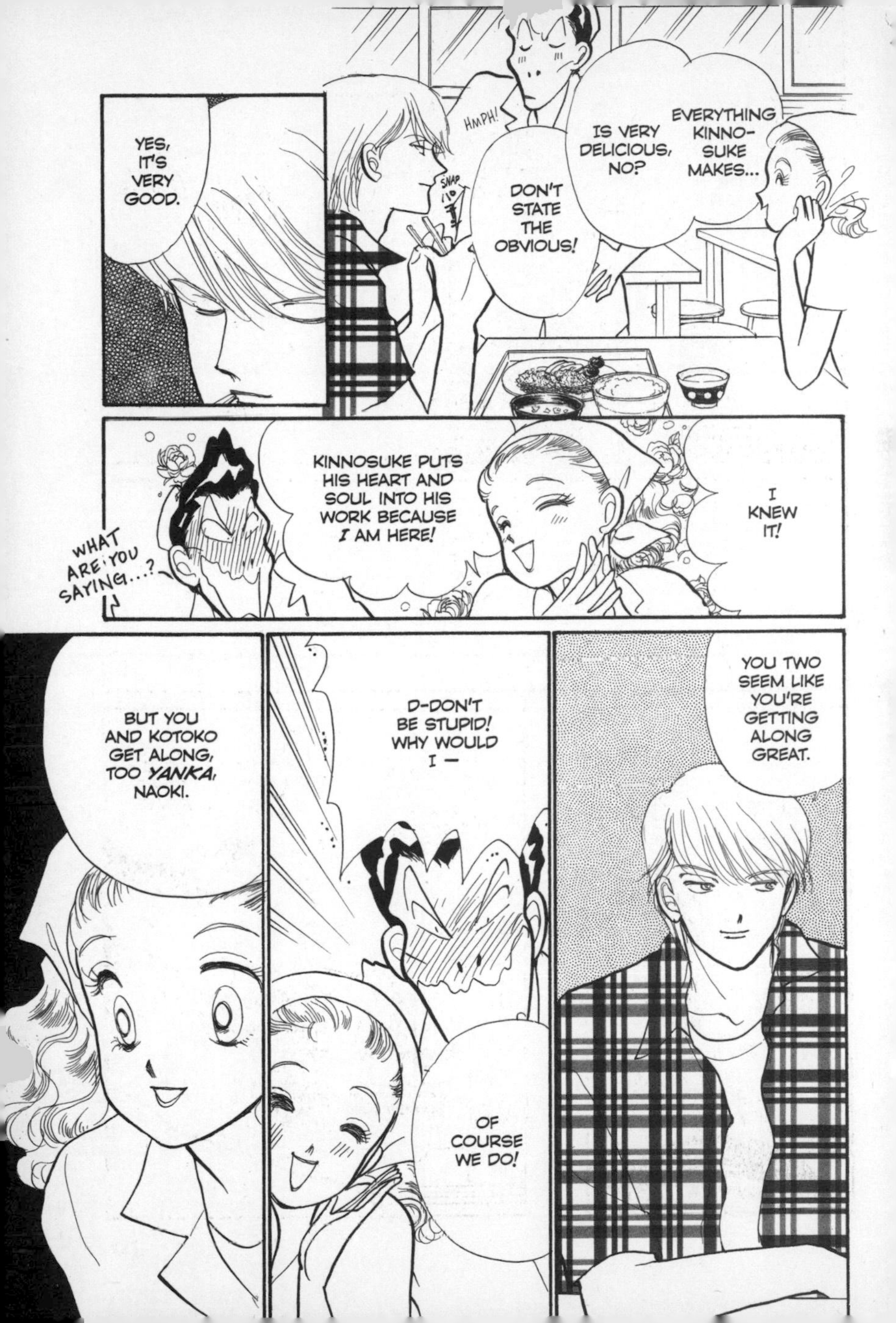
EVERYTHING KINNO-SUKE MAKES...
IS VERY DELICIOUS, NO?
HMPH!
DON'T STATE THE OBVIOUS!
SNAP
YES, IT'S VERY GOOD.
I KNEW IT!
KINNOSUKE PUTS HIS HEART AND SOUL INTO HIS WORK BECAUSE *I* AM HERE!
WHAT ARE YOU SAYING...?
YOU TWO SEEM LIKE YOU'RE GETTING ALONG GREAT.
D-DON'T BE STUPID! WHY WOULD I —
OF COURSE WE DO!
BUT YOU AND KOTOKO GET ALONG, TOO *YANKA*, NAOKI.

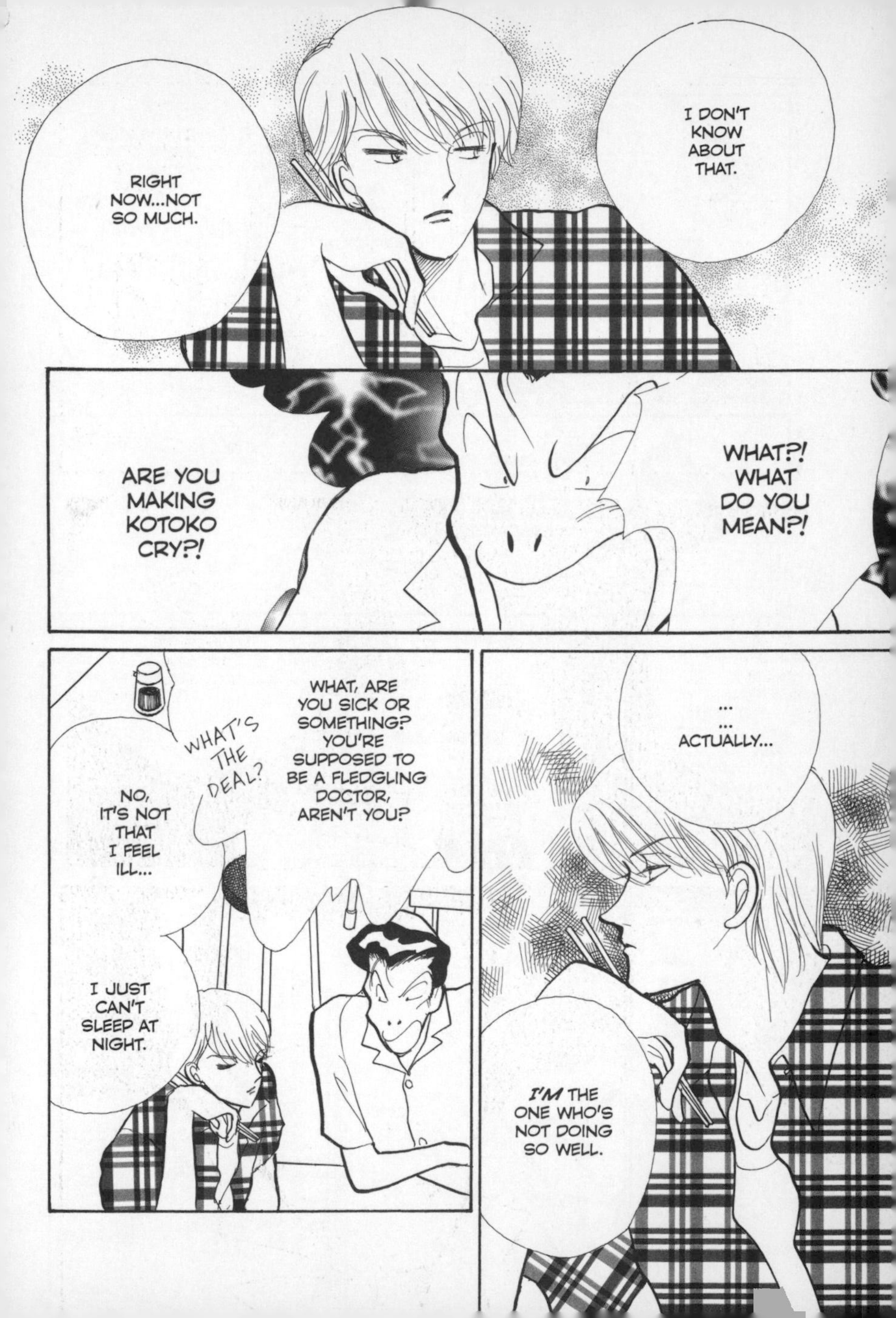
I DON'T KNOW ABOUT THAT.
RIGHT NOW...NOT SO MUCH.
WHAT?! WHAT DO YOU MEAN?!
ARE YOU MAKING KOTOKO CRY?!
... ... ACTUALLY...
I'M THE ONE WHO'S NOT DOING SO WELL.
WHAT, ARE YOU SICK OR SOMETHING? YOU'RE SUPPOSED TO BE A FLEDGLING DOCTOR, AREN'T YOU?
WHAT'S THE DEAL?
NO, IT'S NOT THAT I FEEL ILL...
I JUST CAN'T SLEEP AT NIGHT.

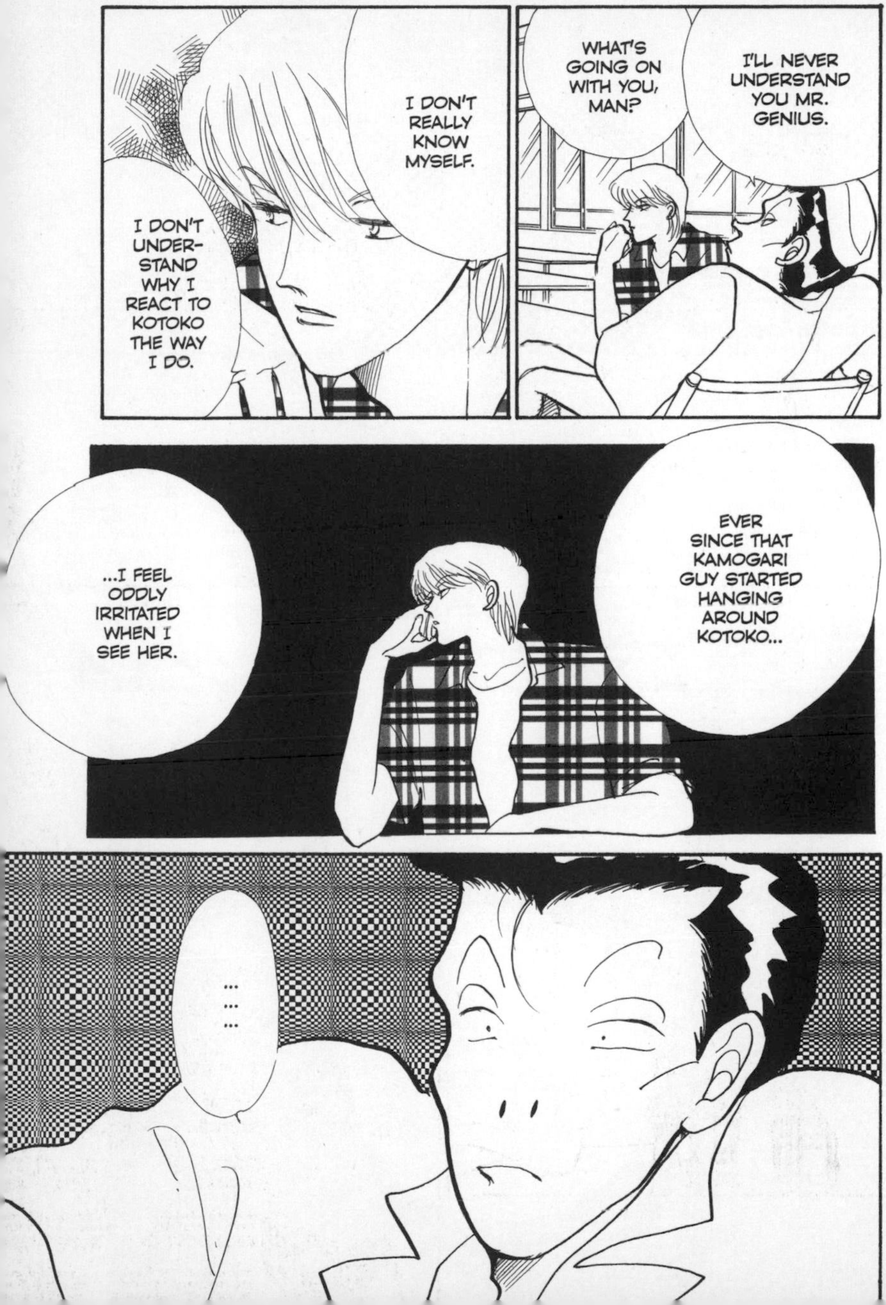
WHAT'S GOING ON WITH YOU, MAN?
I'LL NEVER UNDERSTAND YOU MR. GENIUS.
I DON'T REALLY KNOW MYSELF.
I DON'T UNDER-STAND WHY I REACT TO KOTOKO THE WAY I DO.
EVER SINCE THAT KAMOGARI GUY STARTED HANGING AROUND KOTOKO...
...I FEEL ODDLY IRRITATED WHEN I SEE HER.
...
...
...

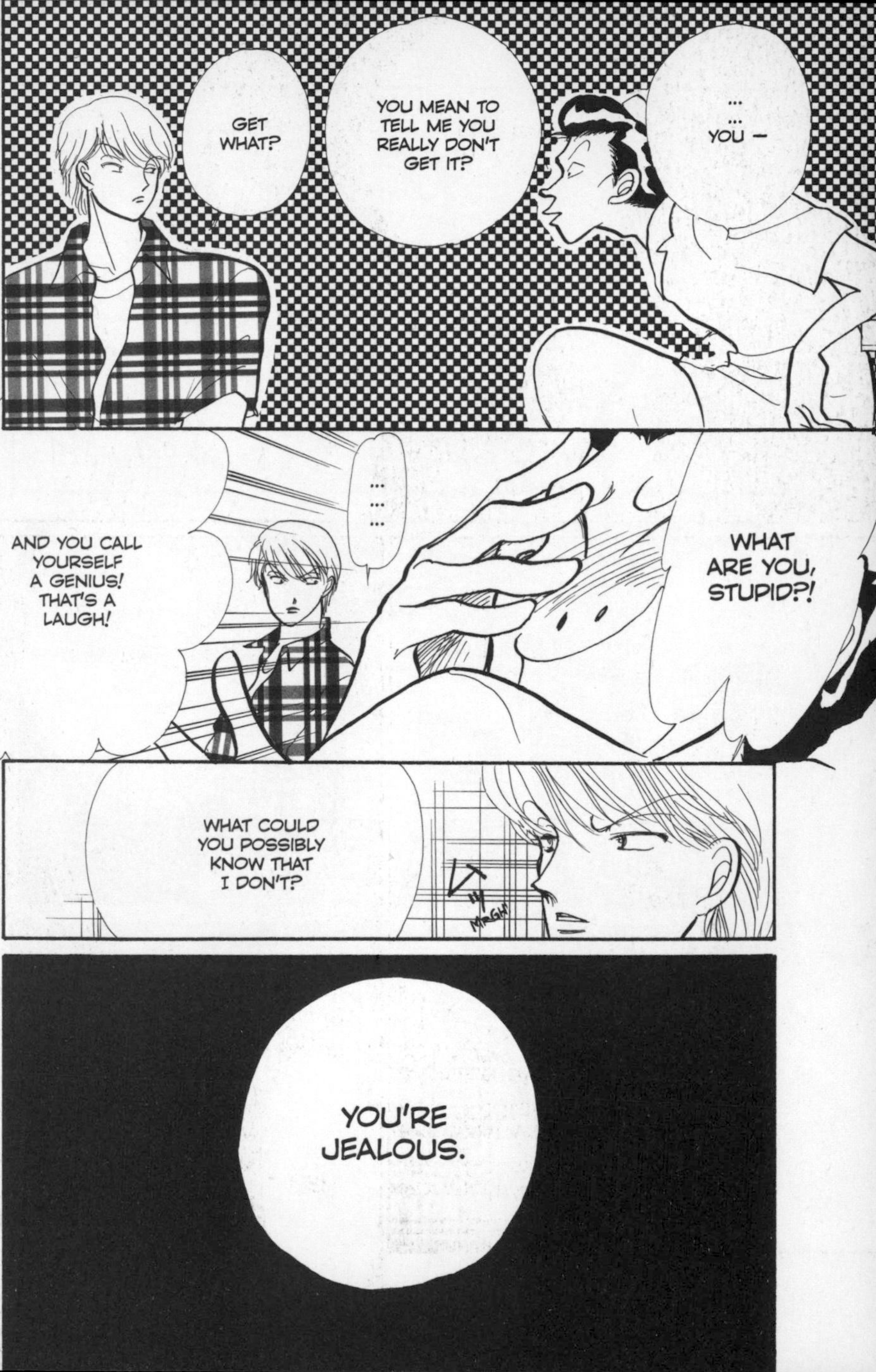
... ... YOU —
YOU MEAN TO TELL ME YOU REALLY DON'T GET IT?
GET WHAT?
WHAT ARE YOU, STUPID?!
... ...
AND YOU CALL YOURSELF A GENIUS! THAT'S A LAUGH!
WHAT COULD YOU POSSIBLY KNOW THAT I DON'T?
YOU'RE JEALOUS.

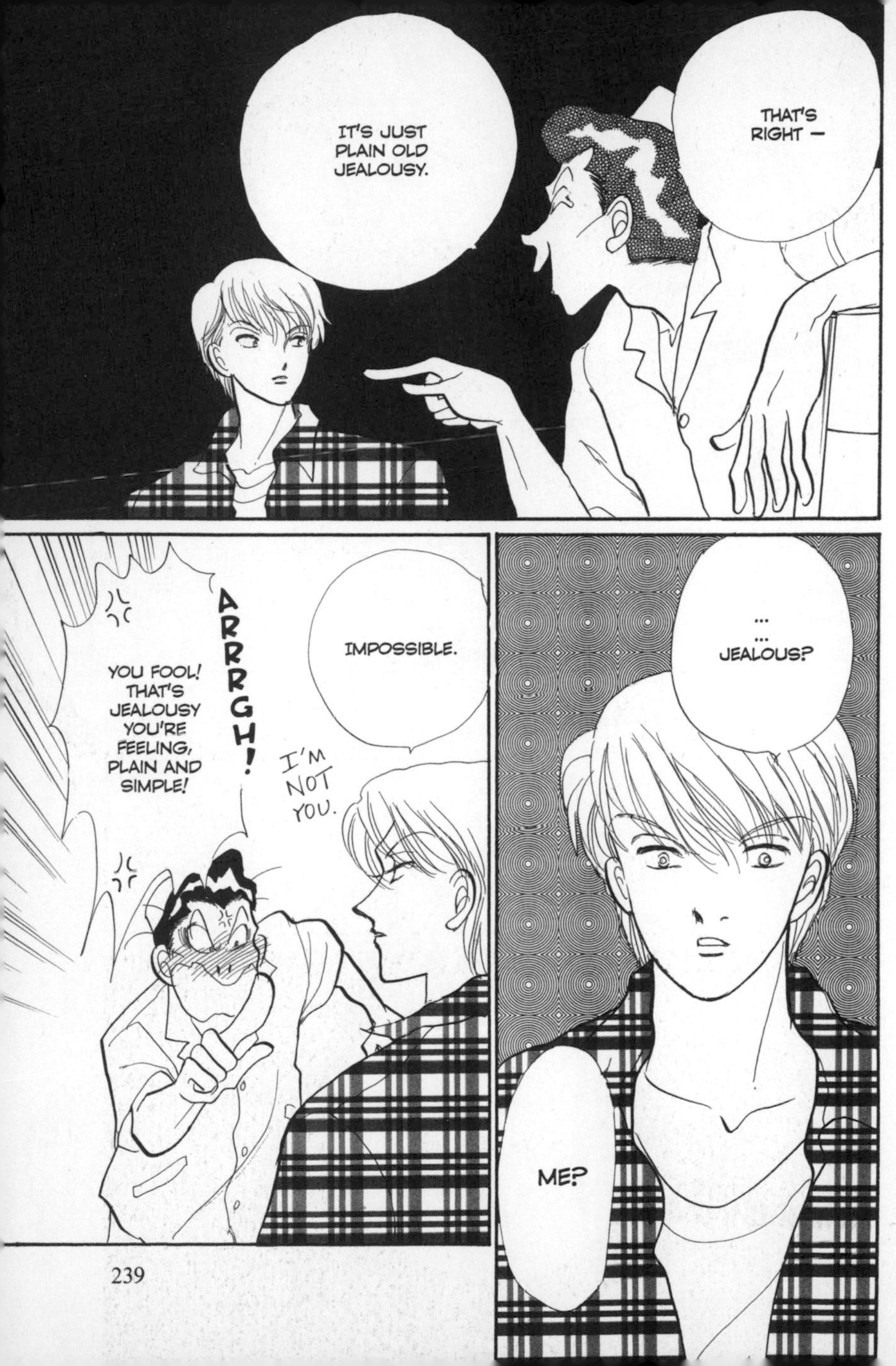
THAT'S RIGHT —
IT'S JUST PLAIN OLD JEALOUSY.
... ... JEALOUS?
ME?
IMPOSSIBLE.
I'M NOT YOU.
ARRRGH!
YOU FOOL! THAT'S JEALOUSY YOU'RE FEELING, PLAIN AND SIMPLE!

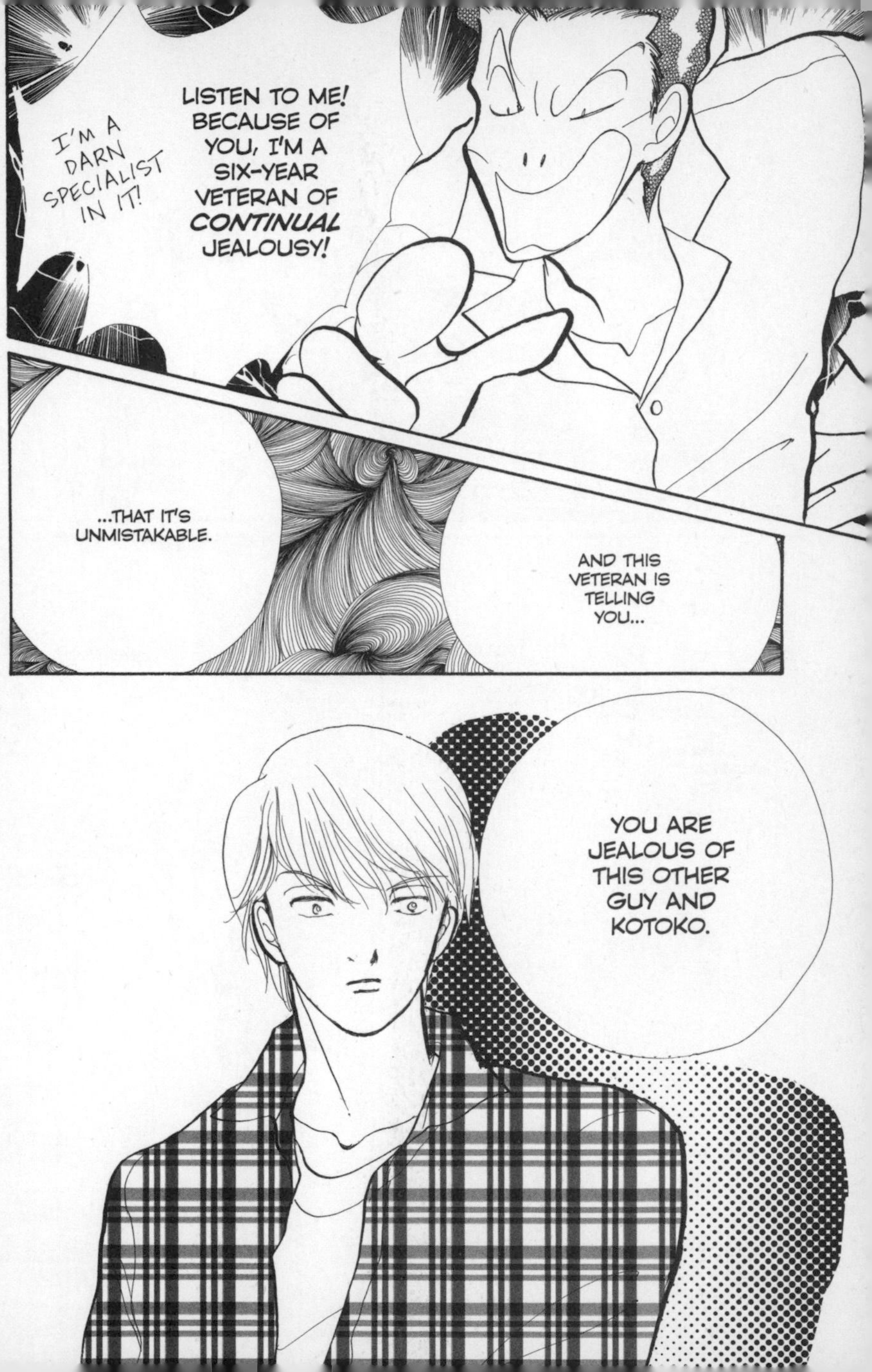
LISTEN TO ME! BECAUSE OF YOU, I'M A SIX-YEAR VETERAN OF CONTINUAL JEALOUSY!
I'M A DARN SPECIALIST IN IT!
AND THIS VETERAN IS TELLING YOU...
...THAT IT'S UNMISTAKABLE.
YOU ARE JEALOUS OF THIS OTHER GUY AND KOTOKO.

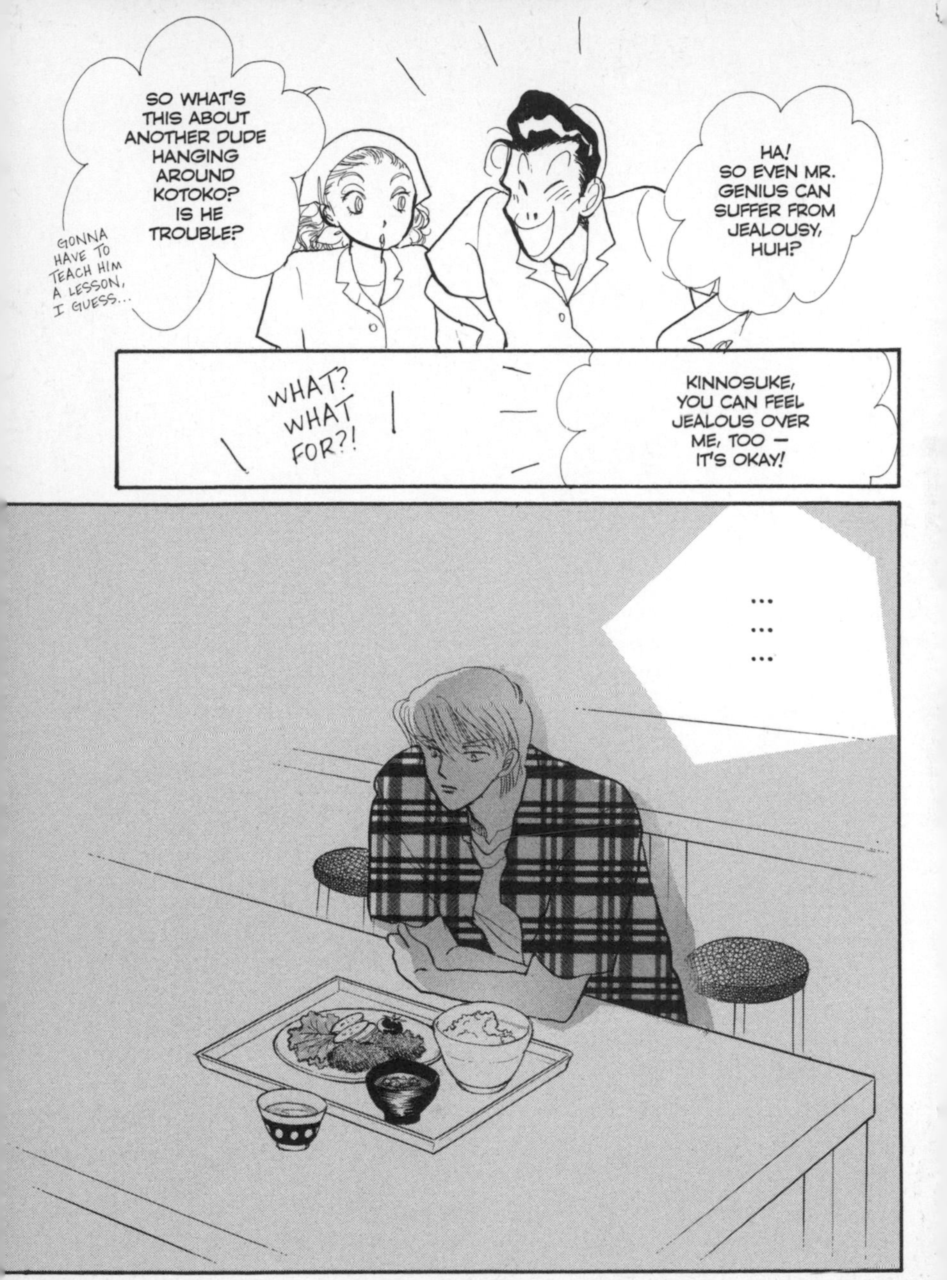
HA! SO EVEN MR. GENIUS CAN SUFFER FROM JEALOUSY, HUH?
SO WHAT'S THIS ABOUT ANOTHER DUDE HANGING AROUND KOTOKO? IS HE TROUBLE?
GONNA HAVE TO TEACH HIM A LESSON, I GUESS...
KINNOSUKE, YOU CAN FEEL JEALOUS OVER ME, TOO — IT'S OKAY!
WHAT? WHAT FOR?!
...
...
...

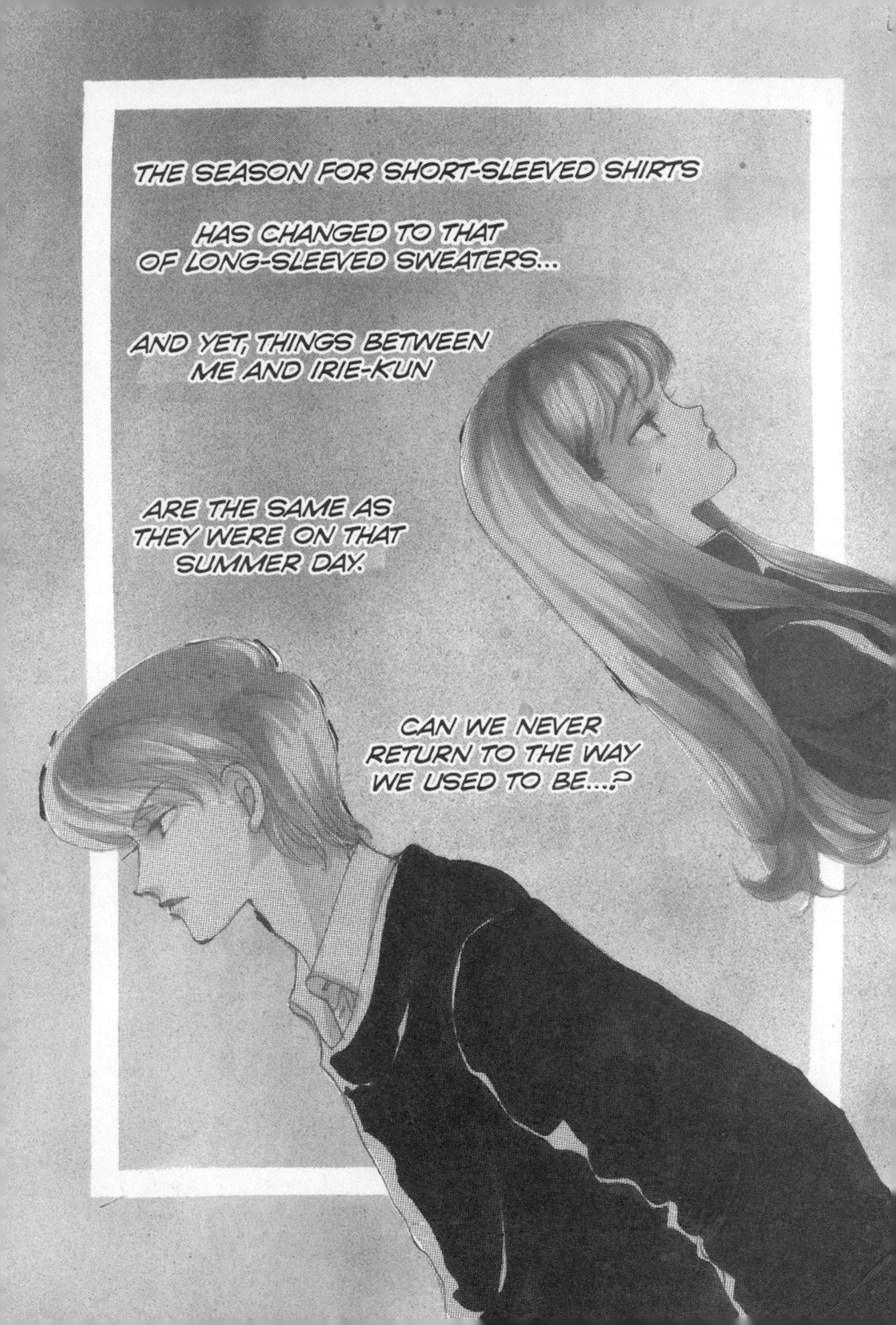
THE SEASON FOR SHORT-SLEEVED SHIRTS
HAS CHANGED TO THAT OF LONG-SLEEVED SWEATERS...
AND YET, THINGS BETWEEN ME AND IRIE-KUN
ARE THE SAME AS THEY WERE ON THAT SUMMER DAY.
CAN WE NEVER RETURN TO THE WAY WE USED TO BE...?

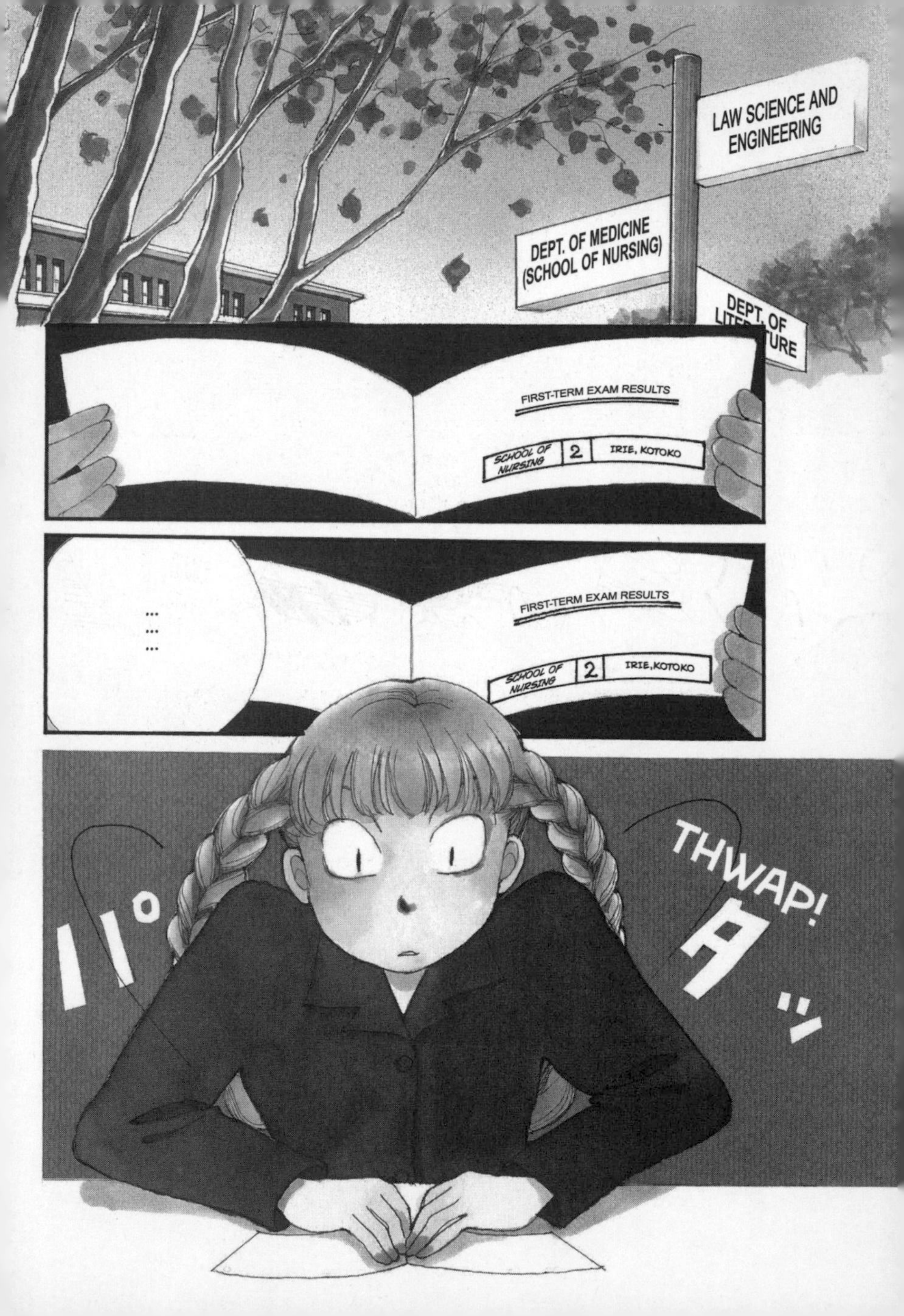
LAW SCIENCE AND ENGINEERING
DEPT. OF MEDICINE (SCHOOL OF NURSING)
DEPT. OF LITERATURE
FIRST-TERM EXAM RESULTS
SCHOOL OF NURSING
2
IRIE, KOTOKO
FIRST-TERM EXAM RESULTS
SCHOOL OF NURSING
2
IRIE,KOTOKO
...
...
...
THWAP!
タッ
パ

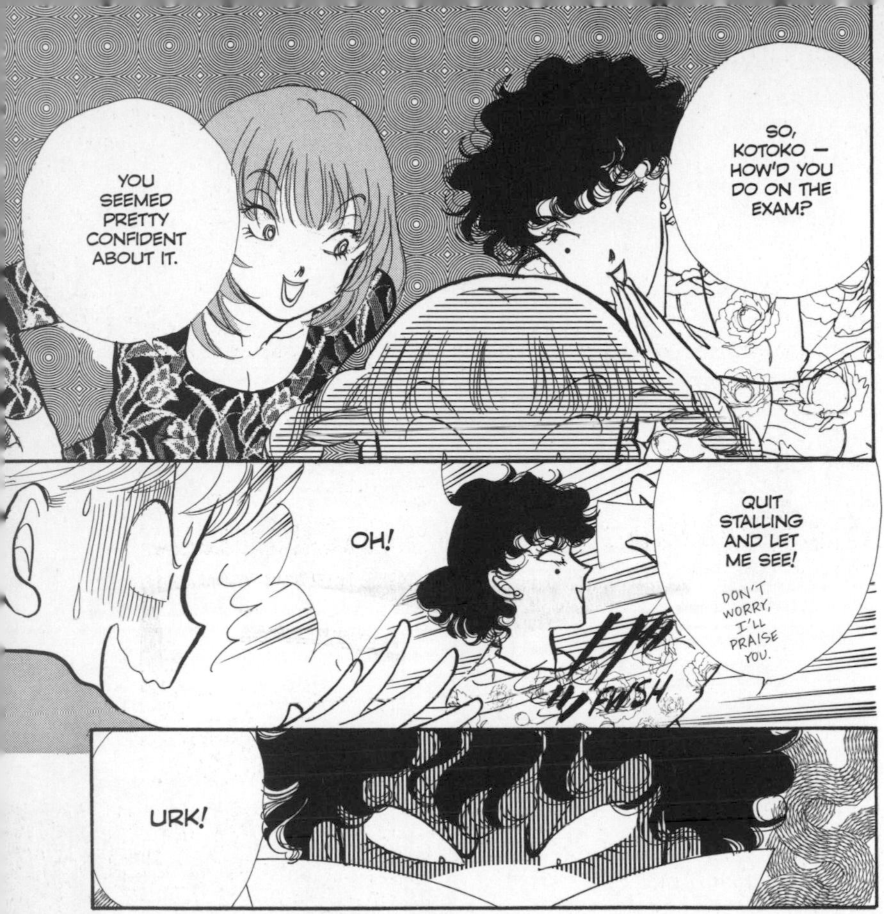
SO, KOTOKO — HOW'D YOU DO ON THE EXAM?
YOU SEEMED PRETTY CONFIDENT ABOUT IT.
QUIT STALLING AND LET ME SEE!
DON'T WORRY, I'LL PRAISE YOU.
FWISH
OH!
URK!

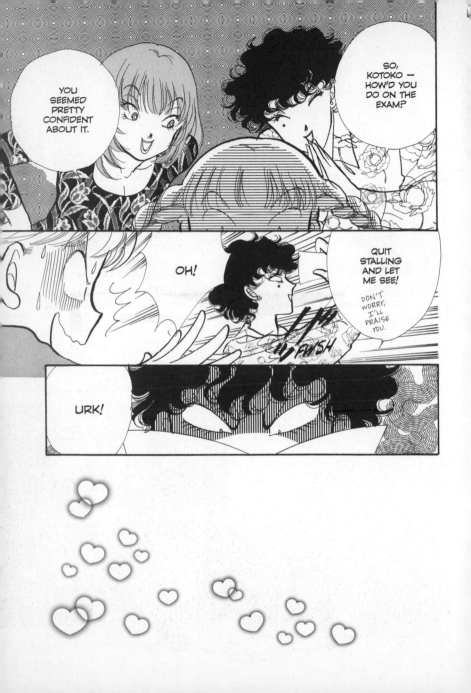

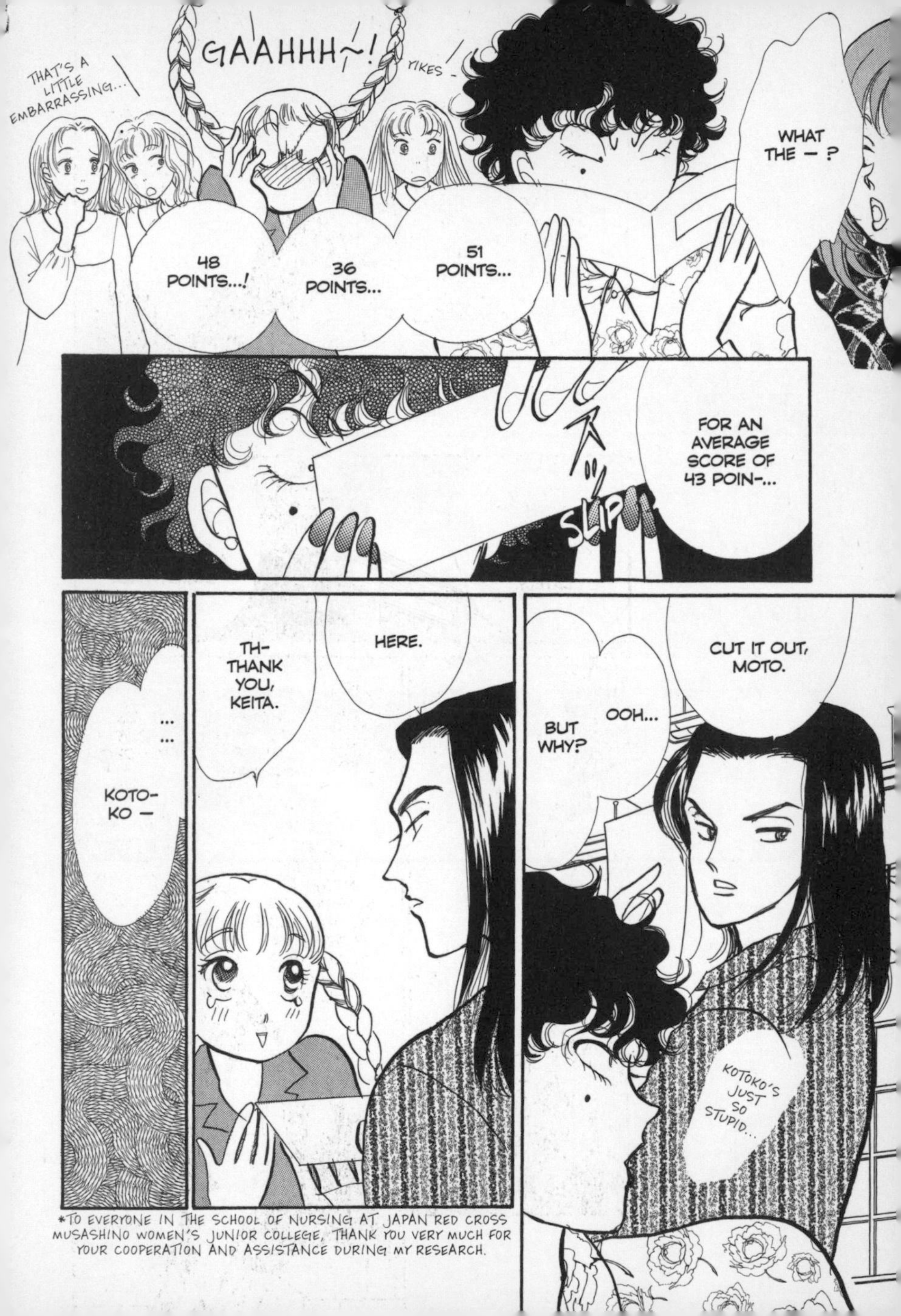
WHAT THE — ?
51 POINTS...
36 POINTS...
48 POINTS...!
YIKES
GAAHHH~!
THAT'S A LITTLE EMBARRASSING...
FOR AN AVERAGE SCORE OF 43 POIN-...
SLIP
CUT IT OUT, MOTO.
OOH... BUT WHY?
KOTOKO'S JUST SO STUPID...
HERE.
TH-THANK YOU, KEITA.
... ...
KOTO-KO —

*TO EVERYONE IN THE SCHOOL OF NURSING AT JAPAN RED CROSS MUSASHINO WOMEN'S JUNIOR COLLEGE, THANK YOU VERY MUCH FOR YOUR COOPERATION AND ASSISTANCE DURING MY RESEARCH.

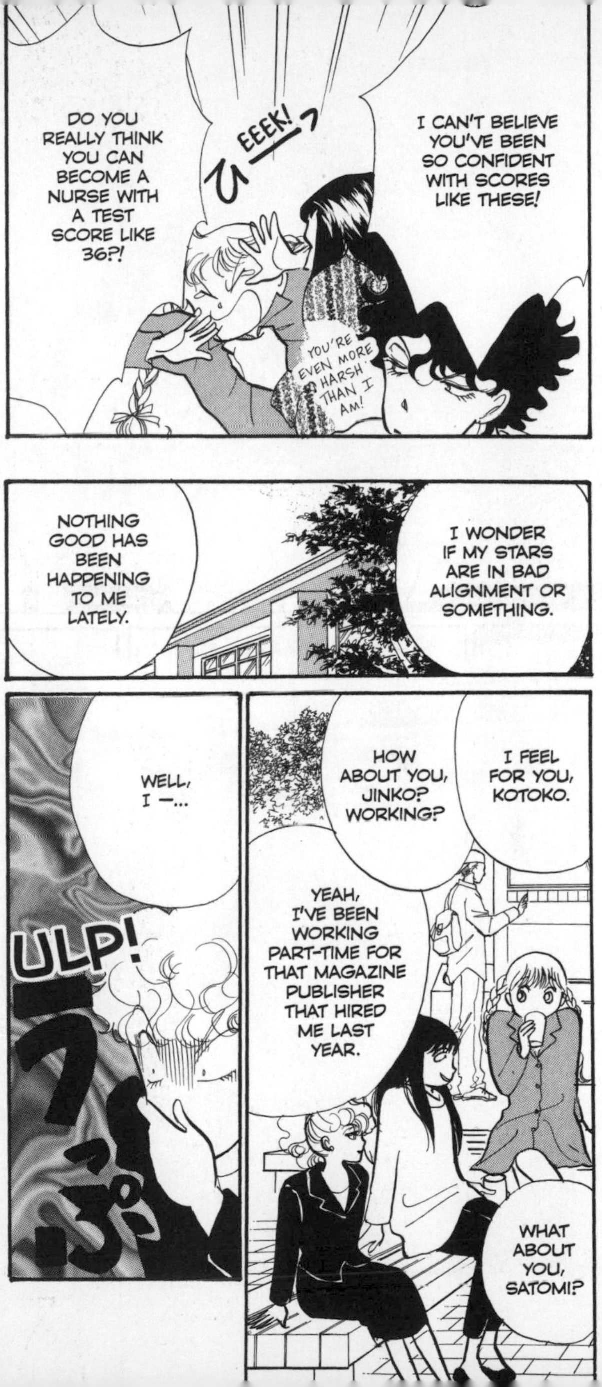
I CAN'T BELIEVE YOU'VE BEEN SO CONFIDENT WITH SCORES LIKE THESE!
EEEK!
DO YOU REALLY THINK YOU CAN BECOME A NURSE WITH A TEST SCORE LIKE 36?!
YOU'RE EVEN MORE HARSH THAN I AM!
I WONDER IF MY STARS ARE IN BAD ALIGNMENT OR SOMETHING.
NOTHING GOOD HAS BEEN HAPPENING TO ME LATELY.
I FEEL FOR YOU, KOTOKO.
HOW ABOUT YOU, JINKO? WORKING?
YEAH, I'VE BEEN WORKING PART-TIME FOR THAT MAGAZINE PUBLISHER THAT HIRED ME LAST YEAR.
WHAT ABOUT YOU, SATOMI?
WELL, I —...
ULP!
ウっぷ

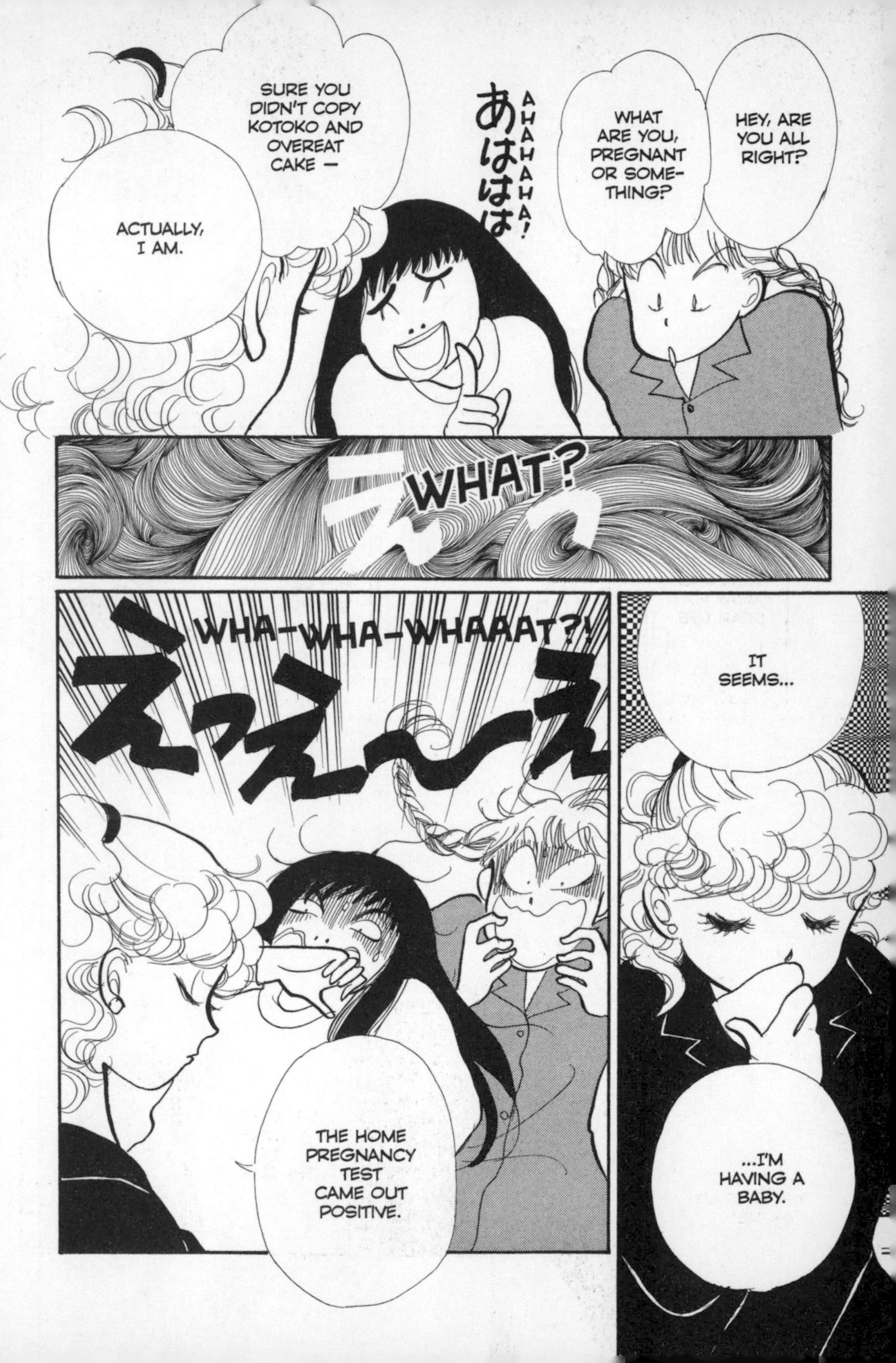
HEY, ARE YOU ALL RIGHT?
WHAT ARE YOU, PREGNANT OR SOME-THING?
あははは
AHAHAHA!
SURE YOU DIDN'T COPY KOTOKO AND OVEREAT CAKE —
ACTUALLY, I AM.
えっ
WHAT?
IT SEEMS...
...I'M HAVING A BABY.
えっえ〜え
WHA-WHA-WHAAAT?!
THE HOME PREGNANCY TEST CAME OUT POSITIVE.

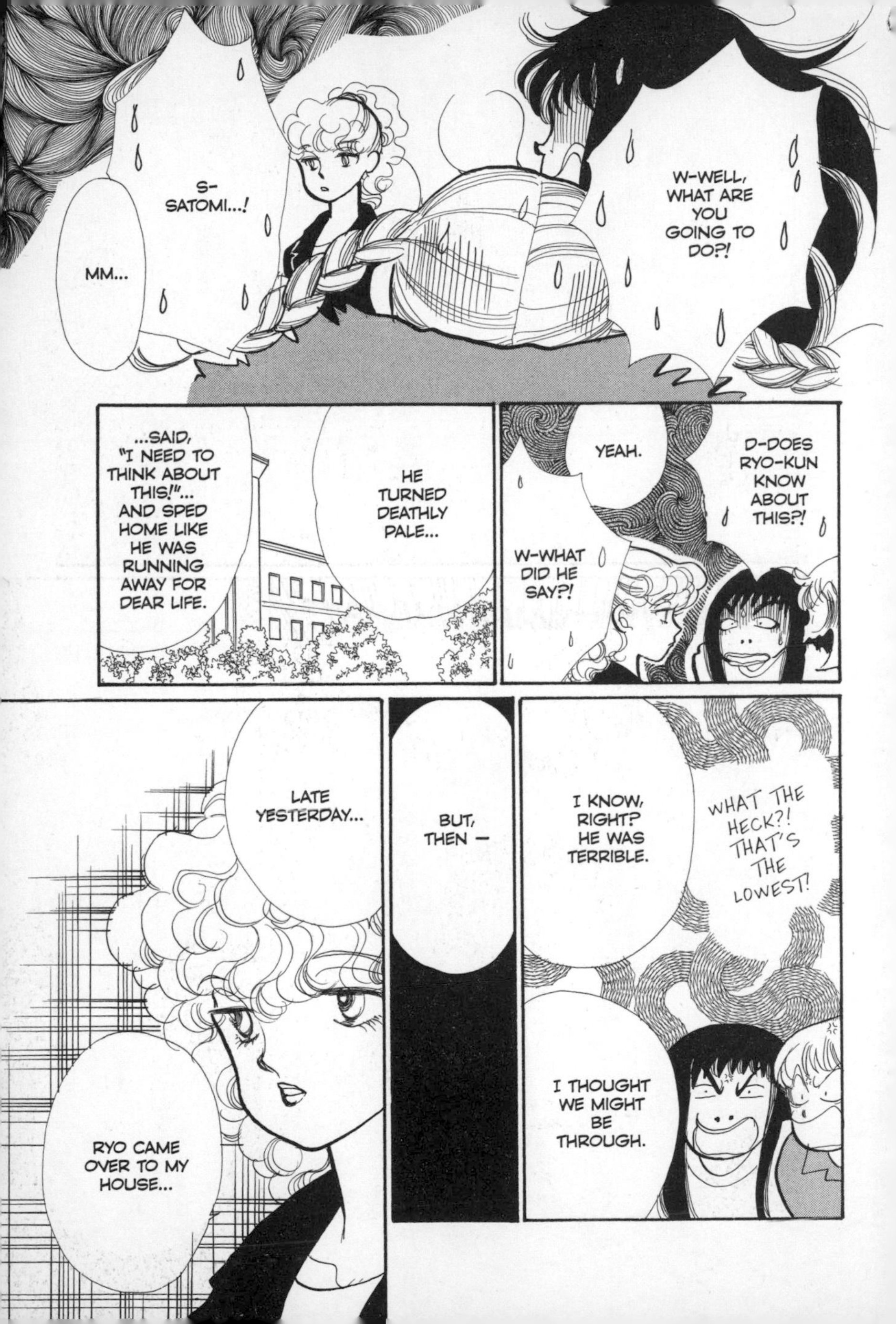
W-WELL, WHAT ARE YOU GOING TO DO?!
S-SATOMI...!
MM...
D-DOES RYO-KUN KNOW ABOUT THIS?!
YEAH.
W-WHAT DID HE SAY?!
HE TURNED DEATHLY PALE...
...SAID, "I NEED TO THINK ABOUT THIS!"... AND SPED HOME LIKE HE WAS RUNNING AWAY FOR DEAR LIFE.
WHAT THE HECK?! THAT'S THE LOWEST!
I KNOW, RIGHT? HE WAS TERRIBLE.
I THOUGHT WE MIGHT BE THROUGH.
BUT, THEN —
LATE YESTERDAY...
RYO CAME OVER TO MY HOUSE...

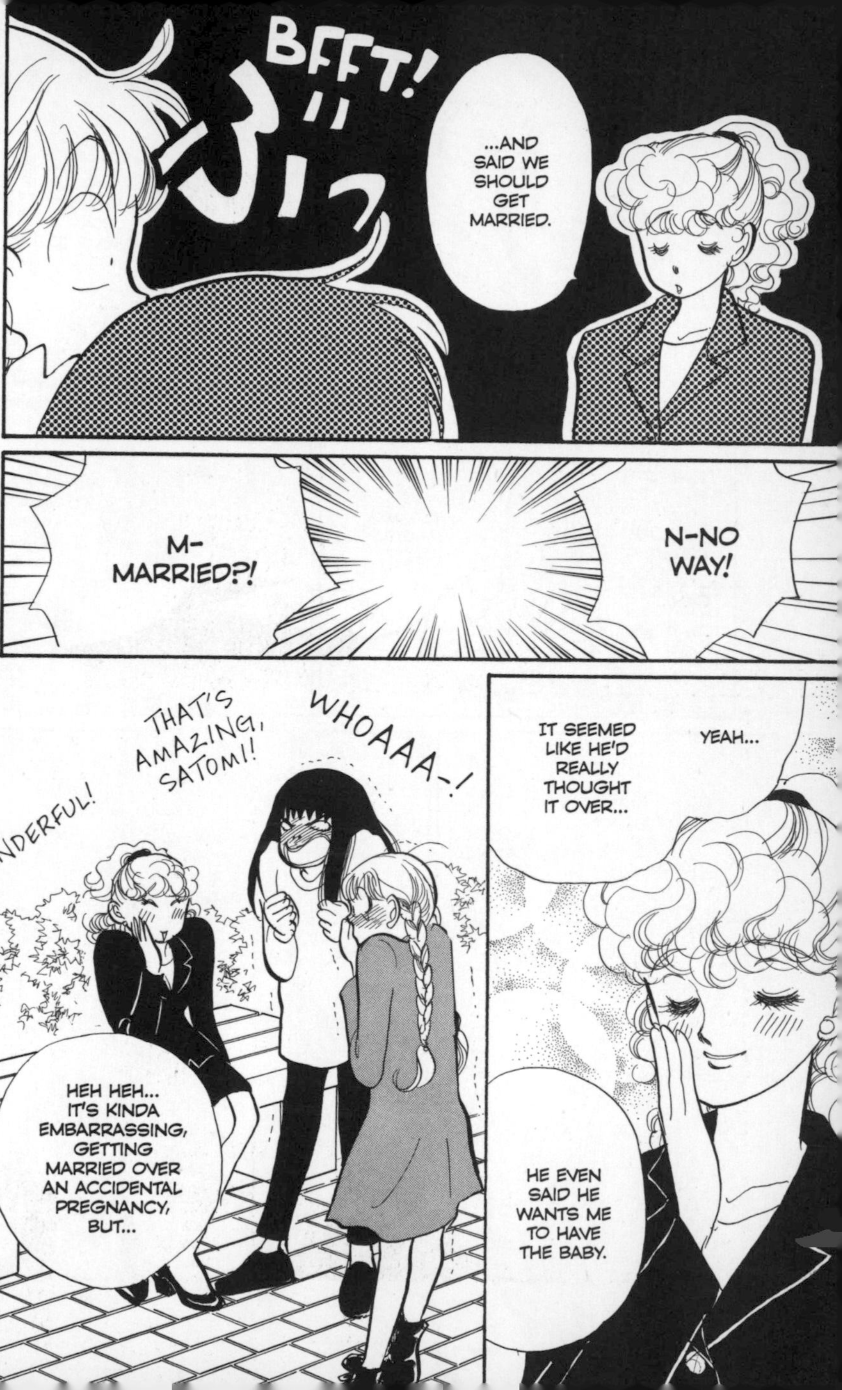
...AND SAID WE SHOULD GET MARRIED.
BFFT!
N-NO WAY!
M-MARRIED?!
YEAH...
IT SEEMED LIKE HE'D REALLY THOUGHT IT OVER...
HE EVEN SAID HE WANTS ME TO HAVE THE BABY.
WHOAAAA-!
THAT'S AMAZING, SATOMI!
WONDERFUL!
HEH HEH... IT'S KINDA EMBARRASSING, GETTING MARRIED OVER AN ACCIDENTAL PREGNANCY, BUT...

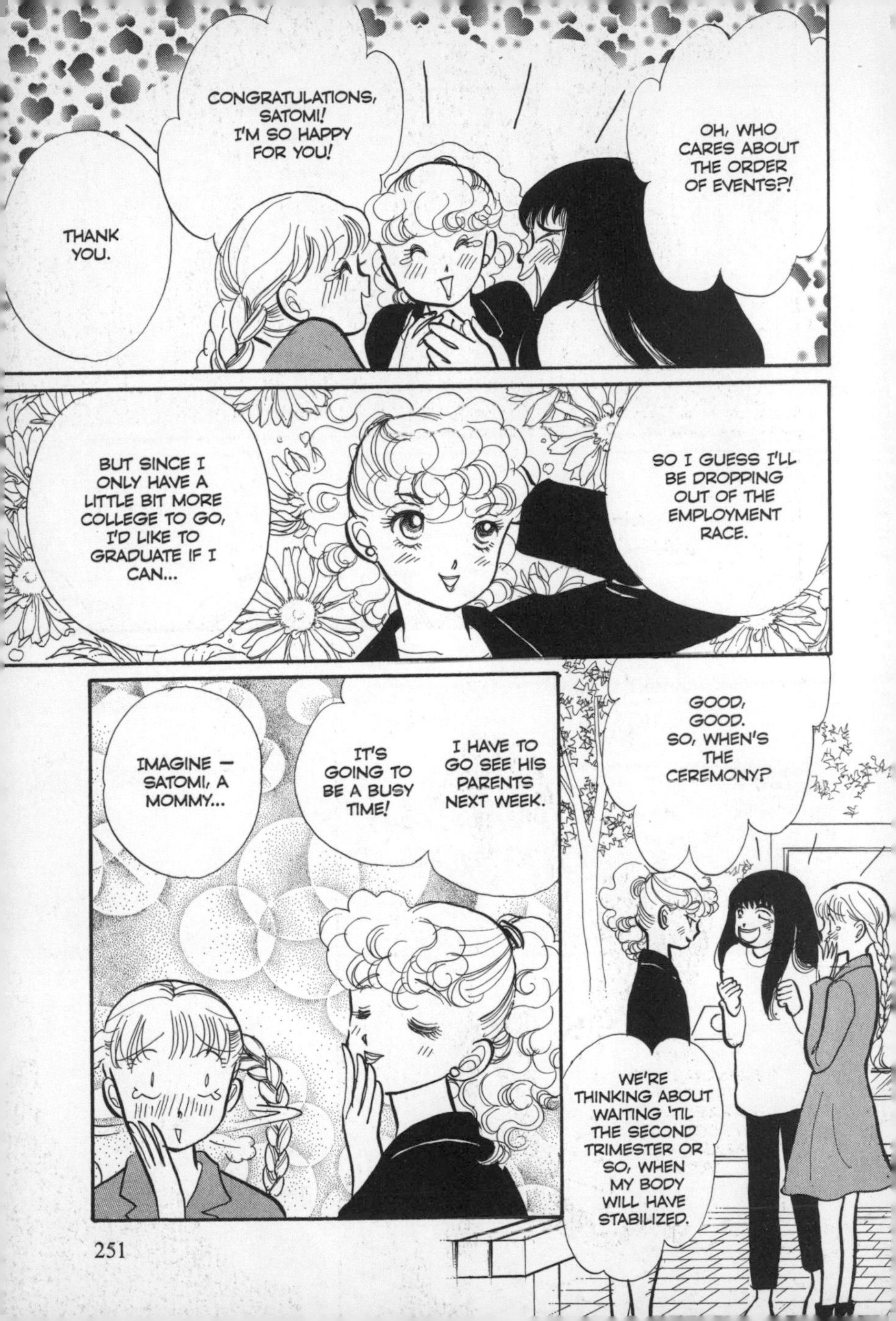
OH, WHO CARES ABOUT THE ORDER OF EVENTS?!
CONGRATULATIONS, SATOMI! I'M SO HAPPY FOR YOU!
THANK YOU.
SO I GUESS I'LL BE DROPPING OUT OF THE EMPLOYMENT RACE.
BUT SINCE I ONLY HAVE A LITTLE BIT MORE COLLEGE TO GO, I'D LIKE TO GRADUATE IF I CAN...
GOOD, GOOD. SO, WHEN'S THE CEREMONY?
WE'RE THINKING ABOUT WAITING 'TIL THE SECOND TRIMESTER OR SO, WHEN MY BODY WILL HAVE STABILIZED.
I HAVE TO GO SEE HIS PARENTS NEXT WEEK.
IT'S GOING TO BE A BUSY TIME!
IMAGINE — SATOMI, A MOMMY...

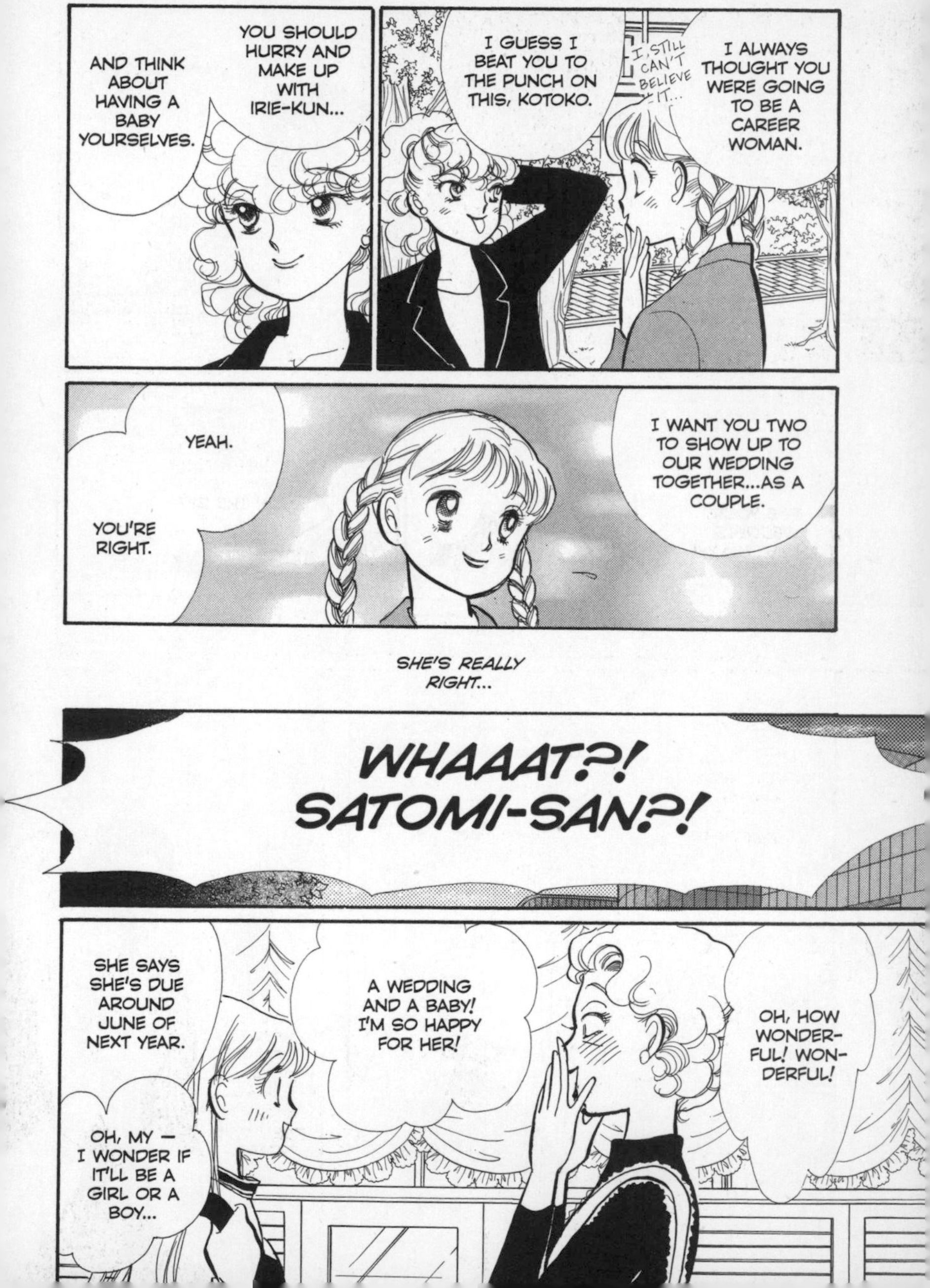
I ALWAYS THOUGHT YOU WERE GOING TO BE A CAREER WOMAN.
I, STILL CAN'T BELIEVE IT...
I GUESS I BEAT YOU TO THE PUNCH ON THIS, KOTOKO.
YOU SHOULD HURRY AND MAKE UP WITH IRIE-KUN...
AND THINK ABOUT HAVING A BABY YOURSELVES.
I WANT YOU TWO TO SHOW UP TO OUR WEDDING TOGETHER...AS A COUPLE.
YEAH.
YOU'RE RIGHT.
SHE'S REALLY RIGHT...
WHAAAT?! SATOMI-SAN?!
OH, HOW WONDERFUL! WONDERFUL!
A WEDDING AND A BABY! I'M SO HAPPY FOR HER!
SHE SAYS SHE'S DUE AROUND JUNE OF NEXT YEAR.
OH, MY — I WONDER IF IT'LL BE A GIRL OR A BOY...

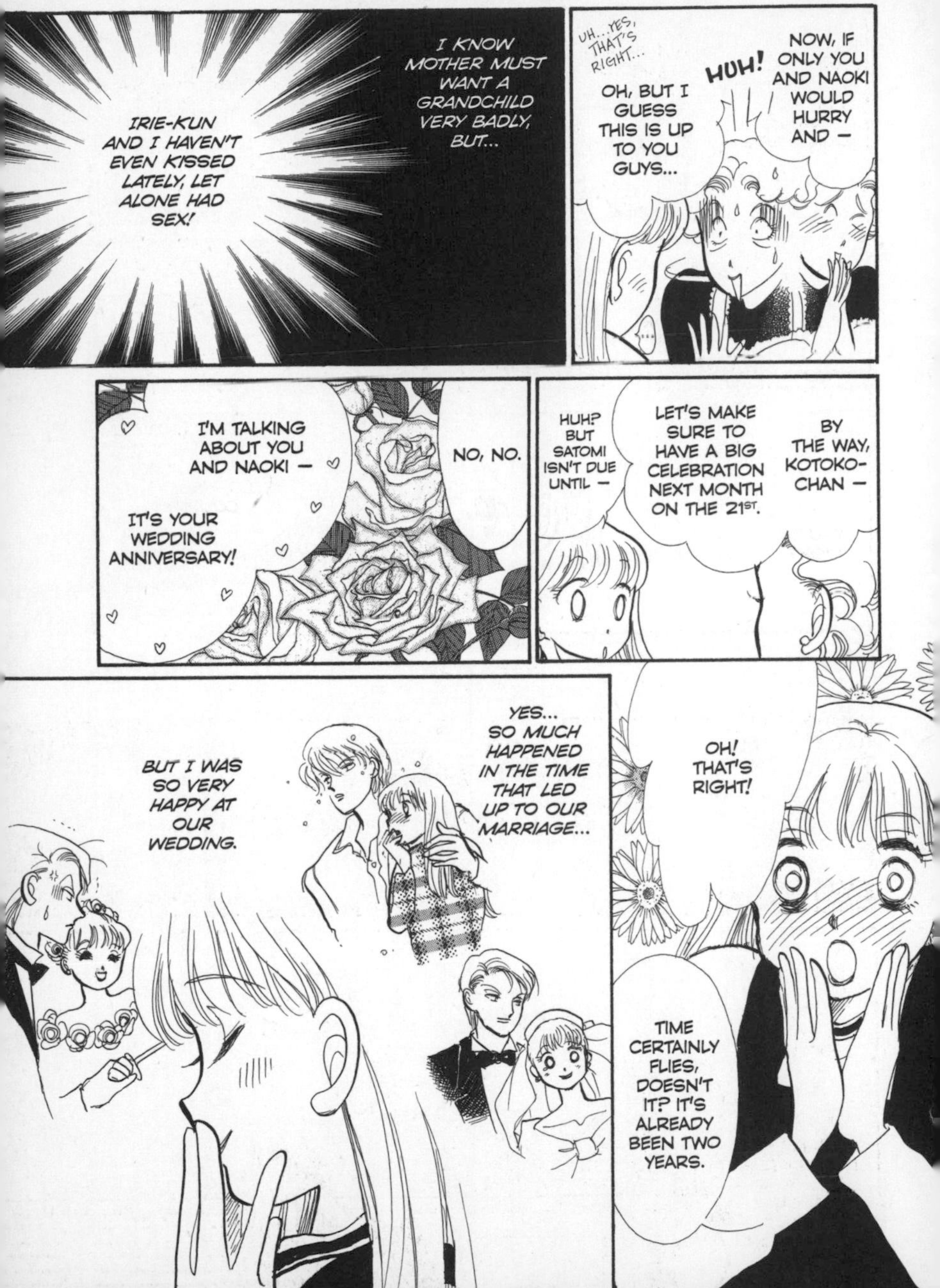
NOW, IF ONLY YOU AND NAOKI WOULD HURRY AND —
HUH!
UH... YES, THAT'S RIGHT...
OH, BUT I GUESS THIS IS UP TO YOU GUYS...
I KNOW MOTHER MUST WANT A GRANDCHILD VERY BADLY, BUT...
IRIE-KUN AND I HAVEN'T EVEN KISSED LATELY, LET ALONE HAD SEX!
BY THE WAY, KOTOKO-CHAN —
LET'S MAKE SURE TO HAVE A BIG CELEBRATION NEXT MONTH ON THE 21ST.
HUH? BUT SATOMI ISN'T DUE UNTIL —
NO, NO.
I'M TALKING ABOUT YOU AND NAOKI —
IT'S YOUR WEDDING ANNIVERSARY!
OH! THAT'S RIGHT!
TIME CERTAINLY FLIES, DOESN'T IT? IT'S ALREADY BEEN TWO YEARS.
YES... SO MUCH HAPPENED IN THE TIME THAT LED UP TO OUR MARRIAGE...
BUT I WAS SO VERY HAPPY AT OUR WEDDING.

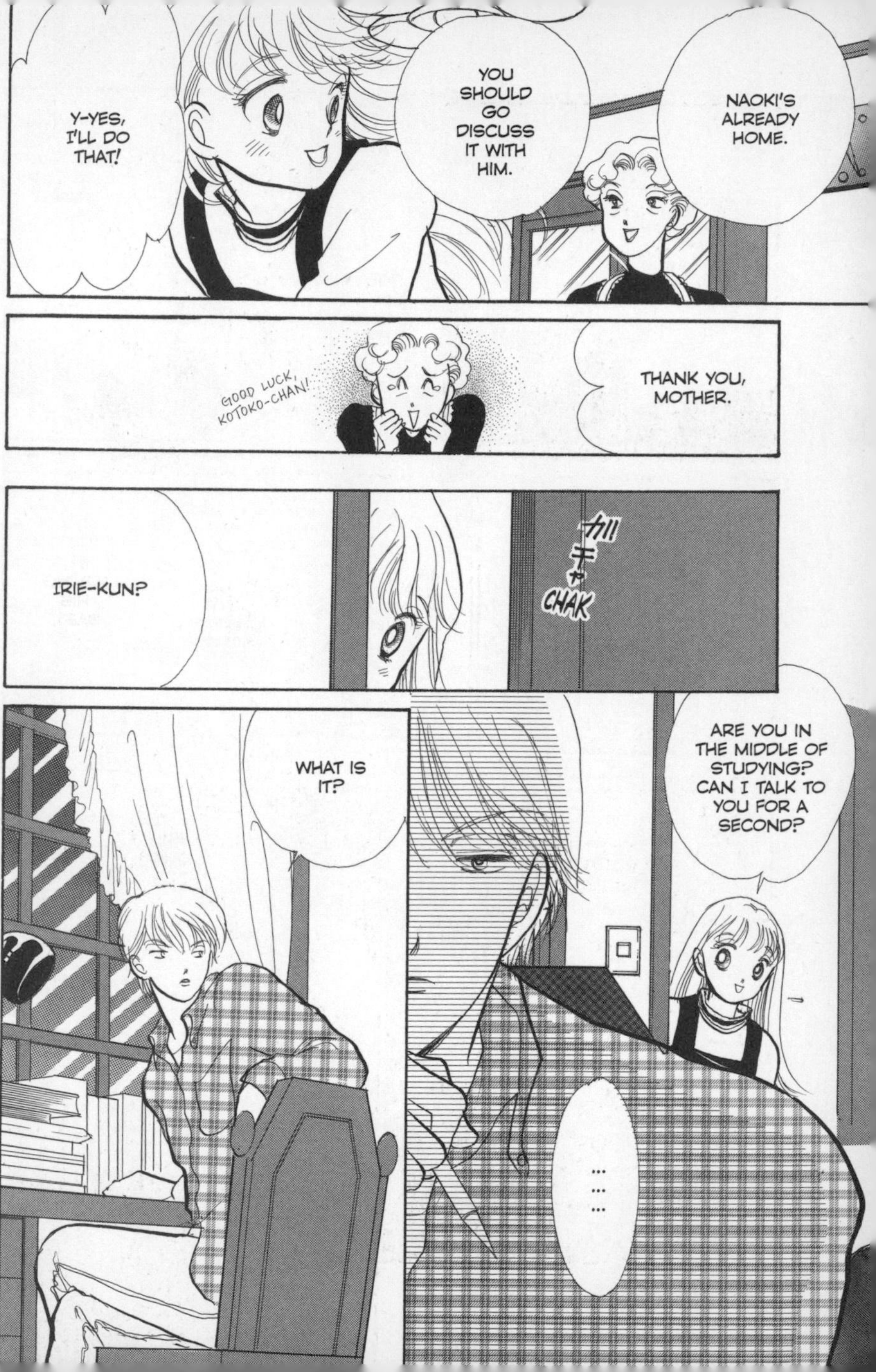
NAOKI'S ALREADY HOME.
YOU SHOULD GO DISCUSS IT WITH HIM.
Y-YES, I'LL DO THAT!
THANK YOU, MOTHER.
GOOD LUCK, KOTOKO-CHAN!
カチャ
CHAK
IRIE-KUN?
ARE YOU IN THE MIDDLE OF STUDYING? CAN I TALK TO YOU FOR A SECOND?
... ...
WHAT IS IT?

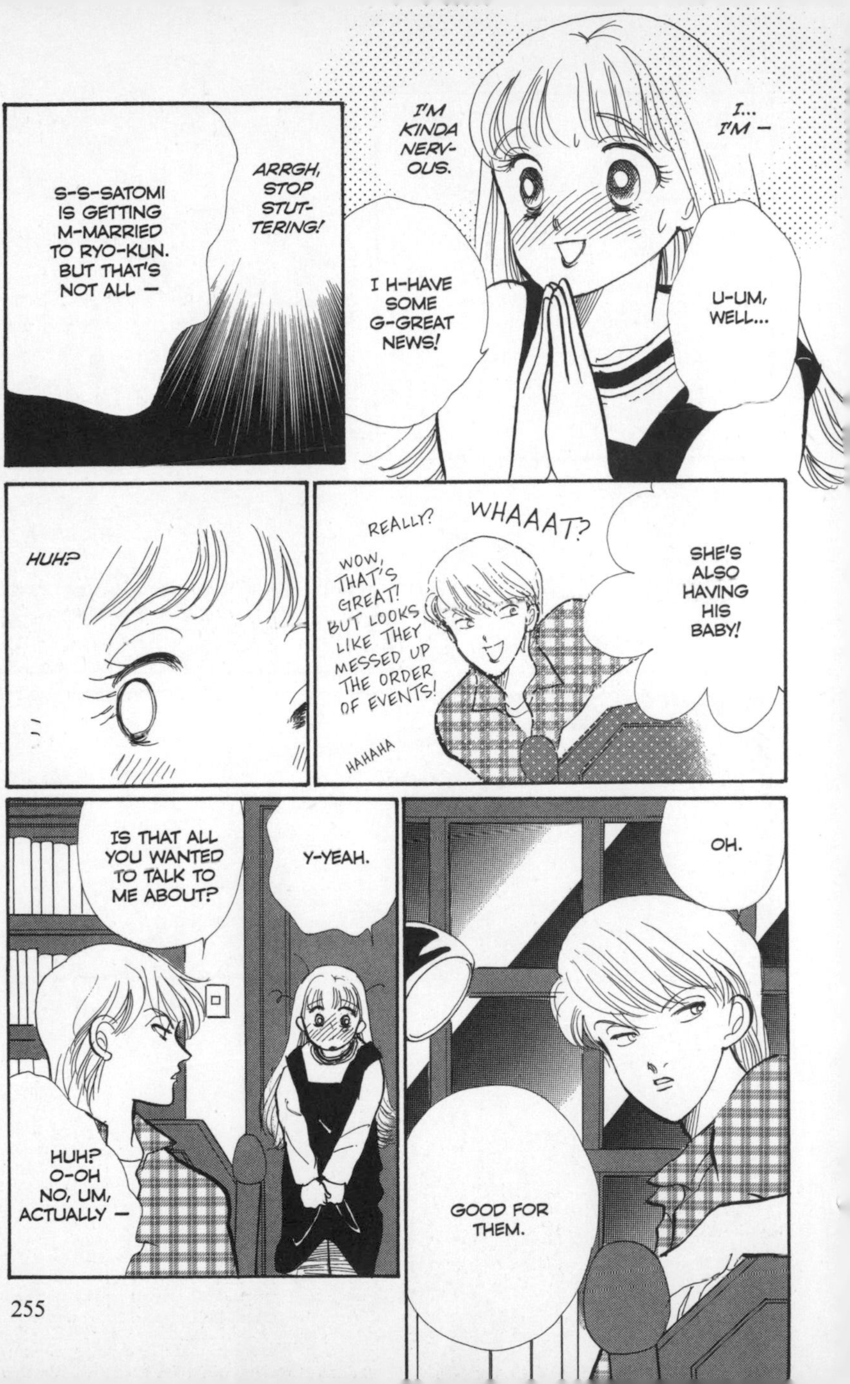
I... I'M —
I'M KINDA NERVOUS.
U-UM, WELL...
I H-HAVE SOME G-GREAT NEWS!
ARRGH, STOP STUTTERING!
S-S-SATOMI IS GETTING M-MARRIED TO RYO-KUN. BUT THAT'S NOT ALL —
SHE'S ALSO HAVING HIS BABY!
WHAAAT?
REALLY?
WOW, THAT'S GREAT! BUT LOOKS LIKE THEY MESSED UP THE ORDER OF EVENTS!
HAHAHA
HUH?
OH.
GOOD FOR THEM.
Y-YEAH.
IS THAT ALL YOU WANTED TO TALK TO ME ABOUT?
HUH? O-OH NO, UM, ACTUALLY —

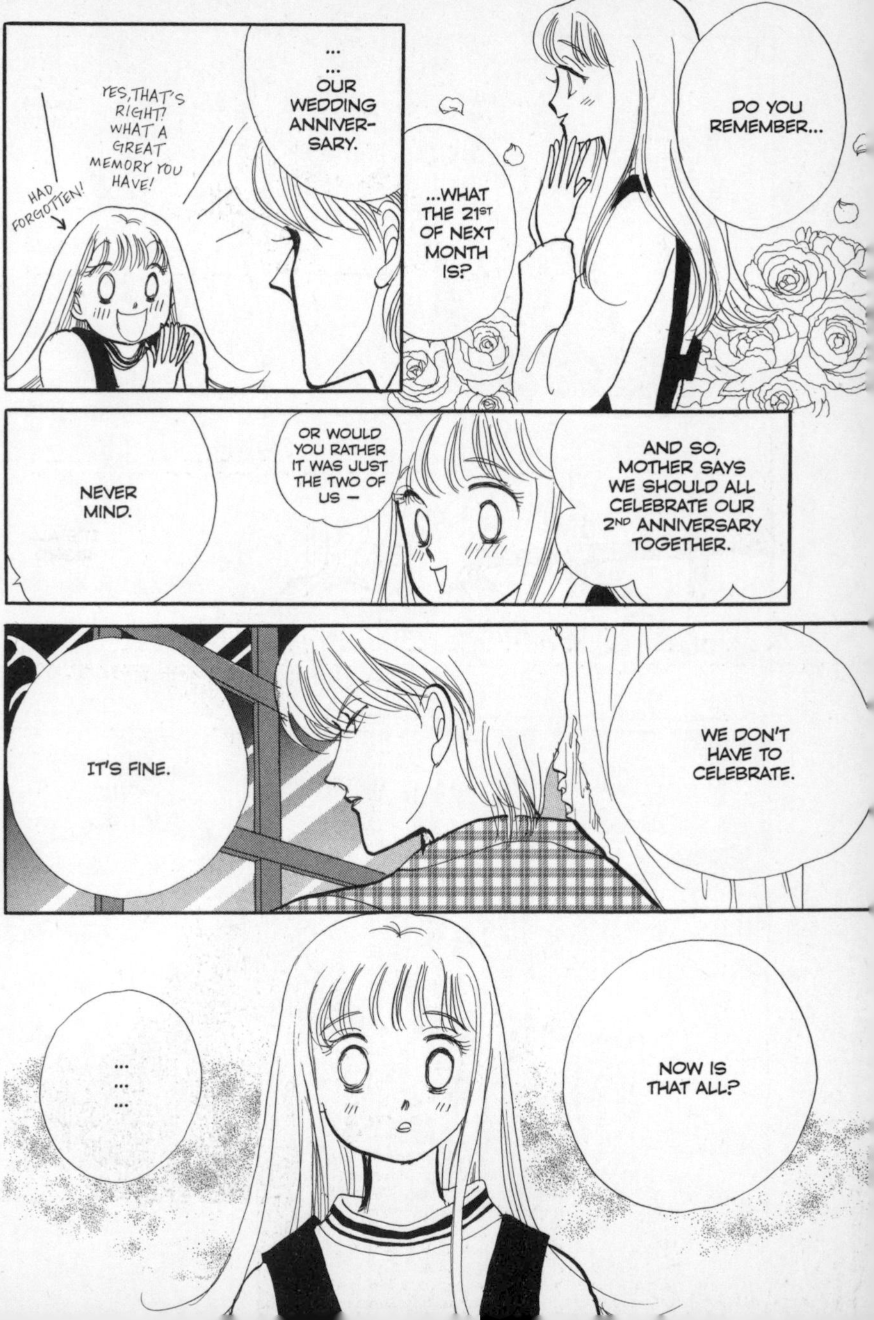
DO YOU REMEMBER...
...WHAT THE 21st OF NEXT MONTH IS?
... ... OUR WEDDING ANNIVERSARY.
YES, THAT'S RIGHT! WHAT A GREAT MEMORY YOU HAVE!
HAD FORGOTTEN!
AND SO, MOTHER SAYS WE SHOULD ALL CELEBRATE OUR 2ND ANNIVERSARY TOGETHER.
OR WOULD YOU RATHER IT WAS JUST THE TWO OF US —
NEVER MIND.
WE DON'T HAVE TO CELEBRATE.
IT'S FINE.
NOW IS THAT ALL?
... ...

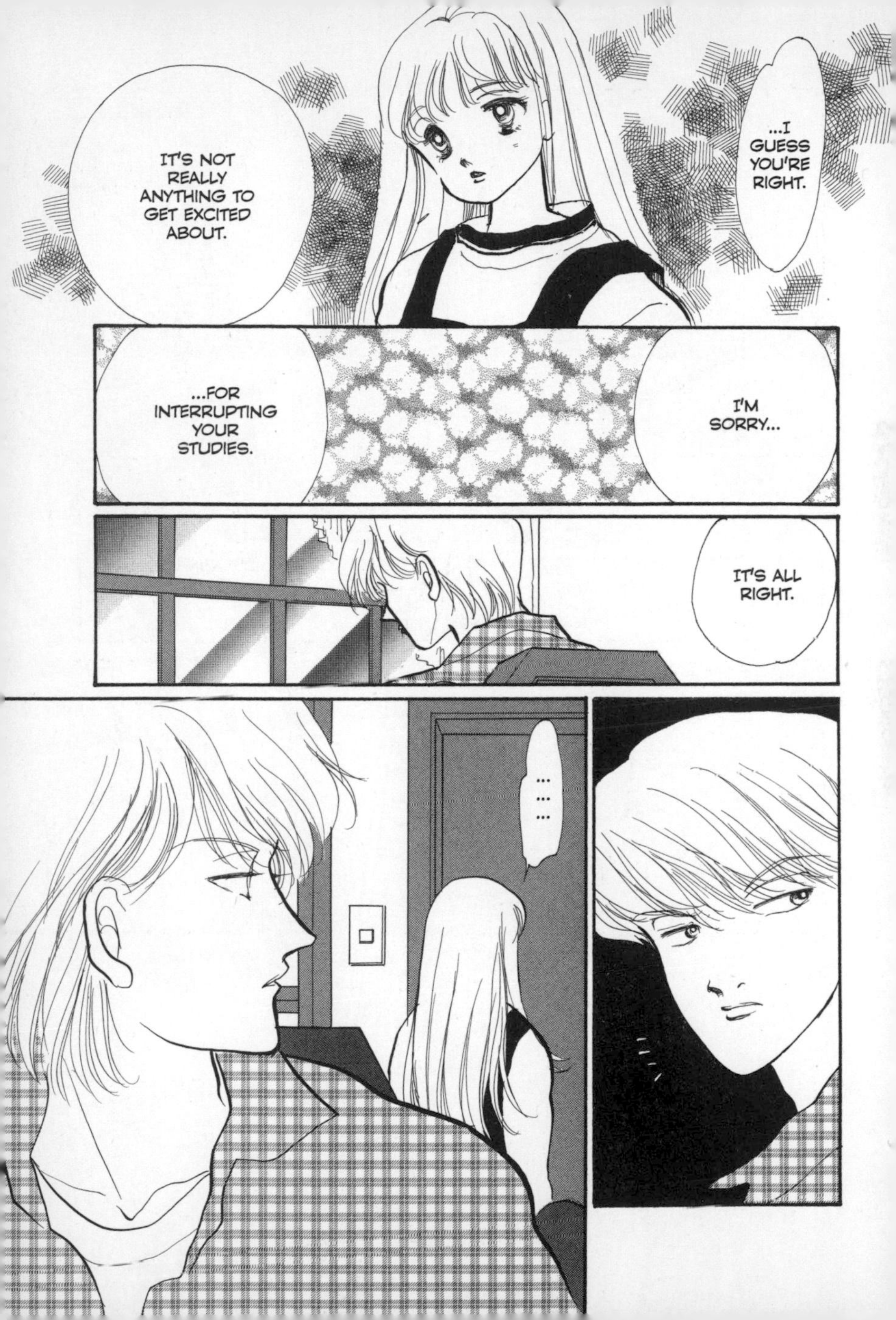
...I GUESS YOU'RE RIGHT.
IT'S NOT REALLY ANYTHING TO GET EXCITED ABOUT.
I'M SORRY...
...FOR INTERRUPTING YOUR STUDIES.
IT'S ALL RIGHT.
... ...

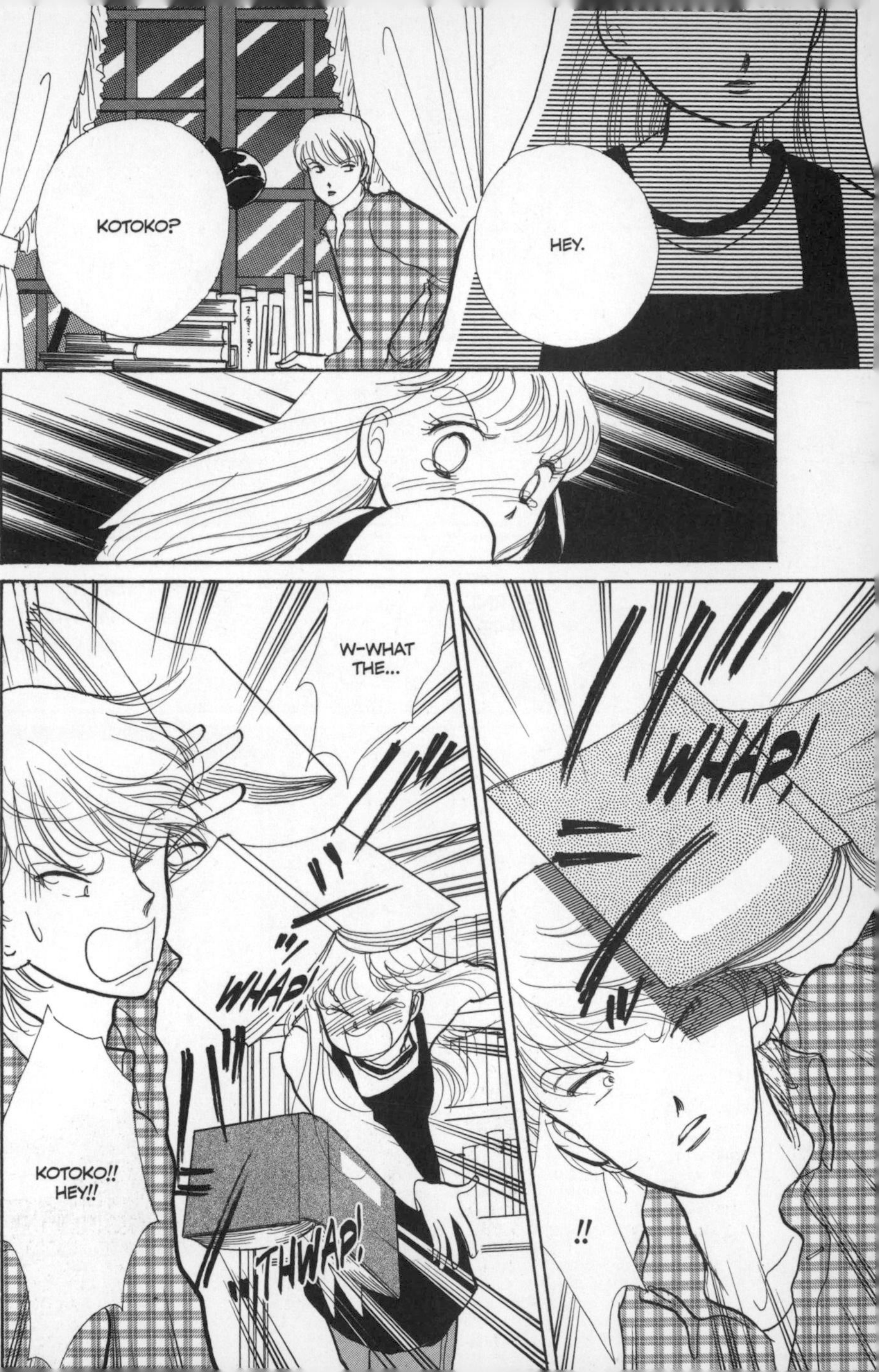
HEY.
KOTOKO?
WHAP!
!!
W-WHAT THE...
WHAP!
KOTOKO!! HEY!!
THWAP!

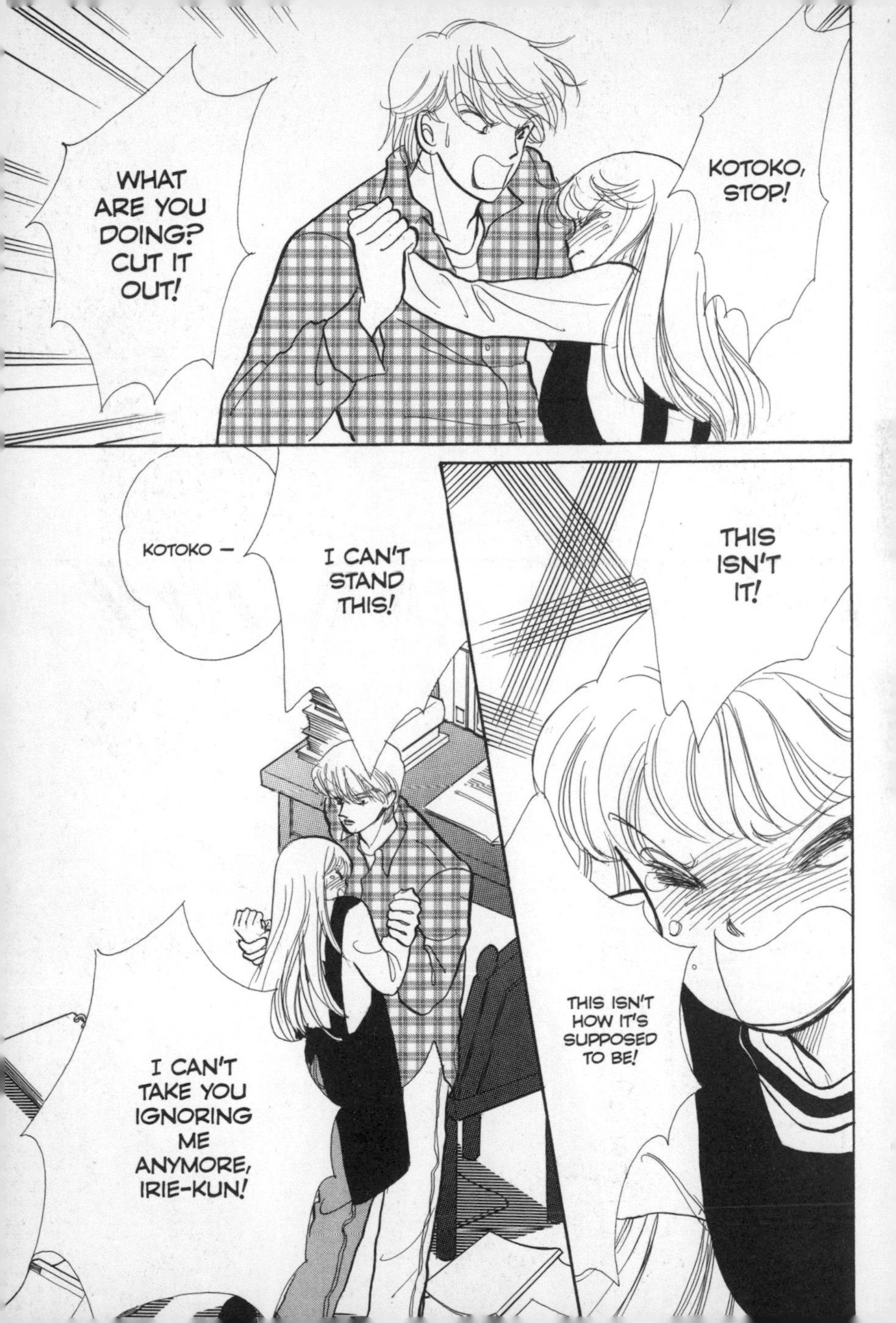
KOTOKO, STOP!
WHAT ARE YOU DOING? CUT IT OUT!
THIS ISN'T IT!
THIS ISN'T HOW IT'S SUPPOSED TO BE!
I CAN'T STAND THIS!
KOTOKO —
I CAN'T TAKE YOU IGNORING ME ANYMORE, IRIE-KUN!

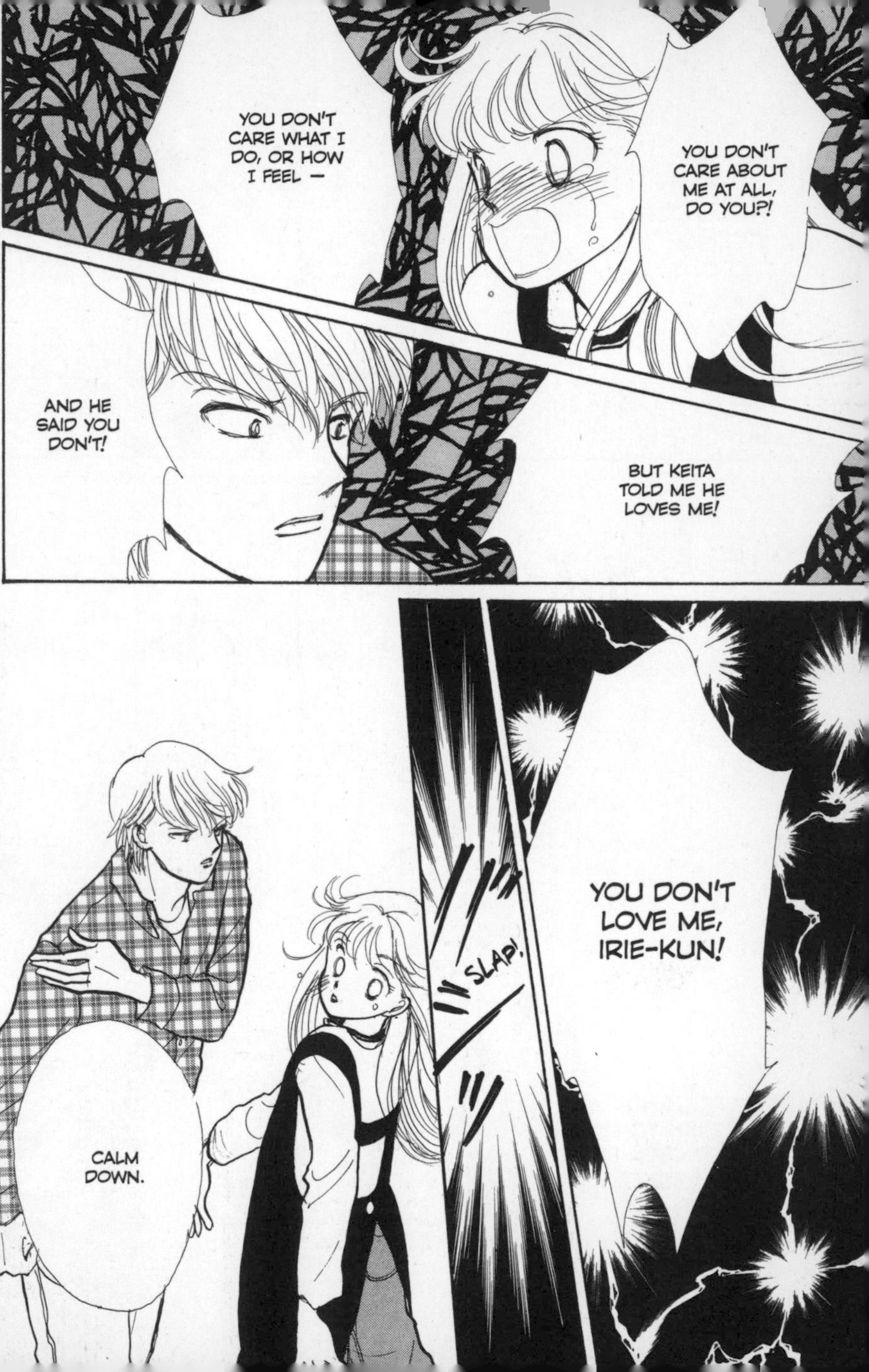
YOU DON'T CARE ABOUT ME AT ALL, DO YOU?!
YOU DON'T CARE WHAT I DO, OR HOW I FEEL —
BUT KEITA TOLD ME HE LOVES ME!
AND HE SAID YOU DON'T!
YOU DON'T LOVE ME, IRIE-KUN!
SLAP!
CALM DOWN.

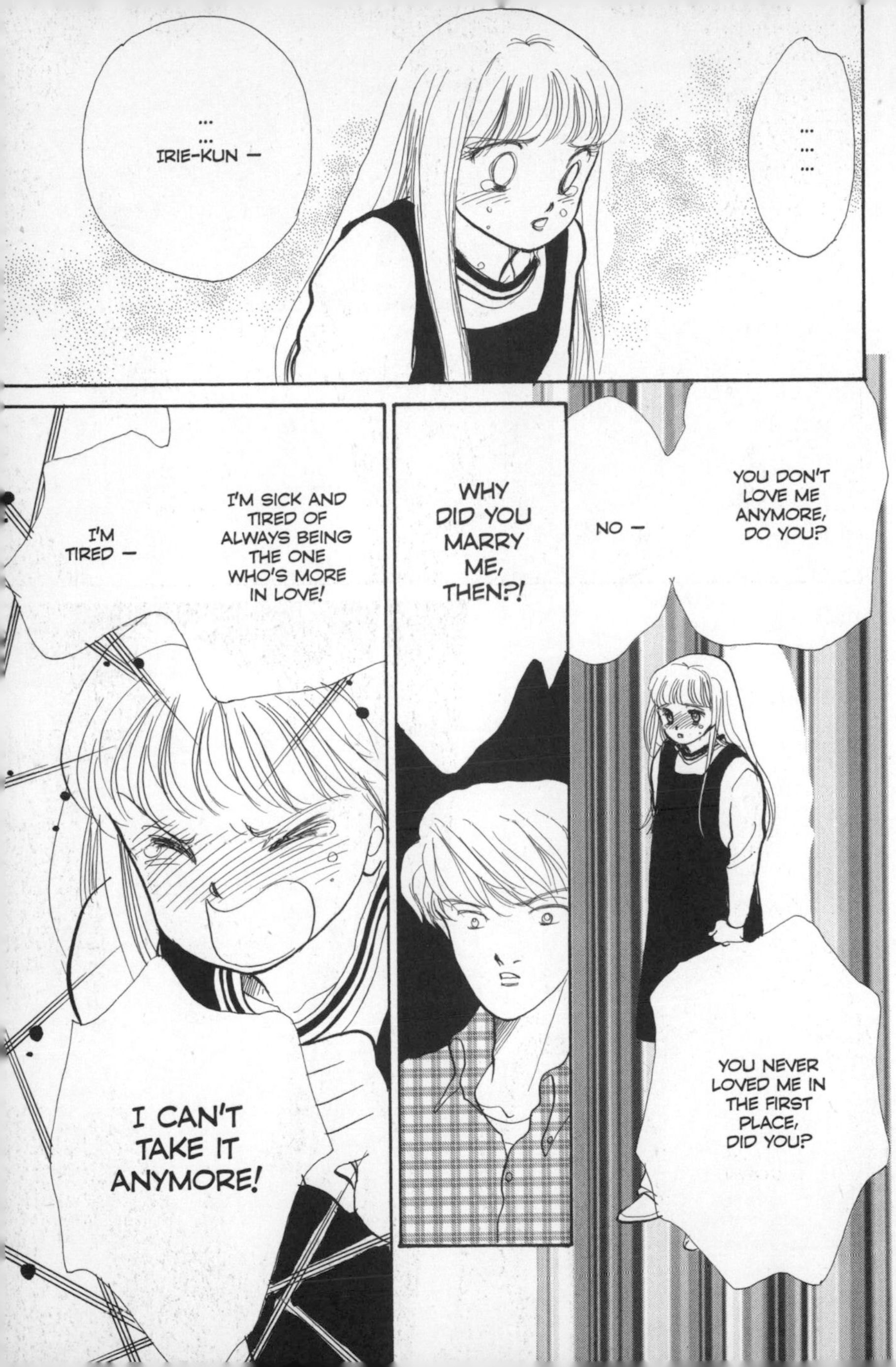
...
...
...
...
...
IRIE-KUN —
YOU DON'T LOVE ME ANYMORE, DO YOU?
NO —
YOU NEVER LOVED ME IN THE FIRST PLACE, DID YOU?
WHY DID YOU MARRY ME, THEN?!
I'M SICK AND TIRED OF ALWAYS BEING THE ONE WHO'S MORE IN LOVE!
I'M TIRED —
I CAN'T TAKE IT ANYMORE!

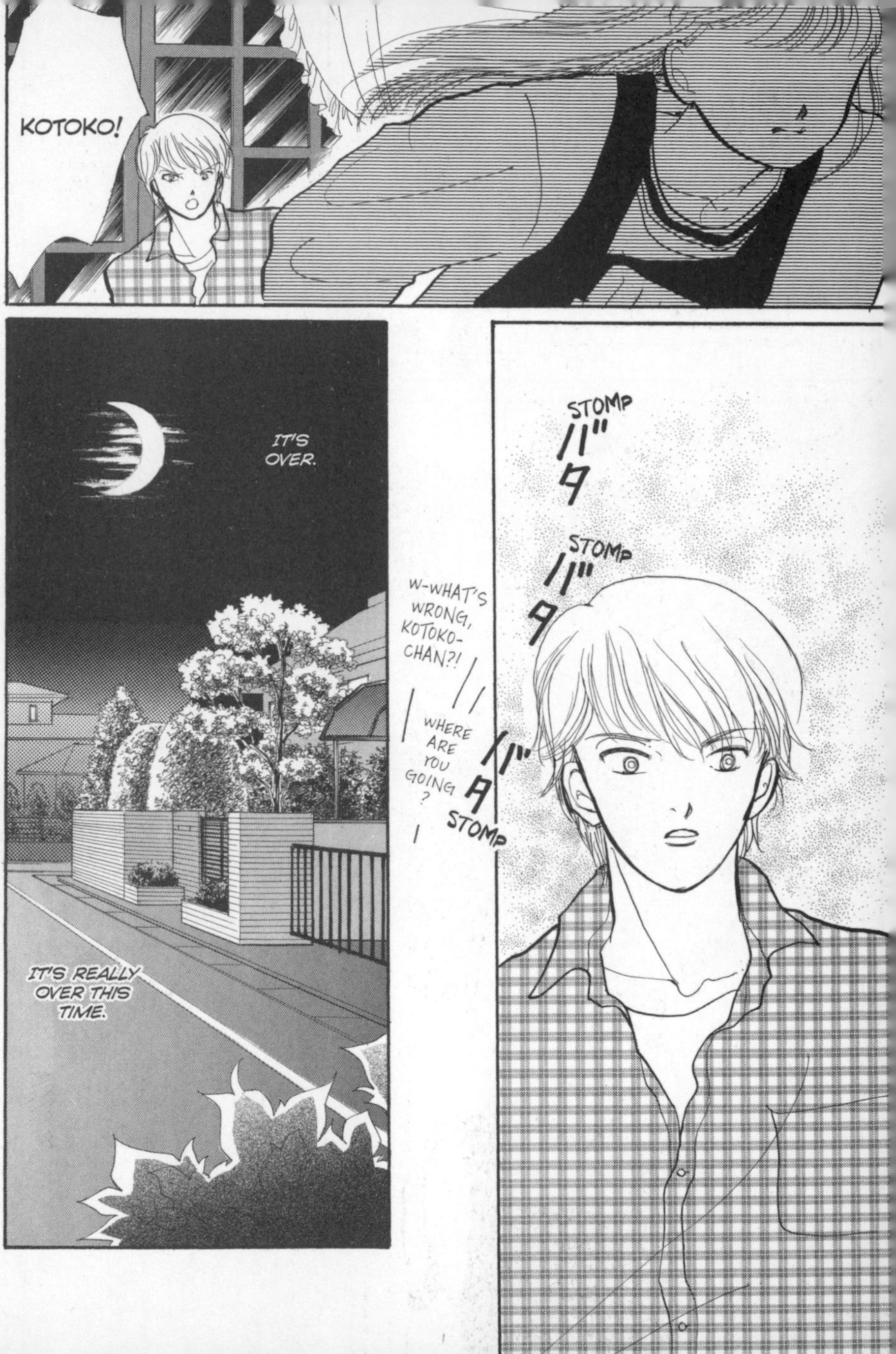
KOTOKO!
STOMP
バタ
STOMP
バタ
W-WHAT'S WRONG, KOTOKO-CHAN?!
WHERE ARE YOU GOING?
バタ
STOMP
IT'S OVER.
IT'S REALLY OVER THIS TIME.

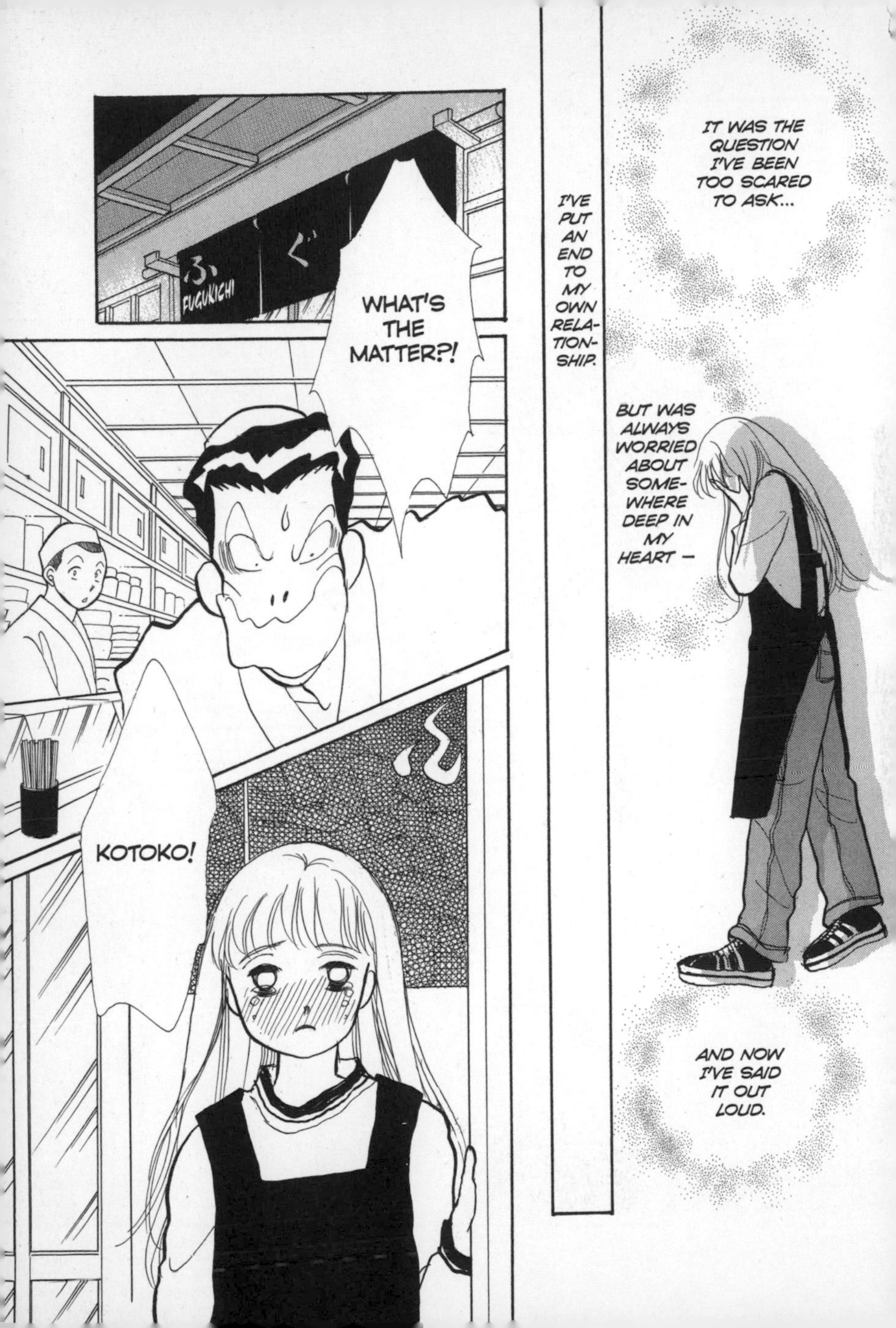
IT WAS THE QUESTION I'VE BEEN TOO SCARED TO ASK...
BUT WAS ALWAYS WORRIED ABOUT SOME-WHERE DEEP IN MY HEART —
AND NOW I'VE SAID IT OUT LOUD.
I'VE PUT AN END TO MY OWN RELA-TION-SHIP.
ふ
FUGUKICHI
WHAT'S THE MATTER?!
KOTOKO!

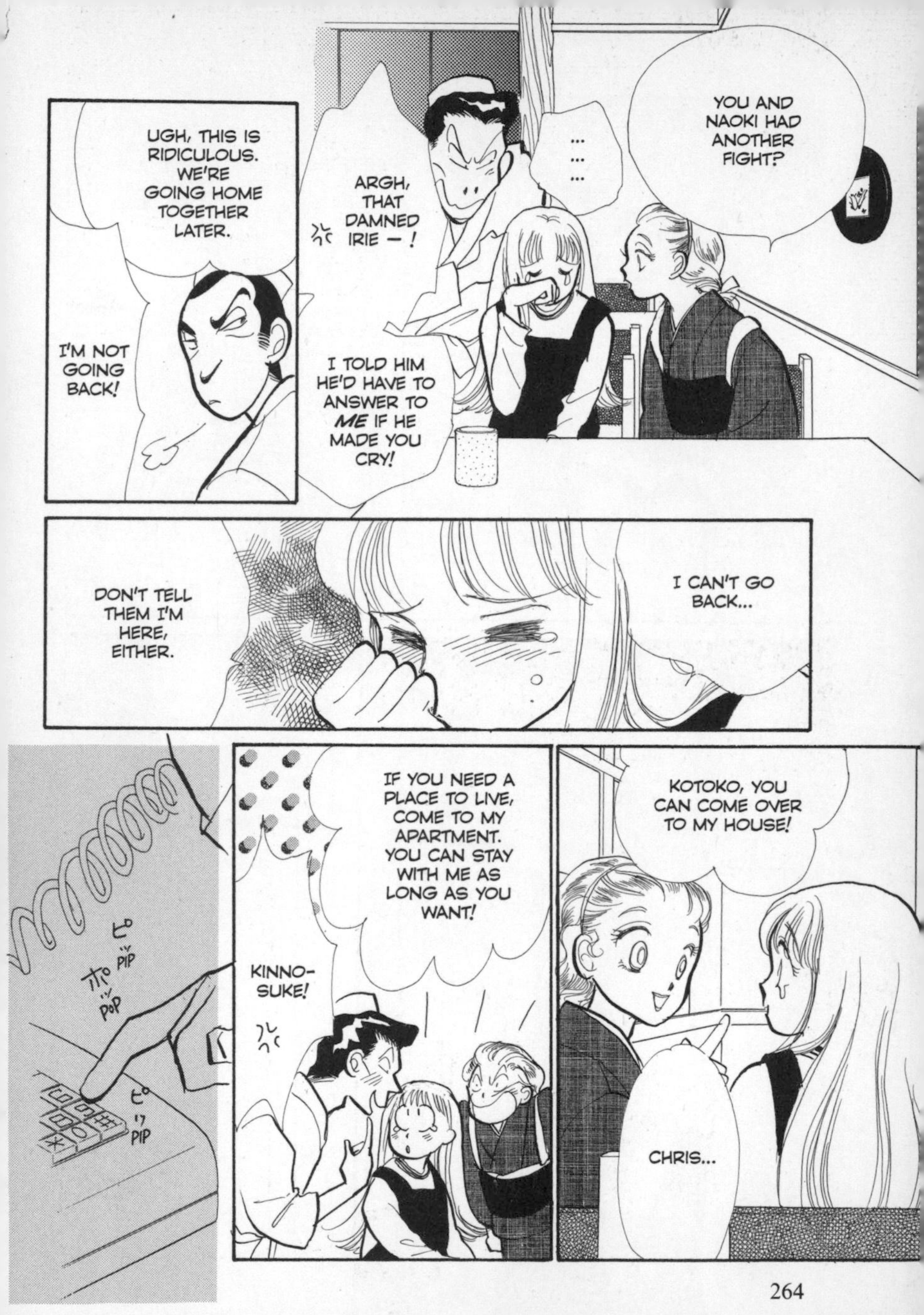
YOU AND NAOKI HAD ANOTHER FIGHT?
... ...
ARGH, THAT DAMNED IRIE —!
I TOLD HIM HE'D HAVE TO ANSWER TO *ME* IF HE MADE YOU CRY!
UGH, THIS IS RIDICULOUS. WE'RE GOING HOME TOGETHER LATER.
I'M NOT GOING BACK!
I CAN'T GO BACK...
DON'T TELL THEM I'M HERE, EITHER.
KOTOKO, YOU CAN COME OVER TO MY HOUSE!
CHRIS...
IF YOU NEED A PLACE TO LIVE, COME TO MY APARTMENT. YOU CAN STAY WITH ME AS LONG AS YOU WANT!
KINNO-SUKE!
ピッ PIP
ポッ POP
ピッ PIP

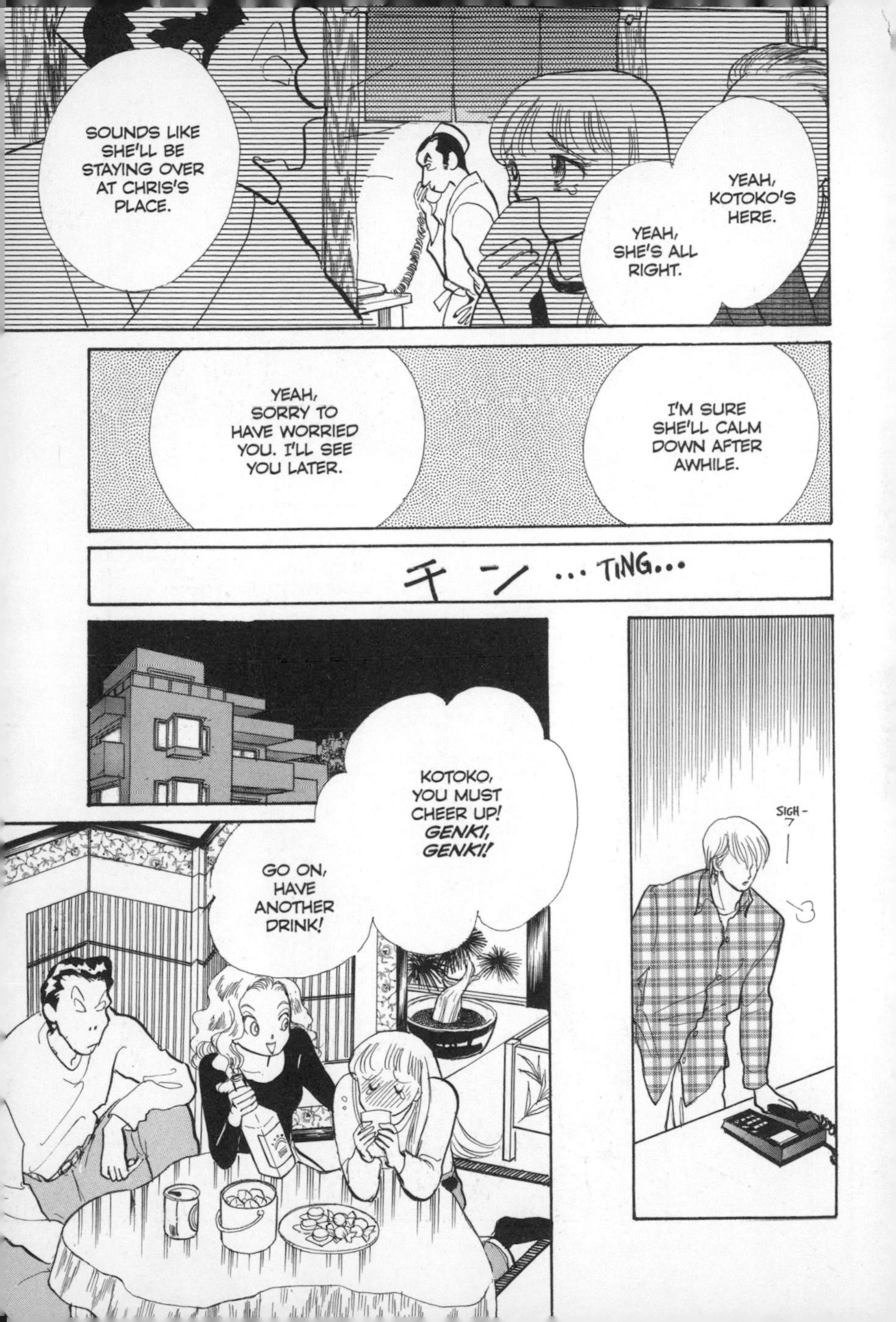
YEAH, KOTOKO'S HERE.
YEAH, SHE'S ALL RIGHT.
SOUNDS LIKE SHE'LL BE STAYING OVER AT CHRIS'S PLACE.
I'M SURE SHE'LL CALM DOWN AFTER AWHILE.
YEAH, SORRY TO HAVE WORRIED YOU. I'LL SEE YOU LATER.
チーン ...TING...
SIGH-
KOTOKO, YOU MUST CHEER UP! *GENKI, GENKI!*
GO ON, HAVE ANOTHER DRINK!

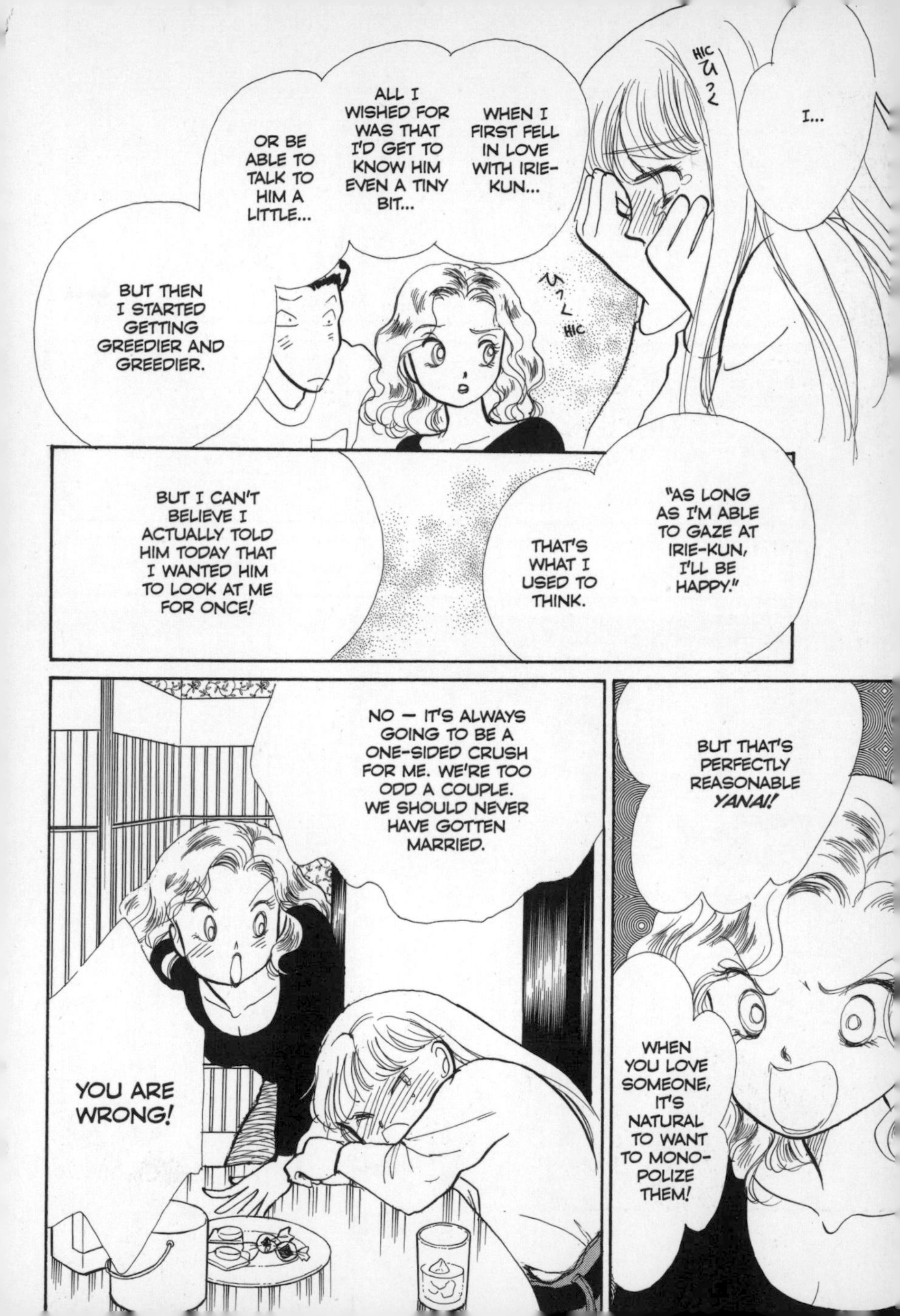

HIC ひっく
I...
WHEN I FIRST FELL IN LOVE WITH IRIE-KUN...
ALL I WISHED FOR WAS THAT I'D GET TO KNOW HIM EVEN A TINY BIT...
OR BE ABLE TO TALK TO HIM A LITTLE...
ひっく HIC
BUT THEN I STARTED GETTING GREEDIER AND GREEDIER.
"AS LONG AS I'M ABLE TO GAZE AT IRIE-KUN, I'LL BE HAPPY."
THAT'S WHAT I USED TO THINK.
BUT I CAN'T BELIEVE I ACTUALLY TOLD HIM TODAY THAT I WANTED HIM TO LOOK AT ME FOR ONCE!
BUT THAT'S PERFECTLY REASONABLE *YANAI!*
WHEN YOU LOVE SOMEONE, IT'S NATURAL TO WANT TO MONO-POLIZE THEM!
NO — IT'S ALWAYS GOING TO BE A ONE-SIDED CRUSH FOR ME. WE'RE TOO ODD A COUPLE. WE SHOULD NEVER HAVE GOTTEN MARRIED.
YOU ARE WRONG!

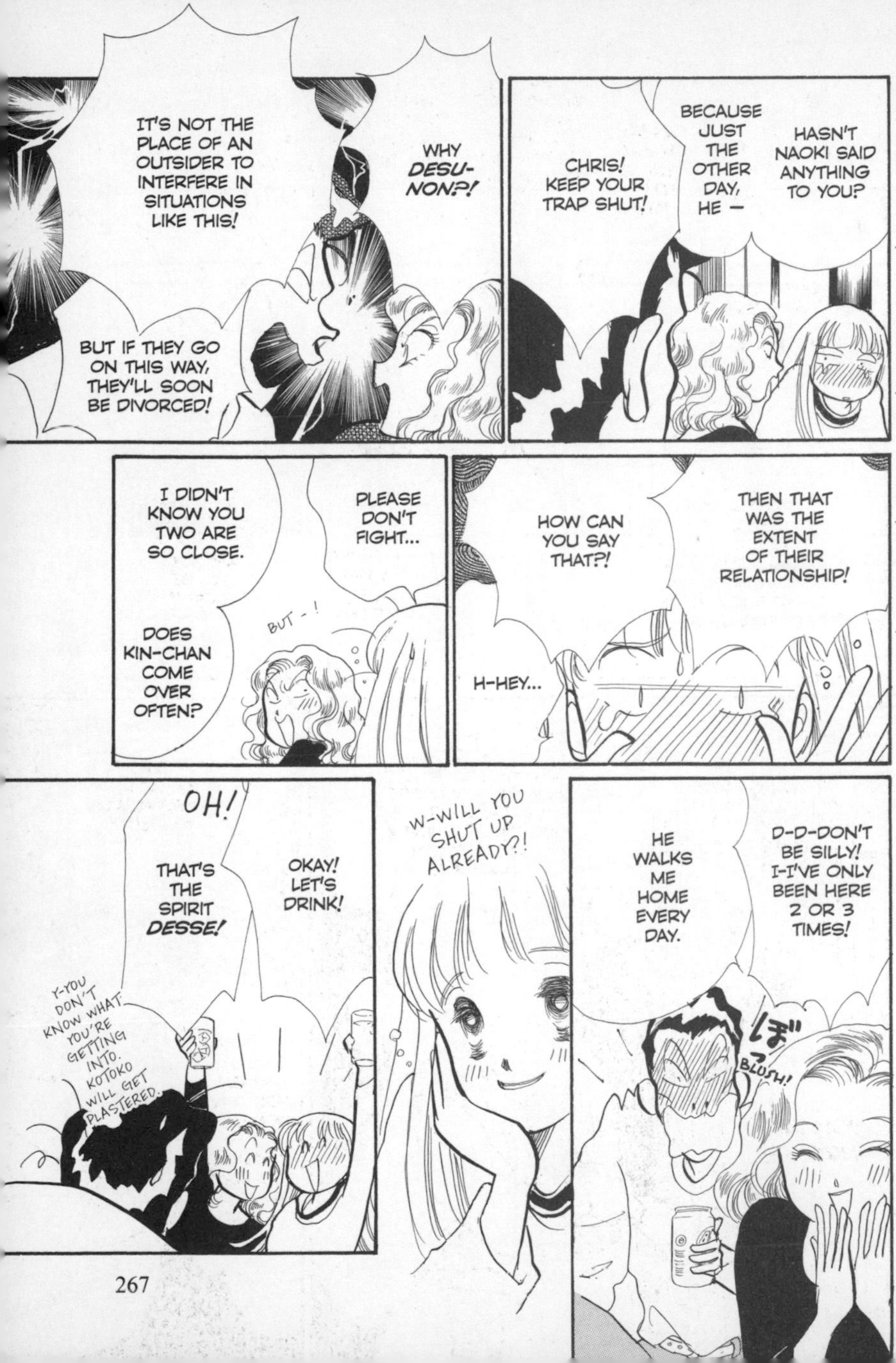
HASN'T NAOKI SAID ANYTHING TO YOU?
BECAUSE JUST THE OTHER DAY, HE —
CHRIS! KEEP YOUR TRAP SHUT!
WHY *DESU-NON?!*
IT'S NOT THE PLACE OF AN OUTSIDER TO INTERFERE IN SITUATIONS LIKE THIS!
BUT IF THEY GO ON THIS WAY, THEY'LL SOON BE DIVORCED!
THEN THAT WAS THE EXTENT OF THEIR RELATIONSHIP!
HOW CAN YOU SAY THAT?!
H-HEY...
PLEASE DON'T FIGHT...
I DIDN'T KNOW YOU TWO ARE SO CLOSE.
BUT - !
DOES KIN-CHAN COME OVER OFTEN?
D-D-DON'T BE SILLY! I-I'VE ONLY BEEN HERE 2 OR 3 TIMES!
HE WALKS ME HOME EVERY DAY.
ぼっ
BLUSH!
W-WILL YOU SHUT UP ALREADY?!
OKAY! LET'S DRINK!
OH!
THAT'S THE SPIRIT *DESSE!*
Y-YOU DON'T KNOW WHAT YOU'RE GETTING INTO. KOTOKO WILL GET PLASTERED.

STAFF: AKIKO ISHIKAWA, ATSUKO SUGIMOTO, MASAKO KATAGAI, SHIUKO AZUNA, SHIZUKO KOIKE

THANK YOU VERY MUCH ♥

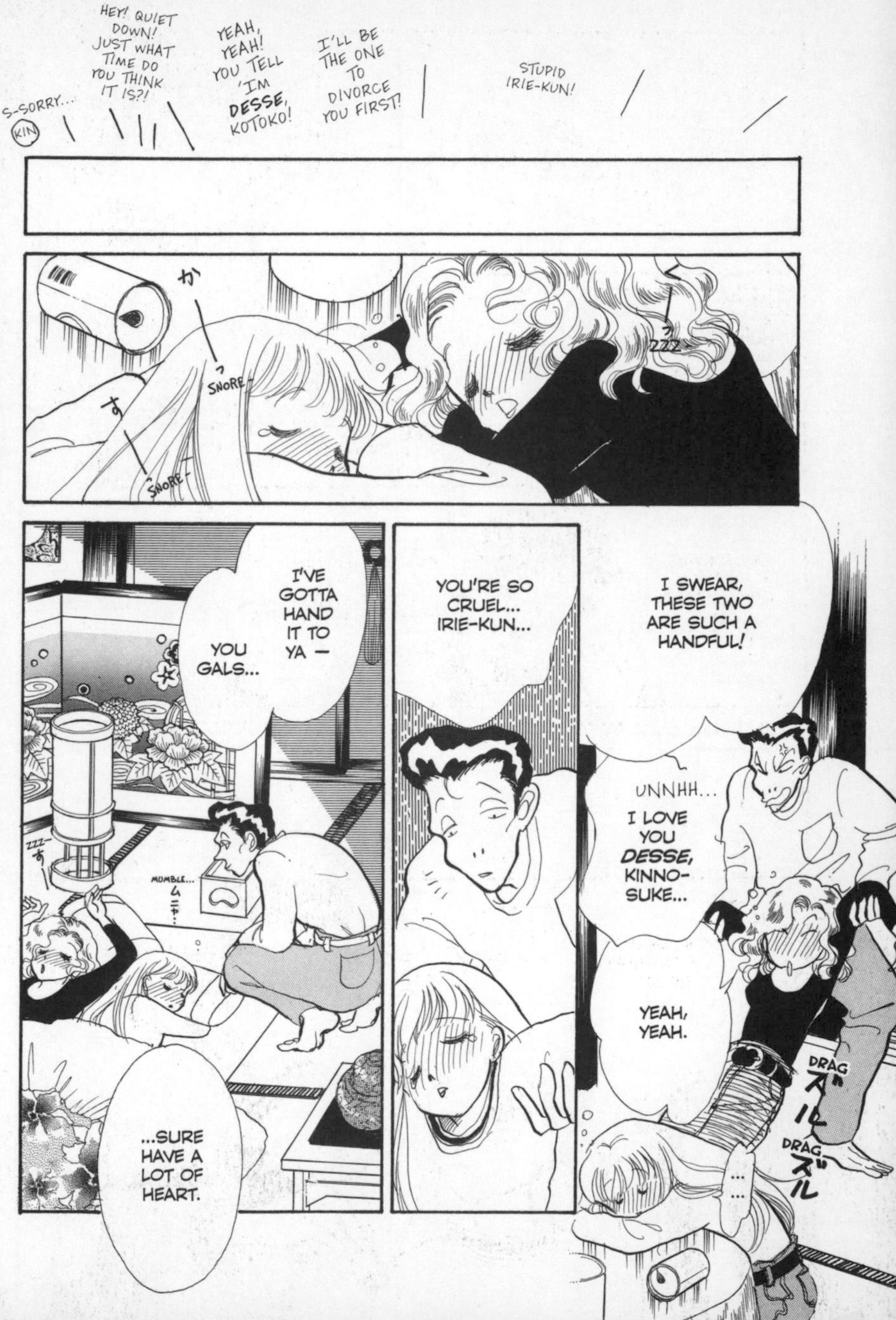
STUPID IRIE-KUN!
I'LL BE THE ONE TO DIVORCE YOU FIRST!
YEAH, YEAH! YOU TELL 'IM DESSE, KOTOKO!
HEY! QUIET DOWN! JUST WHAT TIME DO YOU THINK IT IS?!
S-SORRY...
KIN
ZZZ
SNORE
SNORE
I SWEAR, THESE TWO ARE SUCH A HANDFUL!
UNNHH... I LOVE YOU DESSE, KINNOSUKE...
YEAH, YEAH.
DRAG ズル
DRAG ズル
... ...
YOU'RE SO CRUEL... IRIE-KUN...
I'VE GOTTA HAND IT TO YA — YOU GALS...
ZZZ
MUMBLE... ムニャ...
...SURE HAVE A LOT OF HEART.

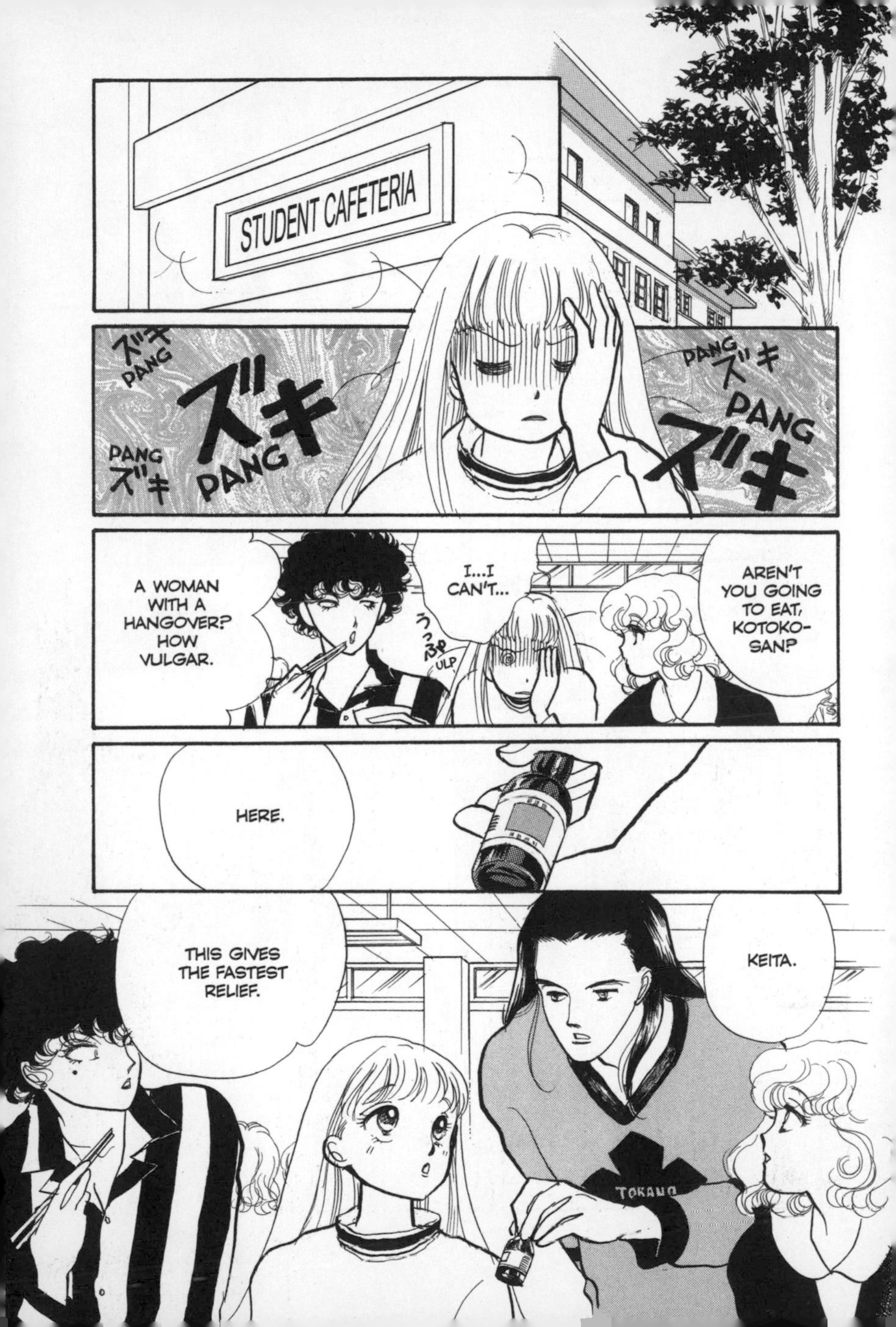
STUDENT CAFETERIA
ズキ PANG
ズキ PANG
ズキ PANG
ズキ PANG
ズキ PANG
ズキ PANG
AREN'T YOU GOING TO EAT, KOTOKO-SAN?
I...I CAN'T...
うっぷ ULP
A WOMAN WITH A HANGOVER? HOW VULGAR.
HERE.
KEITA.
THIS GIVES THE FASTEST RELIEF.
TOKANO

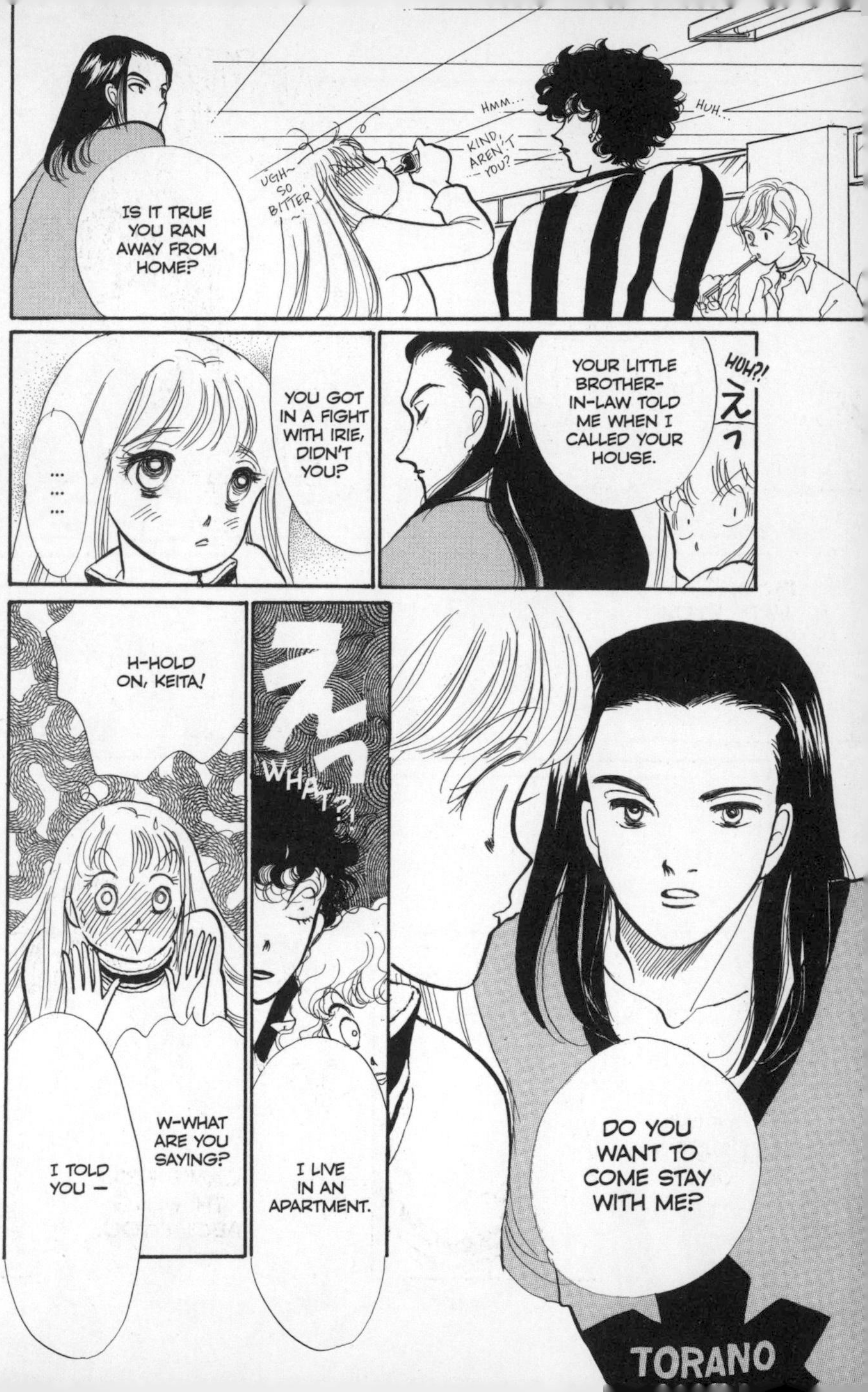
HUH...
HMM...
KIND, AREN'T YOU?
UGH~ SO BITTER~
IS IT TRUE YOU RAN AWAY FROM HOME?
HUH?! え っ
YOUR LITTLE BROTHER-IN-LAW TOLD ME WHEN I CALLED YOUR HOUSE.
YOU GOT IN A FIGHT WITH IRIE, DIDN'T YOU?
... ...
DO YOU WANT TO COME STAY WITH ME?
TORANO
えっ WHAT?!
I LIVE IN AN APARTMENT.
H-HOLD ON, KEITA!
W-WHAT ARE YOU SAYING?
I TOLD YOU —

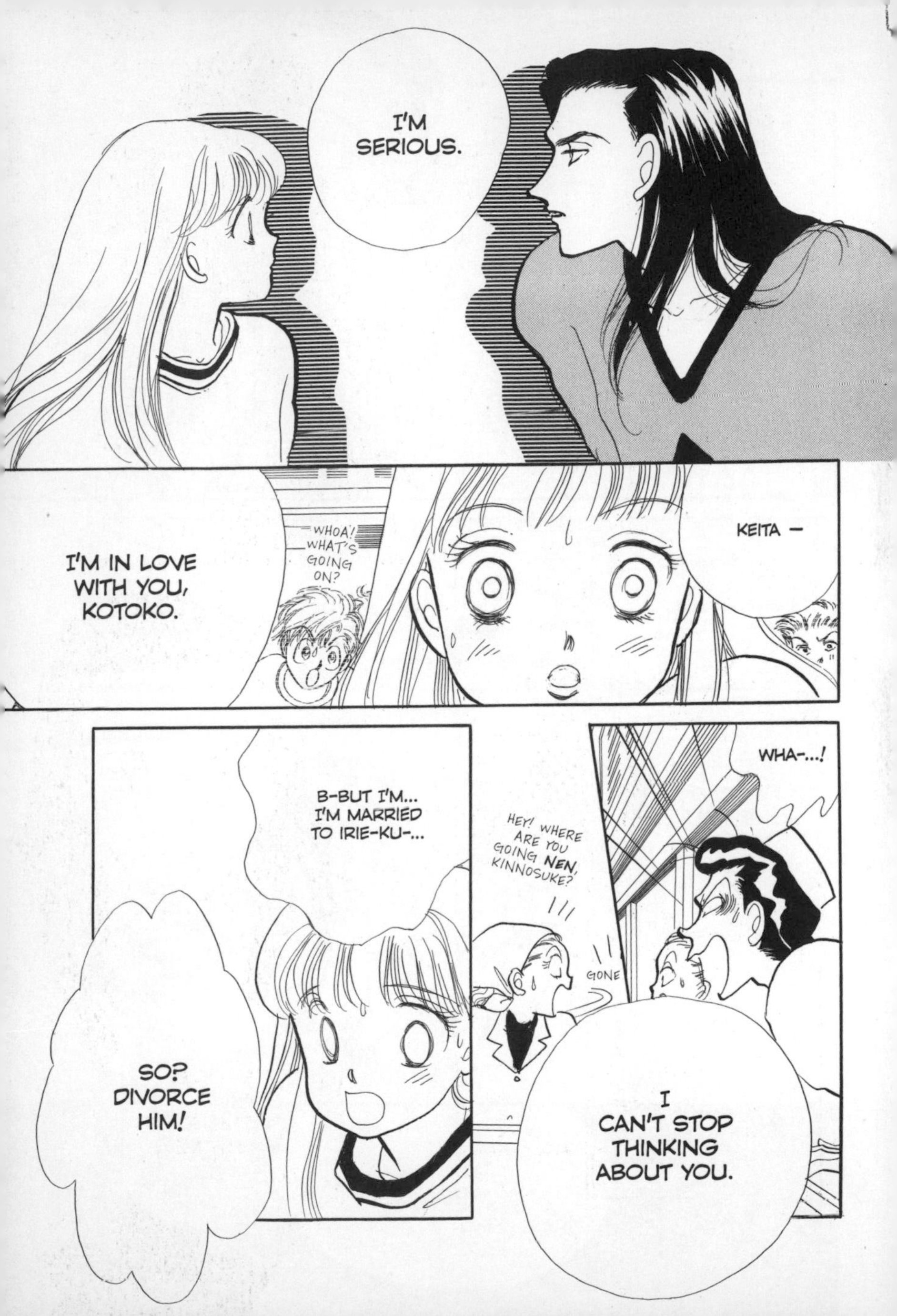
I'M SERIOUS.
KEITA –
WHOA! WHAT'S GOING ON?
I'M IN LOVE WITH YOU, KOTOKO.
WHA-...!
HEY! WHERE ARE YOU GOING NEN, KINNOSUKE?
GONE
I CAN'T STOP THINKING ABOUT YOU.
B-BUT I'M... I'M MARRIED TO IRIE-KU-...
SO? DIVORCE HIM!

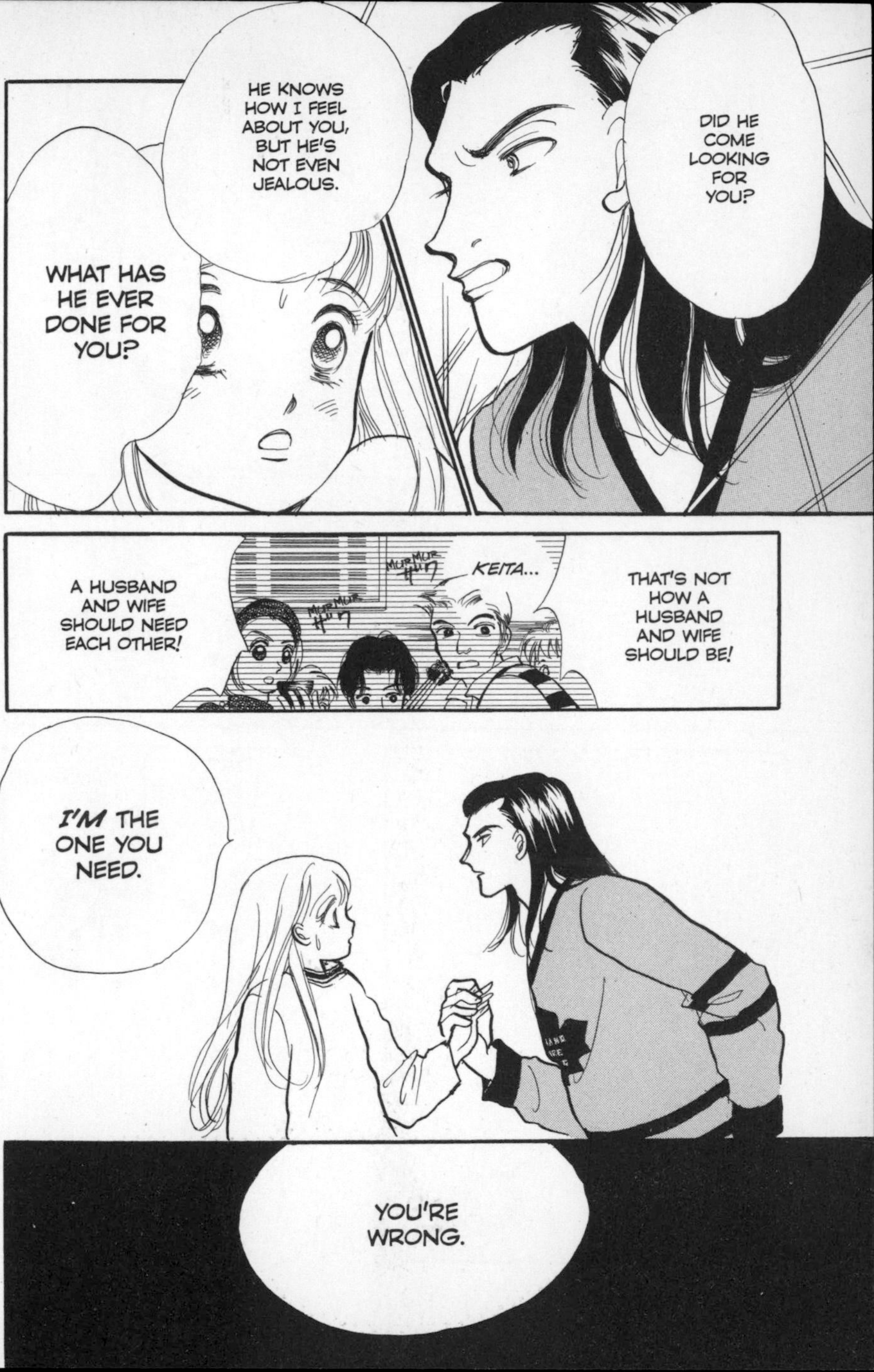
DID HE COME LOOKING FOR YOU?
HE KNOWS HOW I FEEL ABOUT YOU, BUT HE'S NOT EVEN JEALOUS.
WHAT HAS HE EVER DONE FOR YOU?
THAT'S NOT HOW A HUSBAND AND WIFE SHOULD BE!
KEITA...
MURMUR
MURMUR
A HUSBAND AND WIFE SHOULD NEED EACH OTHER!
I'M THE ONE YOU NEED.
YOU'RE WRONG.

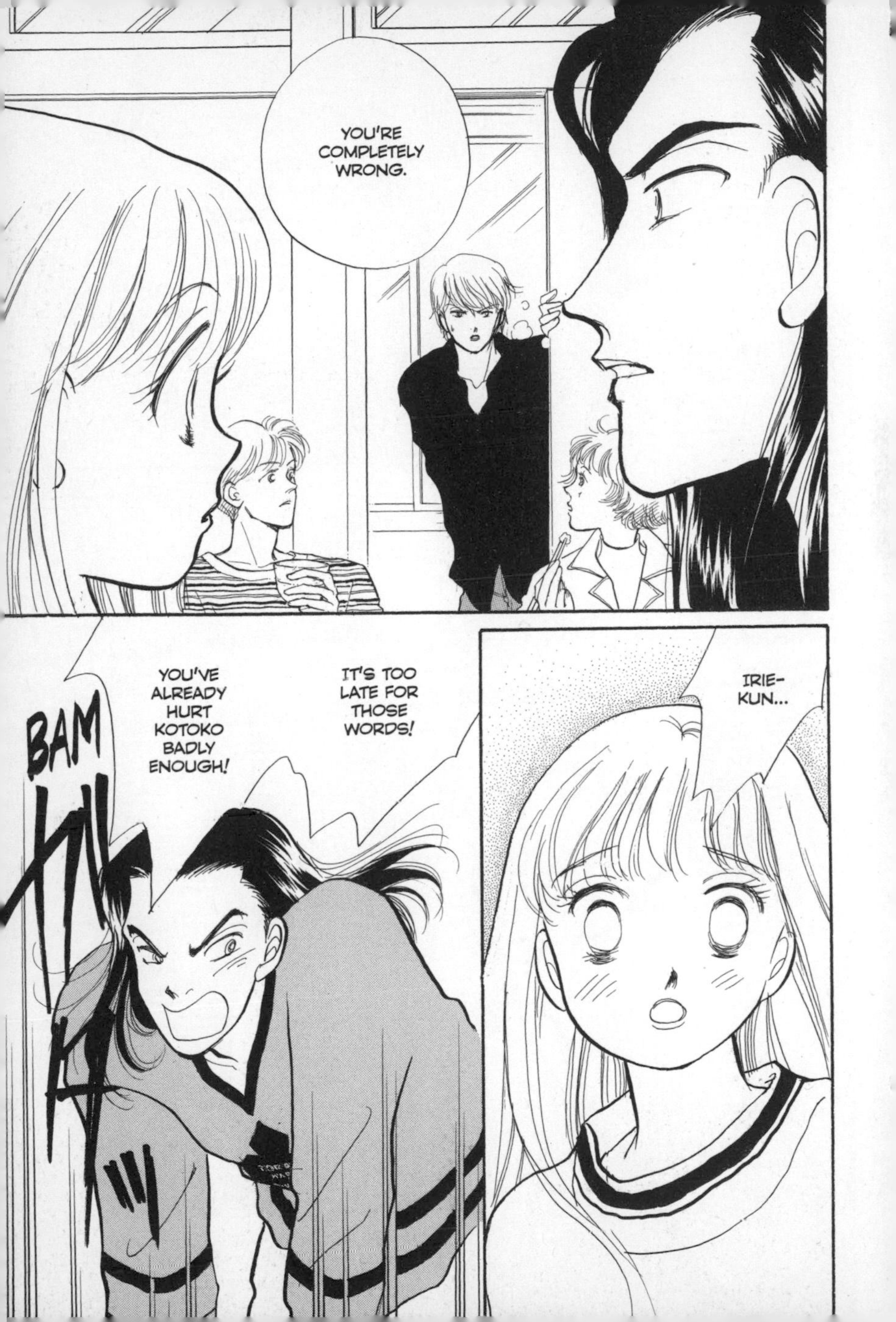
YOU'RE COMPLETELY WRONG.
IRIE-KUN...
IT'S TOO LATE FOR THOSE WORDS!
YOU'VE ALREADY HURT KOTOKO BADLY ENOUGH!
BAM

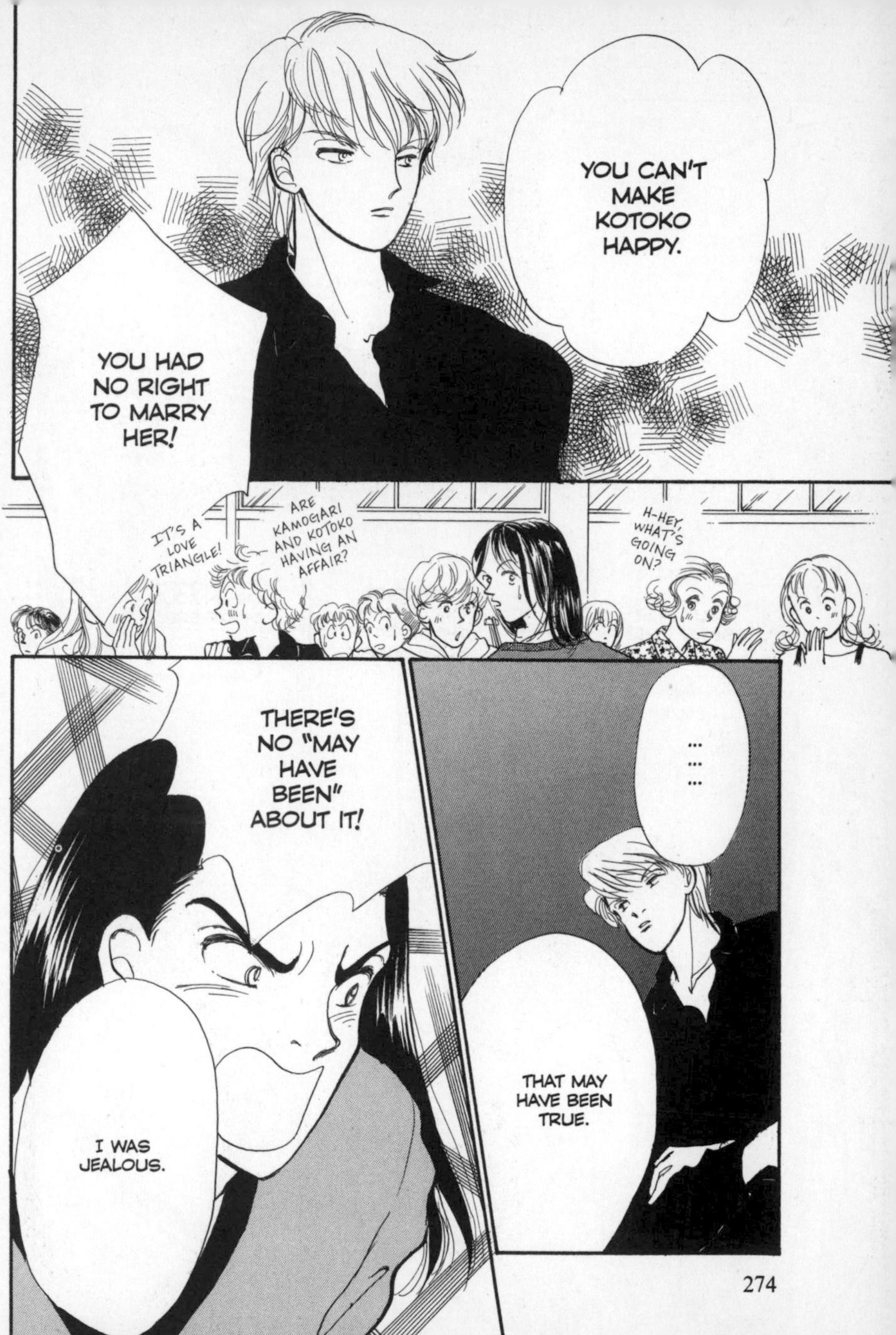
YOU CAN'T MAKE KOTOKO HAPPY.
YOU HAD NO RIGHT TO MARRY HER!
H-HEY, WHAT'S GOING ON?
ARE KAMOGARI AND KOTOKO HAVING AN AFFAIR?
IT'S A LOVE TRIANGLE!
...
...
...
THAT MAY HAVE BEEN TRUE.
THERE'S NO "MAY HAVE BEEN" ABOUT IT!
I WAS JEALOUS.

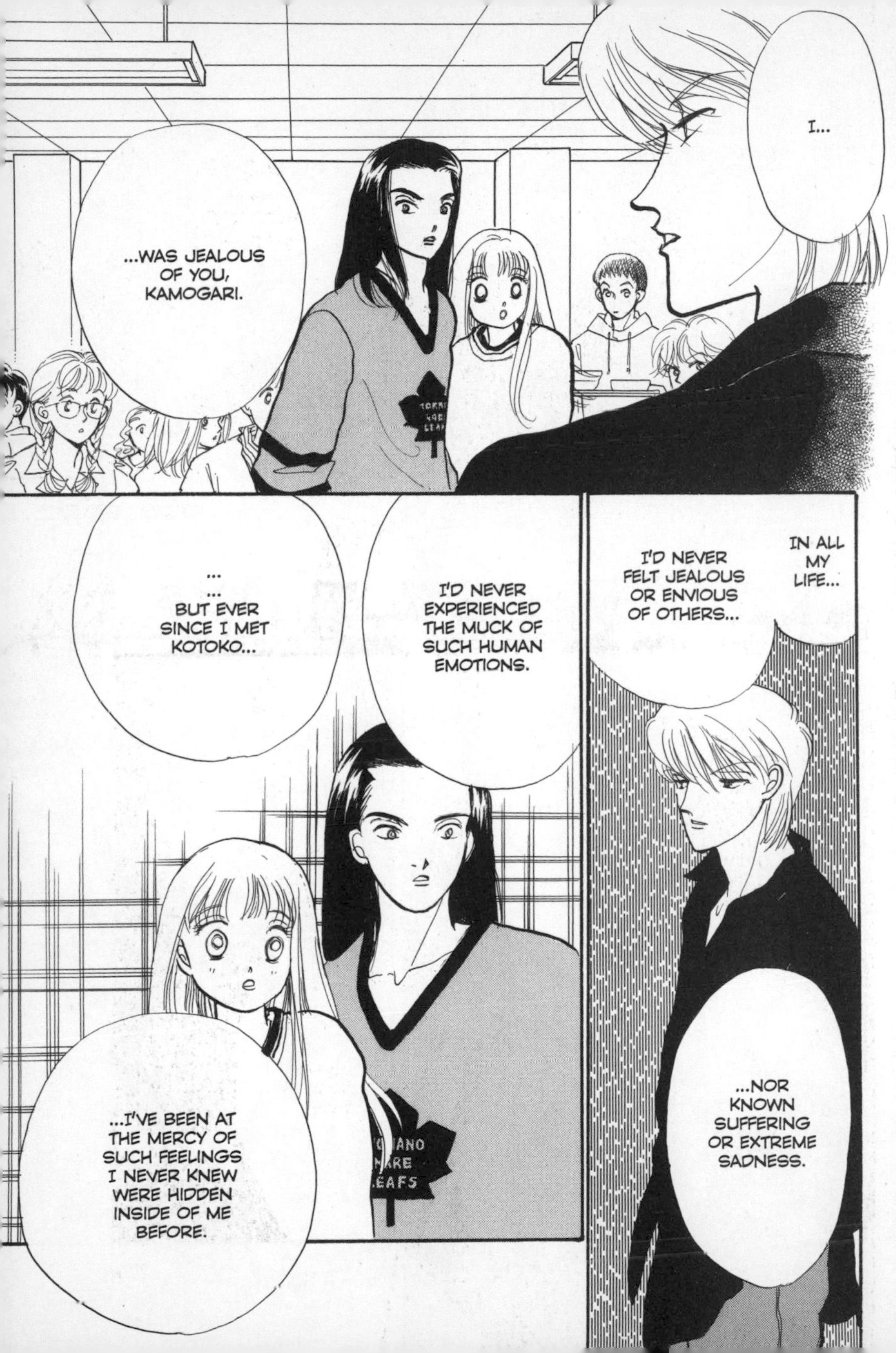
I...
...WAS JEALOUS OF YOU, KAMOGARI.
IN ALL MY LIFE...
I'D NEVER FELT JEALOUS OR ENVIOUS OF OTHERS...
...NOR KNOWN SUFFERING OR EXTREME SADNESS.
I'D NEVER EXPERIENCED THE MUCK OF SUCH HUMAN EMOTIONS.
... ... BUT EVER SINCE I MET KOTOKO...
...I'VE BEEN AT THE MERCY OF SUCH FEELINGS I NEVER KNEW WERE HIDDEN INSIDE OF ME BEFORE.

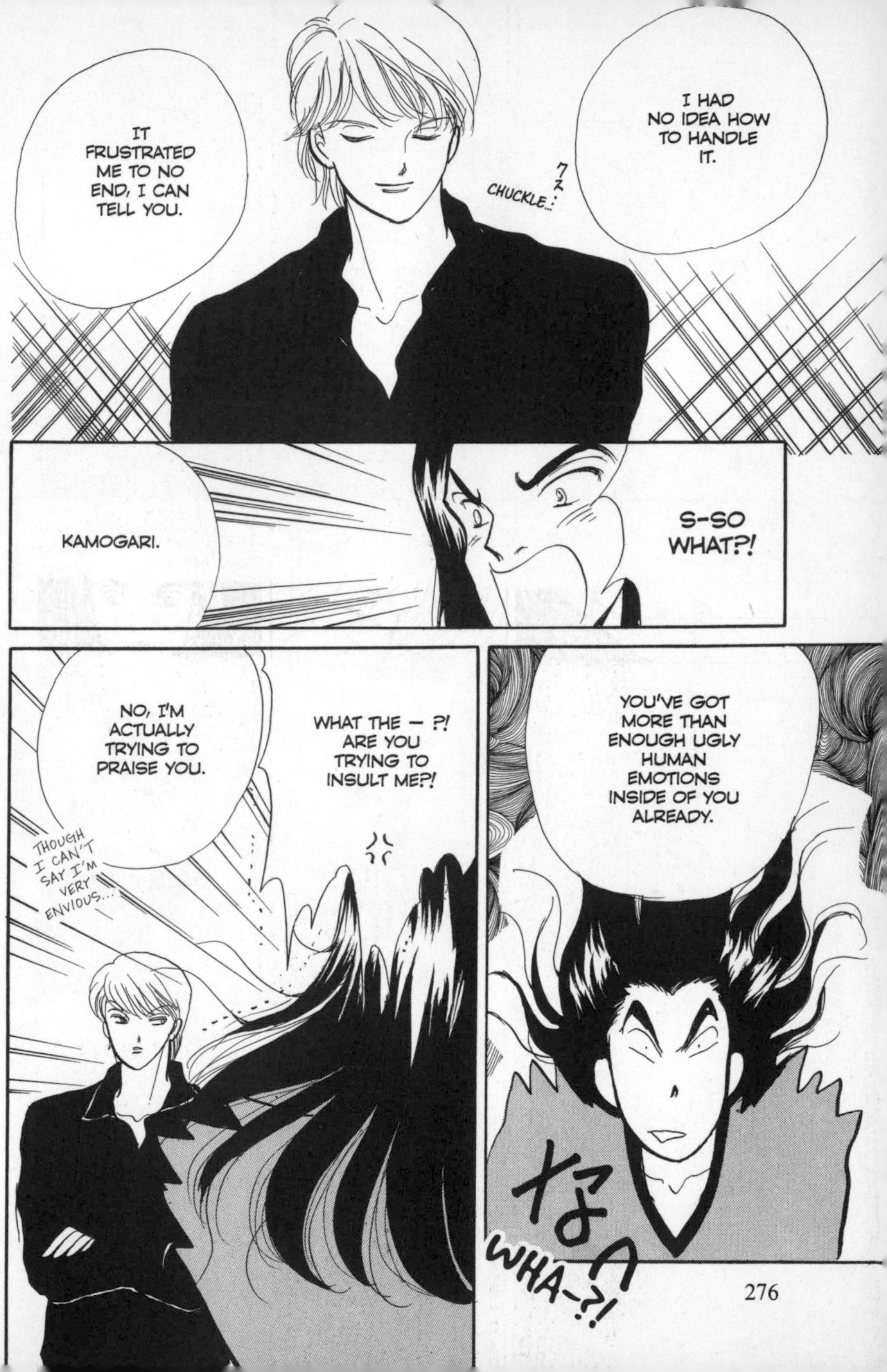
I HAD NO IDEA HOW TO HANDLE IT.
CHUCKLE...
IT FRUSTRATED ME TO NO END, I CAN TELL YOU.
S-SO WHAT?!
KAMOGARI.
YOU'VE GOT MORE THAN ENOUGH UGLY HUMAN EMOTIONS INSIDE OF YOU ALREADY.
WHA-?!
WHAT THE — ?! ARE YOU TRYING TO INSULT ME?!
NO, I'M ACTUALLY TRYING TO PRAISE YOU.
THOUGH I CAN'T SAY I'M VERY ENVIOUS...

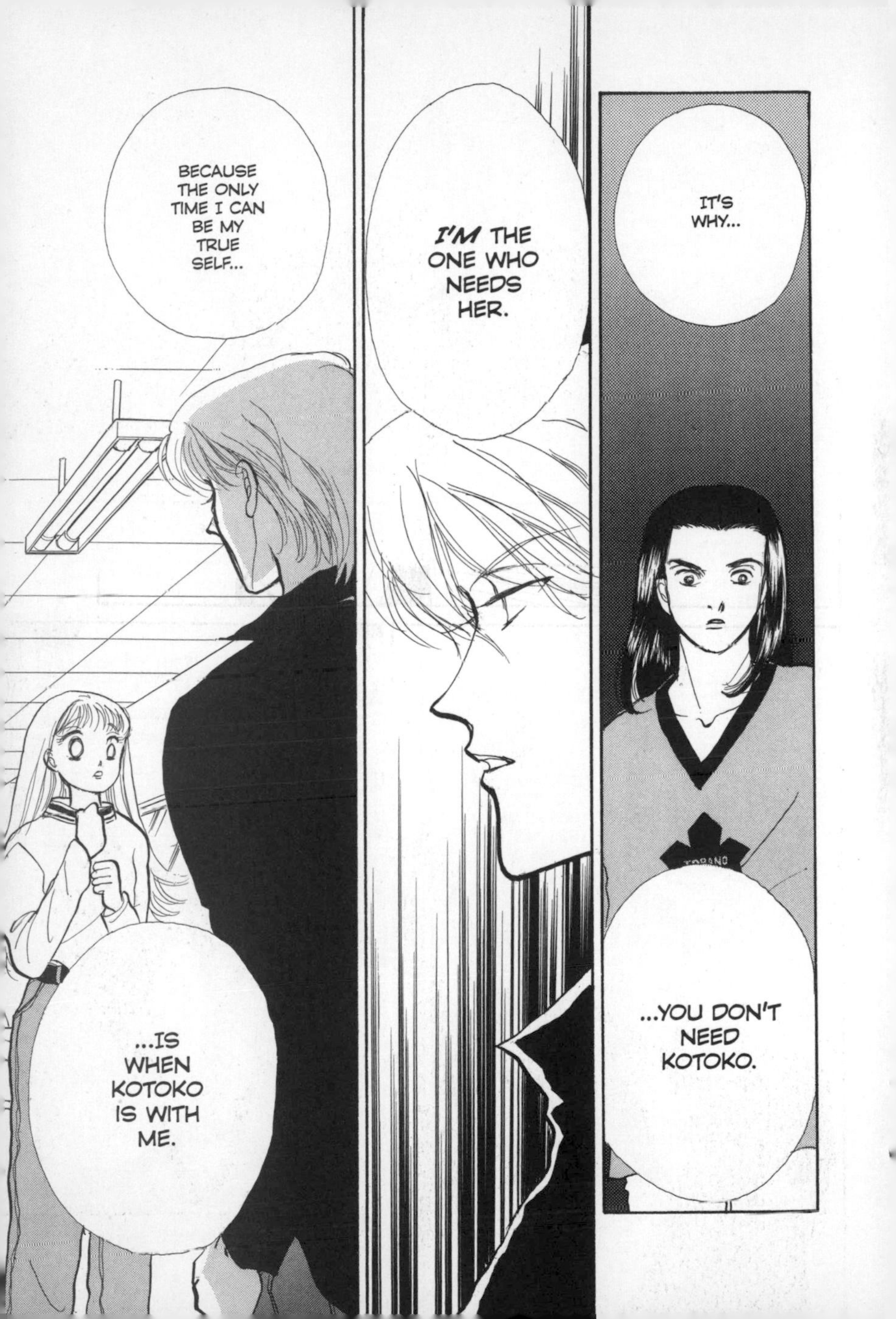
IT'S WHY...
...YOU DON'T NEED KOTOKO.
I'M THE ONE WHO NEEDS HER.
BECAUSE THE ONLY TIME I CAN BE MY TRUE SELF...
...IS WHEN KOTOKO IS WITH ME.

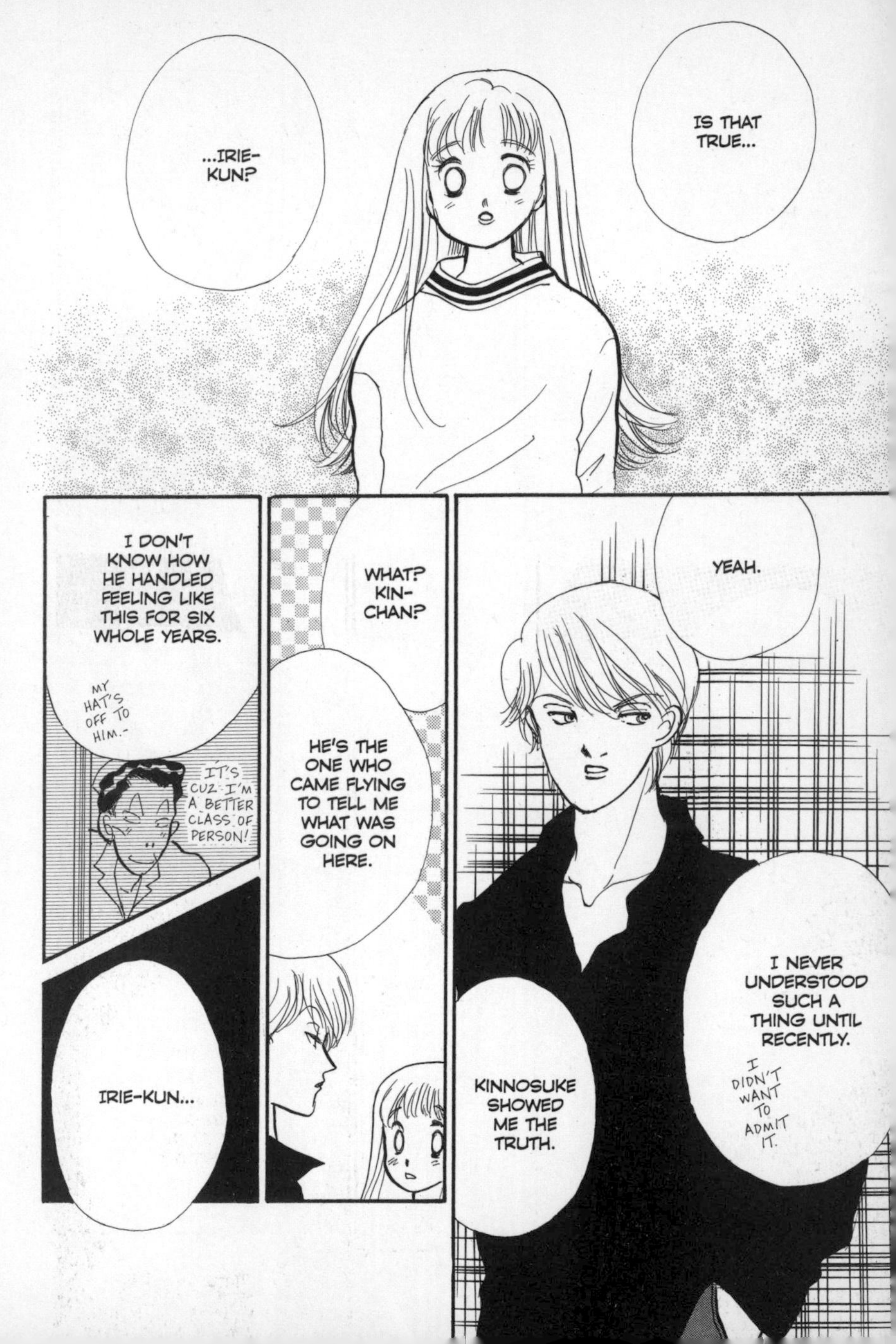
IS THAT TRUE...
...IRIE-KUN?
YEAH.
I NEVER UNDERSTOOD SUCH A THING UNTIL RECENTLY.
I DIDN'T WANT TO ADMIT IT.
KINNOSUKE SHOWED ME THE TRUTH.
WHAT? KIN-CHAN?
HE'S THE ONE WHO CAME FLYING TO TELL ME WHAT WAS GOING ON HERE.
I DON'T KNOW HOW HE HANDLED FEELING LIKE THIS FOR SIX WHOLE YEARS.
MY HAT'S OFF TO HIM.
IT'S CUZ I'M A BETTER CLASS OF PERSON!
IRIE-KUN...

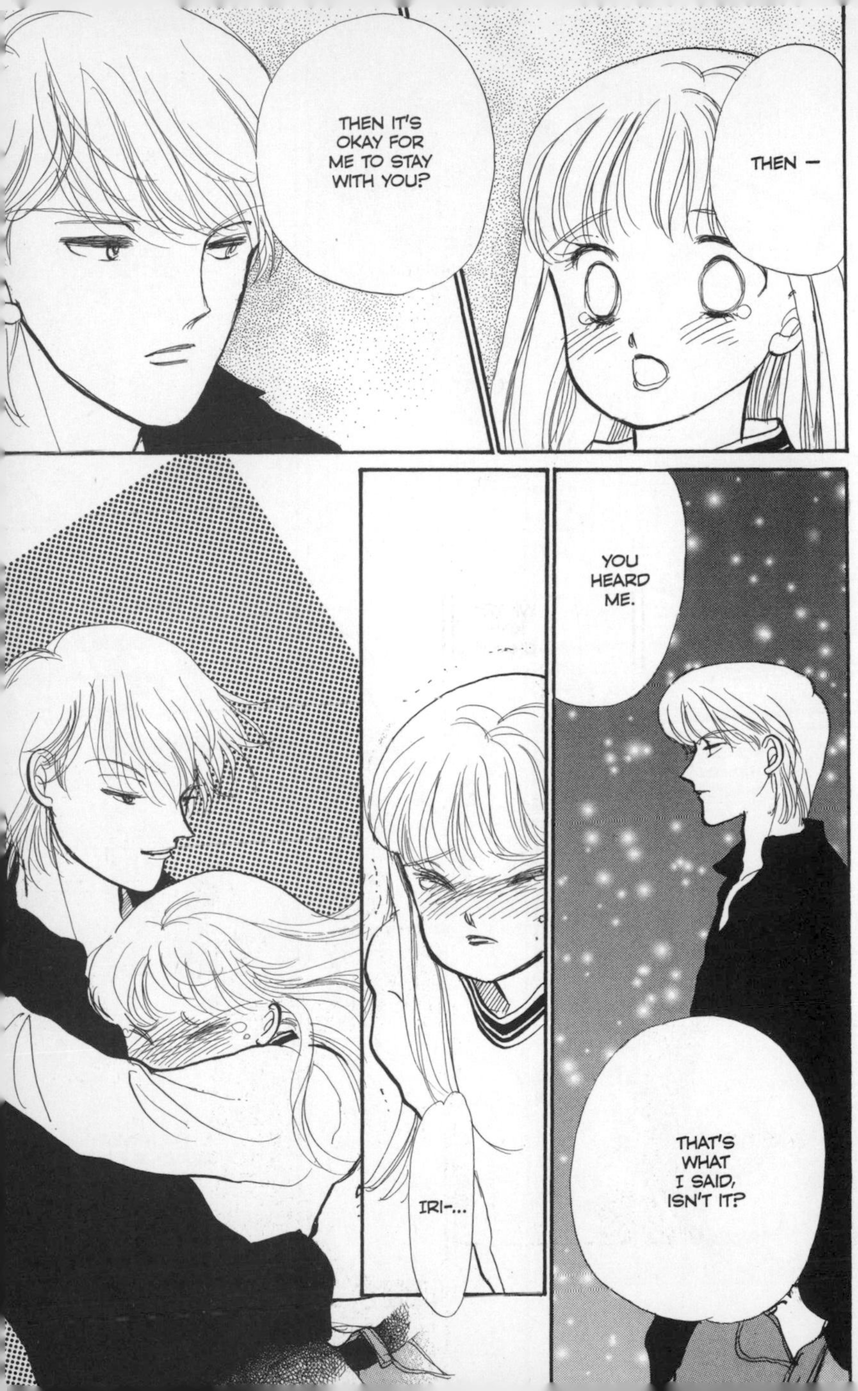
THEN —
THEN IT'S OKAY FOR ME TO STAY WITH YOU?
YOU HEARD ME.
THAT'S WHAT I SAID, ISN'T IT?
IRI-...

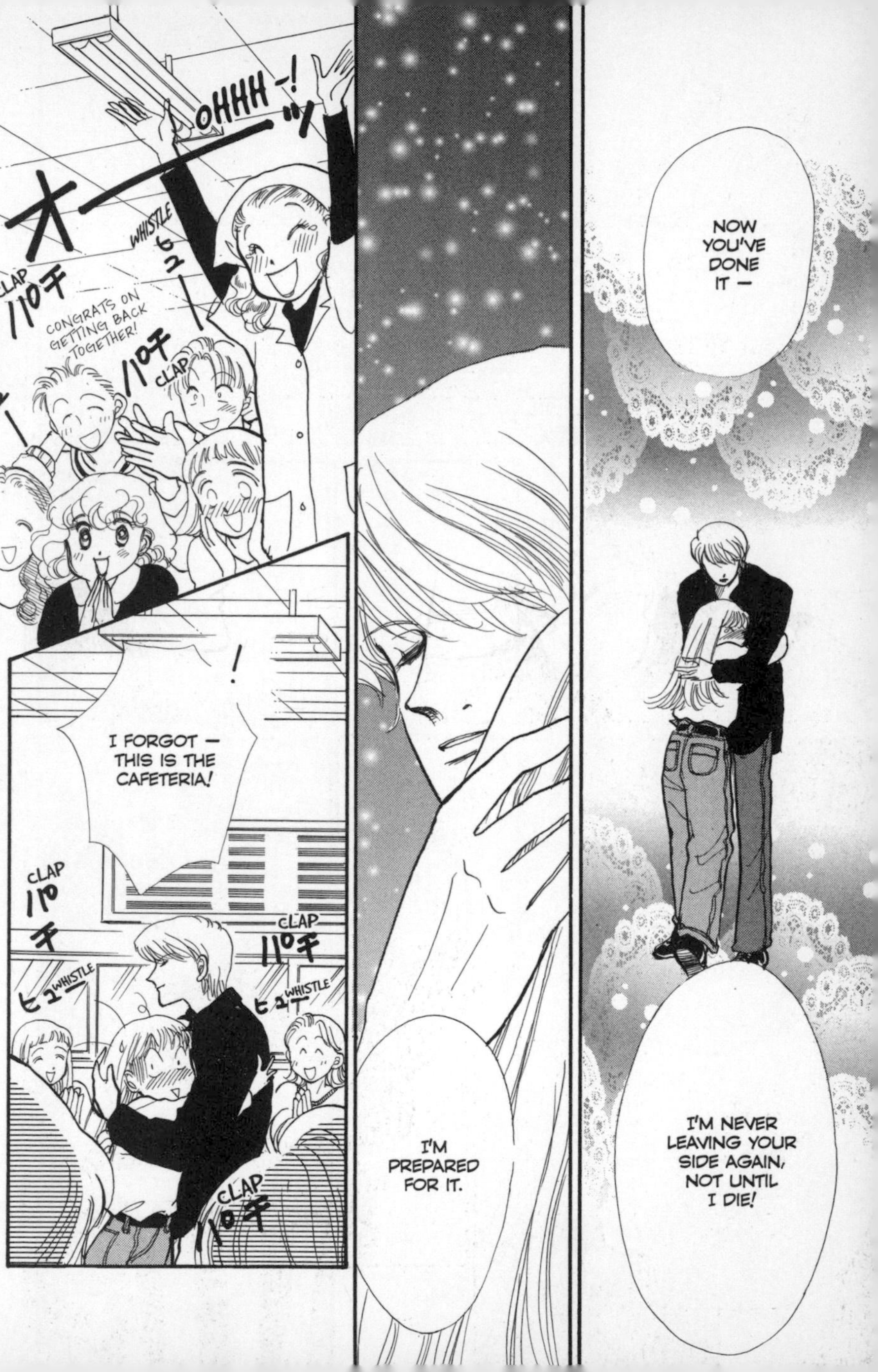
NOW YOU'VE DONE IT —
I'M NEVER LEAVING YOUR SIDE AGAIN, NOT UNTIL I DIE!
I'M PREPARED FOR IT.
OHHH —!
オー
WHISTLE
ヒュー
CLAP
パチ
CONGRATS ON GETTING BACK TOGETHER!
CLAP
パチ
WHISTLE
ヒュー
!
I FORGOT — THIS IS THE CAFETERIA!
CLAP
パチ
WHISTLE
ヒュー
CLAP
パチ
WHISTLE
ヒュー
CLAP
パチ

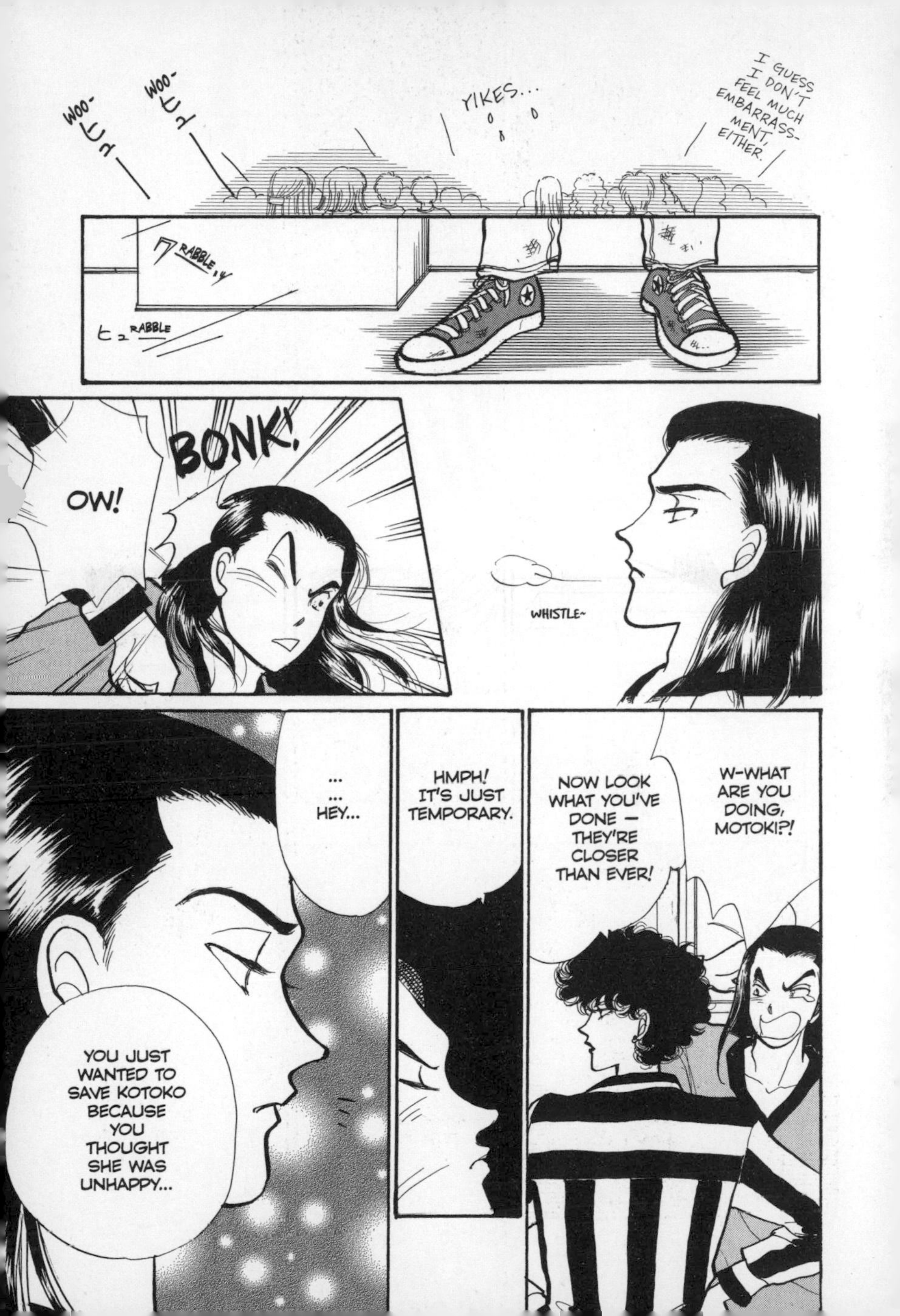

I GUESS I DON'T FEEL MUCH EMBARRASS-MENT, EITHER.
YIKES...
WOO-
WOO-
RABBLE
RABBLE
WHISTLE~
BONK!
OW!
W-WHAT ARE YOU DOING, MOTOKI?!
NOW LOOK WHAT YOU'VE DONE — THEY'RE CLOSER THAN EVER!
HMPH! IT'S JUST TEMPORARY.
... ... HEY...
YOU JUST WANTED TO SAVE KOTOKO BECAUSE YOU THOUGHT SHE WAS UNHAPPY...

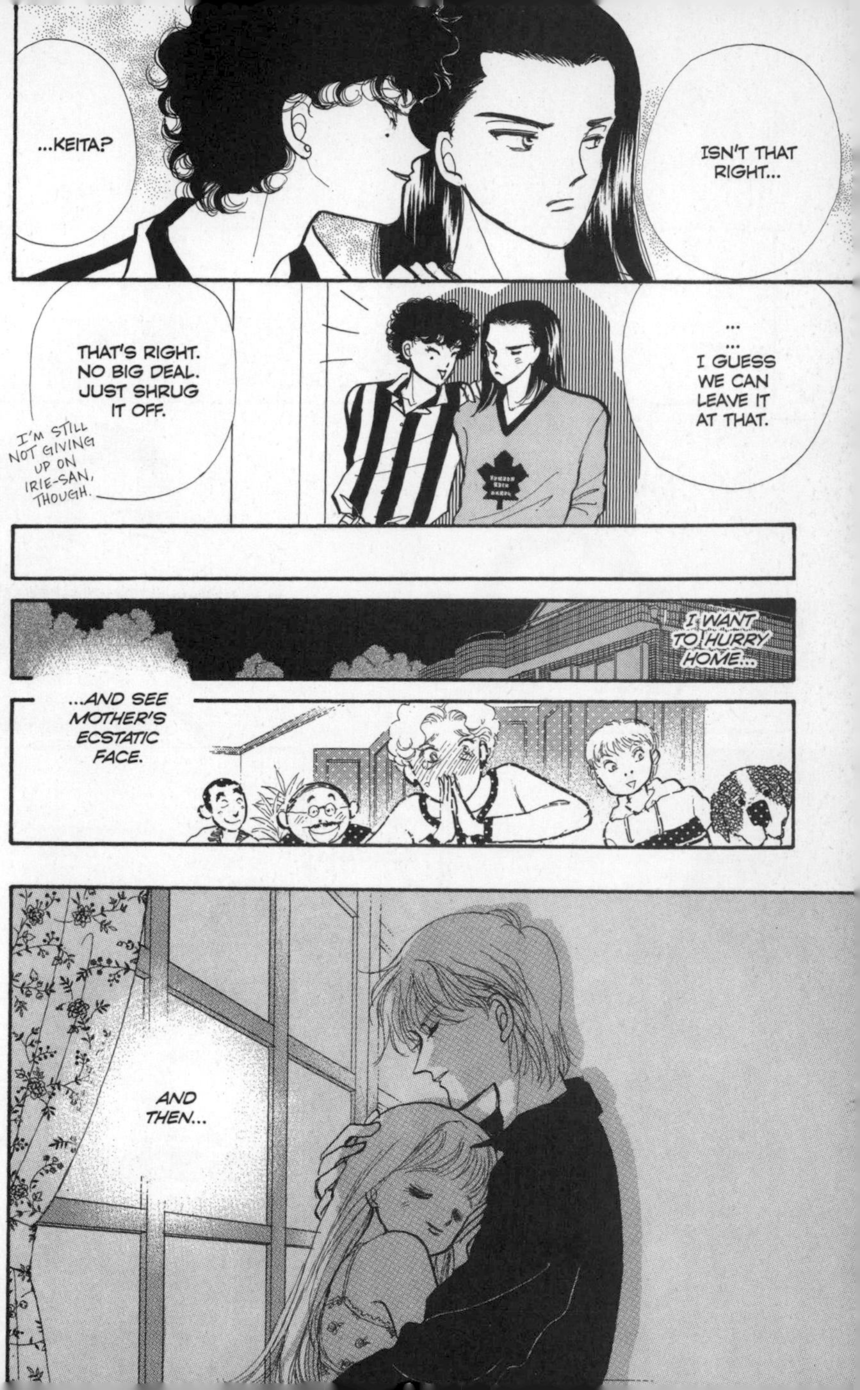
ISN'T THAT RIGHT...
...KEITA?
...
...
I GUESS WE CAN LEAVE IT AT THAT.
THAT'S RIGHT. NO BIG DEAL. JUST SHRUG IT OFF.
I'M STILL NOT GIVING UP ON IRIE-SAN, THOUGH.
I WANT TO HURRY HOME...
...AND SEE MOTHER'S ECSTATIC FACE.
AND THEN...

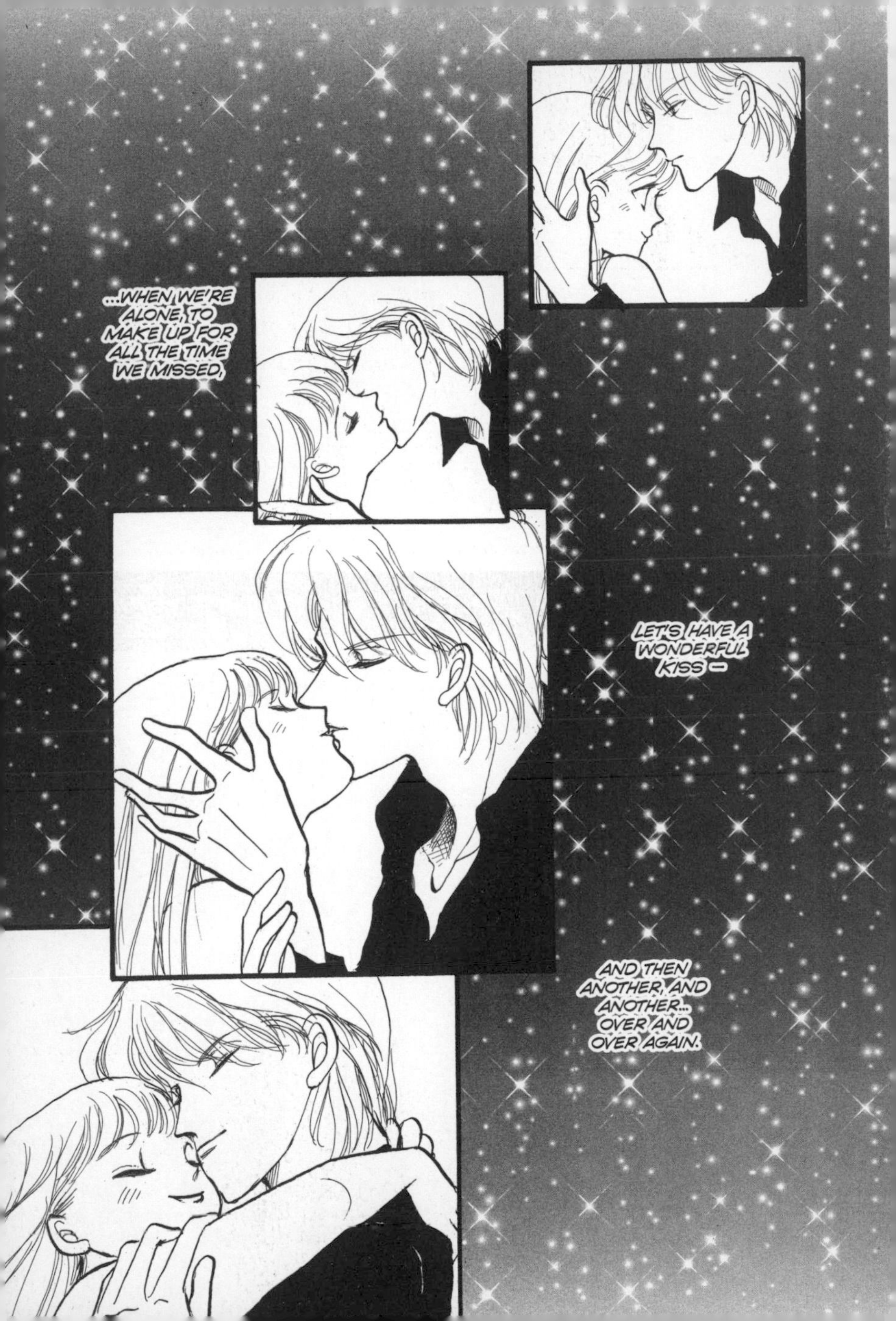
...WHEN WE'RE ALONE, TO MAKE UP FOR ALL THE TIME WE MISSED,
LET'S HAVE A WONDERFUL KISS —
AND THEN ANOTHER, AND ANOTHER... OVER AND OVER AGAIN.

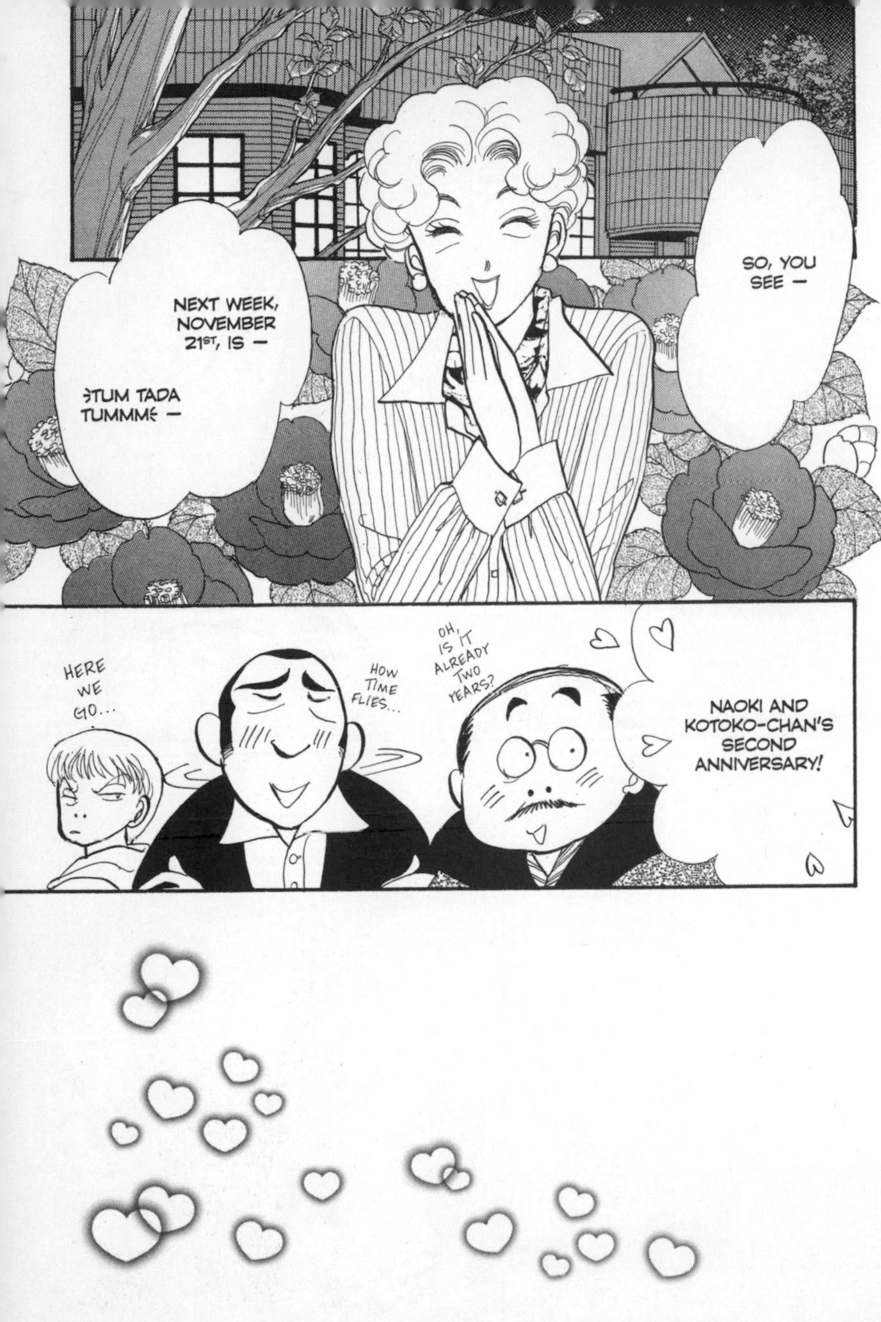
SO, YOU SEE —
NEXT WEEK, NOVEMBER 21st, IS —
≈TUM TADA TUMMM≈ —
NAOKI AND KOTOKO-CHAN'S SECOND ANNIVERSARY!
OH, IS IT ALREADY TWO YEARS?
HOW TIME FLIES...
HERE WE GO...

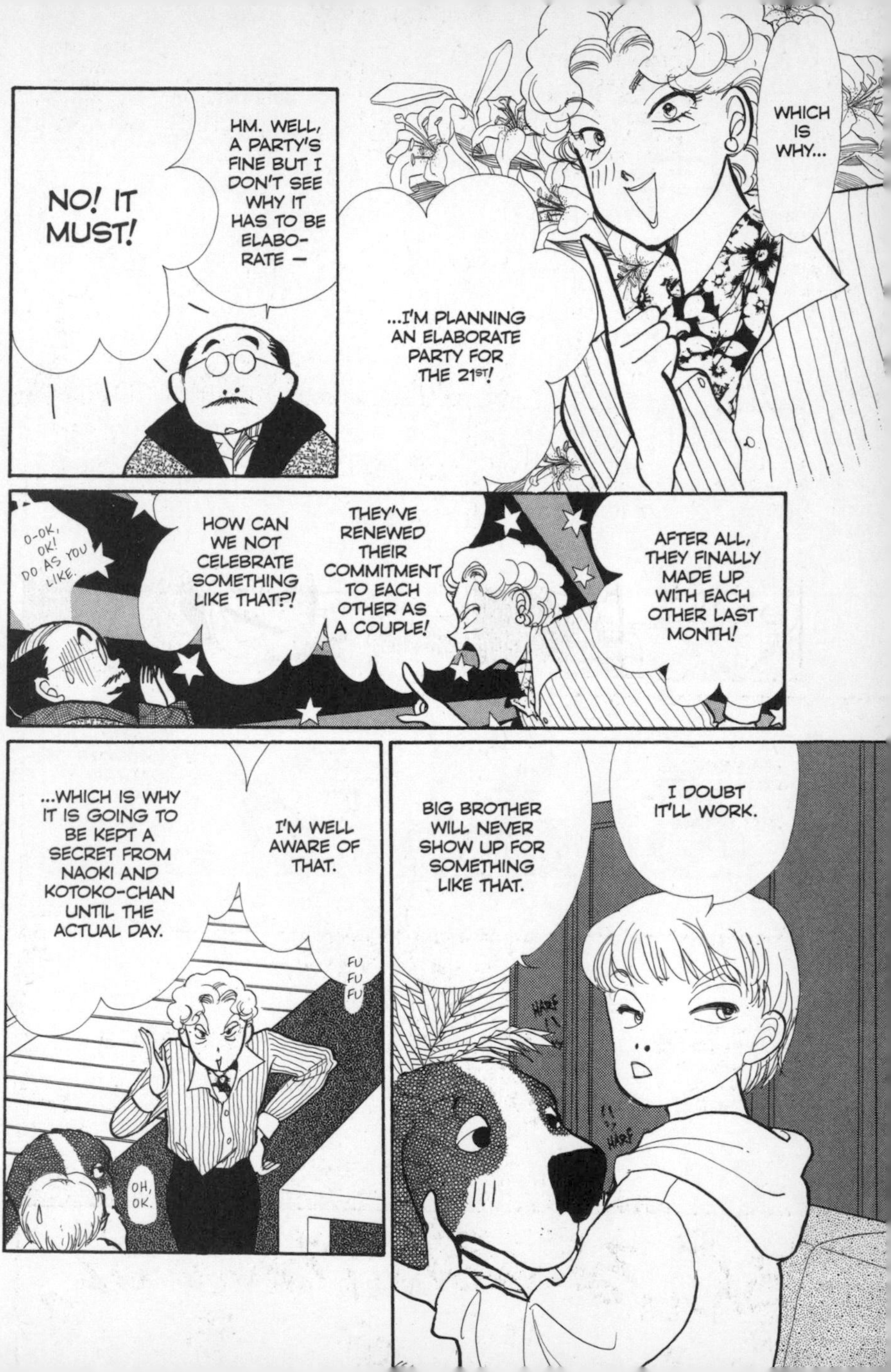

WHICH IS WHY...
...I'M PLANNING AN ELABORATE PARTY FOR THE 21ST!
HM. WELL, A PARTY'S FINE BUT I DON'T SEE WHY IT HAS TO BE ELABORATE —
NO! IT MUST!
AFTER ALL, THEY FINALLY MADE UP WITH EACH OTHER LAST MONTH!
THEY'VE RENEWED THEIR COMMITMENT TO EACH OTHER AS A COUPLE!
HOW CAN WE NOT CELEBRATE SOMETHING LIKE THAT?!
O-OK, OK! DO AS YOU LIKE.
I DOUBT IT'LL WORK.
BIG BROTHER WILL NEVER SHOW UP FOR SOMETHING LIKE THAT.
HARF
HARF
I'M WELL AWARE OF THAT.
...WHICH IS WHY IT IS GOING TO BE KEPT A SECRET FROM NAOKI AND KOTOKO-CHAN UNTIL THE ACTUAL DAY.
FU FU FU
OH, OK.

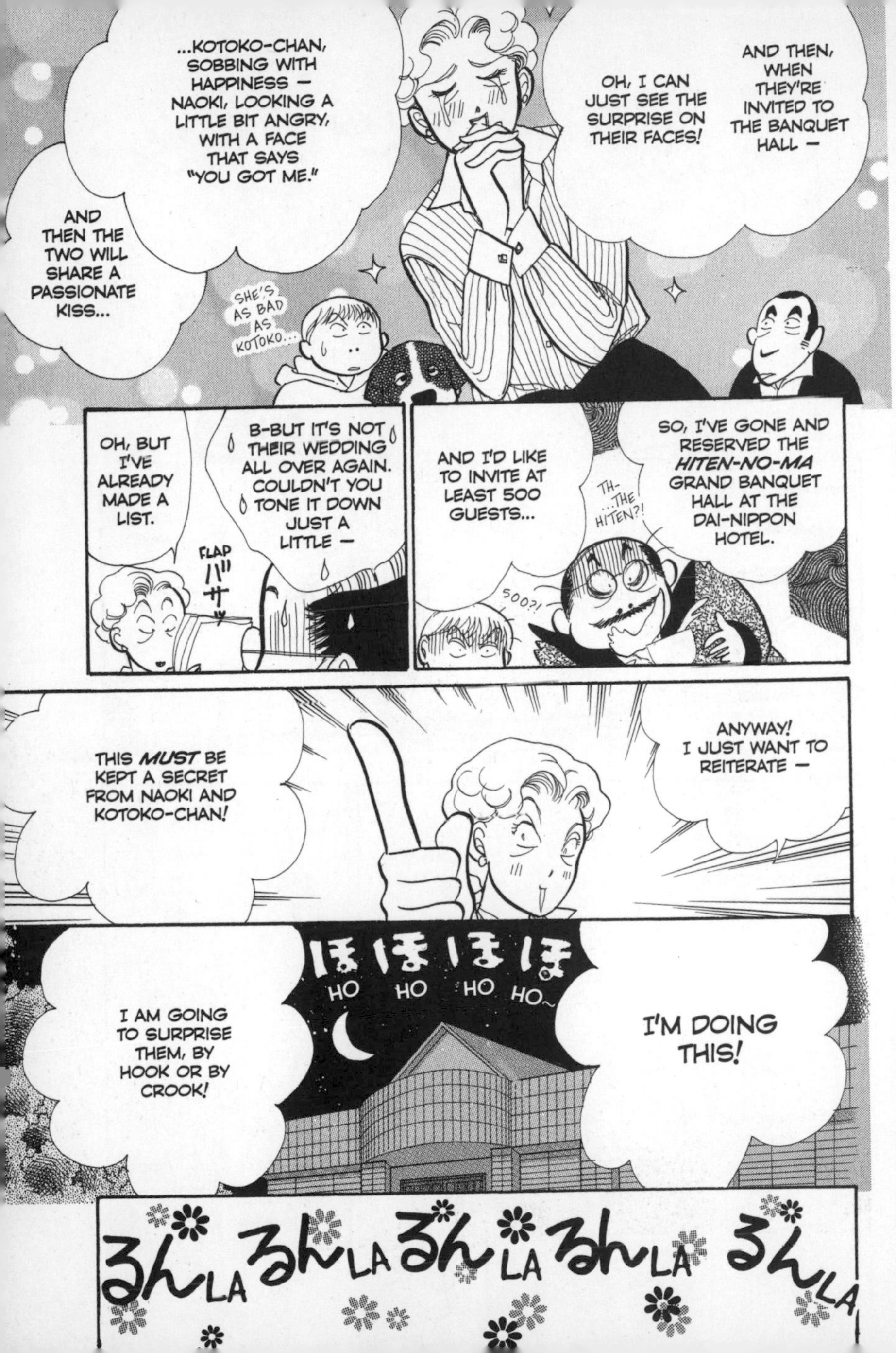
AND THEN, WHEN THEY'RE INVITED TO THE BANQUET HALL —
OH, I CAN JUST SEE THE SURPRISE ON THEIR FACES!
...KOTOKO-CHAN, SOBBING WITH HAPPINESS — NAOKI, LOOKING A LITTLE BIT ANGRY, WITH A FACE THAT SAYS "YOU GOT ME."
AND THEN THE TWO WILL SHARE A PASSIONATE KISS...
SHE'S AS BAD AS KOTOKO...
SO, I'VE GONE AND RESERVED THE *HITEN-NO-MA* GRAND BANQUET HALL AT THE DAI-NIPPON HOTEL.
TH- ...THE HITEN?!
AND I'D LIKE TO INVITE AT LEAST 500 GUESTS...
500?!
B-BUT IT'S NOT THEIR WEDDING ALL OVER AGAIN. COULDN'T YOU TONE IT DOWN JUST A LITTLE —
OH, BUT I'VE ALREADY MADE A LIST.
FLAP バサッ
ANYWAY! I JUST WANT TO REITERATE —
THIS *MUST* BE KEPT A SECRET FROM NAOKI AND KOTOKO-CHAN!
I'M DOING THIS!
ほほほほ HO HO HO HO~
I AM GOING TO SURPRISE THEM, BY HOOK OR BY CROOK!
るん LA るん LA るん LA るん LA るん LA

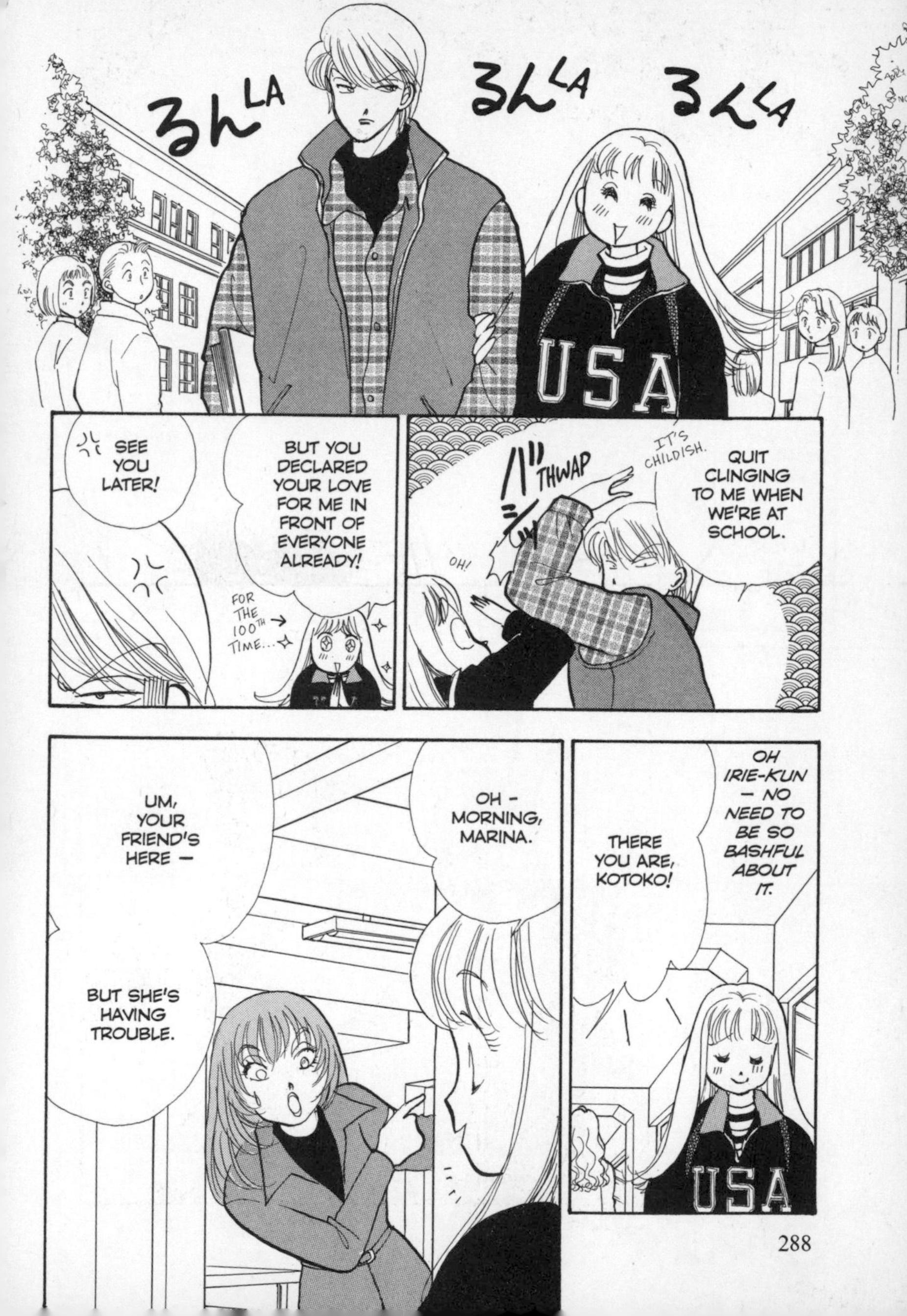
るんLA
るんLA
るんLA
QUIT CLINGING TO ME WHEN WE'RE AT SCHOOL.
IT'S CHILDISH.
バ THWAP
OH!
BUT YOU DECLARED YOUR LOVE FOR ME IN FRONT OF EVERYONE ALREADY!
FOR THE 100TH → TIME...
SEE YOU LATER!
OH IRIE-KUN — NO NEED TO BE SO BASHFUL ABOUT IT.
THERE YOU ARE, KOTOKO!
OH — MORNING, MARINA.
UM, YOUR FRIEND'S HERE —
BUT SHE'S HAVING TROUBLE.

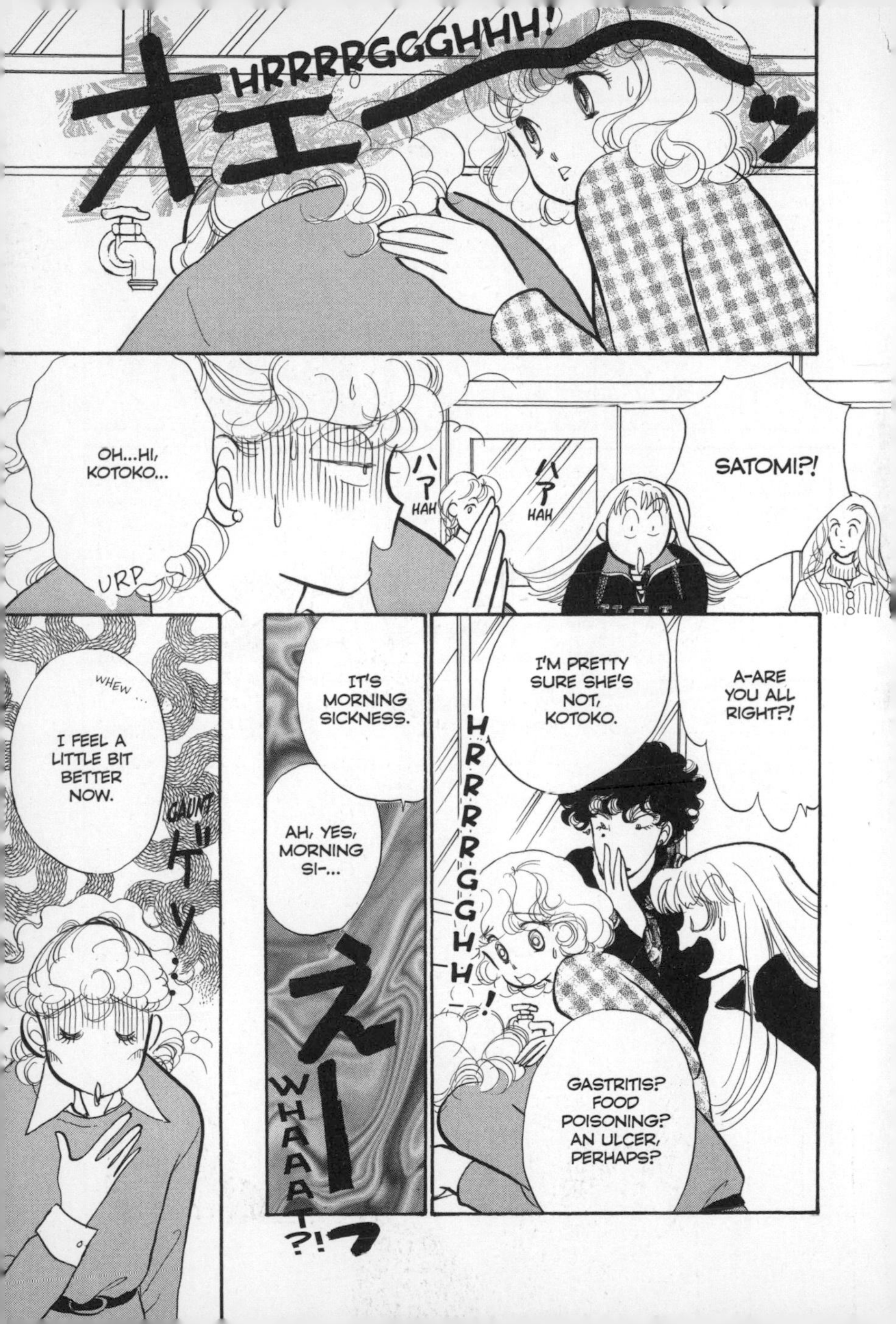
オエーッ
HRRRRGGHHH!
SATOMI?!
ハァ HAH
ハァ HAH
OH...HI, KOTOKO...
URP
A-ARE YOU ALL RIGHT?!
I'M PRETTY SURE SHE'S NOT, KOTOKO.
HRRRRRGGHH-!
GASTRITIS? FOOD POISONING? AN ULCER, PERHAPS?
IT'S MORNING SICKNESS.
AH, YES, MORNING SI-...
えーっ
WHAAAT?!
WHEW...
I FEEL A LITTLE BIT BETTER NOW.
ゲッソ
GAUNT

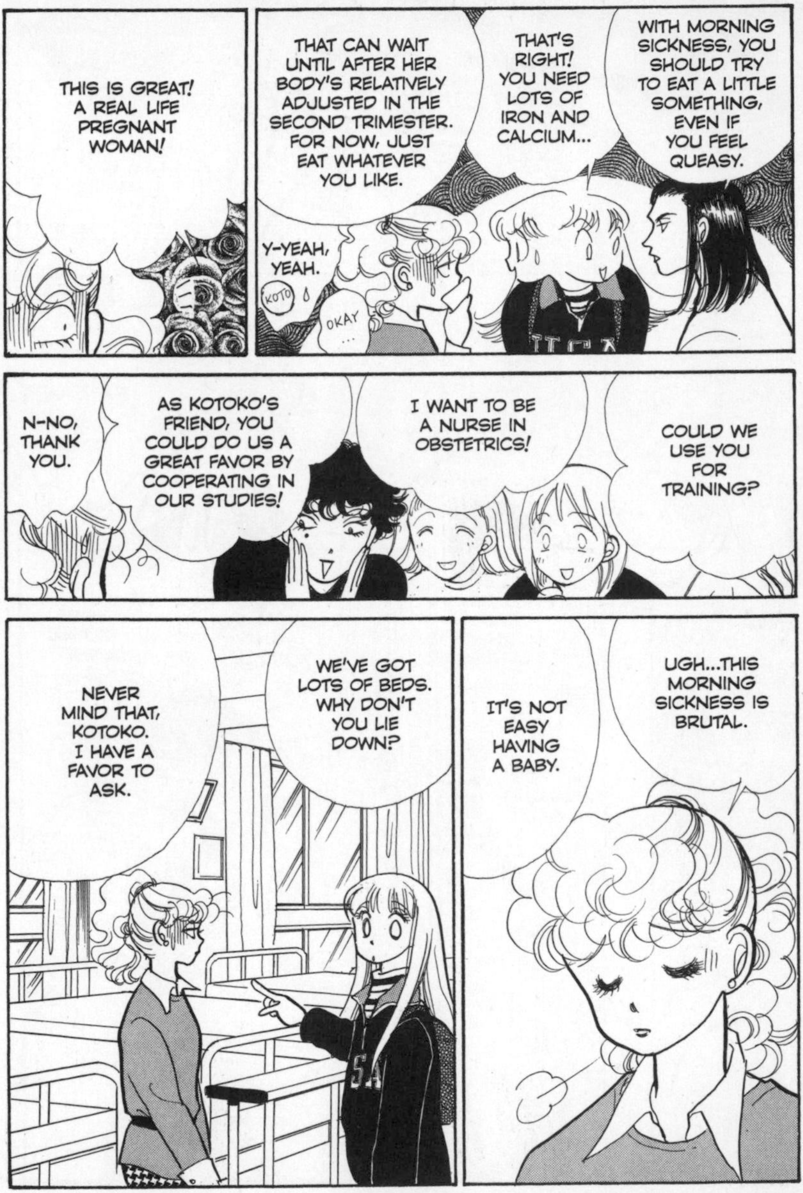
WITH MORNING SICKNESS, YOU SHOULD TRY TO EAT A LITTLE SOMETHING, EVEN IF YOU FEEL QUEASY.
THAT'S RIGHT! YOU NEED LOTS OF IRON AND CALCIUM...
THAT CAN WAIT UNTIL AFTER HER BODY'S RELATIVELY ADJUSTED IN THE SECOND TRIMESTER. FOR NOW, JUST EAT WHATEVER YOU LIKE.
Y-YEAH, YEAH.
KOTO
OKAY ...
THIS IS GREAT! A REAL LIFE PREGNANT WOMAN!
COULD WE USE YOU FOR TRAINING?
I WANT TO BE A NURSE IN OBSTETRICS!
AS KOTOKO'S FRIEND, YOU COULD DO US A GREAT FAVOR BY COOPERATING IN OUR STUDIES!
N-NO, THANK YOU.
UGH...THIS MORNING SICKNESS IS BRUTAL.
IT'S NOT EASY HAVING A BABY.
WE'VE GOT LOTS OF BEDS. WHY DON'T YOU LIE DOWN?
NEVER MIND THAT, KOTOKO. I HAVE A FAVOR TO ASK.

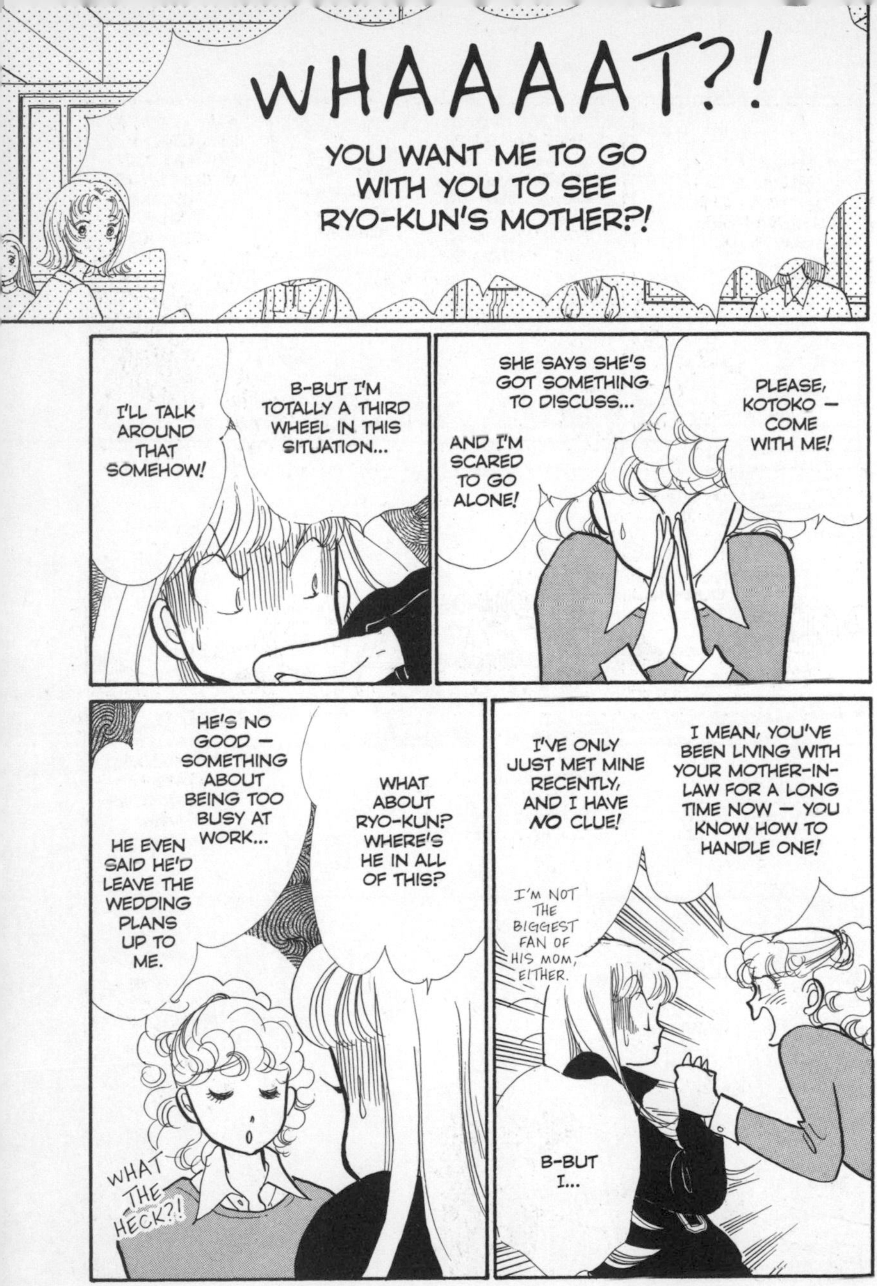
WHAAAAT?!
YOU WANT ME TO GO WITH YOU TO SEE RYO-KUN'S MOTHER?!
PLEASE, KOTOKO — COME WITH ME!
SHE SAYS SHE'S GOT SOMETHING TO DISCUSS...
AND I'M SCARED TO GO ALONE!
B-BUT I'M TOTALLY A THIRD WHEEL IN THIS SITUATION...
I'LL TALK AROUND THAT SOMEHOW!
I MEAN, YOU'VE BEEN LIVING WITH YOUR MOTHER-IN-LAW FOR A LONG TIME NOW — YOU KNOW HOW TO HANDLE ONE!
I'VE ONLY JUST MET MINE RECENTLY, AND I HAVE *NO* CLUE!
I'M NOT THE BIGGEST FAN OF HIS MOM, EITHER.
B-BUT I...
WHAT ABOUT RYO-KUN? WHERE'S HE IN ALL OF THIS?
HE'S NO GOOD — SOMETHING ABOUT BEING TOO BUSY AT WORK...
HE EVEN SAID HE'D LEAVE THE WEDDING PLANS UP TO ME.
WHAT THE HECK?!

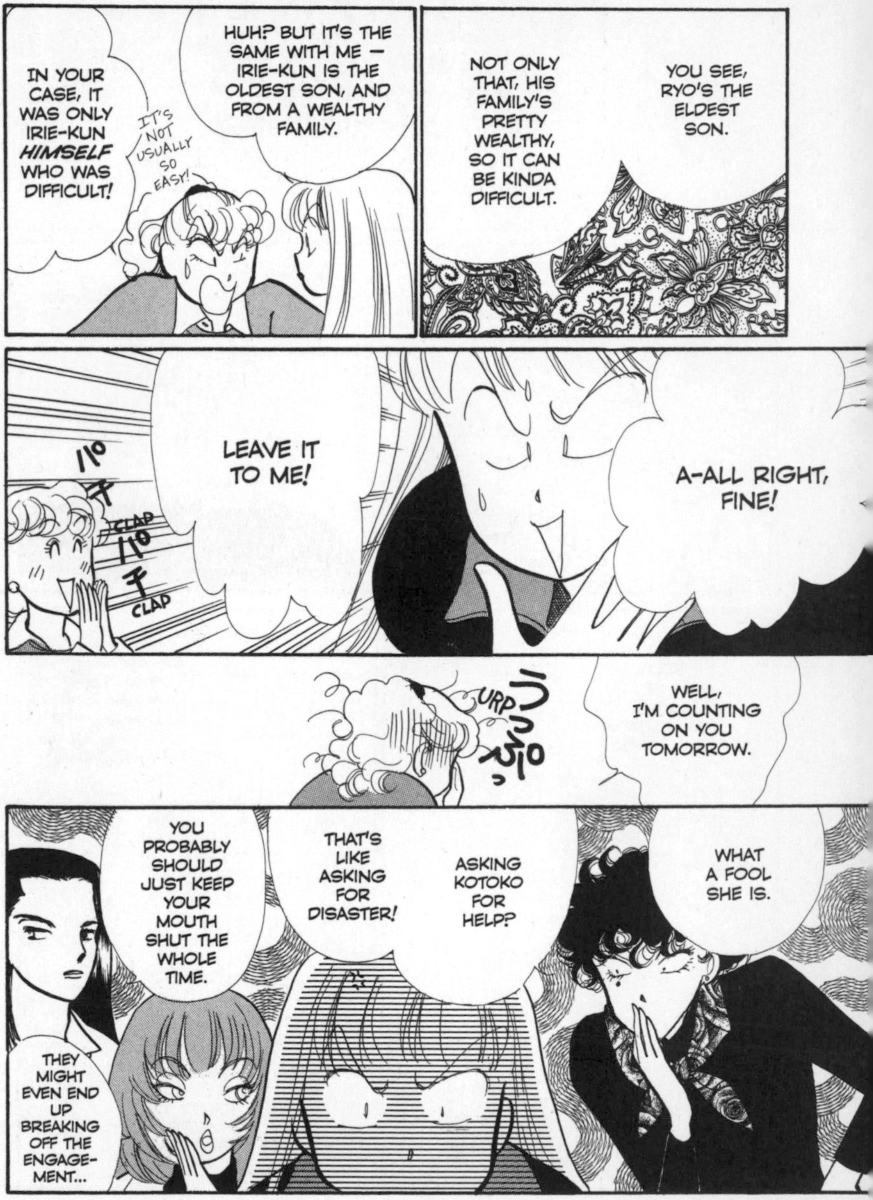
YOU SEE, RYO'S THE ELDEST SON.
NOT ONLY THAT, HIS FAMILY'S PRETTY WEALTHY, SO IT CAN BE KINDA DIFFICULT.
HUH? BUT IT'S THE SAME WITH ME — IRIE-KUN IS THE OLDEST SON, AND FROM A WEALTHY FAMILY.
IT'S NOT USUALLY SO EASY!
IN YOUR CASE, IT WAS ONLY IRIE-KUN *HIMSELF* WHO WAS DIFFICULT!
A-ALL RIGHT, FINE!
LEAVE IT TO ME!
CLAP
CLAP
WELL, I'M COUNTING ON YOU TOMORROW.
URP
WHAT A FOOL SHE IS.
ASKING KOTOKO FOR HELP?
THAT'S LIKE ASKING FOR DISASTER!
YOU PROBABLY SHOULD JUST KEEP YOUR MOUTH SHUT THE WHOLE TIME.
THEY MIGHT EVEN END UP BREAKING OFF THE ENGAGEMENT...

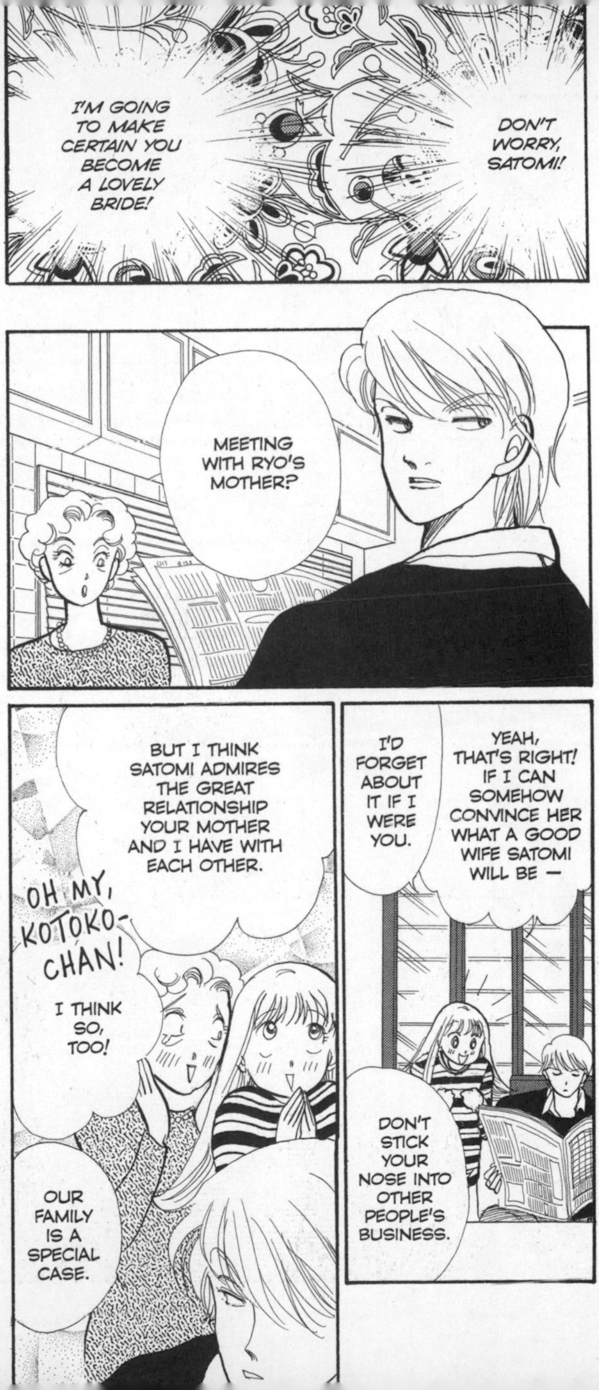
DON'T WORRY, SATOMI!
I'M GOING TO MAKE CERTAIN YOU BECOME A LOVELY BRIDE!
MEETING WITH RYO'S MOTHER?
YEAH, THAT'S RIGHT! IF I CAN SOMEHOW CONVINCE HER WHAT A GOOD WIFE SATOMI WILL BE —
I'D FORGET ABOUT IT IF I WERE YOU.
DON'T STICK YOUR NOSE INTO OTHER PEOPLE'S BUSINESS.
BUT I THINK SATOMI ADMIRES THE GREAT RELATIONSHIP YOUR MOTHER AND I HAVE WITH EACH OTHER.
OH MY, KOTOKO-CHAN!
I THINK SO, TOO!
OUR FAMILY IS A SPECIAL CASE.

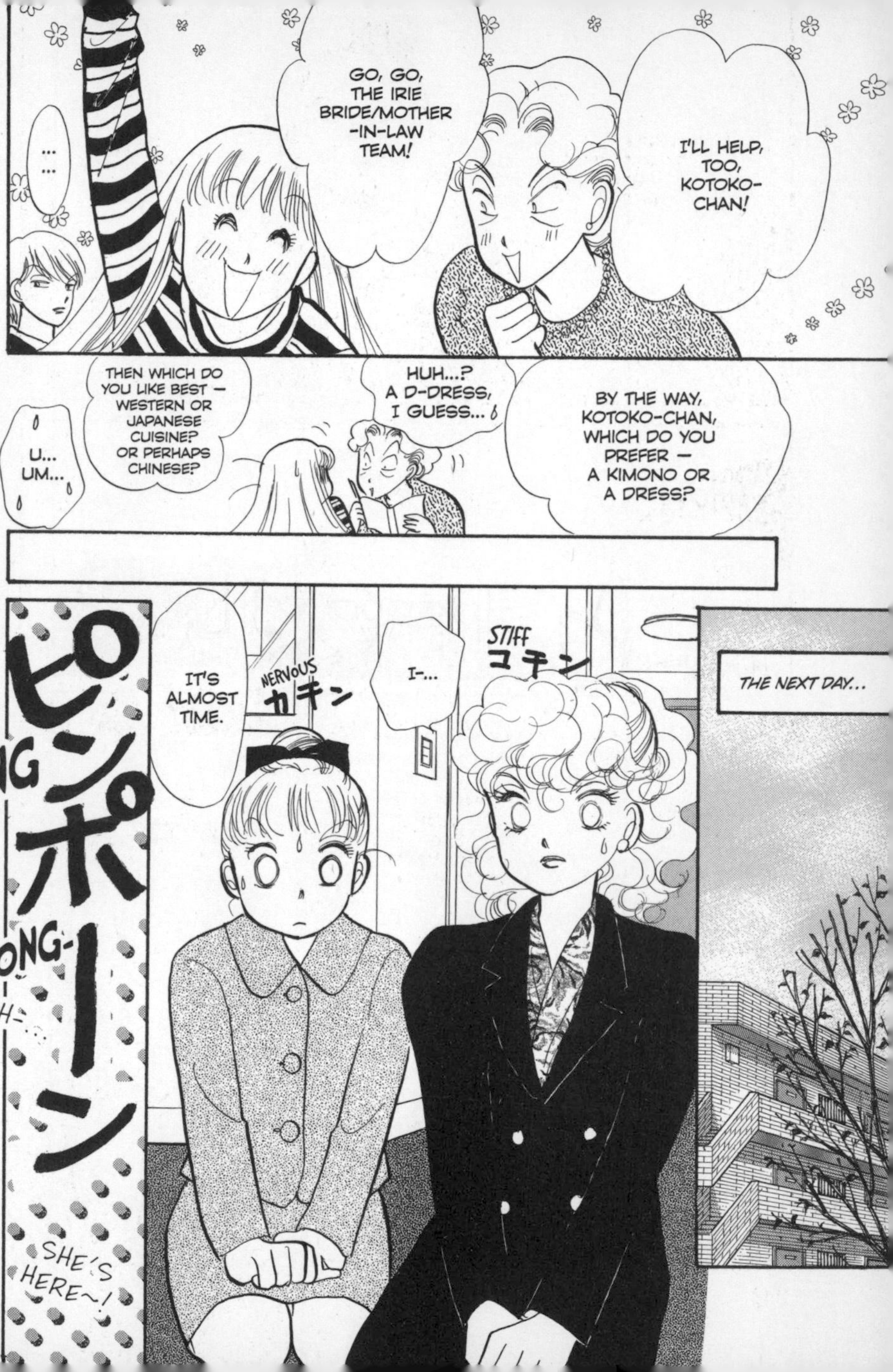
I'LL HELP, TOO, KOTOKO-CHAN!
GO, GO, THE IRIE BRIDE/MOTHER-IN-LAW TEAM!
… …
BY THE WAY, KOTOKO-CHAN, WHICH DO YOU PREFER — A KIMONO OR A DRESS?
HUH…? A D-DRESS, I GUESS…
THEN WHICH DO YOU LIKE BEST — WESTERN OR JAPANESE CUISINE? OR PERHAPS CHINESE?
U… UM…
THE NEXT DAY…
STIFF コチン
I-…
NERVOUS カチン
IT'S ALMOST TIME.
ピンポーン
DING DONG-
SH-
SHE'S HERE~!

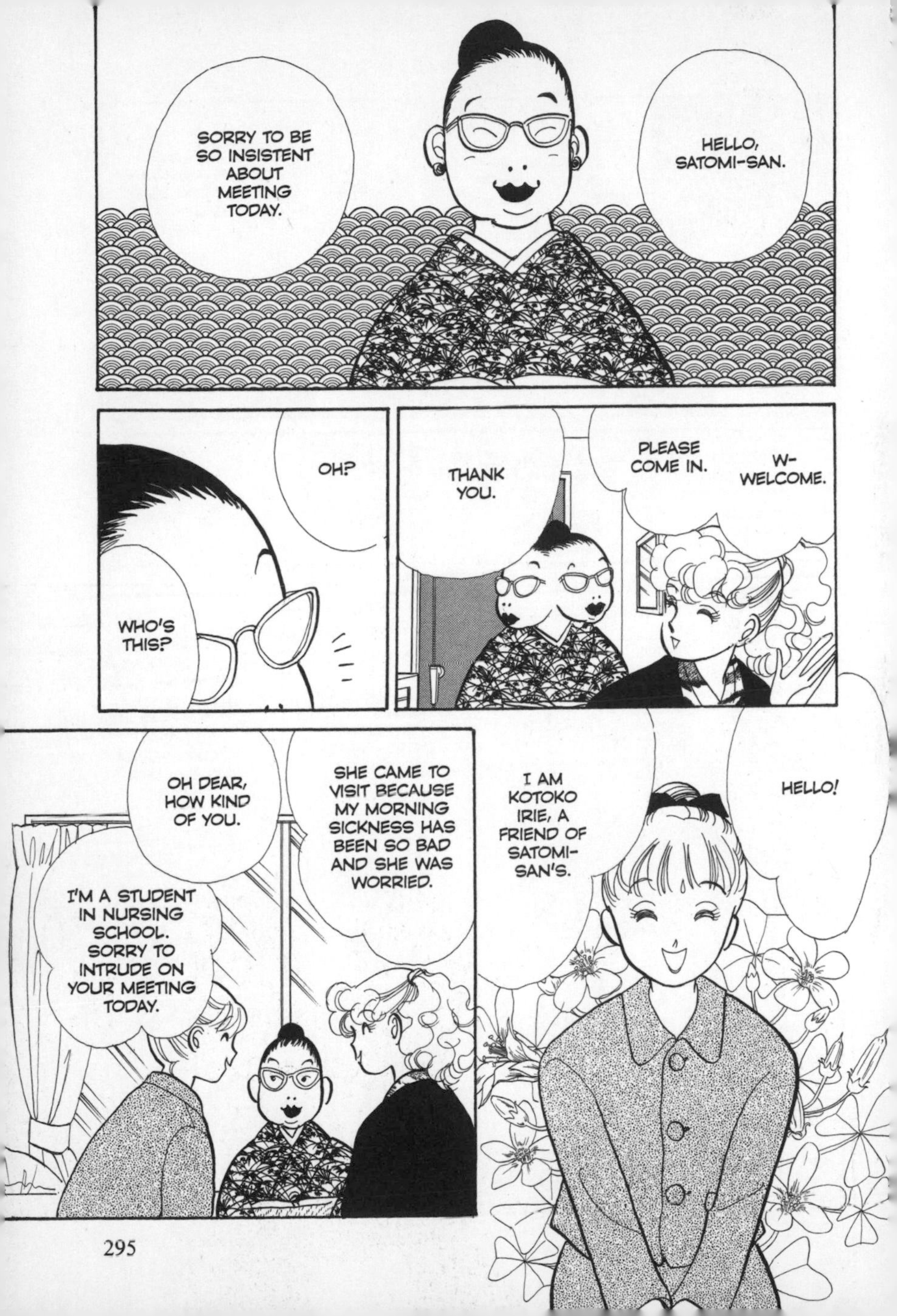
HELLO, SATOMI-SAN.
SORRY TO BE SO INSISTENT ABOUT MEETING TODAY.
W- WELCOME.
PLEASE COME IN.
THANK YOU.
OH?
WHO'S THIS?
HELLO!
I AM KOTOKO IRIE, A FRIEND OF SATOMI-SAN'S.
SHE CAME TO VISIT BECAUSE MY MORNING SICKNESS HAS BEEN SO BAD AND SHE WAS WORRIED.
OH DEAR, HOW KIND OF YOU.
I'M A STUDENT IN NURSING SCHOOL. SORRY TO INTRUDE ON YOUR MEETING TODAY.

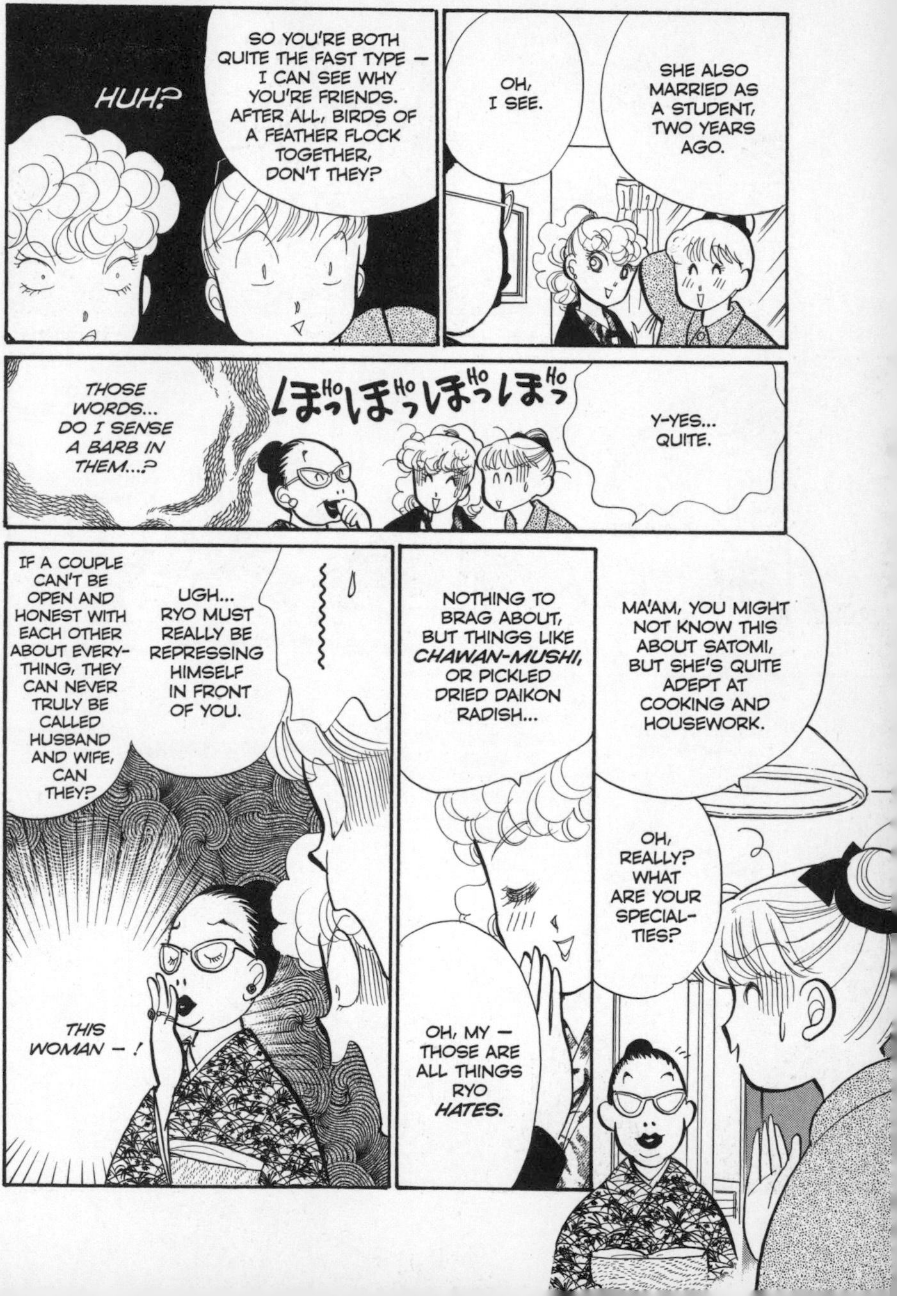
SHE ALSO MARRIED AS A STUDENT, TWO YEARS AGO.
OH, I SEE.
SO YOU'RE BOTH QUITE THE FAST TYPE — I CAN SEE WHY YOU'RE FRIENDS. AFTER ALL, BIRDS OF A FEATHER FLOCK TOGETHER, DON'T THEY?
HUH?
Y-YES... QUITE.
ほっほっほっほっ HO HO HO HO
THOSE WORDS... DO I SENSE A BARB IN THEM...?
MA'AM, YOU MIGHT NOT KNOW THIS ABOUT SATOMI, BUT SHE'S QUITE ADEPT AT COOKING AND HOUSEWORK.
OH, REALLY? WHAT ARE YOUR SPECIAL-TIES?
NOTHING TO BRAG ABOUT, BUT THINGS LIKE CHAWAN-MUSHI, OR PICKLED DRIED DAIKON RADISH...
OH, MY — THOSE ARE ALL THINGS RYO HATES.
UGH... RYO MUST REALLY BE REPRESSING HIMSELF IN FRONT OF YOU.
IF A COUPLE CAN'T BE OPEN AND HONEST WITH EACH OTHER ABOUT EVERY-THING, THEY CAN NEVER TRULY BE CALLED HUSBAND AND WIFE, CAN THEY?
THIS WOMAN —!

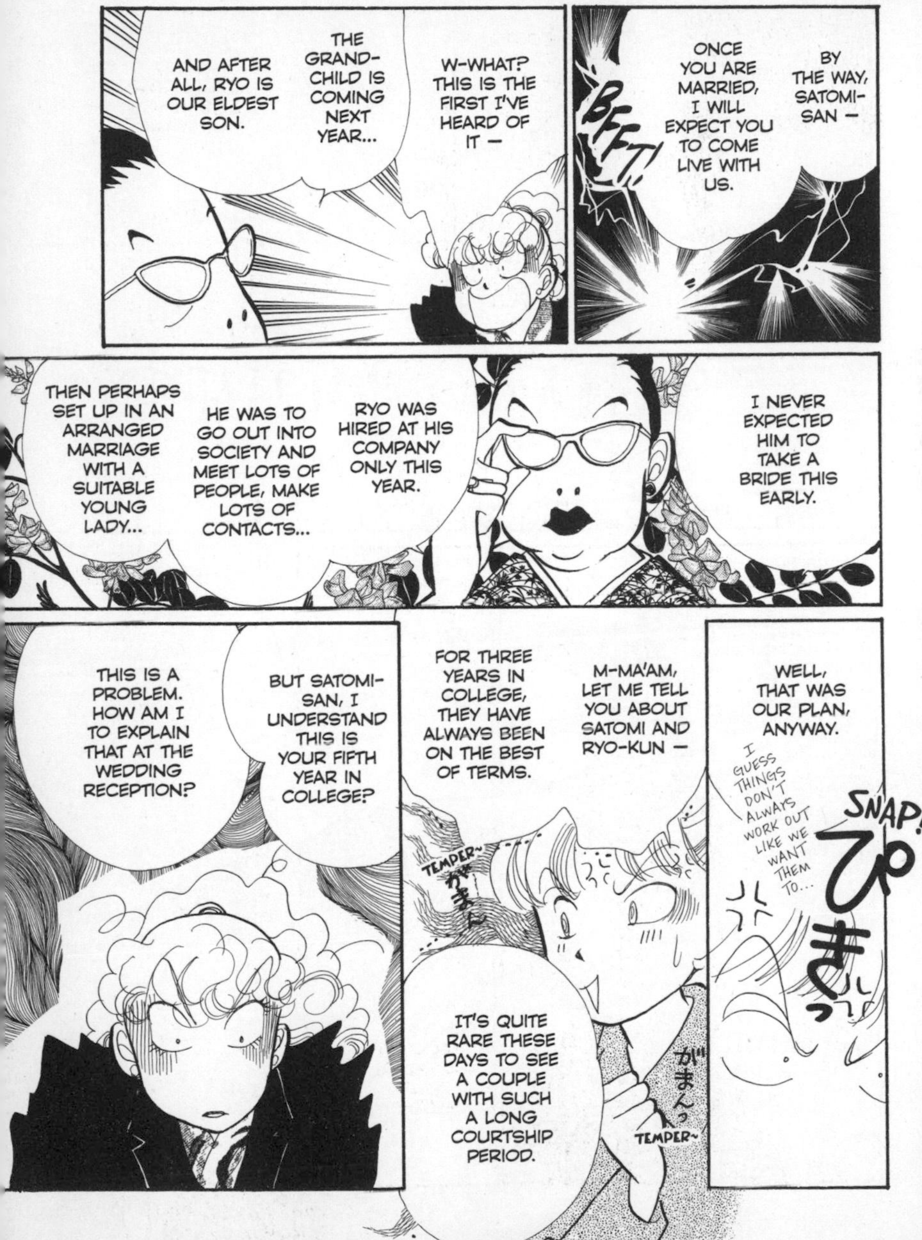
BY THE WAY, SATOMI-SAN —
ONCE YOU ARE MARRIED, I WILL EXPECT YOU TO COME LIVE WITH US.
BFFT!
W-WHAT? THIS IS THE FIRST I'VE HEARD OF IT —
THE GRAND-CHILD IS COMING NEXT YEAR...
AND AFTER ALL, RYO IS OUR ELDEST SON.
I NEVER EXPECTED HIM TO TAKE A BRIDE THIS EARLY.
RYO WAS HIRED AT HIS COMPANY ONLY THIS YEAR.
HE WAS TO GO OUT INTO SOCIETY AND MEET LOTS OF PEOPLE, MAKE LOTS OF CONTACTS...
THEN PERHAPS SET UP IN AN ARRANGED MARRIAGE WITH A SUITABLE YOUNG LADY...
WELL, THAT WAS OUR PLAN, ANYWAY.
I GUESS THINGS DON'T ALWAYS WORK OUT LIKE WE WANT THEM TO...
SNAP!
ぴきっ
M-MA'AM, LET ME TELL YOU ABOUT SATOMI AND RYO-KUN —
FOR THREE YEARS IN COLLEGE, THEY HAVE ALWAYS BEEN ON THE BEST OF TERMS.
TEMPER~
がまん
IT'S QUITE RARE THESE DAYS TO SEE A COUPLE WITH SUCH A LONG COURTSHIP PERIOD.
がまんっ
TEMPER~
BUT SATOMI-SAN, I UNDERSTAND THIS IS YOUR FIFTH YEAR IN COLLEGE?
THIS IS A PROBLEM. HOW AM I TO EXPLAIN THAT AT THE WEDDING RECEPTION?

EVEN WITHOUT THAT, THERE'S THE MATTER OF YOU CONCEIVING A CHILD OUT OF WEDLOCK.
... U- ...
GH...
REALLY, IT'S SO EMBARRASSING!
SHUT UUUPPP!
O-OH...!
OH DEAR, OH MY!
WHAT IS GOING ON?!

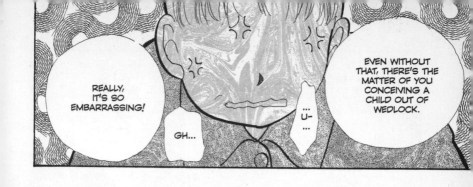

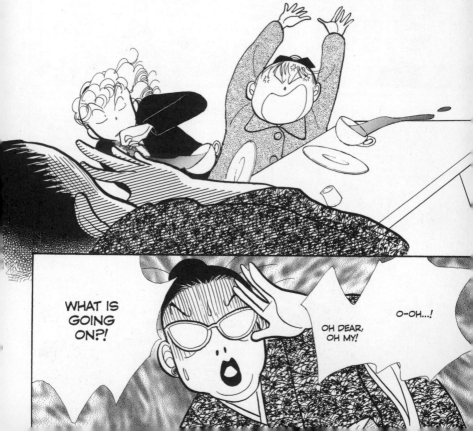

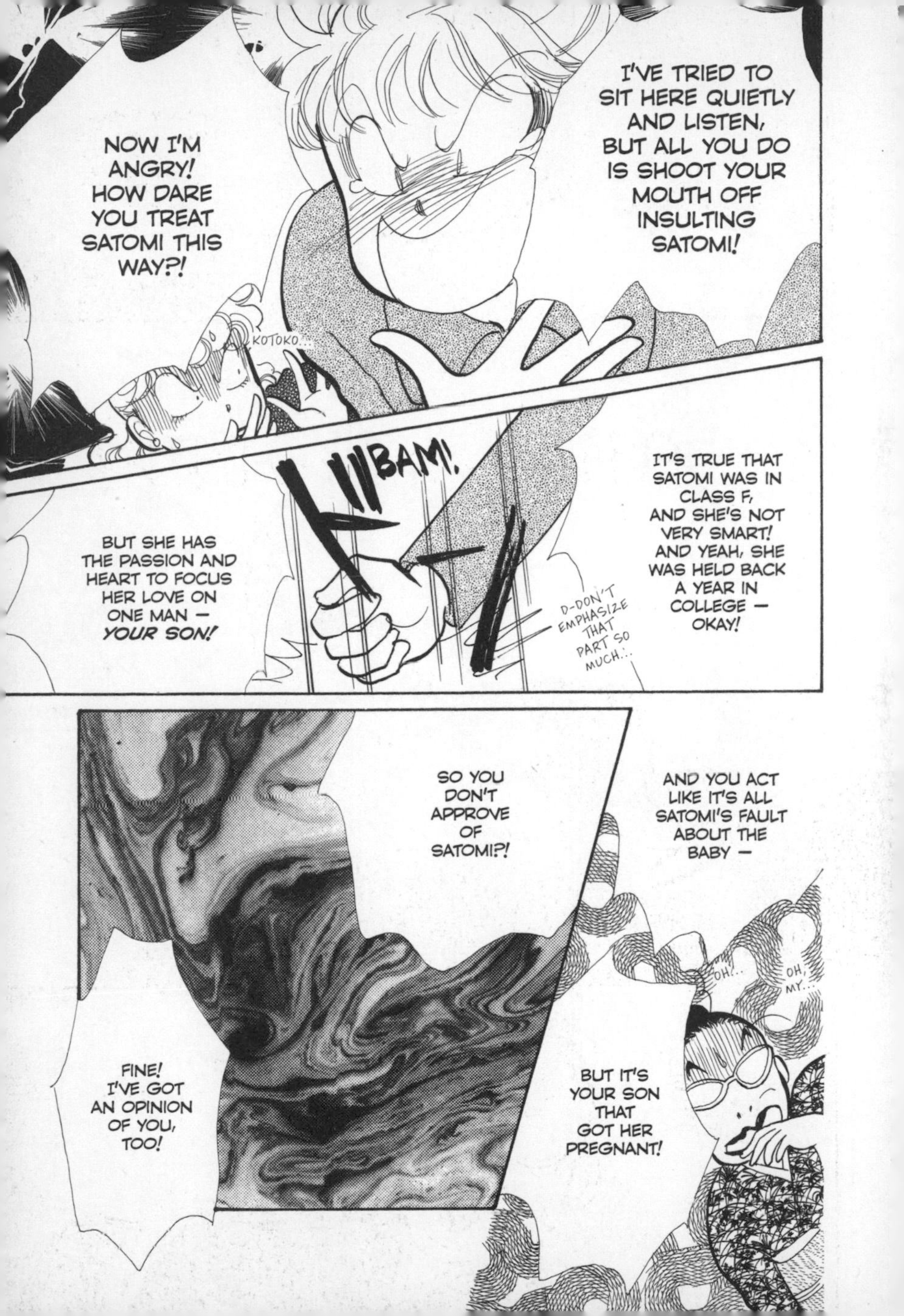
I'VE TRIED TO SIT HERE QUIETLY AND LISTEN, BUT ALL YOU DO IS SHOOT YOUR MOUTH OFF INSULTING SATOMI!
NOW I'M ANGRY! HOW DARE YOU TREAT SATOMI THIS WAY?!
KOTOKO...
IT'S TRUE THAT SATOMI WAS IN CLASS F, AND SHE'S NOT VERY SMART! AND YEAH, SHE WAS HELD BACK A YEAR IN COLLEGE — OKAY!
BAM!
D-DON'T EMPHASIZE THAT PART SO MUCH...
BUT SHE HAS THE PASSION AND HEART TO FOCUS HER LOVE ON ONE MAN — *YOUR SON!*
AND YOU ACT LIKE IT'S ALL SATOMI'S FAULT ABOUT THE BABY —
SO YOU DON'T APPROVE OF SATOMI?!
OH, MY...
OH...
BUT IT'S YOUR SON THAT GOT HER PREGNANT!
FINE! I'VE GOT AN OPINION OF YOU, TOO!

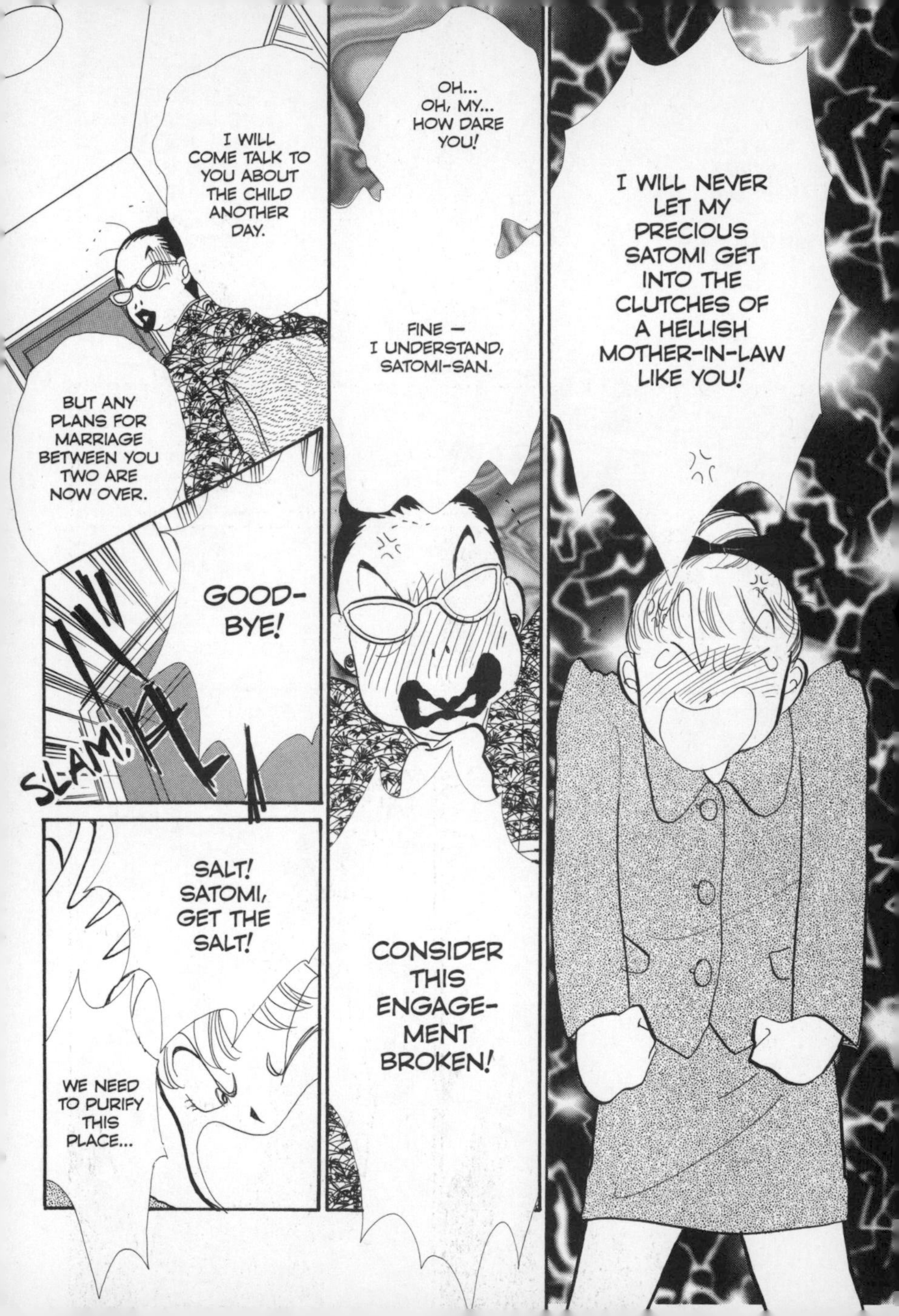
I WILL NEVER LET MY PRECIOUS SATOMI GET INTO THE CLUTCHES OF A HELLISH MOTHER-IN-LAW LIKE YOU!
OH... OH, MY... HOW DARE YOU!
FINE — I UNDERSTAND, SATOMI-SAN.
CONSIDER THIS ENGAGE-MENT BROKEN!
I WILL COME TALK TO YOU ABOUT THE CHILD ANOTHER DAY.
BUT ANY PLANS FOR MARRIAGE BETWEEN YOU TWO ARE NOW OVER.
GOOD-BYE!
SLAM!
SALT! SATOMI, GET THE SALT!
WE NEED TO PURIFY THIS PLACE...

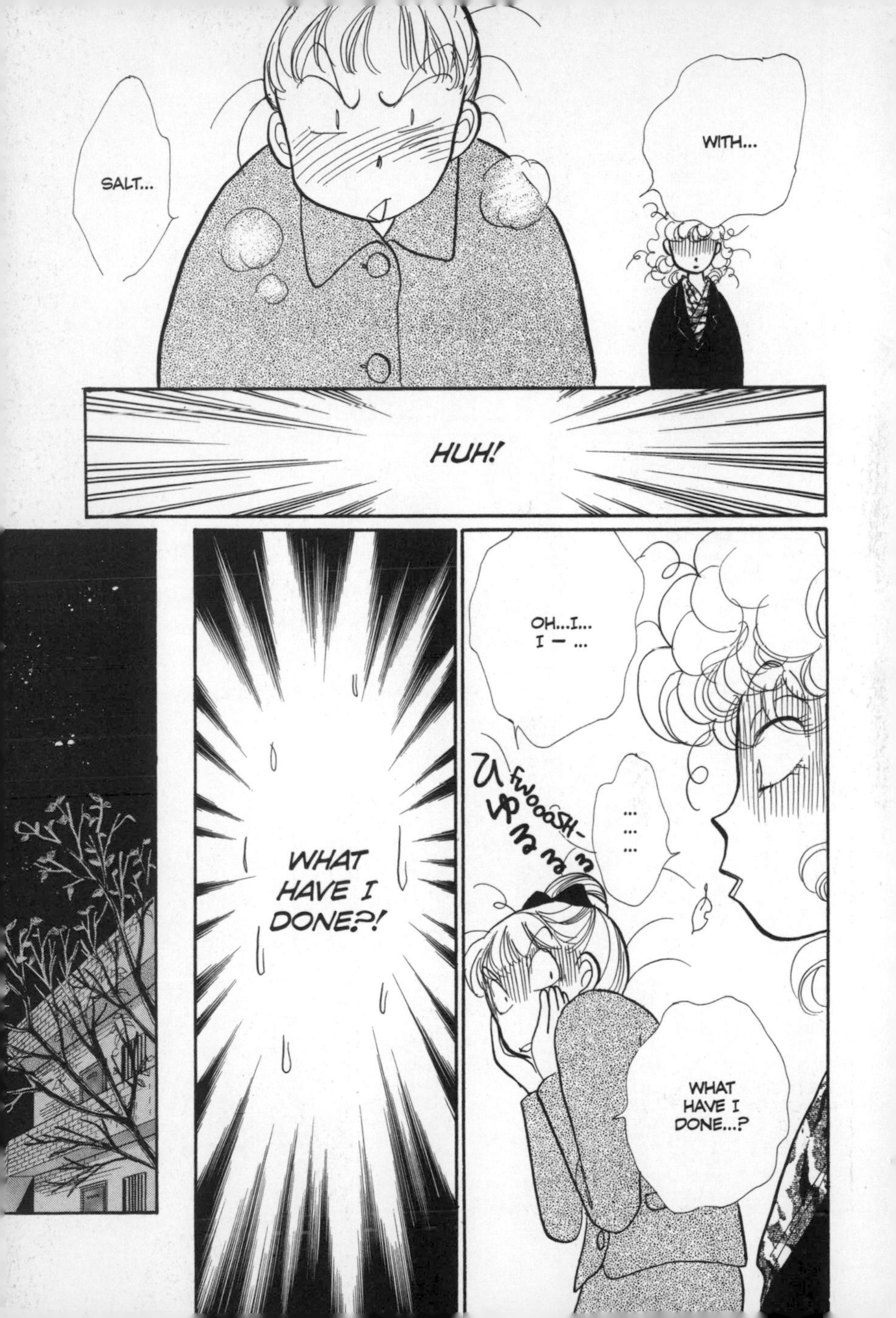
WITH...
SALT...
HUH!
OH...I...
I — ...
FWOOOSH-
...
...
...
WHAT HAVE I DONE...?
WHAT HAVE I DONE?!

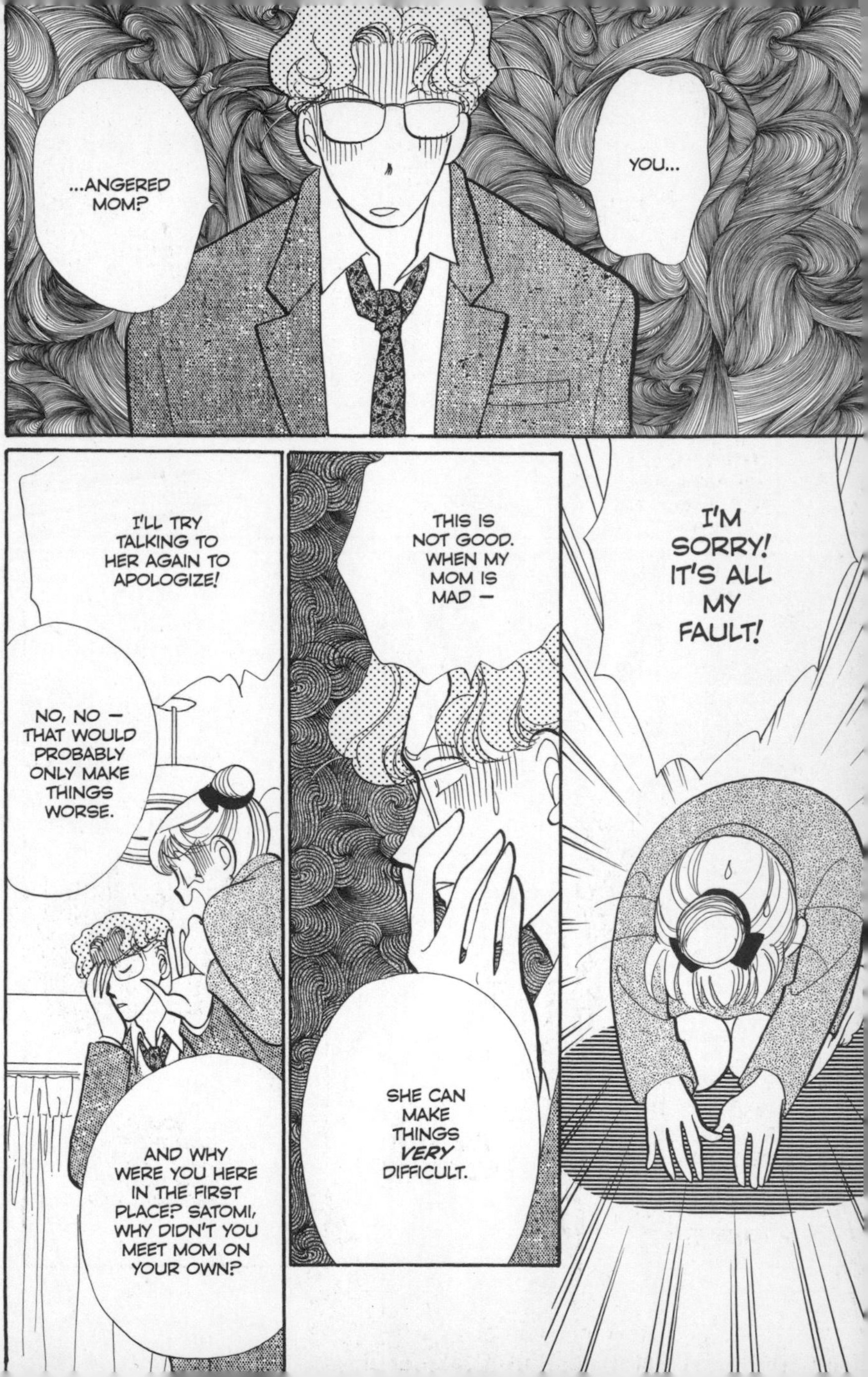
YOU...
...ANGERED MOM?
I'M SORRY! IT'S ALL MY FAULT!
THIS IS NOT GOOD. WHEN MY MOM IS MAD —
SHE CAN MAKE THINGS *VERY* DIFFICULT.
I'LL TRY TALKING TO HER AGAIN TO APOLOGIZE!
NO, NO — THAT WOULD PROBABLY ONLY MAKE THINGS WORSE.
AND WHY WERE YOU HERE IN THE FIRST PLACE? SATOMI, WHY DIDN'T YOU MEET MOM ON YOUR OWN?

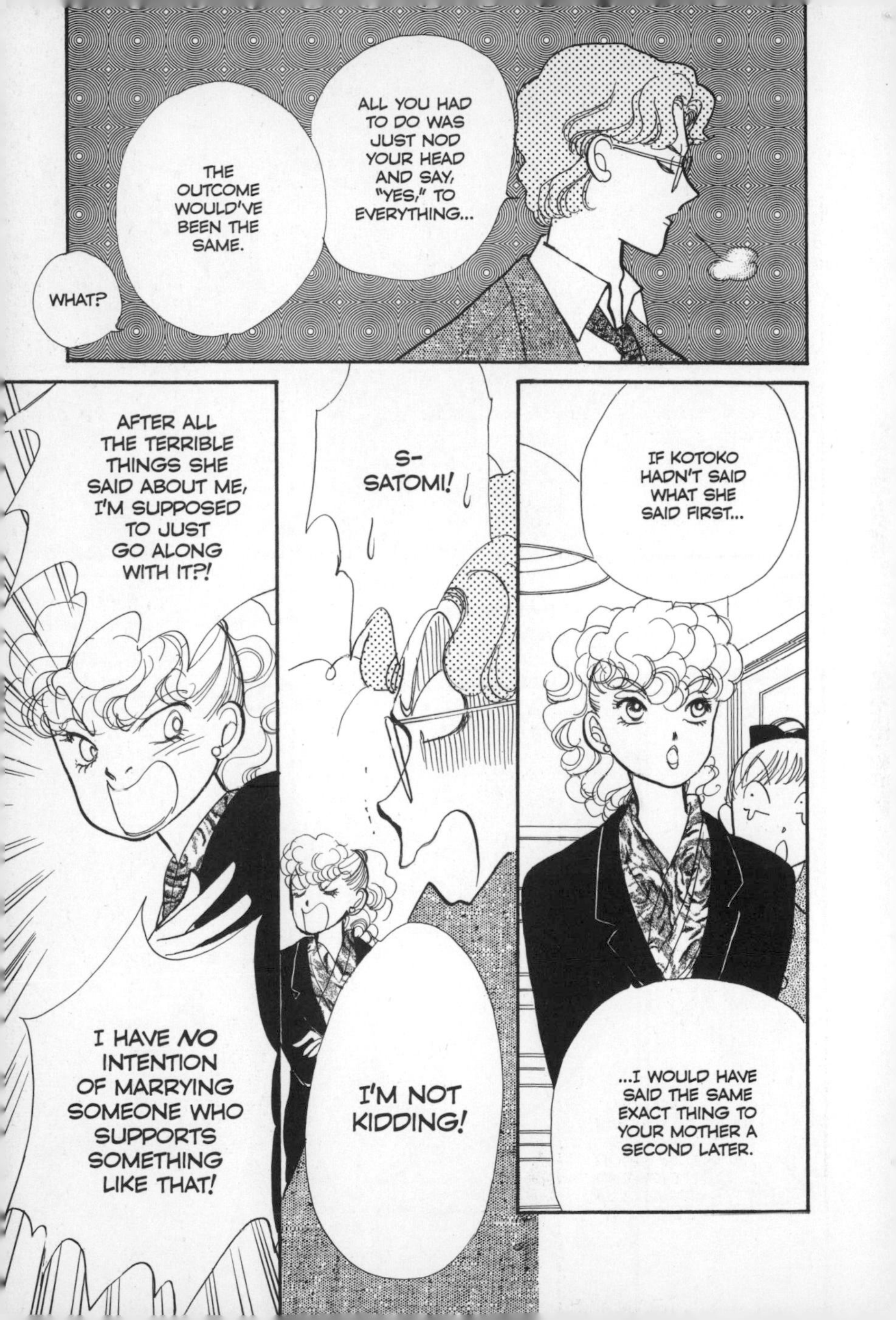
ALL YOU HAD TO DO WAS JUST NOD YOUR HEAD AND SAY, "YES," TO EVERYTHING...
THE OUTCOME WOULD'VE BEEN THE SAME.
WHAT?
IF KOTOKO HADN'T SAID WHAT SHE SAID FIRST...
...I WOULD HAVE SAID THE SAME EXACT THING TO YOUR MOTHER A SECOND LATER.
S-SATOMI!
I'M NOT KIDDING!
AFTER ALL THE TERRIBLE THINGS SHE SAID ABOUT ME, I'M SUPPOSED TO JUST GO ALONG WITH IT?!
I HAVE *NO* INTENTION OF MARRYING SOMEONE WHO SUPPORTS SOMETHING LIKE THAT!

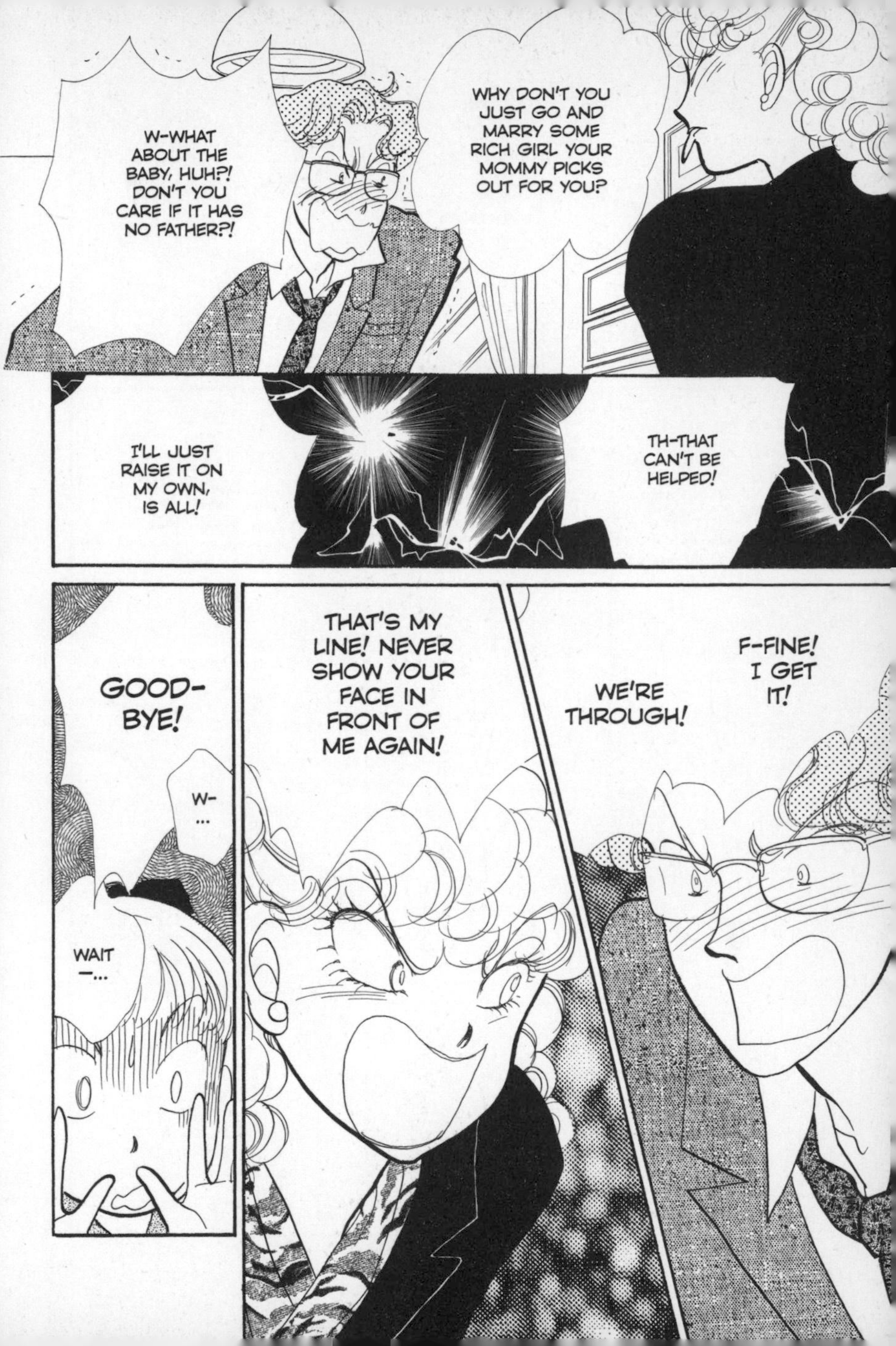
WHY DON'T YOU JUST GO AND MARRY SOME RICH GIRL YOUR MOMMY PICKS OUT FOR YOU?
W-WHAT ABOUT THE BABY, HUH?! DON'T YOU CARE IF IT HAS NO FATHER?!
TH-THAT CAN'T BE HELPED!
I'LL JUST RAISE IT ON MY OWN, IS ALL!
F-FINE! I GET IT!
WE'RE THROUGH!
THAT'S MY LINE! NEVER SHOW YOUR FACE IN FRONT OF ME AGAIN!
GOOD-BYE!
W-...
WAIT—...

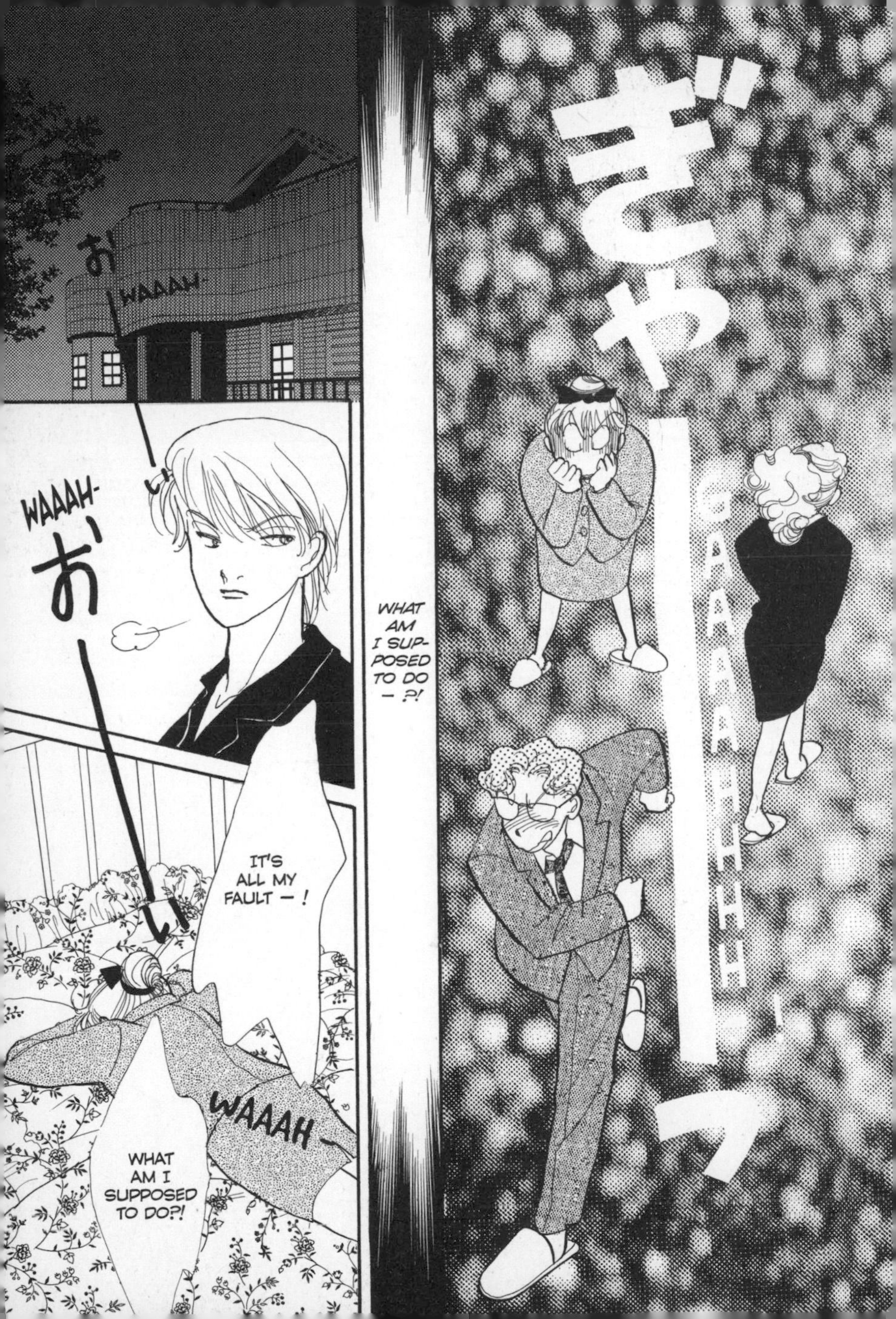
ぎゃーっ
GAAAAHHHH!
WHAT AM I SUPPOSED TO DO — ?!
お
WAAAH-
WAAAH-
おーい
IT'S ALL MY FAULT — !
WAAAH-
WHAT AM I SUPPOSED TO DO?!

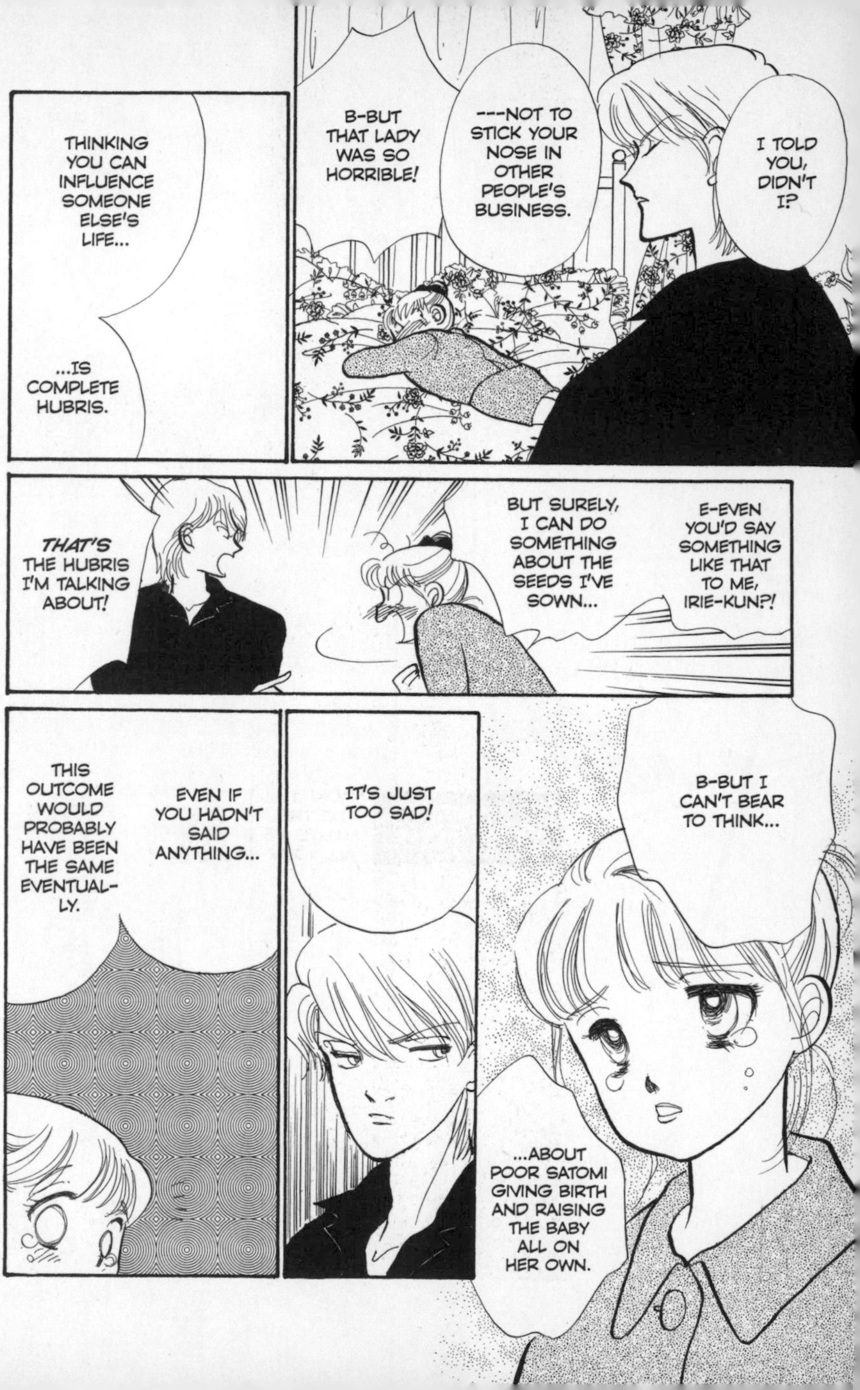
I TOLD YOU, DIDN'T I?
---NOT TO STICK YOUR NOSE IN OTHER PEOPLE'S BUSINESS.
B-BUT THAT LADY WAS SO HORRIBLE!
THINKING YOU CAN INFLUENCE SOMEONE ELSE'S LIFE...
...IS COMPLETE HUBRIS.
E-EVEN YOU'D SAY SOMETHING LIKE THAT TO ME, IRIE-KUN?!
BUT SURELY, I CAN DO SOMETHING ABOUT THE SEEDS I'VE SOWN...
THAT'S THE HUBRIS I'M TALKING ABOUT!
B-BUT I CAN'T BEAR TO THINK...
...ABOUT POOR SATOMI GIVING BIRTH AND RAISING THE BABY ALL ON HER OWN.
IT'S JUST TOO SAD!
EVEN IF YOU HADN'T SAID ANYTHING...
THIS OUTCOME WOULD PROBABLY HAVE BEEN THE SAME EVENTUAL-LY.

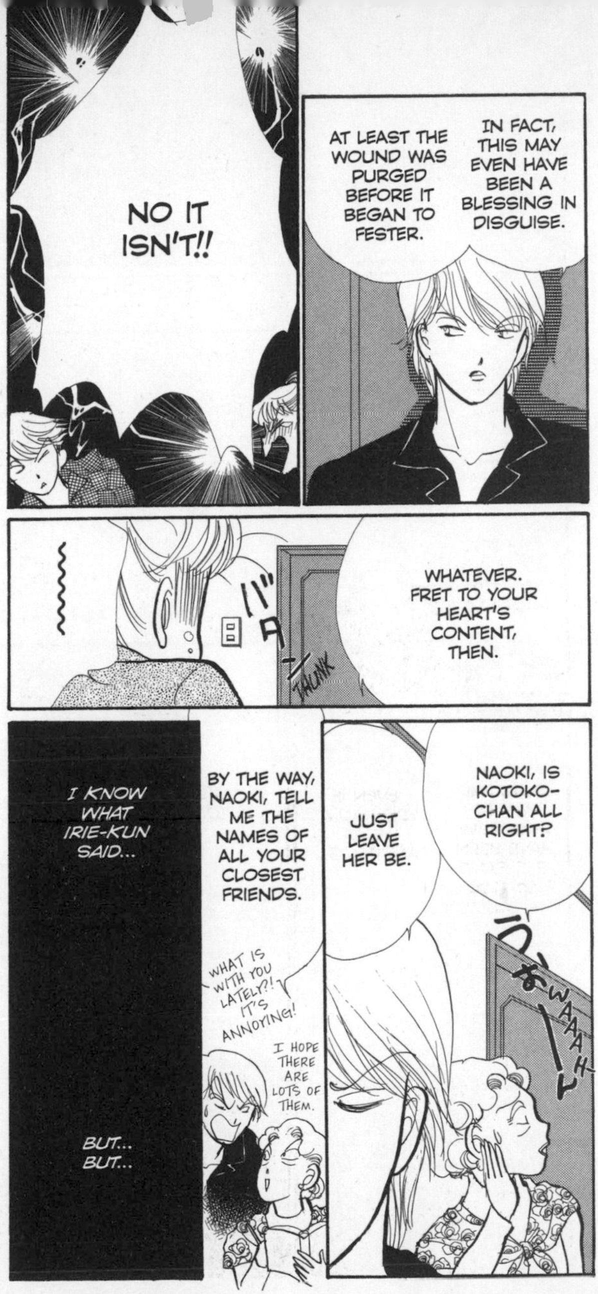
IN FACT, THIS MAY EVEN HAVE BEEN A BLESSING IN DISGUISE.
AT LEAST THE WOUND WAS PURGED BEFORE IT BEGAN TO FESTER.
NO IT ISN'T!!
WHATEVER. FRET TO YOUR HEART'S CONTENT, THEN.
バタ
THUNK
NAOKI, IS KOTOKO-CHAN ALL RIGHT?
JUST LEAVE HER BE.
WAAAH
BY THE WAY, NAOKI, TELL ME THE NAMES OF ALL YOUR CLOSEST FRIENDS.
I HOPE THERE ARE LOTS OF THEM.
WHAT IS WITH YOU LATELY?! IT'S ANNOYING!
I KNOW WHAT IRIE-KUN SAID...
BUT... BUT...

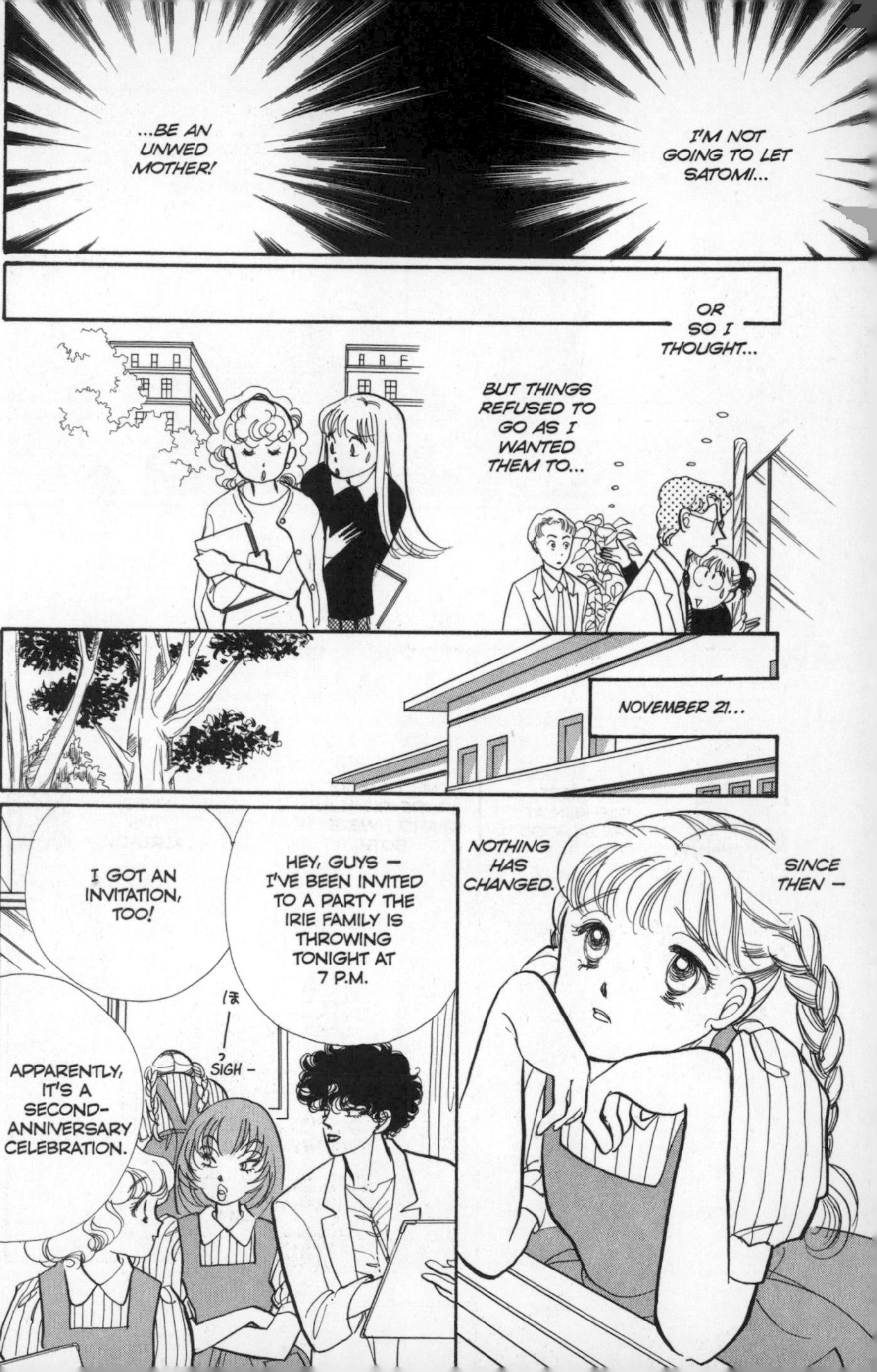
I'M NOT GOING TO LET SATOMI...
...BE AN UNWED MOTHER!
OR SO I THOUGHT...
BUT THINGS REFUSED TO GO AS I WANTED THEM TO...
NOVEMBER 21...
SINCE THEN —
NOTHING HAS CHANGED.
HEY, GUYS — I'VE BEEN INVITED TO A PARTY THE IRIE FAMILY IS THROWING TONIGHT AT 7 P.M.
I GOT AN INVITATION, TOO!
ほー
SIGH —
APPARENTLY, IT'S A SECOND-ANNIVERSARY CELEBRATION.

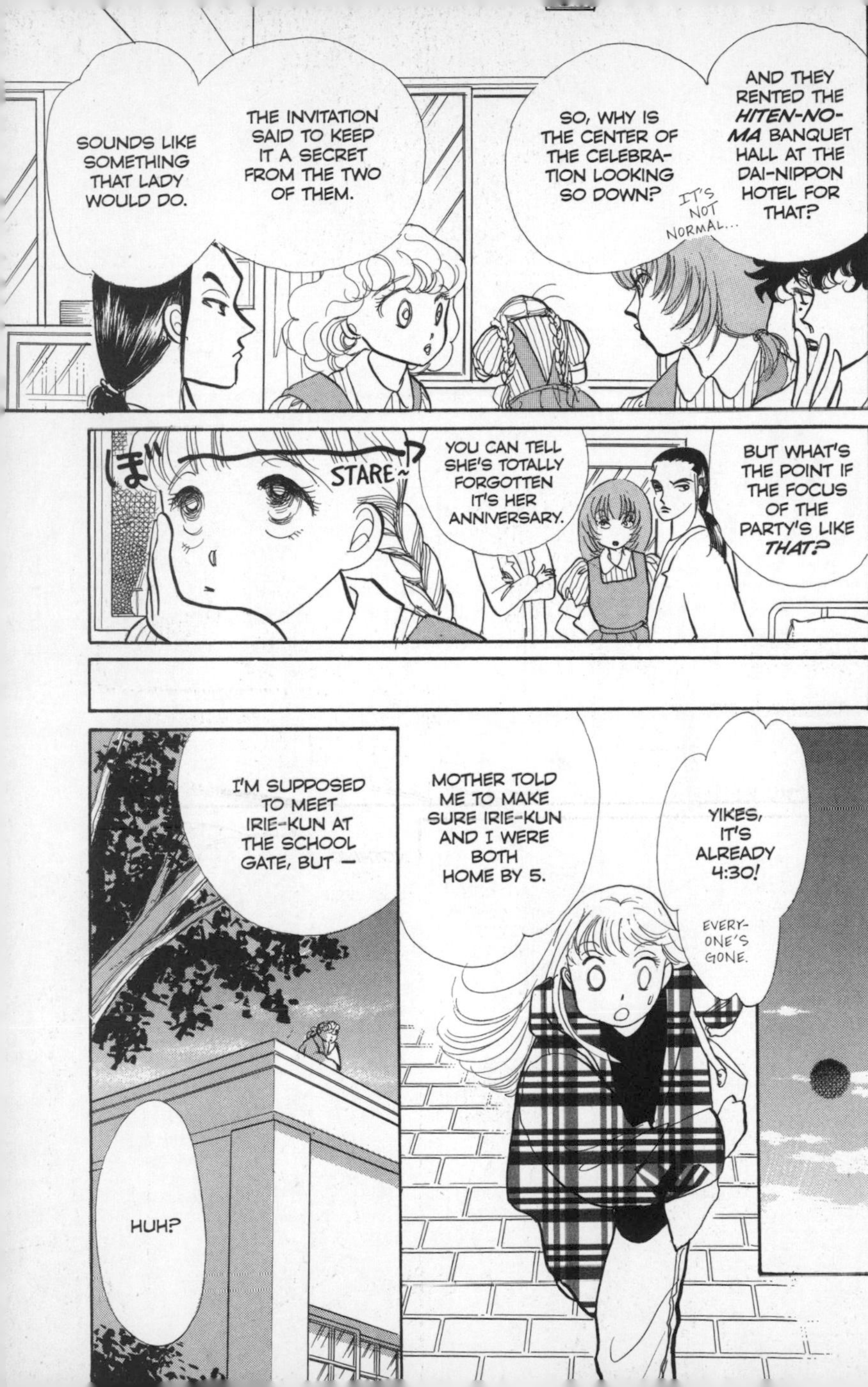
AND THEY RENTED THE *HITEN-NO-MA* BANQUET HALL AT THE DAI-NIPPON HOTEL FOR THAT?
IT'S NOT NORMAL...
SO, WHY IS THE CENTER OF THE CELEBRATION LOOKING SO DOWN?
THE INVITATION SAID TO KEEP IT A SECRET FROM THE TWO OF THEM.
SOUNDS LIKE SOMETHING THAT LADY WOULD DO.
BUT WHAT'S THE POINT IF THE FOCUS OF THE PARTY'S LIKE *THAT?*
YOU CAN TELL SHE'S TOTALLY FORGOTTEN IT'S HER ANNIVERSARY.
ぼ~ STARE~
YIKES, IT'S ALREADY 4:30!
EVERYONE'S GONE.
MOTHER TOLD ME TO MAKE SURE IRIE-KUN AND I WERE BOTH HOME BY 5.
I'M SUPPOSED TO MEET IRIE-KUN AT THE SCHOOL GATE, BUT —
HUH?

STAFF: AKIKO ISHIKAWA, ATSUKO SUGIMOTO, MASAKO KATAGAI, KANAMI SUDŌ, SHIZUKO KOIKE
THANK YOU VERY MUCH ♥

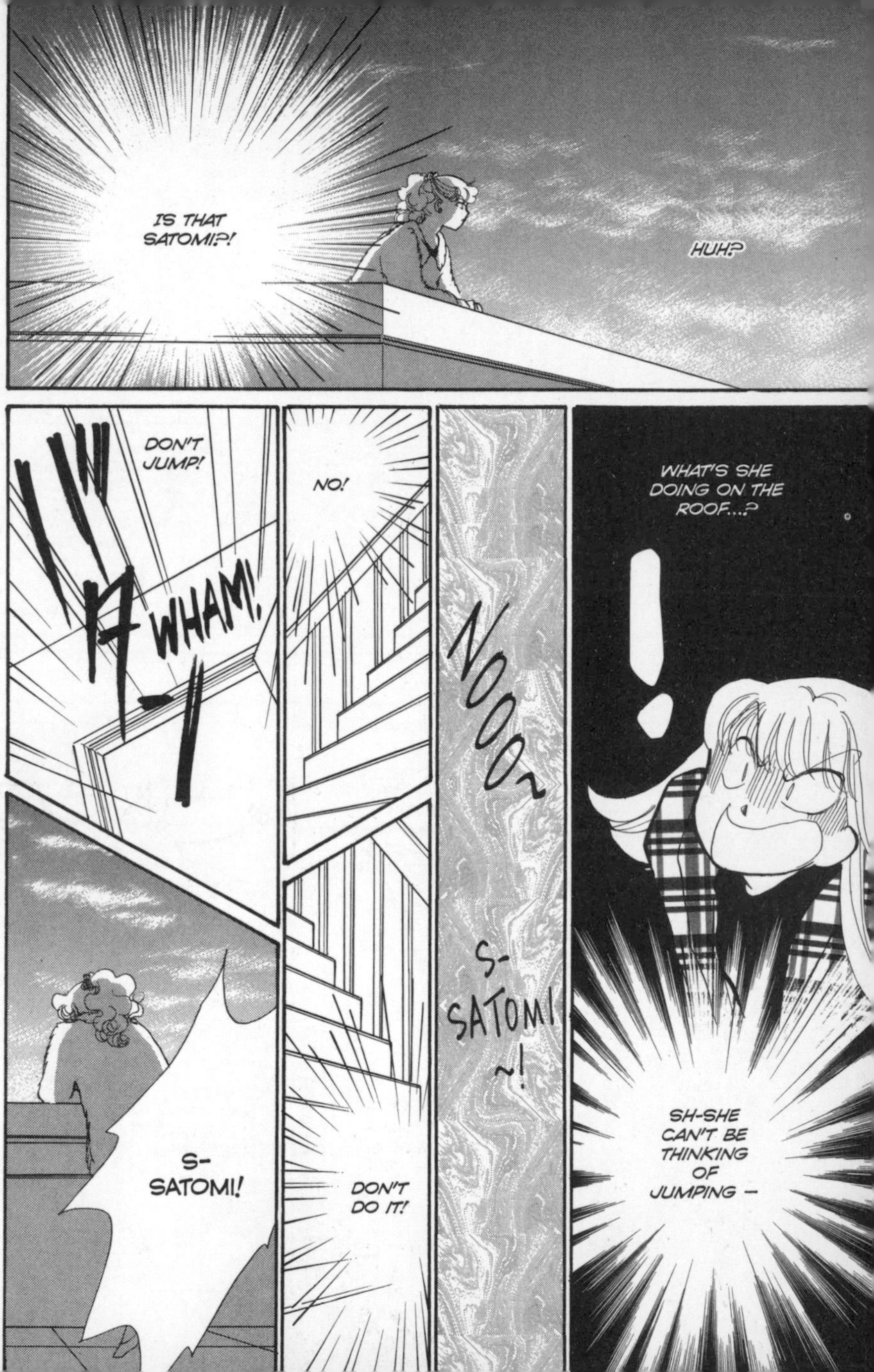
HUH?
IS THAT SATOMI?!
WHAT'S SHE DOING ON THE ROOF...?
!
SH-SHE CAN'T BE THINKING OF JUMPING –
NOOO~
S-SATOMI~!
NO!
DON'T DO IT!
DON'T JUMP!
WHAM!
S-SATOMI!

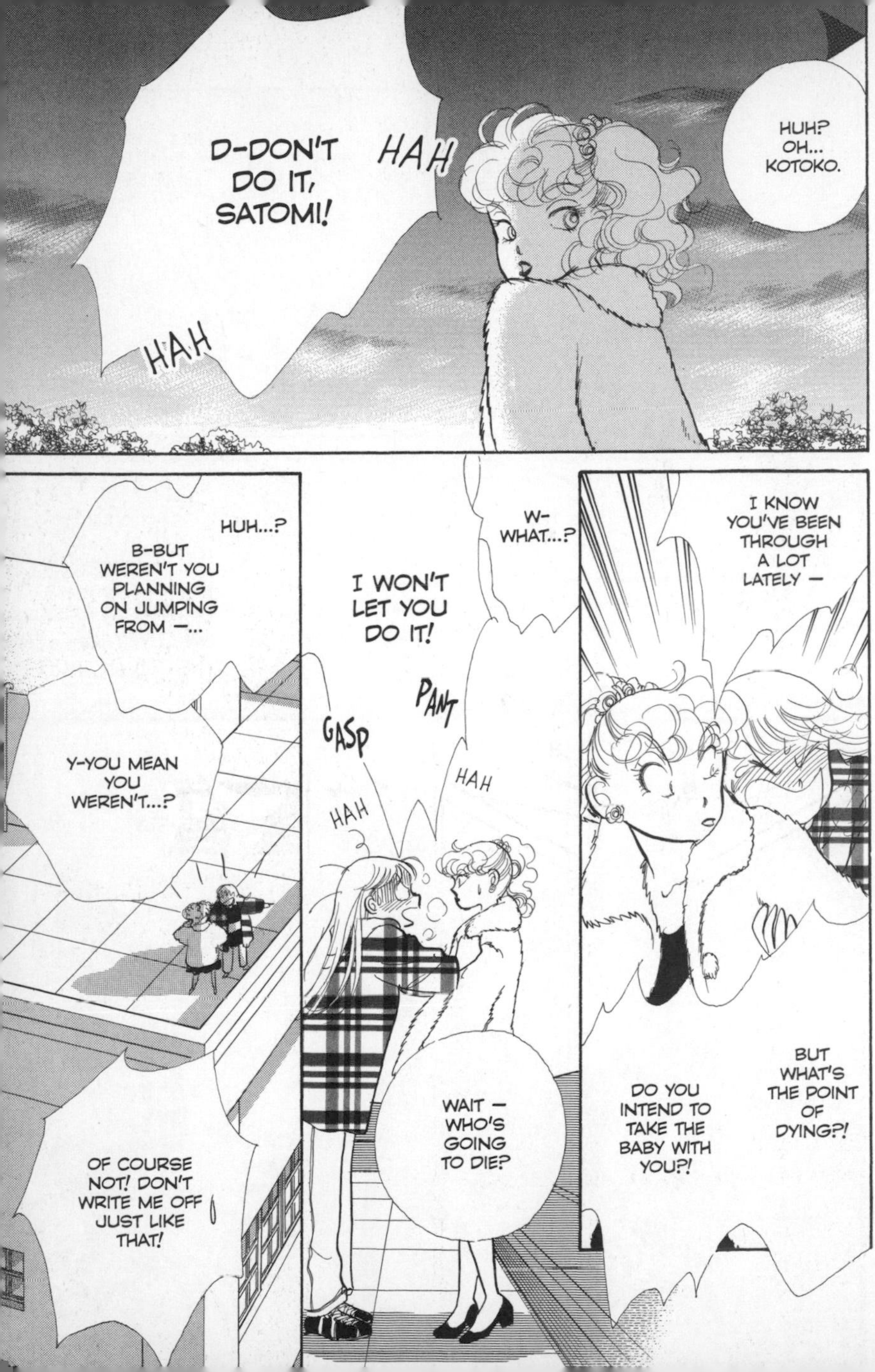
HUH? OH... KOTOKO.
HAH
D-DON'T DO IT, SATOMI!
HAH
I KNOW YOU'VE BEEN THROUGH A LOT LATELY —
BUT WHAT'S THE POINT OF DYING?!
DO YOU INTEND TO TAKE THE BABY WITH YOU?!
W- WHAT...?
I WON'T LET YOU DO IT!
PANT
HAH
GASP
HAH
WAIT — WHO'S GOING TO DIE?
HUH...?
B-BUT WEREN'T YOU PLANNING ON JUMPING FROM —...
Y-YOU MEAN YOU WEREN'T...?
OF COURSE NOT! DON'T WRITE ME OFF JUST LIKE THAT!

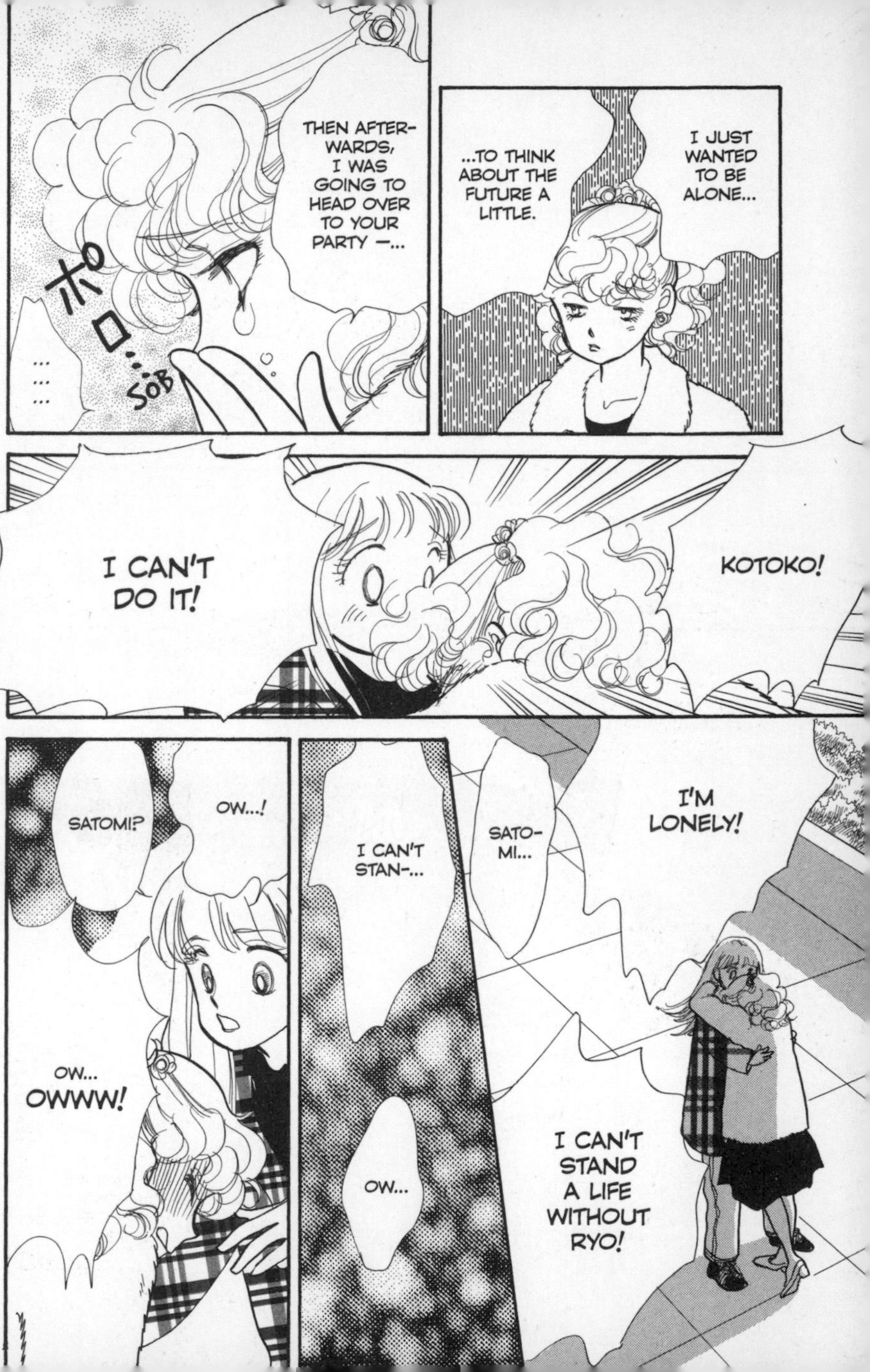
I JUST WANTED TO BE ALONE...
...TO THINK ABOUT THE FUTURE A LITTLE.
THEN AFTER-WARDS, I WAS GOING TO HEAD OVER TO YOUR PARTY —...
ポロ...
SOB
......
KOTOKO!
I CAN'T DO IT!
I'M LONELY!
SATO-MI...
I CAN'T STAND A LIFE WITHOUT RYO!
I CAN'T STAN-...
OW...
OW...!
SATOMI?
OW... OWWW!

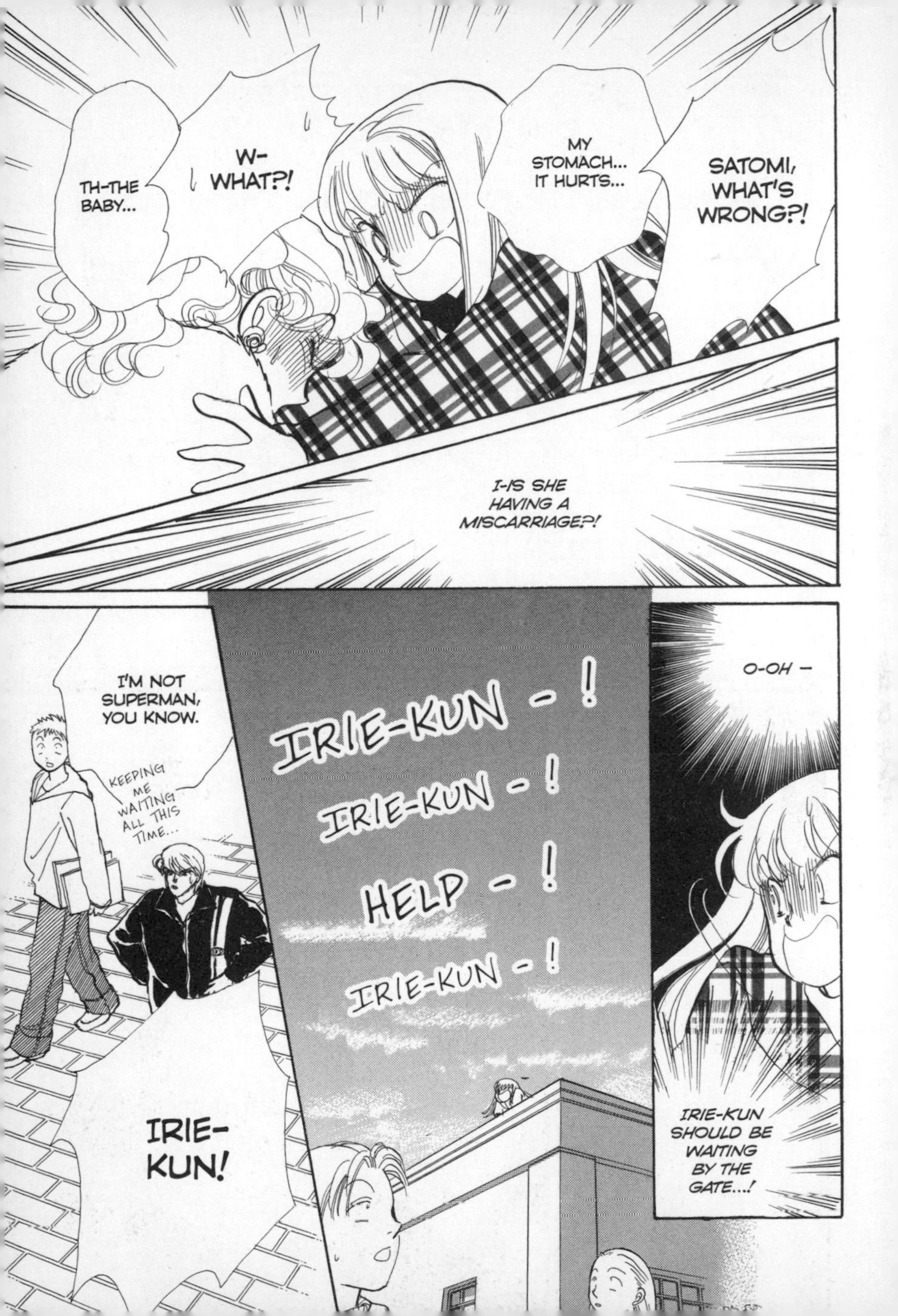
SATOMI, WHAT'S WRONG?!
MY STOMACH... IT HURTS...
W- WHAT?!
TH-THE BABY...
I-IS SHE HAVING A MISCARRIAGE?!
O-OH –
IRIE-KUN SHOULD BE WAITING BY THE GATE...!
IRIE-KUN – !
IRIE-KUN – !
HELP – !
IRIE-KUN – !
I'M NOT SUPERMAN, YOU KNOW.
KEEPING ME WAITING ALL THIS TIME...
IRIE-KUN!

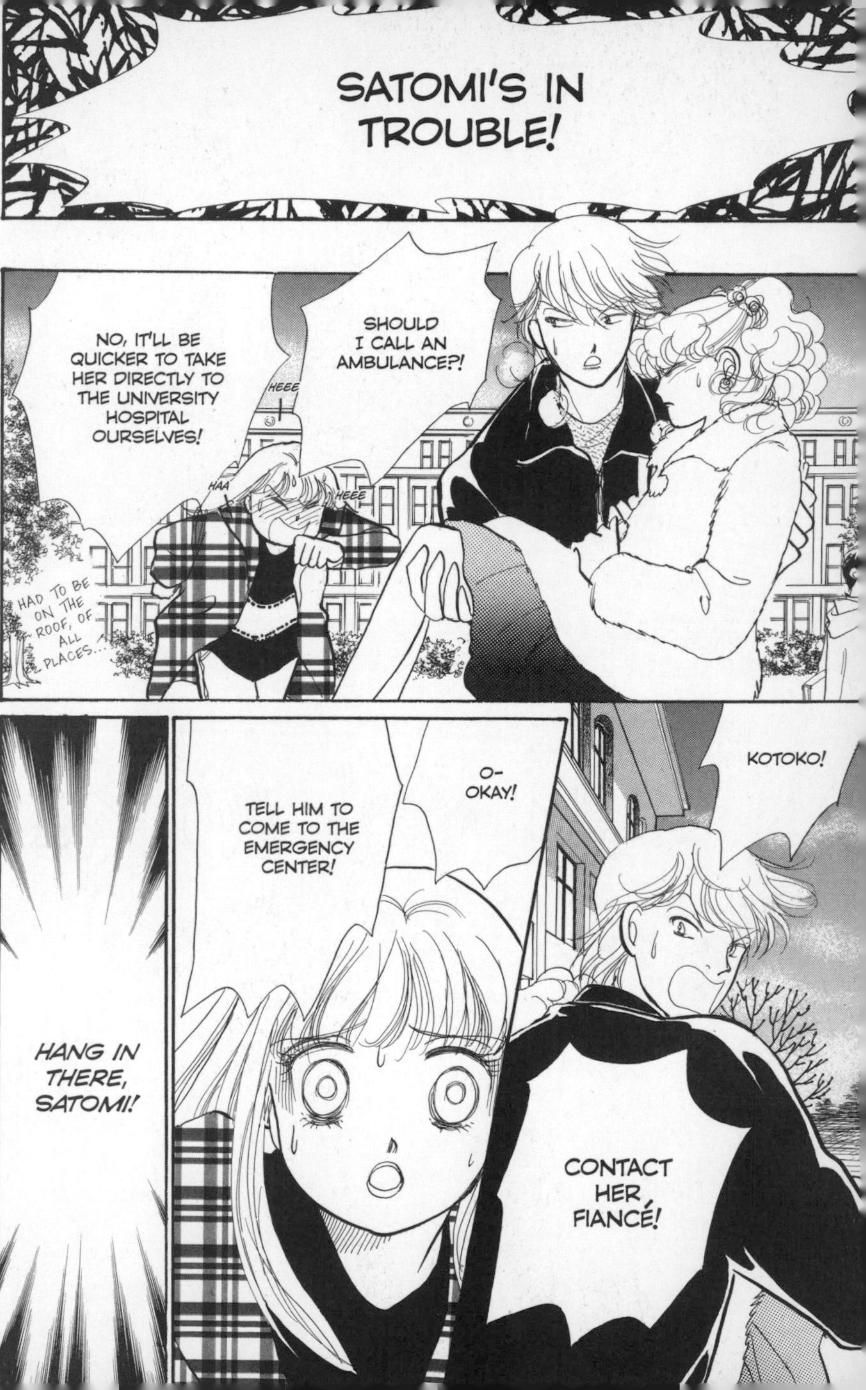
SATOMI'S IN TROUBLE!
SHOULD I CALL AN AMBULANCE?!
NO, IT'LL BE QUICKER TO TAKE HER DIRECTLY TO THE UNIVERSITY HOSPITAL OURSELVES!
HEEE
HAA
HEEE
HAD TO BE ON THE ROOF, OF ALL PLACES...
KOTOKO!
CONTACT HER FIANCÉ!
O-OKAY!
TELL HIM TO COME TO THE EMERGENCY CENTER!
HANG IN THERE, SATOMI!

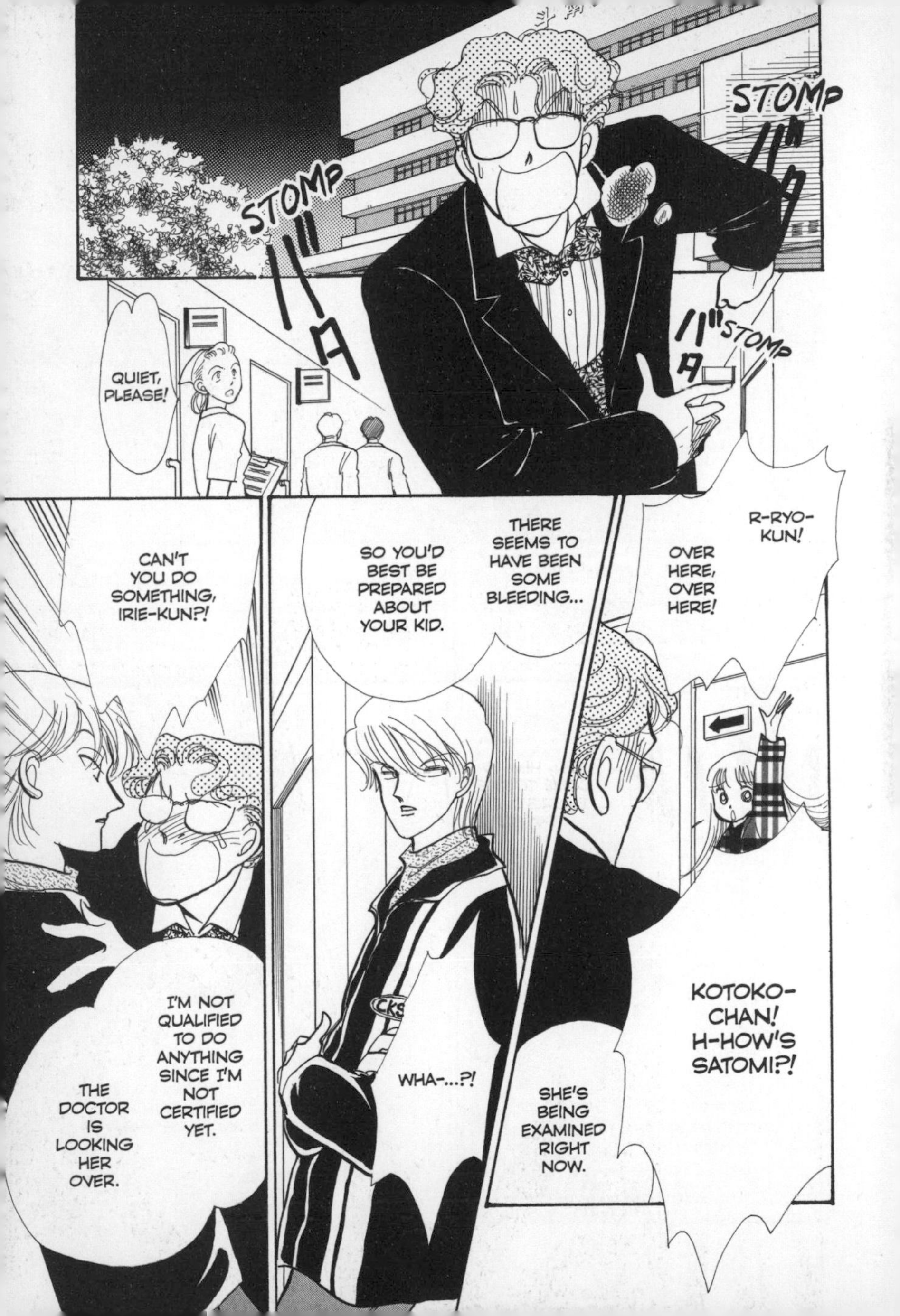
STOMP
STOMP
STOMP
QUIET, PLEASE!
R-RYO-KUN!
OVER HERE, OVER HERE!
KOTOKO-CHAN! H-HOW'S SATOMI?!
SHE'S BEING EXAMINED RIGHT NOW.
THERE SEEMS TO HAVE BEEN SOME BLEEDING...
SO YOU'D BEST BE PREPARED ABOUT YOUR KID.
WHA-...?!
CAN'T YOU DO SOMETHING, IRIE-KUN?!
I'M NOT QUALIFIED TO DO ANYTHING SINCE I'M NOT CERTIFIED YET.
THE DOCTOR IS LOOKING HER OVER.

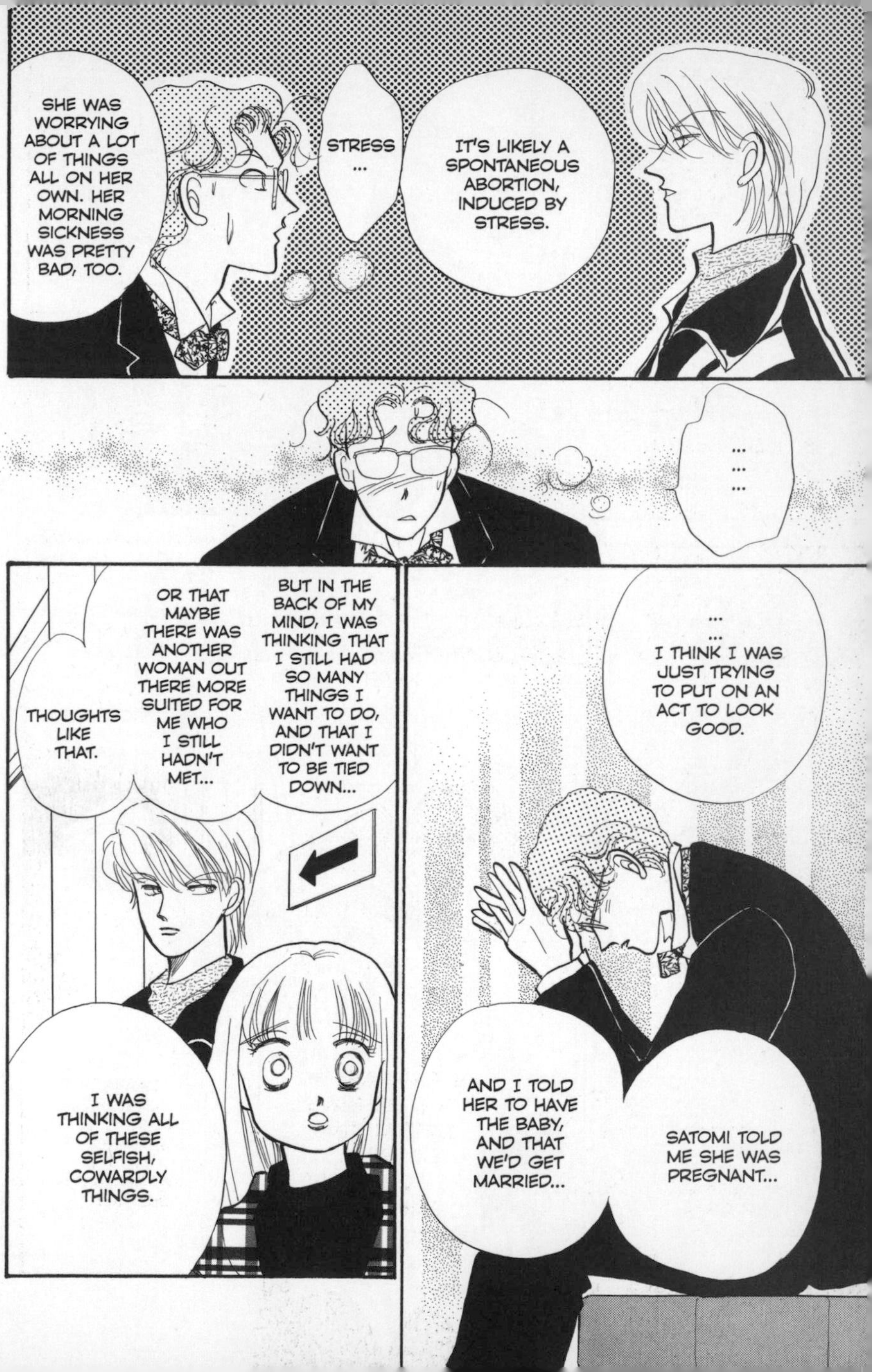
IT'S LIKELY A SPONTANEOUS ABORTION, INDUCED BY STRESS.
STRESS ...
SHE WAS WORRYING ABOUT A LOT OF THINGS ALL ON HER OWN. HER MORNING SICKNESS WAS PRETTY BAD, TOO.
... ...
... ... I THINK I WAS JUST TRYING TO PUT ON AN ACT TO LOOK GOOD.
SATOMI TOLD ME SHE WAS PREGNANT...
AND I TOLD HER TO HAVE THE BABY, AND THAT WE'D GET MARRIED...
BUT IN THE BACK OF MY MIND, I WAS THINKING THAT I STILL HAD SO MANY THINGS I WANT TO DO, AND THAT I DIDN'T WANT TO BE TIED DOWN...
OR THAT MAYBE THERE WAS ANOTHER WOMAN OUT THERE MORE SUITED FOR ME WHO I STILL HADN'T MET...
THOUGHTS LIKE THAT.
I WAS THINKING ALL OF THESE SELFISH, COWARDLY THINGS.

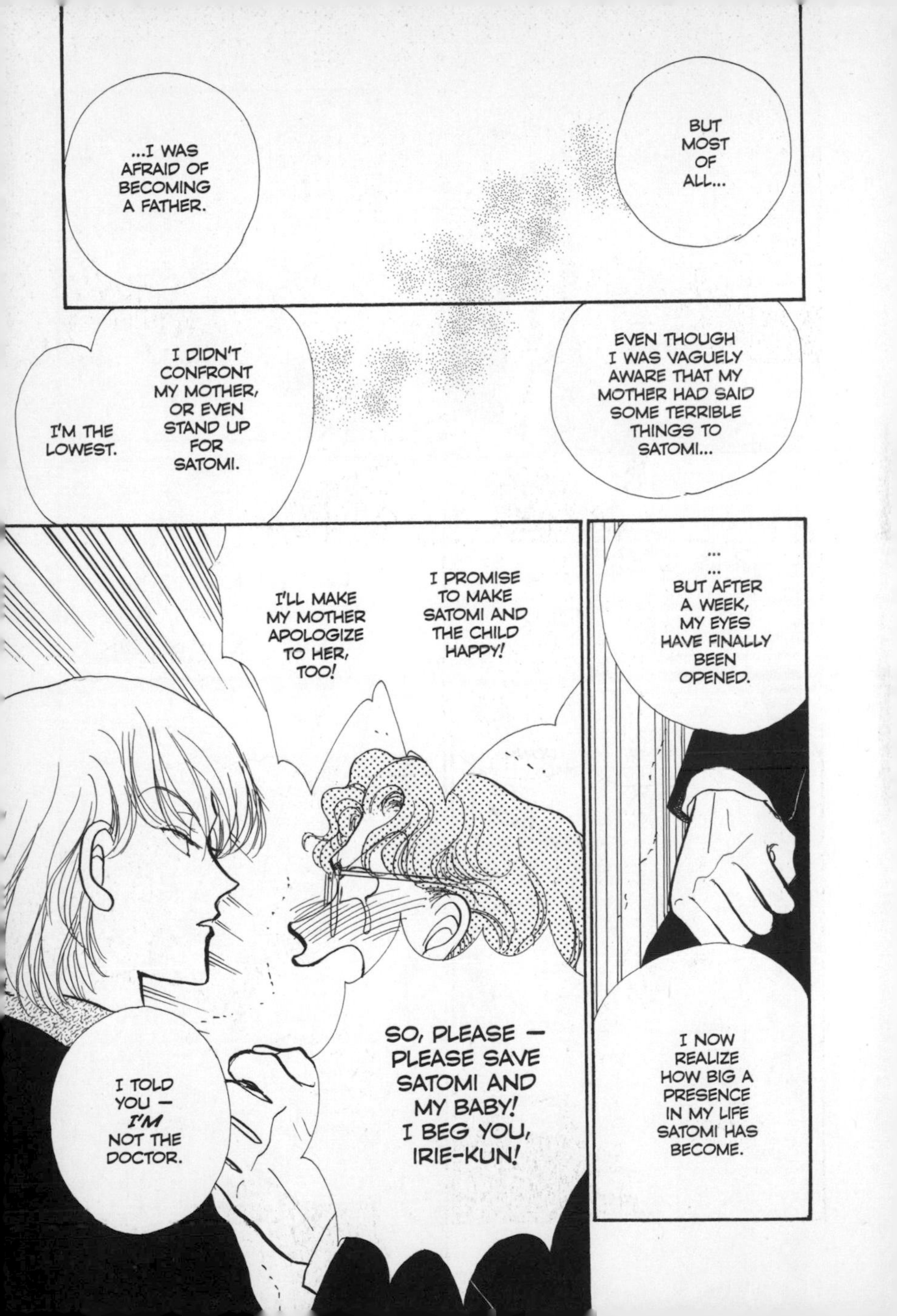
BUT MOST OF ALL...
...I WAS AFRAID OF BECOMING A FATHER.
EVEN THOUGH I WAS VAGUELY AWARE THAT MY MOTHER HAD SAID SOME TERRIBLE THINGS TO SATOMI...
I DIDN'T CONFRONT MY MOTHER, OR EVEN STAND UP FOR SATOMI.
I'M THE LOWEST.
... ... BUT AFTER A WEEK, MY EYES HAVE FINALLY BEEN OPENED.
I NOW REALIZE HOW BIG A PRESENCE IN MY LIFE SATOMI HAS BECOME.
I PROMISE TO MAKE SATOMI AND THE CHILD HAPPY!
I'LL MAKE MY MOTHER APOLOGIZE TO HER, TOO!
SO, PLEASE — PLEASE SAVE SATOMI AND MY BABY! I BEG YOU, IRIE-KUN!
I TOLD YOU — *I'M* NOT THE DOCTOR.

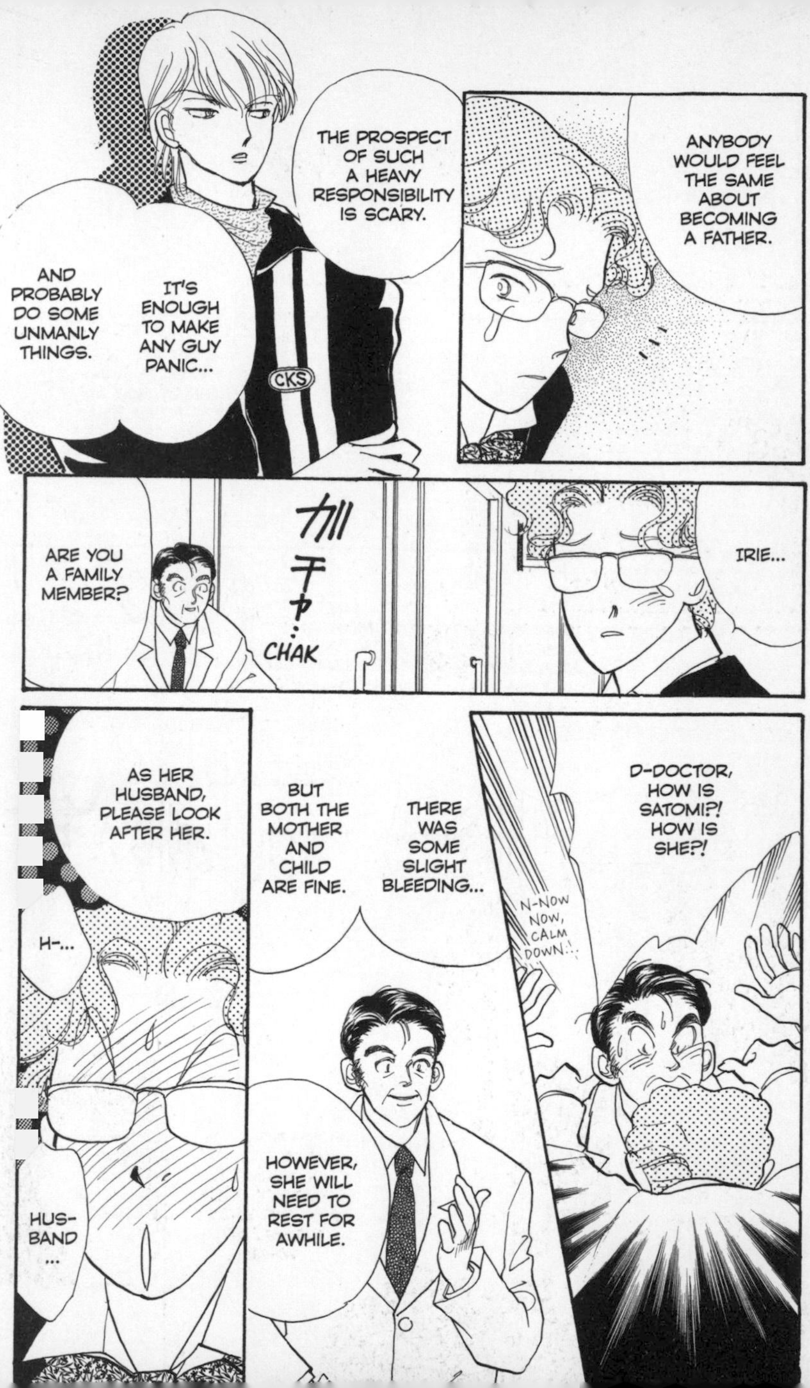
ANYBODY WOULD FEEL THE SAME ABOUT BECOMING A FATHER.
THE PROSPECT OF SUCH A HEAVY RESPONSIBILITY IS SCARY.
IT'S ENOUGH TO MAKE ANY GUY PANIC...
AND PROBABLY DO SOME UNMANLY THINGS.
CKS
IRIE...
カチャ
CHAK
ARE YOU A FAMILY MEMBER?
D-DOCTOR, HOW IS SATOMI?! HOW IS SHE?!
N-NOW NOW, CALM DOWN!!
THERE WAS SOME SLIGHT BLEEDING...
BUT BOTH THE MOTHER AND CHILD ARE FINE.
HOWEVER, SHE WILL NEED TO REST FOR AWHILE.
AS HER HUSBAND, PLEASE LOOK AFTER HER.
H-...
HUS-BAND...

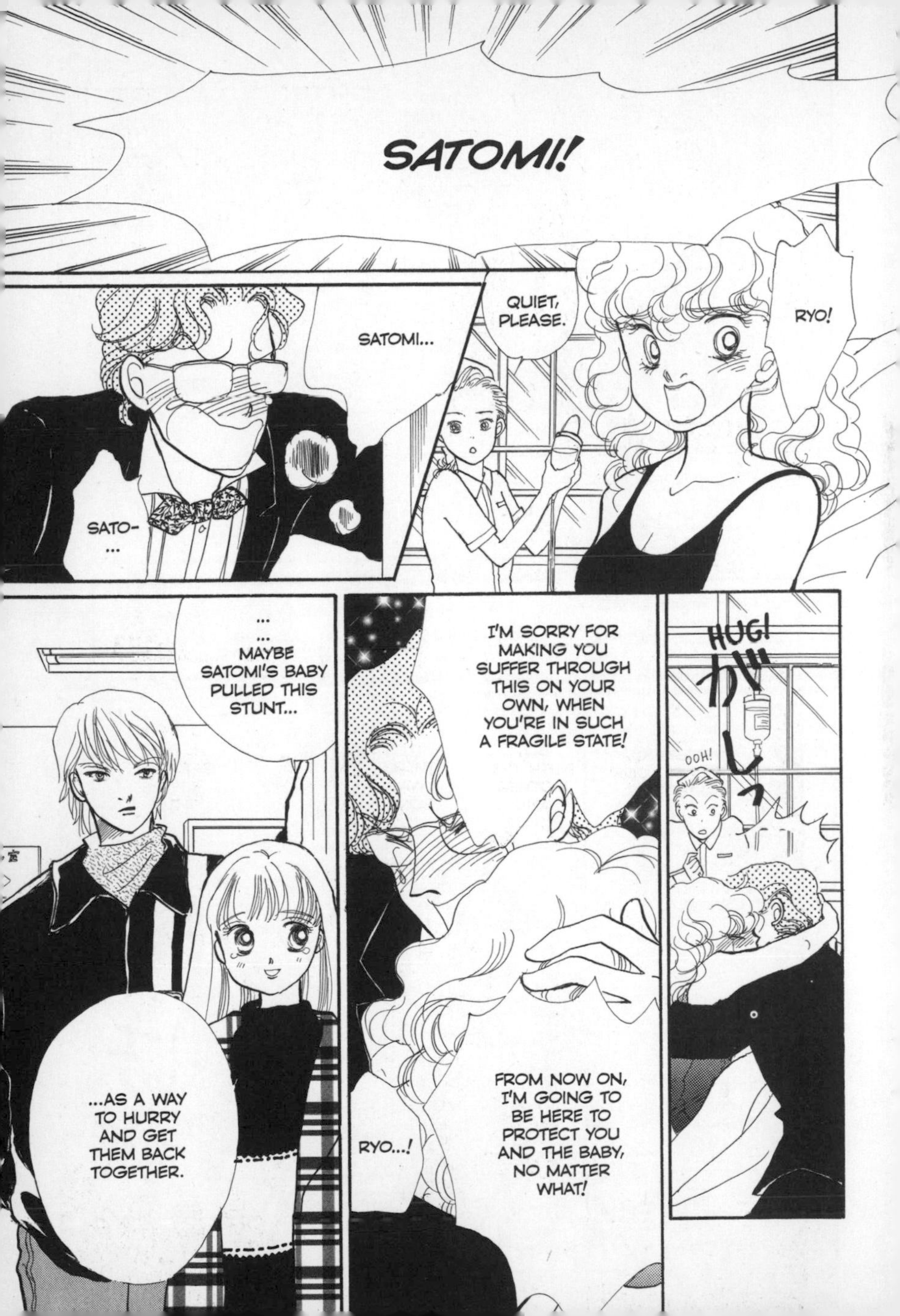
SATOMI!
RYO!
QUIET, PLEASE.
SATOMI...
SATO-...
HUG!
がしっ
OOH!
I'M SORRY FOR MAKING YOU SUFFER THROUGH THIS ON YOUR OWN, WHEN YOU'RE IN SUCH A FRAGILE STATE!
FROM NOW ON, I'M GOING TO BE HERE TO PROTECT YOU AND THE BABY, NO MATTER WHAT!
RYO...!
... ... MAYBE SATOMI'S BABY PULLED THIS STUNT...
...AS A WAY TO HURRY AND GET THEM BACK TOGETHER.

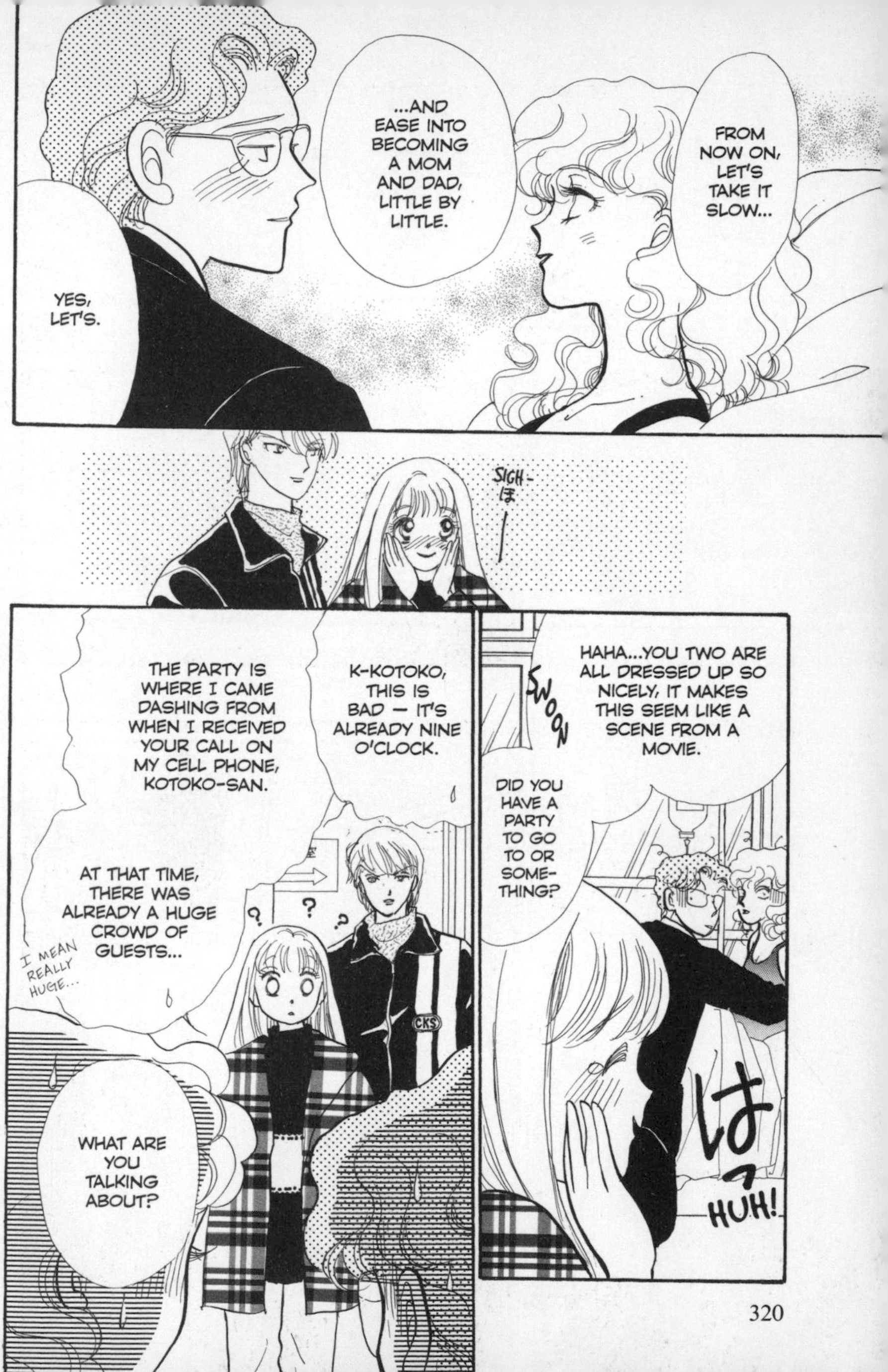
FROM NOW ON, LET'S TAKE IT SLOW...
...AND EASE INTO BECOMING A MOM AND DAD, LITTLE BY LITTLE.
YES, LET'S.
SIGH— ほ
HAHA...YOU TWO ARE ALL DRESSED UP SO NICELY, IT MAKES THIS SEEM LIKE A SCENE FROM A MOVIE.
SWOON
DID YOU HAVE A PARTY TO GO TO OR SOMETHING?
は
HUH!
K-KOTOKO, THIS IS BAD — IT'S ALREADY NINE O'CLOCK.
THE PARTY IS WHERE I CAME DASHING FROM WHEN I RECEIVED YOUR CALL ON MY CELL PHONE, KOTOKO-SAN.
AT THAT TIME, THERE WAS ALREADY A HUGE CROWD OF GUESTS...
I MEAN REALLY HUGE...
WHAT ARE YOU TALKING ABOUT?

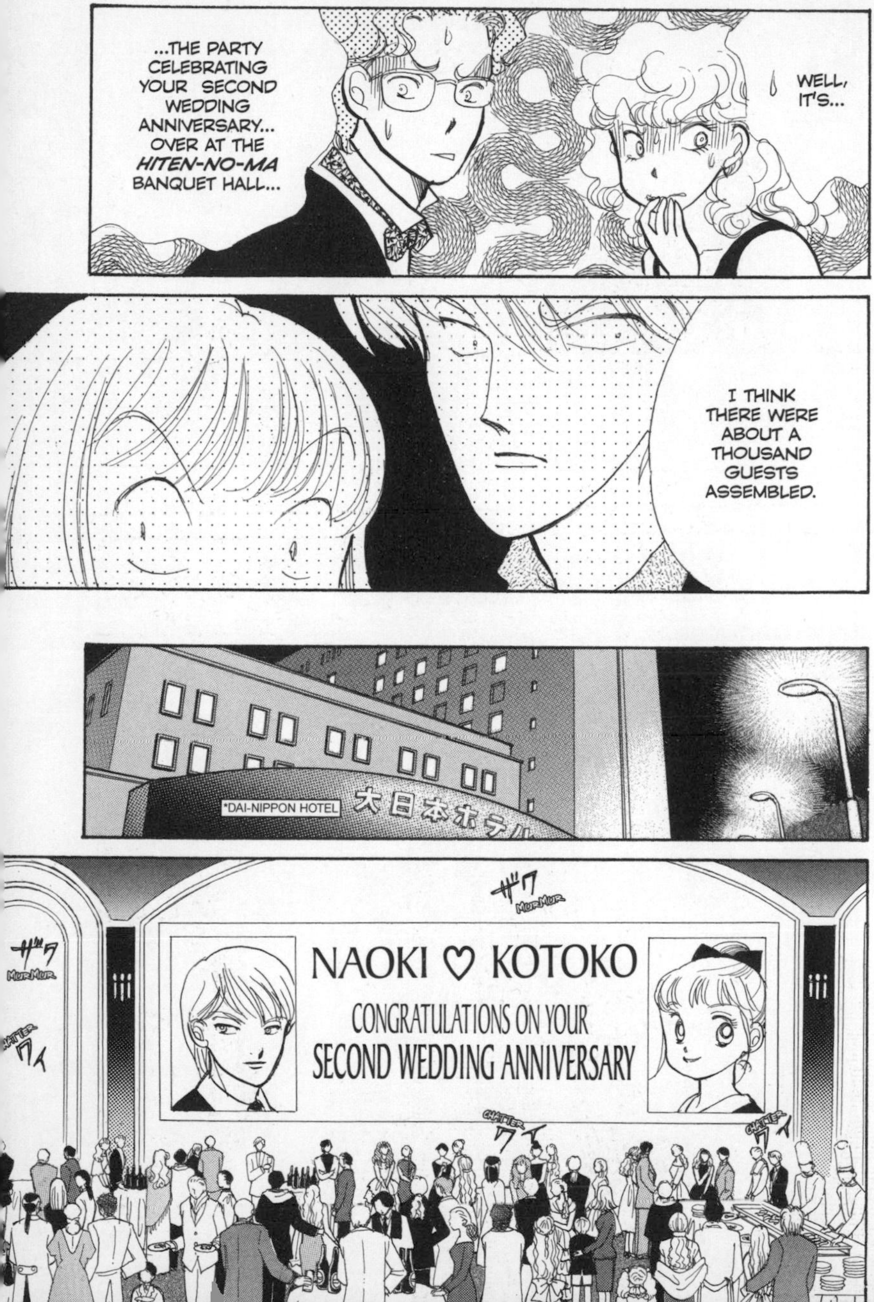
WELL, IT'S...
...THE PARTY CELEBRATING YOUR SECOND WEDDING ANNIVERSARY... OVER AT THE *HITEN-NO-MA* BANQUET HALL...
I THINK THERE WERE ABOUT A THOUSAND GUESTS ASSEMBLED.
大日本ホテル
*DAI-NIPPON HOTEL
ザワ
MURMUR
NAOKI ♡ KOTOKO
CONGRATULATIONS ON YOUR SECOND WEDDING ANNIVERSARY
ザワ
MURMUR
ワイ
CHATTER
ワイ
CHATTER
ワイ
CHATTER

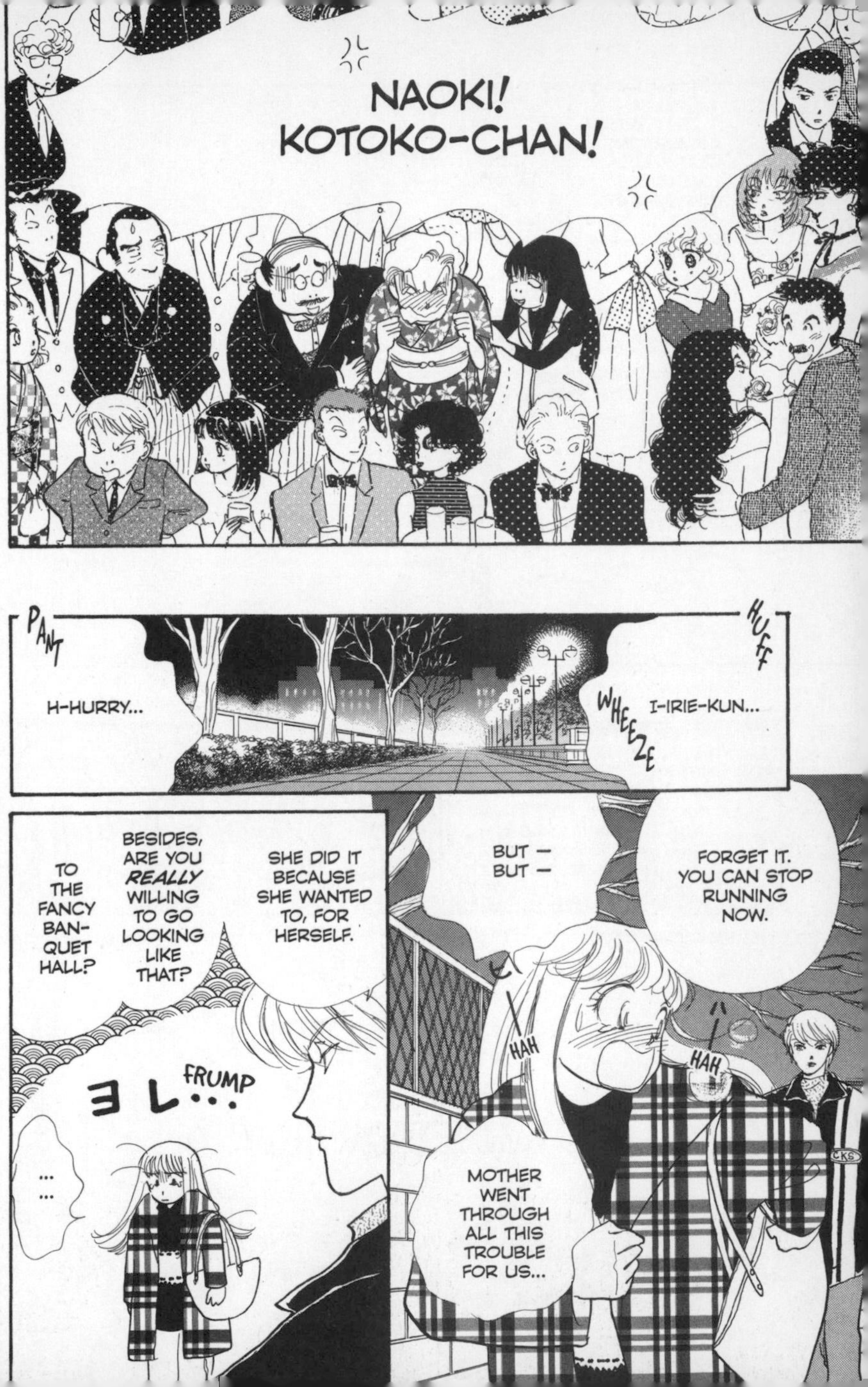
NAOKI!
KOTOKO-CHAN!
HUFF
I-IRIE-KUN...
WHEEZE
H-HURRY...
PANT
FORGET IT. YOU CAN STOP RUNNING NOW.
BUT — BUT —
HAH
HAH
MOTHER WENT THROUGH ALL THIS TROUBLE FOR US...
SHE DID IT BECAUSE SHE WANTED TO, FOR HERSELF.
BESIDES, ARE YOU REALLY WILLING TO GO LOOKING LIKE THAT?
TO THE FANCY BAN-QUET HALL?
ヨレ... FRUMP
...
...

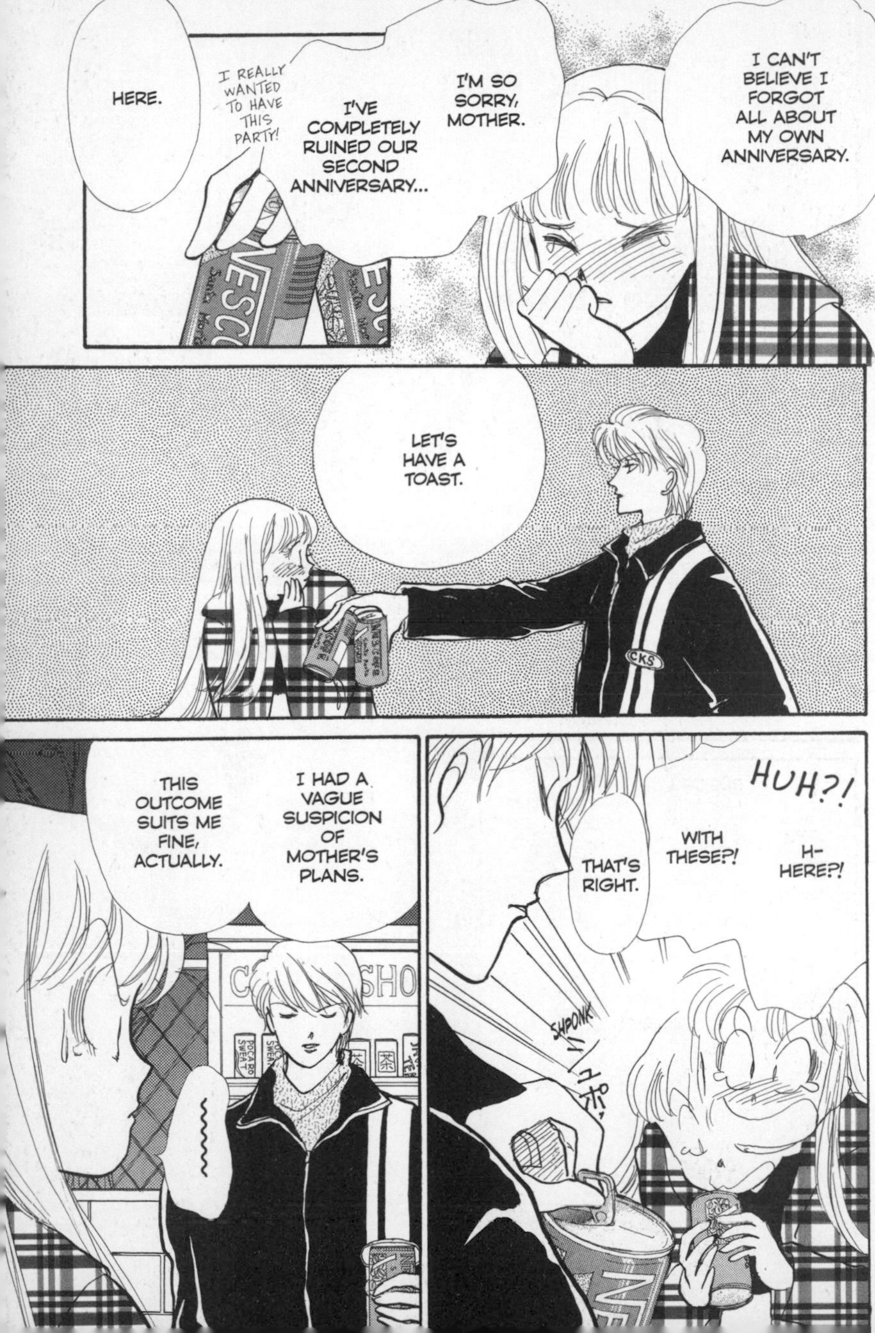
I CAN'T BELIEVE I FORGOT ALL ABOUT MY OWN ANNIVERSARY.
I'M SO SORRY, MOTHER.
I'VE COMPLETELY RUINED OUR SECOND ANNIVERSARY...
I REALLY WANTED TO HAVE THIS PARTY!
HERE.
LET'S HAVE A TOAST.
HUH?!
H- HERE?!
WITH THESE?!
THAT'S RIGHT.
SHPONK
I HAD A VAGUE SUSPICION OF MOTHER'S PLANS.
THIS OUTCOME SUITS ME FINE, ACTUALLY.

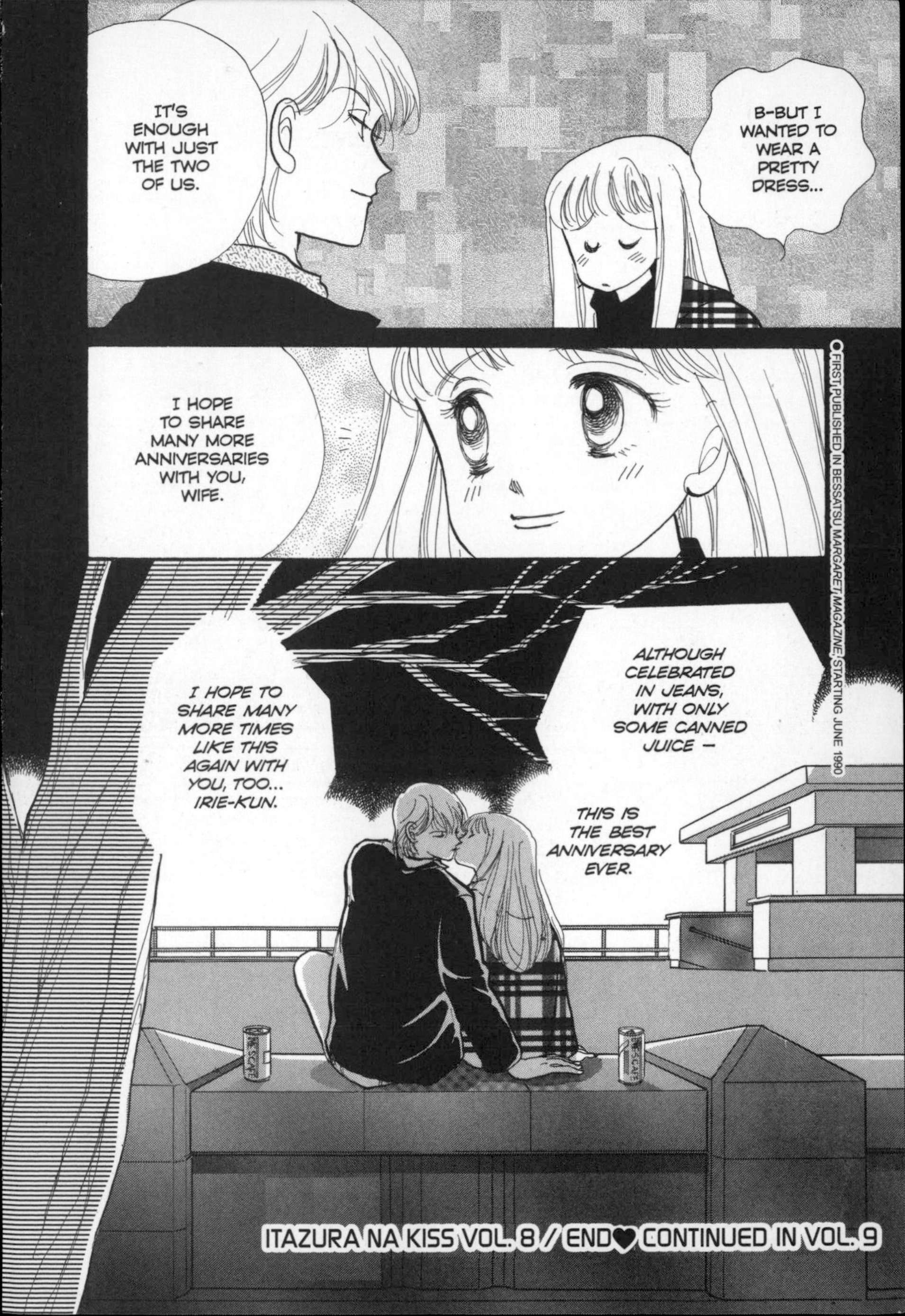
B-BUT I WANTED TO WEAR A PRETTY DRESS...
IT'S ENOUGH WITH JUST THE TWO OF US.
I HOPE TO SHARE MANY MORE ANNIVERSARIES WITH YOU, WIFE.
ALTHOUGH CELEBRATED IN JEANS, WITH ONLY SOME CANNED JUICE —
THIS IS THE BEST ANNIVERSARY EVER.
I HOPE TO SHARE MANY MORE TIMES LIKE THIS AGAIN WITH YOU, TOO... IRIE-KUN.
ITAZURA NA KISS VOL. 8 / END♥ CONTINUED IN VOL. 9

© FIRST PUBLISHED IN BESSATSU MARGARET MAGAZINE, STARTING JUNE 1990

ITAZURA NA KISS

イタズラなKiss キッス

EXTRA EPISODE 番外編

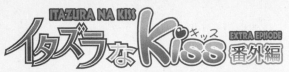

"KOTORINA AND THE PRINCE"

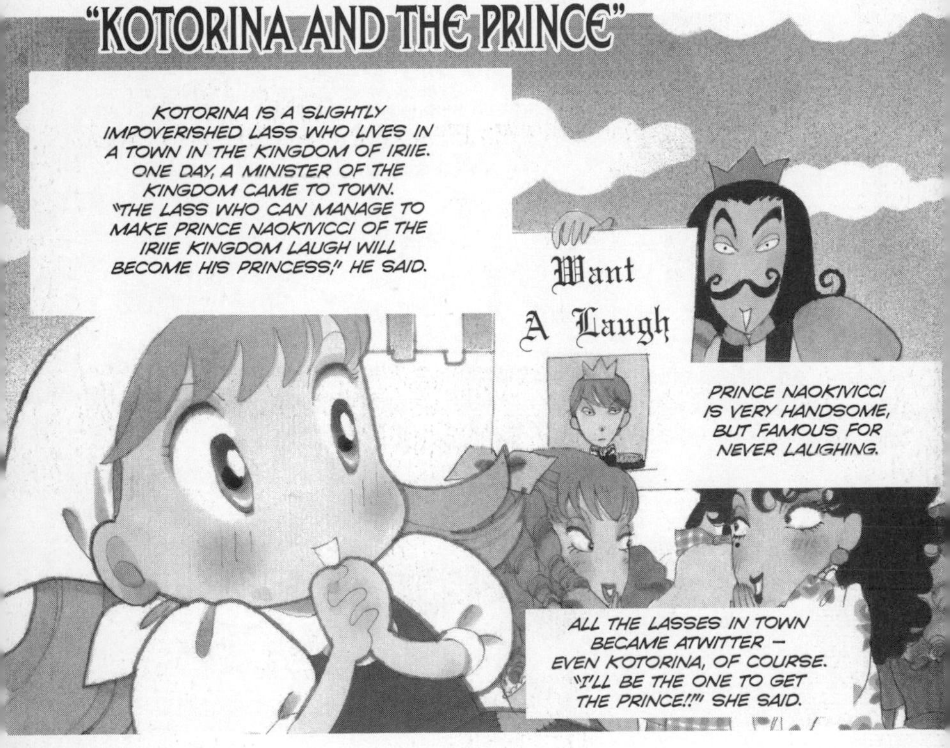
KOTORINA IS A SLIGHTLY IMPOVERISHED LASS WHO LIVES IN A TOWN IN THE KINGDOM OF IRIIE. ONE DAY, A MINISTER OF THE KINGDOM CAME TO TOWN. "THE LASS WHO CAN MANAGE TO MAKE PRINCE NAOKIVICCI OF THE IRIIE KINGDOM LAUGH WILL BECOME HIS PRINCESS," HE SAID.
Want A Laugh
PRINCE NAOKIVICCI IS VERY HANDSOME, BUT FAMOUS FOR NEVER LAUGHING.
ALL THE LASSES IN TOWN BECAME ATWITTER — EVEN KOTORINA, OF COURSE. "I'LL BE THE ONE TO GET THE PRINCE!!" SHE SAID.

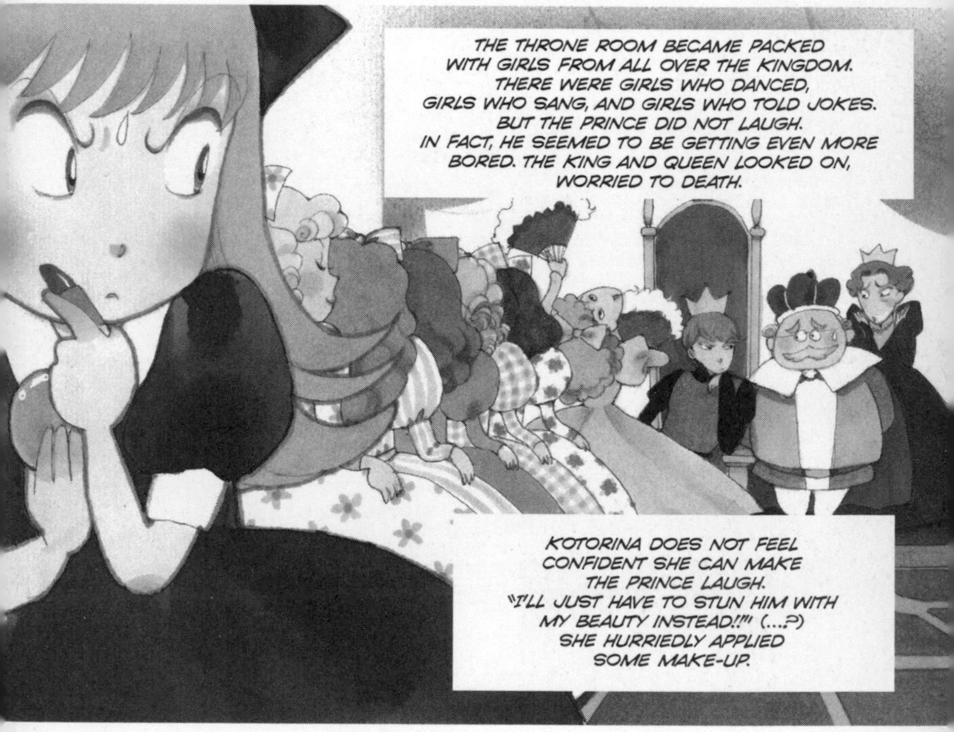
THE THRONE ROOM BECAME PACKED WITH GIRLS FROM ALL OVER THE KINGDOM. THERE WERE GIRLS WHO DANCED, GIRLS WHO SANG, AND GIRLS WHO TOLD JOKES. BUT THE PRINCE DID NOT LAUGH. IN FACT, HE SEEMED TO BE GETTING EVEN MORE BORED. THE KING AND QUEEN LOOKED ON, WORRIED TO DEATH.
KOTORINA DOES NOT FEEL CONFIDENT SHE CAN MAKE THE PRINCE LAUGH. "I'LL JUST HAVE TO STUN HIM WITH MY BEAUTY INSTEAD!!" (...?) SHE HURRIEDLY APPLIED SOME MAKE-UP.

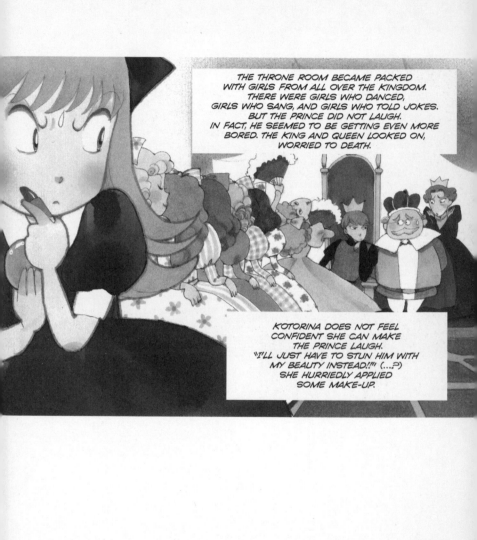

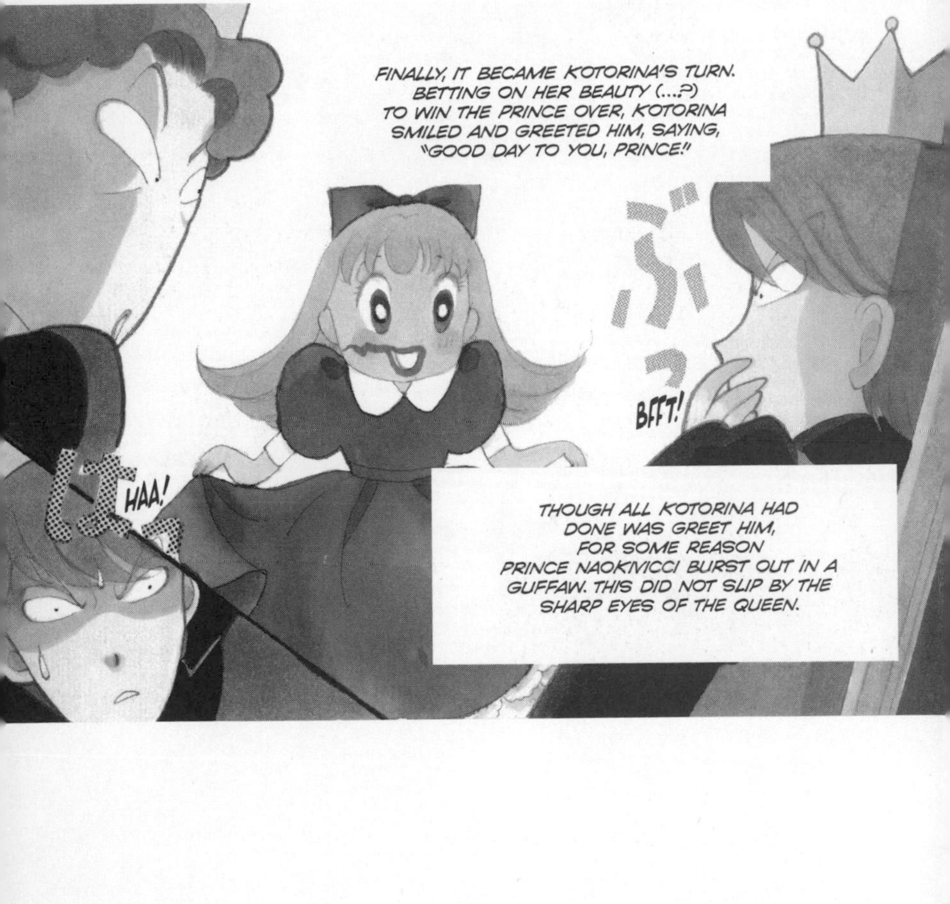
FINALLY, IT BECAME KOTORINA'S TURN.
BETTING ON HER BEAUTY (...?)
TO WIN THE PRINCE OVER, KOTORINA
SMILED AND GREETED HIM, SAYING,
"GOOD DAY TO YOU, PRINCE!"
ぶっ
BFFT!
THOUGH ALL KOTORINA HAD DONE WAS GREET HIM, FOR SOME REASON PRINCE NAOKIVICCI BURST OUT IN A GUFFAW. THIS DID NOT SLIP BY THE SHARP EYES OF THE QUEEN.
HAA!

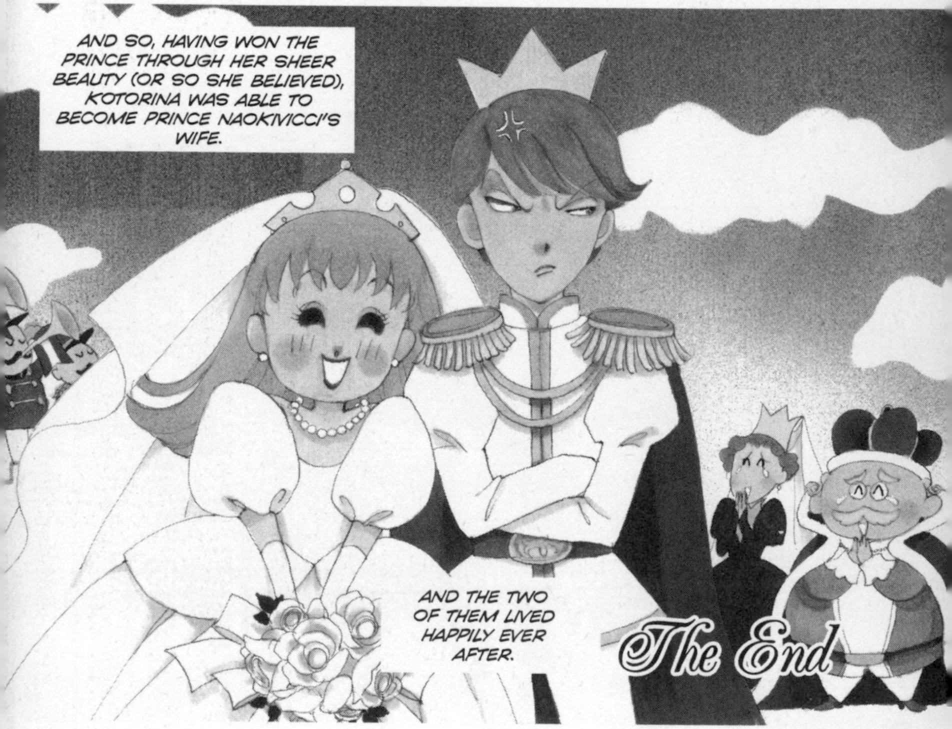
AND SO, HAVING WON THE PRINCE THROUGH HER SHEER BEAUTY (OR SO SHE BELIEVED), KOTORINA WAS ABLE TO BECOME PRINCE NAOKIVICCI'S WIFE.
AND THE TWO OF THEM LIVED HAPPILY EVER AFTER.
The End

●FIRST PUBLISHED IN *BESSATSU MARGARET MAGAZINE*, MARCH 1996

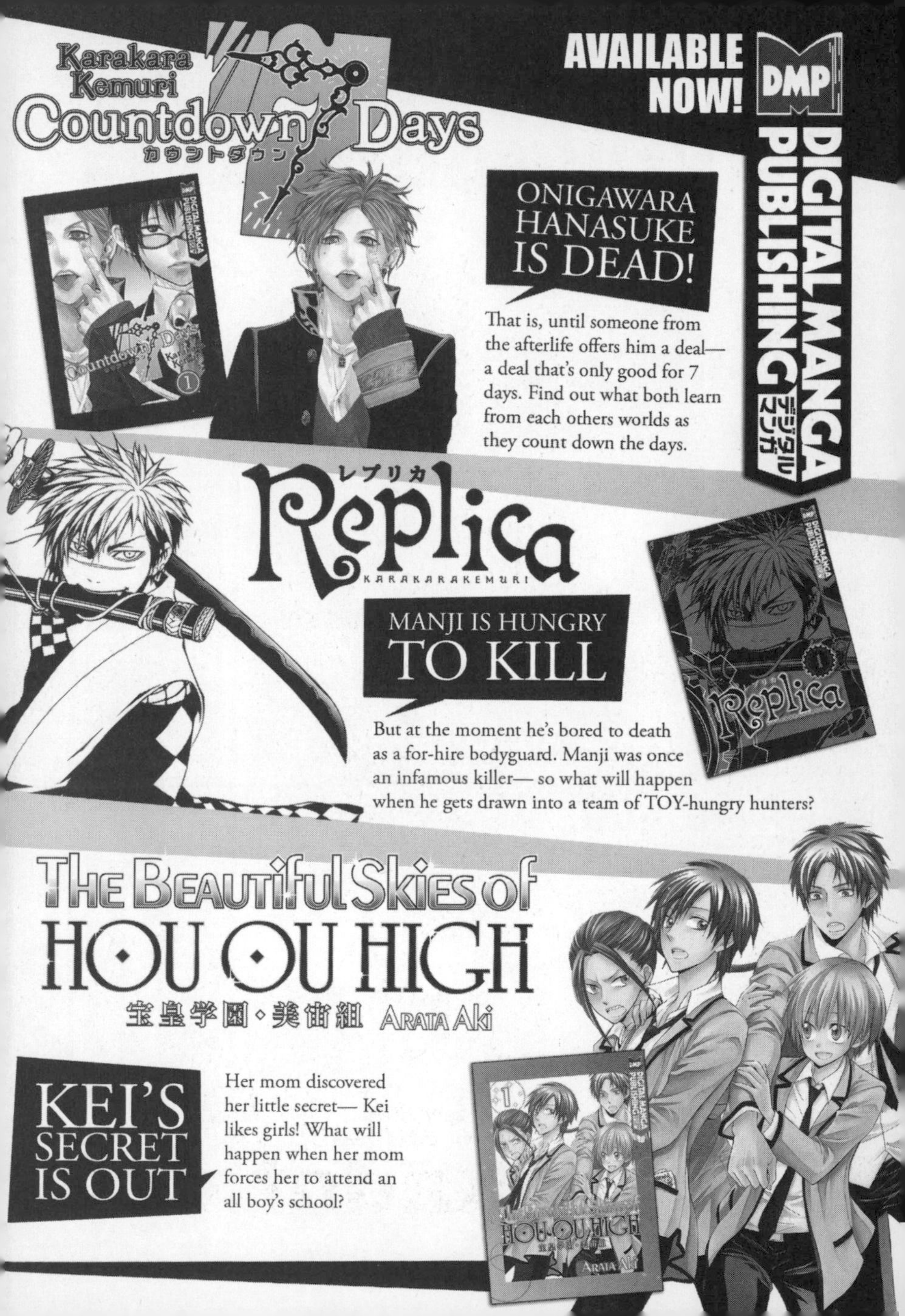

Karakara Kemuri
Countdown 7 Days
カウントダウン
AVAILABLE NOW!
DMP
DIGITAL MANGA PUBLISHING
デジタルマンガ
ONIGAWARA HANASUKE IS DEAD!
That is, until someone from the afterlife offers him a deal— a deal that's only good for 7 days. Find out what both learn from each others worlds as they count down the days.
Countdown Days
1
Replica
レプリカ
KARAKARAKEMURI
MANJI IS HUNGRY TO KILL
But at the moment he's bored to death as a for-hire bodyguard. Manji was once an infamous killer— so what will happen when he gets drawn into a team of TOY-hungry hunters?
Replica
1
The Beautiful Skies of HOU OU HIGH
宝皇学園・美宙組
Arata Aki
KEI'S SECRET IS OUT
Her mom discovered her little secret— Kei likes girls! What will happen when her mom forces her to attend an all boy's school?
HOU OU HIGH
Arata Aki

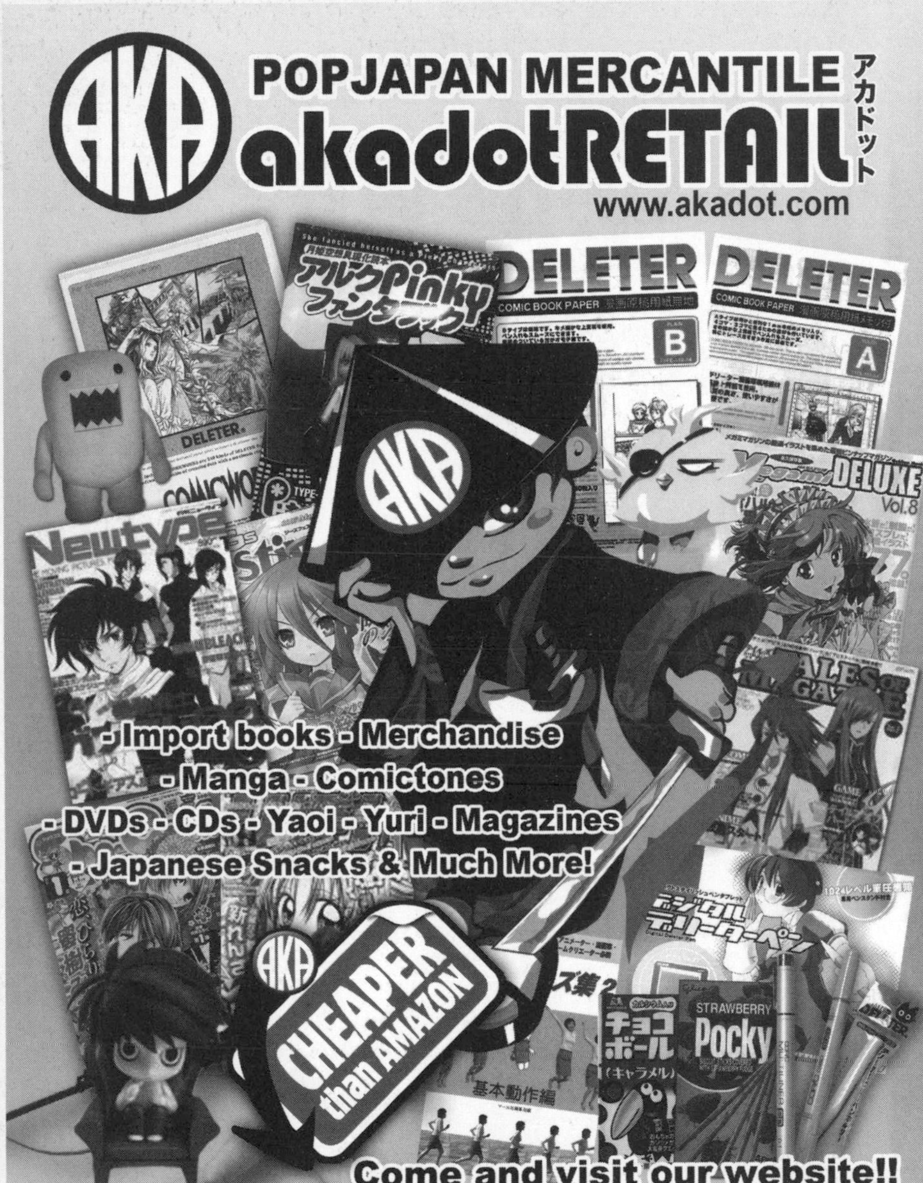
POPJAPAN MERCANTILE
akadotRETAIL
アカドット
www.akadot.com
- Import books - Merchandise
- Manga - Comictones
- DVDs - CDs - Yaoi - Yuri - Magazines
- Japanese Snacks & Much More!
CHEAPER than AMAZON
Come and visit our website!!
www.akadot.com

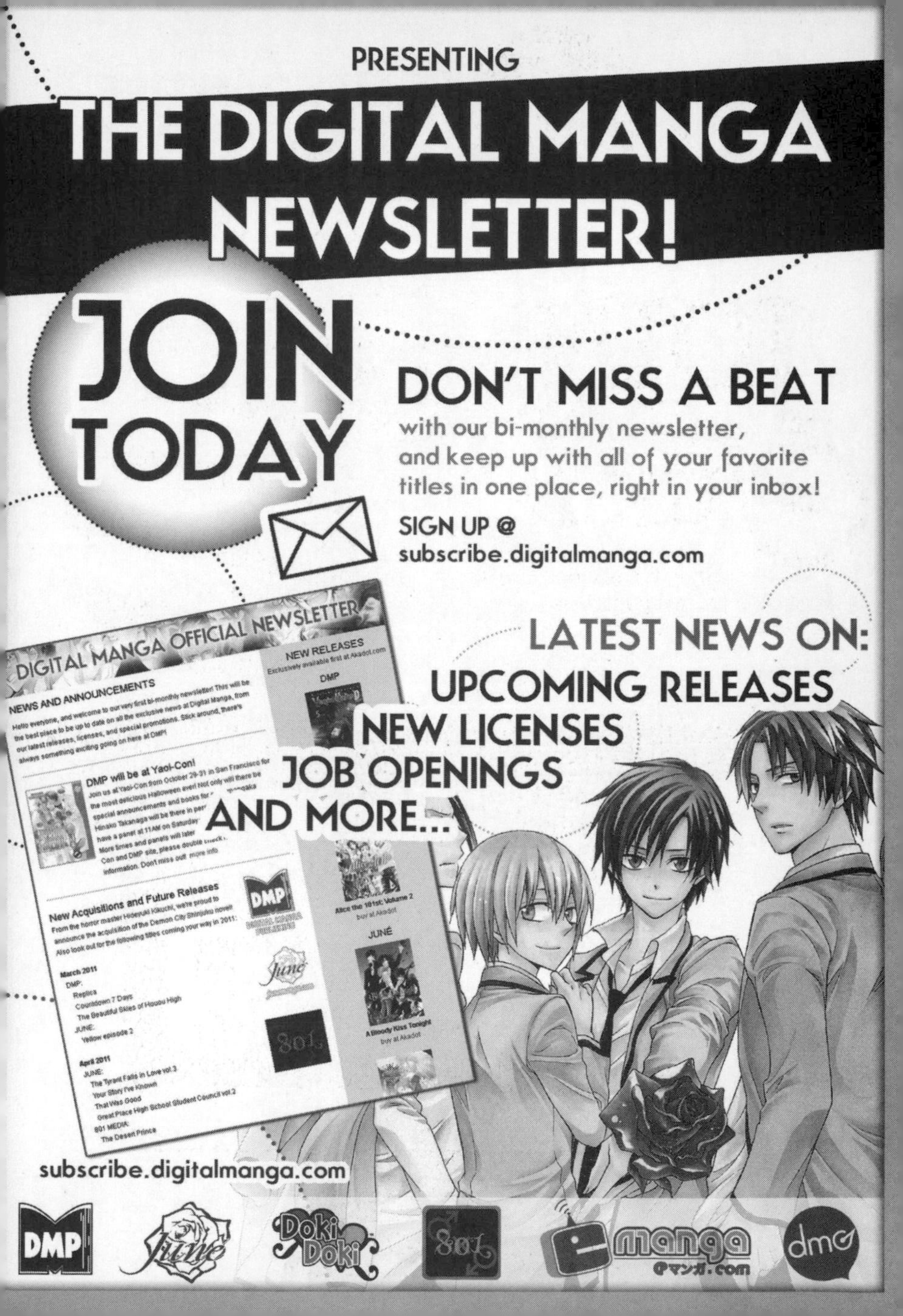
PRESENTING
THE DIGITAL MANGA NEWSLETTER!
JOIN TODAY
DON'T MISS A BEAT
with our bi-monthly newsletter, and keep up with all of your favorite titles in one place, right in your inbox!
SIGN UP @
subscribe.digitalmanga.com
LATEST NEWS ON:
UPCOMING RELEASES
NEW LICENSES
JOB OPENINGS
AND MORE...
DIGITAL MANGA OFFICIAL NEWSLETTER
NEWS AND ANNOUNCEMENTS
NEW RELEASES
DMP will be at Yaoi-Con!
New Acquisitions and Future Releases
Alice the 101st: Volume 2
JUNÉ
A Bloody Kiss Tonight
subscribe.digitalmanga.com
DMP
June
Doki Doki
801
manga
@マンガ.com
dmg

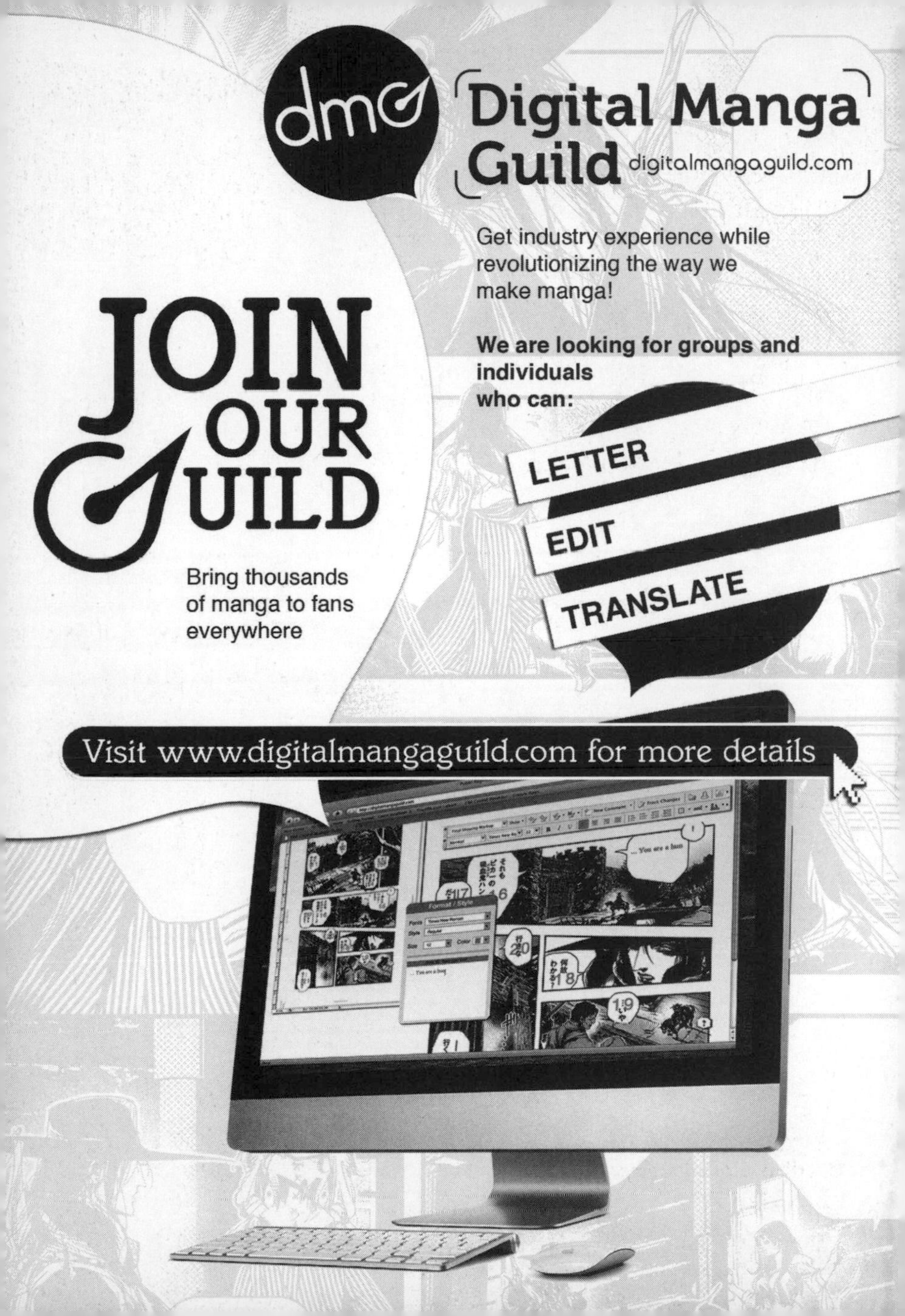

dmg
Digital Manga Guild
digitalmangaguild.com
Get industry experience while revolutionizing the way we make manga!
We are looking for groups and individuals who can:
LETTER
EDIT
TRANSLATE
JOIN OUR GUILD
Bring thousands of manga to fans everywhere
Visit www.digitalmangaguild.com for more details

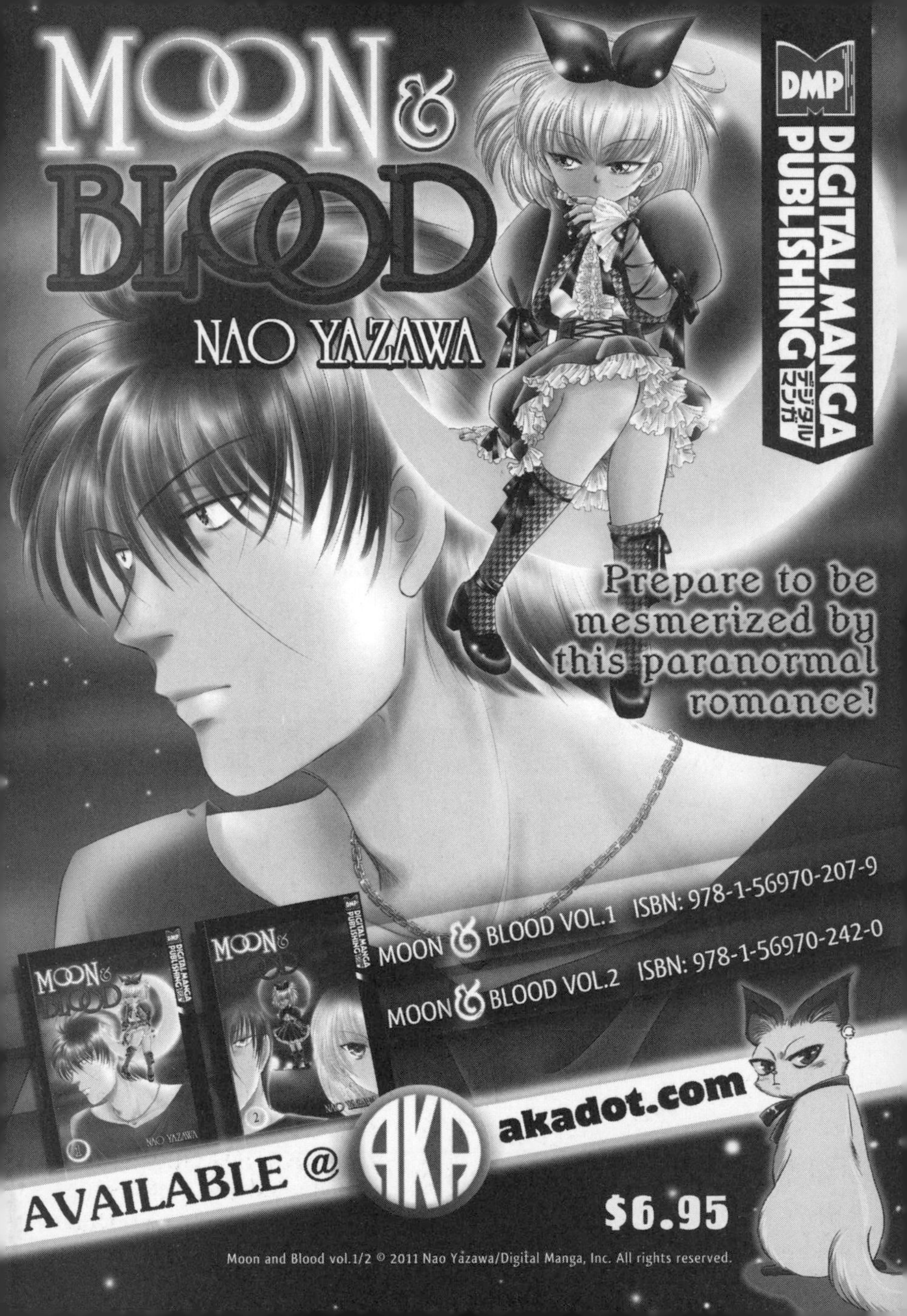
MOON & BLOOD
NAO YAZAWA
DMP
DIGITAL MANGA PUBLISHING
デジタルマンガ
Prepare to be mesmerized by this paranormal romance!
MOON & BLOOD VOL.1 ISBN: 978-1-56970-207-9
MOON & BLOOD VOL.2 ISBN: 978-1-56970-242-0
AVAILABLE @ AKA akadot.com
$6.95
Moon and Blood vol.1/2 © 2011 Nao Yazawa/Digital Manga, Inc. All rights reserved.

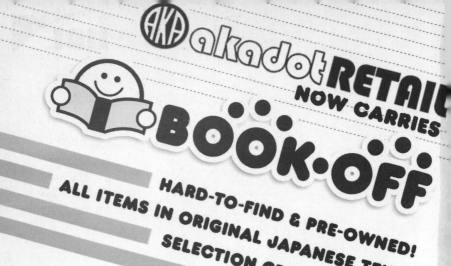

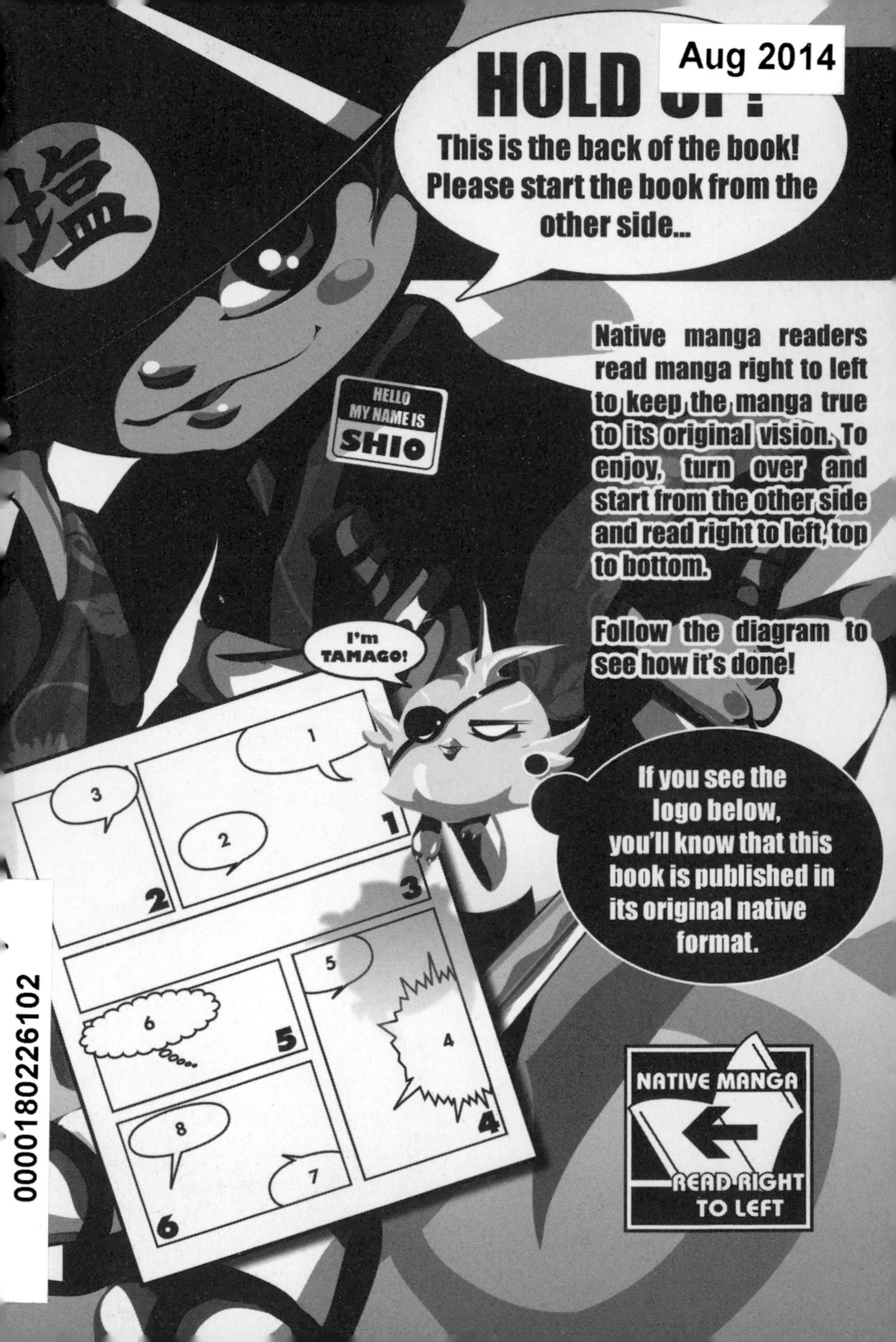
HOLD
This is the back of the book!
Please start the book from the other side...
HELLO MY NAME IS SHIO
Native manga readers read manga right to left to keep the manga true to its original vision. To enjoy, turn over and start from the other side and read right to left, top to bottom.
Follow the diagram to see how it's done!
I'm TAMAGO!
1
2
3
4
5
6
7
8
Oooo
If you see the logo below, you'll know that this book is published in its original native format.
NATIVE MANGA
READ RIGHT TO LEFT